The Enlightenment on Trial

The Enlightenment on Trial

Ordinary Litigants and Colonialism in the Spanish Empire

BIANCA PREMO

OXFORD
UNIVERSITY PRESS

OXFORD

UNIVERSITY PRESS

Oxford University Press is a department of the University of Oxford. It furthers
the University's objective of excellence in research, scholarship, and education
by publishing worldwide. Oxford is a registered trade mark of Oxford University
Press in the UK and certain other countries.

Published in the United States of America by Oxford University Press
198 Madison Avenue, New York, NY 10016, United States of America.

Library of Congress Cataloging-in-Publication Data
Names: Premo, Bianca, author.
Title: The enlightenment on trial : ordinary litigants and colonialism in the
Spanish empire / Bianca Premo.
Description: New York, NY : Oxford University Press, 2017. | Includes
bibliographical references and index.
Identifiers: LCCN 2016041019 (print) | LCCN 2016041169 (ebook) |
ISBN 9780190638733 (pbk. : alk. paper) | ISBN 9780190638726 (hardcover : alk.
paper) | ISBN 9780190638757 (Epub) | ISBN 9780190638740 (Updf)
Subjects: LCSH: Justice, Administration of—Latin America—History. |
Law—Spain—Colonies—History.
Classification: LCC KG495 .P74 2017 (print) | LCC KG495 (ebook) |
DDC 349/.11246—dc23
LC record available at https://lccn.loc.gov/2016041019

For Anna Clair and Alice

CONTENTS

ACKNOWLEDGMENTS

Few books, like few legal petitions in the Spanish empire, are written without agents and patrons. This book has many of both.

Primero, quisiera reconocer el apoyo del personal y de la administración de los varios archivos consultados para este estudio. Aunque este proyecto me requirió cargarlos con preguntas constantes sobre la organización de los archivos y la ubicación de los pleitos, en toda ocasión, los archiveros me han acogido no sólo con profesionalismo sino con entusiasmo. Entre ellos, se destacan el apoyo en España del Archivo de la Real Chancellería de Valladolid, especialmente Carmen Cuevas y el director anterior Pedro Peduelo Martín; del director del gran Archivo Municipal de Toledo, Mariano Ruipérez; y del Padre Miguel Dionsio Vivas, quien maneja el Archivo Diocesano de Toledo. En México, doy gracias al personal de la famosa Sala 3 del Archivo General de la Nación, y la administración, que me proporcionó acceso a la serie de Tribunal Superior de Justicia a pesar de estar en proceso de catalogación. En Oaxaca, los profesionales del Archivo de Histórico de Justicia y del Archivo General del Estado de Oaxaca, especialmente Stella Camargo, fueron muy acogedores. Aunque nunca me siento fuera de casa cuando estoy en el Perú, Marta Chávez y el director Napoleón César Burgos, del Archivo del Regional de la Libertad en Trujillo, me recibieron al estilo criollo cuando entré a su institución para la primera vez. No existe archivo mejor organizado que éste. La administradora del Archivo del Arzobispal de Trujillo, Imelda Solano Galarreta, aseguró que mi trabajo siempre se acompañaba por la música pop del radio. En Lima, donde todo empezó para mí, siento mucha gratitud al personal del Archivo de la Nación del Perú, especialmente Celia Soto y Yolanda Auqui, así como la directora extraordinaria del Archivo Arzobispal de Lima, Laura Gutiérrez, y los encargados de la Sala de Investigadores en la Biblioteca Nacional del Perú. In the US, my thanks go to the staffs of various libraries, especially the Newberry Library, the Huntington

Library, the Nettie Benson Library, and more, for their equally professional and helpful assistance.

Linda Arnold, whose tireless decades of work cataloging and circulating data about the holdings of the Archivo General de la Nación-Mexico and other Mexican repositories quite simply made my work possible. Selene del Carmen García Jiménez and Dr. Amelia Alzamora undertook follow-up work for me in the archives, letting me know where things were and where they weren't. Drs. María Carolina Zumaglini and Paula de la Cruz provided invaluable data coding of cases as research assistants; Isabel Brador ably assisted with the bibliography.

The research and writing for this book required the support of multiple institutions that ultimately are made up of kind people. The College of Arts and Sciences and The Green School of International and Public Affairs at Florida International University, along with my department chair Victor Uribe-Uran and colleagues in History, could not have been more accommodating or generous. The project received funds from a National Endowment for the Humanities Faculty Grant; a Fulbright Senior Scholar Grant; an American Philosophical Society Franklin Research Grant; a National Science Foundation Law and Social Sciences Grant (SES-0921681); and an American Council of Learned Societies Fellowship. The ACLS also later provided a Frederick Burkhardt Fellowship for a year residence at the Newberry Library in Chicago. There, and in Austin with a Fellowship at the Institute for Historical Studies at the University of Texas, I lived the scholar's dream of dedicating myself to thinking, reading, and writing, and I could not be more grateful to Diane Dillon, Courtney Meador, Samantha Rubino, and Seth Garfield for this.

Along the way, many colleagues and friends asked questions or expressed doubts that greatly improved the book. These include my beloved Newberry gang, including but not limited to Susan McDonough, Sarah Pearsall, Leon Fink, and Jeani O'Brien; and the amazing historians at UT-Austin, including Jorge Cañizares-Esguerra, Susan Deans-Smith, Julie Hardwick, Ann Twinam, and visiting fellow Isabel Marín. I am humbled by the interest of those who invited me to share my work and made comments that changed its course, including Tamar Herzog, Karen Stolley, Adriana Brodsky, Richard Ross, Sarah Owens, Susanna Blumenthal, Laurie Wood, José Javier Ruiz Ibáñez, Ramón Sánchez González, and the dearly missed María Elena Martínez. I am also grateful for the company of my archive friends Lucía Crespo Jiménez, Jane Mangan, and the Oaxaca Mamas: Joan Bristol, Nora Jaffary, and especially Yanna Yannakakis, who has accompanied me through this project in many other ways as well. The brilliant Matthew Mirow, an *abogado*, was patient with me, a mere *agente*. Renzo Honores, Trey Proctor, Kathryn Burns, Jamie Melton, Silvia Arrom, David Kazanjian, Pamela Voekel, David Sartorius, Herman Bennett, Judith Mansilla,

Michael Breen, Kunal Parker, António Manuel Hespanha, Stuart Schwartz, Alcira Dueñas, and José Carlos de la Puente Luna provided expertise, shared unpublished work, or asked hard questions. I simply would not have written the book without the intellectual and personal solidarity of two writing groups, one constituted at the beginning of the project with Tracy Devine-Guzmán and Kate Ramsey, and another later organized with Kirsten Wood and Rebecca Friedman, featuring Okezi Otovo. Rebecca, Jody Pavilack, Leslie Harris, and Roy Jeffery showed unending patience as I talked over my writing. I also had the fortune of honing ideas with my students, especially the graduate students who embarked on group endeavors to understand The Birth of Modernity, Is Latin America Non-Western?, and Law in the Spanish Atlantic.

Special thanks are due to Oxford University Press Excutive Editor Susan Ferber and the extraordinary reviewers who read the manuscript so carefully.

This book ultimately represents just a snippet of a decades-long conversation with my mom, Blanche Premo-Hopkins, that inspired the book. As I neared its completion, I began to compose prose in my head to express my gratitude to Barry Levitt. Now that it is time, I realize that words are simply too small for a person so great. Speaking of big and small, Anna Clair and Alice were born with and have grown alongside this book. I am glad to put it down and hold only their hands for a while.

NOTE ON COMPILATIONS OF LAWS

Several major codifications and compilations of Spanish imperial laws are cited in the notes. The oldest is the thirteenth-century *Siete Partidas*, and I use the five-volume English edition translated by Samuel Parsons Scott and edited by Robert I Burns, S.J. (Philadelphia, University of Pennsylvania Press, 2001.) Laws from the *Partidas* are listed by Partida: Libro: Ley(es). The *Recopilación de Leyes de Castilla* (sometimes also called the *Nueva Recopilación de Leyes de Castilla*), compiled in 1567 by Felipe II, are cited by Libro: Título: Ley(es). Likewise the *Recopilación de Leyes de las Indias*, originally compiled in 1680 under Carlos II, are listed by Libro: Título: Ley(es). Laws from the *Novísma Recopilación de Castilla*, (Madrid: s/p, 1805) are listed by volume and page number.

The Enlightenment on Trial

Introduction

Why Is It Enlightenment?

In 1812, when Spanish artist Francisco de Goya used pencil and ink to shade the drawing that adorns this book's cover, a printing press in Cádiz was also working in black and white, churning out copies of a tract called *Complaints of the Americans*. For almost two years prior, constitutional delegates had been huddling in that port city, located on a tiny strip of land jutting out into the Atlantic at precarious distance from the rest of the Napoleon-occupied Iberian peninsula. The French held the Spanish Bourbon monarch Fernando VII imprisoned in exile, and men representing various parts of the vast empire struggled to produce a constitution that could serve as a paper substitute for the missing king.[1] It was in this context that Goya, whose moods swung between optimistic and dark, depicted the apotheosis of law in *The Triumph of Justice*. Questions of law and justice—when it would descend from above, who would bask in its brilliance, and who would be forced into its shadows—were far from academic.

Law was also on the mind of the anonymous Spanish author of *Complaints of the Americans* as he railed against colonial representatives' demands for rights at the constitutional assembly. The very first sentence of his tract accused Spanish Americans of being cheap philosophers with a shoddy understanding of rights: "Let us examine the error that many [make when] they speak of our America and all of the colonies for lack of understanding of the rights of nations (*derechos de gentes*) and of the state; let us examine these plagiarist writers, who without leaving the cabinet, assign character and custom to all nations, aggrandizing some and committing calumny against others." Under the "veil of humanity and equality," the American representatives had cast aside the laws and history of Spain in favor of "fraternity and blood."[2] Reversing conventional claims of metropolitan tyranny, the writer accused creoles, his American-born counterparts, of being the "true despots" who lorded not only over native inhabitants of the empire but, more importantly, peninsular Spaniards. Spain had become "slave" to its colonies.[3]

It may not be surprising that, from a peninsular viewpoint, Spanish Americans had taken advantage of the Napoleonic crisis by deploying the loaded language of the Age of Revolution: fraternity, equality, blood, slavery, despotism. But this tract captured more than the immediate moment. It drew upon a recent history that predated the French invasion, an age without revolution but nonetheless of rights, an age of freedom without calls for liberation from colonial rule. The beleaguered Spaniard repeatedly returned to Spanish Americans' misunderstandings or misuses of law, especially of natural rights. Yet even as he accused colonists of a lack of originality and outright plagiarism, he upturned conventional geographies of cultural superiority in which Europe stands above its colonies.

Spanish Americans, he claimed, had access to cutting-edge intellectual trends of the day and could be considered—indeed, considered themselves—more Enlightened than their peninsular counterparts. He reported that they moaned about Spaniards who immigrated to the colonies for government or business, showing up "uneducated," coming "to civilize themselves."[4] Creoles, especially those in Mexico, "complain, and in this some Europeans join them, that the country is lacking enlightenment [falta de ilustración], and that Spain wants to hold it in a state of barbarity, when only Mexico has countless educational and instructional schools, a laboratory and chair in Chemistry, Physics, Mineralogy, Math, Drawing and a university in which one can graduate from many faculties."[5]

With this, the Cádiz author challenged the version of the Enlightenment that Italian Giambattista Vico had once summarized as "Europe . . . radiant"—that is, a version in which the philosophical, social, and political movement emanated from Parisian salons and London teahouses in weakening concentric circles.[6] Complaints of the Americans civilized the colonies, putting them at the very center of the movement even as they denied their own centrality.

This was, however, more than mere inversion. The writer housed the Enlightenment not in emerging public spheres or reading publics, exactly, but rather in university lecture halls, laboratories, and, especially, courtrooms. All the resources of civilization available in Mexico had resulted in a very peculiar kind of Enlightenment, he observed. "Until now," he wrote, "only good doctors of law have been produced. So many have dedicated themselves to this profession, which carries with it entanglements and discord, that despite the many lawsuits, especially matrimonial, there are too many lawyers."

The Enlightenment on Trial follows this invitation to look into the courtrooms of Spanish America for the Enlightenment. It argues that the movement indeed occurred in the Spanish colonies, brought to life in the everyday "entanglements and discord" that colonial subjects increasingly placed before royal judges.

While the Enlightenment might well have resulted in "too many lawyers," this book argues that ordinary and often illiterate litigants in Spanish America, not their legal representatives, were among its most surprising and skilled legal practitioners.

In the eighteenth century, colonial women, natives, and slaves sued their social superiors before royal judges in increasing numbers. Both the content and the quantity of their civil lawsuits against husbands, native lords, and masters are evidence that the Spanish colonial courts served not as receiving houses for Enlightenment legal concepts as much as their proving grounds. Increasingly as the eighteenth century progressed, colonial Spanish Americans used the civil courts with a zeal that their Spanish counterparts on the peninsula did not match, challenging a traditional legal culture long rooted in notions of justice with a new culture oriented in modern notions of law.

The text of the petitions that subordinate colonial litigants submitted to civil courts animated abstractions such as natural rights, secular civil subjectivity, freedom, merit, and historicism. But more than a philosophy, law-oriented culture was a practice, an empirically observable set of repeated actions surrounding the decision to use the empire's civil tribunals to solve disputes.[7] Thus, beyond the legal arguments they marshaled to their cases, litigants practiced the Enlightenment in the very act of going to civil court. By repeatedly hauling "tyrannical" domestic and community authority figures before royal judges, litigants made space for law as a system of rights and rules that transcended the hierarchical order of colonial society. In short, these litigants produced a movement conventionally understood as the exclusive domain of literate, elite, (northern) European men. Ordinary, unlettered colonial Spanish Americans too produced the Enlightenment.

In recounting this history of Enlightenment in the everyday practice of law in the Spanish colonies, this book is simultaneously a social and ethno-history, and a history of ideas. It is a slave history, a gender history, and a legal history. It employs deep readings of the narratives of texts and explores the circumstances of their production. Yet the architecture of the book—a comparative study of the quantity of lawsuits in six regions of the Spanish empire—follows blueprints from the social sciences more than from the humanities to explore explanations for the increase in colonial Spanish American litigiousness in the eighteenth century. Meanwhile, it maintains a critical distance from those methods, aware that the way that historians think of the past and of what causes change over time is, in large measure, shaped by the very movement that the book seeks to narrate. The Enlightenment is central to this book both because it is the central historical event recounted in its pages and because its legacy so thoroughly infiltrates our way of thinking about that event, where it could occur, and among whom.

Enlightenment without the Eighteenth Century

If it is surprising to discover that, say, an African slave in Lima who could not speak Spanish produced the Enlightenment, we might start by asking why. Why, three centuries after its first stirrings, is there still room to debate what the Enlightenment was and to write new histories of who produced it? The easy answer is that "the Enlightenment" defies consensus. When eighteenth-century Europeans spoke about it by name—in Spanish referring to it as *ilustración* or *"las luces,"* ("the lights") —they often approached it as a question or unresolved problem rather than a self-evident thing.

In this they were not alone. Immanuel Kant's foundational 1784 essay on the Enlightenment responded to a Berlin newspaper's prompt for readers to ponder the question "What is Enlightenment?"[8] Kant offered that it was "man's emergence from his self-incurred immaturity."[9] Provocative enough, but this response hardly helps historians demarcate the Enlightenment as an historical event such as a war or an election; it is an answer that only leads to more questions. French postmodernist Michel Foucault revisited the query two hundred years after Kant's essay was first published, and his response reveals that the Enlightenment continued to be singularly difficult to pin down. Foucault acknowledged that the Enlightenment was a "complex historical event" that occurred at a time, namely the eighteenth century, and in a place, namely Europe.[10] But he also understood it as "an attitude" that marked the shift to modernity. More specifically, it is an "ethos" that links history and human agency. The new, open-ended nature of time embedded in Enlightenment thought meant that humans could be unshackled from authority and tradition, and were free to test the limits of the future. When thinking with the Enlightenment, humans can imagine having a hand in history.

Foucault ultimately was far less interested in what defined the Enlightenment as an event in eighteenth-century history than in its effect on modern thinking about human subjectivity. His brief acknowledgement that the Enlightenment occurred in time is quickly buried under his consideration of its properties as a philosophical attitude. Still, the distinction between event and ethos is helpful, even for those who are primarily interested in what transpired in the past and who have little patience for philosophy. It is a reminder that the understanding of historical occurrences, and perhaps most particularly of the Enlightenment, is never free of philosophy. Or politics. Indeed, Foucault indicates that the Enlightenment is an especially politicized topic because it engages in "intellectual blackmail" by demanding that readers declare themselves "for it" or "against it."[11] Foucault attributes its polemical quality to its very nature as part history, part philosophy, but it might stem more from how the Enlightenment as an event was eclipsed by its use as an avatar for the West itself, in all of its glory and all of its shame.

From Europe's famed post-war Frankfurt School to late twentieth-century post-colonial scholars, particularly South Asianists of the Subaltern School, the Enlightenment's promotion of universal values were linked to modern atrocities, including genocide, fascism, imperialism, and capitalist underdevelopment.[12] Scholarly defenders of the Enlightenment's political virtue are keen to point out that such criticisms sometimes rest more on the imagined properties of eighteenth-century thought than on historical investigation into the actual philosophical debates of the period.[13] Yet, to be fair, many post-colonialist historians demonstrated deep engagement with the past; indeed, the school thoroughly attempted to eliminate the artificial division between "theory" and "history" by documenting how universalism and equality undergirded the violent regimes of Western imperialism. Nonetheless, given the chronology of the New Imperialism—meaning primarily Northern European colonial projects of the nineteenth and twentieth centuries—the version of the Enlightenment these scholars invoked was a "capitalized notion." That is, it was presented as at once a singular, capital-E "Enlightenment" and a gloss for the logics behind modern capitalism.[14] Once again, the eighteenth century and the people who inhabited it were, by force of chronology, somewhat beside the point. The Enlightenment remained more epistemology than event.

Take as an example the canonical work *Provincializing Europe* in which Dipesh Chakrabarty demonstrates how the history of India has been written with a ghostly counterpart in mind—a mythic, developed, and unitary Europe. This is a "clichéd and shorthand form" of thinking by which Europe is imagined as host to historical events and developments that the "non-West" lacks or has yet to experience. Chakrabarty wrestled with the challenges of merely thinking of the history of any place on the globe without recourse to concepts that took their "climactic form in the course of the European Enlightenment and the nineteenth century."[15] He lists no fewer than fourteen historical concepts that make it impossible to think about the past without thinking about the West, including but not limited to citizenship, equality before the law, individualism, democracy, scientific rationality, "and so on." This certainly comes closer to a historical description of the Enlightenment as an event than Kant's philosophical unshackling of human reason or Foucault's emphasis on it as an ethos, but this broad list permits nineteenth-century liberalism to rush in under the cloak of the Enlightenment, indistinguishable from eighteenth-century ideas and occurrences.

At the same time, the concept became stigmatized among European historians, cast out as a relic of intellectual history and replaced with historical-theoretical devices that better hewed to cultural and social history, including "political culture," the "Republic of Letters," and the "public sphere."[16] But, noticing the ground ceded to post-colonialists, European historians kicked off the new millennium with a fresh round of scholarly side-taking.[17] Edited volumes and monographs began to splay before readers the wide range of philosophical thought actually produced in the eighteenth century and aimed to reanimate the philosophers, especially the French *philosophes*, who had been flattened out as one-dimensional Western epistemic conquerors.[18] As scholars began to plumb the depths of eighteenth-century thought, they recovered an Enlightenment that could not be portrayed only as the dark harbinger of imperial inequality or fascist homogenization. Some have found gender inclusive, anti-imperial, and even anti-racist strains of Enlightenment thought.[19]

If historians of the Enlightenment still had to take sides for and against their subject, now allegiance was not so much to a political ideology as to belief in its very existence as a unified entity. Renewed interest in the movement has produced a welter of qualified definitions, including national and global Enlightenments, cartographic Enlightenments, and Atlantic and cosmopolitan Enlightenments. There are enslaved Enlightenments, colonial and postcolonial Enlightenments, cases for the Enlightenment as well as studies of its enemies.[20] The Enlightenment is also an event in the history of "mediation."[21] Predictably, the argument that there were "multiple Enlightenments" has produced, in turn, its own critics: if the Enlightenment has come to mean so much, it has come to signify nothing in particular.[22]

Perhaps no scholar has more valiantly tried to halt the metastasizing of the Enlightenment than Jonathan Israel. Like a modern-day Linnaeus lining up his leaves, Israel employs taxonomy to understand the period's thinkers, including the radical, the moderate, and the anti-Enlightenment varieties.[23] Of all of the philosophers and policymakers in the long eighteenth century, few live up to his standard of radicalism, which involves unfettered religious tolerance, a fearless embrace of republicanism, and a metaphysics that reaches back to seventeenth-century Dutch philosopher Baruch Spinoza.[24] Israel calls this necessary package of philosophy and politics a "Revolution of the Mind."[25]

Israel's intervention is useful for framing the contribution of *The Enlightenment on Trial* in ways both predictable and unpredictable. His reliance on the papers and publications of established philosophers and policymakers makes him a model of an older style of intellectual history in which only a few thinkers are pinned to the wall of the past, like specimens preserved outside their natural context and ordered in relation to a single point of origin (in this case Spinocism.)[26] Such an approach leaves on the shelf a veritable library of recent works on the spread of ideas into popular culture through reading, books, salons, newspapers, coffee houses, and causes célèbres.[27] But Israel's vast command of Enlightenment thought, including Iberian works, makes him a poor straw man from the perspective of the Spanish empire. In fact, though he finds no "Revolution of the Mind" in Spain, he does count nineteenth-century Spanish America as part of the radical Enlightenment.

As scholars considered the value of such old school intellectual history, battle lines for and against the Enlightenment once again shifted.[28] At issue was no longer so much whether the Enlightenment was good or bad, and for whom, but rather what historians mean when they call its story a history of "ideas" or intellectual history.[29] Perhaps the most fruitful result of this new round of debate is the recognition that the Enlightenment demanded no complete revolution at all. Scholars finally delinked the movement from strident anti-monarchism, recognizing that most Enlightenment cultural practices remained largely compatible with, and could even bolster, the social and political structure of the Ancient Regime. This makes it possible to integrate cultural studies of eighteenth-century life with observations about the great philosophical movements of the era without recourse to easy narratives of political revolution. Vincenzo Ferone sums up this new approach succinctly: the Enlightenment "was a complex cultural system . . . made up of more than the circulation of subversive ideas within a circumscribed and elitist intellectual movement." It was, instead, a new way of "living" in society based on the "enthronement of man," defined first and last by its "creation of a distinctive language of the rights of man."[30]

Ferone invites other historians to explore this everyday living in Enlightenment by pushing them to ask not what it *is* but what it *was*.[31] With this, he pulls us back to what Foucault passed over: the event. Ferone calls for Enlightenment scholars to produce work that is ever-more empirical, that is "verifiable in so far as it is falsifiable: i.e., they can get it wrong and they can be shown wrong," "through a rigorous critical study of sources, elaborating new issues and models of analysis and then verifying them."[32]

The Enlightenment on Trial heeds this demand for greater empiricism. But it also is attentive to Ferone's next caveat: precisely because of the sustained attention theoretically inclined scholars have given to what the Enlightenment is, simply explaining what the Enlightenment was is no longer a straightforward endeavor. Goya's illuminated scale can be read as a symbol not only for the new importance of law in the eighteenth-century Spanish empire but also for the difficulty today's scholars face in finding equilibrium between ethos and event in narrating the past. And while this balancing act might be especially tricky for Enlightenment scholars, it is not unique to them.[33] It is in this spirit that this book, even as it tells its story of the Enlightenment, considers what that telling means, especially for Latin America.[34]

Writing, History, and Writing the History of the Spanish Empire

From the vantage point of Latin America—a place one historian refers to as "The Other West"—there could be no simple importation of the post-colonial critique of Western thought.[35] The region's historical experience with European, then later US, imperialism was chronologically and phenomenologically distinct from that of decolonizing nations of the twentieth century.

The initial impulse among some Latin Americanists inclined to post-colonialism was to step backward in time to argue that the founding moments of Western modernity took place in the fifteenth century, with Spanish conquest and colonization of the New World.[36] At that point, Western modernity was predicated on Spain's elevation of its own civilized practices of writing and thinking about history over the New World's indigenous non-alphabetic traditions and temporalities.[37]

The epistemological encounter between writing and non-writing, between history and myth, would prove key to Spanish dominion and endure well into the region's post-colonial history. Uruguayan theorist Angel Rama poetically framed the relationship of power and writing in Latin America as he told the sweeping story of the ongoing concentration of power in the hands of urban elites who used plumes, then pens, then printers to monopolize the region's history and lay claim to its future. He called this space of domination by the literate "the Lettered City."[38]

The denizens of the Spanish imperial Lettered City were not, however, considered first-class citizens of the Republic of Letters. To write Enlightenment histories from Spain and Spanish America is doubly destabilizing to the historicist version of the Enlightenment that places its center not in any Europe but specifically in Northern Europe.[39] Between the seventeenth and eighteenth centuries, Spain drifted from being one of the "privileged sites for the enunciation of European history" to becoming an "object of representation—and symbolic subordination to a newly dominant Europe."[40] This was partly the doing of eighteenth-century imperial rivals in England and France who revived Spanish Catholic missionaries' criticism of the brutality of conquistadors to soften their own colonial pretentions.[41] But Spain too had a hand in writing its empire out of the narrative of Enlightenment.

Spain's *ilustrados*, doubting the capacity of the Spanish people as economic producers, idealized a Europe beyond its borders as more rational and industrious.[42] Historians of Spain sustained this image into the twentieth century by arguing that its Enlightenment was "defective," "hesitant," and "incomplete"—too Catholic, too conservative to count.[43] Gabriel Paquette thoroughly dismantles this historiographical legacy with evidence of Spanish innovation, cosmopolitanism, and Atlantic dynamism under the Spanish Bourbons, who succeeded the Habsburg dynasty in 1711 and came to embody the empire's eighteenth-century experience. While insisting that the Spanish empire "received, used, and modified the ideas of the Enlightenment," Paquette prefers the term "regalism" to describe how the Spanish crown only selectively incorporated "advanced ideas" of other European monarchies into its centralizing measures.[44] Even as Paquette successfully puts to bed, for this generation, the idea that Spain was isolated from the major intellectual and political shifts of the West in the eighteenth century, in the minds of the Spanish Bourbon reformers he studies, the specter of a more advanced Europe hovers.

Jorge Cañizares-Esguerra throws light on that specter in his study of how eighteenth-century Spanish imperial authors engaged in dogged epistemological battles over the past with historians from non-Iberian Europe.[45] In what was once called the "Debate of the New World," creole intellectuals defended the region's past and their own ability to interpret it, skeptical of the eyewitness accounts of early Spanish chroniclers as well as of newer northern European alternatives that degraded Amerindians and American-born Spaniards. Spanish American historians created a new way of writing history based on their proximity to the New World and their mastery of native sources—in many ways, laying the foundation for our own way of writing history—in a dialectic with the rest of Europe.

The Enlightenment on Trial attempts to get beneath the dialectical rivalry among the policymakers and philosophers of empire, to penetrate below the Republic of Letters, to get closer to something like a "lived" or "practiced" Enlightenment among ordinary people, even those who could not read and write.[46] Contemporaries in the Spanish empire often self-consciously struggled to present their Enlightenment as a practice rather than a literary exercise. Take, for example, a 1787 award-winning essay submitted to Madrid's Royal Economic Society, which promoted "utility," one of the hallmarks of Bourbon regalism, and condemned the lack of industriousness in Spain. The prizewinner explained what he meant by the Enlightenment: "The [term] enlightenment has struck a kind of sour note, and this is not without good reason. The presumption, pride and idleness of many intellectuals in this century have given it a bad name. . . . But I do not understand literary arts as enlightenment. . . . By enlightenment, I mean two things: the first, the knowledge of a trade, or a faculty in which each person is instructed; and the second, the true advantages and interests of life."[47]

Even as a broader reading public punctured the aristocratic circles of politics and philosophy, this essayist still needed to justify his notion of the Enlightenment as a practice beyond the world of letters. His interpretation vied, of course, with others that were more exclusionary. The Republic of Letters still had borders. Famous encyclopedist Jean-Baptise la Rond d'Alambert closed its gate by saying "we ought to distinguish the public who reads from the one which only speaks."[48] The distinction between readers and speakers circles back, once more, to Latin America's Lettered City, that ideological space predicated on a literate elite's mastery of the unlettered masses, and forces us to ask whether such a distinction is useful or itself a product of the Enlightenment.

The Republic of the Unlettered

The notion of the Lettered City rests, to a large extent, on the opposition of writing to orality, of materiality to abstraction, of Spaniard to native, of the West to the rest. Rama starkly declared that, with the Spanish conquest "the written word became the only binding one—in contradistinction to the spoken word, which belonged to the realm of things precarious and uncertain . . . Writing boasted a permanence, a kind of autonomy from the material world."[49] Viewed from a certain distance, this may have been true. But closely examining lawsuits, *The Enlightenment on Trial* finds a more complex history of legal writing, reading, and ideas.[50]

The analysis in this book repeatedly shifts from the content of eighteenth-century lawsuits to the question of how the content got onto the pages of the litigation in the first place, and how these pages, in turn, came to constitute a historical archive. In doing so, it reveals that writing, and by extension participation in the law, cannot be reduced only to the wielding of metropolitan or elite colonial power. Even though they did not pen the documents that they submitted in court cases, ordinary imperial subjects displayed remarkable initiative in directing their cases. They took the law into their own hands in multiple ways since writing was the result of lived social interactions between litigants, legal writers, representatives, and judges. As Kathryn Burns puts it in her work on notaries in colonial Cuzco, Peru, the Lettered City had a "much bigger city plan and was much less exclusive than we might suppose."[51]

In making the argument that ordinary people who often could not read or write produced the archive through the law, this book joins a growing number of histories that are recanvassing the lettered world of the Andes, revealing the writing activities of colonial slaves, mestizos and indigenous people as well as a Spanish elite.[52] This complements research in Mexico and Spain, where historians are ever more keen to bring the authors of legal texts—notaries, procurators, and other literate intermediaries—into better view.[53]

The Enlightenment on Trial calls attention to an important but overlooked legal writer, the *agente*. Unofficial and mostly anonymous figures, agentes penned many, if not most, of the petitions in ordinary peoples' lawsuits. Litigants called

Figure I.1 This 1805 *costumbrista* painting from Ecuador is captioned "A mestizo of Quito professing a Liberal Art, accompanied by his pupil," and captures how the Spanish colonial Enlightenment took place out loud, slipping the bonds of literate disciplinary and educational genres. From *The Costumes, of Peru [1805]*, Beinecke Rare Book and Manuscript Library, Yale University.

on a range of writers rather than being limited to court-appointed representatives, who often identified themselves while anonymous writers usually did not, making the petitions they wrote appear to convey petitioners' own, unmediated words. Importantly, the use of legal amanuenses was not limited to subalterns; it was rare to find any parties in a dispute who wrote petitions or other legal documents on their own behalf. Even judges in rural communities who ruled on first-instance cases often could not write, and many high-level judges lacked an education in law and needed the assistance of a legal counselor. This does not mean literacy and writing were unimportant to the inhabitants of the Spanish empire. Rather, accessing writers and, at the same time, making them disappear into one's legal text constituted legal literacy as much as the writing itself did.

By asking not only who penned the pages of a lawsuit but also for whom they wrote, *The Enlightenment on Trial* is a social history squarely situated in the long tradition of "bottom-up" studies of Latin America. While many have associated the Enlightenment with the stridency of Bourbon social control measures, here it appears differently, as much as a popular practice as a state imperative.[54] In this respect, the book brings the Enlightenment to the list of the grand "isms" of Latin America's past produced through ongoing negotiation with the region's impoverished, marginalized populace. It is now clear that ordinary people in nineteenth-century Latin America used the law to shape liberalism and nationalism after independence from Iberian metropolitan rule.[55] Nonetheless, colonial Latin Americans could make "modernity" long before the founding of new republics in the nineteenth century. Scholars of Spanish American Catholicism, notably Stuart Schwartz and Pamela Voekel, argue that key features of modernity such as individualism and religious tolerance could be found in colonial church pews and even the interrogation rooms of the Inquisition.[56]

The Enlightenment on Trial offers a civil counterpart to these arguments about Spanish American modernity that, without resorting to the shibboleth about Catholicism as anti-modern, searches for the kind of popular thinking about the law that appeared in Goya's *The Triumph of Justice*.[57] His scales of justice descended from the sky like the holy spirit, inspiring awe in adherents who cluster on the left, and forcing detractors—notably a cleric on the right—to recoil. If modernity in the Spanish empire was firmly rooted in religion, it was not because its inhabitants failed to imagine secular, civil alternatives to legal selfhood and relations of authority. The soaring number of civil suits in the 1700s testifies to the unique and growing importance of the secular realm to ordinary litigants and the ways historical actors themselves sometimes set royal jurisdiction against the traditions of the Church.[58]

The bottom-up contribution of litigants to broader ideas of the period is perhaps most poignant in the case of slaves struggling for freedom. During the Age of Revolution, enslaved men and women revolted and died for concepts of liberty and equality later trademarked by Europe.[59] In Haiti, slaves produced the Enlightenment even as they were made invisible by its very historical logic.[60] Historian Michel-Rolph Trouillot observed that the Haitian Revolution "entered history with the peculiar characteristic of being unthinkable even as it happened."[61]

Peculiar but not, as this book tries to show, singular. However overlooked it has been, once visible to historians, the Haitian Revolution fits well in the Enlightenment's self-narration as an unshackling from the past. Still, like any event, the revolution actually contained deep continuities. Malick Ghachem argues that the Enlightenment in law proved, more than armed uprising, to be the substance most corrosive to African bondage in the French Caribbean. Legal changes under the Old Regime were "moderate, strategic," and "pragmatic," but nonetheless potent, slowly poisoning the institution of slavery rather than killing it in a single blow.[62] It is precisely by studying regions whose histories were not punctuated by revolutions and major rebellions that this book seeks to show what difference the Enlightenment made without becoming entangled in its own eighteenth-century view of itself as a historical rupture, as a definitive break from tradition.

Thus, this study of the Enlightenment among unlettered colonial litigants draws back from conventional narratives of the event as a revolution, either of the mind or the body politic, and presents the transformation it inaugurated as a more gradual, variable process. It offers verifiable data about changing Enlightenment practices in law while thinking critically about what counts as data in the first place. It pushes beyond the published writings of a privileged few in the history of ideas to ask whether, how, where, and by whom this signal event was lived as an experience. The findings of the book show that the Enlightenment was practiced—not received in Spanish America but produced in it. This production took place, just as the Cádiz complainer indicated, in courts of law, which were textual spaces churning out the papers of lawsuits. Each page turns back to unmask the participation of ordinary people in making a legal Enlightenment even while confirming that colonial hierarchies were real and came to bear on the practice of law, the recording of cases, and, in the end, the documenting of history itself.

A Definition

Foucault's "blackmail" and Chakrabarty's "deep irony" pose a practical conundrum. To label certain ordinary legal practices and arguments as "Enlightened" can easily appear to be a case "for" the Enlightenment and as an implicit capitulation to traditional narratives of the rise of the West. Yet such a critique relies on two unspoken assumptions. The first is that ideas have origins and owners. The second, related to the first, is the "denial of coevalness"—that is, the insistence that place and time are sequenced such that Europe or the West is first and all other places follow.[63]

On the surface, intellectual challenges to the notion that popular or Iberian practices should be considered "the Enlightenment" seem to be perfectly sensible research agendas that call for straightforward methodological solutions. One such agenda would be to ask where Enlightenment ideas came from, to request a genealogy that would prove the Enlightenment bona fides of an idea or practice found in colonial Spanish America. To answer this challenge, the historian might employ what has been called a "circum-Atlantic" approach, focusing on the circulation of people and ideas between the Old and New World, and tracing ideas back to their points of origin in Europe.[64] Another might be to concede that the Spanish colonial Enlightenment was one of "many Enlightenments" rather than "*the* Enlightenment," and to frame it in contrast to the Enlightenment in Europe or even Northern Europe, emphasizing its vernacular elements. Still another approach would be to focus on how Enlightened practices departed from a longer history of ideas that are properly "Spanish," especially Spanish humanism or even longer traditions of "*pactismo*," meaning the contingent nature of royal authority in Iberia.[65] One could argue that there was no Iberian precedent for the practices and ideas captured in eighteenth-century lawsuits or stress their non-Iberian aspects by pointing out analogs in, say, French or English history.

Preempting reflexive challenges to the notion of a popular colonial Enlightenment with the strategies listed above would be wrong not only because it would produce erroneous results but also because the challenges themselves are traps. Each shuttles us back to the Enlightenment's perceived center in an imaginary West; each relies, to some degree, on the "denial of coevalness," making the ontology of Enlightenment a game rigged in favor of an already Enlightened Europe, especially France.[66]

To escape this trap, the book establishes its own proper categories of Enlightenment without recourse to non-Iberian European precedents.[67] This approach is not unique to this book. Scholars of early modern Iberia, rejecting Whig models of history, have been calling for an alternative to the standard rise-of-the-West narrative in which the empires of Spain and Portugal are squeezed in after the fact. Instead, they propose new paradigms in which the Iberian world is essential to the very model.[68]

So to the question of what the Enlightenment was, this book begins with an answer. The list of the chief practices and concepts that are taken to be evidence of the legal Enlightenment in the Spanish empire begins, first, with the expansion of secular jurisdiction and the formalization of legal practice. Litigants as much as royal policymakers promoted the preeminence of secular law as they opted to use the king's civil courts for formal trials rather than suing in other jurisdictions or employing extrajudicial options. At the same time, litigants contributed to the notion that the value of the law was intrinsic, which is to say rooted not primarily in its ability to maintain and facilitate existing relationships of authority but on its very status as law. By seeing the law in this new way, subordinate litigants also saw themselves in a different way: increasingly as juridical subjects possessing a natural right to litigate and to see their suits heard to sentence.

Just as colonial litigants began to reconsider their own legal subjectivity, so too did they begin to see the authority figures closest to them differently: as subordinated to civil law in new ways. So much is evident in the numbers. In the colonies, women, native commoners, and slaves made use of the secular courts against authority figures with a statistically demonstrable enthusiasm. But it was also evident in the kinds of cases they brought, which put pressure on the old pillars of authority in colonial communities and homes, challenging the perks of birthright, privilege, and custom. Instead, litigants made more presentist or even future-oriented arguments about their own merit. They sought to guarantee their freedom from tyrannical excesses by appealing to the "natural right" to self-preservation, and intensified charges of inhumanity and despotism against their opponents. These everyday legal challenges to traditional social hierarchies had a jurisprudential counterpart—a diminishing reliance on the authoritative weight of the great commentators and glossators of Roman law and a rejection of individualized, case-based reasoning in favor of laws and practices of more recent vintage.

In sum, Spanish colonial inhabitants began to imagine the law as a domain separate from inherited social relations and instead as an ambit of action increasingly centered around the royal state, resistant to variation based on judicial discretion, and bound by litigants' rights. Appeals to more current, proximate laws and to notions of natural rights rather than older notions of natural law, the increase of formal complaints against authority figures in secular courts, and the invocation of historicist notions of legal custom and freedom as an end-goal of all human action—this complex of ideas and actions are referred to in this book as the eighteenth-century creation of a modern "law-oriented" culture that competed with traditional "justice-oriented" legal culture.

So why was this the Enlightenment? It was not that going to court, or even going to court to challenge authority figures, was unheard of in the Spanish colonies before the eighteenth century. Instead, this was the Enlightenment because litigants went to royal civil courts more frequently and using new practices against social superiors. It was not the Enlightenment because every idea undergirding these suits was new. In fact, canonical late eighteenth-century philosophers of rights rarely did the heavy lifting in the arguments lawyers advanced in court about natural rights. Instead, it was the Enlightenment because litigants' practices and their lawyers' arguments demonstrated the popularization and everyday reworking, in the moment, of dynamic ideas of rights, freedom, and merit. In turn, those ideas were labeled, often by critics, as "innovations," regardless of their actual geneaologies. Some of these concepts had roots in Iberian legal traditions, developed over centuries. Many others were adoptions of specific seventeenth-century natural rights philosophies that were rocking the basic understandings of justice that had long dominated European civil law systems. Critically, some derived from the minds of Spanish America's own eighteenth-century legal thinkers, such as the conservative creole Peruvian judge Pedro José Bravo de Lagunas y Castillo. Still others, litigants and lawyers made up themselves.

Although the book explores the broader Atlantic context of professional legal education and new philosophies of law, too much focus on these topics risks replicating the notion that the Enlightenment had European origins. In the end, simply finding an analog from a conventional Enlightenment epicenter for historical practices in the Spanish empire—say, discovering a French precedent for the secularization of alimony suits, or arguing that a lawyer in Teposcolula possessed a copy of *Common Sense*—is not really a historical argument. It is a reinforcement of only one part of the Enlightenment, the world historical philosophy that made the West first.

To refrain from searching for the European origins of Enlightenment ideas is not simply to level the playing field. It is to honor the historical evidence. As will become obvious in the chapters that follow, Spanish imperial inhabitants practiced Enlightenment law not after but at the same time as natural rights jurists wrote, French encyclopedists compiled their data, British free market thinkers traded in ideas, and even as Haitian revolutionaries and American founding fathers took up arms.[69] What is more, colonial litigants did not litigate only in response to absolutist crown initiatives but instead often litigated in search of reforms.[70]

The book is built, therefore, on an assertion of the coevalness of the Spanish colonial Enlightenment with Europe's more generally, and a commitment to its popular colonial provenance in everyday action as well as the published word. Even as elite, lettered men of the Spanish empire participated in an Atlantic exchange of ideas, including ideas that increasingly shifted the gravitational pull of history to Northern Europe, ordinary people's daily experiences with law in both Spain and its colonies were unadorned with the conscious cachet of new foreign concepts.[71] The way that some Spanish colonial women, natives, and slaves participated in the wider phenomena of reformulating rights, moving law into its own realm apart from society, and exacting justice from the tyrants whom they hauled before the bench might not have been particularly cosmopolitan, but it was trans-regional. It might not always have been philosophically consistent, but it was commonsensical. And it worked for them, at least until the defendants they sued began to make it clear that the subordinate litigants would not remain the only practitioners of the Enlightenment in the courts.

Methods and Scope

To produce "verifiable and falsifiable" evidence of ordinary colonial litigants generating the Enlightenment, the book entwines two main approaches: one, a comparative analysis of court activity throughout the empire during the period 1700–99; the other, a more cultural-historical reading of legal documents that highlights their creation as well as content. Part I consists of three chapters that explore the lived world of the law in the empire by examining patterns in the process of legal writing, changes in jurisprudence and administrative policy during the century, and the volume of litigation reaching the civil courts in six regions of the empire. Part II focuses on three kinds of cases that increased even more rapidly than most, suits that ordinary colonial litigants brought against their social superiors: women's legal disputes with husbands, native communities' contests over local leadership, and slave suits against their masters.

Even as this book joins other attempts to upset inherited geographies of modernity, and as much as it is in dialog with social histories of women, natives, and slaves in Spanish America, its overall structure and scope derive from legal history more broadly and the history of law in the Spanish empire more particularly. Despite our tendency to echo the frequent complaints about the litigiousness of colonial Spanish Americans, we still lack comparative data on litigation across the empire.[72] To ground conventional wisdom about Spanish imperial litigiousness, *The Enlightenment on Trial* offers a panoramic, comparative view of all colonial civil litigation brought before equivalent jurisdictional bodies across the empire.[73] This comparison yields evidence about ordinary legal practices that encourages new ways of envisioning historical causation.

The comparative method requires special handling. Long implicated in academic imperialism, it can obscure the kinds of messy connections, diasporas, and influences that spill over units of study—the nation, cohesive ethnic groups, the rural—which are themselves sometimes products of politicized, hierarchical ways of thinking.[74] Rather than to jettison the comparative method entirely, believing it has nothing more to offer an age of transnational and Atlantic histories, this study attempts to employ it in a way that makes its units of study and variables overt and adopts comparisons that are more suited to studying events in time and in which cases can influence each other.[75]

In its comparative design, this book offers a chronological and regional survey of the archival holdings of eighteenth-century civil cases in various repositories

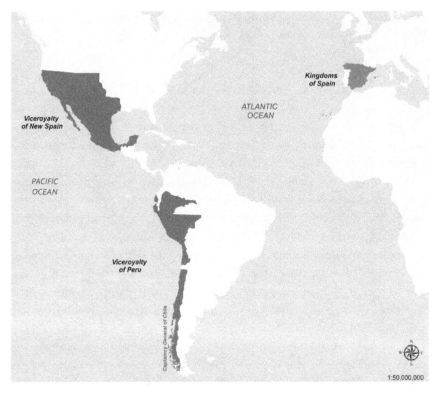

Figure I.2 Spain and the Viceroyalties of Mexico and Peru.

in Peru, Mexico, and Spain. It focuses on the large viceregal capitals of Mexico City and Lima, and two rural regions, Oaxaca, Mexico, and Trujillo, Peru. Castile—New and Old—provides the Spanish region for the study.

Mexico City and Lima were bustling, rowdy, sometimes rough major urban centers that each housed viceroys, the closest thing to a king and his court that could be found in the colonies.[76] They also contained very active high courts called *audiencias*. In these cities, African-born slaves, native migrants from the countryside, and mixed race (*casta*) artisans rubbed threadbare shoulders with the velvety coats of titled peninsular and creole nobility—including some judges and other prominent legal bureaucrats—as well as other elites who dragged behind them a string of distinguished Spanish surnames.

The region of Oaxaca comprised several administrative units that doubled as court jurisdictions, called *alcaldías mayores*. The focus in this book is on two ethnically diverse alcaldías mayores that contained overwhelmingly indigenous populations, that of the predominantly Mixtec district of Teposcolula and the majority Zapotec district of Villa Alta, which are located, respectively, in the northeastern and northwestern sierra surrounding the valley of Oaxaca.

Figure I.3 The Viceroyalty of Mexico before the 1780s.

Although many Spanish colonial courts sat a distance from the native inhabitants of these regions, the law was nonetheless an important part of their world.

Trujillo was a mid-sized provincial city in northern Peru that, at the end of the eighteenth century, competed for recognition with more prominent Spanish colonial urban spaces.[77] Multi-ethnic in its center, it was ringed by populations of natives and people of African descent who toiled on coastal haciendas or lived in hamlets and towns on the western slopes of the Andes. The jurisdictional structure of this region typifies the civil jurisdictional structure in Spanish America. Its civil courts were more or less jurisdictionally concentric, beginning with its active first-instance civil court, moving next to a larger regional court serving a predominantly rural clientele (the *corregimiento*, similar to Mexico's alcaldías mayores). Although Lima's audiencia was not particularly near, many litigants from the north gladly made the days-long journey down the western coastline of Peru to the capital city, where they would shop for the most favorable

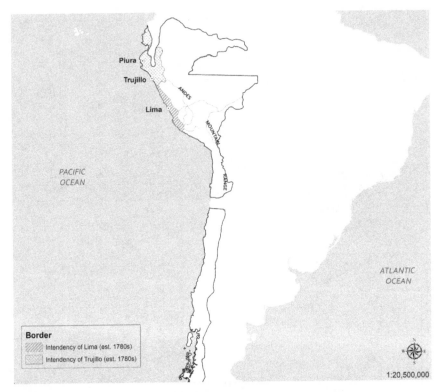

Figure I.4 The Viceroyalty of Peru after the 1780s.

forum in which they could air or appeal their complaints. In 1787, the Bourbon monarchy replaced the corregimiento of Trujillo with a new jurisdiction, the intendancy, as part of a vast reorganization of Spanish imperial administration that affected most mid-level jurisdictions.

The peninsular Spanish regions studied in the book include one rural region in Castilla-La Mancha known as the Montes de Toledo, as well as a high court called the Real Chancellería in Valladolid. The peasants of the Montes de Toledo were mostly ruddy, hardworking types who could have stepped straight out of the windmill-spotted pages of Cervantes. They fell under the criminal and civil jurisdiction of a court that is ideal for comparison with those of colonial Spanish America. Few Castilian archives retain suits from local or lower-level courts—be they seigniorial courts or royal courts. The Fiel del Juzgado series, housed in the Archivo Municipal de Toledo, is an exception.[78] The Fiel was a member of the Ayuntamiento of Toledo (city council and court of first instance; the same as a *cabildo*) who heard appeals from litigants in the Montes, a mountainous region southwest of the city.[79] The city of Toledo had purchased the lands of the Montes in the thirteenth century, making the ayuntamiento, rather than a local *señor*, proprietor of its pasturelands. As a result, there were no seigniorial courts in the

Figure I.5 Spain.

Montes de Toledo. Its residents, like the inhabitants of Spanish America, were direct subjects of the crown who could appeal to the Fiel del Juzgado as a representative of the king to adjudicate disputes even with the city council itself.[80]

The jurisdictional peculiarities of the Montes de Toledo make it ripe for comparison with Spanish America, especially its rural pueblos. At the same time, the inhabitants of the Montes tended to go to court in patterns that were replicated in the Chancellería of Valladolid, a peninsular court with an extensive and diverse reach, which heard appeals and some first instance cases from a large jurisdictional area of central and north Spain. This offsets the chance that the Montes de Toledo represents a singular or aberrant case. As the book makes clear, the court records in both Castilian jurisdictions reveal a common tendency toward decentralized means of adjudicating conflict in the community, making it possible to talk about "Spain" and about early modern justice-oriented legal culture more broadly.

Viewed as units, the six sites of study examined here do stand in for types: the capital cities are dynamic urban centers where inhabitants lived in close proximity to tribunals and thus were at the heart of colonial legal culture; Trujillo is a mixed urban and rural space with a diverse ethnic profile; Oaxaca frequently represents indigenous society as well as rural legal culture functioning at a remove from Spanish tribunals; the Montes de Toledo too is analyzed as a rural legal setting but, along with the high court of Valladolid, is also considered "Spain" and, in some broader sense, "Europe." These regions were selected not only because of their differences but also because they had comparable, relatively stable jurisdictional structures during the eighteenth century.

None of the six regions examined in this book experienced major rebellion during the period 1700–99, with the exception of Villa Alta, where in 1700 a revolt occurred in a Zapotec pueblo after two men turned in fellow villagers to the Dominican priests for their supposedly idolatrous behavior.[81] Certainly, there were riots and violence, but nothing like the sweeping rebellion that engulfed great stretches of the Andes in the 1780s or the uprisings that priests Miguel Hidalgo and José María Morelos led in central Mexico during 1810–16. At most, the inhabitants in these regions were bystanders to the Age of Revolution, thus offering us an Enlightenment story that does not end, at least in the short term, with the emergence of independent republics.

The book mostly stays within the frame of the eighteenth century. The exception is Trujillo, since this is the only region where a major increase in civil lawsuits did not take place in the second half of the 1700s but rather in the first decade of the 1800s. But even though the quantitative analysis in the book focuses on early nineteenth-century Trujillo in spots, its textual analysis is confined mainly to cases from the period 1700–99.

This was admittedly not easy. Enlightenment language and legal practices became more conspicuous at the turn of the century, and it was tempting to dip into nineteenth-century sources because they provide vivid examples instead of the subtle, at times equivocal traces of changing legal culture found in the 1700s. Though it renders the narrative less bold and definitive than would, say, contrasting legal culture and practice in the mid-seventeenth and the mid-nineteenth century, it is precisely by remaining in the eighteenth century that the book illuminates an uneasy process of historical transformation, the production of Enlightenment ideas at their inception, and the way they insinuated themselves into traditional legal practices and ideas. Thus this book, even as it draws a stable "before" to make readable its "after," repeatedly emphasizes that new legal arguments and practices—what is referred to as "law-oriented culture"—did not completely displace older, early modern legal practices, or "justice-oriented culture." Change need not be sudden or complete to be meaningful.[82]

In tackling the problem of change, the book joins legal historians who are strategizing ways to short-circuit a tradition of teleological thinking about the law's development, particularly by exposing how modern legal systems are hybrid and harbor older legal forms and habits, repressed though they may be in portraits of modern law as radically different, more rational, more cogent than law was in the past.[83]

Evidence of the features of early modern justice-oriented culture comes from its endurance in eighteenth-century practice. It also comes from a historiography on the sixteenth and seventeenth centuries that reveals that early modern law was different from modern law in this respect: it was more embedded in society and not a state institution. As historian Tamar Herzog insists, the legal culture dominant at the beginning of the eighteenth century lacked rigid boundaries between the "legal" and the "extralegal." Often oriented toward non-legal or equity outcomes, justice "was not equal to legality, and the legal sphere was not autonomous from other types of knowledge, doctrines or norms."[84] Scholars describe variants of this legal regime using various terms including "infrajustice," "distributive justice," "village justice," and a legal culture rooted in "harmony ideology."

Early modern law was messy. Or, more properly, law in the Spanish empire during this period was pluralistic, emanating from diverse sources and embodied in multiple and overlapping jurisdictions, including royal, ecclesiastical, military, and inquisitorial. It took place simultaneously in high courts and village councils, including those presided over by indigenous judges. Like in other pluralistic colonial regimes, until the end of the eighteenth century, Spanish imperialism did not provide a hierarchy that supported colonial rule as much as "a framework for conflict," in the words of Lauren Benton.[85] Beginning in the late eighteenth century, this pluralistic legal (dis)order came to be replaced by more rigid, state-centered schemata characteristic of modern imperial and national legal regimes.

The Enlightenment on Trial traces a similar arc in discussing the advent of regalist, centralizing practices of law in the Spanish colonies. But, by focusing on the transitional moment of the eighteenth century, it argues that several features of this change, particularly its popular provenance and incomplete nature, can be instructive beyond Spanish America.[86] As one example, the book reveals that the modernizing Bourbon legal regime did not eradicate "custom," a presumably early modern feature of law, but fixed it as a stable feature in an emergent, tentative design of law as a rational system. What is more, the book makes it clear that older practices of justice—socially embedded, pluralistic, and porous in relationship to morality, religion, and local culture—did not quite disappear at the end of the eighteenth century. Thus the rise of a modern state-centered legal regime was not an irreversible step in a march toward modernity. Rather, it was one of multiple, coexisting ways that ordinary people imagined how the law should work and their place in it.[87]

Put differently, the Enlightenment in the Spanish colonial courts was not the product of modernity; it produced the idea of legal modernity. Rather than truly disciplining the hybridity of early modern regimes, it organized that hybridity into cogent stories about systems, science, and release from legal traditions and traditional authority.[88] To be sure, not all Spanish imperial litigants in the eighteenth century saw the law this way. But most of us do. It might be tempting, then, to read this book as a genealogy of ideas, to see the lawsuits that Spanish American colonial litigants placed before judges as the progenitors of our own modern visions of law. But this is no simple origin story. *The Enlightenment on Trial* ultimately seeks to address why some, but not all, Spanish imperial litigants participated in the legal Enlightenment and to explain why this participation is still largely overlooked. In the end, it suggests that modern thinking about history owes as much to defendants' colonial vision of who can generate ideas as it does to the litigants who sued them.

In focusing on the social rank of plaintiffs and defendants, this study is greatly indebted to Richard Kagan's landmark 1985 work on civil litigation in early modern Spain.[89] Investigating the court of the Fiel del Juzgado in the Montes de Toledo and the upper level court of the Chancellería, Kagan demonstrated that litigation in Castile increased during the period 1500–1700, producing a so-called "Legal Revolution" similar to what occurred elsewhere in Europe during the same period. He hinted that royal judges' willingness to hear cases that the poor and powerless brought against the wealthy and well connected contributed to increased legal activity in Golden Age Spain.[90] While *The Enlightenment on Trial* generates a great deal of data about civil litigation more generally, the correlation between volumes of cases and the propensity of legal subordinates to sue superiors is its central concern. Detailed analysis of civil litigation in multiple colonial jurisdictions shows that, as civil litigation rates soared in the colonies, subordinate litigants sued their superiors in greater numbers than before.

To better understand this trend, the book examines in detail three types of secular civil cases in which subordinates took individuals more powerful than they were to court, and finds each increased at a rate even greater than the overall increase in litigation. These, again, are women suing husbands over conjugal obligations; Indian commoners bringing suit against native leaders; and slaves' civil suits against masters. As a control case, the book examines evictions and rent disputes since these suits generally involve more powerful and wealthy property owners suing less powerful tenants. This control case serves to show that, while the eighteenth-century colonial litigation boom involved an increase in a wide array of suits, it especially galvanized subordinates' lawsuits against domestic and community authority figures.

The focus on secular civil cases for this study is deliberate. Since the analytical concern is the degree to which the inhabitants of the Spanish empire produced ideas in the court system, civil litigation is most likely to register this activity.[91] Unlike in Spanish criminal law, where the state often served as plaintiff in trials brought *de oficio*, individuals or communities almost exclusively initiated the cases that appear in the Spanish civil case record.[92] That is not to say that civil suits are examined in isolation. In order to understand litigants' increasing turn toward civil jurisdiction examined in Part II of the book, it is necessary to know whether and how they sought recourse in other courts—or in no courts at all—to solve their conflicts. Thus, in various places, the book compares civil legal activity in secular tribunals to cases heard by ecclesiastical officials or cases tried as crimes. Suits are also read for their "pre-history," or the actions that litigants took prior to entering the formal halls of justice. Indeed, the book begins with a legal action that took place entirely outside a court of law, in a private home in Spain, and without writing. It starts with this informal space of law because it was in leaving such places, in deciding that justice could not be found at home but only in the courts of the Spanish empire, that colonial litigants made the Enlightenment.

PART I

SUING IN THE SPANISH EMPIRE

Felipe Gómez never saw a contract, but he did notice the lemonade. One day in 1789 he went to his friend Manuel's house in the village of Arroba in the Montes de Toledo. There, he observed Manuel call two men who had been unloading some ox carts into his house to share a drink. Felipe later testified that he had figured that the shared lemonade was an *alboroque*, or toast that sealed the deal for the sale of seven carts in total, plus thirteen oxen. The lemonade, it turned out, was not enough. Eleven oxen died and the men refused to pay Manuel what they owed him. The participants in the deal ended up with a case before a judge known as the Fiel del Juzgado in the Spanish imperial city of Toledo, about thirty leagues from their little pueblo.[1]

Business deals gone bad, family squabbles over inheritance, major land disputes, petty debts: this was the stuff of the civil suits that had long piled up on the desks of attorneys, procurators, and judges throughout the Spanish empire. During the sixteenth and seventeenth centuries, suing had become a part of daily life for Spaniards.[2] Yet, even though they racked up considerable debt from legal fees, Golden Age Spaniards were unde-cided about the lawsuit's morality. This was in part because they were still imbued with medieval Christian values that stressed the importance of harmony, and in part because their social world comprised a multitude of corporate relationships that required cooperation—family, town, guild, confraternity.[3]

After the conquest of the indigenous empires of the Americas, crown officials saw a chance to start anew.[4] In 1529, they banned lawyers from

Figure Pt.1.1 Castilian Types–Three Peasants of Toledo, from E. Reclus, *Nouvelle geographie universelle: la terre et les hommes*, (Paris: Librairie Hachette et C°, 1876). Courtesy of the Archivo Histórico Municipal de Toledo.

Peru, hoping the new world would be a more pacific and less petty one.[5] They were wrong. Within a few years there were at least half as many lawyers as priests in Peru. The crown's new indigenous subjects, from Mexico to the Andes, quickly showed themselves to be quite adept at wielding contracts, filing suits against greedy Spanish overlords, and working out long-standing conflicts with rival ethnic groups before colonial judges.[6]

In short, Spanish imperial culture was a suing culture. The first part of this book explores how ordinary litigants in Spain, Mexico, and Peru inhabited this culture in the eighteenth century. It pays close attention to civil suits—who wrote them, how litigants filed them, how they were understood, and how many there were. In part, it aims to subject the courtrooms of the empire to close inquiry: to peel back the layers of authorial voices in suits, to situate jurisprudential ideas within them, and to excavate from the archives of today the legal practices in the past.[7] More specifically, in three chapters it explores key areas of law that can be loosely categorized as papers, policy, and patterns.

The first chapter paces out the procedures, official and unofficial, that constituted suing in the eighteenth century, with special focus on the crafting of the papers of a civil case. The next examines the courtroom as a space of policy and philosophy, specifically as a repository for the changing concerns of intellectuals, jurists, and policymakers. New ideas regarding the nature of justice were manifest in judges' ruling philosophies and in new royal policy associated with the reformist Bourbon government in Spain. The education of lawyers, thoughts about jurisdiction, and principles of jurisprudence all underwent transformation during the eighteenth century.

While lawsuits were made up of written words and sometimes unspoken ideas, courtrooms were also places of numbers. The piling up of legal documents did not occur uniformly throughout the empire or through the years. This much was evident to court officials as they meticulously listed the various fees litigants owed them, and when, as part of their work of administering justice, they fretted over growing case volumes and the slow progress of suits. Hopes that Spanish Americans would be less litigious than peninsular Spaniards was a wistful memory by the eighteenth century, when colonial inhabitants began to sue each other at a furious rate. The third chapter in the section compares the archival holdings and corroborating contemporary statistics on litigation rates in various civil courts in Mexico, Peru, and Spain. It shows that, without a doubt, litigiousness in the colonies was on the rise in the 1700s while lawsuits in Spain stabilized or even declined after a prolonged period of expansion in the sixteenth and seventeenth century.

A central factor in this uneven imperial "legal revolution" is also a recurring theme in the history of procedure and policy during the period: the ways that legal papers, judicial philosophies, and patterns in suing were shaped at the margins: by unlettered litigants, by the colonies, by practice rather than rules. As the first chapter, on procedure, shows, imperial legal culture and the strains of colonial Enlightenment that grew within it, cannot be reduced to the ruminations of an educated, literate legal elite. As Chapter 2, on policy, demonstrates, it cannot be pegged to a specific reform or new philosophy generated by the Bourbon monarchy, no matter how important royal reforms were to the changes in legal culture during the century. As the third chapter on the volume and numbers of lawsuits reveals, reasons for legal change cannot be plotted onto neat charts, no matter how clear the trends toward greater litigation in the colonies over the course of the century are. This section of the book ends by showing that, while there are undoubtedly multiple explanations for the increased litigiousness in the colonies in the second half of the 1700s, one surely has to do with changing cultures of authority in the eighteenth century. And lemonade.

1

Agents and Powers

Litigants and Writers in the Courts

Ordinary Spanish colonial litigants reshaped concepts of authority by suing more in the eighteenth century, and particularly by suing "tyrants" to whom they were subject in homes and communities. They also reshaped legal culture as they opted for formal practices of conflict dispute, and as they favored the impartial application of the law over traditional notions of justice. They forced themselves, as rights-bearing subjects, into new jurisprudential spaces that were formerly too narrow to allow them entry or that simply had not previously existed. They presented themselves as secular juridical subjects in cases drawing from emerging notions of natural rights, time, and freedom. Such a complex argument about the multiple ways litigants created an Enlightenment legal culture from below depends, of course, on a clear understanding of whether ordinary people were speaking for themselves.

Or, perhaps better put, writing for themselves. The Spanish imperial courtroom was more a textual than physical place. Until its final stages, the lawsuit transpired mostly through the exchange of petitions, interim judgments, notary notifications, and witness testimony written up in various sites, including the streets, homes, and offices of imperial cities and villages. Many, perhaps most, lawsuits—rejected as groundless by judges, abandoned by litigants, or settled out of court—never even got to the later stages involving a hearing. Litigants and lawyers only rarely gathered in the lavish halls of government buildings called *salas de justicia*, crowned by the judges' bench.

Although the law could happen anywhere, its location still mattered. Litigants exercised different degrees of power over their suits depending on whether their legal practices took place in the street or the *sala*. In the picaresque scene in Figure 1.1, illustrated by an Italian traveler who traversed the early Mexican republic in the nineteenth century, a woman crouches with a scribe in the capital's central plaza. Inside his ramshackle, traveling "office"—consisting of

Figure 1.1 Claudio Linati's 1827 rendering of a Mexico City public scribe, whom he describes as holding all of the secrets of the country. "Escribano público" reproduced by permission from *Trajes Civiles, militares y religiosos de México (Distrito Federal: Instituto de Investigaciones Estéticas, Universidad Nacional Aútonoma de México*, 1956), pl. 9.

a woven mat, or *petate,* propped on some sticks to block the sun—the woman lifts her index finger to make her point. The bespectacled legal agent, *mestizo* by all appearances, poises his plume above paper, translating her perspective into the written word.[1] In contrast, the parties to the civil dispute do not even appear in Figure 1.2, of the high court of the Chancellería of Valladolid. Had they shown up, most would have occupied the corners of the courtroom. With the magistrates and their own lawyers elevated above them on risers, litigants were pushed to the margins of the scene. They, like the judges, were probably hearing for the first time the eloquent, impassioned arguments put forward by their attorneys.

These illustrations capture a distance between the physical and textual space of the Spanish imperial "courts," a distance paralleled in the historiography of the law in the Spanish empire, where litigant voices either emanate from below or the hands of legal officials shape the case from above.[2] Legal testimony and petitions written in the first person and signed in the name of litigants provide

Figure 1.2 In this 1667 etching, the ministers of the Chancellería de Valladolid gather for a civil case, performed with extensive ritual and ceremony. The ministers are flanked by the licensed court attorneys (*abogados de número*), who were permitted to argue before the bench while remaining seated. Only the most prestigious male litigants could sit below them, in chairs at floor level, and only with prior permission. Otherwise, most litigants sat at the margins of their own cases. The foreground of the *sala*, or courtroom, is lined with various court officials, including the Protector of the Poor, the Crown's Attorney (*agente fiscal*), and court notaries. From Representación animada de la Sala de los Oidores de la Real Chancillería y Audiencia de Valladolid, added to Manuel Fernández de Ayala, *Chancellería de Valladolid. Dirigido Presidente y Iueses della* (Valladolid: Imprenta de Iospeh de Rueda, 1667), fol. 48, reprinted in José María Vallejo García-Hevia, *El Consejo Real de Castilla y sus escribanos en el siglo XVIII* (Madrid: Junta de Castilla y León, 2007), Lámina VII, 279.

rich information on ordinary life, attitudes, and social relations. But these documents were mostly written by "scribes," meaning both court notaries and a range of other legal writers, and the words they wrote derived from textual formulas set out in laws and in legal manuals.[3] Take, as an example, the boilerplate for a civil case from the popular 1736 *Instruction for Scribes in the Judicial Realm, Also Useful to Procurators and Litigants*, reprinted several times during the century. It seems to demonstrate that an opening petition was one-size-fits-all. Litigants might pin and tuck a bit—inserting their names, adding detail about their conflict to the narrative, asking for something extra like special status before the court. But this was highly generic writing.

> [I], J. Doe, vecino of such a place, appear before Your Mercy and according to what is most fitting in Law, and say that N[ame], vecino of this City or Village, is obligated to pay me, give, do or complete such-and-such a thing for such reason, and I, having requested its compliance several times, have not been able to achieve it. Thus I ask and beg Your mercy to demand that said N[ame] to appear before you and to swear and declare as to the tenor of this petition . . .[4]

The seeming contradiction between litigant agency and the power of protocol can be reconciled if the lawsuit is viewed not as a singular entity reducible to its outcome but a staged process.[5] This process followed a typical sequence in which the litigant was active in the creation of the initial petition and early motions of the suit, later to be increasingly crowded out by legal officials. Therefore, rather than focus on the lawsuit as if it were a single-authored text such as a diary or a novel, or even a drama with multiple actors, the lawsuit can be analyzed in stages and pages.

This chapter reads lawsuits precisely in this way, as a series of various phases and as a sequence of papers. The argument that unlettered litigants produced the Enlightenment through the practice of law rests, in the first instance, on knowing just how much litigants were able to participate in the law as an everyday practice. Holding the processes of suing still momentarily instead of focusing on change over time, it analyzes how petitions were submitted, who represented litigants, whether litigants authored or authorized various papers of their suits, and who paid for the cases. Within these topics, the discussion tacks back and forth between explaining how lawsuits were supposed to occur and how they actually happened. The point is to provide a history that accounts for both the limits the legal system imposed on ordinary litigants and the authority they managed to exert over their cases. In this history of "powers" and "agents," litigants might not have written their suits but nonetheless are their main protagonists.

Powers: The Paper and the Protocol

Remaining in control of a suit was no easy task. In the Spanish empire, written laws and legal manuals tightly scripted, down the minutia, the procedure for suing. They specified how parties should be notified of accusations against them, the number of days that could elapse between actions, formal procedures and regulations for appointing legal representatives, and even how much a judge should say about the rationale for his decision. Certainly, laws were ignored and rules flouted, and procedure and wording varied by region. But litigants and legal representatives in the empire followed prescribed procedure for civil suits with impressive uniformity. Those basic rules dictated not only what a suit would say but also on what and by whom.

If it began according to plan, a civil suit started on a piece of paper, preferably paper bearing the royal seal. *Papel sellado*, as it was known, came in various stocks, each to be used for different kinds of official business. Judges' rulings (*autos*) and interim and final sentences (*fallos* or *sentencias definitivas*) were to be written on the highest grades of paper, as were some of the pages of witness testimony. But initial petitions came in on paper of the third degree of quality, which in the eighteenth century cost a peso a page.[6] If the plaintiff was one of the "solemn poor," the official category of poor determined by the court, or was considered an "Indian," the cheapest official paper, of the fourth grade, or paper simply stamped with the "*sello de oficio*" of a notary would suffice.[7] A special decree in 1639 stipulated that native complaints could not be nullified on the grounds that they had been submitted on regular paper.[8] The first page of each subsequent filing, most consisting of back-and-forth motions, also were to be made on grade-four papel sellado, but the follow-up pages could be composed on ordinary paper (*papel común*).[9] The official design of the seal on the paper changed every two years and thus always bore two dates, ensuring both that it presented the most current royal insignia and that its sale would bring steady royal profits. While officials in most districts made efforts to keep the paper current, a shortage of papel sellado plagued more remote areas of the empire. For this reason in 1807 the town officials of Tontontepec in Villa Alta submitted a complaint on old sheet of papel sellado dated 1794.[10]

As illustrated earlier, the writing of the petition, as the opening "act," or *auto*, frequently took place outside the court.[11] The plaintiff (or her representative) would then submit the document produced there—called by various names, including a *memorial*, a *demanda*, and a *pedido*—to offices generally located in the central plaza of a city or town. Yet even in a capital city like Lima, the "court" could still be a metaphor. In a 1794 guide to the city of Lima, José Hipólito Unanue listed the names of all court personnel, including lawyers and court

officials, as well as "the streets and houses where they live in the places corresponding to their employment, and they should be sought out there."[12] Thus,
although the physical building of the courts sat in the city square, the point was
to put the petition in the hands of the proper person. That judges were said to
have "seen" (*vistos los autos*) rather than to have "heard" most motions in a case
reveals how law was conceived of as the circulation of texts.

If the court was in a sizable and important district, the opening petition
would be turned over to an official whose job it was to receive such paper (the
receptor); otherwise, it would to go to the court notary. The official verified the
procedural accuracy of the petition with the words "before me" and his signature. Most litigants submitted initial petitions that reached almost to the bottom of the back of one sheet of paper, leaving space for the notary to sign on
the verso side. This kept papel sellado costs low. The court notary also might
enter a few lines on behalf of the presiding judge, who, if the complaint was
provisionally accepted, would generally order that the petition be communicated to the opposing party (*dar traslado*). The opposing party, in turn, had the
opportunity to respond within a period of three days. If, for established legal
reasons, the opposing party needed more time, she could submit a petition for
an extension.

Unless the judge ruled that the initial complaint "has no place [in law]" (*no
tiene lugar*, or *no ha lugar*), the suit began once the defendant responded.[13] Along
the way, the judge or panel of magistrates rendered interim decisions in the margins of the first pages of petitions and motions, facilitating the efficient review of
what could become lengthy paper exchanges. For the parties involved, the objective eventually was to accumulate evidence in the form of documentary proof
and witness testimony (*probanzas*) and to discredit the opponent's evidence
and witnesses. At this stage, holding onto the collected papers of the suit was an
effective way to commandeer a case. At the end, lawyers for the two sides would
make grand final arguments resting their cases upon towers of cited written law
or revered works of legal commentators. These final arguments were sometimes
delivered before a public audience of the judge or panel of judges. In the civil
law tradition, in which justice was to be fitted to the particularities of each case
rather than precedent, judges were not supposed to divulge too much of their
legal thinking. So the magistrate rendered his ruling with a few curt words stating which side best proved its case and spelled out the general details of the
settlement.

Still, getting to the end of a suit took a while, to say the least. Roughly two-
thirds of cases registered in the empire dragged out for over a year. At least a
tenth of them would go on for more than a decade.[14] A sentence would be rendered only after a great deal of delay and wrangling, during which at any point
the case might simply slip into the category of "*casos olvidados*" (forgotten suits).

Part of the reason suits took so long was procedural. Each petition and each response had to be communicated to the opposing party, and the judge ruled on each of these individual motions and requests, again usually on the margins of the pages. High court magistrates presided over public hearings only for three hours during set workdays, usually in the morning, hearing oral arguments and considering written motions, and they returned in the afternoon to make rulings. However, judges enjoyed quite a few holidays for saints' feasts, holy days, civil processions, and the like.[15] What is more, the court notary signed each new motion and went personally to the parties to read them any interim decisions that came down from the bench.

Perhaps the majority of motions in a case were requests for more time or complaints about the failure of the opposing side to respond. Spanish law itself allowed for the fact that ignoring a suit was a standard strategy and had a built-in tolerance for a certain number of instances of "*rebeldía*," or failure to respond to the court.[16] One had to "rebel" against the court quite a few times before being considered "in contempt."[17]

It was obvious why defendants might dodge a summons. Yet plaintiffs sometimes let their own suits fizzle out because they were not an end in itself but rather maneuvers to bend opposing parties into quicker, if exasperated, out-of-court settlements.[18] In this respect, many suits were what might be called "nuisance suits." In any event, if just one of the parties was persistent, paper would pile up, calendar pages would fly by, and entries would multiply in the account ledgers of the various legal officials who collected fees for their work.

Not just anyone could be a litigant. There was a detailed list of who could go to civil court, established primarily in the thirteenth-century law code the *Siete Partidas* of King Alfonso X of Castile. Slaves were only supposed to appear in civil courts on their own behalf for their freedom. The excommunicated, the demented, the mute, and the "totally" deaf were excluded, just as they were restricted from becoming lawyers.[19] The exclusion of the mute and the deaf, residuals from Roman law, signal the continued importance of orality in the legal culture in the Spanish empire.[20]

While law did not necessarily transpire in the courtroom of modern imaginings, it did take place out loud as well as on paper. Parties and legal personnel quite literally talked over the writing of the suit; judges made verbal orders or suggestions and called in opposing parties for semi-formal chats; court notaries went out to inform litigants of a development in a case and might become embroiled in a conversation that had bearing on the suit. Petitions, then, were not always inaugural texts but often surrounded by unwritten legal encounters— a toast with lemonade that sealed a business deal, for example. Spanish imperial inhabitants had a word for this parallel legal world of speech and summary judgments: *lo extrajudicial.*

Remaining prejudices about who could sue were less about speaking and writing than about the patriarchal order of society. Written law limited the civil juridical personality of several categories of dependents—minors under the age of 25, married women, slaves, and eventually natives. But Spanish law did counter legal constraints on categories of people who were considered less than full juridical subjects by providing them some advantage in their clashes with superiors. Married women could sue their husbands for mismanagement of dowries or abuse in civil courts; minors could go to court against parents to be emancipated or to bring charges of mistreatment; and slaves could sue for mistreatment or for false enslavement. If petitioners fell into a protected category known as "*casos de corte*," which included the "solemn poor," widows, slaves, and minors, their civil suits could bypass the lower courts and be heard by the highest court available, the audiencias.[21]

After conquest, medieval legal categories of dependency, grouped under the status of "*miserables*," provided the basis for natives' special legal treatment in court, and eventually slaves' legal protection as well.[22] In the sixteenth century, special institutional channels were established as alternatives for indigenous litigants, called the General Indian Court in Mexico and the Defender of Natives in Peru, replete with named personnel for representing native cases.[23] Most of these legally dependent groups also had other jurisdictional privileges, were to receive counsel pro bono from designated legal representatives, and were to be exempt from certain court costs.[24]

Thus the experience of being a "litigant" could vary. It could involve invoking justice by right or seeking protection and gratis representation. It could range from a long-term commitment to a temporary move in protracted disputes that mostly took place outside tribunals. Even after a case entered the legal system, the litigant usually had to exhibit active engagement to ensure it was carried through.

That is not to say that litigants represented themselves. After the initial petition had been submitted, legal personnel increasingly determined its future. Their control was even more pronounced if the litigant fell into one of the protected legal categories of imperial subjects, such as the indigenous and minors, who were to be represented pro bono. But both paying and nonpaying litigants needed lawyers to direct their cases. Soon after the opposing party responded to the initial petition, litigant and defendant were to turn their cases over to legal representatives.

Two types of lawyers handled cases: procurators (*procuradores de número*) and attorneys of the court (*abogados de número*).[25] While both were licensed to practice law and both occupied a limited number of posts in each district court, abogados were more highly educated professionals, holding post-baccalaureate degrees, and thus enjoyed greater prestige and pay. The abogados stepped in at the end of the suit to offer final arguments, drawing from their broader command of Roman, canon, and Spanish written law and local legal practice. Procurators, on the other hand, steered cases through to this final phase. After being named, they drew up the majority of the documents that clients submitted, set the strategy of the suit, and often composed the questionnaires used to interview witnesses.

Litigants turned authority over to legal representatives in official documents called *poderes* (lit: "powers," or powers of attorney).[26] Poderes for lawyers usually were specific to the case while general powers-of-attorney were used in other instances, as when someone who lived in the countryside named another to take care of his legal business in the city. Technically, litigants naming a legal representative—whether lawyers or others—were to submit an official, notarized power-of-attorney to the court to be included with the rest of the autos. In practice, it was not unusual for these poderes to be kept separately from the case, filed in the tall ledgers of the public notary who authored the contract.

Litigants sometimes began suits with no idea who would represent them and frequently found reason to switch legal representatives in the middle of a suit. As a result, they conveniently failed to turn over their "powers" in writing, saving themselves both the pesos the notary would charge for contracting a representative and the trouble of formally naming a new one.

Official representatives did not have a monopoly on the written legal word, and various other writers milled around the courts. The very diversity of amanuenses available to potential litigants has made it difficult to figure out who did the writing in many parts of legal cases, especially the first pages. In the Italian's picaresque scene of the Mexican woman and the "public scribe" in Figure 1.1, the artist indicates that the scribe was a licensed professional, but the transient nature of his office is less suggestive of a licensed public notary than of the numerous unlicensed petition-writers who operated in the cities of the empire.

The highest-ranking official legal writer was the court notary (*escribano de corte, de cámara, del cabildo*). His job, in a manner of speaking, was to make the case as he collated papers into *los autos*, the lawsuit.[27] He testified to the legitimacy of petitions, motions, and judges' interim rulings by co-signing them. He personally often went out into the community to notify the parties of developments, took witness depositions, and kept the archives of the case. The position of court notary was coveted: even the high court of Lima only had two official *escribanos de cámara* in each of the single criminal and civil salas. But it took far more than two men to accomplish all the legal work of a high court, so their offices employed assistant writers, variously called *escribanos habilitados* (authorized scribes), *plumeros* (quill-men), and *escribientes* (scriveners).

In addition to the court notaries and their assistants, most larger cities and towns counted a number of public notaries. They had been trained and certified

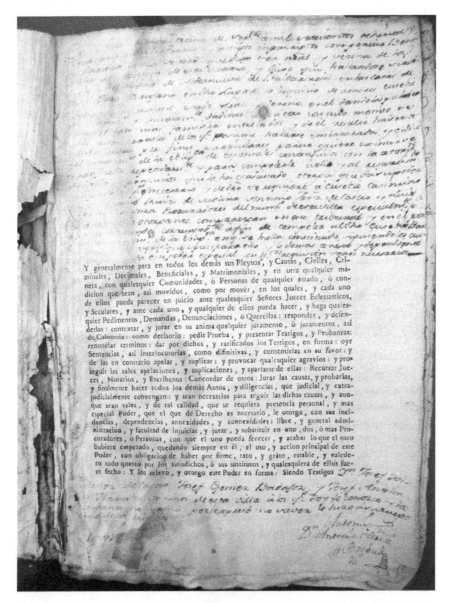

Figure 1.3 The increasing use of print in the late eighteenth century meant that many standard notarial documents came ready-made, as did this 1785 *poder*, or power of attorney, for a Church suit over the fulfillment of marital vows aired in the Bishopric of Toledo. Note the amount of additional information that the notary added above and below the printed standard formula, making this document an excellent example of the interplay between the particular and the generic in legal writing. Reproduced by permission from Esponsales de Aldeanueva de Balbarroia, Talavera, Procesos, 1785, Archivo Diocesano de Toledo.

to produce the thousands of pages of contracts collected in every archive in the region. The functions of public notaries included filling out wills, bills of sale, and I.O.U.s—sheets of thin white paper containing millions of written lines that drew the various regions of Spain's vast empire into one legal system. The expertise of public notaries was such that procurators often trained at their sides, especially in the eighteenth century as practical experience was increasingly integrated into legal education.[28] In areas of the empire where legal personnel were scarce, such as Trujillo and the Montes de Toledo, public notaries frequently functioned as de facto procurators for litigants.[29]

Indeed, the lack of literate and trained personnel in the countryside meant anyone associated with the legal system might be roped into writing a petition.[30] Even Spanish judges in isolated regions could be called upon to help craft or accept an initial petition opening a suit. When natives representing the pueblo of Choapán showed up one December day in 1742 in the district capital of Villa Alta, Oaxaca, to file a suit claiming their community elections had been rigged, they found that there was no public or court notary within twenty-four leagues of the city. The personal assistant of the magistrate of the jurisdiction, the *alcalde mayor*, served as their scribe and the magistrate himself formally received the suit.[31]

Theoretically, the natives of Choapán should have had access to a scribe earlier. Each indigenous town council was supposed to count among its officials a notary responsible for recording local records and annals, and in Mexico these often were kept in indigenous languages.[32] Native-language criminal testimony and some civil cases in Oaxaca reveal that there existed a cadre of indigenous intellectuals well trained in Spanish legal procedure.[33] While the role of writer/advocate for native communities varied by region and differed between the Viceroyalties of New Spain and Peru, in general the indigenous scribe can be viewed as a combination of court and public notary and legal adviser. He kept the records of the community, but he often also served as the primary counsel for its people, shaping petitions and complaints for Spanish jurisdictions. Many were called upon to sign edicts and other documents for native community officials. For example, the governor of the pueblo of Tabáa, in Villa Alta, inartfully signed a document in 1783 only because, he reported, "my scribe is sick."[34]

Native scribes' intermediate position between community advocate and colonial functionary drew the suspicion of more than one village in the eighteenth century.[35] Indigenous notaries, in this respect, were similar to non-indigenous notaries and procurators, whose control over legal papers gave them margin to play with the truth and, as a result, opened them to depiction as shady characters.[36] At least in theory, however, a strong code of honor bound licensed legal writers.[37] Handbooks for scribes, notaries, and lawyers of all stripes—produced throughout the centuries but appearing with ever more frequency in the eighteenth century—universally emphasized the importance of professional integrity.[38]

Manual writers had an interest in ensuring that litigants as well as professionals followed the rules, particularly the rules that pointed to their own indispensability as official, licensed personnel.[39] For example, Josef Juan y Colom, writer of the popular 1736 *Instruction to Scribes*, felt he could not overemphasize the critical importance of the official poder to name a procurator.[40] Another eighteenth-century manual writer, this one a Mexican, neglected to provide the formula of a civil petition at all, but in his list of formats for various legal documents he put the power of attorney for a procurator at the very top.[41] Alonso Villadiego Vascuñana y Montoya's *Instruction in Judicial Policy and Practice, Conforming to the Style of the Councils*, perhaps the most widely-known legal manual in the empire, stipulated that naming a procurator constituted one of only five elements that legitimized an initial petition, though other manuals omitted the requirement to name a procurator as part of an opening petition and prescribed it for a later point in the suit.[42]

Both the formulaic nature of legal writing and these manuals' insistence on the centrality of official personnel give the impression that litigants fed their complaints to the paper machinery of the imperial justice system rather quickly. However, looking closely at the lawsuit as a series of phases, many initiated or shaped by the litigant, shows that this was not necessarily true. Litigants could control many aspects of their cases, from the forum in which they were heard to who penned them, and from the naming of an attorney to the pace of subsequent filings.

Agents: Litigant Options and Authorship

The first decision that litigants faced was where to file a complaint. The Spanish legal system comprised several competing jurisdictions, and litigants could claim privileged access to courts based not only on belonging to a protected legal category, as with widows and natives, but also on their corporate membership in bodies such as the military or the clergy.

A hypothetical woman of an indeterminate amount of indigenous ancestry, living on the outskirts of Mexico City and married to an *español* militiaman, could activate a range of options that did not involve going before a judge to settle her domestic dispute. She could complain to his parents, to her female neighbors, to their parish priest. However, if these options failed to bring peace to her marriage, she could take her husband to court. If she presented herself as an "*india*," she could appeal to Mexico's General Indian Court for free.[43] If she presented herself as a mestiza, she would gain access to a court that did not hear cases involving natives: the Holy Office of the Inquisition. But here her case would have to involve crimes against religion, so she might lodge a complaint about, say, how her husband's mistress seduced him with love magic. She could go to a royal criminal judge to report her husband for being physically abusive, or she could sue him in royal civil court for dissipating her dowry. In both of the prior scenarios involving royal courts, she would have to choose whether to file before a municipal authority (*alcalde*) or a district judge (*corregidor* or *alcalde mayor*). And she had still more options. She could complain to her husband's superior in military court where he enjoyed the privilege of jurisdictional membership (*fuero*) based on his participation in the corporate body. Finally, she could decide to end the marriage altogether by entering ecclesiastical court, where she would face the further option of filing for either a marital annulment or *divorcio* (Church-sanctioned separation).

The variety of judges and types of suits available to litigants meant that they could pit jurisdictions against each other in order to gain advantage in a dispute or search for the court where they could achieve their best outcome—practices sometimes referred to as "jurisdictional jockeying" or "forum shopping."[44] Conflict over jurisdiction was a pronounced feature of Spain's peninsular legal culture, but it reached particular intensity in the legal culture of the Spanish American colonies. Fighting over jurisdiction was, in a sense, how colonial inhabitants practiced politics.[45] Through jurisdictional disputes, the powerful gained access to resources and labor, and symbolically refortified, time and again, the hierarchy of authority between the crown, the Church, and various other corporate powers.

Beyond jurisdictional choices, litigants also had options in the medium for submitting their complaints. Until now the complaint has been referred to as an "opening petition." However, in Spanish, there were several names assigned this piece of paper or act: *demanda, pedimiento, memorial, libelo.* Although legal manuals locked in the generic constraints of the opening petition, and although most petitions submitted to the court came in on the appropriate *papel sellado* and accorded with prescribed form, this obscures the multiple ways that imperial subjects actually produced them.

Some litigants showed up at the court with a complaint to voice but otherwise empty-handed. In fact, many plaintiffs lodged their complaints verbally. The authors of legal manuals tried, of course, to undermine the legality of verbal complaints since they eliminated the middlemen—namely, them. Manual writer Juan y Colom, in treating the broad category of a *"demanda,"* or complaint, allowed that there existed a law that permitted judges to admit verbal complaints, "but the [current] practice is to only admit it if it is in writing, which we commonly call a *pedimiento.*" Thus he attempted to fix the definition of a *demanda* to paper, defining it as "a brief writing that the plaintiff presents in court against a defender."[46]

Court personnel were responsible transferring verbal complaints to writing when litigants came in without a petition.[47] In some instances, they drew up the documents themselves; in others, they sent the litigant to local writers whose professional expertise and grasp of law ran the gamut. The original petitions in some suits were penned as letters to the judge—primarily complaints from rural areas where access to papel sellado, official legal writers, and the cash to pay for either was in short supply. It is often easy to detect the creases where they had been folded up into a small square for delivery to a far-away magistrate.[48] Informally called "*esquelitas*" (notes), after these papers were accepted as legal petitions they were known as "*memoriales*." Court notaries and receptors sometimes helped align these documents with legal protocol.

Literate litigants might, from time to time, pen their own papers. For example, when in 1799 the Spanish immigrant Don Antonio de Espineira was thrown out of his room in a Lima boarding house for falling behind on rent, he himself seems to have written most of the petitions he filed to reclaim his seized belongings.[49] Having been employed as an accountant of rare gems earlier in life, he probably had more exposure to official writing than the average imperial inhabitant. Most litigants came ready to sue armed with papers written by someone else.

The identity of those petition writers is often hidden. The memorial for the indigenous litigant Juan Francisco of Villa Alta shown in Figure 1.4 contained only the name of the litigant. However, that signature matched the handwriting of the text, indicating that the litigant could not write and that the writer signed it for him.[50]

While this Oaxacan memorial was quite typical in that it ends in the name of the litigant alone without revealing the identity of the writer, this was only one of many possibilities. Sometimes the petition writer signed his own name, occasionally accompanied by "*a ruego de*," or "at the request of" the petitioner. This most frequently happened when the writer was a legal counselor, namely, a procurator. It is also easy to see which petitions procurators or attorneys wrote by analyzing the text since they usually referred to clients in the third person.[51] Alternately, both the petition writer and the litigant might sign their own names to a first-person petition, or the litigant would etch out a cross ("+") as a signature. Other times, the petition writer explicitly stated that the client "*no sabe firmar*" (does not know how to sign), whether or not the writer was identified.[52]

In one other category of written petitions, the petitioner would sign an anonymously composed document in her own hand. Consider a petition in the case of Doña María Micaela Vega (Figure 1.5), who was in a Mexico City court suing her husband. This was the end of a motion she submitted well after her case was underway. Like the initial petition, it was written in the first person and it

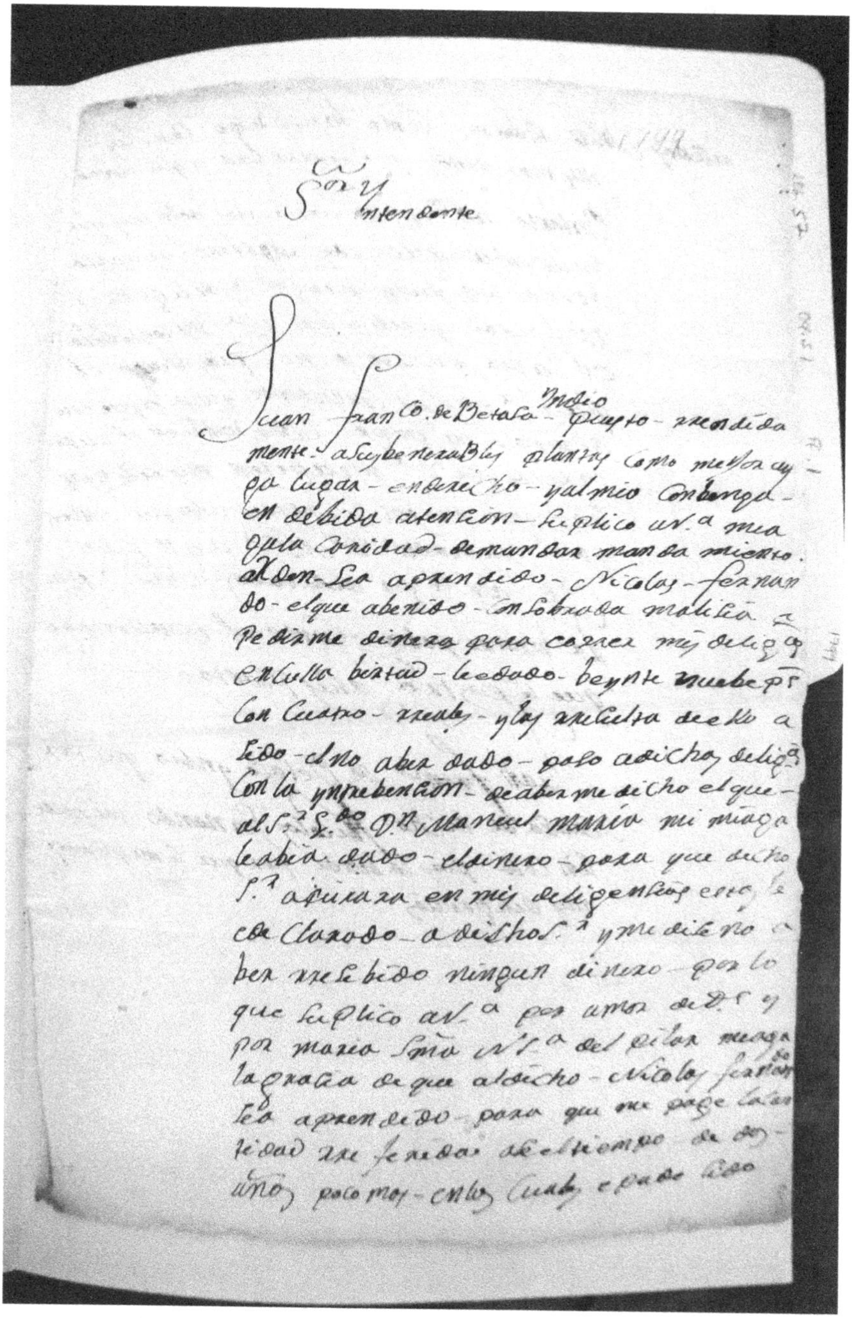

Figure 1.4 Native litigant Juan Francisco addresses a memorial to the intendant of Villa Alta, Oaxaca, in a unfolded, letter-like petition on ordinary paper. Note the absence of a last name but the regional identifying marker "from Betanza"; also note the writer (or reader) added the word "*Yndio*" (Indian) above the initial script. Reproduced by permission from Juan Francisco del pueblo de Betaza solicita, que Nicolás Fernando sea aprehendido, por pedirle dinero para seguir sus diligencias y no le ha pagado, Archivo del Poder Ejecutivo del Estado de Oaxaca, Intendencia, Villa Alta, Legajo 57, expediente 51, f. 1, 1799.

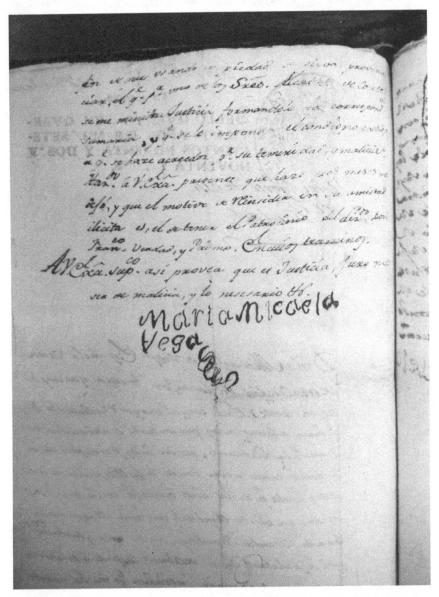

Figure 1.5 A female litigant's shaky signature on a petition. Reproduced by permission from Doña Micaela de Vega, contra su marido D. Pedro Camaño, por malos tratamientos, Archivo General de la Nación-Mexico, Civ, vol. 2045, exp. 11.

contained no traces of the identity of the individual who penned it, though this person clearly was not María Micaela, whose clunky signature reveals her discomfort in wielding the quill. That she signed the petition is no guarantee that she knew how to read it.[53]

The insistent imperfection of María Micaela's signature at the bottom of almost every petition in her case enhances rather than diminishes their legal integrity. Although literacy conferred cultural mastery to urban *"letrados,"* this did not mean that all authority flowed from artful ink.[54] A shaky signature or a weak grasp of writing and even reading certainly was no barrier to possessing power in the eighteenth-century Spanish empire. Consider Figure 1.6. It displays the middle of a court process that village authorities in Navalpino, Spain, brought against a man for living with a woman out of wedlock. Bernardo Pérez's poor signature makes María Micaela's look like a Michelangelo. He was not a party in this case but the *alcalde pedeano,* or magistrate of first instance in the village.

In the broader Spanish legal culture, then, even legal officials could have difficulty writing, and in its writing culture, it was common to delegate to a third party the writing of not just petitions and contracts but also love letters and notes. As a result, writers for hire were everywhere, especially in the cities. Litigants' use of unlicensed, often anonymous legal agents to craft their initial petitions clashed with the notion that writing petitions was the job of licensed procurators. Even the manual writer Villadiego Vascuñana, who otherwise insisted on the

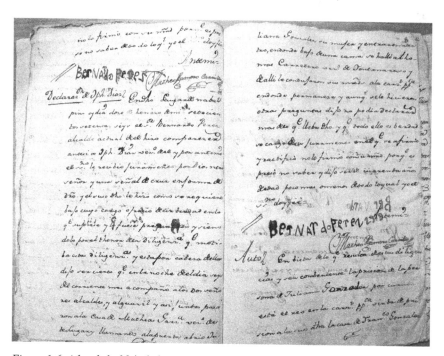

Figure 1.6 A local alcalde's shaky signature in a criminal case brought by town authorities. Reproduced by permission from Proceso por amancebamiento abierto de oficio contra Tomás Carretero, Archivo Histórico de la Municipalidad de Toledo, Criminal, Navalpino, 6328/3769, 1776, ff. 3v–4.

importance of court-appointed official writers, conceded that litigants could not be compelled to hire a *procurador* against their will.[55]

In the seventeenth century, King Felipe IV tried to rein in anonymous amanuenses by replacing them with a restricted number of supervised "business agents" (*agentes de negocios*).[56] But unlicensed legal writers would not disappear. Disparagingly called "*agentes intrusos*" (intrusive agents), "*tinterillos*" (little ink spillers) or "*picapleitos*" (pettifoggers), their numbers in the cities grew throughout the eighteenth century.

Given how much of the archive these shadowy legal agents created as they scratched out petitions and motions before the lawyers got involved, it is remarkable that most parties remained silent about their identities. The narrative practice that reigned throughout the empire made many legal documents, particularly those submitted at the beginning of suits, appear as the unmediated words of the litigants. It is true that Spanish officials repeatedly insisted that petition writers sign their names to the papers they filed.[57] Court notaries and receptors were reminded not to accept filings where the name of the writer did not appear. Yet no one paid much attention; receptors and court notaries kept taking petitions without the names of the writers appended.

Sometimes, however, the identity of the agent peeks through. When agents signed their own names, they often demonstrated that they held bachelor's or master's degrees by using their title as a prefix, usually as "*licdo*," or "*licenciado*." Many of these educated men were ad-hoc procurators, trained in the law and engaged in piecework paperwork but not officially assigned to a case. Among those who displayed their titles, they typically demonstrated a level of education that matched, and at times surpassed that achieved by official procurators of the court, who by the eighteenth century often held only a bachelor's degree.[58] Thus these educated individuals occupied a kind of parallel legal world where they were legal agents but technically not "procurators" by trade.[59]

Agents who failed to sign their names to petitions could be of more humble background. When a group of agentes de negocios moved to convert their positions into official posts in Mexico City in 1747, they excluded several kinds of petition writers known to be working in the city, including the *mulato* slave of an older, respected agente de negocio who could no longer work, four natives, a person of "unknown quality," and five priests. Indeed, priests of the regular orders seem to have provided a good deal of legal advice to commoner litigants. In 1668, King Carlos II complained of cloister-breaking monks who were "introducing themselves in the business and dependencies of the secular world (*el siglo*), under the title of agents or procurators or solicitors of the Realms, communities, relatives or unrelated persons."[60]

These diverse writers operated in a kind of underground legal circuit, or what Kathryn Burns calls "the back alleys of the 'lettered city.' "[61] The African-born slave Agustín Carabali, who charged his owner with abuse in civil court, wandered through these literary alleys in Lima in 1790, though how he navigated them is unclear. When a court notary quizzed Agustín about who had written the petition he submitted to the alcalde of Lima, he found the slave's explanation to be as labyrinthine as the capital's back streets. The notary did his best to render intelligible what the slave, who was "entirely *bozal* [African-born] and *chacarero* [field-worker]," said.[62] What he could piece together is that Agustín slipped away from the Hacienda of Collique, which his mistress owned, and had a petition drawn up accusing her of the "most cruel tyranny." The slave claimed that he did not know the original petition writer at all, not even his name, and only knew that he lived somewhere on a main street in the city. Apparently, the rough language or legal faults of the petition caught the eye of the court receptor when Agustín attempted to submit it, so the receptor told the slave to have the petition re-written by an escribano. He also gave him an accompanying note to take to the scribe.

Somehow, Agustín ended up on the other side of the Rimác River, knocking on the door of a one-room corn beer tavern run by a black woman from Trujillo. A *negro criollo* named José, who rented a room in the house of one of the city's licensed attorneys, was a frequent customer. Presumably, José's residence with the lawyer gave him access to legal knowledge, and he told Agustín he could re-write the petition and make it more formal. He rendered the petition in the third person and signed at the end with squiggles and flourishes that replicated the coat-of-arms a public notary might use to distinguish his signature. It appears that the receptor accepted this second, more elaborate but still rough copy, making a few amendments and grammatical corrections. And it would have sufficed if Agustín's owner had not challenged its legality.

To be sure, anonymous writers were not always anonymous to the litigant, as Agustín claimed his first agent was. The writer might be a relative, acquaintance, or patron who chose not to sign. A *negra criolla* named Andrea testified the year after Agustín's suit that when she filed a civil case over the custody and purchase of her enslaved daughter, she had asked the husband of her daughter's caretaker, Don Tomás Domínguez, to craft her petitions for her until the court appointed her a pro bono lawyer. She swore:

> that neither Don Tomás nor his wife had provided her other protection than to draw up, at the many pleas of the litigant, the said writings, and the testifier does not know how to write and thus cannot sign, but neither does she know who signed them for [her] but [does know] that she was in charge of the case since it concerns her . . .[63]

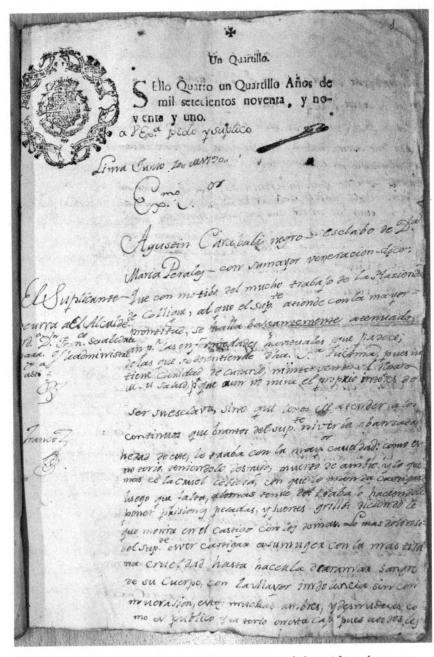

Figure 1.7 An opening petition submitted by Agustín Carabeli, an African-born, non-literate slave, who sued his owner for abuse. Note the minor corrections in spelling and the insertion of formalities such as "A V[uestra] Ex[celenci]a" (to Your Excellency), presumably placed by the court receptor who had originally turned back Agustín's first petition. Reproduced by permission from Autos seguidos por Agustín Caraveli [sic], esclavo de Dna. Mariá Perales, sobre sevicia, Archivo General de la Nación-Perú, RA, Civ., Leg. 289, C. 2568-B, 1790, f. 1v.

Andrea's insistence that she still was "in charge of the case since it concerns her" even though she did not write or sign her petition is key. Again and again, litigants made sure to emphasize that, even when others did the writing for them, they managed their lawsuits. More than the mere words written in them, lawsuits were coordinated events requiring their involvement. In a sense, the litigant could be the author of a suit but not its writer.[64]

Sometimes writers were relatives, especially the fathers or brothers of female litigants. In one instance, a woman suing her husband later claimed that she purposely refrained from signing a petition because it had been written for her under duress from her father.[65] Others were family intimates such as a local priest or lower-level official who had an interest in a case. More than once, women divorcing men or bringing abuse charges against them were accused of conspiring with local officials or notaries.[66]

In fact, when a man wrote up legal papers for a woman, it often aroused suspicions about the woman's sexual propriety. In at least one case, the suspicions were founded. The slave Juana Portocarrera admitted that she had been having an affair with a mulato surgeon named José Ferrones. She claimed it was only after their romantic encounters that she discovered from talking to a washerwoman that he was knowledgeable in lawsuits and had helped various slaves in the city take masters to court for abuse. Juana asked him to write her petitions for her so that she could be sold to a new owner. José responded that "it would cost her some dough (*plata*) because when he wrote for the others he was compensated with their work."[67] Since she had no money he agreed to write hers for free, "moved by charity and without any interest."

The possible exchange of romance for writing between Juana and José might seem to call into question the authenticity of Juana's allegations of abuse or even the "truth" of the suit overall. Juana was aware of this. She took pains to explain that José had read the contents of the petitions to her out loud, that after he began to work as her legal agent they no longer carried on their sexual affair, and that he never promised to free her, only that he would help her achieve sale to another owner. These claims were intended to mitigate the seeming partiality that her relationship with her writer implied and to emphasize that the substance of the suit was not the intellectual work of another but her own.

Thus even if protocol dictated that lawyers were to take over early in the case, legal agents—unlicensed, unidentified, sometimes hired counselors-cum-penmen, some priests, others lovers, a few drinking buddies—remained involved well into the middle of the case. Together, litigant and agent worked out strategy and filed motions until, or even in some cases beyond, the point when a power of attorney was signed. In the back-and-forth of the early phases of the suit, when it was uncertain how the case would proceed—Was the suit itself lawful? Would a slave litigant be bonded during the course of the case? Would a wife enter a convent during a marital dispute?—naming lawyers got lost in the shuffle, leaving litigants as both the initiators of the suit and their textual protagonists.

Litigants were the textual protagonists of lawsuits in another sense. Many legal narratives in a civil case, especially the early ones, were written in the first person, even though everyone in the legal system understood that very few litigants or defendants would write their own briefs or petitions. Yet amanuenses persisted in writing in the voice of the litigant. The narrative consequence of using the first person was to portray litigant and defendant as acting as free-willed actors.[68] So while petitions did not necessarily contain litigants' exact words, the inhabitants of the Spanish empire nonetheless held fast to the notion that these texts represented litigants' legal position.

In part, that legal position was predicated on the virtue of their legal argument. Traditional jurisprudence in the Spanish empire was founded on the notion that the "*yo*" on each side of a lawsuit possessed a "truth" and a "justice" to himself or herself. The judges' role was not to "apply the law," as in modern formalist systems, but rather to find in written law and commentators' analysis the source of justice that best nourished each side of the case, based on the position of the litigant.

The legal position implied in the "*yo*" at the beginning of a petition was also a reference to the litigant's social placement. The proclamation of personhood in the first lines of a petition was followed by other identifying coordinates on which the reader/judge could locate the social place of the speaker/litigant— namely, genealogical, sacramental, social caste, and regional markers. It was always "I, Juana, *española*, legitimate wife of so-and-so of such a trade, natural of such-and-such a place, appear before you . . ."[69]

Whatever the preset formula for positioning oneself as litigant, official, licensed legal writers came to rely quite heavily on the groundwork legal agents and litigants laid in those early petitions written in the first person. Petitions on papel sellado frequently repeated the exact wording that a litigant had been presented in a prior, more informal letter or memorial accepted by the court. In the Chancellería de Valladolid, lawyers submitted many formal demandas in marital disputes that copied verbatim the wording of an earlier narrative.[70] The procedure for this high court seems to have followed quite closely the notarial protocol that held a first-person pedimiento to be distinct from an attorney-authored demanda, and that not until the second was submitted was a case kicked off. Even in this more formal order of things, the lawyers' words depended on the litigants' words, not the other way around.

Consider the case a slave brought against his master for abuse shown in Figure 1.8. The uneven fading of the ink over time and cramming of letters into a small space exposes the fact that the writer clearly had written a version

Figure 1.8 An anonymous legal writer subsequently fills in, with different ink, the names of the parties and signs for the slave litigant in a lawsuit that slave Luis Mariano Amusquibar brought against owner Don Mariano Rodríguez, Reproduced by permission from Causa seguida por Luis Mariano Amusquibar, esclavo de Don Mariano Rodríguez, sobre sevicia, Archivo General de la Nación- Perú, RA, Civ.; Leg. 192; C. 1628-A, 1775, f. 14.

of the petition without having knowledge of the names of either the slave litigant or the master defendant, which got filled in later. This petition did not appear until the fourteenth page of the suit. It was written in the voice of the slave, and an attorney who had already been assigned to the case did not sign it. There were so many pens on this slave's suit by the fourteenth page that the writer appeared to have access to the details of the case—the abuse that the slave Luis Mariano claimed and the story of his incarceration in a bakery— but not his name. Where did he get this information? Presumably from the very first petition ever presented in the case: a small piece of ordinary paper addressed to the viceroy of Peru, requesting a superior decree to name the slave an attorney.

In lower-level courts throughout the empire, many original petitions appear at the beginning of the autos, or they are tucked in alongside statements re-written by court scribes or presented in the name of high-powered attorneys. Such was the case with Doña Inés de Matamoros's letter to the alcalde of Mexico in 1790. Though an official demand signed by her and endorsed by her procurator is

filed at the front of her autos, thirty pages into the case dossier her original petition appears, written at an earlier date, seemingly in her own handwriting. It
is in the form of a letter, signed "your surrendered servant," and it contains an
almost identical version of the statement that she and her procurator later had
drawn up and signed.[71] Don Antonio Ruiz's case against his wife for attempting
to poison him was similar. His original letter to the first-instance criminal judge,
written on ordinary paper and dated August 1800, appears deep within his legal
dossier, next to the more formal complaint he lodged a month later. Yet even
this second petition is something of a hybrid, an artifact of the transition from
informal letter to formal petition: the part of the paper bearing the seal of papel
sellado is actually sewn with thread onto this otherwise informal original missive to the judge.[72]

An assigned or hired lawyer might not even bother to pull out a fresh sheet
of paper when taking on a case. This included the lawyer of one woman who
initiated a suit before the Audiencia of Mexico against her Spanish immigrant
lover after he won the lottery in 1799. Her lawyer simply changed the "I's" in her
original petition to "my clients," and altered the ending of the verbs, originally
written in the first person, to match the third person. He did not catch all the
verbs, however, and thus left the petition a grammatical garble.[73]

While litigants had the greatest room for agency in the early part of a suit,
that space did not contract completely after a lawyer had been appointed.
A few cases reveal that litigants took, and retook, their cases into their own
hands when their representatives failed to move quickly enough for them or
made decisions that they disagreed with. In some instances, litigants simply
submitted motions penned by an agent to move matters along. Most of the
time, it seems that they were following the procurator's or lawyer's advice, as
in Figure 1.9 where the defendant Antonio Araburúa placed above his own signature the words "for my procurator" and signed the name of that procurator,
Baltasar de los Reyes. (The procurator's more flowery and practiced auto-
graph appears elsewhere in the case.) An indigenous petitioner from Santiago
de Cao on the north coast of Peru likewise signed his own name and "for my
procurator Alberto Chosop," the Procurador de Naturales for the Audiencia of
Lima, in a 1769 petition.[74]

Even when a procurator was doing the work, it could be clear that a litigant
was still in charge. A common practice in petitions was that a series of "tachas,"
or corrected errors made in the writing of a petition, would be noted at the end,
a practice especially common in Mexico City. Often, the tachas simply represented the corrections to errors in copies that a writer caught on his own. The
corrected words or letters would be listed at the end of the petition in a non-
sensical string, such as "on=8=v=r=gn=rro=vis=s=fi=x" preceded by the words
"amended" and followed by "okay" (vale).[75]

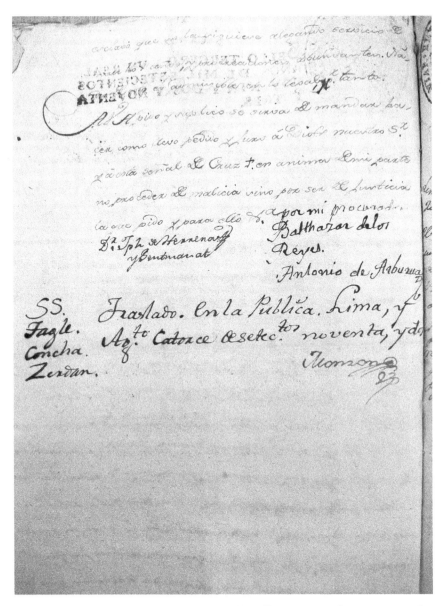

Figure 1.9 Litigant signs for procurator. Reproduced by permission from Autos seguidos por don Antonio Arburúa con su esclava, Andrea Escalante (sic Arburúa), sobre la libertad de ésta (sic; su hija), Archivo General de la Nación- Perú, RA Civ, Leg. 203, C. 2616, 1791, 19v.

The more substantive of these corrections reveal an ongoing narrative negotiation between litigant and legal counselor. As part of the process of reviewing a prewritten petition and signing off on it, a lawyer or court notary might correct the spelling or the names of litigants, which often could be mistaken or confused in an agent's version. Or a lawyer would reconcile breaches in the use of honorific titles for judges by making sure the right "your excellencies" and "your superiorities" were used with the proper magistrates, as Lima's receptor seems to have done with the African Agustín Carabali's second petition shown in Figure 1.8. But if a petition or motion was already composed, the lawyer was limited to making only a few small alterations or additions. Licenciado Manuel Fernández Pantaleón added the phrase "speaking with all due respect" to the petition the inhabitants of San Pablo de Cajones brought against the subdelegate of the Intendancy of Oaxaca in 1791. This was the best he could do to soften the defiant tone of the native community's already-composed petition, whose writer remained anonymous.[76]

When the writing of a petition was finished, it often was read aloud to the litigant, either immediately upon completion or after filing. In the former instance, this gave an involved petitioner the opportunity to make the writer go back and change features of the statement. Doña Marcelina Gutiérrez seems to have forced her petition writer to amend a motion to emphasize the illegal foundations of her opponent's case against her. The writer had to add whole phrases for this apparently literate and forceful litigant.[77] In other instances, after a petition had been submitted to the court, court notaries sought out the litigants to confirm that the petition belonged to them, ensuring they were "read [aloud] word-for-word."[78]

Many litigants continued to have access to agents and their writings even after a procurator and attorney had been named to their case. As a consequence, they could continue to direct the course of disputes by filing motions. It was possible, if rare, for a litigant to file legal papers against the advice of their attorneys. Doña María García of Mexico City, for example, peeled off from her Church divorce to appear before civil officials to accuse her husband of "*rebeldía*," or failure to turn over the documents of a conjugal suit in due time. She did this apparently without any advice from her chosen counsel. For various reasons, the legal move jeopardized her Church suit for divorce. Her lawyer attempted to clean up her legal mess before ecclesiastical authorities, but he never fully admitted that she had filed the secular suit without his approval. He withdrew the rebeldía charge, calling it "a spawn of my ignorance and brought to life by the seduction of a subject uninstructed in the law," and he called the petition "of little importance."[79]

By calling the petition "of little importance" and using such sexualized language, the lawyer was trying to minimize the impact of his female client's commandeering of her case. In a way, he was right. Doña María's renegade move into the secular court was not of monumental significance in that it did not undo her entire case. But Doña María's suit was important in other ways, namely because she explicitly argued that her husband should foot the legal bills for their marital dispute. Thus, in addition to revealing litigants' power to direct and even jeopardize their own suits, her case also draws attention to the contentious issue of who paid court costs and attorney fees. This was a matter of more than a "little importance" in the legal system of the empire.

"God Isn't Paying"

The fact that civil lawsuits cost money obviously meant that the law was more accessible to the rich than to the poor. This bias in the legal system deserves exploration with special, though not exclusive, attention to indigenous litigants. Because Spanish colonial officials often portrayed Indians as both wanton litigators and as hapless victims coerced into the court system, their lawsuits prove especially instructive for separating discourses about the cost of suits from the actual money exchanged.[80] Native lawsuits also illuminate whether money, like demands for legal literacy and generic rigidity actually prevented social subordinates from becoming litigants.

At the high court level of the Audiencia of Lima, an eighteenth-century inventory of cases from 1793–94 attests to the elevated social rank of litigators. The use of the high court was self-selecting, favoring corporate groups such as monasteries and Indian communities suing over hefty amounts. Among individuals, "dons" and "doñas" made up the great preponderance, and the vast majority of cases involved substantial sums of money. Out of a total of 620 hearings, only 23 involved cases brought forward by litigants who did not use an honorific title, and the presence of titled nobility such as marquis and counts is notable.[81]

So few ordinary litigants show up in the Audiencia inventory because many of this court's cases were appeals, and several had lasted until the very final stages of a dispute. Litigants undoubtedly weighed what they stood to gain in seeing a suit through to the end against the possibility that they would lose and be forced to pay court costs as a penalty.[82] A standard ending of opening petitions perfunctorily read " *ytem pido costas*" ("I ask for [the opposing party to pay] legal fees.") Litigants who persisted to sentencing or appeal were those who were willing to risk seeing this request denied and having to pay at least the legal costs they themselves incurred, not to mention potentially being penalized with the costs of their opponents' legal fees. Even a favorable sentence could be costly. As the famed Spanish Enlightenment thinker Benito Jerónimo Feijóo put it, in courts of law "the winner can end up the loser."[83]

Losing could cost a litigant indeed. Whether it was a marriage or real estate dispute, an average formal civil case brought to sentence in the Spanish empire would run most litigants around 200 pesos, including the various writings of scribes, judges, and lawyers.[84] By the late eighteenth century, when *litis expensas*, or court costs, became contentious grounds for secular civil suits between spouses in marriage disputes, 200 pesos was judged the standard fee that would cover a divorce or other civil domestic issues. This amount of money would purchase an African slave child in Lima, buy some 200 casks of Andean wine, or furnish a physician's salary for a month or a wet nurse's pay for a year.[85]

Of course, the actual cost litigants incurred ranged from a few pesos for a petition to hundreds of thousands for a decades-long civil suit. Quite a few litigants skipped out on their bills.[86] But once the case was taken into the formal system, prices were set in official pricelists (*aranceles*) issued for different regions and updated periodically. These lists spelled out the exact value of each written item or action, from the cost the receptor of the court levied to the judge's fees, from the delivery of motions to opposing parties to procurator's rates.[87] In Spanish these fees were called "*derechos*," which, being the same word as "rights," poetically underscores that justice could be contingent on paying up.

One of many examples of a litigant penalized with court fees as part of a sentence can be found in a dispute between a husband and wife in Guadalajara, Spain.[88] The wife lost her case on her husband's appeal and was charged 78 pesos, distributed in a manner represented in Table 1.1. Most legal charges went

Table 1.1 **Distribution of Legal Fees, Spanish Marital Dispute, 1799**

Court scribes' office (escribanía de camara)	54 reales (rs)
Courier (relator)	16 rs
Delivery and return of papers (de llevadas y bueltas de autos)	20 rs
Royal Scribe for notifications (Al Escribano real por notificaciones)	4 rs
To the attorney for the review of the autos and assistance and for the report he presented at the hearing (Al abogado por reconocimiento de los autos y asistencia al informe [que] el da de la vista)	260 rs
Procurator for two petitions, two "tomas," notification and paper (Al procurador por dos pedimientos dos tomas y aviso y papel)	42 rs, 12 maravedís (ms)
Copy of power of attorney (una copia de poder)	22 rs, 12 ms
Judge's fees for reversal (Derechos de esta casación)	61 rs, 14 ms
Total	**630 rs, 4 ms**

From Juan Francisco Udaeta con María Josefa Molero, su consorte, sobre divorcio a orden de la demanda que le puso ésta. Una pieza. Guadalajara, AHN, Consejos, 29387, exp. 12.

to the attorney and procurator. The attorney's services are clearly delineated as advisory and in making final arguments, not in having a heavy hand in writing the pages that filled up the autos.

Still, the fees that individuals other than lawyers charged added up. When the Lima procurator Felipe Useda was sued for back rent, he wrote all of his own petitions and arguments, yet he still owed 95 pesos in court costs.[89] Aside from the costs on the official price list, there were potentially other fees, some legal and some illegal, that could raise the price of a suit, particularly for indigenous litigants. For example, Mexico's minor court officials demanded "tips" for their services until a 1713 ruling by Mexico's viceroy attempted to put an end to that illegal practice.[90] There were translation costs for those who did not speak Spanish, with petitions or witness testimonies costing around 20 pesos.[91] Even pressing charges for violent crime could leave a victim in hock. A *teniente*, or lieutenant magistrate, in a rural region of Mexico charged 6 reales to pursue a domestic violence case, and the female victim owed this on top of the 12 reales (usually 1½ pesos) she had to pay to the barber who tended to her wounds.[92]

Clearly, there were plenty of people around who tried to make a coin or two by serving as mediators between litigants and the law. In fact, royal rulings and administrative complaints about legal agents abusing unsuspecting litigants abounded, especially in the colonies. Colonial discourses about indigenous peoples portrayed them as wasting their money on suits and vulnerable to the legal predations of pettifoggers, unscrupulous Spanish landowners, and abusive community leaders.[93] For example, in 1798, a priest in the Mixe village of Tontontepec, Villa Alta, sounded a familiar refrain when he complained about native legal counselors stirring up legal trouble. The pueblo's "*apoderado*," or the representative from the community with power of attorney, fomented unrest by "tricking [Indians] into bringing their suits before the Señor Intendant, taking advantage of these unhappy ones and [making them] contribute [to court costs], in their fickleness to believe anything."[94] Others complained that theoretically pro bono representatives, such as the Protector of Naturales in Peru, drove up the cost of official paper by filling up the page with big handwriting or charged for services when they should not.[95]

Yet these concerns cannot be accepted at face value. Indigenous litigants, like other subordinate peoples throughout the empire, turned discourses about their legal vulnerability to their advantage.[96] When Juan Francisco traveled from the village of Betanza to the capital of Antequera in Oaxaca to protest being duped out of 29 pesos for a lawsuit that never materialized, his informal memorial, submitted on regular paper, pointed out that he was "a poor Indian unsheltered in a strange land" (Fig. 1.4). He asked not only for the arrest of the man who took his money to "take care of his [legal] errands," but also for the intendant of Oaxaca to pick up his original case for free.[97] Juan Francisco, in short, went to court for being tricked while trying to go to court. While his case could be seen as evidence of a "poor, unsheltered Indian" duped in the law, it reveals a legal tenacity and dexterity in manipulating stereotypes to gain favorable rulings.

Although the structure of Indian justice varied by region, natives throughout the empire had access to appointed legal representatives at both the community (native) and colonial (Spanish) levels. They also were theoretically exempt from fees except those collected communally for the salaries of native scribes and interpreters.[98] Using this access, ordinary native inhabitants of the empire played politics by pitting Spaniard against Spaniard, or Spaniard against native community leaders, and they judged those leaders by how well they directed the pueblos' disputes.[99] Throughout Spanish America, indigenous people regularly gave a contribution, called "*derramas*," to be spent on the fees for lawsuits, just like they contributed to funds for the celebration of saints' days or for tribute.

Spanish officials who portrayed natives caught up in the court system as victims had to admit that natives sometimes were willing legal participants. Take the objections of one corregidor on the Peruvian North Coast, who at mid century was engaged in an intense battle over water rights with the native town council and the priest of San Pedro del Virú. In typical form, he proclaimed that his opposition funded its case by twisting the arms of poor indigenous villagers, collecting between two and four and a half pesos per Indian. Even then, he conceded that the issue was not so much that the community demanded that indigenous inhabitants kick in for legal fees as it was that ordinary natives opposed the particular suit.[100]

When other colonial officials likewise worried about the extortion of legal costs from indigenous communities, their concern was similarly nuanced with acknowledgement that indigenous litigants entered courts of their own accord. In fact, at times officials portrayed Indians as unbridled litigators. An official in Xochimilco, in central Mexico, reported to the viceroy that the judges in his jurisdiction spent all of their time working for free on Indian suits and on negotiating the debts that they ran up with surgeons after drunken fights. Indeed, the officials of that same central Mexican district bemoaned natives' longstanding exemption from certain legal fees in at least three separate cases involving domestic abuse in the 1770s. A local Spanish official there tried to pass on a legal bill from two other officials in Mexico City to a native villager, complaining, "God isn't paying for all this."[101]

Since it could be unclear how much a suit might end up costing, a contingent approach to justice was especially prevalent among ordinary litigants, including natives, who could not afford to risk being sentenced to pay for a complete case or who had privileges that provided them special summary proceedings. In Peru,

Viceroy Manuel Amat y Junient issued an order on Indians and lawsuits, spelling out how native inhabitants were to incur fees at no more than half the rate of other litigants. But what is important is that his ruling—contrary to much official discourse lamenting that Indians wasted their money on lawsuits—cautioned that charging steep legal fees made ordinary natives (*atunrunas*, in Quechua) drop their suits mid-way.[102]

In one of the Xochimilco suits, the corregidor reminded another judge that since the plaintiffs in the case were natives, the suit "did not demand the observation of the formalities that in other cases should be observed."[103] But many native litigants also joined other litigants in practicing a more open-ended kind of law than the formal suit that Amat and this Mexican judge envisioned. Beginning a suit but not ending it was part of traditional Spanish imperial legal culture. The value of the lawsuit, as a written object, could derive as much from its initiation as from its conclusion.

The correlation between lower social rank and the short duration of a legal action is clear from eighteenth-century cases before the city court judge (*alcalde ordinario*) and the corregidor in Trujillo.[104] Recall that in Lima's Audiencia in 1793–94, fewer than 4 percent of individual litigants lacked the honorific "don" or "doña." The Trujillo courts, by contrast, heard cases in the first instance and were more accessible to ordinary litigants. In the city court from 1700–99, almost 14 percent of individual litigants whose status could be determined were non-dons. A review of the dates the suits were opened and closed in the corregimiento suggests that cases involving more elite litigants appear far more likely to have lasted beyond one year. The suits brought by slaves and *castas*, or ordinary free people of mixed ancestry, tended to last only a month or so, or no dates were provided in the archival description, indicating that these are merely opening petitions.

This does not even count all of the oral exchanges that might never have materialized into a written petition at all. One local official from Xochimilco, where Spanish colonial officials were beginning to balk at natives' special legal status, sought to formalize the payment structure for those who took on Indian cases. Nonetheless he still saw his role of arbiter of indigenous cases as settling cases out of court. He defended his performance as a judge by stating that the "due completion" of his "obligation" as a judge was to swiftly rule in the "extrajudicial realm" (*lo extrajudicial*).[105]

The official's comments underscore just how often the law took place outside of the written world of formal lawsuits, especially in the first instance. When cases were transformed into the written word, it could be a tentative step rather than a commitment. Thus the fees litigants paid were often only small sums rendered to agents, particularly at the beginning of suits. Only later did the tab begin to fill up with formal charges for formal personnel.

This piecemeal payment system is evident in several stories already discussed. When the native community leaders of Choapán in Oaxaca showed up ready to initiate a lawsuit in 1747 and the judge assigned his own assistant to draw up their opening petition, they were charged three pesos, one of which went to pay for the papel sellado. This means that the cost of an opening petition was not prohibitive. A litigant could, say, take his mother's best clothes to the pawn shop in Mexico City and end up with enough money to initiate no fewer than five civil suits.[106]

Social subordinates who believed they might qualify for pro bono representation as *miserables*—whether because they were widowed, poor, or enslaved—only had to find someone to pen a petition or two until a lawyer was named to their case. At the end of Lima slave Antonina Guillen's lawsuit against her master, someone (perhaps the presiding judge) meticulously crossed out each itemized legal expense and wrote a "0" next to her name.[107] If Antonina was personally liable for any expenses, perhaps she paid the person who wrote the first two petitions in her suit, which briefly summarized her case and requested gratis representation from the court.

Recall that the mulato surgeon José Ferrones told his ex lover, Juana Portocarrera, that he did precisely this kind of work for enslaved washerwomen in Lima. When she asked him to write her petition to help her find a new owner, as he had for the other women, he pointed out that those women had paid him in labor. Yet Juana went on to emphasize that her former lover ended up writing her petition free of charge because she had no money to pay him, portraying his legal counsel as a disinterested act of kindness. Though litigants rarely spoke of the identity of those who wrote their initial petitions, when they did, they often claimed their legal writers picked up a quill out of charity or as a favor.

Surely this was sometimes true: certain writing patrons undoubtedly acted out of pity or a sense of justice. But others might have had an angle in mind that would reward them with the labor of the litigant, as José Ferrones did. Some might have worked on contingency fees, being paid if the litigant was successful.[108] For their part, litigants quite routinely objected to the idea that they were being manipulated in suits, and they remained silent about the identity of their petition writers. For example, Andrea, a Lima slave, had forcefully reported that she "was in charge" of her suit "because it concerned her," even though the husband of her former mistress wrote up her petitions. She was sure to point out that he did this without her "having to pay anything, given that her constitution as a slave would not permit [her to pay.]"[109] Clearly, for Andrea, she had neither to pay for nor to pen a petition for a lawsuit to belong to her.

By regarding the lawsuit as a series of moments rather than only an object, this chapter has shown that the degree of control a litigant had over a civil case could vary over the life of the suit. To be sure, laws and legal manuals provided a general script for litigants and legal writers to follow and a template for their petitions and motions. Indeed, one of the striking things about lawsuits from across the empire is their general uniformity in following the outlines of prescribed procedure. But following forensic rules does not necessarily mean that litigants could not claim their lawsuits as their own or direct them in multiple ways.

"Agentes" (agents) and "poderes" (powers) were legal terms-of-art that referred, respectively, to unofficial writers who drafted legal papers for litigants and to the official process of naming a representative. Questions of agency and power also have underlay diverse approaches to Spanish colonial law in recent decades. In both their legal technical and theoretical connotations, the terms capture the dynamic relationship between official and unofficial writing that drove the legal system of the Spanish empire, a fluctuation between process and people that propelled every lawsuit forward. By focusing on the early phase of the suit, it becomes clear that the imperial archive is made up not only of papers authored by literate individuals but also the legal practices of unlettered subjects. Close attention to the issue of authorship in papers and the exchanges—both verbal and material—that created opening petitions in civil cases reveals the lawsuit as far more than an artifact of imperial or state power. But, of course, it was that too. Lawsuits also were affairs that concerned lettered men and royal officials. As such, they were subject to the shifting philosophies of law and legal authority that underwrote them.

2

Derecho and Law

Legal Enlightenment in Philosophy and Policy

There is no better guide to the top-down legal changes in the empire than Benito Jerónimo Fejióo y Montenegro, arguably the greatest Enlightenment intellectual in eighteenth-century Spain. When turning to the topic of law, Feijóo, a polymath Benedictine monk, shared his thoughts as a piece of fictional correspondence from a judge to his son upon becoming a magistrate.[1] The letter, entitled "Astraea's Balance: Or the upright administration of justice," stressed judicial impartiality. The father tells his son that, by donning the toga, he had shed country, friends, and relatives, and become a "slave" to "the public."[2] In this way, Feijóo helped construct a modern notion of law as a realm unto itself, part of a public sphere above and apart from private society.[3] Friendships and family attachments, he admitted, might be unavoidable. But this meant only that a magistrate should have a "soul of wax in private life, and a spirit of bronze in public administration."[4]

If Feijóo was relatively rigid in his demand that judges had a public duty to separate from their social selves, he was more flexible when it came to judicial method. In the first part of a section on judicial sentencing, he made the traditional pronouncement that a judge's job was to interpret rather than apply the laws. Invoking principals of distributive justice, he wrote that interpretation should "follow from the needs of the public good and according to the judgment of natural equity," or judicial compassion. Feijóo was quick to clarify that he did not envision benches full of bleeding hearts, but he did believe judges had the responsibility, "by the virtue that they call *Epikeya* [Greek for "rehabilitation"], to reduce and even omit in some cases the penalties that the Law decrees. This is not kindness but rather justice because we are obligated to follow the mind of the Legislator rather than the letter of the law."[5]

Were he to have stopped there, Feijóo's description of judicial method might have fit as nicely in the mid-seventeenth century as the mid-eighteenth. Though he subjected judges' discretion to larger considerations of the public good and to nature, Feijóo retained the conviction that they needed to exercise equity and adjust laws to circumstances.[6] Magistrates should parcel out justice to each party, choosing which laws spoke to the particularity of the situation and interpreting them in a way that would give each side its rightful due, in a method known as "casuism" (or more derogatorily, as "casuistry"). Any distinctions Feijóo might have wished to draw between public and private duties, between rational legal judgment and compassion, end up blurred—the judge's soul of wax melts a bit onto his bronze armor.

But Feijóo did not stop there. He also insisted that the modern magistrate should be an impartial public servant, a follower of laws rather than purveyor of arbitrary opinions. He wrapped up his fictional missive with what at first might appear to be a jumble of ideas about law and compassion.

> . . . Piety, as is demanded from subaltern Judges, [is] improperly called such, since it conforms to the Law rationally understood, and otherwise is injustice. In cases omitted [from legislation] and when the Law is unclear, there are general laws to interpret it or complement it which have the force of Law. Thus, in the subaltern Judge, there is no medium between justice and injustice, because there is no middle ground between working in conformity with the Law and working against the Law.[7]

Here, the Benedictine philosopher stepped tentatively into a new field of thinking in which jurisprudence would follow from the rational understanding of the Law as an abstract concept. The invocation of "general laws" was not incidental. It captured a centuries-long transition away from judicial interpretation, culminating in the eighteenth century in an "anti-hermeneutic politics of Enlightenment."[8] This new way of regarding law, elaborated into a method and system, would eventually be known as formalism, a theoretical rejection of judicial equity and a departure from particularlistic, casuist models of judgment.[9] Feijóo strains toward this when he presents law is as a unified whole, with no variation permitted. In essence, he argues that the law rises above any judicial interpretation that might vary from case to case.

Feijóo notably never uses the Spanish word "*derecho*" in his discussion of method. This single word would have pointed to the vast constellation of laws and legal interpretations in the early modern tradition of *ius commune*, which comprised what one historian aptly calls a "universe of opinions."[10] Like his European contemporaries, Feijóo instead opts to use the word "*Ley,*" or "Law," which nodded toward law as a system.[11] Often articulated by using the phrase "general and fixed law," this new law-driven culture stabilized justice, aiming for a system where outcomes could be predictable, and perhaps more equal, rather than variable and pegged to the status of each litigant, as they were in a distributive justice system.[12] Feijóo, while cautious about exactly which system he would support, nonetheless expressed a resolute willingness to follow "any system" that was sound and free of "grave difficulties."[13]

Other Spanish imperial Enlightenment legal thinkers might better embody the transition to formalism than Feijóo. In a 1783 treatise dedicated to a highly influential Bourbon royal adviser, Antonio López de Oliver described causism as an "antiquity" and called for magistrates to be "not arbiters but precise executors" of the law.[14] A famous Mexican penologist even went so far as to argue that judicial discretion should be done away with entirely in criminal sentencing in favor of strict interpretation of "fixed" laws.[15] Still, Feijóo's judicial epistemology is a useful example of Enlightenment legal thought in the Spanish empire precisely because is earlier and more eclectic than those presented in such late eighteenth-century texts.

Historians have long drawn schematic distinctions between early modern justice and modern law to convey the epochal shifts taking place in judicial thought, whether the shift was from causism to system, or from polycentric to state-centered legal regimes.[16] But these different epistemologies and regimes of law were not necessarily inimical. An older, cobbled version of early modern law did not crumble as a sleek, modern version of universal law rose.[17] As a historically lived experience, the advent of modern law probably felt more tentative and less monumental. Despite official dabbling in Napoleonic-like codification, including recompilations of Castilian and colonial laws at the turn of the nineteenth century, no single "universal law"—no version of Feijóo's "general laws" for judicial interpretation—ever emerged in Spain.[18] Or, it must be stressed, anywhere.[19] In other words, the idea that law could be a predictable science with universal application should be approached as a historical aspiration rather than a realization.[20]

Given this, rather than portraying this story as an actual clash between legal modernity and tradition or as a showdown between an emergent state and society, this chapter narrates the highly recombinant nature of Spanish imperial Enlightenment legal thought and exposes its deep origins in humanism—*contra* those contemporaries who construed it as radical or new in order to defend legal traditions. In doing so, it offers an alternative to a narrative in which peninsular Bourbon royal reformers pushed new, modern imperial legal ideas on colonial subjects who defensively clung to old ways and customs.

Instead, the Spanish imperial Enlightenment entailed the trans-Atlantic co-production of a new legal culture, a new "law-centered culture," among lettered men.[21] The elements of this culture included the circulation and creation of new legal epistemologies hostile to causism and favorable to royal law. It also embraced a vision of natural rights that departed from the kinds of privileges and duties that accreted to individuals in earlier natural law theories. While lofty ideas about legal truth and rights mostly were the provenance of erudite jurists and legal theorists, law-centered culture also touched imperial ground in multiple places, such as university classrooms and the sentences judges rendered every day. New ideas about law also became law through multiple Bourbon royal orders and administrative reforms that brought greater court efficiency, impartiality, and accessibility to the empire's civil courts. As a result, the law emerged as an autonomous, increasingly secular field of action based on rational state institutions, whose efficient operation fostered broad access to the courts, which in turn hosted new notions of rights.

"*Ley*" never completely triumphed over "*derecho*." Formalistic, rights-based ways of imagining the law did not come to dominate all legal thinking in the empire, where older concepts of custom, casuistic legal practices, and calls for judicial equity endured. Rather than seeing this as a shortcoming or failure, the chapter starts from the premise that the experience of Iberian legal modernity, as with modernity everywhere, was dynamic and partial. It involved as much the invocation of innovation as the reality of a break from the past, as legal minds and practitioners came to associate new ways of doing law with "modernity" and "novelty," choosing sides for and against the new legal culture.

The Transformation in Philosophies of Law

There was no magic Enlightenment ingredient that transformed early modern Spanish imperial law into modern law, despite the temptation to represent the shift to formalist law systems in terms of clear philosophical positions—faith-based understandings of law disappeared, law became a rational science, law became less corrupt. A metaphor might help avoid overdrawing the distinction between early modern and modern law, and give a more nuanced portrayal of concepts of justice before the Enlightenment.

Taking Felipe Gómez's story of lemonade as a metaphor for justice-oriented culture, law can be imaged as a lemon tree, with the tree representing a legal system and the fruit it bears representing justice. In early modern legal culture, the lemons grew from multiple branches of law: Spanish legislation, codified laws, local laws, custom, Roman and canon law. For jurists in the civil law tradition, the aim was to choose the most appropriate lemons on the tree, suited to the circumstance and status of the litigating subject. In the rest of the book, terms that should call to mind this early modern approach to law include casuism, distributive justice, ius commune, and probabilism.

In the eighteenth century, Enlightenment jurists produced a law-oriented culture by shifting focus away from the lemons to the tree. As with so many other aspects of Enlightenment thought, jurists busied themselves studying, dissecting, and classifying the "law" as a concept apart from "justice," focusing on the tree rather than its fruit, attempting to come up with a science of law that would engineer the production of the best and most uniform kind of justice useful everywhere. The key legal history terms that evoke this new culture of law include formalism, regalism, and jusrationalism, or natural rights theory.

The Spanish empire had laws budding on many branches, making its experience with legal formalism and rights theories instructive for larger processes of legal change in the West. The laws of the multiple kingdoms united under Castile and Aragon in the fifteenth century, already pluralistic, proliferated in the new overseas kingdoms during colonial expansion. Centralizing and rationalizing law would be a real challenge in such a setting.

Early Modern Law in the Spanish Empire

In the Spanish empire, subjects looking for civil laws to support justice in everyday lawsuits could turn to the medieval *Siete Partidas*, to Castilian legislation that had been compiled in the sixteenth century, as well as to local legal privileges, known as fueros, applicable to specific corporate groups, which could be as large as the diverse kingdoms making up "Spain" and as small as guilds.[22] They could draw on local laws issued by high courts or promulgated by town councils. Colonial litigants also had at hand the flurry of written imperial legislation directly issued for the Americas, eventually assembled in the late seventeenth-century compendium known as the *Recopilación de Leyes de Indias*, a casuist masterpiece that drew together laws written in response to unique situations that had developed in the New World from the time of contact forward.[23]

And then there was custom. Given the Spanish monarchy's longstanding cultural respect for the rights of towns and the slow, two-centuries-long process of political unification under the Castilian crown, regional custom held a great deal of legal sway in situations that were not addressed by written, royal laws.[24] In a book-length analysis of custom, Víctor Tau de Anzóategui cautions that custom was no mere placeholder for absences in written law but rather an entire "dimension" of judicial thinking. It could be an epistemology, a method, or a concrete popular practice; it could refer to legal cultural traditions at the level of the town or indigenous pueblo, or to precedent. In the colonies, it could be identified by means of consulting erudite written works on colonial law, known as "*derecho indiano*," such as Juan de Solórzano's *Política indiana* or Peruvian viceroy's Francisco de Toledo's wide-ranging *Ordenanzas*, which applied to Andean native populations from the late sixteenth century on.

These diverse sources of civil Spanish peninsular and colonial law, including royal edicts, local law, and unwritten custom, were not, technically speaking, the focus of the university education of professional jurists and lawyers, at least not until the eighteenth century. Instead, lawyers attended fundamentally religious institutions—most dominated by Jesuits, but some directed by other religious orders—where they were trained in ius commune. Ius commune created a civil law tradition for Catholic Europe based on a body of law and legal commentary merging canon law with Roman imperial law, which both fell under divine law.[25] Students imbibed ius commune as they listened to chaired professors in canon and civil law deliver lectures from polished wooden podiums in the universities of Spain and Spanish America, as they engaged in mock trials, and they presented their own arguments in order to graduate.[26]

Mastering ius commune meant concentrating on two corpuses of texts: the *corpus iuris canonico* and the *corpus iuris civilis*. In canon law, professors exposed students to Gratian's *Decretum*—a kind of canonical legal textbook from the twelfth century—along with versions compiled by two twelfth-century popes that included updates to the collected canonical opinions. In other words, eighteenth-century law students studied canon law that was fundamentally late medieval in orientation. In turn, law students studied civil law that was, in a sense, fundamentally Roman. Their legal education mostly focused on emperor Justinian's sixth-century compilation of Roman civil laws, the *Corpus juris civilis*. This corpus comprised three parts: the Digest, which contained Roman jurists' brief opinions; the Code, which was a list of legislation; and the Institutes, a set of lessons that redacted civil laws. Until the mid-eighteenth century, students closely studied the Digest to ground or supplement Spanish law.

In reality, most working lawyers in the Spanish empire did not page through the huge tomes of the *Decretum* or memorize the Digest. Rather, they consulted the reflections of many glossators and commentators that had been published over the centuries, principally from the late fifteenth century on. They referred to these jurists and theologians deferentially as "the Authors" or "the Doctors." Indeed, the reliance on others' interpretation of canon, Roman and even Spanish law was a hallmark of early modern legal argumentation, known as "*interpretatio*" or the "Italian method" (*mos italicus.*)[27]

The hegemony of ius commune did not mean that lawyers and legal professionals trained in a vacuum or that their education entirely neglected peninsular and Spanish colonial law. Law students in Mexico had various, though perhaps informal, channels to study derecho indiano.[28] The arguments lawyers and procurators put before judges manifested an ease in citing peninsular law and its commentators, especially Gregorio López's annotation of the *Siete Partidas*. Yet Castilian law, which furnished a great deal of lawyers' understanding of broader Spanish law, was itself often established in circular reference to Roman law, particularly in the sphere of private law, or the kind of litigation between individuals over ordinary relations of authority that underwent significant transformation in the colonies. Treating topics ranging from monarchical power to child custody, the *Siete Partidas* functioned as a—maybe the—primary touchstone of civil law in the empire.[29] Its heavily Roman foundation tightened the legal cultural attachment to ius commune among university-trained professionals.

Eclectic Enlightenment

The Spanish imperial preeminence of ius commune began to face its first serious challenges after the Bourbon dynasty replaced the Habsburgs on Spain's throne in the early eighteenth century. In a 1713 royal instruction detailing the sequence in which judges should apply royal laws, Felipe V complained that lawyers and judges had come to rank "foreign" glossators of canon and Roman law over Spanish commentators, customs, and written royal law itself.[30] Bourbon officials began to mount a regalist campaign to shift the focus of legal education to what was called *derecho patrio*, or the laws of Spain and its empire. College and university administrators, along with other high-placed intellectuals, resisted this early initiative.[31] Adherents to the traditional teaching of law succeeded in delaying the king's attempts to elevate the empire's own laws to a status on par with (or even above) canon and Roman law for two decades. By 1741, however, the crown was able to introduce systematic study of derecho patrio in imperial universities, a move that culminated in the 1768 abolition of peninsular Jesuit colleges, the religious order's ultimate expulsion from the empire, and a royal take-over of its educational institutions.[32] Subsequently, students at universities granting law degrees took formal classes dedicated to Spanish sources such as the *Siete Partidas* and, in the colonies, learned from derecho indiano sources such as Solórzano.[33]

Legal historians tend to view the introduction of royal law into professional lawyers' education as an act that launched the Spanish empire into the modern age. The language of Spanish peninsular *ilustrados* and royal communications seem to support to this view, since they often denigrated the Roman basis of Spanish law as "barbaric" and promoted national law by diminishing the influence of non-Iberian glossators and commentators.[34] Still, for other scholars, the overwhelming regalism of Spanish thought and the tentativeness of curricular changes in universities in the eighteenth century disqualifies state sponsorship of this reform as the "Enlightenment." Indeed, only a few colonial Spanish American jurists' libraries contained the works of writers normally associated with the French Enlightenment, such as Voltaire or Jean-Jacques Rousseau. Even fewer contained contemporary British or Scottish thinkers' works, though the seventeenth-century works of John Locke and Thomas Hobbes did frequently pop up on their shelves.[35]

This apparent lack of engagement with the European republic of laws seems to confirm the judgment of scholars like Israel, who describes Spanish

Enlightenment thinkers as willing only to "embrace the New Philosophy from an eclectic ... standpoint rather than one of whole-hearted commitment."[36] Israel's categorization of the Spanish Enlightenment as "eclectic" might betray the stringency of his criteria for what counts as radical Enlightenment, but other historians less apt to view Spain as philosophically deficient also choose the same word to describe jurisprudential and political thought in the eighteenth century.[37] They generally employ the term "eclectic," along with others such as "hybrid" or "amalgamated," to indicate that Spain's Century of Lights was dappled with old and new influences. These references pave the way for a consideration of an important, though little known, aspect of the Spanish imperial legal Enlightenment.

Eclecticism, it turns out, was a conscious feature of regalist thought. As a philosophy, eclecticism refers to the eighteenth-century natural rights theory espoused by the German Christian Thomasius, a student of the theorist Samuel von Pufendorf.[38] Thomasius's eclecticism envisioned law as a formal system divorced from moral philosophy and metaphysics, and it contained an emphasis on practice and reason rather than revelation as the basis for natural law.

Profound wrestling with the concept of natural law was, of course, not new to this period or to Spain. The great sixteenth-century Spanish natural law theorists, including Francisco de Vitoria, Luis de Molina, and Francisco Suárez, merged Catholic theology with Aristotelian ideas in the halls of the famed School of Salamanca.[39] For these theorists, *jus naturae*, or natural law, was a plane of theorizing about human reason and the capability to discern God-given "first principles" of morality. Such thinkers dedicated significant attention to philosophical-theological questions that had bearings on rights, notably the questions of whether there existed first principles that applied to every individual and what the relationship between the soul and the body was. In that sense, natural law theorists surely were concerned with "individuals," but they believed moral and natural law were one and the same. They subordinated any rights that accrued to individuals in social systems to the first principles: if a social system violated larger first principles, the rights disappeared.[40] Working lawyers in the empire paraded Salamanca School natural law theorists, along with Aristotle himself, through the civil courts of the Spanish empire as they delivered legal arguments in the mos italicus, with the Jesuits frequently pushing Suárez to the front of the group.

At the end of seventeenth century, there was a major shift in focus among philosophers of civil law from "natural law" to "natural rights."[41] Jusnaturalists at the helm of this change, especially Hugo Grotius, were highly indebted to Spanish scholars, but he, along with Hobbes and Pufendorf, began to use *jus* to describe not what was "traditionally right, law, or what is objectively just and fair," but rather as a "subjective right, faculty or power of action possessed by the individual."[42]

Whether the emergence of natural rights theory constituted a whole new path of legal thinking or a simply a bend in the long road of Western legal philosophy, the shift entailed working on a constellation of problems that were distinct from those of "first principles": what were the rights humans possessed by virtue of being human; did those rights only follow from the duties imposed by natural law or did they stand alone; and how could those rights be protected by legitimate rulers or overstepped by tyrants?[43]

Eclecticism emerged in the seventeenth century amidst such secularizing, increasingly individualized questions of natural right. According to Thomasius, God may have created natural law, but he did not dictate it.[44] Taking this as a starting point, Thomasius worked through three aspects of a new law-centered paradigm. First, he argued that jurisprudence was chiefly an expression of human achievement; when determining justice, the truth that was revealed was less important than the rational faculties that one used in trying to determine it. This concern for the process or procedure of administering law and the place of human reason in its application pulled emphasis away from reliance on authorities as a means of proving truth. Second, Thomasius held that natural law was a science separate from moral philosophy. Finally, he, like many of his humanist contemporaries, was deeply invested in historicizing law. Thomasius advocated for a kind of legal education that would lead to the greatest openness to new ideas, and in particular to an attitude that would return the creation of laws, particularly Roman laws, to their historical context.[45]

Thomasius's ideas did not amount to a particularly large movement, but eclecticism is nonetheless critical for understanding law in the eighteenth-century Spanish empire for several reasons. It points to the existence of historical exits to the seeming contradiction posed by the rise of modern individual rights-oriented notions of law and the persistence of more traditional, corporatist, divine-law oriented cultures.[46] Moreover, it makes it clear that imperial subjects could adopt natural rights theory that displaced but did not deny divinity, and shows us that "secularization" in law did not have to mean radical rejection of Catholicism. Finally, eclecticism was a circuit that ran through Protestant and Catholic moral and civic philosophy, demonstrating that the philosophy of law in Northern Europe and the Spanish empire did not develop in isolation.

One textbook traveled this circuit. A disciple of Thomasius, Johann Gottfried Heineccius (in Spanish, Heineccio) wrote a guide to natural rights theory that became highly influential in the Spanish empire.[47] *Elements of Natural Law and the Law of Nations* found its way into the personal libraries of jurists in Guatemala and Mexico, making its author famous in his own time.[48] Various imperial law schools both on the peninsula and in the American colonies adopted or recommended this text. *Elements of Natural Law* was, for example, listed in the revised curriculum of the University of San Marcos in Lima in 1771 as well as in Cuzco in the Colegio de San Bernardo Abad.[49] *Elements of Natural Law* also provided, ironically, the basic understanding of rights that Gregorio Mayans Siscar, eventual philosophical favorite of Bourbon king Carlos III, used to attack natural rights theorists in his 1746 work *Christian Philosophy*.[50] Meanwhile, reformed syllabi integrated Heineccius's historical treatments of Roman law and his parsing of the Institutes and Digest.[51]

Notwithstanding Mayans's warnings to the king about the dangers of jusrationalist thought, university reformers wanting to expose budding lawyers to natural rights theory thought Heineccio's text fit the bill perfectly. Spanish educational reformers believed that, in circulating texts like his, they could promote a kind of cosmopolitan homogeneity in imperial legal thought that deracinated *ius commune*.[52] Curriculums in colleges and universities dedicated specifically to the study of "Derecho Natural y de Gentes" adopted Heineccius's *Elements of Natural Law* as a textbook. The first chair of the institution of San Isidro in Madrid justified the choice by overlooking Heineccius's flirtation with more individualistic and secular philosophers, and deeming him to be "the most modest and pacific" among the options.[53]

In *Elements of Natural Law*, Heineccius proposed a jusrationalist vision edging toward an individualized, human-based notion of rights, deemphasizing the role of God and pondering the limits of the rule of kings. This was a version of natural law in which reason generated love for God, other humans and, critically, oneself. Heineccius posited a kind of "axiomatic equality" between all humans, and he spent little time wondering whether different degrees of rationality bestowed legal privileges onto different groups.[54] His focus was on the distinction between the internal and external duty of individuals, their natural rights, and how a government could reconcile individual rights to self-preservation and security with its own need to secure and defend the body politic. The theme of self-preservation, of the boundaries between the subject and society, and the degree to which any ruler or community could require a subject to submit to rule in a way that violated nature, was a puzzle that particularly preoccupied Heineccius and his natural rights theorist contemporaries.

Even beyond its complex philosophical content, *Elements of Natural Law* joined other jurisprudential works that opened natural rights to new popular legal understandings, indeed to a new lexicon. By the mid-eighteenth century, there was an increased instability in Spanish imperial courts of law around the term "*derecho natural*," which could mean, in Spanish, both natural law and natural right. It was often unclear whether lawyers and litigants were using it to refer to divine law or individual rights. They shared this ambiguity with more lettered men: clear articulations of passive natural rights derived from duties ordered by

God and those active, individually held rights ordered by reason are nearly impossible to find until the nineteenth century.[55]

When lawyers and litigants invoked "derecho natural" in Spanish American
lawsuits in the eighteenth century they nonetheless often clearly meant to index
the debates about self-preservation and the power of tyrants that so concerned
emergent natural rights theorists such as Heineccius. But wading into new questions about rights was not the only way lawyers and litigants participated in the
legal debates of their time. They also summoned a notion of law as a system that
no longer drew its authority exclusively from the Authors.[56] The new emphasis
on rights as one of the principal elements of a system of law accompanied, then,
emergence of formalism as a framework. So much is obvious from the new title
George Turnbull gave Heineccius's treatise on natural rights when he translated
it to English: *A Methodical System of Universal Law.*[57]

Simply learning about this or any "methodical system" of law or focusing on
rights did not render casuism or the interpretations of Authors obsolete in the
Spanish empire. But it did provide an alternative to the old way of doing law. The
challenge to authoritative interpretation in law and closer attention to royal legislation affected epistemologies of moral truth as well as justice. In a process that
ran parallel to the challenge to judicial interpretation in legal thought, regalist
professors took on one of its theological corollaries, probabilism, in the lecture
halls of the empire.[58]

A Jesuit-inspired style of moral reasoning, probabilism maintained that an
argument could be proven valid as long as a sufficient number of written authorities supported it, no matter the size or strength of arguments advanced by an
opposing group of authoritative experts. Regalist reformers viewed probabilism as an epistemological haven for rebellious Jesuits whom the king could not
control. By the second half of the century, Bourbon reformers sought to eradicate this style of moral reasoning from the universities—no easy task given the
Jesuits' deep roots in colonial education.[59] The Viceroy of Peru banned its mere
mention in courses on theology at the University of San Marcos around the
same time that students were being directed into new courses on modern philosophy and the history of laws.[60] Such educational reforms, along with greater
attention to Spanish legislation in courses on jurisprudence, marked an epistemological break from the scholastic past.[61] Spanish imperial jurists and lawyers
now could legitimately participate in a mode of legal reasoning in which laws
were scrutinized and ranked by proximity to themselves in time and place as
well as content.[62]

By the end of the eighteenth century, criticism of traditional juridical and
moral epistemologies freely floated around the empire. Legal professionals wandering the bookstores that increasingly lined the streets of the cities of the empire found publications that excoriated ius commune interpretative traditions

as outdated and ultimately detrimental to imperial modernization. In addition to Antonio Muratori and Juan Francisco de Castro, perhaps the most widely cited critic of the old ways was Luis Antonio Verney, known as "el Barbadiño," whose 1746 Catalan work, *True Method of Studying in Order to Be Useful to the Republic,* betrayed its regalist orientation. Readers might also skim the same books that royal advisers did—political tracts like López de Oliver's *True Idea of a Prince,* in which the author claimed that traditional casuism had produced "Anarchy in the Republic of Laws."[63] Even the archbishop of Mexico, Francisco Antonio de Lorenzana, circulated a 1772 tract about the perils of Jesuit-style argumentation.[64]

Criticisms of the old order took place out loud as well as in print. In Spain, crowds gathered in 1780 to hear Gaspar Melchor de Jovellanos, one of the chief Enlightened royal advisers to the Bourbon monarchy, give a speech upon induction into the Royal Academy of History that condemned ius commune for not only obstructing the understanding of Spanish law but at times even contradicting it.[65] Such speeches often contained covertly anti-clerical overtones. Seven years later, before his colleagues at the University of San Marcos in Lima, the jurist José de Baquíjano y Carillo argued priests should not be permitted to occupy the chair of Prima de Leyes, the most prestigious teaching position in civil law.[66]

Changes in legal thought in the empire were not swift, unopposed, or complete. By the end of the century, one could find counter-Enlightenment tracts that attacked the new culture of law as dangerously radical on shelves next to works that invoked natural rights, condemned tyranny, and conceptually built rational systems of law. Stirred by revolutions in North America, France, and Haiti, counter-Enlightenment thinkers increasingly portrayed natural rights theories as jejune, a dangerous fad that threatened the social order and venerable intellectual traditions. One old-school priest writing under the pen name "Aristotle" in early nineteenth-century Spain worried that eclectic philosophy merely masked atheism and popularized the act of thinking and writing about ideas. In the old days, he complained, it took years to write a philosophical work; today, "in a half an hour a work of *eclectic* philosophy is written," slapped together with overly long citations and full of partisan, "pre-emptive responses to the criticism of the author, his teachers and his disciples."[67]

Beyond dangerously democratizing the law, the opposition claimed that natural rights theory also threatened religious tradition. Vicente Fernández Valcarce, adviser to the Count of Floridablanca, began the fourth of six volumes in his counter-Enlightenment corpus *Philosophical Disillusionments* (1790) by flatly rejecting formalism and its relationship to emergent concepts of natural rights. He denied the fundamental principle of legal "Innovators," which was that a system of "Natural Right" existed separately from "Natural Morality."[68]

Valcarce's indictment of natural rights theory settled on the likes of Pufendorf, Wolf, and especially Heineccius, who, he reported, had attracted a following among many "modern Critics" because of their repugnance for casuism.[69]

Like many counter-Enlightenment tracts, Valcarce's invective actually provided a more succinct definition of the new legal culture than could be found among its adherents. His disdain for "the famous" Heineccius was particularly pronounced as he focused on the German's idea of natural right as an individual's right to conserve life. Valcarce pondered Heineccius's claim that individuals could defend themselves against any law, whether purported to be divine or man-made, that endangered human life without just cause and the necessity to conserve a larger common good.[70] Valcarce rejected the idea outright, mostly because it seemed radically disengaged from morality and overly secular: "In place of solid and Christian maxims, purely political and natural maxims will enter and reign over the conscience of men, under the pretext of Derecho Natural and good society." In law-centered culture, men would be governed only by "flesh, convenience and human interest." If adopted, he predicted that Christian piety, faith, and religion would "disappear from the world."[71]

As counter-Enlightenment thinkers rejected natural rights theory as too radical and secular, new approaches to jurisprudence faced strong—if not quite so apocalyptic—opposition in the universities, particularly from longstanding adherents to probabilism. Baquíjano lamented their success in paralyzing education in the University of San Marcos. Early plans to rid Lima's university of "the servile respect that has been transmitted age after age to the ancient gods of philosophy and morals" had "produced only a cold winter of inaction" in terms of curriculum changes.[72] The leadership of the newly established Real Convictorio Carolino in Lima, a hothouse for cultivating regalist though, even removed from syllabi Heineccius's *Elements of Roman Law*, a relatively tame explication of the Institutes, and replaced it with a text that prompted less critical thinking and more memorization.[73] In addition, while "national" (Spanish imperial) law now claimed chaired professorships, it was taught in a way that continued to subordinate it to Roman law.[74]

Counter-Enlightenment opposition to the new law-centered culture was ultimately successful in a couple of respects. It nurtured the popular belief that there was something inherently anti-religious, foreign, and radically novel in natural rights theory. Second, pointing repeatedly to events in France, it nudged the crown into a 1794 law that suspended the teaching of Derecho Natural y de Gentes in the empire, convincing Carlos IV that even the censored versions of texts such as Heineccio's undermined monarchy.[75] The two decades or so during which the discipline was an official part of the curriculum in Spanish imperial law schools had hardly been long enough to completely change ordinary modes of argumentation. In the courts of the empire, lawyers continued to put into full use their training in ius commune, consistently listing the names of authoritative, classical, and medieval commentators in their arguments well into the nineteenth century.[76] Nonetheless, the old practice of tracing the sources of law backward through the Authors was no longer the only, or even the most privileged, way to make a legal argument. Budding lawyers had enjoyed the legitimate ability to question and ponder the origin of law and the basis of rights, and jus-rationalist university officials dragged their feet in implementing the 1794 order.

Focusing on the rights of legal subjects and breaking with the interpretation-centered past had great potential for changing things outside of lecture halls and courtrooms as well as within. When Napoleon forced Spanish King Fernando VII into exile, leaving each local governing body in the empire to deliberate on its rights in the absence of the monarch, some Spanish American jurists departed from their compatriots, who were grounding their rights in older Salamanca School natural law theories, and instead invoked principles of sovereignty, consent, and natural rights they had learned from Heineccius's *Elements of Natural Law*.[77] The book had agitated the status quo enough in Spain itself that one historian cites it—even in the somewhat defanged version that had been approved by the Inquisition—as the principle textual inspiration for liberalism on the peninsula in the nineteenth century.[78]

Still, by the 1800s thinkers interested in natural rights theories could choose from more radical alternatives. The Mexican José Servando Teresa de Mier ultimately decided that moderate natural rights doctrines such as Heineccius's thwarted rather than facilitated his country's movement for independence.[79] But the eclectic approach—one that angered the "ancient gods of philosophy and morality" but did not provoke the ire of the monarchy—ended up appealing to creole republicans after independence just as it had to reformists who put it on law students' syllabi in the century before. Heineccius's *Elements of Natural Law* was among the first legal textbooks published in the newly independent Republic of Peru, rolling off of one of Cuzco's presses as early as 1826.[80] In Mexico, his works remained the standard texts on Roman law until the 1940s.[81]

Colonial Jurisprudence

Working lawyers generally refrained from citing any contemporary works—including the works of new natural rights theorists—in ordinary cases.[82] But occasionally new authors did join the exalted ranks of the pantheon of the Authors cited in everyday lawsuits in the empire. One of these new authors was a Lima-born creole jurist, and attorneys referred to his published writing in legal arguments aired in both the capital city and in Trujillo in the 1780s and '90s.[83] He was José Pedro Bravo de Lagunas y Castilla, an *oidor*, or high court minister, of the Lima Audiencia, who published a collection of his legal opinions in 1761 entitled *Legal Collection of Letters, Rulings, and Other Law Papers* [*Colección legal de cartas, dictámenes, y otros papeles de derecho*].[84]

In general, magistrates in the Spanish empire did not explain their decisions, whether they were interim judgments or final sentences.[85] They issued simple verdicts: "we find that the claimant proved her case and the defendant did not prove his." Ruling rationales can sometimes be gleaned from recommendations made by the high court crown's attorney, the *fiscal*, and, at the lower-court level, from the opinion of an educated *asesor*, usually a lawyer in residence called upon to assist a judge lacking a legal education. But most ordinary decisions lacked judicial justification.

This is what makes Bravo de Lagunas's compendium of his legal opinions, originally written in 1740s and '50s, so valuable.[86] The *Legal Collection* is a particularly rich artifact of colonial legal thought since Bravo de Lagunas possessed a deep legal education as well as experience in various positions in Peru's judiciary, including the Defender of Natives and legal adviser to the viceroy.[87] His opinions provide a glimpse of the kind of jurisprudence that hid beneath judges' brief sentences in Mexico and Peru, and can be read as vectors through which lettered philosophies expanded the legal horizons of unlettered litigants. When colonial judges accepted as valid new kinds of suits, they abetted lawyers and litigants who decided to question authority—jurisprudential as well as social—in their cases.

Bravo de Lagunas's opinions show that even the most conservative of colonial judges actively generated new philosophies of law when faced with challenging cases. For this judge, participating in the Enlightenment did not mean picking sides in a preexisting European debate between "ancients and moderns." While he was part of a cosmopolitan intellectual republic, making reference to the same humanist sources that inspired other eighteenth-century thinkers as well his own Enlightened contemporaries in Spain such as Feijóo, all of his opinions date from the first half of the century. This testifies to the fact that his ideas were not reactive. Penning his opinions at roughly the same time as Heineccius published his *Elements of Natural Law*, Bravo de Lagunas was at once part of a broader European conversation and a colonial jurisprudential pioneer.[88]

Bravo de Lagunas garnered notoriety in his own time for the first opinion in the book, a reprint of a 1755 pro-creole commentary in favor of state regulation to benefit Peru's coastal hacienda owners, who had been pushed out of the grain market by an alliance of the Church, a new merchant elite, and Chilean wheat. According to one historian, this text dressed a defense of the Habsburg status quo in the garb of Bourbon modernity by using fashionable words, including "reason," "public good," and "tyranny."[89] But this is not the only way to read the text or its author.[90]

The other items he published in the *Legal Collection*, which have received far less attention, reveal that judicial thought in mid-century Lima was far more than gussied up old ideas. The opinions include departures from traditional jurisprudence both in their novelty and uniqueness. In terms of novelty, Bravo de Lagunas rejected casuism and probabilism in legal epistemology; in terms of distinctiveness, he formulated what can be called a "new creole jurisprudence," which combined a defense of custom with Spanish Enlightenment sources and a heavy emphasis on natural rights theory. The idea that a jurist could be at once part of the Enlightenment and a defender of custom might seem strange, since custom is normally set up as contrary to modernizing thought.[91] But indeed they coacted in Bravo de Lagunas's mind.

Three of the six opinions in the *Legal Collection* and its appendix treat specific points of law of the type that commonly appeared on the docket of a city judge or of the high court of the Audiencia, including a reflection on women's dowry rights and two considerations of the rights of slaves, capped by an appendix that treated the topic of royal jurisdiction. In a style typical among citizens of the Republic of Letters, he formulated most of the opinions as letters written in response to queries from various of Lima's luminaries, especially other high court judges. A "receipt" from a correspondent, usually another creole legal magistrate, commenting on the opinion and praising its quality, precedes each letter in the compendium.

There was nothing that made Bravo de Lagunas's innovative approach to the law inevitable; to the contrary, he had every reason to cling to older interpretative models of legal thought. For thirteen years after earning his doctorate, he had held a chaired position teaching the Digest at the Colegio Real y Mayor de San Felipe and later was appointed the Chair of Prima de Leyes at San Marcos.[92] Yet, despite his mastery of the foundational civil laws of ius commune, Bravo de Lagunas did not revere the commentators and glossators who had parsed huge and complicated Roman laws, and he disapproved of advocates and judges who over-relied on these secondary texts. He clucked at young lawyers who acted "as if Jurisprudence did not have fixed laws" and did not understand that "the authorities on Law are not [themselves] laws [and their] words should not be taken as rules."[93]

Beyond rejecting the old methods of interpretation, Bravo de Lagunas also believed that if lawyers and judges would turn to the original sources and to Spanish and Roman law as written, a predictable, stable system of law would emerge. Interpretative authorities lacked the "generality" that was necessary for law and thus should only be used in a limited fashion to illuminate a specific legal issue, or else "the Interpreter would say what the Law does not."[94] For his formalist vision, the jurist found inspiration in older natural law schools of Luis de Molina, one of the founders of the School of Salamanca, and the critical method of Pietro Marcellino Corradini (*Crítica e interpretación*, 1707), both of whom

Figure 2.1 A portrait of Bravo de Lagunas, possibly by Crisóbal Lozada. From Guillermo Lohmann Villena, *Los ministros de la Audencia de Lima (1700–1821)* (Sevilla: Escuela de Estudios Hispano-Americanos, 1974), Lámina II.

he refers to in his 1746 opinion on slavery, discussed below. He also drew from Pufendorf and especially Grotius, whom he openly cited despite an Inquisition ban.[95] Beyond his jusrationalist sources and "anti-hermenutic politics," Bravo de Lagunas's notion of law was rooted in the importance of creole jurisprudence, which derived from royal law and local precedent in equal measure.

Bravo de Lagunas on Secular Jurisdiction

To understand how Bravo de Lagunas could simultaneously promote both regalism and custom as precedent, it is helpful to begin at the end, with this colonial jurist's last opinion, "Discord over the concordance." In it, he responded to a 1749 publication condemning early Bourbon assertions of royal prerogative in jurisdictional matters.[96] Bravo de Lagunas defended the crown's ability to review the decisions of ecclesiastical tribunals and to determine whether they had overstepped their bounds in hearing or denying certain kinds of cases, a royal jurisdictional privilege known as the *recurso de fuerza*.[97]

Bravo de Lagunas criticized the supporters of ecclesiastical authority for narrowing what had once been a wide spectrum of judicial opinions about the crown's right to trump the Church in hearing certain civil cases. The Lima jurist showed his facility with the Doctors as he considered the case that had triggered the dispute, but he claimed that, although one or two supported the Church in such jurisdictional disputes, the greater number did not. Unlike those who thought that opinions "should not be counted, but rather weighed"—meaning probabilists—Bravo de Lagunas preferred to extract "generalities" from diverse doctrines known as "common opinion." Warning against the tendency to follow the Authors "like sheep," he read commentaries as objects to be rationally approached, eventually subordinating interpretation to law as written and, critically, as practiced.

Ultimately, his regalist argument rested both on Spanish royal law itself and on custom. Perhaps the clearest Spanish law on the matter was compiled in the Castilian *Recopilación,* which set forth the idea that the king would be a kind of referee in disputes over what were called "mixed things," or jurisdictionally contested matters.[98] At the same time, Bravo de Lagunas argued that even if the law were unclear, practice would take precedence, and practice had been to respect royal authority in such matters. What, in custom, he asked, could be "more legitimate, rational, and exercised with the most justification than the practice [of royal prerogative] long accepted. . . . by the Holy See"?[99]

Bravo de Lagunas on Slavery

In his opinions on slavery, Bravo de Lagunas's rejection of casuism and probabilism were a bit more subdued than in his writings on secular jurisdiction. But in these opinions, his defense of custom as a privileged source of law is even more pronounced and landed closer to home. The two opinions on slavery dealt with unique legal features of Spanish American bondage and manumission: slaves' civil right to self-purchase and conditional liberty, a contractual practice in which an owner freed a slave pending death, the passage of time, or the completion of a certain service. Bravo de Lagunas displayed a kind of creole eclecticism regarding slave law in a 1746 opinion entitled "Letter in which it is considered: if, because of the favor of liberty, a master can be obligated to receive the price of his servant," referred to here as the "Letter . . . of liberty."[100]

The main body of this text is a consideration of various sources—Roman, Spanish, and customary—concerning whether, if masters were forced to sell their slaves, the slaves should be given the first option to purchase their own freedom.[101] The jurist reverse-engineered his consideration of each basis of law according to its ultimate significance, and local practice came out on top.

He began his exploration of whether slaves possessed the right to purchase freedom by systematically poking holes in the understandings of the commentators and *tratadistas* who surmised that a master could be forced to sell a slave. Departing from older models of interpretation, he cast commentators aside and immersed himself directly in Roman laws on bondage and the conditions under which they were promulgated, ultimately deciding that, when considered in historical context, none permitted the courts to force a master to sell his slave.

Bravo de Lagunas paused from his historical consideration of Roman law only to directly address the concept of equity. The colonial jurist wrote about equity in a way reminiscent of Feijóo but, in the end, he more easily dispensed with judicial compassion than did his peninsular counterpart. Equity, he claimed, had become a way for judges to put "crowns on their heads" and "scepters in their hands." Invoking equity made it appear that judges were ruling out of compassion for slaves but, in fact, this tendency was "an equity against the Law (*Ley*) and against reason, on which it is founded."[102]

Pitting "equity against the Law" served as the coup de grâce in Bravo de Lagunas's treatment of Roman law. After demonstrating his deep knowledge and ability to historically contextualize the *corpus iuris*, he turned to perform the same kind of surgery on Spanish laws. Again, he condemned popular commentators, who he believed had misconstrued a Spanish law that appeared in the *Recopilación de leyes de las indias*. This law granted the free fathers of slave children precedence in buying freedom for their offspring in the event they were to be sold. Bravo de Lagunas pointed out that this law did not address the issue of whether slaves should be able to purchase themselves and that it said nothing on whether a master might be forced to sell a slave to the father.

The jurist finally made his ruling: in a certain instance, slaves could be legally considered to have the right to precedence in purchasing their liberty. He noted that both Roman laws and the *Siete Partidas* expressly stated that a master convicted of mistreating or prostituting his slave would suffer the punishment of being compelled to sell the slave, losing all rights over his human property.[103] It was here, Bravo de Lagunas indicated, that the law favored slaves by permitting them to search for a legal avenue toward freedom.

Bravo de Lagunas's decision to favor slave rights to self-purchase in cases of abuse derived from a particularly creole deployment of precedent and custom. First, he spent considerable time considering Corradini's description of a customary practice in Naples that was later extended to other Spanish realms.[104] When the king wanted to sell a town that he owned, Bravo de Lagunas explained, the laws held that the town had a right of "*prelación*," or precedence in purchasing its independence, rather than to step aside and cede control to another nobleman or prince.[105] Drawing parallels between pueblos' and slaves' privileges to be free and independent, Bravo de Lagunas reasoned that slaves should be given precedence to purchase their own freedom.

Second, Bravo de Lagunas drew from the legitimating weight of precedent.[106] For this, he turned to Juan Bautista Larrea, a late sixteenth-century Spanish "*decisionista*" whose works compiled opinions on diverse legal matters, and who gained increasing popularity in Spanish America during the second half of the eighteenth century.[107] No particular decision in Larrea's compilation captivated Bravo de Lagunas or lent weight to his opinion favoring slaves in cases of abuse, merely that decisions could be sources of authority in and of themselves. "The style of judging in Superior Tribunals, [when] justified," he proclaimed in a common refrain, "is the best interpreter of the law."[108]

The comments of one of his correspondents, Antonio de Borda, pushed the argument even further by calling for a "national" codification of Peru's laws. Borda, a fellow law professor from San Marcos, reported that Bravo de Lagunas had encouraged him to contribute to the *Legal Collection* a statement advocating for the systematic modernization of imperial law. To Borda, this meant more than an update of the *Recopilación de las leyes de Indias*. He proclaimed that Spanish conquest had not "established two Colonies but two Empires" in Mexico and Peru that required codified laws for each "nation," and pointed out the best jurisprudence drew principally not from Rome, Spain, or Europe more broadly, but rather from the "patria," where laws should be molded to the diversity of its population, including Indians and "negros."[109]

A local colonial, even "national" rationale for ruling in slave suits undergirded Bravo de Lagunas's final, and most radical, opinion in the "Letter . . . of Liberty," which concerned the issue of a master's intent to sell a slave. Since, like pueblos, slaves had the right of precedence to purchase themselves, they also had precedence if a master intended to sell a slave but only resisted because the slave had made her own arrangements with a purchaser. The basis for his opinion was simple: "According to the practice of our Tribunals, the serious intention of a master of a servant is sufficient [to force a sale]."[110] The jurist went on to consider earlier practice in Peru that might have better served as precedent, including a custom described to him by an elder judge of forcing the *tasación*, or establishing the official price, of slave brides in order to free slaves as a kind of "dowry," although, the judge said, "I don't have an example before me."

Thus Bravo de Lagunas's 1746 "Letter . . . of Liberty" mixed natural rights theories with early formalist notions of law as a generalizable system. It rejected the commentator-obsessed casuistic Jesuit juridical and ethical method that had long supported customary, local colonial control, but it was not intended to undermine local custom as a legitimate source of law. Indeed, Bravo de Lagunas worked into his decision on slave rights an endorsement of a pueblo's right to liberate itself, and he elevated the practices of his home tribunal, the judicial history of his city, and even his colonial "nation's" experience with slavery above the commentators and glossators long revered by his counterparts. That all of his legal opinions were patriotic exercises in asserting the place of Spanish American Enlightenment legal thought was clear in his choice to quote from Feijóo in the preface to his published collection. The "culture of human arts," the Benedictine monk had observed, ". . . flowers more in America than Spain."[111]

This would not be the jurist's final word on slavery. In 1758, he drew back from this position on slave rights, advancing a more restrictive view of slaves' legal avenues toward freedom. The "recipient" of the new letter on slavery, fellow creole high court minister Domingo José Orrantia, hints at what might have inspired Bravo de Lagunas's change of heart. He pointed out that Bravo de Lagunas's indictment of the legal profession no longer centered on young lawyers but on the entire legal profession. The problem was to be found in classrooms and, ultimately, the courtrooms of the city. In the *colegios* where young lawyers were trained, it was almost mandatory to be a probabilist. "They take every doubt as a probability . . . their genius finds doubts in every suit . . . In this way, the [number of cases] grow, and the Republic suffers the evils, lamented by all, of a multitude of suits."[112] Bravo de Lagunas too watched this "multitude of suits" swell. He reported on ruling on at least one slave case that brushed up against the very type of issues he addressed in this letter. More, he claimed, were on the docket awaiting trial.

As civil cases, including those slaves initiated, increasingly filled the dockets of judges like Orrantia and Bravo de Lagunas in the 1750s, they no longer approached the question of freedom as one that reflected back on the rights of the pueblo or the jurisprudence of the Peruvian "empire." The ministers, Orrantia reported, were awaiting a remedy for the "many and slow suits" making their way through Lima's high court. The solution could not, he was sure, come from the judges themselves but rather "must come from a hand superior to ours, the monarch." The creole oidores called for royal reform responsive to the particular legal needs of the colonies. They would not have to wait long.

Laws on Laws

Like any practical-minded Enlightenment thinker, Benito Feijóo had some concrete ideas about how best to administer justice. Lawsuits took too long and royal reform was needed to shorten them. His essay "On the Grave Importance of Shortening Cases" was inspired by Peter the Great of Russia, who, deciding that court cases in Russia dragged on excessively, decreed that all pending cases be decided in eleven days. Still a legal pluralist committed to jurisdictional competition, Feijóo did not recommend rushing in the manner of the czar; after all, he said, this eleven-day period did not include "appeals and judgments in different Tribunals."[113] But the Russian reform prompted Feijóo to enumerate the multiple inefficiencies of Spain's imperial justice system.

As he did this, Feijóo provided a panoramic view of the contemporary court system in the empire. Slow lawsuits comprised one problem, impeding the economic productivity of litigants and diminishing revenue for the crown. He detailed the excessive cost of suits, the manner in which suing drew litigants into the cities away from their homes and work, and the unregulated activities of legal amanuenses. Feijóo guessed that at least a hundred thousand men were employed in legal activities in and around the courts of Spain, all of whom, "with a new policy to shorten suits will be more useful to the whole Kingdom, employed [instead] in Agriculture, the Militia, the Navy and the liberal and mechanical arts."[114] Caging one of the central preoccupations of the century—the inefficiency of the legal system—in a regalist framework, Feijóo presaged many of the legal reforms that Bourbon royal officials would implement over the remaining half of the century.[115] In the final decades of the 1700s, efforts to improve the administration of justice increasingly came to mean asserting the primacy of secular jurisdiction.

No judicial body remained untouched by the sweeping administrative reforms and new institutional mechanisms for meting out justice implemented during the most active years of Bourbon Reforms, which spanned the reigns of Carlos III (1759–88) and Carlos IV (1788–1808). Even the Council of Indies, the jurisdictional pinnacle of Spain's American empire, underwent significant reorganization in the 1760s. Administratively, the establishment of the intendancy system, which replaced the former system of alcaldías mayores and corregidores, or mid-level jurisdictions, was a move with potentially wide-ranging consequences for litigants.

These royal programs of legal centralization fit nicely with the image of the Spanish Bourbon dynasty as a rigid and universalizing modern state that sought to promote law over justice. Yet regalist reforms of legal practices did not originate only from the minds of the reformist bureaucrats ensconced in the rooms of royal ministries but also from dynamic interactions with the colonies. Indeed, colonial litigants were frequently the initiators of the changes.[116]

"Unencumbered and Free": Laws on Judicial Efficiency

A clause in the 1788 *Instructions to Intendants*, issued as royal reformers put into place new administrative and judicial structures throughout the empire, summed up the new legal orientation of the empire. Judges were specially instructed to ensure that cases receive "brief dispatch" and that litigants not be "bothered with useless delays."[117] This prodding of magistrates to move cases along capped a series of earlier efforts to speed cases through the secular courts, frequently crafted in response to colonial complaints about the slow pace of the justice system.[118]

The *Instructions to Intendants* suggested that lawyers, procurators, and the "rest of the judicial officials" served as a drag on the court system. In this, it echoed a 1768 order demanding that the customary practice of explaining sentences, which had developed in some regions of the peninsula, be ended so that all sentences followed an abbreviated form and were issued in Spanish rather than Latin to promote "uniformity of language." Reading more deeply, the documents also implied that litigants shared the blame for creating bottlenecks in the justice system by dragging out suits and making them more complicated than they had to be.[119]

A law aimed at litigant practices issued in 1774 was designed to force parties in a dispute to respond to motions by the opposing party more quickly.[120] Because litigants often missed or ignored deadlines, many lapsed into "rebeldía" of the court. They either filed nothing in response, which prompted repeated requests from their opponents to judges to enforce the deadlines, or made unending requests for more time. Litigants usually faced no consequences for this foot-dragging. Carlos III's 1774 royal order—importantly, issued in response to a colonial case from Cartagena—shortened the number of lapses that would be legally tolerated from three to one. Citing laws in both the *Recopilaciones* of Castile and the Indies, the order called the three-time practice an "abuse" and "corruption" that drove up court costs. The edict limiting the lapses to one was to be placed on a placard to ensure that all litigants of the "Dominions of America" would know about it.[121]

Three years later, the king further cleared the clogged channels of colonial courts with an edict ensuring that cases heard by first-instance courts would not be delayed while litigants appealed to superior courts for rulings on secondary details of the suits, even if it was the king himself who was seeking clarification on a judicial matter.[122] Citing "the repeated insistence" of Spanish American litigants and officials, Carlos III directed litigants to respect the "admirable order" of the jurisdictional hierarchy of appeals to promote the "briefest determination of Suits and their appeals and recourses, conforming to law so that the Vassals enter the appropriate court and tribunals unencumbered and free to air and conclude their actions and rights (*derechos*)."[123]

These plans to hurry cases through to sentences according to an "admirable order" suggest that the crown was formulating a new science of suing by minimizing jurisdictional conflict and maximizing the efficiency of the courts to bring cases to resolution. This new science of suing involved gathering vast amounts of information to ensure that existing laws about legal practice once ignored were now followed, and that new laws could be created to enhance the technologies of the state. Among these was the March 20, 1790, royal order, promulgated by Carlos IV, requiring all of the high courts in the colonies to provide a summary accounting of the cases pending and sentenced in their tribunals during the year.[124] Sent to the audiencias of Spanish America and the Philippines at the request of the regent of Santo Domingo, the order was "in favor of the public interest and for the benefit of my vassals and their privileged [legal] business, that they not be exposed to notorious delays."[125]

These legal information-gathering efforts are significant, but developing new technologies of the state and promoting more formalist approaches to the law was not an exact science. In some instances, royal policy seemed to entrench or expand longstanding practices of justice-oriented legal culture. For example, even as the crown attempted to accelerate the pace at which formal lawsuits worked their way through the justice system, many royal reforms also permitted the controlled growth of the extrajudicial sphere of unwritten activity of court officials, albeit with some measure of judicial accountability attached. Such was the case with a 1777 royal order tackling the fact that, in Lima, sentences were being concluded with the decisions of fewer judges than normally required at both high and low court levels. While Carlos III superficially encouraged compliance with sentencing requirements and reiterated that existing rules must be followed, he also tacitly accepted the continued functioning of the extrajudicial, unwritten role of legal officials in verbally solving less weighty disputes.[126] In the 1788 *Instructions to Intendants,* the crown explicitly encouraged judges to use their benches for extrajudicial settlements in minor cases and to foster in litigants a spirit of "friendship and spiritual freedom (*voluntariedad*)." Thus, the Bourbon goal was not rigidity for its own sake but rather promoting judicial accessibility and efficiency.[127]

Bronze Ministers

Bourbon reformers' primary interest was in court access and efficiency, but promoting judicial impartiality ran a close second. The signal administrative reform of the Bourbon period was the creation of the intendancy system, headed by an official appointed by the king and paid with a royal salary. The new system was intended to be less rooted in local communities and more impartial than the embedded justice system of the Hapsburgs, in which judges paid for their posts.[128] Intendants were to embody the spirit of the public servant—the bronze ministers of Feijóo's imagination.

The creation of the position of regent in the late 1770s constituted another ambitious reform at the high court level. The office of the regency responded to trenchant criticisms leveled against the audiencias, complaints made chiefly by José de Gálvez, whom Carlos III sent during the early years of his reign to assess the state of royal administration in the American colonies. The regency was to provide a royal counterweight to the outsize influence of the high courts over judicial matters and regulate the perceived overreach of viceroys into lawsuits. Regencies were established as discrete official posts in the Audiencias of Mexico, Peru, and New Granada; in other smaller audiencias, the post was combined with the post of president of the audiencia.

Procedurally, the main job of the regent was to ensure smooth operation of the courts, squelching unnecessary jurisdictional conflict and ensuring that justice moved quickly and cleanly without the usual personal entanglements and work stoppages. One of the regent's primary tasks was to provide reports on the "state of the Suits in the Audiencias, to avoid anything that impedes their course, or their determination by illegitimate means ... so that Justice is exercised in the due and prompt way it should be."[129] The regent also was required to ensure that, when a case was appealed to the audiencia, the tribunal did not impose sentences that might "defraud" and instill "terror" in litigants or to "intimidate the parties to refrain from pursuing their justice."[130] While the functions delegated to the regent leaned toward a formalist vision of law, this did not mean that his job was to formalize all suits that reached him. The regent could hear verbal complaints from litigants who were considered "miserables," though he did not exercise exclusive jurisdiction over those suits.[131]

The establishment of intendancies and regencies revealed a fundamental lack of faith in the traditional judicial institutions of the audiencias and the viceroy. Bourbon policymakers deemed the legal knowledge of judges and lawyers to be lacking and their commitment to impartial justice weak, and Bourbon edicts about how to practice law often contained a subtext about the perceived ineptness or corruption of legal professionals.

A longstanding problem in systematizing the use of law was that judges themselves often did not know the laws and were not university trained. In 1789, Carlos III confronted the issue of whether a lack of education exempted judges from responsibility if their advisers provided them bad advice.[132] While the crown found judges to not be accountable for failings based on poor counsel, the edict made it clear that royal concern was less about the individual judges than in instilling some kind of regularity in sentencing. The order explicitly discussed the royal desire to align "old" and "modern" laws and to produce a "general and fixed rule" to remedy the variation in judicial rationales for rulings.

Another pressing issue for Bourbon reformers concerned litigants' ability to challenge biased ministers of the law. Royal policy here had a kind of whiplash quality, first limiting then endorsing litigants' right to challenge potentially partial judges or legal advisers. A ruling in 1766 limited to three the number of times a litigant could ask to recuse judicial advisers, stating that a major impediment to the "brief expedition of cases" were litigants' endless requests for recusal at lower-court levels.[133]

Still, royal policy did not treat litigants' claims to judicial bias as unfounded. In 1777, the Peruvian viceroy complained to Carlos III that litigants had been bombarding him with requests to recuse judges and their advisers because of perceived prejudice. Viceroy Manual Amat y Junient had, in fact, tried to curb rampant recusals with a decree of his own, but one in which he defended the obviously suspect practice of naming "secret" advisors to judges. Litigants legitimately claimed that these secret advisors often had an interest in the disputes. In fact, the viceroy's ruling revealed that anonymous advisors might be the very same lawyers representing one or the other party in the dispute.

In his 1777 royal cédula, the king attempted to explain how such an obviously dubious legal practice had developed, and quarantine it from more modern judicial procedures aimed at expediency and impartiality. The royal order recounted how, at one time, it had made sense to double up on legal counsel in regions without lawyers but, the king pointed out that, even then the advisors did not work anonymously. Despite the fact that the initial request from the viceroy was to squelch emboldened litigants' requests for recusals, the king rejected the viceroy's protection of secret advisors, sided with litigants, and ultimately called for greater transparency in the practices of judicial advisement.[134]

The Growth of Secular Jurisdiction

Jurisdiction had always been contested in the empire and especially so in the colonies. But, as Bravo de Lagunas's writings reveal, contests between church and crown intensified the 1700s. A review of cédulas issued in the late 1780s and early '90s suggests that the king and his advisers spent a great deal of the time attempting to put in a more modern order the traditional disorder of jurisdictional jockeying by making royal authority supreme.

Peninsular jurists defended the crown's jurisdictional prerogatives by updating their interpretations of traditional mechanisms of royal oversight (*patronazgo*) of the Church. Continuing in the same regalist vein as Bravo de Lagunas, Spanish writers such as José de Covarrubias attempted to categorize and institutionalize the institution of royal sovereignty embodied in the practice of the *recurso de fuerza,* or the right of crown courts to force ecclesiastical courts to hear or re-hear a case.[135] His *Maxims about* Recursos de fuerza, published in 1790, married natural rights theory with regalism, intending to show that royal protection of subjects from the arbitrary and unlawful abuses of ecclesiastical judges aligned with the larger protections that the sovereign owed his subjects.[136] Covarrubias suggested that the right to appeal was a "natural right" (Derecho Natural). He advanced a secular notion of society when he claimed that by "natural law" men are subjected to society, and "men are born Citizens; and Ecclesiastics do not cease to be such."[137] In short, the new Bourbon legal order was not only more formal and more purportedly impartial but also decidedly more secular and natural-rights driven.[138]

During the second half of the eighteenth century, the Spanish Bourbon monarchy asserted civil jurisdictional control over various ordinary legal matters that had formerly been the domain of ecclesiastical courts. These included parental dissent over children's choice of marriage partners; extramarital affairs (concubinage) and bigamy; and the civil aspects of divorce suits.[139] Much as these jurisdictional changes comprised a larger regalist drift toward legal secularization, they also responded to concrete challenges from litigants.

The colonial origins of new Bourbon laws on law are especially obvious in the history of alimony and child support cases, which, in 1787, were placed under secular, rather than ecclesiastical, jurisdiction. This ruling was the culmination of multiple jurisdictional disputes that resulted from the "forum shopping" strategies of quarreling Peruvian spouses. On June 17, 1786, Carlos III was asked to consider a jurisdictional dispute between Peru's viceroy and the intendant in the provincial city of Arequipa. These two colonial authorities sparred over who held competence to rule on a vicious marital dispute between Doña María Romero and her husband Don Ygnacio Salgado.[140] The puppet master behind the controversy was the bishop of Arequipa, Fray Miguel de González de Pamplona, who had been the first to rule on the conflict.

The bishop at first had tried to reunite the pair by calling on the couple's friends and relatives to persuade them to get back together, forcing them into a face-to-face encounter (careo), and even leveling a very steep—and decidedly unorthodox—extrajudicial fine of 1,009 pesos against Don Ygnacio for failing to comply with his orders. Don Ygnacio, a friend of the civil judges, scoffed at the fine and, it seems, resumed a longstanding affair with a local woman, sending his wife to live in a lay spiritual house. That is when Doña Maria returned to Bishop Miguel to complain that her estranged husband had tried to poison her. The bishop called on the intendant, and the two worked together to demand that Don Ygnacio pay for his wife's upkeep and court fees during a trial, as well as answer criminal charges of infidelity and attempted murder before the intendant. But Don Ygnacio had had enough of the bishop's meddling. He went to the Real Audiencia in Lima and then to the viceroy, seeking secular intervention to remove the case from ecclesiastical jurisdiction. The high court and the viceroy agreed that poisoning was a criminal offense and thus beyond the Church's reach, but Bishop Miguel appealed to the Council of Indies to retain jurisdiction over the embattled couple.

The case stumped the Council and perplexed the king. Some of it was clear: the divorce case fell in the domain of the ecclesiastical judge, while poisoning and the "dishonest life" of Don Ygnacio's lover were secular matters. But the crown was at a loss concerning jurisdiction over Doña María's dowry, alimony, and court fees (litis expensas.) The king issued an order shuffling the case back to the Council of Indies, whose ministers in turn only indirectly addressed the jurisdictional complications by reminding Spanish American bishops that they had no ability to level fines on parishioners and warning them "in the future to proceed with more regularity and not meddle in matters that are proper to Royal jurisdiction."[141]

The following year, upon facing another such dispute—this one based on a Lima divorce case—the crown could no longer avoid the colonial pressure to decide on increasingly complicated jurisdictional issues in marriage disputes. The king issued a groundbreaking cédula that placed conflicts over the material aspects of divorce under royal civil courts.[142] This edict effectively split jurisdiction over divorce and annulment suits between secular and Church authorities. No longer were Church judges to issue interim, executive rulings on dowries, alimony, or court fees as marital disputes wended their way through the ecclesiastical court system. The order corralled Church judges into hearing only the root causes of divorce or annulment suits, described as purely "spiritual," and were forbidden from "becoming mixed up . . . in temporal and profane matters concerning *alimentos*, court fees, or the restitution of dowries, which are rightful and exclusive to secular Magistrates." Not until 1804 was the order extended, by a royal disposition, to Spain itself, based on colonial precedent and a desire to make imperial practice uniform.[143]

As it muscled the Church out of its traditional role in managing many aspects of marital discord, the 1787 royal order flexed secular control over a new area of contention, that is, colonial women's demands that husbands pay the costs of going to court in the first place. By shifting the matter of litis expensas to secular courts, the cédula signaled the crown's general hospitality to the colonial women who chose to file formal suits against husbands before civil authorities, even as the crown discursively promoted the informal resolution of conflicts. While observers fretted about litigiousness in the Spanish empire, the royal ruling on alimentos demonstrates that the Bourbon crown's default response was to take advantage of colonial litigants' insistence on greater jurisdictional clarity by widening the channels through which they could enter royal courts, often at the expense of the Church.

Agents and Powers Revisited

The outcome of eighteenth-century debates concerning the licensing of legal agents, or informal writers-for-hire, serves as a final example of how Bourbon policy expanded access to civil courts and, in doing so, contributed to a general shift toward a new law-oriented culture. The battle to defend litigants' "liberty" to be represented as they saw fit found allies even at the highest echelons of royal policymakers, including the king himself.

The legal agents who set up makeshift offices and proffered their services to potential litigants in the arched halls of the empire's bureaucratic buildings had always been a source of trouble in the empire, prompting royal efforts to control their activities in the seventeenth century. In the eighteenth century, the trouble seemed to reach a critical juncture, especially as agents rankled professional lawyers in Mexico City. During the first half of the century, the official procurators of the high court in the capital city of New Spain worried that agents' anonymity, slim education in the law, and lack of accountability for the suits they initiated on behalf of clients posed serious risks to the justice system. Naturally, procurators were also concerned that agents siphoned off some of their income.[144]

It is probably not a coincidence that the most energetic efforts to limit these unlicensed legal writers began at mid-century, as the number of cases in the tribunals of Mexico City began to climb. In the 1740s, Viceroy Pedro de Sastro Figueroa y Salazar, Duque de la Conquista, proposed a program to license and register agents and force them to pay the *media anata*, a tax on royal posts paid by all officials or guild members. His efforts amounted to little, although a few rogue writers did face penalties and hefty fines of 200 to 500 pesos for acting as unregistered agents, or an *agentes intrusos*.

Mexico City's procurators worried about more than these unregistered agents. Throughout the second half of the eighteenth century, they repeatedly sought to reduce the number of officially registered agents as well, and to deny them the ability to purchase, hold, and pass their offices to successors, as other official personnel of the court could. For their part, the official agents protested that procurators wanted to monopolize not only formal petitions to initiate formal lawsuits but even petitions designed to bring about quick—perhaps verbal—resolution. The more the procurators scuffled with the registered agents, the greater the number of unregistered agents grew.

In the 1770s, Visitor General José Antonio Areche revived the flagging idea of an agent registration system. As a former high court judge in the Audiencia of Mexico who had been appointed as a visitor by the new Minister of the Indies, José de Gálvez, Areche understood well that legal representation functioned without oversight in most colonial tribunals. He capped the number of licensed agents in the Mexican high court at fourteen, and forbade agents from filing formal cases.[145] This did little to stop litigants from seeking outside agents, and indeed Mexico's viceroy abetted their search by continually appointing supernumerary agents as official *agentes de negocio*, exceeding the limit of fourteen. Soon, successive viceroys, audiencia ministers, and crown attorneys began to clash over the matter of agents both official and unofficial, all supporting some system of licensing but failing to agree on how best to institute it. Finally, the issue was sent to the Council of Indies in 1784, where it sat for over a decade, awaiting a decision.

In the meantime, in Madrid a similar set of problems surrounding colonial cases cropped up in courts that heard cases from the Indies. In the 1770s Carlos III had become concerned with the freewheeling work of agents representing colonial litigants in peninsular tribunals. The quantity and diversity of such legal amanuenses available for colonial litigants to hire in Spain's courts had prompted the king to issue a circular in 1778 that named thirty approved agents—a process of licensing in which agents would be "numbered" (*agentes de número*) similar to procurators or attorneys. In subsequent years, several of the thirty posts became vacant, giving rise to questions regarding the procedures for new appointments and revealing that the numbered agent system functioned more on paper than in reality. By 1793, Carlos IV increased the number of numbered agents to fifty, possibly in response to the increasing number of suits from the colonies reaching Spain. The next year, he formalized the agents' work with published ordinances that required the representatives to be disinterested professionals.

In 1795, the Council of Indies finally ruled on the issue of agents for Mexico's audiencia and shortly thereafter the king tried to solve, once and for all, the problem of the Madrid agents. Both rulings championed the rights of colonial litigants to use agents of their choosing. In a decision rendered on the Mexican dispute on April 14, the minister overseeing the case before the Council of Indies ruled against the procurators and in favor of the registered agents of the audiencia and, ultimately, the litigants who contracted their services. His decision did not start out auspiciously for the agents and their clients: "for a long time," he wrote, "it has been clear that the arbitrary occupation that various vassals have taken of the title of Agentes de Negocios is odious and prejudicial, and the result is that vice-ridden and lazy [individuals] hide beneath the cape of Agents."[146] But he went on to say that, although the issue appeared to be one that was urgent, and despite the insistence of procurators that they should hold exclusive monopoly over court cases, in fact the matter should be "left to the free will (*voluntad*) of the parties" of a dispute. The solution was for registered agents to be made available to all litigants while freeing litigants to choose to use them or not.

It should be noted that the sentence was based on more than only litigant rights in an abstract sense. The judge detailed the various ways that the crown would lose income by restricting Mexican litigants to select only among agents who owned their titles and could sell them to others. But whatever his motivation, litigants, he said, had the "liberty of availing themselves of any other person" to represent them in court.[147]

Less than two weeks later, on April 24, Carlos IV issued a cédula that mirrored this decision in the Mexican case. In it, the king detailed precisely how colonial litigants were to select counsel in the peninsular courts of Spain.[148] It came up with rules to ensure that royal courts could facilitate litigants' access to "loyal, disinterested, and pure" legal representation through loose licensing laws protecting their freedom to name their own counsel. That counsel included unregistered agents. The crown order specified that colonial Spanish American litigants were not bound to use only the select fifty numbered agents in metropolitan courts. Rather, as in Mexico, the agents would be made available for litigants to choose if they desired, and they would serve as a kind of reserve in the event that a private, unnumbered agent selected by the litigant was deemed unfit. While the courts were responsible for ensuring that private agents were fit to serve, the king was unequivocal on the point that colonial subjects enjoyed liberty in selecting their own legal representatives for the early parts of suits, along with other legal business.[149]

While the licensing and registration of agents can be rightly interpreted as an attempt to rein in agents who had informally offered their services to colonial clients for centuries, Bourbon legal reforms also balanced regulation with clear support for litigants' freedom to select their own legal representation. Thus the "modern" legal process at work involved both imagining the litigant as a rights-bearing, independent subject and engineering state mechanisms through which that independence would be ensured.

During the annual elegy of the Spanish king at Madrid's Economic Society in 1787, a member of the society referred not to a republic but an "Empire of Letters." Royal reform had ensured that Spain "will no longer experience that alternation of darkness and light that has led Foreigners to believe that we were by nature condemned to perpetual shadows." Through the monarchy's promotion of reform, "a general system of principals has been unveiled, perhaps for the first time, and the art of discovering the truth has been reduced to a method; because, with him, reason is recovering rights that authority had usurped."[150] With this, the elegist made it clear that regalism comfortably harbored the kinds of legal concepts about methods, reason, and rights that constituted the lettered legal Enlightenment.

Top-down versions of Spanish Enlightenment legal thought reached litigants in multiple ways. They came in the books their lawyers read, in the decisions their judges rendered, and in the laws their king promulgated. A new culture of law emanated from rarified spaces such as university lecture halls, economic societies, and judges' chambers, where once-dispersed sources of "derecho" narrowed to a more state-centered focus on "law" as a formal and impartial system. But this was no leviathan rising from among metropolitan intellectuals and policy-makers in Madrid, extending across the Atlantic to the far reaches of places such as southern Mexico. In multiple cases, colonial subjects themselves demanded royal reform of the legal system. These demands came in the published opinions of the Lima jurist Bravo de Lagunas and his fellow high court ministers;

they came as requests from colonial authorities for greater efficiency in the court system; they even came as the result of backfiring official requests to bolster more traditional ways of practicing the law. And these demands came from colonial litigants and their legal agents who challenged the flexible jurisdictional boundaries and justice-oriented culture of the empire, inspiring the king to buttress royal prerogatives and open wider channels for litigants to freely access his courts.

Although the advent of legal modernity in the Spanish empire involved a transition from derecho to law, it would be misleading to imagine this period as one in which formalist, rationalist versions of law became incontestably dominant. The history of the Spanish legal Enlightenment reveals a need to think beyond tradition and modernity as inimical categories in eighteenth-century history. Recognizing the importance of eclecticism is one route to a more nuanced understanding of the legal thought of the era, as is expanding the definition of modernity to accommodate the lived experience of litigants in the Spanish empire and beyond.

The dynamic way Spanish imperial jurists, royal advisers and Bourbon kings generated eclectic and novel ways of thinking about laws and rights in dialogue with colonial exigencies also serves to challenge versions of intellectual and legal history that read as a succession of learned books and lettered correspondence that propelled modernity forward. Beyond the printed tract or edict, this more dynamic intellectual history also belonged to litigants who never published a thing but did submit handwritten petitions and papers to the court. As they did this, they lodged their own history of ideas in the legal archives of the empire.

3

Numbers and Values

Counting Cases in the Spanish Empire

Clogged court dockets. Peasants quick to run to judges. Suit-wielding city-dwellers. An overabundance of lawyers. These are standard descriptions of sixteenth- and seventeenth-century Spain during its so-called "legal revolution." Deep in the eighteenth century, Spanish royal officials again complained of cities crawling with "multitudes of lawyers of uncertain birth and bad habits," scribes recounted working through the day and night "with an incessant and daily fatigue," and priests complained that native peasants would rather spend their days suing their superiors than working in the fields.[1] The descriptions now came, however, from Lima and Mexico City rather than León and Madrid.

Comparative analysis of the eighteenth-century civil case record from various judicial archives in the Spanish empire confirms that lawsuits in the Spanish American colonies indeed were on the rise in the 1700s while they stabilized or declined on the peninsula. Of course, the "civil case record" might be a measurable historical object only in the same way that the imperial "courtroom" was a real place. Knowing whether the story it tells is reliable entails paying attention to how cases were compiled and preserved. It involves considering a range of factors that affect how often people appeared before judges in the past, including demographics, economics and the bureaucracy. It also means revisiting the question of how much control ordinary litigants possessed over their suits.

Surprisingly, eighteenth century litigants who were presumably the least familiar with the lettered world of the law—subordinate colonial subjects who often could neither read nor write—increasingly entered civil courts against the powerful men and masters who held authority over them. Subordinate colonial litigants brought cases against their social superiors in numbers that outstripped the overall growth of civil litigation in the colonies, while more powerful litigants merely kept pace.

The outsize participation of subordinate litigants in the expanding civil court system of the Spanish American colonies is a significant finding. But it must be approached with caution. The numbers presented in this chapter—first about the rising tide of Spanish colonial civil suits in the eighteenth century and then about the current running within it of subordinates' lawsuits against superiors—should not be mistaken for an argument about direct causation. In order to nuance the understanding of what causes legal change, the chapter breaks up the quantitative analysis of civil lawsuits in various regions of the empire with a descriptive consideration of early modern legal practice in rural Spain, proposing an approach to historical causation in which culture counts.

Numbers

Legal historian António Manuel Hespanha, declaring that it is time for "facts again," encourages historians to examine large-scale empirical data without forgetting that legal facts themselves are representations.[2] What follows is a first cut at doing just that by analyzing civil litigation rates from roughly 1700–99 in the six regions under study: Lima and Trujillo, Peru; Mexico City and Oaxaca in New Spain; and the Montes de Toledo and the high court of Valladolid, Spain. (Appendix I describes the methods used to obtain this data and Appendix II contains the results organized in tables for each series examined.) This assessment is accompanied by reflections on reliability of these numbers and consideration of possible causes for patterns in them.[3]

Counting Cases

Overall, the archival catalogs of various Spanish American courts reveal an exceptionally clear pattern. Almost all of the civil case archival series in Mexico and Peru show a vertiginous rise in lawsuits during the second half of the eighteenth century. In Spain, however, civil litigation seemed to stabilize or even decline over the course of the century.

Figure 3.1 illustrates the general pattern of colonial litigation growth by isolating trends in five lower-level provincial and city courts. In the Montes de Toledo, cases heard by the Fiel del Juzgado dropped in the eighteenth century while in every colonial Spanish American series except the first-instance Peruvian municipal court of Trujillo the number of lawsuits skyrockets in the 1700s. And Trujillo did not lag far behind. Though not shown in Figure 3.1, there too cases would almost triple in volume in the first two decades of the nineteenth century.

Imperial inhabitants had a highly variable degree of access to formal judicial institutions. Rural inhabitants sometimes lived several days' treacherous journey from tribunals, and many rural indigenous subjects did not speak Spanish.

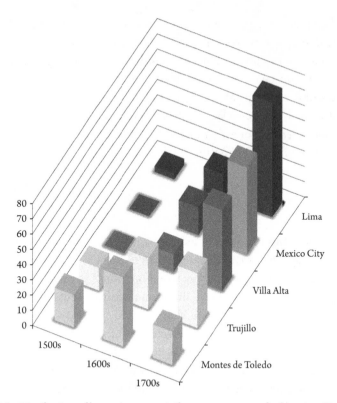

Figure 3.1 Distribution of lower-instance civil cases per century by location. Data represents percentage of total suits heard in each jurisdiction out of the total over three centuries. The actual number of suits on file for each jurisdiction and period ranges widely, from 4 to over 9,000. Data for Montes de Toledo from AMT series Fiel del Juzgado, Pleitos, Civiles, Ejecutivos. Data for Trujillo from ARL series Cabildo, Justicia Ordinaria, Civiles. Data for Villa Alta from AHJO, series Villa Alta, Civiles. Data for Mexico City from AGN-M series TSJ, Civiles. Data for Lima from AGN-P series Cabildo, Civiles.

Residents of native pueblos technically had access to interpreters, and like inhabitants of other rural villages, including in Spain, they could turn to trained notaries to write up petitions to submit to district judges. But given notaries' frequent absences in rural regions and village-level judges' common inability to write, most community justice probably took place verbally. Only if a litigant coordinated with the notary or interpreter, often under the watchful eye of a local justice, could a suit be put in writing and sent on to a magistrate such as the Fiel del Juzgado in Toledo or the alcaldes mayores and corregidores who presided over district seats in rural Mexico and Peru.

City dwellers and urban migrants, especially those in capital cities, could enter an array of tribunals that teemed with personnel—official and unofficial—ready to write a petition for a prospective litigant. But even in the large capitals such as Mexico City and Lima, written and verbal legal practices still frequently overlapped. Sometimes litigants approached magistrates to complain out loud rather than to open a formal, written dispute, and a judge of any rank in a bustling city might solve a dispute without a formal, written sentence or by mediating a face-to-face encounter between parties.

Yet, regardless of jurisdiction or region, the sheer number of written civil cases on record the colonial sites examined increases at the turn of the century. While proximity to colonial cities, particularly viceregal capitals, correlated to the highest numbers of cases, the surge in civil lawsuits also took place in rural areas quite distant from Spanish tribunals.[4] It occurred in the courts of traditional Hapsburg administration and in the newly created jurisdictions of Bourbon judges. In almost all instances, the 1770s mark the beginning of the growth and, in every region, the increase continues into the first decades of the 1800s, until the wars for independence in Spanish America.

By contrast, Spanish peninsular courts—the courts of the imperial metropole—do not present any significant growth in civil caseloads during the eighteenth century. In the Montes de Toledo, a decline in the numbers of civil cases registered with the Fiel del Juzgado that began at the end of the seventeenth century continued into the nineteenth century. At the same time, the number of cases heard in the Castilian high court of the Real Chancellería de Valladolid stabilized, failing to show the intense growth that is visible in civil lawsuits in the colonies. In this respect, the Spanish peninsular civil courts examined reflect a broader European trend that historians call the "great litigation decline" of the eighteenth century.[5]

Before accepting the argument that the colonial litigation boom and Spanish peninsular litigation bust were real, it is worthwhile to reflect on whether numbers generated from eighteenth-century archives should be used to ascertain historical trends at all.[6] The organization and unique histories of the various national and regional archives holding these cases undoubtedly affect the reliability of the statistics they can generate. Indeed, one ready explanation for the increase in colonial civil cases is simple archival preservation: the more recent the lawsuit, the greater the chance it survives today. However, if this were true, each archive's holdings, regardless of document type, regardless of region, should increase steadily over time.

Gradual growth certainly is not the rule in every archive or series examined here. It is not manifest in certain of the first-instance series of civil cases in Mexico, or in any jurisdiction in Trujillo, where litigation rates undulate in the eighteenth century before cresting in the nineteenth. And it does not pertain to any series in the two Spanish regions examined. Other kinds of legal documents beside civil cases heard in royal courts, such as certain types of ecclesiastical disputes and even ordinary notary records such as apprenticeships and legal guardianship contracts, diminish over the course of the eighteenth century.[7]

More to the point, contemporary documents detailing the volume of civil cases in various jurisdictions tend to substantiate the patterns in today's archival holdings. Complaints of overwork among court personnel constitute one type of corroboration. For example, several procurators in the city of Lima protested that they were far too busy to take on the pro bono case of slave Liberata de Jesús, who was suing her owner for excessive cruelty in 1791. No fewer than three procurators begged off representing her, stating they were saddled with too many suits. One said he was steering at least 30 pro bono cases through court in addition to the suits of his paying clientele.[8]

Obviously, lawyers' laments, especially those designed to get out of working for free, might be considered highly problematic historical evidence. Yet other, less self-interested sources also solidify contemporaries' observations that colonial civil suits were on the rise. For example, the regent of Guadalajara proposed moving some civil cases to the criminal bench of the city's audiencia in 1778, since the civil cases had grown in number while criminal cases declined.[9] Even more helpful are eighteenth-century recordings of caseloads such as the list that the court notaries of the Audiencia of Lima compiled for each year between 1790 and 1796, detailing the suits that the high court heard, concluded, and sentenced.[10] These reports make it possible to compare the amount of material in the archive today with the activities of the high court in the past.

Court notaries reported, for example, that the Audiencia of Lima heard 626 cases in 1791, rendering a final sentence on 199 suits, with 427 still pending final determination. The number of civil suits from this jurisdiction that remain on file for the year 1791 in the national archive of Peru is 125. The cases in the archive do not seem to have survived according to any particular logic. Most are petitions and motions or stray arguments rather than full dossiers capped by sentences, including some written petitions to initiate formal lawsuits over small sums. They also contain the formal, written cases of slaves, Indians, and widows, who could use the audiencias as a first-instance court—that is, if they could find someone to pen a petition on the proper paper and submit it. If the cases captured in the archival series can reasonably be compared to the "pending" and "sentenced" cases in court notaries' 1791 inventory, today's archival holdings would represent around 20 percent of all suits actually heard and should capture the ebbs and flows of litigation rates and types in the eighteenth century, although not the total universe of cases.

If high court records are reasonably reliable, repositories holding judicial records from lower-instance courts generate even more trustworthy numbers. An inventory undertaken in 1793 of civil and criminal disputes filed over seventy years in the Oaxacan district of Teposcolula lists all the cases that had been heard since the tenure of district magistrate Francisco Rodríguez Franco, dating back to the mid-1720s.[11] Cross-referencing that eighteenth-century inventory in the Archivo Histórico de Justicia de Oaxaca today yields a reassuring fact about colonial early modern litigation statistics: there are not fewer but more cases on file for Teposcolula in today's archive than were registered in the 1793 inventory.

From 1729–93 there are 793 civil cases on file in the Justicia Ordinaria section of the judicial archive for the Spanish colonial magistrate district of Teposcolula.[12] In contrast, the inventory taken in the eighteenth century counts 713 cases. It is possible that the extra 90 cases came in during the first and final years of the century, and therefore were not captured in the 1793 inventory. The inventory also includes an aggregate reference to "*legajos*," or bundles, of various other top-down kinds of documents described by the compiler as "superior decrees and municipal orders, and papers and letters from scribes." Some of these items undoubtedly found their way into the case file today, and the integration of these materials into the series might have enlarged the present-day number of cases such that they undercount the actual number of cases aired in the tribunal. But even if the current case record for eighteenth-century Teposcolula is not perfect, it does appear to contain most lawsuits actually aired before the Spanish district magistrate.

The Teposcolula inventory, which is organized by the tenure of the district judge rather than individual years, also indicates that a crucial turning point in colonial litigiousness occurred in the second half of the century, and particularly the 1770s.[13] Between the tenure of the first six magistrates who presided over the region during the period 1725–53 and the next six who presided from 1753–76, cases almost tripled, from 101 to 288 suits. The Spanish district magistrate who served from 1771–76 oversaw the greatest growth in cases during his tenure. He heard three times more cases per year than did his predecessors—26 per year rather than around 8—and the volume of civil litigation passing through this tribunal would be sustained or even grow after he left office. In short, the inventory aligns with the archival catalog, with both capturing a growth in colonial civil litigation from the 1770s on.[14]

If the archives of the present contain traces of a real increase in colonial judicial activity in the past, this raises the question of why that increase happened. Historians, perhaps by impulse, often first look to isolate a cause that might explain such change—some structural change that corresponds to the quantitative shift or some precipitating event to give coherence to the historical record.[15] No such unified factor emerged in my research. A number of causal factors surely impinged on the rise in Spanish colonial cases and the stability of in the number of Spanish civil suits, including the shifts in official and elite legal philosophy previously explored, as well as demography, economics and bureaucratic developments in the courts. Abandoning the search for a single cause does not, however, meaning eschewing historical explanation.[16]

Counting Causes

Demographics would provide most logical structural explanation for the growth in civil litigation during the last decades of the eighteenth century. There were simply more people living in colonial Spanish America than ever before, making it logical that more people entered the courts. Lima and Mexico City, for example, underwent significant population increases over the course of the century, which surely contributed to rising litigation rates in the cities.

But the growth in litigation does not necessarily keep perfect pace with rate of growth in population.[17] For every one inhabitant in Lima in 1700, there were 1.4 inhabitants in 1790. Yet, according to the archival record, for every one civil case filed in Lima's Cabildo during the first half of the eighteenth century, 4.2 cases appear in the civil court records during the second half of the century (Appendix II, A.3).[18] Even if the archival record for Lima's first-instance civil court were to hold all of the cases actually aired in the city rather than the 20 percent suggested by the 1791 Audiencia of Lima report, this would still mean that litigiousness ran far ahead of population growth. As for Mexico City, for every one person residing in the capital city in 1697 there may have been up to 1.6 by the early 1800s, a rate that was roughly equal to overall population growth in the Viceroyalty of New Spain between 1749 and 1808 (1:1.8).[19] The combined numbers from the two series from Mexico City's first-instance city judges indicates that for every one civil case filed in the period 1710–19, a staggering 15 appeared on judges' dockets during the period 1790–99. As Appendix II relates, the organization of Mexico's national archive surely exaggerates this number, but the stunning growth of cases it registers is not unique: the district magistrate (corregidor) of Mexico City heard 2.4 cases per year in the 1710s but 25 per year in the 1790s.

In rural areas of colonial Spanish America, the number of lawsuits also grew faster than the populations who brought them to court. In Villa Alta, Oaxaca, the population grew by one-third over the course of the century, yet civil litigation more than doubled during the same period.[20] Civil litigation in the Oaxacan district of Teposcolula likewise doubled at roughly the same time, even though this region had reached a population equilibrium at mid-century, exhibiting little growth until the latter half of the 1700s.[21] In sum, litigation grew more quickly during the eighteenth century than did the population in colonial capitals as well as in rural regions where inhabitants were more isolated from Spanish colonial tribunals.

Figures for the Spanish region of the Montes de Toledo further demonstrate that population change—while surely linked to litigation growth and slow-downs in certain instances—does not always neatly map onto litigation rates. Civil suits in the Montes had achieved previous highs in the sixteenth and seventeenth centuries precisely when the population declined. While population records for the region are spotty at best, it does appear that after the city of Toledo lost its medieval crown as the capital of Castile in 1561, the city and its rural hinterland, which included the arid Montes, began to reverse an earlier history of demographic explosion and to show signs of significant depopulation and pauperization, with peasant incomes falling.[22] Thus the Golden Age of litigation in the region occurred in a context of demographic thinning and economic decline. In the eighteenth century the population of the Montes, like Teposcolula, was relatively stable. Unlike Teposcolula, however, there was no great surge in litigation in this rural Castilian region; civil case numbers stalled and fell in a pattern typical throughout eighteenth-century Europe.[23]

Beyond a direct relationship in which population growth might spur litigation simply because there were more people to sue, demographics and suing can be related in less direct ways. Given the kind social phenomena that attends population growth, including land pressure, residential overcrowding, and migration, it is easy to imagine that the more people there are, the more they conflict. Or, perhaps the very immiseration of peasants in the Montes de Toledo in the seventeenth century produced social conflict, which then found its way into the courts. Though historians of Spanish America have not carefully correlated lawsuits and economic pressure per se, many have viewed increased litigation as a bellwether of the tense economic relationships that precede rebellion.[24] Evidence that economic hard times breed lawsuits, however, is mixed. For example, historian Juan Miguel González Fernández shows that during times of economic scarcity in eighteenth-century Galicia, first-instance civil suits went up, often instigated by more powerful plaintiffs seeking to collect on debts. When things got better, such as immediately following a harvest, civil cases slowed but criminal demands rose. Such fluctuation only affected the region's lower courts; litigation and criminal prosecution rates in the Audiencia of Galicia were impervious to the economic roller coaster outside the tribunal's doors.[25]

Hard times for some folks, of course, were not necessarily hard times for all. Perhaps nowhere was this as true as in eighteenth-century Mexico, where commercial expansion based on mining pushed natives and other peasants from their lands and created greater conflict over resources, not to mention urban overcrowding. Compounding these economic tensions were a series of serious droughts and food shortages, culminating in the so-called "year of the famine" in 1785–86.[26] At the same time, multiplying market opportunities in Mexico created a growing middle sector.

Indeed, many historians suggest that it is not downward economic pressure but rather commercial expansion that propels lawsuits. Kagan argued that Spain's early modern economic dynamism in part led to the growth of a professional class and to more commercial interactions, creating both more opportunity for conflict over business deals and more lawyers ready to argue over those deals in court. Historians of the contemporaneous legal revolutions in early modern England and France concur.[27] In fact, it was precisely women of the middling sort in colonial cities like Mexico City —the wives of artisans, shop owners, and merchants—who were most likely to sue in civil courts over alimony and child support. Likewise, aspiring indigenous elites brought many cases against native authorities, and American-born urban slaves were most likely to sue owners.

This should not lead to the conclusion that disputes among the middling classes are alone responsible for rising litigation rates.[28] During the sixteenth- and seventeenth-century heyday of litigation in Europe, the range of social groups participating in litigation was far too wide and the range of suits far too varied to be reduced to the activities of any single class, even if the middling classes were especially drawn to the courts.[29] The same can be said for litigation in the eighteenth-century Spanish empire, although, as explored below, commercial expansion conceivably could have swelled the ranks of legal professionals ready to represent litigants in court.

Professionalization can affect litigation rates in various ways. More systematized record-keeping during the Bourbon years, for example, probably led to the better preservation of existing cases for more recent periods. Yet it should be noted that the same official personnel, including public notaries and lawyers, who worked in the secular legal sphere also often worked on ecclesiastical cases, which do not present uniform growth during the period. It seems doubtful that administrative or record-keeping changes would have affected only secular legal records.

Could a surplus of legal personnel have contributed to the growth of litigation? This seems more likely than the explanation based on record keeping. Many official commentators bemoaned the growing number of Spanish American lawyers—men who, they suggested, might try to drum up business by inciting people to sue one another. In Lima, the reported number of *abogados,* or attorneys educated beyond the level of the bachelor's degree, grew significantly over the century, from 15 to 91 between 1700 and 1790.[30] In 1817, Lima's newly created Colegio de Abogados listed 111 legal representatives in the city (including two *procuradores de los pobres*).[31] As lawyers' numbers grew, their opportunities in colonial administration contracted. Historian Víctor Gayol suspects that official procurators and attorneys in the Audiencia of Mexico may have lost revenue from appeals with the creation of the intendancy system during the Bourbon Reforms, forcing them to search for first-instance business in order to make up for the loss.[32] A proliferation of legal personnel, including abogados, procurators, and agents of all kinds also might have been related to a declining sense of the importance of advanced education in the law and more emphasis on experience, especially through clerking.[33]

Still, greedy lawyers had long been stock characters in the Spanish imperial imagination. Rogelio Pérez-Perdomo maintains that, despite feverish official rhetoric about a glut of legal professionals in the colonies, the numbers of lawyers in Spanish America remained relatively low with respect to the population at the end of the eighteenth century. He further argues that the cultural dictates of honor constrained many lawyers, preventing them from seeking out potential plaintiffs for profit.[34] It is also difficult to tell whether more lawyers led to more litigation or the other way around, with the increase in lawyers responding to rising demands of litigants.[35]

Official auxiliary personnel, such as court notaries and deputy notaries certainly seemed overtaxed by the colonial surge in litigation. In late colonial Mexico City, there were hardly sufficient numbers of these officials to serve the communities to which they were appointed, and in the case of criminal trials, scribes reported having to serve twice as many districts as normal.[36] Again, all provincial regions outside of the capital cities, including rural districts of Oaxaca and Trujillo as well as the Montes de Toledo in Spain, experienced a chronic shortage of court scribes and educated legal personnel.

If the numbers of official agents could not keep pace with litigation in the colonies, *unofficial* agents did appear to be everywhere, as the earlier discussion of debates about licensing of legal representatives in Mexico City and Madrid reveal. Colonial inhabitants could shell out lower fees for the rogue petition-writers, who then could fish around to see if a judge would accept the plaintiff's case. If, and only if, the case went somewhere would the plaintiff hire an official procurator from the court to steer the case through the judicial maze, and an attorney to pull the case together at the end with learned arguments. Or, if the plaintiff were of the class called the "miserables" or "unprotected," they later would be named a pro bono representative. In sum, if demographic trends, economic factors, and bureaucratic practices in the civil courts affected the colonial litigation boom, they do not seem to have done so in a systematic, replicable way.

Another avenue to understanding the change is to center on the law itself, making the variable of "legal culture" worth considering more closely.[37] The fact that litigants were in court over money or over land is itself a cultural phenomenon that warrants interrogation.[38] How much was too little to sue over? Did debtors ever sue lenders? How did litigants originally strike a deal?[39] Answering such questions entails imagining the court not so much as legal culture's showcase but rather as one of its workshops. It means counting legal culture, like demography, economics, and bureaucratic changes, as a factor influencing the increasingly formal use of the courts in the colonies. It means returning to the Spaniard Juan Gómez's testimony about lemonade to see what it tells us not about numbers of cases but about values of a different sort.

Values

When Felipe Gómez recounted his lemonade story in court, he both revealed and reproduced a broader "justice-oriented" legal culture within the Spanish empire. Justice-oriented legal culture had a top-down version, manifesting in early modern philosophies of law that favored casuistic jurisprudence, customary law, jurisdictional competition, and distributive justice. The bottom-up version was characterized by its community-centeredness, flexibility, and extrajudicial nature. These elements served to limit, if not always prevent, lower-level disputes from extending beyond the local community, particularly by restraining social subordinates from litigating against social superiors. To be sure, justice-oriented culture encouraged all kinds of dynamic legal interactions among diverse groups, but it tended to concentrate formal civil litigation among powerful individuals, corporate groups, and institutions.

The Montes of Toledo and Justice-Oriented Culture

The Montes de Toledo serves as a useful example of the broader lived experience of justice-oriented culture in the empire. Its jurisdictional structure, as well as the region's economic subservience to the city of Toledo, makes it very similar to rural indigenous districts in Spanish America. What is more, the way inhabitants in the Montes de Toledo interacted with the law exemplifies a deep-rooted and durable early modern legal culture found in both cities as well as the countryside, on the peninsula, in Europe more broadly, and in the New World.

"Culture," in this instance, refers to litigants' repeated, patterned decisions to use or not to use the courts, especially for formal, written disputes. The decision not to use the courts is key. Throughout the Spanish empire and throughout the centuries, social exchanges that were technically legal often played out according to extrajudicial cultural scripts. Although the pueblos of the Montes de Toledo sorely lacked inhabitants who knew how to read or write, frequently including its pueblos' own first-instance judges, it was nonetheless a highly legalistic place. This legalism often was symbolic rather than written or procedural, and could be expressed in a wide repertoire of gestures: double-fisted handshakes, a hand lowered to one's side where a sword dangled, the tipping of or knocking off of hats.[40] Such symbolism revealed a creative tension between vertical, royally sanctioned authority and the horizontal ties of community. Even the common way of greeting authorities in the Montes de Toledo captured this contradiction. When Navalmoral's town officials encountered a villager while making their nightly policing rounds, they would greet him "in the name of His Majesty," and follow this with the question, "What people [go there]?" to which the individual was to respond "People of peace."[41]

This same tension infused the interactions between local, often unwritten ambits of justice and the more formal world of the king's courts. The legal culture of the Montes de Toledo emphasized communal self-sufficiency and stressed local authority in legal affairs—being able to close a financial deal with a toast of lemonade rather than a formal notarial contract. When Montes inhabitants did decide to go to court, they could count on a jurisdiction set up just for them. The Fiel del Juzgado, a chief magistrate who sat on the city of Toledo's council and first-instance court (*ayuntamiento*), exercised special authority over criminal and civil disputes in the region because Toledo, as a corporate body, "owned" the Montes such that the court combined royal and seigniorial jurisdictional modes.[42]

Time and again, when litigants brought civil lawsuits to the Fiel, they began by recounting extralegal, verbal arrangements that had gone awry, much like Gómez's lemonade deal. As such, written contracts and lawsuits appear as villagers' second, not first, resort in practicing law.[43] Indeed, in the Montes, this combination of legalism and independence from outside authority also profoundly shaped religious practices, as villagers made compacts with patron saints as if they were arrangements between friends, and without intervention from priests.[44]

Villagers preferred for such local legal cultural practices to run parallel to, rather than cross with, the formal justice system. In one dispute between a stepfather and stepson in the Montes de Toledo, a lawyer explained that the injustice the stepfather had committed in withholding his stepson's portion of inheritance was not just economic. By prompting a formal legal dispute, he also threatened the community as a whole. The stepfather had failed, the plaintiff's argument read, to the uphold the principle "that every person should live with the peace and tranquility that Christians hunger for."[45]

Even as they contributed to Spain's Golden Age of litigation in the sixteenth and seventeenth centuries, the inhabitants of the Montes de Toledo valued local authority and informal mechanisms for keeping the peace, and they generally sought to keep outsiders at bay. At the most basic level, communal protectiveness wrote itself on the faces of the local officials who suspiciously peered at newcomers to the villages, frequently accusing them of crimes and of being "gypsies" and "Jews."[46] But in the eighteenth century, the outsider that villagers most conspired to keep at arm's length was the city judge under whose jurisdiction they fell: the Fiel del Juzgado.

A shroud of secrecy covered not only extralegal community action in the villages of the Montes but even official, legal affairs.[47] When a faction of one Castilian town council met to set meat and grain prices without calling together all officials, as was required, they instructed the local notary not to make a record of any of their verbal dealings. When he responded that he feared being fined by the Fiel for dereliction of duty, the conspiring village officials assured him they would pay for any fine he incurred.[48]

Village officials were not alone in stiffening when faced with the Fiel's oversight. Frequently, ordinary villagers stuck together to resist his uninvited judicial interventions. The entire town of Navalucillos stopped talking to the Fiel during his investigation of a pueblo revolt after the parish priest tried to move a statue of the Virgin Mary out of its church.[49] In another instance, a court notary arriving in the pueblo of Marjaliza, armed with papers informing village officials of an unfavorable outcome in their land dispute with a neighboring pueblo, confronted head-on the force of community cohesion. A local woman hid a town official in her house so the court notary could not deliver the Fiel del Juzgado's sentence and complete the case, and several other female villagers played dumb when asked of his whereabouts.[50]

Therefore, although Castile possessed a legalistic culture in general, "justice" did not always entail appeals to impartial judges bound to transcend the interests and entanglements of the community and blindly administer the law. Rather, justice-oriented practices of law involved a wobbly balance between calling for the contingent mediation of outside magistrates and protecting the community, where first-instance magistrates concatenated local and royal power as they exercised unwritten authority.[51]

To be sure, in most archives, complete civil cases, recorded from opening petitions to sentences, mingle indiscriminately with the various other documentary artifacts eighteenth-century imperial inhabitants left behind. Attention to the actual content of a "lawsuit"—whether it was a request to sue someone and see the case through to sentence or was a plea for summary legal intervention of a different kind—is key to both establishing the baseline of legal culture in the empire and to understanding how it changed in the eighteenth century.

When villagers did appeal to formal courts of law, they often wished for intervention to be verbal and summary, just as their original dealings with each other frequently had been.[52] Josef Martínez, who sued two men from the Montes before the Fiel, recounted making several trips to the city of Toledo in order to collect on a debt; but he did so not by filing a suit but rather by lodging verbal complaints.[53] The hassle and cost of formal suits was not worth it to many of the region's inhabitants. When tenants sued the Cruz family for renting them a house in Navalmoral that was dilapidated and dangerous, the family chose to neither fix the house nor go to court. They sold part of the structure to avoid the legal mess entirely.[54]

Even if they did find themselves initiating formal suits before the Fiel, litigants often opened their cases by lamenting that they had to enter the courts at all. Several cases meticulously recount the steps litigants took to resolve disputes before involving a judge.[55] And, once a suit was underway, it did not have to stay that way. Even in a tribunal as expensive and elevated as Spain's Real Chancellería of Valladolid, an entire section of the court notaries' records were reserved for "forgotten suits," which, in the eighteenth century, outnumbered cases brought to sentence.[56] In the Montes de Toledo, litigants frequently abandoned cases with formal "*apartamientos*" (separation from the suit) or "*fees de amistad*" (statements of friendship). Even with these options available, plaintiffs did not always find formal desisting necessary. Just as they made deals over a glass of lemonade, they often ended suits with a handshake rather than a formal legal document.[57]

This is not to say that ordinary folks' reticence to involve official justice in their disputes or to see suits through to sentencing implied village egalitarianism. Local authority figures—primarily men commissioned as town officials, but also heads of household, elders, and priests—regulated community life and worked to determine which disputes would reach district courts.[58] It is obvious that in the Montes, much of the activity that reached the Fiel del Juzgado had first passed through unwritten judicial processes at the lower level, processes that reinforced local (male) authority. In a 1793 report on criminal cases from the region that were pending before the judge in Toledo, only one had come without prior local mediation. Either village officials or the imperial city's guards who roamed the countryside, checking on city-held lands, brought all but one of the 19 suits.[59]

In general, then, early modern inhabitants of the Montes preferred to resolve issues by relying on local hierarchies, social codes of public esteem and relatively rigid gendered normative prescriptions. In this formulation, the operational distinction is not between "extralegal" (or "illegal") and "legal" activity, which would imply that actions were either illegitimate or legitimate by virtue of being unwritten or written. Rather, written and verbal appeals operated in overlapping fields in which local custom competed with the official intrusions of legal representatives of a growing absolutist state.[60]

The legal culture of the Montes de Toledo looks quite similar to other places in Spain, such as Cantabria, where Tomás Mantecón-Movellan reports local authorities retained their hold over the legal activities of the villages well into the nineteenth century. If these local strongmen overstepped their limits or acted in a way deemed to infringe on the community as a whole, which they often did, "there were ways to resist tyranny outside the courts."[61] Justice-oriented legal culture stretched from Paris to Neapolitan villages, from the Montes pueblo of Ventas, Castile, to Villa Alta in Oaxaca, where rural inhabitants generally shrank from external mediation unless a crisis that threatened community stability made it unavoidable.[62]

Of course, people did sue one another in Spain. During the sixteenth and seventeenth centuries, they sued each other a lot. And some of these people were ordinary folks.[63] Throughout Spain, peasants, women, and other social subordinates sometimes found their way to the courts, even if their cases never reached the same proportion of overall litigation as they would in eighteenth-century Spanish America.

Although local officials and elites exercised a great deal of control over disputes in the villages of the Montes de Toledo, they could never completely dominate legal practices. It was possible for subordinate villagers from the region to appeal to the Fiel del Juzgado to curb the excesses of the powerful inhabitants of their villages, whom inhabitants referred to nakedly as "*los ricos*," or "the rich." Their cases certainly were not unchanging through time, and shifted according to the concerns of Bourbon officials and Enlightened elites. But even when social subordinates in the Montes denounced their social superiors before the Fiel del Juzgado, their legal actions generally reproduced justice-oriented culture.

Take the conflict between the rich and the poor that the Fiel del Juzgado attempted to mediate in the pueblo of Las Ventas de Peña Aguilera in 1776, a dispute that prompted him to leave his bench in the city's council and tread the rocky ground of their village, listening to peasants' complaints.[64] The peasants protested los ricos' pasturing practices and seizure of natural resources. Their complaints touched a nerve among an Enlightened elite in Toledo that worried about the deleterious economic effects of depopulation and the unequal and inefficient distribution of land in rural Castilla-La Mancha.[65]

This was not technically speaking a "case," however. The peasants did not bring suit; the suit was brought to them. A member of Toledo's city council and one of the most prominent members of its new economic society, the Sociedad Económica de los Amantes del País, invited the Fiel del Juzgado to gather the peasants' testimony about the wasteful and unfair concentration of resources the hands of the rich.[66] The Fiel listened as poor witnesses complained that community justice was stacked against them, that legal officials, including a particularly corrupt notary, dominated los ricos and formed a powerful alliance. The collusion had, they reported, disrupted the normal "peace and obedience," and "good correspondence and Christian peace" that reigned in their pueblo. Even while they complained, they stuck to the principle of community peace and opened no lawsuit.[67]

Ordinary peoples' reticence to litigate was common in many other regions in Europe and was perhaps even a growing phenomenon explaining its "great litigation decline."[68] As secular jurisdiction grew, village authorities in the Montes de Toledo drew justice inward, creating what one contemporary observer called "formal resistance" to Bourbon governance and "public imperiousness" in the face of their most proximate authority figure, the Fiel.[69]

The inhabitants of the pueblo of Arroba had become so intransigent against judicial intervention from the imperial city that, in 1797, a local notary wrote to the Fiel to complain that village officials were "secretive and useless" and that they continually thwarted "Royal Jurisdiction." In this case, the notary objected not to a single event but the overall legal culture of the town. He presented royal jurisdiction as personified in the Fiel del Juzgado himself. "Royal jurisdiction" was forced to stand by and watch itself "denied obedience, its respect abolished, its sentences shredded with formal resistance and public and scandalous imperiousness, and [with] continual insults and injurious and offensive civil disagreement among its subjects."[70] In other words, villagers fought each other but refused to do so in the Fiel's courts.

By the end of the century, the Fiel's slipping purchase on jurisdiction in the region turned into a free fall in the wake of one seemingly insignificant case. In this suit, an ordinary villager complained about the business practices of a merchant who sold trinkets and staples in the pueblo of Yébenes. The Fiel del Juzgado found shop owner Vicente Marín guilty of cheating his customers by using a rigged scale, and imposed a small fine. Marín, smarting at having been bested in court by his peasant customer, appealed the case to the Council of Castile and questioned the very basis of the Fiel's jurisdiction. The Council decided that Marín had indeed fiddled with the weights of the scale but that the punishment the Fiel levied against him was too small to be of concern. However, the Fiel had overreached in hearing the case of an ordinary peasant and ruling against the shopkeeper. Reinforcing the discourses of peace and community cohesion so characteristic of justice-oriented culture, the crown's attorney stated that, "For the peace and quiet of Yébenes, it is indispensable to fix just and orderly limits [on the Fiel del Juzgado's authority] and to conserve the political order and gradations of different classes of jurisdiction."[71] The Council even went so far as to demand an accounting of the Fiel's jurisdictional prerogatives in order to restrict them. Upsetting the delicate balance of justice between local and state authorities was a violation far worse than rigging scales.

This suit contained traces of all kinds of eighteenth-century change, including the increasing hostility among Bourbon officials to the practice of cities owning *"propios y montes"* such as the Montes de Toledo, as well as the belief that such outmoded medieval arrangements impeded economic productivity and challenged centralized rule.[72] Even so, the Council's sentence did little to threaten justice-oriented legal culture in the region or disrupt legal practices that kept disputes from spilling outside the community. In fact, it expressly aimed to "conserve" local jurisdiction and to limit the superior, formal authority of the Fiel del Juzgado's tribunal.

In contrast, in the colonies, ordinary litigants' civil cases had more corrosive effects on justice-oriented culture and traditional authority figures, including household patriarchs, slave masters, and noble indigenous leaders, who themselves acted as local magistrates. The civil lawsuits that women, native commoners, and slaves initiated in colonial royal courts lifted the extrajudicial shroud that covered the exercise of authority in the household, neighborhood, and community, increasingly exposing the actions of social superiors to the scrutiny of royal magistrates.

Thresholds and Doors: Colonial Subordinates' Suits

Placing the eighteenth-century increase in colonial civil suits against the background of justice-oriented culture rather than locating it within economic or demographic contexts might seem to reproduce the old opposition in historical explanation between culture and structure. Culture—legal or otherwise—is notoriously difficult to measure, and, some would argue, more appropriately considered a dependent rather than independent variable.[73] But as global legal historians have recently observed, the old structure-versus-culture divide seems to have outlived its usefulness.[74] Approaching the impulse to sue as simultaneously (or, perhaps, neither) structural or cultural—again, looking at the courts as places where legal history is made rather than merely displayed—leaves it unclear whether the historian's task is to seek causation at all.[75] In other words, legal historians stand at a threshold when thinking about what causes historical change.

One way to cross this threshold in the history of litigation in the Spanish empire without either falling forward into endless contingency or backward into hard structure is to pay greater attention to what litigants and defendants themselves were reporting about causes and changes. New approaches to historical causation propose that humans must see a social condition as "meaningful" before it can transform into a structure and, in turn, act as a cause in history.[76] Historical actors' recognition of change, in other words, can lead to lasting structural transformations that constitute a historical event.[77] Historians are not alone in rethinking causation. Similar reconceptualizations of causation also are taking place in the social and biological sciences.[78] Boiled down to a practical method for explaining change, such new approaches call for historians to take seriously what contemporaries said they were witnessing, to pinpoint historical actors' own analysis of the schema in which they lived, and to trace links between how they surveyed the horizon of the possible and the actual events that occurred.[79]

Briefly doing just that, consider what eighteenth-century contemporaries were saying about suing in one region, Trujillo. In 1741, the master of slave María Gabriela Ponce de León warned the city judge that the "neighborhood" was watching the case she had brought against him over her right to purchase herself. He urged the judge to "shut the door" to similar cases.[80] Seven years later, indigenous commoners of a nearby community decided to bypass the jurisdiction of a possibly corrupt official called the Juez de Aguas in a dispute with their pueblo's native leadership over water rights. The Juez de Aguas warned his superiors that entertaining suits from natives of "minor privileges with little comprehension . . . leaves the door open to a multitude of problems, which are [already] being seen."[81] Some forty years later, in 1789, a poor woman of African descent from Trujillo named Segunda Montejo was embroiled in a divorce case with her abusive husband. In light of the royal order two years prior that asserted secular jurisdiction over certain aspects of divorce cases, she took her case to a civil judge in a royal court rather than the church courts. Her husband's lawyer prodded the ecclesiastical judge to do something, since if civil judges got in the habit of listening only to "the simple narrative of women, no marriage would find itself safe . . . and a door would be opened that would prejudice" matrimony itself.[82]

With their panicked metaphors about the cracked doors of the royal courts, these Trujillo defendants registered a significant change. The fact that others observed the event was important to the defendants. The "neighborhood," as María Gabriela's slave owner warned, was watching. The crisis that judges would create by permitting commoner natives to bypass lower officials and challenge their higher-ups "was being seen." Following these historical actors' own analysis, it is notable that what observers witnessed was slaves, indigenous people, and women slipping through the courthouse doors to sue their most proximate social superiors.

The Trujillo defendants had a point. As the number of cases grew in the colonies over the course of the century, less powerful members of society increasingly watched as their counterparts formally sued defendants more powerful than them, and some then did the same (Fig. 3.2). Comparing the social ranks of plaintiffs and defendants in Spain during its litigation revolution and in Spanish America during its later litigation boom reveals that a unique feature of the colonial surge was an increasing propensity for subordinate litigants to sue social superiors.

Correlations between litigant social status and litigation rates in Castilian litigation suggest that the act of suing was not, in the early modern period, normally a practice for challenging social superiors. Kagan's numbers suggest that, during the so-called "legal revolution" in the sixteenth century, cases in which peninsular Spanish plaintiffs and defendants were from different social ranks did grow.[83] But even at the apogee of litigation in the high court of the Chancellería de Valladolid, plaintiffs whose social standing was equal to the individual they sued brought the vast majority of civil cases—75 to 90 percent. And in cases between socially disparate plaintiffs and defendants, more powerful individuals sued inferiors more often than subordinates sued superiors. Only 8 percent of all litigants were social inferiors suing superiors; 17.6 percent were superiors suing inferiors. Later, when litigation slowed, plaintiffs and defendants equalized in social rank, and, if parties in court were of different social ranks, plaintiffs still tended to be socially superior to the defendant.

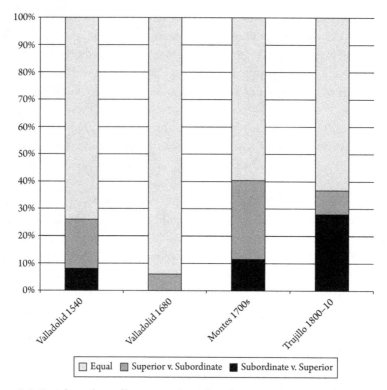

Figure 3.2 Social standing of litigants in Spanish and Peruvian jurisdictions. Data on
Valladolid from Kagan, *Lawsuits*. Data on Montes de Toledo from AMT, Fiel del Juzgado,
Pleitos, Civiles, Ejecutivos. Data on Trujillo from ARL, Cabildo, Justicia Ordinaria,
Civiles.

A similar pattern emerges from examining 51 civil disputes from the Montes
brought before the Fiel del Juzgado from 1700 to 1799. These are all of the
instances in a sample of formal civil disputes in which the social status of litigants could be determined with certainty. In this court, there was a greater dis-
crepancy in the social standing of litigants than is evident at any point in the
high court of Valladolid. This is understandable since, as a lower-level court, it
was more accessible to ordinary litigants than was the venerable Chancellería.
But, critically, in legal actions involving parties of different social statuses in the
Montes de Toledo, powerful litigants sued social inferiors far more often than
the other way around (27 as opposed to 11 percent of total).[84]

Patterns in Trujillo's first instance courts during the period 1800–19 contrast with trends in Spanish litigation. To reiterate, civil litigation had doubled
in volume here from the decade before.[85] So this small, comprehensive data set
serves as a tidy colonial counterpoint to Castile's legal revolution. Examining all
civil cases in the first-instance civil court of Trujillo in which the social status of
litigants could be determined shows that subordinates suing superiors brought

a remarkable proportion of cases (27 percent). Over a third of that subset comprised a new kind of case: slave civil suits for freedom or to change owners. Whereas social superiors sued subordinates with more frequency during Spain's legal boom, in the colonies subordinate legal subjects took advantage of the boom by leveling a growing number of cases against superiors.[86] In other words, not every legal revolution mobilizes the same troops.

Again, this is not to say that suits in which subordinates sued superiors alone or even primarily account for the surge in colonial litigation in the 1700s. While the work of producing a complete classification of civil litigation in the Spanish colonies awaits future scholars, a control case indicates that much of eighteenth-century growth in Spanish American litigation was likely composed of a proportional swelling of the same kinds of lawsuits that had always occupied civil judges, such as inheritance cases, debts, and other commercial transactions— lawsuits in which the social rank of litigants was either equal or favored social superiors. Cases in which landlords took tenants to court for back rent or eviction (*desocupe*) are a good example since we can be relatively certain that the plaintiffs in rent disputes were socially superior to defendants.

Examining landlord-tenant disputes in Peru provides a useful contrast to the increasing number of lawsuits initiated by social subordinates. In the first-instance civil court of Lima, back rent and eviction cases numerically increased over the course of the century. However, unlike the cases that subordinates leveled against superiors, the growth in eviction suits did not outpace the overall rise in litigation. More concretely, landlord-tenant disputes consistently constituted around 2–3 percent of all ordinary civil cases in Lima. In Trujillo, the proportion of rent cases at various jurisdictional levels shows no clear increase over time and perhaps indicates a decrease in the proportion of superiors who took subordinates to court.[87] So even if everyone in the colonies, whether superior or subordinate, grew more enthusiastic to enter civil tribunals in second half of the 1700s, colonial subordinates were especially keen to go to court. In their enthusiasm, they did more than participate in a general colonial litigation boom. They broke with a longer, durable legal cultural tradition in the Spanish empire that functioned to contain justice within the hierarchies of the community.

Defendants' evocations of "opening doors" were, to be sure, age-old colloquialisms meant to warn Spanish colonial judges to be cautious about the larger consequences of permitting individual suits into their tribunals. But in the legal arguments of the Trujillo defendants, the door was an even more precise kind of referent. It conveyed the prospect that socially subordinate individuals in particular might rush the courts and destabilize longstanding practices of justice that maintained traditional authority. The Trujillo defendants' use of the metaphor of the door also indicated something even more. Their words evoked an event in history as much as the act of entrance into the courts, bearing witness to a change in subordinate litigants' perception of their own legal possibilities.

At the end of the century, Spanish colonial magistrates' increasingly formal role as impartial stewards of the law crowded in on their traditional role as informal, moral mediators. Meanwhile, legal formalism and regalism shifted emphasis from justice, which could be adjudicated in the community and without a formal trial, to law, which took place in formal tribunals. Spain appears to have weathered this change in judicial philosophy without a concomitant rise in individual suits against local authority figures, and even without a rise in civil litigation overall. If there was change in Spain, it resulted in rural communities such as the Montes de Toledo pulling inward, restricting interaction with the royal judge closest to them, and expanding the extrajudicial sphere. In the colonies, in contrast, some litigants circumvented traditional, local channels of justice and rejected extrajudicial resolutions to their conflicts. As they insisted on clarifications about the role of the royal courts in domestic disputes, as they exercised the liberty to name their own agents at law, and as they sought greater legal access, efficiency, and judicial impartiality, colonial litigants separated the law from the social world of community-based justice, and contributed to its emergence as an ambit dictated by its own logic.

In a sense, by commenting on this, the Trujillo defendants reverse the normal chain we attribute to causes and events. Rather than deciding between structural or cultural explanations for the increase in litigation in the colonies, it might be more fitting to observe that each individual lawsuit itself fed a concept of the law as a practice that could be autonomous from social relations of subordination. In other words, the event begat one of its causes; the opening of the courthouse door in Spanish America helped build the structure of modern law itself.

PART II

LIGHTS FROM LITIGANTS

As colonial subordinates brought lawsuits against superiors at an accelerated pace within the overall colonial litigation boom, their arguments and actions revealed shifting cultural understandings of the purpose of the law. The second part of this book closely examines three types of case: the suits that women, natives, and slaves brought against their social superiors. Each displayed elements of an emerging Enlightenment legal culture, including a new secular legal subjectivity, new understandings of natural rights, notions of legal custom as historical and changing, an emphasis on merit over birthright, and freedom as a progressive human phenomenon rather than a categorical condition. Beyond excavating these broader ideas from the texts of the arguments in the suits, the chapters analyze the human activities that created the lawsuits, asking how and why suits ended up in royal civil courts rather than in other courts, and how they ended up in writing at all.

But before turning to the cases, an additional word about culture and causation is in order. While it is not the purpose of the book to explain the eighteenth-century increase in litigation in Mexico and Peru more generally, a brief consideration of the control case in this study helps further reveal the larger relationship between litigation rates and legal culture during the period. The parties involved in rent disputes provide more evidence that litigants' changing perceptions of the law could generate more legal activity, even in cases subordinates did not initiate.

Again, rent disputes and eviction cases in Peru—cases in which residential landlords were the primary litigants suing tenants who were either their social equals or inferiors—represent average types of civil disputes in the eighteenth century. These suits can be considered "average" in part because they did not typically involve subordinates suing superiors, a subset of civil disputes that always constituted a statistical minority even within the colonial surge in litigation. Rent and eviction cases were also average in terms of change over time, making up a relatively steady proportion of all suits over the course of the century in Lima and Trujillo.

This steadiness does not, however, indicate stasis. Rent and eviction suits brought against tenants kept proportional pace with the general increase in litigation, increasing in real numbers in the 1700s. In other words, as the number of all lawsuits grew, so did these cases. Just as in the new kinds of civil cases that women, slaves, and Indians would bring before judges, these suits reveal changes in how litigants conceived of law. Arguments in rent and eviction cases did not typically focus on overcrowding in cities or economic hard times—though these and other structural pressures might have motivated them. Instead, the parties debated the role of the courts, whether the disputes should be formal suits at all or should be settled extrajudicially with equity in mind, and whether informal legal arrangements were binding. In other words, their focus was on the parameters of law and on legal culture itself.

It was the defendants—the more subordinate parties in the suit— whose arguments tended to draw judges toward older models of justice. Tenants like José Tomas Carillo, who was two years behind on his 17-pesos-per-month rent for a relatively fancy second-story residence on the corner of Animas and Acabas streets in Lima, seemed puzzled by the fact that landlords were taking rent disputes to judges. He faced off against Don Felipe Sancho Dávila, a prominent man who held the prime post of regidor on the city's town council.[1] José Tomás responded to his landlord's formal petition to obtain back rent by calling it silly, an insult to his status as a gentleman, and claiming that the dispute was over such a small amount that legal recourse was unnecessary.[2] Even procurator Felipe Useda, who made his living in the courts, seemed quite surprised when his landlord went straight to the city's audiencia over the debt he had accrued on the home he rented with his family below the Rímac River bridge. "I am not by nature one of those defaulting and malicious debtors who do not satisfy and fail to pay their credit," he claimed.[3] In fact, Useda said, before his family had fallen on hard times, he usually had been prompt with his rent. He did sometimes divide the annual amount he owed into installments of different amounts, but he reported that, if he tried to pay his rent in advance he was told not to worry about it, that there was no hurry.

Useda echoed a more general dismay, common among defendants, over the harsh reality that renters no longer could count on the accommodations of the extrajudicial world of informal arrangements to protect them from being hauled in court and then put out on the street. Landlords' new penchant for formal rental arrangements and timely payments left tenants in the cold, Useda lamented, and instead of being treated with "charity and humanity," he found himself "embittered by the rigors of justice."[4]

Renters like Useda had every reason to expect that judges would be lenient and landlords patient. The medieval laws that governed rental arrangements for residences were incredibly favorable to tenants. Property owners could evict tenants in only four circumstances, two of which—if the owner had no other residence in which to live or if the residence was in such total disrepair that it had be unoccupied in order to fix it—required the landlord to secure an equally suitable residence for the renter. Tenants had to fall egregiously behind on rent before they could be evicted: the *Siete Partidas* gave a vague example to explain what kind of payment structure should guide a lease for a residence, stating that a tenant renting for a period of "four or five years" would have to lag behind for two years on payments before he could be evicted.[5] In practice, rental contracts in eighteenth-century Lima continued to leave things rather open-ended, stipulating both a minimum number of years in which the renter was bound to the contract and another period set as "voluntary."[6]

Since written laws and legal practices had long encouraged flexibility and informality between tenants and landlords, renters believed that "derecho" worked in their favor. They appealed to judicial compassion, and they overtly pitted calls for "equity" against landlords' claims that it was their right to throw out deadbeat renters.

The broke procurator Useda constructed his entire defense around judicial equity, calling the plan he had concocted to pay his (reduced) debt to his landlord over time a "proposal founded on balance and equity."[7] Equity likewise was strewn throughout the defense of a master coachman evicted from his workshop in a decaying mansion by the marquis who owned it. The coachman had informally agreed to maintain a number of the nobleman's coaches as a substitute for rent, but the marquis later signed a contract with a new renter and went to Lima's alcalde to kick the coachman out. The coachman's defense called for judicial compassion, claiming "it would conform to the equity that should always be a priority for Judges in their frequent sentences on this kind of matter."[8]

Maybe the coachman should not have mentioned other cases. His landlord also had built his own argument around recent rulings the courts were making in similar eviction disputes.[9] The owner cited recent precedent in which judges had supported landlords based on their basic property rights. Landlords promoted the idea that their right to evict tenants derived from simple dominion, that their ownership trumped claims to equity, and that the common way for courts to proceed was in support of landlords. The landlord in Useda's case even denied that there was any room for judicial discretion at all in such cases.[10] And they were often successful. The coachman was thrown out of the crumbling mansion. The procurator Useda had to pay up, even if on his own timetable, and moved out. José Tomás Carrillo had nothing to offer his landlord for his debt except a silver-threaded woman's skirt, and the landlord took it.

Rent and eviction cases thus reveal a weakening of extrajudicial, informal practices of law, as tenants found that they could not trust handshakes and toasts to keep a roof over their heads. These disputes also indicated that a broad range of litigants—property owners, as well as middling-class women, commoner natives, and slaves—were drawn to the lettered sphere of the law over disputes that their opponents believed could be solved in the unwritten world of social interaction. The increasingly common references to precedent in these cases propelled the growth in civil lawsuits in the colonies in a kind of feedback loop: the more landlords sued tenants, the more landlords could point other cases as proof that judicial compassion did not override their legal rights.

If rent cases serve to illustrate how a growing tendency to litigate undercut the assumptions of justice-oriented legal culture in average lawsuits during the Spanish colonial litigation boom, they also serve as a reminder that new legal ideas and strategies were not the exclusive property of ordinary women, Indians, and slaves. Still, these litigants would prove extraordinarily adept at producing them.

4

Pleitos and Lawsuits

Conjugal Conflicts in Civil Courts

In Spanish, "*pleitos*" are lawsuits, specifically civil lawsuits. In the parlance of the inhabitants of the empire in the 1700s "pleitos" also meant domestic quarrels.[1] A doña in Mexico City, for example, mentioned that from time to time she and her husband had "certain *pleitos de voces.*" A cacique, or native lord, in the village of Yogevo, in Villa Alta, Oaxaca, complained that after his granddaughter married her husband "she got nothing but pleitos and disagreements."[2] Neither the doña nor the cacique meant that the spouses had gone to court. But in the second half of the eighteenth century, particularly in the cities of colonial Spanish America, the formal legal definition of "pleito" increasingly absorbed its domestic meaning. Many women seemed increasingly interested in lodging formal suits against their husbands and lovers in the royal civil courts of the colonies, and in doing so forged a new Enlightenment legal culture.

This chapter examines women's use of civil courts in domestic disputes during the eighteenth century, drawing on hundreds of cases of divorce, adultery, abuse, and alimony aired throughout the Spanish empire. In the larger story of how litigants made the colonial Spanish Enlightenment, the spotlight is primarily on civil cases, but this examination of women's suits also draws extensively from criminal complaints and ecclesiastical suits.[3] This is because the question of where litigants sued in domestic cases mattered. The issue of jurisdiction (Church or crown) and court (criminal or civil) proved critical to women's participation in the imperial legal Enlightenment.

Focusing on their choices before the law, it becomes clear that women in domestic disputes with men tended to reinforce justice-oriented-culture, maneuvering on the edges of formal law, seeking verbal mediation and the instrumental aid of a range of authorities, even beyond official judges.[4] Yet, in the second half of the century, rather than go to Church courts or the police, rather than rely on extrajudicial or village arbitration, some female litigants—particularly middling-class women from the colonial cities—turned to civil judges in royal

courts to formally sue husbands and lovers. One particular type of case represents the widening possibilities for women within secular jurisdiction: women's
suits over alimony and child support (both called "*alimentos*"). Through these
cases, female litigants emphasized the civil aspects of domestic unions, and many
began to overtly reject extrajudicial solutions to marital disputes. Instead, they
approached the bench as civil legal subjects, bringing formal suits over issues
extending beyond dowries or inheritance and more centered on independence
and ordinary material life.

When female litigants appealed to royal courts at the end of the century, they
did not create from whole cloth new legal selves. They drew on longstanding
legal statuses as faithful, free-willed Catholic subjects, and they did not abruptly
abandon their sacramental identity when they advanced civil marriage cases at
the end of the 1700s. In turn, the Church cases that women continued to pursue
were in many ways touched by the larger legal and philosophical currents of the
age.[5] What is more, many, perhaps most, women in the empire continued to engage in justice-oriented practices throughout the 1700s, which involved seeking
informal mediation of priest-judges as well as initiating formal lawsuits in the ecclesiastical courts.[6] In fact, women who sued husbands and lovers in civil courts
could simultaneously turn to Church magistrates for divorces and rely on local
police to impose moral discipline on wayward husbands, engaging in the venerable Spanish imperial practices of venue shopping and jurisdictional jockeying.

Nonetheless, casting the spotlight on colonial women's activities in royal civil
courts reveals that colonial women were not simply reading from multiple jurisdictional scripts. As they increasingly entered the civil forum, women's cases
emphasized the contractual bases of matrimony and suggested that their rights
were not contingent on their subjugation to men in the conjugal home. Even
colonial women who left their husbands without Church approval seem to have
believed that this should have little bearing on their claims of rights or their
status as civil subjects.

The way women presented themselves in lawsuits became intimately tied
to an expanding notion of "natural rights," rights that positioned them as legal
agents whose subjectivity lay beyond marriage, with the king. The concept of
self-preservation, fundamental to women's arguments in civil domestic cases,
relied on the idea that no law could compel them, as natural-rights-bearing individuals, to submit to tyrannical authority at home. Such a concept of rights fell
squarely within the jusrationalist ideas introduced in the empire's universities.

Spanish imperial policies expanding secular jurisdiction, especially over marriage matters, could work to foster women's sense of civil legal subjectivity.[7] This
might make it temping to chalk up women's active use of the civil legal sphere
to Bourbon regalism or the circulation of new legal philosophies alone. But the
vibrant regional and demographic differences among the women likely to bring

formal civil suits over domestic discord make it difficult to attribute their litigation to empire-wide policy, or indeed to any force entirely exogenous to their
own actions. Through the end of the eighteenth century, most rural women involved in conflicts with their husbands and lovers relied on the traditional procedures and practices of justice-oriented legal culture. It was women in cities, and
specifically cities in the colonies, who tended to insist on the use of civil courts
in marital disputes. The explanation for this is to be found in the women's own
petitions and motions, which employed arguments about the natural right to
self-preservation to advocate for the freedom to live independently from men
and close to the courts, as well as to argue for procedural rights related to legal
representation and relief from the financial cost of exercising those rights in the
first place.

Any study of women's legal activities surrounding marriage joins a near-
canonical historiography on Spanish colonial gender norms, especially notable
for Mexico, where historians have revealed the legal dynamism at the heart of
colonial marriages through studies of divorce, parental objections to their children's marriage choices, and other family conflicts.[8] Women had always possessed a broad range of "rights"—*derechos* (rights), *acciones* (actions), or *fueros*
(privileges)—rooted in very specific civil and ecclesiastical laws, which in
turn were believed to be reflective of divine order.[9] These laws, springing from
sources ranging from codes, compilations and local *fueros*, through canon law
and Spanish American Church conciliar decisions about divorce, had long permitted women to take their partners to court. Women could enter ecclesiastical
courts to sue their husbands for annulment and *divorcio* (separation without the
ability to remarry). At times, men sued their wives for divorce or over adultery,
and, in these and other suits, husbands asked judges to imprison their consorts
or place them under residential supervision (a practice known as "deposit.") But,
in the vast majority of domestic disputes examined, women rather than men
were the primary litigants or aggrieved parties in Church suits. This had been
true since at least the late sixteenth century, when women—mostly elite women
of Spanish descent—sought divorce or annulment far more frequently than did
husbands.[10]

Women from more diverse origins went to criminal courts with charges of
sevicia, or excessive physical abuse. They also used the criminal courts to report
husbands' dalliances, though their rights to bring secular charges of adultery
were more restricted than men's.[11] Beyond cases of conjugal conflict, women
were charged for criminal offenses like theft or occasionally for physical aggres-
sion with other women, and they were both accused and accusers in Inquisition
trials.[12]

Whether women ended up suing in the courts of the empire depended
not only on their class position but also their place in the lifecycle. Widows

and elite women were active litigators over ownership, debts, inheritance, and other financial matters. Less frequently than their widowed counterparts, elite married women could use civil courts to claim their living husbands mismanaged their dowries or the property they brought into marriages.[13]

That changed in the eighteenth century, as diverse working- and middling-class married women, especially in Spanish colonial cities, turned to the civil courts to engage in disputes with their living husbands. In order to fully grasp what this turn entailed, this chapter first details how women traditionally interacted with the legal system both in civil litigation writ large and specifically in instances in which they sought justice against their husbands and lovers. Understanding what was new about these women's claims to rights first requires understanding what was traditional about their search for justice.

Justice

In traditional justice-oriented practices, the community and those who held authority in it all could serve as judges for women involved in domestic conflict. In turn, many women appealed to actual judges not necessarily for the sentences that they could hand down but rather as simply another link in a chain of authority figures that could swiftly rebuild broken homes. Achieving an immediate objective and finding a solution to a domestic conflict were often more important than assuming the status of litigant and winning a case. In addition, within justice-oriented practice, verbal, unwritten interactions between plaintiffs and judges easily flowed into written petitions that constituted a legal act but not necessarily a "suit." Even when women formally sued husbands and lovers, their pleitos admitted ample space for informal resolution and unwritten mediation in lo extrajudicial.

Women and Village Justice

Rural women were, comparatively speaking, far less likely than urban women to appear as civil litigants in all types of disputes, and the few cases they did put before judges reveal a vibrant extrajudicial culture that kept them out of court. Women in the rugged Castilian region of the Montes de Toledo, as one example, only infrequently filed civil cases. It was especially rare for a married woman of the Montes to initiate a civil case without her husband listed as primary litigant. Such gendered judicial inconspicuousness was not confined to married women; in over two hundred formal civil cases (pleitos and causas civiles) and legal injunctions handed down by the Fiel del Juzgado (ejectuorías), in fewer than a dozen instances were women of any status registered as the sole plaintiffs.[14]

Those women who did sue or were sued as individuals in the Montes de Toledo were overwhelmingly widows, and they generally sought to settle inheritance matters.[15] A few were property owners in disputes with tenants or potential real estate buyers. Reading through these civil cases to the social world behind them, it is clear that widows' everyday exercise of authority was not reducible to their subordination as women.[16] They fought with each other and with male neighbors, loaned money, and were on the front lines when their pueblos revolted against local priests or new taxes.[17] But no matter how economically or politically active they were, rural women often conducted a good deal of their legal business outside the courts.

Antonio García certainly believed he faced a formidable legal opponent in the widow María Rodríguez in 1776. Both litigant and defendant were described as *vecinos* of the pueblo of Horcajo, a designation that conveyed relatively elevated status within the town.[18] The widow Rodríguez had, by "her own authority"— meaning without a contract—given García planting privileges on the lands of her late husband. Ten years later she decided to move stones to indicate her ownership of neighboring properties. The move shaved down the size of García's plot considerably. Though he attempted to settle the matter with the intervention of one of Horcajo's local alcaldes, García became frustrated because he believed this local official was in league with the widow in carrying out the enclosure.[19]

Until seeking the intervention of the Fiel del Juzgado in the city of Toledo, whose judicial authority was superior to that of the local alcalde, García was clearly outmatched in terms of his real power to maintain access to the fields he cultivated. Yet it is also clear that the widow Rodríguez's alliance with the alcalde was not accidental. She needed his help to begin the process of land enclosure and, indeed, the alcalde himself supervised the replacement of the landmarks in defiance of an early ruling by the Fiel. Like Rodríguez, elite widows might have held significant power over men in everyday relations, but even they tended to rely on notable men from the community as interlocutors if not procurators when involved in legal disputes.

The title a court scribe gave to the case, "Antonio García, *vecino* of Horcajo, versus María Rodríguez," reveals that it was García, not she, who initiated the suit. The widow Rodríguez never seems to have brought a formal claim against García to limit his usufruct rights to the lands she inherited from her dead husband, relying instead on the extrajudicial authority of the village. Her methods were "legal" but they were also informal and unwritten, at least until her opponent sued her. Rodríguez, statistically exceptional in that she was a rural woman involved in a civil dispute over property in the Montes de Toledo, was typical in another regard: she was technically not a plaintiff.

Like Rodríguez, women in the heavily indigenous rural districts of Teposcolula and Villa Alta, Oaxaca, show up relatively infrequently on the rolls of formal litigants in civil cases. A panoramic view of the titles and descriptions of all the civil cases before the Spanish colonial district judge of these regions gives the impression that women in Teposcolula, particularly widows and single women, were more active in property disputes than they were in Villa Alta, despite the fact that both regions were overwhelmingly indigenous.[20] Yet even women in Teposcolula constituted only a small proportion of the overall numbers of litigants and defendants in the eighteenth century. The inventory undertaken in 1793 of civil and criminal disputes in Teposcolula reveals that from roughly 1724–93, women constituted only 13 and 14 percent of registered litigants and defendants, with "doñas" making up a high proportion of those who sued (44 percent) and of those who were sued (29 percent.)[21] Unfortunately, the inventory does not permit us to know if these women were widowed or single, but the fact that so many were doñas in this poor, indigenous region underscores how self-selecting the group of litigating women could be.

Of course, there were rural women who defied the odds by walking or bumping on mule-back along dirt roads over long distances and the rugged terrain of the Montes de Toledo or the Sierra Zapoteca in Oaxaca, aiming for a city or town where they could initiate a suit over property, inheritance, and other civil matters. Nonetheless, in sheer numbers, women's presence as litigants is much more pronounced in cities than in rural regions.

Although it might seem intuitive that city dwellers sued more than rural folks, a number of factors aside from sheer population density affect litigation rates, and rural people sometimes can be more litigious than urban inhabitants.[22] Thus it is significant that, in 1790, the viceregal capital city of Lima, Peru, had roughly the same population as did Teposcolula in 1742 (around 50,000), yet Lima's inhabitants put lawsuits on the bench of the city's first-instance court five times more often (50 versus 10 per year).[23]

Perhaps it is unfair to compare isolated little villages in places like the Montes de Toledo and rural Oaxaca to the lively civil courts of huge capital cities such as Mexico City and Lima, where everyone lived in close proximity to a wide assortment of agents and institutions of colonial justice. In this respect, the suing habits of women in Trujillo, Peru, a district with haciendas and rural pueblos flanking a sizeable provincial city, is worth examining. Before the first-instance court in the sizeable city of Trujillo, female litigants composed almost a third of all civil plaintiffs (140 of 448) from 1700–99.[24] In the corregimiento of Trujillo, a jurisdictional district that comprised the city as well as surrounding countryside, the percentage of female litigants was even higher, at 41 percent.[25] Thus, women in Trujillo were far more active as litigants than were women in both the Montes de Toledo and Oaxaca, indicating that Spanish tribunals at even medium range distance could serve as magnets drawing women into courts.[26]

Figure 4.1 Two peasant women ride through the rugged hills into the imperial city of Toledo. Illustration by Auguste Boruet in Maurice Barré, *Gréco ou Le secret de Tolède* (París: Les editions d'Art Devambez, 1928). Courtesy of the Archivo Histórico Municipal de Toledo.

If, compared to urban women, rural women can best be described as hesitant civil litigants in suits against debtors, renters, or rival heirs, as litigators in civil suits against husbands and lovers, they were downright spectral. In only one case examined did a woman in the Montes de Toledo sue her husband in the civil court of the Fiel del Juzgado. Likewise, from a review of over 1000 civil cases in districts of Villa Alta and Teposcolula, only a small number of women initiated written civil suits in matters pertaining to divorce, adultery, alimony, court costs, or female "deposit." Here again, the cases that do survive tend to involve elite women. Of only two civil cases against husbands identified in the records from

Teposcolula, one was filed by an *española* (ethnic Spaniard)—in a district where the Spanish population never topped 5 percent.[27]

Women as Criminal Accusers

That relatively few female civil litigants from the countryside were registered as plaintiffs did not mean that these women were not in the courts. In fact, in both rural Oaxaca and the Montes de Toledo women's vivid appearances in criminal disputes with male partners—mostly as victims, but sometimes as accusers—contrast with their shadowy presence when it came to taking husbands to civil court.[28] In these rural areas, women appeared in one quarter to a third of cases of violent crime, though statistical generalizations here prove somewhat tricky.[29]

This tendency might owe to the distinct nature of the two types of suit. Specific individuals or groups filed civil suits while representatives of the royal state could file criminal cases labeled as "de oficio," or brought by authorities.[30] It is the distinction of being registered as a litigant or accuser rather than victim that deserves analytical attention. The part women played in criminal cases over abuse provides an illuminating counterpoint to their civil activities and helps sharpen the contours of women's civil juridical subjectivity in the late eighteenth century. Looking at a series of types of complaints and suits, including abuse (*malos tratos*), extramarital affairs, seduction, and rape, reveals how much initiative women exhibited by entering the justice system against men.

The line between criminal and civil cases could be hazy in the Spanish imperial legal world, particularly for litigants whose first-instance resource was a magistrate who held authority in both salas, or benches.[31] Yet even within all this jurisdictional fluidity and with the vaguely inclusive references to both civil and criminal "*acciones*" that might correspond to a complaint, for most of the seventeenth and early eighteenth century, civil suits traced back more directly to litigant initiative than did criminal claims. In criminal claims, judges' discretion and notions of public order heavily impinged on the opening and formalization of a case. In rural areas of the empire, many, if not most, criminal cases on file were brought "de oficio."[32]

Peering in at instances when husbands from the Montes de Toledo were accused of spousal abuse reveals that a mix of factors beyond women's individual legal initiative produced formal criminal suits. When Juan Gómez Gordo, from the pueblo of Navalmoral, became the target of a criminal prosecution one testy summer night in 1736, it was not exactly because his wife, María López, had decided to officially denounce him as a wife beater. True, she verbally complained about his violence to local officials. But this was only after they heard a ruckus in the house while making their nightly rounds policing the town. Four town officials stood in the doorway to the couple's home and announced that they intended to throw Juan in the local jail to prevent him from making further scenes. Juan responded to their reprimand by stabbing the alcalde. It was this, not María's complaint, that landed him before the magistrate in the city of Toledo.[33] Otherwise Juan would have cooled off for the night in the local jail and gone back home in the morning—perhaps resentful, perhaps regretful—and no paperwork would have been filed in the case.

In this instance, the "crime" of spousal abuse clearly did not lead to the "case." The adjudication of contentious matters between husband and wife—unwritten, local, and informal—did not necessarily or even mostly produce suits, and it certainly did not require women to take the role of a litigant or accuser. Furthermore, justice often hinged on concerns for public order and deterrence rather than on procedure and codified law, and it was dependent on the discretion of the justices involved in considering it an offense, not necessarily on the act committed. Indeed, Juan Gómez Gordo himself was acutely aware that justice operated this way in his pueblo. When one official asked him why he did not quiet down and make peace with his wife, his cantankerous reply was to point out to the officials that "your homes do not lack for disagreements either."[34]

Juan Gómez Gordo's case illuminates two central features of justice-oriented culture as it operated in domestic conflicts. First, many of the cases women seemingly leveled against men were in fact brought de oficio, casting them as victims rather than subjects. Second, Juan's case reveals the importance of a sphere of judicial activity that was informal and community based, a locus of law that generated an unwritten history preceding the instigation of official, formal cases.[35]

"De oficio": Men behind Women's Suits

That a case was filed de oficio did not mean that women were somehow absent or powerless in the realm of law. Juan's wife, María, had verbally shared her complaints with town authorities, but they, not she, charged her husband. Even the legal protagonism of unmarried women such as the widow Rodríguez of Horcajo, who got the local alcalde to act on her behalf informally in her land dispute, could be hidden behind the actions of male authority figures acting as guardians of public order.[36]

Though they transpired mostly on paper, legal proceedings nonetheless could be considered public affairs.[37] In order to protect the honor of women in this forum, male relatives represented women in all manner of suits. In small rural communities, protecting reputation and honor meant that, unless they were widows, women's names would not be attached to lawsuits. In the Montes de

Toledo, an alcalde might cryptically state that he "received notice" of domestic trouble when he opened a case de oficio against a husband. This is exactly what an official in Yébenes did in a 1722 prosecution of vecino Francisco Moreno. He wrote that he was compelled to register a formal complaint on behalf of the court because "he had been notified" that Moreno's home was filled with "disagreements, questionable words, and fights."[38] In one Church divorce from the city of Toledo, a husband was surprised to find out that it was actually his wife who had initiated a formal complaint with a criminal judge against his lover, since he "presumed [the case] had been filed de oficio."[39]

Documents omitted women's names to protect propriety not only when they were accusers but even when they were perpetrators of moral crimes. In the ecclesiastical tribunals of the Archdiocese of Toledo, which received cases and appeals from throughout central Spain, it was not uncommon for the Church's attorney to level formal charges of extramarital relations against men while suppressing the names of the women involved from the record, "for the sake of honor."[40] Often, the secrecy was not to protect the honor of the woman herself but rather the reputation of her male relatives or lovers, including even priests engaged in sexual affairs.

In cases over rape, seduction, or unfulfilled marriage promises, abstract community notions of "outrage" and "scandal" often did the legal work for women. Local justices such as Marjaliza's alcalde Fernando de Arce took the authorial lead in single women's lawsuits, wrapping the cases they passed to the Fiel del Juzgado in a language of official responsibility to uphold community gender norms. For example, de Arce reported in 1781 that it had "come to his notice as a public and notorious thing" that a single woman named Paula Esteban had gotten pregnant. His statement made no reference to Paula's "right" to have the father of her baby support her and their child—though in a sense this is ultimately what she sought. Rather, the local judge's knowledge of the affair, as well as the gossip and scandal it caused, propelled the suit.[41]

Parallel processes were at work in criminal suits leveled against husbands in Oaxaca in the 1700s. In criminal cases against men for domestic abuse or public adultery aired in the alcaldía mayor districts of Villa Alta and Teposcolula, it is obvious that women were not always the prime movers behind formal suits against men. Indeed, the larger legal culture of these communities filtered out disputes considered less serious, such as domestic disagreements, before they could reach Spanish authorities. In the inventory of written criminal cases in Teposcolula, over a third were serious violent offenses, and of this group half were homicides or death investigations brought de oficio.[42] In addition, indigenous officials in head villages had a certain amount of jurisdiction over non-violent crimes. Before cases reached Spanish officials, many first made their way through the community, frequently passing beneath the staffs (*varas*) of native village justices.[43]

María de Yllescas, from the Villa Alta pueblo of San Miguel de Talea, presents an extreme case of a woman who, although the sole victim of her husband's violence, was nonetheless only a bit player in the suit against him. Two native authorities of San Juan de Yae, the head town in the region, rushed to the Spanish subdelegate in Villa Alta in 1707. They reported through the court's interpreter that, during the weekly market held in their town, María's husband had stabbed her in the torso and "spilled her guts."[44] Local authorities were permitted to handle light crimes in the community, but homicide or serious assault had to go before Spanish authorities.[45] No doubt it was the gravity of María's injury that prompted indigenous community officials to report the event to the subdelegate. After taking the testimony of seventeen witnesses, the Spanish official threw Francisco in jail, where he remained for two years. Finally healed from her wounds, María presented a petition that begged the court to release her husband from prison so that he could return to her and "quietly and pacifically make a married life."[46] Critically, the request was made on ordinary paper that failed to bear the official royal seal, and the petition carried her father's name beside her own.

As in the Montes de Toledo, in rural Oaxaca the formal practices of law often took place between male authorities. María's part in the legal, as opposed to the social, drama was informal and instrumental, and the only element of the criminal case in which she appeared as an agent was cosigned by her father. Even in women's petitions that are not cosigned, it is easy to excavate strata of various male authorities—some Spanish, some indigenous; some associated with the state, others with the Church or the community—that existed and competed with one another as mediators in village life. In fact, many women who by themselves brought criminal cases against husbands recounted having tried many other means to rectify their unhappy home lives before formally submitting written petitions to the Spanish courts. Some used gossip or enlisted female neighbors to come to their defense. The more "legal" aspects of their actions involved appealing verbally to judges.[47]

Lo extrajudicial

Along these lines, a second lesson extracted from the alcalde-stabbing Spanish wife-beater Juan Gómez Gordo involves the verbal nature of justice-oriented legal culture. Women's formal cases against husbands often contain evidence of an informal, local, and unrecorded prehistory that provides insight into the operation of law beyond the courts. This was a culture of justice often aimed at least discursively at peace over punishment, at resolution rather than rights.

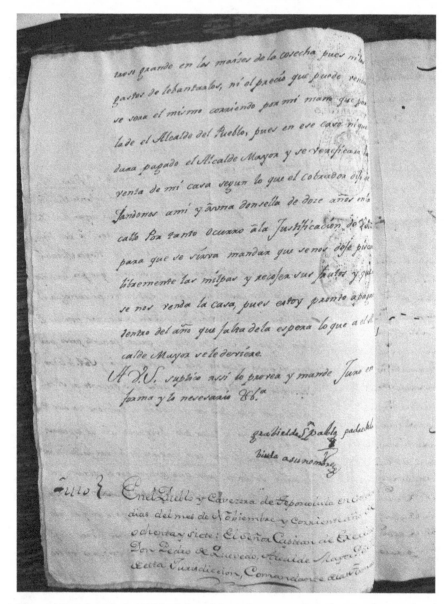

Figure 4.2 Gabriel de San Pablo, father of the indigenous widow Clara María, signs "in her name" (*a su nombre*) in a 1787 first-person petition to the intendant over the alcalde mayor's demands that she pay tribute for her dead husband. From Instancia de Clara María, natural de San Pedro Mártir, en el partido de Teposcolula, para que el alcalde mayor no la moleste, por el dinero de repartimiento que tomó su difunto marido, hasta que se cumpla el término del despacho de esperas que obtuvo de la Real Audiencia, APGEO, leg. 60, exp. 3, 1787, f. 1v.

When judges throughout the empire unfolded the letter-like papers that women such as Juana Sánchez, the wife of the Indian *gobernador* of Juxtlahuaca in Teposcolula, presented to them, tales of verbal legal interactions tumbled out with their complaints. Juana's husband had been cheating on her for two years with a woman from a neighboring pueblo. Her petition outlined the steps that she took to try to remedy her dismal domestic situation before formally petitioning the court: "I have desired peace, quiet and calm, even though I could have complained criminally for his punishment, especially since when I caught him with his lover I cut the *tlacollales* [hair ornaments typical of Mixtec women] out of her braids as proof. [But] I [instead] have availed myself on various occasions only of parish priests and their vicars specifically so that they would remind him of his obligations . . . and I have done the same in this court."[48]

Juana reported having visited priests informally before coming to court to file a written complaint. The small number of eighteenth-century divorce cases that remain in the ecclesiastical archives of Trujillo, Peru—21—provide a concise data set that illustrates the larger pattern in Juana's story, in which women appealed first to parents, indigenous authorities, priests, and even civil magistrates *en lo extrajudicial*. Fourteen of the litigants began their suits by cataloging the verbal complaints they had made before deciding to file an official suit.[49] Priests could be a first stop for rural women who wanted to tamp out sparks, though they often pushed reconciliation doggedly.[50] For native women, another alternative was indigenous officials, who could arrest and punish wayward husbands locally and mostly verbally, even in places where Indian authorities kept native-language records of criminal cases.[51]

Juana also revealed that earlier she had availed herself specifically "of this court," meaning the alcalde mayor's court of Teposcolula. In the justice-oriented legal culture of the Spanish empire, not every pleito was a pleito. In other words, not every complaint to a secular judicial authority was a lawsuit, and not every piece of paper passed to the bench was a lawsuit. To understand how the domestic and the legal pleito mingled on the margins of the formal justice system, the tales of two different doñas from two different cities, Oaxaca City (Antequera) and Mexico City, are instructive.

When the first instance civil judge in Antequera received Doña Petronila de Muñar y Puente's formal petition (*demanda*) dated October 5, 1731, it was not the first he had heard from her.[52] She had appeared two days earlier requesting that the judge warn her second husband, a local storeowner, to keep his hands off the property she had brought into their marriage. The alcalde complied with her request and issued a verbal warning to the husband, sending her to be confined (*depositada*) in her sister's home. None of this was written down. Not until two days later, after her husband disregarded the judge's warning and broke into her empty house to remove several valuable items, did Doña Petronila return to the judge with a formal petition initiating a civil suit against her husband over the possession of her belongings.

Unlike Doña Petronila's original verbal complaint, Doña Inés María Fernández's justice-oriented interaction with the royal courts in Mexico City began in silence. Noticeably bruised in the face, she wordlessly slipped a petition—a memorial written on ordinary paper—into the hand of the city's lieutenant magistrate. Still, the written nature of her complaint did not quite make it a lawsuit.[53] In the statement, she explained that her husband had hit her simply because one of her hens had pecked his inexpensive little psalm book.[54] The magistrate dismissed her initial petition, convinced that "this was one of those common *pleytos* that occur between spouses, and although passionate at the beginning and later they calm down, I worked in due completion of my duties with the end of reuniting them." He enlisted their parish priest to reconcile the quarreling spouses. The clergyman's efforts were, however, unsuccessful, and when Doña Inés's husband openly bristled at the priest's meddling, the priest had him thrown in jail for insubordination.

The dispute wound up at the bench of the Church's attorney, whose recommendation reveals a great deal about how magistrates understood women's civil complaints against husbands within the framework of justice-oriented law. There were, he deduced, two suits being pursued simultaneously: the spousal abuse charge and the priest's complaint against his recalcitrant parishioner. The Church's attorney found no grounds on which the abuse case against the husband could continue, even though a surgeon had testified to the wife's wounds. His reasons for this were threefold: there was "no petition or formal writing at all of a complaint"; Doña Inés had not appeared before the lieutenant as a judge but rather as a "paternal resource"; and finally, even in more formal and severe cases of spousal abuse, such charges, even if formal, were easily dropped.[55]

Thus, in 1775, a key figure in Mexico City's Church judiciary carved a bold distinction between a "lawsuit" and an informal (even if written) appeal to a judge as yet one more in a chain of paternal community authority figures. He also signaled that women's tendency to drop marital suits made their complaints somehow distinct from real lawsuits. That distinction was one that many litigants themselves also made not only when they registered verbal rather than written complaints but also when they turned written petitions over to magistrates without ever intending to receive a formal sentence.[56]

The conclusion of most petitions was the place where litigants and accusers detailed a concrete request for a specific judicial action. But in line with justice-oriented practice, many women's petitions against husbands and lovers ended with vague language that seemed to leave it up to a judge to decide how to proceed. For example, Josefa Dolores of Chilapa, in Teposcolula, recounted in a criminal case in 1797 that her philandering, physically abusive husband had taken her, pregnant, before indigenous community authorities to have her whipped for insubordination, causing her to miscarry. Her petition to the sub-delegate of the district closed by simply asking that the judge "carry out what you find fitting." The judge decided that the case merited the initiation of formal charges. But he first ordered the court notary to certify that the petition was hers. She responded that it was but hastened to clarify that "her intention was to ensure that her husband did not return to offend her with his adultery or mis-treat her, and giving guarantees, asks that he [be permitted to] leave prison."[57] Josefa had filed a petition without intending to start a suit.

Even the rare Montes de Toledo peasant woman who did file suit—for ex-ample, María Antonia Díaz de la Cruz of Yébenes, who took her fiance to Church court for breaking his marital promise—might suddenly drop a suit mid-process. María Antonia vaguely referred to being "moved by just causes" to cease in her ecclesiastical suit.[58] Those "just causes" could have been social pres-sures from family members or the community, as well as the financial hardships that men's long imprisonment created for women. In fact, some women reported that they continued to perform their gendered responsibility to provide their husbands food in jail, even when the women themselves were responsible for their incarceration.[59]

Still, cases did not always remain informal or end abruptly because female liti-gants wanted it that way. Some royal magistrates discouraged marital litigation, and Church judges, charged mostly with putting couples back together, refused to hear divorce suits.[60] Often, however, the decision to drop a suit came from a woman, even (or perhaps especially) when the suit had originated from inter-action with another male authority figure. Doña Inés, whose husband scuffled with a local priest after he beat her over his psalm book, ended up downplaying the formality of her earlier written memorial recounting the hen pecking. Four months imprisonment seemed to her excessive since the "light pleitos that move married people are not [the equivalent of] a criminal suit."[61]

If their own written complaint had set the wheels of justice in motion, women often had to draw up a second petition to put the brakes on the process.[62] María Oloya Pérez, from Yanhuitlan in Teposcolula, had sent a petition to the subdel-egate to complain of the trouble her husband gave her whenever he got drunk (which was, by all accounts, frequently). Shortly after her husband was impris-oned, she issued another petition dropping the case. It indicated that she had wanted only to teach her husband a lesson. Indeed, her initial petition did not call for punishment as much as announce her desire that her husband appear be-fore the judge to state for the record that she was a good wife.[63]

Cases such as these prompted the ecclesiastical judge in an indigenous parish north of Mexico City to blame dropped suits on native peoples' unfamiliarity with the law. "Since Indians did not know how to follow through with various judicial actions, it is easy to return [the women] to their husbands, no matter how great the offense," he reported.[64] Yet, obviously, native women were far from ignorant of the law. They understood well enough how they were using the legal system—as an instrument to coax their husbands back home, to break up an ex-tramarital relationship, or to try to ensure that beatings would stop. Contrary to the judge's opinion, dropping suits did not indicate the failure to pursue justice properly. Instead, it exposed an instrumental, outcome-oriented legal culture in which the process of suing was not necessarily the point.

Justice-oriented legal culture extended from the eastern Sierra Norte of Mexico to the Montes de Toledo, from Pamplona to Peru to Puebla.[65] In 1796, Josefa Dolores of Chilapa, when questioned about her written complaint against her husband, clarified that she was not so much interested in going to court as in ensuring that "her husband not return to offend her." The very same year that she made this statement from Southern Mexico, María Asunción of Pamplona, Spain, dropped the suit for alimony she had leveled against Pedro Ignacio in the high court of Valladolid. Also in 1796 Doña Juana Luna of Lima withdrew the suit she had lodged against the father of her illegitimate daughter for child support, and Cayetana Alberta, the wife of an español gold weaver from Puebla, Mexico, dropped the abuse charges she had leveled against her husband.[66]

These women from diverse regions had as many reasons for dropping these cases as they had for bringing them in the first place. Both the indigenous women from Oaxaca and the artisan's wife from Puebla indicated that their husbands' incarceration caused them financial hardship. The Pamplona couple's reconciliation remains unexplained in the judicial record, but it seems their parish priest had encouraged it. Doña Juana dropped her case because she had reached a settlement with her lover: he agreed to pay her six pesos a month so that the child did not take his name and sully his reputation in the tribunals of the city.[67]

In sum, the women of the Spanish empire who appealed to judges were not always "suing" their husbands, and even if they were, the outcome they sought often could be achieved without a formal sentence. Though they formulaically referred to what "corresponded to my right" (*como más conviene a mi derecho*) or appealed "in the jurisdiction that befits in law" (*como más ha lugar en derecho*), this was a connotation of "derecho" different from "rights."[68] These phrases conveyed that justice could reside in many places and be produced from the fluid interactions between women, men, and a range of authority figures.

It was not that the women in the Spanish empire who entered the informal, flexible, and often unwritten field of justice called "lo extrajudicial" failed to imagine the possibility of filing formal suits against husbands. After all, women throughout the empire, especially elite women, annulled marriages or sued over the return of their dowries all the time. But a divorce or a civil case with a concrete sentence and outcome was not what many ordinary women were after. A native woman named Felipa Huesca, from the coastal pueblo of Xicochamilco near Veracruz, Mexico, appealed all the way to the viceroy in Mexico City after her husband sold some of her cows without her permission. Yet even she, a determined petitioner, clearly saw a distinction between her petition and a formal suit, which she equated with divorce. In a mix of third and first person common in legal petitions, her statement reads that she petitioned the viceroy "to pursue the case, and asks not to divorce since there is law for that (*hai lei pa eyo*)" but rather that "Your Excellency orders that they send [her husband] to a presidio and that he declares to whom he sold my cows so that the buyers can pay me."[69]

For Felipa, there was the law and then there was her pleito. Invoking rights or assuming the status of a litigant was unnecessary in order to achieve a just outcome. Lo extrajudicial was not a space or practice beyond law; it was the site of its very production. Nothing could contrast more with the attitude of some of the urban women in the colonies who hauled their husbands into court at the end of the century.

Rights

On June 17, 1786, the puzzling lawsuit from Arequipa, Peru between Doña María Romero and Don Ygnacio Salgado over alimony, adultery, poisoning, and divorce sat before King Carlos III.[70] Until this point both the king and his Council of Indies had avoided becoming tangled up in María and Ygnacio's jurisdictional thicket. But the next year another colonial lawsuit over divorce would force the monarch to pronounce a separation between the spiritual and material aspects of divorce in a cédula moving alimony to civil jurisdiction.

While justice-oriented culture might have encouraged extrajudicial solutions, female litigants nonetheless sued their husbands in civil court, divorces happened, and moralizing officials prosecuted sex crimes. A legal culture that facilitated appeals to multiple authority figures meant that, at times, litigants made complaints in multiple jurisdictions, repeatedly forcing competition between judges. This competition sometimes resulted in *competencias*, or formal disputes over jurisdiction appealed to high courts, especially between ecclesiastical and royal authorities. Sometimes a husband would complain to a criminal judge that his wife was having an affair while a wife sought a divorce from the Church. At other times, an unfavorable ruling in one court led a litigant to seek a more amenable judge in a different one.

But if competition between jurisdictions and forum shopping were hardly new to early modern Spanish legal culture, the jurisdictional legal tactics that spouses and lovers employed in colonial domestic disputes reached an unprecedented intensity by the mid-eighteenth century.[71] At the largest scale of analysis, jurisdictional order was coming to replace fluidity and unchecked competition. By issuing rulings such as the 1787 cédula, the crown eclipsed Church power in a range of domestic disputes. Lawyers and judges were undoubtedly chief players in the intensification of jurisdictional centralization, shaping how the Enlightenment looked from the top-down. But the origins of the 1787 royal cédula on alimentos are a reminder that there would be no lawyerly ruminations or sentences—or even new laws—if litigants like María and Ygnacio of Arequipa had not been in the courts in the first place.

As litigants entered secular courts over marital issues in the last decades of the eighteenth century, a more formal legal culture pressed in on conventional justice-oriented practices. The remainder of this chapter explores this transformation in women's suits at two scales. It first surveys the chronological and regional patterns in one particular kind of case, suits over alimentos, or alimony and child support. This examination reveals that the shift to royal jurisdiction, bumpy though it was, emanated from the choices that colonial women made when they asked secular judges to accept their petitions and, at times, formally admit lawsuits against husbands and lovers.

Next, a broader vista of marital disputes of various kinds, including alimony as well as divorce and adultery cases, highlights various features of the new legal culture these litigants created. One of these features was the contractualization of marriage, or an emphasis on the civil as well as sacred character of the rights and duties marriage implied. As backdrops for larger jurisdictional struggles between the crown and clergy, women's lawsuits against husbands became stages for dramatic duels between Church and crown authorities. More germane to the women themselves, Bourbon-era jurisdictional wrangling opened space to forge a specifically civil juridical subjectivity, one that they began to exercise without deep prehistories and prior appeals to community authorities or multiple jurisdictions.

Concretely, this meant women defined themselves as bearers of "natural rights," which they translated into the legitimate ability to claim gendered legal prerogatives in civil jurisdiction, including separating from husbands without Church approval, suing their husbands for financial support, and naming their own lawyers. In making this shift, women's petitions to judges became inaugural acts rather than extensions of prior verbal interventions. What is more, they pushed to see their suits brought to sentence. Women's cases also frequently contained jurisprudential challenges to older ways of determining justice. At times, the very sources of justice that women and their representatives cited changed, moving away from the diffuse, casuistic interpretations of Roman and medieval laws. Rather than justice revealed in practice, law sprang from either "natural rights," defined vaguely but always beneficially for the women, from precedent, or from recent positive laws such as the king's 1787 cédula on alimony.

A Brief History of Alimony

To understand how the inhabitants of the Spanish colonies came to define marriage as increasingly secular and contractual, a brief history of the meaning and legal practices associated with alimony proves useful. Through the sixteenth and seventeenth century, women in the empire were sometimes compelled to go to civil courts to sue husbands—often husbands on the other side of the Atlantic—over inheritance or fiduciary matters.[72] But in its most general legal usage in civil courts, the term "alimentos" referred to financial support among family members but not necessarily between living spouses.[73]

While alimentos cases between living spouses were rare in secular courts until the eighteenth century, they long had been a standard part of divorce and annulment proceedings in Church courts, where they were considered worldly details to be dispensed with quickly so priest-judges could ponder the more important canonical issues related to annulment and divorce.[74] When a couple separated and one partner initiated Church proceedings, the ecclesiastical judge was called on to make a series of executive, summary decisions concerning where a woman would live and how she and the couple's children would be supported during the course of the suit.

Thus "alimentos" was in many ways synonymous with the practice of "*depósito*," which referred to placing women in private homes or in institutions such as lay spiritual houses or convents during the course of a suit to protect their honor and, of course, the honor of their husbands.[75] Don Antonio Catalán's conflict over alimentos with his wife in Lima in 1786, a year before Carlos III issued his royal cédula on the matter, typifies how alimentos usually entered divorce cases. His wife sued for divorce and had herself deposited, on his peso, in an institution for women called the Casa de Desamparadas. He submitted an accounting of his finances to demonstrate that the 12 pesos a month required for her upkeep in the lay spiritual house ate up too large a share of his monthly salary.[76]

As they haggled over amounts in divorce cases, men such as Don Antonio tended to argue that their contributions to their wives were "voluntary," and thus not a right to which their wives were entitled. Gertrudis Herrera's husband, accused of adultery in Teposcolula, for example, successfully argued that a court could not "make something obligatory that has been voluntary," and was permitted to pay her "what he wished" as the adultery suit against him made its way through the Church courts.[77]

This broad and flexible approach to alimony changed during the final decades of the 1700s, particularly in Mexico City and Lima. During these years, "alimentos" cases began to refer primarily to women's civil demands against men for alimony and child support, and women argued it was a right rather than a favor. Though produced in diverse legal contexts, their cases can be grouped as "spousal alimentos" suits. In some instances, one spouse was pursuing divorce in the Church courts simultaneously with the civil suit; others were based on spousal abandonment, or were suits brought by mothers against the living fathers of illegitimate children to force them to provide them daily child support.[78] In some cases, women expected ongoing alimony payments during a permanent separation; in others they wanted only payments during the course of the suit.

While not statistically massive, alimentos cases are nonetheless compelling because of their timing and their placement. Of the 23 suits exclusively over spousal alimentos identified in the Mexican national archives and 37 in the courts of Lima, women filed the vast majority (18 and 29, respectively) after the year 1750.[79] Many women filed between 1750 and 1787, the year of the real cédula. In Lima, 13 purely civil cases over alimentos reached Lima's secular courts before the cédula was issued; in Mexico City, at least 12 suits were submitted to secular authorities or involved jurisdictional conflict on the subject of alimentos during years preceding the ruling.

In contrast, in the Chancellería of Valladolid in Spain, the slim proportion of eighteenth-century civil clashes between living spouses that involved alimentos took on a very different hue.[80] The majority of spousal alimentos disputes that reached the Spanish high court ministers were not, strictly speaking, requests for secular magistrates to rule on alimony or child support but instead attempts to reignite stalled ecclesiastical cases through the recurso de fuerza.[81] When divorcing women—and, it must be emphasized, frequently men—had reached a dead-end with Catholic authorities, they turned to this high court to enforce royal patronage, which meant forcing an ecclesiastical judge to accept cases or admit appeals.

These recurso de fuerza petitions reveal Spanish women as legally engaged and jurisdictionally savvy. They actively used ecclesiastical courts and often appealed to multiple judicial authorities in order to get favorable outcomes in their conflicts with husbands and lovers.[82] Yet however active or independent Spanish women were, the peninsular legal culture that emerges from these cases looks different than the law-centered culture evident in the alimony cases in the colonies. While the amount of alimony a woman was to receive during a divorce case might figure prominently as a point of contention during an appeal to the Chancellería de Valladolid, in almost all instances, "winning" a recurso de fuerza request simply meant that Church judges were required to reopen the dispute. With only a few exceptions, litigants and magistrates unquestioningly accepted that ecclesiastical authorities had the jurisdiction to determine how much alimony women would receive, showing little of the muscular development of royal jurisdiction evident in the colonial cases.[83]

Spanish American litigants involved in domestic disputes also sometimes requested recursos de fuerza before their own high courts when the Church courts had let them down. But this was only one maneuver in a wider repertoire of moves they used to pit secular and Church jurisdictions against each other.[84] Legal gamesmanship of this type was easier for city-dwellers with access to multiple levels of the justice system: local courts (alcaldes), regional tribunals (corregidores and, later, intendants), high courts (audiencias), and large, active ecclesiastical tribunals. Middling-class women who lived in or near colonial capital cities—mostly doñas, but some entrepreneurial indigenous or *casta* (mixed race) freewomen—pressed especially hard to expand the limits of royal jurisdiction through their domestic disputes. In a jurisdiction such as Trujillo, civil suits exclusively over alimentos were infrequent, numbering only four, all dating after 1750.[85] In the more remote peasant districts of Mexico and Spain, such cases were virtually absent.[86]

The women in Lima and Mexico City who brought these suits were frequently the wives of artisans such as carpenters or musicians, lower-ranking bureaucrats, shop owners, and occasionally merchants. The average amount they asked for (and typically received) was between 10 and 30 pesos a month.[87] Though most could be categorized as middling-class women, the status of litigants varied. There was the doña who fretted that, with the confiscation of her husband's property in a related suit, she had lost use of her horse and carriage and would be forced walk Mexico City's cobblestoned streets. Then there was the woman who supported herself during her separation from her husband by living with her mother and washing and mending clients' clothes.[88] Several came into their marriages with no dowry, and most did not have employment outside the home, thus having little on which they could subsist if not for the aid of their husbands. Claiming poverty was an important strategic move, of course, and one that men also engaged in in alimentos disputes.[89] However, as the century progressed, many women of diverse backgrounds, including the working-class castas of the colonies, slipped demands for financial support into domestic suits that were chiefly about something else, such as abuse or adultery, making the request for financial support an increasingly standard part of suing husbands.

Secularization and Self

The largely urban and middling-class profile of women who used the courts to forge a new law-oriented culture might be attributed to the fact that city women tended to be more independent financially and that capital cities teemed with agents and Bourbon-era legal institutions and policing efforts.[90] But Bourbon legal institutions did not predictably promote women's interests in their disputes with men, as the records of one city criminal judge illustrate.

Corregidor Antonio Bassoco of Mexico City was an especially eager Bourbon magistrate who assumed responsibility for marital disputes, drawing them into secular jurisdiction, increasing his own authority, and further contributing to the emerging contractual character of marriage at the end of the 1700s.[91] The complaints Corregidor Bassoco heard could have been adjudicated en lo extrajudicial, but he took them on in formal, abbreviated criminal cases.[92] In his resolutions, the corregidor at times solicited specific promises from men as preconditions for reunions, including, in one case, a promise to provide financial support in the same manner that a separated woman might receive alimony.[93] Still, Bassoco showed himself quite determined to reunite Mexico City's couples, even at times against women's wishes. Thus, the legal ménage à trois between a married couple and a Bourbon judge could be a complicated affair, sometimes benefitting a wife, sometimes a husband, and sometimes leaving everyone dissatisfied.

The new Bourbon position of intendant established in the 1780s did provide a more accessible judicial forum for women, if not a consistent ally, especially for ordinary female litigants. For example, in Trujillo from 1700–84, doñas had comprised 85 percent (119 of 140) of all female litigants in first instance courts of the city's cabildo and 75 percent (95 of 132) of women suing in the rural corregimiento. Yet, during the period 1785–1810, in the new jurisdiction of the Intendency of Trujillo, doñas comprised only 52 percent (144 of 274) of female litigants. The rest of the female litigants were non-white women, identified as "mulatas," "mestizas," or "negras" who did not preface their name with "doña." What is more, Trujillo's intendant oversaw the majority of the small number (13) of civil alimentos, dowry, marital dissent, and custody suits aired during the period 1700–1810. This indicates that access to the bench of this state official, representing a new, more impartial regalist legal order, might have attracted women who otherwise would not have submitted formal cases in domestic disputes.

Judges and litigants did not exactly rush into expanding secular jurisdiction over domestic matters. The 1778 petition to the alcalde mayor of Teposcolula in Gertrudis Herrera's case—over alimony and separation, heard by a civil judge yet still tightly enmeshed with ecclesiastical jurisdiction—was chronologically and jurisprudentially positioned midway in the rise of law-centered culture. Gertrudis was an older widow of Spanish descent, who had lived apart from her second husband for almost two decades after failing to obtain a divorce from a Church judge. She was inspired to submit a petition only after a local priest had ordered her husband to pay her 12 pesos a month. Her husband refused and retaliated by filing a case against her for adultery in the Church courts.[94]

Gertrudis stated in a quintessentially justice-oriented fashion, "if my husband had complied with God and with me as he should, it would seem that I wouldn't have a right (*derecho*) to anything."[95] Not only did Gertrudis construe her right to sue for alimentos in civil court as contingent on her husband's behavior, both she and her husband presented their obligations to one another through a sacramental prism, and the original ruling for financial support in Gertrudis's case came from their village priest.

In a string of similarly transitional cases from mid-century Mexico City, men too made overtures to secular judges to hear marital disputes. When, in 1754, Don Josef Muñoz's wife successfully demonstrated to Church authorities that he had abused her and so was granted a divorce, the ecclesiastical judge required him to pay a peso a day for her upkeep in a lay spiritual house in Mexico City. Don Josef found the amount excessive and had his lawyer threaten to take the matter before secular judges. Such a jurisdictional move, his wife's lawyer countered, would be patently "illegal" since there were no grounds on which to contest the definitive sentence of the Church judge in matters of alimentos.[96] In another case, an indigenous noblewoman from Cuernavaca named Doña María Luisa Hinojosa had arranged for ecclesiastical authorities to have her husband thrown in jail for abusing her. The first thing the husband did when released was to petition the viceroy in Mexico City to force her to return to their marriage. She responded, in turn, to the General Indian Court, worrying that "if he takes me [back], he might kill me." Yet still she held out hope that the judge's oversight of a reunion might calm her husband's passions. The judge agreed to mediate.[97] Thus, some women ended up appearing before civil judges circumstantially, often prompted by their husband's own jurisdictional maneuvering.

Soon enough women would bring their cases before civil authorities more deliberately. Doña Ana Rosel of Mexico first complained about her husband's abuse to Toluca's corregidor, but the magistrate repeatedly referred her to ecclesiastical authorities. Church officials unsuccessfully attempted to persuade him to change his ways time after time, at one point even requiring him to put his money behind his promise to be a better husband through a formal, written guarantee (*fianza de indemnidad*).[98] When the abuse continued, Doña Ana decided that she wanted more than a guarantee; she wanted him to provide her alimentos and to live apart from him. Her husband and the priests of Toluca demanded they reunite. When in 1768 the ecclesiastical court notary came and showed her an order to return to her husband, Doña Ana refused, claiming she was in royal jurisdiction. Over cries of outrage from the Church magistrate in Mexico City, the Audiencia of Mexico forced the ecclesiastical court to turn over its papers on the case. Ultimately, however, the secular high court attempted to make peace between both the jurisdictions and the spouses.[99]

So, while secular authorities had begun to admit formal cases over alimentos in New Spain at mid-century, they were not quite ready to consistently rule that women possessed a secular right to spousal support or to defy the Church's long-standing prerogative to hear all elements of divorce cases. By the time the crown issued its cédula on alimentos in 1787, a handful of women in the colonies had already decided to begin their interactions with the law directly with secular judges; after the cédula such practices became firmly entrenched. In 1795, Doña Mercedes Zegarra of Lima made an official appeal to a civil judge for financial support as the first, not last, stop on her legal journey with her husband. When she brought the case, she narrated no long tale of appeals to other authority figures of to patch up her broken marriage to a struggling musician who offered to pay for her upkeep only if she entered a convent.

In fact, it seems that Doña Mercedes sought alimony from secular judges without filing for divorce. Although the crown ruling passed eight years prior to her lawsuit had moved alimony disputes from Church to crown jurisdiction, it presumed that alimony disputes would arise from formal divorce demands.[100] The case was eventually passed up to the high court ministers of the Audiencia of Lima, who determined that there were no legal grounds for the two spouses to have separated in the first place and called on the provincial alcalde to reunite the discordant duo. Quickly, Doña Mercedes's lawyer responded that she indeed had a divorce case pending before the Church judges of the city, a fact that would have permitted secular judges to proceed with the alimony suit. But the timing of the divorce case was suspicious, seemingly filed only after the high court ruled.

In addition to starting with royal judges rather than the Church, Doña Mercedes engaged in another law-oriented practice that diverged sharply from earlier justice-oriented culture, with its wide space for extrajudicial reconciliation. She recounted how the judge unsuccessfully tried to persuade her that this kind of matter should be worked out off-the-record (*hablando a solas*) rather than in a "*pleito público*."[101] She refused.

In the last decades of the century, other tenacious women from colonial cities likewise ignored judges' attempts to keep their cases en lo extrajudicial and struggled to get their cases sentenced.[102] Even if some Bourbon-era secular judges such as Mexico City's Corregidor Bassoco seemed enthusiastic to take on marital disputes, this was not so everywhere. In the end, litigants' initiative was just as important as judges' actions in creating a new legal culture. Perhaps even more important.

Like Doña Mercedes, many women wanted their cases to be formalized. In 1794, Doña Petronila de Cal filed a criminal complaint with the intendant about her husband's ongoing affair in addition to the civil case over alimony she had brought before the village alcalde of Axtlico, Mexico. When the criminal case stalled, she personally presented herself before the intendant and his legal advisor who, she later reported, "told me not to bother them."[103] Unwilling to see her petition dismissed and incensed that the intendant would not return her legal filings so she could pursue her civil case for alimony, she traveled in person to Mexico City to present the viceroy with a petition that directly addressed her subjectivity as a civil litigant. "I submissively plead," it reads, "not that you punish my husband and his lover but instead that you make the necessary rulings." What Doña Petronila meant is that the informal interventions of justice-oriented culture, in which judges might "do what they found fitting" by tossing a wayward or hotheaded husband in jail for a night or a month or a year, would no longer do. Like other women, she might have worried that his imprisonment would only punish her with a lack of resources.[104] Whatever the motivation, she wanted not castigation but a case.

Doña Petronila's desire to formalize her complaint and see it brought to sentence was inextricable, for her, from her right to receive financial support during the course of the suit. Financial support was a decidedly civil rather than religious affair, and Petronila pursued her case in the secular court "so that I, having already suffered so much injustice, might have some quiet in my conscience and that my husband might sustain me, giving me and my little ones what is necessary; and if this means I must present myself before the ecclesiastical [tribunal] to file for Divorce, I am prepared to do so; but so that Your Excellency might proceed according to law, may it dignify you to order that the Intendant turn over my *autos* [legal papers] in the return mail without delay."[105] Gone was the sense that extrajudicial maneuvers or unwritten appeals were enough to bring about justice. Gone too was the subordination of the alimony suit to the Church divorce. It had become its own, discrete realm of legal action and rights, which she suggested could be independent of a divorce.

To enter this realm of law, Doña Petronila made the journey to Mexico City and assumed the status of full-time litigant. Women had long moved to cities to conduct legal business. If that business involved marital disputes, they often were placed on deposit with honorable families or in large lay spiritual institutions. Whereas earlier in the century some women complained that jurisdictional entanglements were keeping them in capital cities far from home, by the end of the century, women suing for alimentos were gladly making the journey and arguing that they needed freedom from being placed on deposit while in the city to supervise the progress of their cases.[106] At times their parish priests aided their attempts to formally sue in city courts, including in secular suits, as did a priest who actually loaned a woman money to pay legal fees.[107] One woman, who had gotten nowhere with the adultery suit she had filed with the intendent of Puebla, moved with her mother to Mexico City where she made her money by sewing and spent it by suing her husband in civil court.[108] At other times, "city justice" could follow the women back home. When Trujillo's intendant was not able to resolve a case between a provincial couple while they were visiting the city, he promised that he would do so during his next official tour through the provinces.[109]

Natural Rights and Sources of Law

Women's new legal practices—deliberately entering only civil jurisdiction, insisting on formal suits, nudging alimony to center stage, moving to cities to pursue cases—generated a law-centered culture as much as any argument their lawyers advanced. Still, the narratives in women's petitions and the disquisitions of their learned legal representatives also reveal important aspects of law-centered culture. These arguments help explain why some but not all women participated in the shift to secular, formal disputes. Indeed, the power of legal narratives was not lost on women's legal opponents. One husband facing a Church divorce suit implied that judges in all jurisdictions were accepting formal cases in marriage disputes too easily. "If such cases are admitted because of the simple narrative of women, no marriage will be secure."[110]

The keywords that appeared in women's petitions and their lawyers' arguments turned traditional relations of authority into potential ties of oppression. Terms like "tyranny" and "despotism," "inhumanity" and "barbarity" appear frequently in women's cases in the latter part of the eighteenth century, as did frequent references to "slavery," which served women metaphorically when facing oppressive husbands. It might be easy to dismiss these words as nothing new. Even in earlier suits over adultery or abandonment, women complained, for instance, of their husbands' cruelty since sevicia, or abuse, was a canonically acceptable reason for divorce. "Tyranny" and "inhumanity" certainly had long been key entries in the colonial and early modern Spanish lexicon.

But the words seemed to crop up everywhere in late colonial cases. In 1795, Margarita Zegarra's lawyer called the father of her children "barbarous and inhuman" before the provincial alcalde of Lima.[111] Another woman from Trujillo said that instead of being a "companion of one flesh" her husband was "the most Barbaric and atrocious tyrant, putting his hands on me and treating me with a continual sevicie [sic] as if I were his slave."[112] In 1788, a lawyer for Mexico City resident Don Antonio Sotomayor predicted, correctly, that his client's wife would portray him in court as "the most criminal, cruel and abhorrent of husbands," and would "[paint] my client's slightest slips with the blackest of colors."[113] He moved preemptively to take the sting out of any such accusations by himself accusing his opponent's mother of "inhumanities."

More than empty or pro-forma accusations, these terms had begun to attach themselves to a larger critique of patriarchal (and, by extension, monarchical) authority. Certain of these keywords had regional overtones with unique political connotations. Trujillo had assumed a regional identity of loyalty after the great Andean rebellions of the 1780s, and the threat of treason and anti-royal activity saturated the late-colonial political culture of the area. This inflected the language used in all kinds of lawsuits, including women's abuse cases against their husbands. The criminal complaint of *trujillana* María de las Nieves against her husband described how he "manifested a seditious inquietude toward our marital union."[114]

The pedigree of "tyranny" or "sedition" can be traced not only to their lexical meanings but also to their discursive associations. Women's petitions began to gesture toward more erudite linkages between tyranny and natural rights theory, including offering arguments in line with natural rights philosophers including Pufendorf and Heineccius, whose work had been introduced to Lima's law students around this time. Among other concerns, these jusrationalist theorists pondered how the natural right to self-preservation fit within a larger rational legal order. In a divorce dispute, the petition of Ana Cárdenas directly invoked her right to self-preservation and freedom from tyranny. It claimed her entire marriage had been filled with "tyrannical *sevicia*" and "barbaric cruelty." "By natural right," she should be permitted to separate from her husband, since marriage should not "amount to a life in tyrannical captivity."[115]

The way litigant petitions invoked natural rights and natural law sometimes conceptually separated sacramental and human law, a separation as likely to turn up in petitions to Church judges as to secular authorities. In some instances, this distinction simply expressed the growing jurisprudential division between civil and Church jurisdictions. One woman's petition explicitly divided "Divine law" and "humanity" as discrete foundations for law, arguing that her husband had "abandoned the respect owed to the sacrament of Marriage and [showed] contempt for what is owed by Divine Laws and even what humanity itself dictates." [116]

The term "derecho" in this petition could be taken to mean both "law" and "right," an instability in meaning that was itself meaningful. References to "derecho" and "derecho natural" increasingly crowded out more traditional references to women's "action" or "privilege" in law. Sometimes the shift was tentative and its significance hard to attribute to any larger legal change. But after 1787, derecho often referred to a specific right based in written law: the right to sue for alimony, which was the basis for many women to invoke a general right to sue. Several suits expressly mentioned the real cédula of 1787 as a source of rights. Doña Trinidad Guzmán started her petition not with the traditional phrasing "using my actions" or "rights," but rather stated that she was "using my right before Royal Justice in conformity with the recent real cédula of His Majesty."[117] Female litigants did not view the 1787 cédula as just a fancy piece of paper whose significance was restricted to temporarily moving part of a divorce suit to

a different judge. Instead, it appeared in their petitions and cases as royal validation that they possessed a broad set of rights that could dwarf the pretensions of
Church judges to claim jurisdiction over marital matters.

The same year that Carlos IV issued the cédula on alimentos, he repeated
an order from the prior decade asserting royal jurisdiction over concubinage
cases.[118] In 1792, a woman drew on this law not as a litigant but as a defendant,
and in doing so invoked a strident secular subjectivity. Doña María Niño Ladrón
de Guevara had been thrown into a home for wayward women without being
told of the charges against her, though her petition to the intendant of Trujillo
indicated that she suspected it was because she had been having an affair. It conceded she was "no [Saint] Clare, or Teresa ... or even Catherine, Virgin and
Martyr," but took full advantage of the legal culture that placed "national" law
above foreign commentators and interpretations. The petition assured the intendant that she wanted nothing "more than to reveal the vigilant zeal of Our
Sovereign to [ensure] that your Royal Supreme authority and jurisdiction that is
found in Hispanic and American law are not usurped."[119]

Although the intendant physically presented the 1787 cédula demonstrating
royal jurisdiction over such matters to the Bishop of Trujillo to force her release
from prison, the ecclesiastical judge would not budge. This only inflamed Doña
María's sense that her rights, founded in a concrete secular civil law, had been
trampled.[120] She petitioned again with a bold statement concerning her secular
subjectivity. "The ecclesiastical judge is," the petition announced, "in terms of
the Monarch, as much a Vassal as I."[121]

Even if they were not as bold as Doña María, those women who construed
their rights as the ability to voluntarily leave their husbands without Church approval and still receive alimony in secular jurisdiction promoted a civil notion of
freedom that sent up a chorus of protests by men and their lawyers.[122] A common defense was to claim that the women were simply trying to achieve "liberty" and throw off the "yoke of marriage" by filing suit. This claim appears so
often yet so unadorned in men's arguments that it seems that all parties would
agree that "liberty" was a negative aspiration for women. One husband argued
that the entire alimony demand his wife embedded in a divorce dispute was a
ploy for her to keep herself out of deposit and in a state of "liberty" for as long
as possible.[123]

Women also attempted to impose contractual obligations on husbands,
making the union itself as well as its dissolution something that need not be
overseen by the Church. In a case aired in Lima's ecclesiastical tribunal, Don
Anselmo Pino admitted that he had agreed, out of court, to pay his wife alimony
for nine months when she first moved out of their home. He later thought twice
about their special negotiation, arguing "the woman has no authority (*potestad*) to enter into such deals but should live subjected and subordinated to the

husband at his expense."[124] Don Anselmo's admission of making a deal with his wife highlights the rising culture of contract increasingly pervading marriages. One husband hauled into court lamented this new culture, recounting in his divorce case that when he needed to borrow money from his wife, she had forced him to sign an actual contract with her "as if I were a stranger."[125] The culture of contract even seeped into marriages where spouses considered reconciliation. A Mexico City woman, separated from her husband of six years, initiated an alimentos suit before the first-instance city court in 1790. She admitted she had not gotten around to suing for divorce in the Church but nonetheless wanted her husband to be civilly obligated to support her. She also said that before she would even entertain reconciliation with her husband, she wanted him to contractually guarantee that he would pay her upkeep.[126]

Just as female litigants took secular jurisdiction over alimony to be a contractual right to alimony, they also imagined it to imply a right to court costs.[127] It is worth recalling that the 1787 cédula extended beyond spousal and child support; it also stipulated that secular officials hear conflicts over court costs (*litis expensas*) and dowries. Don José de Eslava from Tepoztlán, Mexico, whose wife had sued him for alimentos the year after the promulgation of the royal order, objected not so much to her request for alimony as the injustice of being forced to pay court costs for the very civil case she had leveled against him. In doing so, he indirectly validated her claim that alimony was a natural right rooted in self-preservation. His attorney, José Lisla, was adamant that a right to court costs was not a natural right:

> Although the terms *alimentos* and *expensas* tend to be analogized or confused by many professors of Jurisprudence, it is certain that these are very different and distinct[;] alimony is rooted specifically in justice because it is founded on natural right, which demands the conservation of the living; the same is not true of court costs since these are normally voluntary (*de gracia*), and when, in rare occasions, they should be administered, it should be under the conditions and circumstances that the Authorities stipulate, however little they treat this material.

Lisla went on to point out that his client never denied Doña Gertrudis alimony, "but he cannot do the same with the litis expensas because, for court costs, it was necessary for Doña Gertrudis to prove that she has a right to his voluntary assistance, which she never has and never will."[128]

Thus female litigants construed the royal law that conferred the ability to sue in secular courts over court costs as a right to receive from their husbands funds to support their suits. Put differently, they construed their right as men's duty to facilitate the defense of their rights in court. But the emphasis did not shift completely to male duty; women continued to submit complaints that drew rights into themselves as civil subjects. In fact, the right to have husbands pay court costs could blossom into other, subsidiary gendered rights. Doña María García of Mexico City invoked a new right in her divorce case: the right to name her own legal counsel.[129] It is, perhaps, not a surprise that she would make this argument. She was the especially smart and skillful litigant who demanded to name her own lawyer and got into some trouble by filing her own petitions.

Doña María's legal theatrics with her husband, militia member Don Josef Pila, had played out almost like one of the dramatic French *teatro lacrimosa* plays that Mexico City residents had been crowding into their new coliseum to watch.[130] The opening scene to this lawsuit involved a young male university student and some downed sangria. Later, her husband found love letters to the student written in Doña María's handwriting. The first act closed with a military judge left standing alone, rebuffed and insulted, in the courtyard of the offices of Mexico City's chief ecclesiastical magistrate, Juan de Cienfuentes. The military official had come to discuss jurisdiction with the priest-judge, believing that the Church should cede the alimony and court costs portion of the divorce dispute to his court since the husband was in the militia. Cienfuentes breezily dismissed his request, stepped into his carriage, and rode away.

The jurisdictional drama surrounding this divorce case provided Doña María the opportunity to push her role as a litigant to its limits. Since the ecclesiastical judge clung to jurisdiction, she would give him what he wanted. She submitted to the Church court detailed petitions concerning the alimony she was receiving while on deposit, and she argued that her husband should cover court costs "since it is *de derecho*." In a relatively unusual move, she demanded to name her own lawyer even though the court would provide her one.[131]

Her petition requesting to choose counsel was cosigned by one of the men whom Doña María singled out as her choice for representation. It argued, in essence, that the right to name a legal represented was rooted in the growing separation of Church and royal authority. While lawyers in the empire were always trained in both canon and civil law and could represent parties in either jurisdiction, the petition argued that it was likely she would receive a lawyer with "little or no knowledge" of the rules and laws of the ecclesiastical tribunal, which might be an "unfamiliar forum" for the lawyer.[132] Church-state tensions created the space in which Doña María was able to argue that civil and ecclesiastical tribunals and the laws they supported were so separate as to require technical, specialized knowledge. While her assertion of the freedom to choose her own counsel was unusual, it was also resonant with larger jurisprudential developments in the colonies, particularly the 1795 ruling by the fiscal of the Council of Indies backing litigants' freedom to select their own legal representation, including uncertified agents.

Women thus interpreted the 1787 cédula as a broad ratification of rights to alimony, court costs, and even to name counsel in cases involving alimentos. Such construals of "natural rights" were not limited to divorce and separation cases. For example, Lima attorney José Dávila complained in a 1796 case that women had come to believe that they had a right to alimentos even when they had committed adultery.[133] His fears eventually materialized into a most striking case, in which a woman convicted of having conspired with her lover to poison her husband was awarded alimony by a Lima civil court in 1800. Her right to alimony was even upheld on appeal.[134]

An indigenous woman named Tomasa Maldonado certainly employed a capacious notion of the variety of civil actions that a wife could bring against a husband, as she sued her spendthrift, wandering husband over a diverse array of offenses. This woman, who hailed from the Peruvian coastal town of Lurín, threw a request for a daily stipend (*diario*) into her opening petition to the Intendant of Lima in 1796. But she then proceeded to continually change the basis of her complaint from neglect to robbery to adultery. At the same time, she repeatedly recused lawyers and judges for partiality and appealed all the way to the Council of Indies—to the outrage of the subdelegate who had tried in vain to put the marital dispute to rest with several rulings in her favor.[135]

Tomasa initially traveled to Lima to appear before the subdelegate because she was convinced that the local justices were all in league with her husband. Throughout her case she complained of the partiality of local officials, and eventually turned the same complaints against the magistrate in Lima. Women like her began to dedicate considerable space in their suits to the assertion that judicial authority was to be administered impartially, even impersonally.

Within this new legal culture, female litigants denied lo extrajudicial as a valid space for the revelation of justice and instead portrayed it as a haven for "sinister" dealings favoring their husbands. This was especially true of provincial women like Doña Petronila de Cal from Axtlico, Mexico, and Doña Melchora Oyos, from Chota, Peru, both of whom made the long journey to larger cities to escape biased local magistrates.[136]

A petition one women from a pueblo in Veracruz submitted made a patchwork of arguments that stitched together many of the dominant strains of law-oriented gendered culture, tying the natural right to self-preservation to the idea that urban courts might be more impartial than village judges, and attaching this, in turn, to her right to separate from her husband on her own accord: "I came with others [to the court of Mexico City] to the defense that is very natural and which God concedes even to brutes, so that in the course [of the dispute] they can free themselves from enemy oppression, whose disorderly passion hides itself in the smoke of detracting voices."[137]

In making women's cases, lawyers such as Angel Rodríguez Baldo struggled with the transition from traditional justice-oriented emphasis on judicial flexibility, equity, and distributive sentencing to a new stress on procedure, impartiality and recent law. Rodríguez Baldo was engaged in one of many intense battles with the Church attorney for the Archbishopric of Mexico City in a divorce suit. Since the ecclesiastical official would not remit the alimony part of a case to secular authority, the lawyer took the opportunity in his statement before the court to make a case for the greater justice of law-oriented practice. Judges should "administer and distribute justice with impartiality," he claimed, continuing that "even when there are no conclusive laws on which [judges] can base their rulings, there are other [laws] dictated by prudence to which they should submit their decisions, guaranteeing that they are in good order and in conformity with Law of Nations (*Derecho de Gentes*)."[138]

To both administer and to distribute justice: the former implies the application of the law, the latter judicial flexibility to achieve equitable outcomes. Both terms were, perhaps, standard parts of Spanish imperial legal thinking, but the tenor of the lawyer's argument shifted positive emphasis to the former and negative emphasis to the latter.[139] Rodríguez Baldo warned of the dangers of the flexible interpretation of laws. Moving away from casuistic rulings and toward unwritten, universal laws of "good order" and the "Law of Nations" would ensure that rights would not be compromised if litigants faced unscrupulous judges since, in a system of purely distributive justice, "the litigant has no recourse but the rectitude of the Judge . . . [who might] deviate from the unchanging maxims of Jurisprudence"[140]

Even the less erudite opening petitions in women's cases suggested that rights proceeded not from authoritative sources but rather from unwritten natural rights. Paula Soriano of Lima complained that her husband acted as if "laws were subject to his whims," and she founded the legitimacy of her case against her husband and her freedom to live separated from him in what Rodríguez Baldo had called "unchanging Maxims." "There can be no law that obligates me to make a married life with a lion, being [that] I am a lamb, when the laws themselves favor me."[141] Here, Doña Paula's petition invoked a refrain common to women's cases at the end of the eighteenth century: "there exists no law" (*no habra ley*). "To [make me] return to the dominion of a tyrant?" Ana Teresa Cárdenas's opening petition in a divorce suit rhetorically asked before responding, "There can be no law."[142]

Evocations of unchanging maxims might be helpful to women who wanted to argue that their claims against husbands should be heard in court, but if they could point to a recent a law or ruling, all the better. To legitimize their formal, civil suits, women's petitions specifically referenced local practices in colonial tribunals, as well as from more recent rulings in marriage cases, heightening the

historicist character of legal cases and fixing local colonial precedent in an emerging system of law.[143] The argument put forward on behalf of Doña María García,
who contended she had the right to name her own lawyer, drew primarily from
precedent. Her petition did mention canonists and commentators on civil law
but expressly named them "last" behind "many examples that can be found in
this court, other tribunals of this city, and other Countries."[144]

Doña María's lawyer seemed to have a lot invested in his argument about judicial precedent. When her lawsuit took another turn and it benefited her case to
be heard in ecclesiastical jurisdiction rather than secular courts, her legal counsel
stated, "it would be enough" to move the case back to the Church based on the
jurisdictional affirmations of "Canons and Pontifical Bulls." But even when making this argument, he found canons and bulls to be less important than practice.
For this lawyer, the attack on the Church's prerogatives emanated not from abstract jurisdictional designs in Madrid but rather from corrupt colonial practices,
which had built up in the courts. "In the end," he reminded the judge, "[to accept
the case in ecclesiastical jurisdiction] is in line with your own opinions and observable rulings; and as a result you have extirpated the abuses and pretexts
of custom, and the practices that have been introduced into the Ecclesiastical
courts [by] the judges who govern them and the professors who seek to enter
them, since there has been no new development in the methods of the past."[145]

This was a tough sell. To reclaim the case in his jurisdiction, the Church judge
would have to flatly ignore the 1787 royal cédula on alimony and court costs,
turn his back on the fierce debates about moral and legal reasoning that dominated the Bourbon era, and agree that there had been "no new development in
the methods of the past." But, critically, this lawyer did not argue that keeping
the case in ecclesiastical tribunal was the right thing to do only because it was
a time-honored practice or upheld older epistemologies of justice. Instead, he
argued that it squared with the judge's own recent rulings in similar cases—in
other words, precedent. It was not the "introduction" of new policies in the court
alone that was the problem; it was that they were dressed as "custom" by "judges
and professors" who presumably had secular agendas.

Dionisio de Lima, the lawyer representing Doña María's husband, countered
this by invoking the more practical, streamlined, and orderly system of jurisprudence that was coming to replace the justice-oriented reliance on a thick corpus
of commentators and authorities for legal sources. De Lima contemptuously
responded that the sources that Doña María's counsel cited were "not practical
authors but canonists."[146] Canonists would have been just fine to cite in decades
past, but in a legal culture obsessed with practicality and in which casuism was
waning, the great minds of the Church were facing challenges as legal sources.

This description of legal arguments in the dramatic case of Doña María
simplifies the complex legal maneuverings of the couple's lawyers, who often

grabbed at an array of sources and deployed a range of logics, sometimes contradicting themselves as the case took new twists and turns. But more ordinary cases also registered a shift toward precedent and a belief that cases should be classified with like cases in order determine sentences.

Take the suit between Doña Melchora Oyos and her husband Don Pedro Francisco Albarez, in which neither litigant signed an official power of attorney but rather used unidentified agents.[147] Don Pedro objected to the fact that his wife received a loan from a priest to travel to the city of Trujillo to sue him. He specifically pointed to codified laws that prohibited married women from entering into contracts without their husband's license, as his wife had done when taking the priest's loan.[148] Doña Melchora, for her part, marshaled practice and precedent to her case: "I have never needed a license" before for business dealings, she retorted.[149] She also cited a ruling that the intendant of Trujillo had made in a case of a "priest [named] Risco from San Agustín against the shop owner" as precedent, though the context of that case was not clear.

Even husbands' arguments contrasted recent practice and precedent to antiquated laws, shifting the temporal pull of judicial decisions to more contemporary criteria. When a husband objected to the fact that his wife was on deposit with her mother during their legal dispute while he wanted her in an institution, her lawyer defended her choice to live with her mother, citing the Third Mexican Council, held in 1585, which stipulated that women could be deposited in "honest homes." Her husband's response was that the Council had taken place over 185 years before, when there were no institutions for housing women in Mexico City, and confidently stated, "I assure you the thinking would change in the present time."[150]

Women's Civil Cases as Enlightenment

Without explicit reference to European trends or intellectual debates, women, men, and their lawyers in Spanish America made emergent law-centered culture central to their domestic pleitos. But how did their legal actions and arguments connect to the Enlightenment as a specific historical movement? Contemporary observers made the connection obliquely: To identify how civil lawsuits between colonial spouses fit within the larger movement, recall the words of the anonymous author from Cádiz who in 1811 complained that colonial Spanish Americans had all of the advantages of the Enlightenment (*las Luces*) but seemed to channel them mostly into "discords and entanglements, especially matrimonial." Among the many features in these discords and entanglements that mark them as Enlightenment, a few stand out, particularly their marshaling of new notions of natural rights, the reliance on new epistemologies of law, and their participation in larger processes of secularization.

Women's claims to alimony and litis expensas articulated with broader natural rights theory, specifically a preoccupation with the boundaries of the individual and the right to preserve oneself against against tyranny. This language clearly nodded to the jusrationalist philosophies that had infiltrated legal education and official policy at the end of the century. Did civil governments possess the ability to make laws that would defy an individual's right to conserve life? Heineccius's treatise on natural rights, widely circulated through Spanish imperial law schools, provided an answer: yes and no. A fundamental feature of just laws was their ability to protect (a greater number of) subjects, but too much infringement constituted tyranny. Such philosophies led many a litigant or legal amanuensis to proclaim that "there could be no law" requiring a woman to return to a home of a despotic husband. At the extreme, women's cases could extrapolate this natural right to self-preservation into rights applicable to "humanity" or "the Laws of Nations" at large.

The invocation of natural rights in women's cases was deeply bound up with the introduction of new ways of knowing and arguing about the law. One historian of European law asserts that "natural law"—referring to seventeenth-century jusrationalism and its later iterations—was the "first modern philosophy of law." It necessarily required new epistemologies of justice because it "reduced the whole complex of rules regarding outward behavior under a systematic structure."[151] That systematization was evident in spousal disputes as litigants and their lawyers engaged in Enlightenment methods of argumentation, at times rejecting traditional authorities or commentators as outmoded. One lawyer offhandedly dismissed canonists as "impractical" sources of law, while another fretted that casuistic interpretation bound a litigant's rights too tightly to a magistrate.

This new thinking about the law had a definite temporal dimension, especially drawing on recent practice and precedent to guide judges' decisions. The push and pull in court between wives and husbands often boiled down arguments about which side was newest, most systematic or most innovative. While one lawyer argued that older laws had to be rethought "because thinking would change in present times," another lawyer tried to assure a Church judge that his own "recent rulings" trumped the 1787 royal cédula, which was not even an "innovation."

Arguments in colonial domestic suits indicated that justice should be based on legal foundations not only closer in time to the cases but also closer in proximity to Spanish America. After colonial litigants forced a royal ruling on secular jurisdiction over the financial facets of divorce cases in 1787, female litigants could point to positive law designed especially for the colonies to bypass the tradition of interpretation and connect their rights directly to the civil sphere. They increasingly appealed to precedent and to laws closer in place and time to the litigants—to "Hispanic and American law," as one woman's petition framed it.

These experiments with new epistemologies of law in eighteenth-century Spanish American colonies' courts were, in a word, secular. This is not to say that quarreling spouses or their lawyers were losing their religion.[152] It is to say, however, that the colonial spouses who entered royal civil courts over alimony actively contributed to the secularization of marriage, a process that by its very nature curbed the ecclesiastical contribution to marital justice. Even rural priests participated in this process, loaning women money to take their abusive husbands to civil court.

Exactly how conscious litigants and defendants were of their participation in this process could vary. At times, secularization was the result of colonial forum-shopping strategies. Many litigants made sure that they left the appropriate argument at the appropriate bench as they moved through a revolving door of jurisdictions, flattering both ecclesiastical and secular magistrates along the way. But in some instances, women's intentional preference for the civil courts is hard to miss. Doña Ana of Toluca, tired of Church authorities' ceaseless attempts at extrajudicial mediation and reunion in her abusive marriage, patently refused an ecclesiastical order to return to her husband by claiming to be in "royal jurisdiction." An admitted adulteress in 1792 confessed to being no saint but insouciantly claimed the bishop of Trujillo was "as much a Vassal" as she. Perhaps this litigant or her lawyer purposely borrowed these words from the regalist jurist José Covarrubias's *Maxims on Recursos de Fuerza*, published two years earlier, in which the author explicitly marshaled natural rights theory against "arbitrary" Church judges, pronouncing that "men are born Citizens; and Ecclesiastics do not cease to be such."[153] In any case, the words are mere echoes of those in the petitions that scores of women filed in civil courts without even setting foot before an ecclesiastical judge, pushing their civil rights in marital matters far beyond what the king intended in the royal cédula of 1787.

Whether the result of short-sighted forum shopping or more historically conscious participation in the construction of civil law on marriage, women's entrance into royal jurisdiction undeniably advanced a more contractual, utilitarian vision of marriage than had existed before. This could not help but have repercussions in the way in which litigants saw themselves and their place in law.[154] To some extent, this development presages the so-called "categorical" identity commonplace in modern nations and analytically contrasts to the fluctuating "relational identity" more characteristic of early modern societies or those based on kinship.[155]

To accept that eighteenth-century women in the Spanish American colonies produced categorical juridical identities through civil marriage litigation does not mean that they embraced a unified, singular individualism, as the concept of citizenship would later.[156] The eighteenth-century production of secular legal selfhood among women in colonial Spanish America is perhaps best understood as a dawn of new horizons rather than of the replacement of one form of subjective legal identity with another. It was an experiment in presenting a new kind of gendered self to judges. In the eighteenth century, secularization did not mean the death of the sacramental self as much as "the opening of other possible sources" of identity.[157] Competition between jurisdictions, which had defined Spanish imperial legal practice throughout the early modern period, was one thing. The elevation of royal authority over the spiritual power of the Church on the matter of marriage was another. It provided a platform for a new source of women's legal selfhood, built on rights at law distinct from the moral authority of the faith.

"It is not right," mused don Antonio Sanz, that "I would foment a Pleito against myself." He went on, "I do not believe there is a law that says in a voluntary disunion undertaken by the woman" that the husband owed alimony. Technically, he had a point. He also had a point about the injustice inherent in his wife's request that he pay for the lawsuit she had leveled against him in royal court.[158] Yet, by the end of the eighteenth century, colonial Spanish American women appealed to royal civil courts to force their husbands to do just that, requesting that men provide alimony indefinitely and pay the expenses women ran up suing them in the first place. In the Enlightenment legal culture of the Spanish American colonies, having a pleito with one's wife came at a cost, monetary as well as legal.

When Don Antonio made this statement before the royal court of the Corregidor of Trujillo in 1780, there indeed existed no law that compelled him to pay for either alimony or court costs. The promulgation of the royal order on the temporal nature of alimony, dowries, and litis expensas was seven years away. Yet that ruling was less a statement on women's rights than a pronouncement on jurisdiction. It did not endow women such as Don Antonio's wife with the legal right to initiate a marital separation outside the Church courts, obtain alimony indefinitely rather than only during a divorce suit, and push the legal costs to sue over this right onto their husbands. In fact, the king's policy was as much a response to the changing nature of colonial domestic litigation—to suits like the one initiated by Don Antonio's wife—as it was an impetus for this litigation. In Spanish America, the litigants involved in domestic lawsuits had been straining the edges of jurisdictions for decades, forcing the expansion of royal authority.

Secular judges' willingness to entertain such arguments coincided, of course, with a larger shift toward regalism in the political and legal order of the empire. But simultaneity should not be mistaken for causation. When colonial civil judges considered domestic disputes before the 1787 real cédula, particularly those concerning alimony, they were generally cautious to respect the Church's longstanding dominion over marital matters. It was colonial women and their legal representatives, particularly in the colonies, who pressed the matter, invoking new natural rights and demanding to defend those rights in court.

5

Then and Now

Native Status and Custom

Beginning only shortly after conquest, indigenous people adopted their conquerors' legalistic culture and streamed into Spanish courts.[1] They used the courts not just to limit the devastating effects of colonial labor regimes and exploitation but also against other indigenous communities. To that extent, the law can be viewed as a tool of Western imperialism that fractured indigenous peoples into an internally divided peasantry compromised by its reliance on a colonial state.[2] Yet native legal history is more than simply a tragic tale of increased dependence on state institutions.[3]

As a unified legal category, the "Indian" was of course a colonial invention. But Spanish colonial law simultaneously recognized and authorized varied ranks, ethnicities, and origins of native peoples.[4] Thus, native identity—who claimed or was assigned "indigeneity," and when and how—was itself produced through and around the law. As the meaning of the native before the law changed over time, so too did the meaning of law for the native. Indigenous law, as any other law, could be "modernized."[5] That process is the focus of this chapter, which is neither a history of heroic resistance to an encroaching capitalist order nor a sad tale of capitulation to the forces of a racialized Enlightenment. Instead, it is a story of how indigenous people's contests over the law simultaneously shaped native tradition and legal modernity.

The chapter first examines the ongoing production of indigenous and Spanish colonial legal culture at the level of the native community in the seventeenth and early eighteenth centuries. It was from that dynamic that an indigenous legal Enlightenment emerged. With this in mind, the chapter then turns to its central argument, examining how two phenomena attributed to Western modernity, merit and historicism, were bred in Indians' suits, particularly in increasingly contentious intra-community suits over status and custom in the eighteenth century. As a final plot twist, elite native defendants and Spanish judges met these new articulations of status and custom—these new ways of conceiving of rank within communities and new articulations of local history—with a retreat into the ahistoricity of custom and a concept of Indian law that remained rooted in distributive justice. In other words, it was precisely because some native litigants began to conceive of and express law in new ways that others entrenched visions of Indian justice as old.

Part of the difficulty in searching for innovations and transformations in legal concepts such as status and custom is that their very meanings signify tradition and stasis. The mere invocation of "custom" in a lawsuit can be taken, prima facie, as evidence for continuity, especially in indigenous legal history. Historians have often understood native culture to be "localocentric," "deeply conservative," and focused on a "primordial We-ness," all characteristics that contrast to the cosmopolitanism, radicalism, and individualism that define the Enlightenment and Western modernity.[6]

Indeed, native litigants never stopped talking about community, custom, local tradition, and inherited status in lawsuits. As a result, their cases only sometimes pivoted on key concepts that had taken on new meaning in the Age of Enlightenment—say, "tyranny" or "equality"—in comparison to such traditional notions. What is more, other terms typically associated with the radical form of political Enlightenment, such as "republic" and "liberty," had a life in indigenous people's lawsuits long before the end of the eighteenth century, making it easy to overlook indexical change in how they imagined and practiced the law.[7]

So rather than just using the appearance of certain words in legal arguments to measure native participation in the Enlightenment, the analysis here focuses on status and custom as motivations for lawsuits in practice as much on the page, beginning with a statistical analysis of the transformations in the number and types of civil cases in native communities during the century. As the volume of litigation in Spanish courts coming from native pueblos rose alongside the increase in all civil litigation across Spanish America, more native litigants brought suits centered on a notion of status as earned and accessible to all, and more suits imbued custom with an immediacy and historicity that it had not previously possessed.

Then

It is important to establish what the practices of justice-oriented culture were like for native litigants before and during the rise of Enlightenment practices during the eighteenth century. Legal practice in indigenous communities was not simply a direct inheritance of pre-hispanic practices. Nor did natives possess a legal culture wholly apart from European culture.[8] Rather, in indigenous pueblos, officials and villagers built local legal practices through ongoing interaction with early modern Spanish legal concepts, particularly those that favored local custom and conciliation. In other words, what native law was—its limits, its features, its culture—might sometimes be defined in contrast to Spanish law, but it just as often could adopt and magnify its features, contributing to a broader imperial legal culture. Knowing this means that there is no empirical answer to the question of which party in a dispute had indigenous tradition or custom on its side. In fact, these very terms could be capsules for dynamic ideas about status, law, and time, even as their repetition provided a veneer of stasis.

Harmony and Justice

Native litigants across the Spanish empire promoted local cultures grounded in discourses of harmony. In fact, this tendency toward conciliation within native communities long outlasted Spanish colonial rule—a cultural attitude anthropologist of the Zapotec people Laura Nader calls "harmony ideology," in which justice is achieved through mediation among diverse authorities and through compromise rather than retribution or winning a case in formal processes of law.[9] This emphasis on harmony is rooted in a collective notion of morality and serves multiple functions, not least of which is to contain conflict and to insulate native communities from the intrusions of outside mediators, particularly legal officials representing the Mexican state.

Harmony ideology shares commonalities with the justice-oriented culture that the rural Castilian Felipe Gómez witnessed when he saw peasants toasting a legal deal with a cup of lemonade. Considering native justice within this broader imperial framework raises an important question: Was the justice-oriented approach to law in native communities a version of a generic "early modern" mode of thinking about the law? Or was it uniquely "indigenous" in its expression?[10]

Not long after conquest, the Spanish established a conceptual and administrative distinction between the politico-legal entities of the Republic of Spaniards and the Republic of Indians, providing an institutional structure through which peninsular concepts of authority, governance, and justice could be translated into local cultural vernaculars. In the colonies, early modern legal pluralism meant more than simply recognizing that native customs could fill the silences in written, royal law. More concretely, pluralism meant that indigenous cultures of status and descent merged with Spanish practices of town governance. Native officials often came from the ranks of hereditary rulers (*caciques*) and notables (*principales*), and served on town councils with judicial functions in the capacity of governors, mayors-cum-judges (*alcaldes*) and sheriffs (*alguaciles*). Native notables also trained in the Spanish language and were exposed to Spanish jurisprudence and Catholic theology in order to serve as notaries, interpreters, and procurators for their communities.[11]

Balancing local and imperial cultures of law was an ongoing process. Conflicts over leadership and status—meaning nobility by inheritance and the right to political leadership in the community—certainly drew from and reinforced local concepts of descent and varied by ethnic group. Countless pages of lawsuits were dedicated to ascertaining the legitimacy of birthright in individual communities in order to settle competing claims to native chiefdoms and their corresponding economic perks in possessing land and commanding labor.[12] At the same time, the judicial authority native leaders exercised and their relationship to Spanish administration were regulated by written colonial law, from comprehensive corpuses of administrative orders such as Peruvian Viceroy Francisco de Toledo's late sixteenth-century *Ordenanzas*, and the individual royal laws issued for the New World compiled in the late seventeenth-century *Recopilación de las leyes de Indias*.

Thus the interaction of imperial judicial structure and local hierarchies of status, and the interplay of unwritten tradition and written law, all informed justice-oriented culture in native communities. This legal culture also took on a special kind of vibrancy as the actual languages used to express and implement the law intertwined. Legal terms were among the swiftest and most numerous words to infiltrate native languages after conquest.[13] A Zapotec-language election record from 1751 shows clearly how community legal and administrative terms were expressed using Spanish loanwords: *rey* (king), *justicias* (justices), *alcalde, botos* [sic] (votes), *elección* [sic] (election), *confirmar* (to confirm), *firma* (signature).[14]

Establishing a colonial legal and administrative structure and lexicon was not the same as providing it constant oversight: Spanish officials were spread thin in the countryside and, as a result, they often left native community government to function on its own.[15] Barring a disturbance in tribute remittances to the crown or the need to squelch political conflict between communities or with neighboring Spaniards, native pueblos could administer justice on local terms.

In places like Oaxaca that possessed rich indigenous-language writing cultures and relative isolation from secular authorities, natives surely administered law and governance in some decidedly "Indian" ways.[16] Compared to Peru, elected native authorities in Mexico possessed somewhat greater legal autonomy, and indigenous cabildo officials held clearer jurisdiction over land disputes and minor crimes.[17] In contrast, from the time that Peruvian Viceroy Toledo issued his organizing *Ordenanzas* regulating almost all aspects of native life and governance, Andean natives were technically required to use Spanish courts and were assigned Spanish as well as Indian representatives for their cases.[18] Yet native authority in both Peru and Mexico was "judicial." Community elders in both regions who might not have any particular administrative title exercised extrajudicial authority, attempting through unwritten means to make peace between divided community members or spouses, and even administering corporal punishment to those who transgressed community norms of morality.[19]

Native leaders' formal legal authority functioned on two scales: it implied their own power to mete out justice and adjudicate customs in the community, as well as their responsibility over any community suits that did reach Spanish courts. Beginning as early as the sixteenth century, natives expected their leaders to effectively shepherd their communities through the imperial judicial system.[20] Not all were good at it. A man from San Agustín Tlalotepec, Teposcolula, reported in 1707 that a neighboring pueblo had leveled so many lawsuits against him during his tenure as alcalde that he was left with a hefty debt for defending himself. This, in addition to some sloppy accounting he had undertaken with his own pueblo's funds, forced him to flee the area. When he finally appeared before the Spanish district alcalde, he asked the colonial judge to carefully read him the text of this suit against him to be sure he understood the Spanish.[21]

Even if eventually revealed to be incompetent, shifty, or problematically unfamiliar with the Spanish language, colonial officials regarded native leaders as the appropriate legal representatives of their communities, endowing them with ability to litigate in the "*voz del común y república*" (voice of the community and republic). In fact, when litigants from a community in the Valley of Oaxaca tried to tuck into a 1750 dispute with the elected officials a statement from their lawyer saying that "anyone from the pueblo can litigate on behalf of the common good or the republic, [and] they should be heard even if they are not parties to the dispute," the Spanish alcalde mayor flatly rejected the idea.[22] Instead, governing doctrine was that a suit should be brought by a person with recognized authority to speak on behalf of the pueblo, be it a cacique, a native legal representative, or an elected official.

Given that community elites served as principal litigants in much of the legal action coming from native pueblos until the middle of the eighteenth century, many internal conflicts surely were handled without appeal to Spanish judges. For example, elections to the governing body of San Juan Yae in 1751, mentioned earlier, were recorded in Zapotec, and the record of votes would have remained in the community had it not been material to a suit a villager brought against local officials fifteen years later.[23]

Local ethnic practice rather than universal rules governed many features of elections like the one in Yae. The question of who got to vote and how consensus was achieved could differ significantly between communities located relatively close to one another. The Spanish crown reinforced and permitted the flourishing of such differences by maintaining a relatively light grip over confirmation of elected native leaders. Until the end of the eighteenth century, the official line was that native leaders received legitimacy directly from the highest body

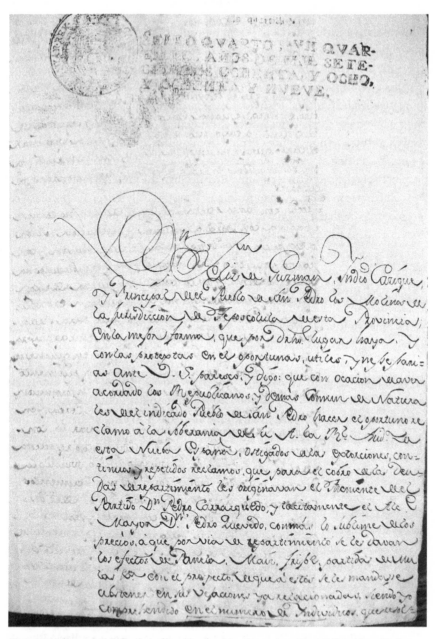

Figure 5.1 In a typical display of legal leadership, the cacique Don Felipe Guzmán is the named plaintiff in a case against a Spanish official for abuse of power and brings suit on behalf of the voting members and the rest of the native community (*"republicanos y demás común de naturales"*) of his pueblo, San Pedro de Molinas, Teposcolula. From Félix de Guzmán, indio cacique principal del pueblo de San Pedro de los Molinos, de la jurisdicción de Teposcolula, representando a su pueblo, se queja de las extorciones ocasionadas en el cobró de las deudas de repartimiento, originadas por el teniente del partido, Pedro Carrasquedo y el Alcalde Mayor Pedro Quevedo, APGEO, Intendencia, Teposcolula, leg. 60, exp, 12, 1788–1789, f. 1v.

of royal administration in the colonies, namely, the audiencias, rather than from district officials such as corregidores or alcaldes mayores. A 1715 order from the viceroy of Mexico to the Spanish alcaldes mayores in his jurisdiction neatly summed up the qualifications that elected officials should have: they were to be good Christians, of "good enthusiasm and conscience, not drunks or rebels, or men of bad living, but rather persons who work for the Service of God, of his Majesty, and the good of their peoples."[24]

Notably, the viceroy also warned Spanish colonial district magistrates in native jurisdictions to refrain from intervening in local elections. They were only to see to it that the elections had received confirmation from the Audiencia in Mexico City before outgoing officials handed their *varas*, or staffs of justices, to the newly elected government. According to the Toledan *Ordenanzas*, Peruvian corregidores could be called upon to break a tie in elections, as happened in the contested election that pitted the twin pueblos of Santa Ana and San Sebastián in Trujillo against each other in 1723. But even in such a case, higher royal officials in Lima looked upon the district official's intrusion with suspicion.[25] Of course, many Spaniards and creole elites found the prospect of doing politics in native communities to be irresistible, whether to promote the election of business allies or simply because they held a paternalistic attitude toward native governance. Priests in particular came to believe that they were the proper authorities to oversee elections and to direct community legal affairs; many were present at voting, while others got involved in collecting funds for community civil suits.[26]

Still, theoretically, Indians were to be left to conduct legal business in the community according to their "*usos y costumbres*"—a standard phrase in a Spanish pluralistic legal order referring to legitimate local practice that could coexist with written, royal law. Overall, native legal culture fit within an imperial legal culture that promoted particularism, casuism, and decentralization.[27] As a result, for most of the colonial period, there was no need to separate local customs from the realm of Spanish law. In fact, as the 1690 case of Zapotec official Juan de Illescas illustrates, the two were not just compatible but perhaps even coeval.

The Law's Language: A Zapotec Legal Dispute

Trying to glimpse native legal cultures at work is perhaps easiest when there is a written record left in native languages. Such is the case of instances when native officials punished "disorderly" villagers locally without the intervention of Spanish officials. One seventeenth-century Zapotec-language document detailed, in a highly repetitive and poetic indigenous style, local rituals surrounding the sanction of a villager who betrayed his community. Evidence of this native legal process might never have reached the archive had litigants in a subsequent suit not used it as evidence in a suit aired before Spanish district magistrate.[28]

Indigenous people also kept their legal business to themselves in other ways. For example, native legal writers converted a purely colonial genre of land documentation known as "primordial titles" into their own secret instruments, sometimes marking the paper with the warning "Do not show to the Christians."[29]

In commandeering written Spanish forms for internal native purposes, indigenous people sustained a dynamic interdependence between local and imperial legal cultures. A 1690 clash between a beleaguered native alcalde named Juan de Illescas and the grandson of a local notable in Tanetze, Villa Alta, shows this interdependence in action.[30] The conflict took place in an environment that favored village justice—from the authority Illescas held as alcalde to physically punish and incarcerate an insubordinate youth, to the central place of the local priest as a kind of judge of first resort. Few in the village of Tanetze spoke Spanish, and local authorities had ample room to maneuver without civil oversight when keeping pueblo order.[31] But in this case, the conventional channels for containing conflict had become blocked. Juan de Illescas had run afoul of his community before, and they had gone on record against him. So he was already on shaky ground when later, as native alcalde, he assumed responsibility for a local celebration.

As the celebration preparations began, Illescas criticized the work of a young man who was making a bouquet of roses to welcome a priest to the village. The youth cheekily retorted that the official should make the flower arrangement himself. In their ensuing argument, typical early modern Spanish insults mixed with affronts of a more local flavor, registering the importance of age hierarchies in the community. Having been cursed with Spanish words like "rascal," "horse's ass strap" and "broken old horse," Illescas threatened to perform a humiliating native punishment by cutting the side locks and ears of youth, whom he called "a boy" (in Zapotec, *bini cuiti nii*).[32]

When Illescas ordered the young man to be whipped and jailed by the village sheriff for his insubordination, the youth's grandfather, a notable in the community, intervened. The ensuing conflict reignited the nobles' ire against Illescas and raised old resentments from the outgoing curate. Knowing he could not take a traditional route to seeking intervention from the village's priest, the native alcalde brought his predicament to the Spanish colonial magistrate, the alcalde mayor, in the district center of Villa Alta. There were technically no civil grounds to sue his insubordinate villagers, so Illescas claimed that the faction against him had engaged in a kind of treason against the Spanish king.

Just as the insults in this case mixed native and European languages, authority itself was linguistically and procedurally constituted simultaneously at the local and imperial scales. Illescas did not speak Spanish, and his petition—drawn up on ordinary paper rather than the official paper—was written in the Nexitzo dialect of Zapotec.[33] Although his informal petition was not in Spanish, Illescas presented himself as a royal representative and repeatedly alluded to possessing the "staff of the king" (in Zapotec, Spanish loanwords were mixed in: "*bara queh Reii*").

The colonial magistrate appointed a translator who began his Spanish rendering of the complaint on the same page as the original report. Rather than developing in a parallel fashion, the Spanish version of the complaint had some curious changes. One linguistic swap affected the very name of the native alcalde. In the original complaint, the alcalde's name was Hispanicized as "Iglesias"—a Spanish surname—whereas in the Spanish translation his surname was rendered as "Yllescas"—a native name.

After receiving this hybrid complaint, the Spanish judge commissioned the translator with gathering the previous complaints against the native alcalde to contextualize the conflict. The Zapotec originals of the villagers' testimony, when read alongside their Spanish translations, provide further documentary evidence of the cultural complexity of "native law" or "village justice" in late seventeenth-century Spanish America. While the administrative structure of native governance was Spanish in structure, in practice the interpenetration of Zapotec and Spanish notions of justice was clear. Illescas used a highly indigenous emphasis on communal membership to convey his authority even as he was attempting to link his own power to the Spanish king's authority over the larger community of the empire. He twice described himself as being from the "people of your pueblo" (*gente de tu pueblo*), a construction that really conveyed nothing special in Spanish but was more meaningful in Zapotec as "*neta na bene* [*bene* = people] *yetze* [*yez* = pueblo]," an expression of belonging or citizenship more locally rooted than other choices available, such as "vassal," or "natural."[34]

The testimony against the alcalde that the court dug up from years before was called a "*memoria*" of his "sins." This memoria is written in an inventive legal genre with no real Spanish analog, and its repetitive style was consistent with the exaggerated and rhythmic gestures that composed appropriate social interaction in native society—a ceremonial style known as *libana*.[35] In it, elected officials as well as notables in the town enumerated infractions including Illescas's misappropriation of tribute cloth, his disrespect for and violence toward elected officials, and his betrayal of fellow community members for purported idolatry. To cap it off, villagers complained that Illescas "had no right to be an officer in the audiencia [cabildo], that he is a commoner [as were] his father and grandfather."[36]

In addition to genealogical privilege, the legitimacy of a legal authority figure sprang from the promotion of order and harmony and the ability to shield villagers from the scrutiny of outsiders such as the priest. The witnesses against Illescas referred repeatedly to his transgressions against the pueblo as "*xi tolae coyag yoo la hui*," translated into Spanish as "*su pecado que fue contra la comunidad*," or "his sin that was against the community." The translation signals that judicial guilt was highly communal and harmony-based rather than procedural.[37] Legal transgressions might be considered "indigenous" in that they could defy direct translation into the secularized legalese of colonial civil courts, and they were only partially rendered intelligible to Spanish authorities. But, at the same time, Zapotec concepts of legal transgression as sin were also related to a Christian-rooted sense of community peace.[38]

If we can generalize from the single case of an alcalde from the pueblo of Tanetze in 1690, then, there existed a semi-autonomous realm of justice among natives and unique local vernaculars of justice, even if law was not "indigenous" in any essential way.[39] The ideology of harmonious native community order fit snugly within the broader justice-orientation of Spanish imperial law, Christian mores concerning peace, and local inheritance practices, all of which were retro-fitted to the needs of town governance. This was true even of the rural peoples of Oaxaca, whose language culture and geographical isolation from the seats of co-lonial administration created a palpable gulf between the local and the imperial.

Since very little native-language legal documentation was produced in the Andes, we might expect native authorities in Peru to have been dependent on Spanish legal protocols and more likely to appeal to colonial judges. But native officials in Peru too handled legal matters according to local custom and with the tacit approval of Spanish officials.[40] As discussed in the last chapter, native women in Peru sometimes complained that village officials had a lock on local justice and tried to circumvent their authority by appealing directly to Spanish magistrates in cases against their husbands.[41] At the same time, even when aired before colonial judges in the Spanish language, native lawsuits in Lima and Trujillo depended so heavily on knowledge of local customs and descent pat-terns that the most experienced of colonial magistrates turned into confused anthropologists, struggling to make sense of things such as the relationship be-tween "upper" and "lower" districts (*anansaya* and *urinsaya*) within moieties called *ayllus*, or the succession of leadership positions that varied widely across the region, such as the *pachaca* chiefdoms of the North Coast of Peru.[42]

To the question, then, of whether native legal custom and practices that favored conciliation, community adjudication, moral balance, and the multi-centricity of legal authority were, properly-speaking, "indigenous" or "early modern," the answer seems to be that they were both. Indigenous law—as much as it can be conceptualized as an ambit apart from "sin" or "disorder"—developed within a larger European legal framework that set its parameters and values. Native con-cepts of justice displayed and at times amplified those early modern values, espe-cially those that made local notions of order compatible with empire, expressing them both in their Spanish forms and in vernaculars—sometimes literally, by presenting them in native language, and sometimes figuratively, as when native concepts such as *"gente de tu pueblo"* or the *anan/urinsaya* division lodged themselves into the colonial practice of law. Justice-oriented legal culture discursively emphasized the mutual legitimacy of native and royal authority. That legitimacy was grounded in birthright and predicated on the maintenance of village peace administered from within, even if under the staff of the Spanish king.

Now

Whatever placid surface of community harmony indigenous peoples were able to maintain under Spanish colonialism increasingly showed cracks in the second half of the 1700s. While surely Bourbon reform measures aimed at centralizing control over native pueblos created greater conflict between Indians and Spanish colonial elites, internal political battles in the communities also produced an uptick in natives' lawsuits.[43] These intra-pueblo struggles demonstrated two major tendencies that pulled the villages and their legal maelstroms into the currents of rationalizing Bourbon governance and the broader historical sweep of the Age of Revolution: a tendency to challenge birthright with arguments about merit and new articulations of custom and history.[44]

Scholars have observed the intensification of native litigation over status and authority but rarely provide statistical data. John Chance has perhaps come closest to showing an actual increase in the numbers of intra-community lawsuits over these kinds of matters. He identified 38 disputes over noble status from eighteenth-century Villa Alta, Oaxaca, with the vast majority dating from the final decades of the century.[45] Eighteenth-century observers in Mexico certainly believed there was an acceleration of conflict between commoners and nobles or between nobles and cabildos. Chance adds to his numbers the comments of a lawyer who remarked that such cases were becoming "much too common" in Villa Alta.[46]

Litigation of all types—not just suits over authority, status, and custom—increased in the second half of the eighteenth century in the primarily indigenous districts of both Teposcolula and Villa Alta. Table 5.1 shows that, although the number of civil suits cataloged in the Archivo Histórico Judicial de Oaxaca database is much higher in Teposcolula than in Villa Alta for almost all periods until the first half of the nineteenth century, the overall trend is the same in both regions. The number of cases on record doubles or triples for the second half of the 1700s. This increase mirrors the rate of increase reflected in an eighteenth-century inventory of cases provided by the alcalde mayor in Teposcolula.[47]

In both regions, the real number of intra-community cases over community obligations, native authority, elections, and noble status, while never voluminous, nonetheless rose at an even greater rate than the overall increase

Table 5.1 **Average Number of Cases Per Year, Alcaldías Mayores de Teposcolula**
and Villa Alta. From Computerized database, Civil Cases, AHJO.

Region	1650–99	1700–49	1750–99	1800–49
Teposcolula	3.78	7.02	14.64	13.18
Villa Alta	1.46	2.9	9.46	13.94

Source: Computerized database, Civil Cases, APJO

in civil suits.[48] Six suits over native authority and status could be identified from 1700–49, whereas from 1750–99, that number rose to 27.[49] A sampling of cases from three-decade-long intervals across the century for Teposcolula turned up only one case of contention over native authority and status from 1700–9 but 12 for each periods between 1750–59 and 1790–99. In general then, cases of intra-pueblo strife in indigenous Oaxaca appear to have grown faster than the overall increase in civil litigation.

There is a similar surge of native litigation in the Corregimiento of Trujillo during the final years of that district's existence in the 1780s. The volume of cases native communities brought more than doubled in the four years leading up to the replacement of the corregidor by the intendant.[50] Once the intendancy system was in place, it especially attracted intra-community disputes over status and authority. Eleven of the 35 disputes native communities brought before the intendant were lawsuits directly against their own caciques.[51] Undoubtedly, the generic titles of many other kinds of disputes in all of these majority-Indian districts—vaguely recorded as "over pesos" or even "over land"—also concealed disputes that pivoted on important legal issues surrounding native authority and the perks of status.

In each area under study, local developments can be tied to the increase in intra-pueblo litigation. The aftermath of an uprising in turn-of-the-century Villa Alta, the subsequent search for "idolaters," and the replacement of Dominican missionaries by parish priests created flashpoints for conflict in that region.[52] In the northern Peruvian regions surrounding Trujillo, such as Lambayeque, a series of agricultural crises in the early 1700s—plagues, infestations, floods, and droughts—was followed by a push from a new class of Spanish merchant elites onto communal native lands, triggering clashes between and within Indian communities.[53]

Yet while native litigation over rival concepts of authority and custom undoubtedly looked local from the perspective of the pueblo as local events and disasters drove litigants into court, when viewed from a more panoramic angle, it is obvious that Indians from diverse regions were bringing disputes to court. In part this was because of colonial reform. The Bourbon state introduced new policies during the second half of the century that inflamed rivalries and brought long-simmering contests between village factions to a boil. Most notable among these was a 1786 royal cédula that required native officials elected to village government to be literate in Spanish and permitted secular authorities to intervene in pueblo voting.[54] This measure was overtly aligned with the more abstract "utility" orientation of many Bourbon policies, particularly to ensure that elected leaders in native communities supported the economic productivity of village inhabitants. At the same time, it is also notable that Carlos III issued the cédula "with the objective of avoiding the disruptive lawsuits and uprisings that frequently originate among natives because of their elections."[55] Once again, a Bourbon order followed, and did not precede, legal conflict from below.[56]

Merit, Or the New Science of Status

Rebounding from depopulation after conquest and the attendant epidemics of the sixteenth and seventeenth centuries, the number of Indians living in rural regions climbed in the 1700s. At the same time, inherited power waned. Most historians continue to agree, at least in broad strokes, with the observations that Charles Gibson made in his classic 1964 study of colonial Aztec society: over time, nobles who claimed authority by birthright increasingly lost their political power to Indians of more ordinary extraction who gained power through service in rotating offices and religious positions in the community.[57] Of course, elite status based on inheritance did not disappear altogether and remained the bedrock of indigenous leadership in the Valley of Oaxaca and the North Coast of Peru.[58] But at the end of the eighteenth century, even noble Indians from these regions could not take for granted that their lineage would mean what it had before.[59]

Status in native communities under Spanish rule traditionally had emanated from two sources that often, but not always, overlapped: inherited status as a native lord (cacique) or notable (principal), and election to village government. Although election to the most prestigious positions was predicated on the elite lineage of the candidate, eighteenth-century lawsuits demonstrate that native litigants increasingly considered other issues, such as occupation, past experience, and economic utility as merit-based criteria for judging the legitimacy of political authority and social status. Lawsuits over elections to rotating positions in village government and clashes over individual responsibility for communal labor or possession of property tugged at native hierarchies formerly firmly grounded in genealogical claims.

Commoners increasingly demanded the vote in elections for village councils, sued if they were excluded, and sometimes insisted on filling elected offices themselves. Such demands challenged nobles' monopoly on the higher positions of village government—typically around six to seven posts ranging from the position of *regidor* up to native alcalde and gobernador.

An incident in Choapán in Villa Alta serves as an early example of the social leveling that complicated elections. Choapán was divided in multiple ways, including between the head village and a subject pueblo, and between commoners and notables, who both had voting rights. By the eighteenth century, so many men had moved into the more prestigious rank that their numbers were nearly equal: 120 to 111, respectively. All of these tensions conspired to make the municipal election of 1742 a rocky one. When the officials of the outgoing government secretly gathered a band of fifteen principales and counted ballots inside the community house behind closed doors, a group of commoners objected in the name of the community. The basis for their objection embedded local practices within royal laws. The litigants reminded the Spanish magistrate that they expected elections to follow procedure drawn from the "custom that we have, which you are well familiar with, as [it follows the] commands [of] the King our Lord . . . in his royal Provisions."[60]

It was not enough for the litigants to impress on the Spanish alcalde mayor the faulty nature of the election by creating a discursive allegiance between local custom and written royal sanction: the men, they also said, had not earned the positions. They described the newly elected men as inadequate based on behavior and called for the election of men of "good qualities" who "merited" the positions.[61] They also accused the aspiring officials of stealing silver items from the bishop and misappropriating village cloth, which was generally used as currency in the tribute system. Lineage was not missing from the argument—they pointed out that "none of their line had served in community office before"—but this referenced progenitors' prior service to the pueblo and not nobility per se.[62]

Although in Choapán native nobles had unsuccessfully attempted to shut commoners out of their 1747 election, it usually was the other way around, with commoners pressing for greater political power or greater access to the privileges of caciques, who claimed authority by birthright.[63] In San Juan Yae in the 1750s, a coalition of commoners and principales had gathered and voted without the participation of the local caciques—a move within a longer set of electoral power plays between the village and its rival twin pueblo, Yagallo.[64] Again in 1774 and 1775, the caciques of Yae found themselves having to appeal to Spanish judicial authorities because elections were held without them and, in one case, not a single cacique had been elected to office. "It does not seem good," they observed in one of their petitions, "that having Noble Persons in the Pueblo, those who are not [noble] fill honorific offices."[65] The electors countered that voting was the prerogative of a small group who had cycled through the various offices of town governance, and that none of the "caciques were elders (*ancianos*)." This was a crucial argument since, with it, the community claimed that experience in town governance rather than birthright qualified candidates for town government.[66]

Many litigants seemed to be aware that their legal contests were part of a general trend, at least regionally.[67] Lawsuits emanating from below especially plagued caciques in Teposcolula during the 1770s. In fact, there, a group of caciques tried to hijack community funds to pay for the multiple civil cases they had to fend off within their own pueblo in 1777.[68] Noble natives such as these only had to look to the repeated court rulings favoring ordinary Indians to realize commoners were prevailing in the courts. For example, a noble married couple claiming cacique status in Yanhuitlan and the surrounding communities of the Mixteca Baja suffered a major legal loss to the inhabitants of their community. In the final ruling over the privileges of their nobility, the Audiencia of Mexico sided with the "liberty" of the commoners and their right to treat as communal the property the caciques claimed for themselves, including lands and the community building called the *tecpán*. By turning the cacique's house into the people's house, the high court merely gave its imprimatur to a process already under way. As historian Kevin Terraciano points out, these rulings from the high court "undercut the cacicazgo only after its caciques had lost their base of support."[69]

Another case over the contested reelection of a gobernador in the district capital village of San Juan de Teposcolula indicated that widespread strife around the transfer of authority was common at election time. The lawyer for the deposed native official claimed that it was well known that commoners had united against principales throughout the district, regularly causing rebellions and uprisings when votes were cast.[70] This gobernador did not clash with his opposition by claiming that his people had turned against him; rather, he was a man of the people, an official supported by the "*común*" against powerful adversaries, including the Spanish public notary of the pueblo and other principales. Caciques in Peru also appear to have felt pressure to ground their claims to status in popular support rather than the privileges of status.[71]

Beyond claiming popular support, noble natives defended themselves with a series of arguments that shifted legitimacy off genealogical ground. For example, many pointed out that living relatives rather than ancestors were considered honorable enough to occupy positions in the Church or in "literary careers," and this included relatives by marriage not just blood.[72]

For their part, the native commoners challenging the prerogatives of the nobility or elbowing their way into higher social ranks expressed a preference for leadership based on experience and skill acquired during one's lifetime. The election of one Santiago Bacón to a council position in the coastal Peruvian fishing village of Huanchaco produced stark declarations on the importance of experience as a qualification for holding municipal office. The post to which Bacón had been elected in 1777 was the native "*alcalde de aguas*," a unique position in town government on the arid Peruvian North Coast and a critical one given the need for communal access to clean water sources. A 1778 petition, written on behalf of the "Indian común" of the village with the collaboration of the Spanish alcalde de aguas, objected to their native cabildo's tacit approval of Bacón. Some of the complaints about Bacón were typical—he was an outsider to the community, or a *forastero*; he was rebellious and criminal; he was in league with others to divert water to their personal lands and away from community use. Even more important to his opposition, who represented themselves as agriculturalists, the current village officials were "only qualified in the management of the net and fishing, in which they had always been employed, and they have not the least skill or experiences with Agriculture and the work that it requires." Native council members' own lack of aptitude in the "science of agriculture," the petition claimed, disqualified the officials from determining who should serve in the position of the alcalde de aguas.[73]

Crucially, the privileged place given to natives as agriculturalists in this argument came in advance of the royal cédula of 1786 concerning secular governmental intrusion into native elections and the requirement that native officials read and write in Spanish. A close look at the cédula reveals that, as important as Spanish-language skills were, he was also concerned that candidates for elected office fit the reigning notion of "utility," that is, officials in natives communities should "distinguish themselves in the commendable employment of agriculture or industry."[74]

Official discourses prizing native agricultural utility presented a real challenge to traditional native elites. Consider the 1795 case of a noble Indian named Don Jacinto Asavache who claimed possession of lands corresponding to a prehispanic sacred site (*huaca*) in the Moche Valley in northern coastal Peru—lands that potentially contained buried treasure. Asavache found himself unable to persuade both native officials and royal officials of his property rights in the new order of things. He tried everything from arguing that the lands were part of the "tradition of my elders" dating from "gentility" (the common term for the time prior to conquest), to dropping the "don" from his name and proclaiming himself a loyal tribute-payer. He lost his suit to the cabildo officials, who instead supported the usufruct rights of a common, poor widower with many children who had productively worked the lands for twelve years. Asavache, they suggested, should be satisfied with the relatively vast lands he inherited from the community by virtue of his nobility alone.[75]

Rulings like this chipped away at native nobles' material perks and hold over political power by shifting weight to skill—in some cases meaning agricultural skill or productivity, in others, legal skill, particularly Enlightened legal literacy. A fascinating 1782 case involving the native cabildo of Lima illustrates the point.

A rebellious group of brothers with the surname Cochacín had called a junta of native officials from throughout the metropolitan area. Their proclamation in the "voice of the people" centered on the position of *"procurador de naturales,"* the post of legal representative for the indigenous population. Normally, two procuradores de naturales handled the work of filing lawsuits for the city's native litigants when the suits were between Indians, and in 1735 a royal cédula confirmed that indigenous candidates should be preferred over all others for the posts.[76] In 1781, the elected officials of the native cabildo appointed Toribio Ramos to fill a vacancy. But the rebel junta objected, claiming Ramos was a *"chino"* or *"sambaigo,"* both caste designations implying he was of mixed ancestry. Even beyond violating the 1735 royal order, they said, the cabildo's appointment of Ramos contravened the will (*voluntad*) of the native community of Lima.

In response, the elected officials of the native cabildo directly located their legal actions within a broader Enlightenment legal culture. They claimed that no indigenous candidates offered up by the community were qualified for the office: "Their scant training has led to this lack [of acceptable native candidates]. The very applicants are so devoid of Enlightenment (*escasos de Luzes*) in issues related to lawsuits that they are entirely ignorant of the basic principles and barely know how to write."[77] The officials went on to divert discussion of Ramos's native ancestry to more contemporary and achievement-oriented criteria. "To be a procurator requires no *hidalguía,*" their petition reminded the court, choosing a term for elite status more European than native. Instead of proving his inherited status, cabildo members accumulated various examples of effective arguments Ramos had made on behalf of his native clientele in recent cases.[78]

By the end of the century, it had become so accepted that experience and skill—the opposite of a "scarcity of Enlightenment"—were the chief criteria to serve as native procurador in Lima that the candidate Vicente Jiménez Ninavilca had to find a way to cleverly slip a reference his illustrious ancestry into his bid for the position. He deserved the post, he said, based on his education and mastery of the "language of his nation" alone, "without even taking into consideration his noble descent nor the services that his ancestors had undertaken for the Sovereigns as faithful vassals."[79]

In addition to overt debates about how and what kind of skill and experience qualified native officials for their positions of authority, many other cases revolved around the material and labor resources claimed either by caciques for themselves or by the community in the name of the "common good"—which increasingly meant favoring ordinary Indians as laborers against their noble, and presumably abusive, superiors. As historians of Spanish Bourbon law stress, "the public good" was a highly specific historical concept often glossed as promoting "utility."[80] Applied to native communities, "utility" hinged on the idea that Indians could be rescued from the abuses of a pluralistic legal order that had given too much power to native lords and Spanish landowners. Royal policy aimed to undercut such middlemen and see to it that each vassal was directly tapped as potential economic producer for the empire.[81]

Indian litigants who believed they held inherited privileges—and consequently a right to land and the tributary labor of common Indians, as well as exemption from the community service that commoners performed—thus bucked against opponents who often counted on the support of royal officials who sought to promote the "liberty" and "utility" of ordinary natives. At the same time, the rising number of individuals who claimed some elite status in places like Oaxaca put a strain on local communal labor practices and the statuses that came with them.

Recall the case of the contested Choapán election in the 1740s, where principales outnumbered commoners by only nine voters. This was not unusual. In the Oaxaca Valley pueblo of San Gerónimo de Tlacochuaya in the 1730s, the town council attempted to force the swelling number of those calling themselves caciques to perform communal labor. The Audiencia of Mexico upheld the caciques' exemption but, aware that this would thin the labor supply, it also ruled that should the number of caciques rise above the number of commoners in the community, the caciques would be forced to produce written evidence of their status within 24 hours. The order was read before a gathering of drunken commoners and cabildo officials, who met official support for the exemption with threats, shouts, and jeers.[82]

It was not so much that crowds like these rejected outright inherited claims to privilege; it was that they saw birthright as only one path to status. Juan López, a principal in the village of San Juan de Yaviche, Villa Alta, found out the hard way that genealogy alone no longer secured privilege—in this case, exemption from community work called *tequíos*, which included tasks such as gathering firewood or sweeping the plaza. When he sought to prove his status as a principal in court, the native cabildo countered that achievement in service in local governance counted as much as, if not more than, inherited status.[83] It sought to limit those achievements to the lifetime of the claimant and successfully dissuaded López from founding his argument on the service his father and grandfather had performed for the community. At first, López clung to his hereditary argument, even arguing that the custom in his mother's village, Lachincha, was to exempt principales from service and implying that this local custom should be universally respected throughout the area.[84] But finding this inheritance argument to be increasingly ineffective, he switched tactics and tried to claim that the service that he himself performed as a sacristan for the community priest was a merit-based activity that permitted him exemption.

In response, the officials of Yaviche's cabildo contracted a Mexico City lawyer resident in Oaxaca City, the former chair of Primas Letras of Antequera,

Dr. Joseph Alejandro de Miranda, to push their case.[85] Miranda's argument on behalf of the cabildo emphasized that rank in the indigenous community derived from more than just the accident of birth. "Your Mercy knows," he stated to the magistrate, "that in the style, practice and custom of Our Pueblo"[86] there are two ways of deriving the status of a principal: "One is through the origin of sanguinity. . . . The other is through merit of serving the Republic in lower and laborious offices."[87] Pitting birthright against merit, the lawyer favored the more democratic of the two since ascension to special status through achievement made the native pueblo an orderly organization no different from the clergy or the military. To skip ranks would be an "injurious inequality [meaning] that some work more than others in one single Republic."[88] Such an outcome could not possibly be acceptable in an atmosphere that favored the utility of every royal subject.

Caving in to the intense pressure to do their fair share for "one single Republic," even temporarily, could have long-term consequences for nobles, especially principales occupying the middling stratum of the communities. In the pueblo of San Pedro Apostól in the Valley of Oaxaca in 1734, three brothers found themselves on the defensive because their relatives had agreed to help commoners with communal labor in the past.[89] The result was that subsequent generations had lost their privileges of exemption. In this case, as in others, town officials seemed to shift the proof of nobility to those who claimed it, demanding that the men produce concrete evidence in written titles.

Not all natives had access to such written proof, and they instead relied on public memory of the status of their ancestors. Another group of three brothers from San Juan Yae in Villa Alta argued that, by virtue of their birth, they were exempt from serving in servile positions called *gobaces* in town governance or from performing communal labor. Their arguments about their privileges turned, for the most part, on basic genealogical criteria—in fact, they adopted the Spanish term "Old Christian" to categorize their status. (In this case, however, their lineage was said to be clean from the "stain" not of Jewish or Moorish ancestry, as it would be for Spaniards, but rather from the idolatry that had only forty years before been a major concern in the area.) Like the three brothers in San Apostól in the Oaxaca Valley, these plaintiffs relied on the testimony of notables in the community rather than paper proof to make their claims.[90]

During the course of the eighteenth century, traditional methods for deciphering the "truth" about status and how it was inherited in native legal cases increasingly fell under suspicion. Indeed, often it was the lawsuit itself that became the most valued piece of evidence for a pretender to noble status. For example, in the pueblo of San Pedro de Lloc in the corregimiento of Zaña, the cacique Francisco Xavier de Lloc had for years been dispossessed of his role and the office of village governor. His opposition, a group including the sacristan of the local church and various Indians, wrested a strongbox containing the autos of his lawsuit over his status from the village scribe, greased the lock, and hid all of the pertinent documents in the case. His petitions only partially focused on the inheritance claims that were contained in the papers; instead, the very fact that he had a lawsuit over his status lodged in court seemed to come to represent, in an abstract sense, his legitimacy.[91]

As far as native status was concerned, what paper said was coming to matter more than what people said. The Corregidor of Trujillo knew as much as early as 1723. When he was called on to break an electoral tie, he told the voters that he was supporting one candidate but later crossed out that candidate's name in the village's record book and wrote the name of the other without the electorate's knowledge. By the time the case reached Lima, the crown attorney had to perform a handwriting analysis in order to determine whose claim to alcalde was legitimate.[92] Such was the power of the written documentation of status in native communities; so strongly had inhabitants of the empire come to rely on records that recollections of who was who in the village could become the equivalent of disappearing ink.

Custom Today

The rise of an alternative to casuistic, pluralistic, and justice-oriented early modern practices might seem to have weakened native communities' reliance on legal custom as a principle of order. But upon closer inspection, local practice and custom often held a privileged place in law-centered culture. This is obvious not only in erudite jurisprudential writings, the decisions rendered by Spanish colonial and imperial judges, or new educational programs in the colonies' universities. The pivotal place of custom in law-centered culture is also evident in the arguments some native litigants made in contentious eighteenth-century lawsuits over local authority. In a sense, litigants sought to systematize custom, to make it a predictable part of the functioning of a modern legal system.

Given the importance of custom to Indian governance, its modernization had unique consequences in native communities. Indigenous litigants and their legal representatives imbued custom with new temporal dimensions in their multiplying lawsuits. Custom became, for them, a vessel for historicity, precedent, and immediacy—all elements that contrast sharply with the presumption that "custom" refers to stasis and tradition. Increasingly, legal competition for status centered around not only what customs were but also how they were constituted in time and by what method they could be determined.

Custom had never been a singular or stable concept. If in Spain it had long held multiple connotations, it evoked even more meanings in Spanish America, where it became a key feature of native jurisdiction.[93] An ever-evolving legal concept, custom had bifurcated by the time of Spanish conquest to contain two principal meanings, dubbed by Paola Miceli as "romantic" and "primordial."[94] The first gestured toward the spontaneous popular will of the community; the second harkened to a tradition dating from the distant (often Roman) past. These two conceptual renderings of custom served indigenous populations well throughout the colonial period, as natives bent them to meet their legal needs. By the late eighteenth century, custom could gesture either toward remembered practice (which is to say a practice that people recalled as being widespread in the community) or toward tradition (that is, a repeated practice with a definable origin). Sometimes natives suggested the practices were pre-hispanic, but increasingly they referred to only one or two generations before, during Hapsburg rule, as a way of challenging Bourbon reforms.[95]

For early modern Europeans and, by extension, colonial Spanish Americans, custom not only referred to temporal practices but also a judicial method. During the late medieval and early modern period, custom referred specifically to the use of Roman law in jurisprudence. Medieval thinkers became highly concerned with measuring classical time, using their knowledge of Roman history to judge the applicability of its law to contemporary situations. This historical concern turned into a near obsession among humanist civil law jurists in the early modern period.[96] In the eighteenth century, some jurists in the European civil-law tradition retreated from this hyper-historical method centered on the Roman past into a more ahistorical or transhistorical concept of custom as existing outside of time. Custom became the quality or historical character of a community or people rather than a practice that could be pinpointed somewhere in Roman history.[97] As a result, by the eighteenth century, *"derecho consuetudinario"* (customary law) promiscuously mixed invocations of practices made legitimate by their popularity in practice, a juridical method fixated on the classical past, and newer notions of custom as the spirit of a people transcending history.[98] In many ways, what custom meant by the late eighteenth century was a free-for-all, but in any permutation, it contained highly complex allusions to time and history.

A compelling example of debates about the temporal parameters of custom appeared in a longstanding conflict on Peru's north coast between two native families, the Fayso Ferrochumbis and the Temoches, over the cacicazgo of Ferreñafe, a conflict that was eventually adjudicated by the Council of Indies. The arguments the two families advanced instantiated two different historical sources of political authority, one historical and one contemporary, one based on blood and the other on merit. The Fayso Ferrochumbi line founded their claim to legitimacy in antiquity, which they dated to their loyalty to the Spanish during the period of conquest.[99] The Temoche clan based its claim of loyalty on its very recent service in village governance and its family members' more contemporary track record of keeping peace in the community.[100]

When Juan Damaso Temoche, who sought the Audiencia of Lima's confirmation as cacique, made reference to his fidelity to the crown, it was more than rote allusion to historic loyalty to empire. In the early 1780s, indigenous Peru was rocked by a chain of bloody uprisings touched off by a local cacique from the Cuzco region, José Condorcanqui, who claimed Inca descent and christened himself "Tupac Amaru II." In swift reaction to the uprising, José Antonio de Areche, visitor general of Peru, obtained a royal cédula that placed a moratorium on the colonial audiencias' confirmation of caciques, with special emphasis on halting the confirmation of any native who claimed Inca lineage.

Soon officials in Lima realized that cases like the Ferreñafe dispute made the moratorium problematic. Although unrest had ignited broad swaths of the Andes, native royalism doused any sparks of rebellion along Peru's north coast. As a result, Areche's 1781 ban on confirming caciques risked alienating loyal natives who made no claim to Inca descent. The depth of the dilemma dawned on Areche a year after issuing the moratorium. He tried to backtrack by conceding that "Indians who had shown themselves to be faithful and resisted the rebels" were "deserving of reward." Their "right" to the cacicazgos was "acquired" and thus valid.[101] While fidelity to the Spanish still served as a source of legitimacy, the visitor's ruling moved the temporal frame of that fidelity from conquest to present royal service.[102]

The Audiencia of Lima, which traditionally confirmed claims to cacique status, refused to proceed in the dispute without clarification from Madrid about its authority over native leadership. The Council of Indies responded with an opinion unfavorable to very idea of inherited succession among native nobility. The entire practice of recognizing caciques was, it proclaimed, a "detestable custom" that drew from the improper validation of the nobility of "Gentile Kings" rather than Spanish royal sanction. Because Indians put stock in native genealogical claims, men like Tupac Amaru II exercised a "quasi-despotic dominion" over the Indian population.[103] In this way, the Council endorsed the growing belief that caciques had become tyrants who had held Indians back from realizing their full potential to the crown.

José de Cistué y Coll, the fiscal of the Council of Indies responsible for Peruvian suits, then rendered his opinion, tempering the Council's hostility to the very notion of native nobility. In one sense, he reaffirmed the legitimacy of the inherited nature of cacicazgos. Areche's moratorium, he said, was essentially illegal—that is, devoid of reference to any source of written law except in the case that caciques were proven rebels. Citing the *Recopilación de las leyes de Indias* and the writings of Spanish American jurist Juan de Solórzano, the fiscal pointed out that caciques could not be deprived of office even if they mistreated their own native subjects, and he further argued that it was in the interest of "Your Majesty, equity and the Laws" that his vassals be able to bequeath royal acknowledgment onto their descendants.[104]

Beyond pinning the legitimacy of cacicazgos almost exclusively to royal favor—a move that had a particularly strong resonance in light of the Andean uprisings and general Bourbon efforts to promote the utility among natives— the fiscal also made a series of arguments about how to read the history of the New World.[105] There should be, he surmised, few heirs to the Incas left in the Andes, and thus any new claims to Inca status would be, ipso facto, false. But how could he know this? What was his source for Inca history? The fiscal, a peninsular bureaucrat with experience in Mexico, Guatemala, and Ecuador but none in the region for which he was serving as crown attorney, located his logic in written texts rather than ethnographic mastery.[106] (Indeed, he consistently misspelled the name "Ferreñafe" throughout his opinion.) Instead of citing the written histories of the Incas as authoritative, he challenged the accuracy of what was then arguably the most popular published work of Andean history.[107]

The sixteenth-century *Comentarios reales* had become so identified with the history of native people in Peru that its author, noble mestizo chronicler Garcilaso de la Vega, was known simply as "*el Inca.*" Garcilaso's claim that there were not one but several branches in the Inca bloodline troubled Cistué y Coll. By applying emergent standards of objectivity and internal consistency in judging the reliability of historical texts, the crown's attorney claimed that el Inca was overly impassioned and biased in his reasons for exaggerating the number of royal lineages, and that the *Comentarios reales* was itself internally contradictory on the matter. Using what Cañizares-Esguerra has called a "new art of reading history" to discredit the sole written source he had for native practice, the fiscal briefly alluded to other (unnamed) historians and pronounced that they were "uniform" in their agreement that the Incas should be mostly gone.[108]

The fiscal's historical epistemology contained traces of anti-probabilistic and anti-casuisic thinking. For him, one source, however popular or venerated, was not enough. As the creole jurist Bravo de Lagunas would have put it, opinions should be counted rather than weighed. Consensus overruled singular cleverness. By putting this method into effect, the fiscal proclaimed that the Incas were the only true nobility in the Andes and then quickly moved them into a distant past. All remaining cacicazgos were emptied of their antiquity; all Indian nobles essentially derived their status from an ongoing grant from the Spanish king. Although native leadership could be inherited, its legitimacy took place in a kind of perpetual "now" in which heirs would be constantly judged on their merit and utility to the Spanish crown. The Temoches, with their presentist claims to meritorious lineage, won the day with the fiscal. His final recommendation was to award them the cacicazgo.

Not all of the articulations of custom as immediate, politicized, and subject to change came from the plumes of high-level Spanish administrators. Indeed, in many—perhaps most—instances, native litigants could persuade Spanish officials to rule in their favor by seeming to promise them certainty about local custom. This fostered officials' hopes that native traditions could be lodged in a more predictable, universal legal system. In one critical case from mid-century Villa Alta, the Audiencia of Mexico sought legal papers to prove what native custom dictated in a struggle between two pueblos, believing a written document could serve as a master key to the multiple, mutable versions of customary practice that varied from pueblo to pueblo.[109]

If Spanish officials had to struggle with native custom that was regionally variable, they also faced Indian litigants who claimed it could be temporally variable, as well. The Oaxaca city lawyer Miranda represented the native village government of Yagallo in Villa Alta against Juan López, who sought to escape demeaning labor for his pueblo, and helped craft a questionnaire for witnesses that wrote historical variability directly into the very meaning of "costumbre." One question asked witnesses to verify that, even if López could prove that a custom exempting him from labor had existed at the time he was born, custom changed over time. Is it not true, the questionnaire posed, that "today there is a different custom" than there was then?

Juan López's argument about custom eventually implied that it changed with each passing generation. After arguing about his ancestors, he finally shifted entirely away from past practice as a basis for his exemption from service, and he went so far as to criticize the use of testimony of village elders, an established legal method of ascertaining custom in native communities.[110] He accused witnesses of following a "premeditated pattern (sermón)" in testimony, revealing their lack of veracity.[111] If the word "sermón" here suggested the influence of Zapotec ceremonial styles on the actual sermons of Catholic priests in the region, the argument becomes even more radical, suggesting that native oral testimony was by its nature untruthful.[112] Even if not, López's dismissal of witnesses is important because it challenged the use of recollections rather than written proof in court. Witnesses' memories were too "fresh" to reliably recount his father's identity since he had been dead for eleven years. In the end, then, both parties to this suit were willing to cast doubt on custom as a practice or concept rooted in a static past and accepted as valid on its face, and went so far as challenge the methods of drawing on memory long used to ascertain its content. Yesterday, there was one custom; today, another.

Arguing that custom could be subjected to political whims, misunderstandings, and mistaken memories would have deep implications for longstanding constructs of native history. In the city of Trujillo, the remaking of the native past manifested itself in a reassessment of militia customs, particularly regarding the battalion of *forasteros*—a designation indicating native immigrant status of great importance in Andean pueblos, where indigenous relocation had drastically reshaped the social landscape throughout the colonial period. In 1733, a representative of the captains of the battalion of forasteros argued that they were the most privileged within the native militia of the city and that they held the greater claims to "*antigüedad*," or ancientness, than the militia of "*originarios*," or original residents. His logic went that, since no natives existed in the city before Spaniards had founded it in the sixteenth century, all Indians were immigrants to the region, and "thus the forasteros are the most venerable (*ancianos*) in the militia."[113] In this argument, the temporal meanings of "originario" and "forastero" were turned on their heads, and so too were the presumptions about the Indian past that came with them.

Recall the case from Lima discussed in the last section, in which the city's elected authorities argued on behalf of an experienced, "Enlightened" candidate to the post of procurador of natives despite his questionable status as an Indian. In that case, the council itself put forward arguments that wrote historicity into custom. They argued that the junta of leaders who opposed the "chino" procurador Toribio Ramos, mistakenly "believe that the Royal Law"—a 1734 ruling that privileged native candidates for the position of procurador over all other claimants—"confers them the ability [*arbitrio*] to decide who gets to be procuradores." Such an interpretation, their argument went, was not a custom but a *cisaña*, a vice or "bad habit" that could nestle inside good custom.[114] It was an interpretation, they argued, that rested on the faulty notion that custom was an expression of a pueblo's "*voluntad*," or will. Instead, they proposed, customs were better ascertained according to royal precedent.

The cabildo located its authority to choose a procurator, with the help of a trained Spanish lawyer, directly in the field of recent court rulings. As a corporate body, the officials claimed, the cabildo possessed sufficient "representation to speak for the Indians and deduce what is fitting to their Right (*Derecho*). . . . Having sought the counsel of a *Letrado*, it conducted itself in the terms that precedent in similar cases dictates."[115] The cabildo placed the gravitational pull of native law not in the "spontaneous will of the people" or in time-honored practice but rather in recent court rulings. Discourses of antiquity and repetition were replaced here by a custom constituted in recent rulings and supplanted by politics itself, in the present tense.

As a final move to drain the past of its legal significance and invest a politicized present with the power of custom, Lima's native cabildo went on to point out even its own historicity as an institution. Confronting the fact that the elected officials who formed the council the year before had themselves referred to the candidate Toribio Ramos as a "chino," the cabildo dismissed the admission as mere politics. "At that time," their statement reads, "there were applicants for the

post among the cabildo members." As if it were generations and not a year before, the cabildo suggested that certain former elected officials who themselves
sought the position of procurador had an interest in undermining Ramos's candidacy. "But today," they assured the court, "the Cabildo proceed[s] impartially
and with no particular interest . . ."[116]

As the Fiscal of the Council of Indies had implied when reflecting on Garcilaso
de la Vega's *Comentarios reales*, the past was not impartial, histories could be biased, and custom was open to corruption.[117] Only in the present moment could
impartiality, legitimacy and, ultimately, justice be assured. Put differently, the
temporal juridical argument of both Lima's indigenous cabildo and the fiscal in
Madrid was that, as far as customs go, that was then and this is now.

Native Civil Cases as Enlightenment

The early modern political order in Europe relied on social and temporal pre-
dictability in which individual or community status could be determined by
tracing backward into a stable past. In the late eighteenth century, the story goes,
the revolutionary bourgeoisie of Europe attacked privilege and, in an intersect-
ing development, German world-historical philosophers advanced a historicist
vision of the past that destabilized the foundational accounts of genealogical legitimacy among the artistocracy.[118] That similar concepts also emanated simultaneously, rather than consequently, from native lawsuits in remote reaches of
the Spanish empire goes a long way toward challenging arguments about natives
as peoples whose traditions "survived" time. Native litigants did not survive
modern times; they made them in the courts.

The idea that revolutionaries and republicans uniquely venerated skill and
virtue over inherited status was, at least partially, a post-Revolutionary myth.[119]
Merit had long been part of the European aristocracy's own calculus of status,
and in the eighteenth century nobles had begun to experiment with rewarding
commoners, especially those serving the state in corporate bodies such as the
military, with status based on performance. Nonetheless, the myth of early
modern privilege and modern merit is itself a kind of historical evidence. By the
late 1700s, privilege by birthright and earned merit were cleaving into two, distinct concepts, one cast as old and one as new, one as corrupted and the other
as just.[120]

In Spain, the eighteenth-century notion of merit developed within the more
complicated mode of foreign "emulation," in which international rivalry and intense self-consciousness about the historical character of the Spanish people
infused discourses about status earned rather than bequeathed.[121] Nonetheless,
an equalizing notion of achievement based in economic utility to the state lodged

itself securely within the Spanish Enlightenment lexicon. Feijóo pronounced on merit this way: "I venerate for his own sake and for his own merit he who serves the Republic usefully, be he illustrious or humble."[122]

Increased emphasis on merit was evident preceding Spanish American independence, especially among creoles who increasingly demanded political parity with their peninsula-born Spanish counterparts. It was also evident among militiamen, artisans, and the laboring classes in early republican Peru, Colombia, and Mexico.[123] Socially, these individuals drew from the late colonial development of a language of honor that would shadow elites' pretensions of superiority by birth. For ordinary Spanish Americans, however, the term of art was "to be honored" ("*honra*" rather than "*honor*"), a term that conveyed recognition earned, an achievement distant enough from elite concepts of inherited birthright that it could be accessible even to slaves.

Outside the classes of laboring urban castas and slaves, among native communities in both cities and in the rural reaches of the Spanish empire, merit had a different but arguably even more important function. In the sixteenth and seventeenth centuries, it had implied noble status and came with concrete political and economic benefits for those who enjoyed it, endowing some Indians with the special royal commendations (*méritos y servicios* and *gracias*) that the crown had issued to faithful servants since the late Middle Ages. These privileges had to be defended, and in some cases even relinquished, in the atmosphere of native social leveling in the eighteenth century.

In the 1700s, the number of indigenous subjects who considered themselves "principales" expanded rapidly in many regions, as commoners pushed for expanded rights as political members of their pueblos. The lawyer who argued that there were two ways to become a native noble in Villa Alta spoke directly to this transformation, specifically invoking "merit" as a product of actions in one's own lifetime, not just a matter of bequest and decent. If merit could be earned, so could status be changed in an orderly, rationally organized Indian republic. This republic looked, not coincidentally, a lot like a military or similar corporate body in which rank was not a permanent state but rather a rung on a ladder of achievement.[124] The native cabildo of Lima put it in their own way, claiming that court posts should be based on experience rather than "hidalguía."

Status was not the only concept that became more contingent and less tethered to a fixed and knowable past in late-eighteenth-century native pueblos. In several lawsuits during the period, indigenous litigants and legal advisors began to promote a historicist notion of custom, to view it as subject to change depending on the present. What is more, utility to the state rather than local tradition could determine legitimate custom. The power of this other custom was not in its allusion to antiquity or even in its repetition.[125] Rather, its force derived from its "nowness," an awareness of the passage of time long recognized to have marked a transition to modernity in the eighteenth century.[126] This awareness is based on a perception that time is accelerating and a belief in the subjectivity and temporalization of history, "in the sense that, by virtue of the passing of time, [history] changes at each given present."[127] It is this nowness that makes modern time unique.[128]

Most native litigants probably did not intend for the temporal dimensions of their arguments about merit and custom to align with a movement called "the Enlightenment," but some testimony in cases indicates that it was certainly fully within their capacity. The cabildo of Lima made the association overt when it promoted the candidacy of a purported non-native to the position of Lima's procurador de indios. Indeed, the cabildo's statement about his qualifications—based on his experience in the courtroom rather than his Indianness—clearly situated the dispute in the larger environment of the Age of Lights: they complained that the other candidates were unqualified because they were "devoid of Enlightenment in lawsuit matters" (*escaso de Luces en materias de pleitos*).

The phrase "devoid of Enlightenment," as it appears here, was a relatively recent formulation (with "luces" indicating "Enlightenment")—a complex concept containing references to attitudes and practices of urbanity, literacy, and education held to be new and distinct from those of the past. This was a phrase in wide circulation in the empire. In 1788 Madrid, a writer littered his appeal for the establishment of a periodical publication in the city of Burgos with the language of lights plentiful and scarce. Burgos was, the author claimed, isolated from the trends of the day, with no exposure to printed materials, and suffered a "scarcity of lights." Concretely, this meant that its inhabitants clung to "old opinions," keeping them in a state of dark "barbarity."[129] The educational and literary connotations of the "scarcity of lights" was made clear again only a few years later, when, on the opening of a new high court in Extremedura, Spain, a speaker lamented the region's "scarcity of lights" and its long struggle to "enlighten itself" (*ilustrarse*).[130] After the collapse of colonial rule in Spanish America, Mexicans repurposed the phrase "scarcity of lights" to describe the lack of preparation in some regions for the "science" of elective governance, while others applied it backward in time, to discuss early independence leaders' failure to comprehend the depth of Spanish colonial tyranny.[131] Thus, when the cabildo of Lima advocated on behalf of a legal representative who possessed "Lights," it meant not only an advocate who was educated and literate but also one with a kind of modern historical consciousness, whether that history was indigenous or not.

Native litigants who advanced concepts of merit and custom as politics in the present tense ultimately faced defendants who entrenched the idea that modern forms of formal law were alien to native culture. Such a notion pivoted on the presumption that natives were, by nature, pacific and disinclined to lawsuits. Many cases brought in the name of native communities intensified the notion that cooperation rather than conflict was the natural state of indigenous affairs. Take, as one example, a 1771 petition from the pueblo of Lambayque in Peru. In a contest over the possession of a cacicazgo, a group of Indians partial to one candidate opened the suit by praising their leader for his wise counsel, which always had the effect of promoting "peace and harmony."[132] On the other hand, legal foes were often characterized as "disturbers of peace." One of the most common words used to describe legal opponents in native communities was "*caviloso*"— or litigious and quarrelsome.[133] As the Council of Indies expressed it, native leaders had become "quasi-despots"; as multitudes of rival Indian litigants put it, they had become cruel "tyrants."[134]

As a result, some native leaders refrained from calling attention to their effective handling of village legal affairs and instead boasted that they had steered their gullible Indian subjects away from lawsuits, "to which they are easily led for [outsiders'] particular ends, which they cannot perceive because of their rustic comprehension."[135] It was the fault only of "inhuman" outsiders who had insinuated themselves in the community—including but not limited to opportunistic native leaders—that Indians went to court at all.[136] Even officials whose express job it was to provide legal counsel to natives began to pride themselves on keeping cases out of court. When Tomás Collaysos found himself defending his hold on the title of *quipocamayo*, or native court notary, of Lima, he responded that "in the ten years that I have had this post there have not been lawsuits and disturbances among the natives as there had been before," and he wondered aloud who was influencing his opponents.[137] The unspoken assumption was that it was an outsider, perhaps even a powerful Spaniard.

Spanish officials had to be cautious lest they too be cast as master manipulators behind native commoners' cases. In a dispute in Lambayeque over support for a candidate to a Spanish colonial post of legal advocacy for Indians known as the protector de naturales, natives easily shifted accusations of puppetry from outsider Indians to Spanish officials. A group of native defendants claimed that the candidate and his powerful cronies had duped other natives into supporting him. The hyperbole was astounding. A predator who incited Indians to litigation, this colonial official was no less than a villain against humankind. According to the faction's lawyer, the Spanish legal adviser was

> the principal mover in the restlessness of the miserable Indians, and far from protecting and sheltering them, keeping them in peace as is right, he moves them to lawsuits and disagreements, so that they bring various cases into your superior [court], preventing the Unhappy Ones from earning from the labor the sustenance of their families, making

them spend on trips to Trujillo and Lima, because he is not only a capital enemy of the Indian nation, but also of all humanity.[138]

Two years later and not so far away, the intendant of Trujillo, Juan Bazo y Berry,
turned accusations of stirring up legal trouble back onto native leaders. He fretted to the Peruvian viceroy about a litigious rabble-rouser named Chumbi, who
had moved into the pueblo of Chocope and rigged the electoral process so he
would be voted in as native alcalde. The description that the intendant offered
of the normal relationship between Spanish officials and Indian villages entrenched the idea that natives were by nature pacific unless manipulated by outsiders.[139] Chumbi, he wrote, "fomented and sustained lawsuits and appeals." He
was the first Indian "of this class" that Bazo y Berry had encountered in his six-
teen years as intendant, since the official had always tried to ensure that Indians
"had been left in absolute liberty for their elections, only taking care to avoiding
the spoiling [of votes] and nullifications by sending [special] commissions." The
intendant characterized his intervention in this case as "outside of the common
rules," even though recent royal law conceded him the power to supervise village
elections. The idea was that Indians, under normal conditions, needed no official
oversight, no legal mediation.

Thus both Spanish legal officials and native leaders squirmed under accusations that they had disturbed the putatively pacific natural state of the native
pueblos by inciting legal conflict. Indeed, this kind of argument moved a
Spanish subdelegate to attempt to eliminate the position of the Spanish protector de naturales from the courts of Lambayeque altogether in 1798. The
outcry from the native community at the loss of their colonial legal representative was intense, but they were in a tough spot. The court-appointed native
procurator in Lima's Audiencia, Isdrio Vilca, had the difficult task of trying to
frame the protest in terms consonant with notions of the litigation-adverse nature of indigenous pueblos. His made sure to state that his clients only sought
"the tranquility and calm of the Pueblos," and "the good regimen of the inhabitants and the judges who govern them . . ." But inside this argument, he deftly
summarized the way that all the talk about native peace set a trap for litigants.
Using a familiar metaphor, he argued that eliminating the post "closed the door
to the Indians of Lambayeque to defend themselves from the hostilities that this
[policy itself] presents." Without recourse to legal aid, "these Poor Natives find
themselves completely persecuted and have nowhere to go, not one of them,
lest [they take] some action that might stand out in the mind of a Spaniard as
an uprising. If an Indian defends himself and presents a petition, he is a rebel
and troublemaker."[140]

Viewed as part of a larger Enlightenment turn in the legal culture of the
Spanish empire, and particularly understood as an "indigenized modern" movement toward merit and historicism, this predicament peels back the layers of

discourses in native lawsuits during the Bourbon years, laying bare the hand-iwork of rival indigenous litigants and Spanish officials in manipulating ste-reotypes of harmonious natives and litigating tyrants.[141] The "common rules," as intendant Bazo y Berry had put it, had come to be conceived as a policy of colonial nonintervention in communities that, left on their own, privileged au-tonomy, harmony, and peace.[142] Litigation, in this view, was a phenomenon ex-trinsic to native society and was tantamount to rebellion.

It was not difficult to move from saying that the natural order of native so-ciety was pacific to saying that their concepts of justice derived from earlier times. One native litigant after another lamented the coming-of-age of a new generation of disturbers of the peace. An elder cacique decrying the litigious-ness of his pueblo's outgoing elected officials, whose lawsuits were bankrupting the community, put it this way: this was a "generation of troublemakers," who "rather than maintain the pueblo in peace, stir them [*sic*] up and force them into lawsuits." "The whole reason there are elected officials," he said, was "to main-tain community peace." In other words, good native rulers did not guide their subjects through the Spanish courts; they kept them out of the courts in the first place. And legitimate rulers did not engage in dangerous legal argumenta-tion; they preserved the peace through the status quo. The Indians in his village were neither "rebels nor friends of novelty."[143] By casting litigation as a pastime among the impetuous and young, peace became a tradition and litigation an innovation.

In the meantime, one Spanish official after another also struggled to find a place for native custom within an emergent modern concept of law as a rational system, and they did so by imagining that they were protecting Indians against the "friends of novelty" who led natives into the courts. In the end, Spanish offi-cials like Bazo y Berry would come to see themselves as the true defenders of custom in native communities, protecting them from formal lawsuits against their leaders, including complaints against leaders who had failed to litigate for their communities.[144]

That is what happened in 1789, during a series of extremely contentious cases over elections and community labor in the pueblo of Tabaá in Villa Alta.[145] The affair turned on a conflict over whether the community should litigate to pro-tect itself from a newly instituted mine labor draft. The faction supporting labor resistance through litigation tried to cast its position as one of natural rights, of protection of the community against slavery, as grounded in the "love of Patria" that had been displayed by no less a people than the Romans. Though they sought lawsuits against the labor draft, they simultaneously attempted to portray their adversaries as the true disrupters of "public peace and quiet."

The faction was turned back by the opinion of a legal adviser (*asesor*) to Villa Alta's alcalde mayor, who founded his argument on the fifteenth-century jurist Bobadilla, a thinker squarely within the jurisprudential tradition of intepretatio.

If this were to be a formal suit over the unsuitability of the elected officials, the asesor said, native litigants would surely be within their rights to pursue their cause. To claim, however, that the officials were unsuitable only because they would not litigate on behalf of their community was not good enough, and the proof that natives seeking litigation had presented was, in the asesor's opinion, nothing more than a "simple complaint" rather than a lawsuit proper.[146]

Those Indians who insisted on moving forward with litigation proved undaunted, and kept filing objections and blocking elections and the exercise of office in their community. Five years later, and three years after the 1787 cédula permitting district officials to oversee the election of native officials, the crown attorney in the Audiencia of Mexico nudged the district alcalde mayor to settle the protracted dispute. They instructed him to find and appoint a native governor who spoke Spanish and had proven himself useful in "agriculture or industry." The alcalde mayor, however, took the charge as a call to pin down, once and for all, what the local custom concerning elections was, seemingly certain that there was a correct answer to the dispute. He enlisted community elders to tell him about their electoral traditions. In their statements, some witnesses testified that they had tried to mediate between the Indian parties "extrajudicially, exhorting them to make the peace that they should have in the pueblos," but to no avail.[147]

This was exactly what Spanish officials wanted to hear. Both the alcalde mayor and the fiscal became transfixed by testimony that suggested that the traditional course of affairs in native communities was extrajudicial. They seized in particular on the testimony of the only village elder who spoke Spanish. The fiscal decided that this witness should be governor of the divided people. The rationale for this derived not only from the authority recent Bourbon law had bestowed on district officials to intervene in elections but also from "considering the ideas of the natives [and] distributive justice."[148] In other words, native law was best understood within the traditions of early modern law, of a piece with the paradigm of distributive justice, which could favor community mediation rather than laws and courts.

Where did the Spanish officials get such an idea? It came from the arguments put forward by the other native faction in the dispute, which had stated that their rivals had flouted the custom of the community of achieving consensus in elections before the vote was taken. Their opponents, they proclaimed, were more interested in lawsuits than living together.[149] Given that native litigants themselves reported to the Spanish officials that their customs supported peace and harmony and discouraged litigation, perhaps it should not surprise us that native law came to be synonymous with traditional forms of justice. This historical outcome was not preordained. But it was, in the end, still a matter of time.

Being and Becoming

Freedom and Slave Lawsuits

Josefa Piñeda was almost halfway there. Her owner had specified in a will that her heirs could not sell Josefa for more than 350 pesos, and she and her husband had scrimped and saved to amass 150. But now, five months after her master's death, Josefa's new mistress was demanding 500 pesos as her price. Josefa went to Lima's alcalde in 1791 to protest. In the initial petition she submitted to the court, which explained both her first owner's intention in setting her price and her own efforts to save up enough to purchase herself, an expression appears twice. "This got me closer," it reads, "in a certain way, to freedom."[1]

The idea that all humans strive to be free—and that slaves do so most of all—might seem obvious.[2] The concept of liberty has become so central to Western thought since the Enlightenment that it is almost unthinkable that oppressed humans ever acted out of anything other than a quest for more of it. But even if "liberty" has been around forever, its meaning and the practices people employ to attain it have varied.[3] In Spanish America, slaves' legal drive toward liberty through law was a historical event, not a historical inevitability.[4] Josefa Piñeda's movement "closer to freedom" captured a watershed moment in the legal definition of slavery in Spanish America.

Exploring slave lawsuits against masters in the three regions studied in this book where slavery was a significant part of daily life, namely Mexico City, Lima, and Trujillo, this chapter shows that, although certain possibilities had always existed for slaves to use the law, it was in the eighteenth century that they really began to take advantage of royal courts as a forum for challenging owners. As they filed lawsuits in greater numbers and forged a civil subjectivity as litigants, they were doing more than simply drawing on preexisting laws to ameliorate the harshness of their condition. Slaves were making Spanish law on slavery. Beyond making law, they were also making Enlightenment thought. Slave litigants put flesh on abstract philosophical questions that had become more pressing during the century, such as the meaning of natural rights, tyranny, and humanity. Among these concepts, one stands out: in these suits, slaves brought to life the modern conception of freedom as the objective of human action.

Such a conceit might send up warning signals of being caught in the very Enlightenment mindset that sets up history as an unswerving march toward liberty. But slaves created civil definitions of freedom, alongside other Enlightenment conceptions, in a specific context. Their propensity to sue in civil courts over their condition in general and, at times, to be freed altogether, can be dated to the eighteenth century. It was then that slavery generated philosophical clashes in the civil courts that turned on the meaning of natural and human rights, legal personhood and possession, and liberty—the very same debates that raged at the very same moment among the brightest minds of Europe, and that would eventually transform the debate about slavery throughout the Atlantic world.[5]

This is not to say, of course, that slaves did not want to be free until the eighteenth century. But slaves brought to the secular courts notions of humanity, rights, and freedom that departed in key ways from their prior legal practices around bondage. In order to appreciate the novelty of their creations, the chapter begins by briefly reviewing the rich historiography on slavery in Latin America. Next, a statistical overview of the number of slave suits heard in various civil jurisdictions in the colonies as well as specific courts in Lima demonstrates that when slaves entered royal courts in unprecedented numbers in the 1700s, they, like the female litigants suing husbands, were not simply turning their backs on the magistrates of the sacred to face the magistrates of the king. In fact, the king's magistrates were far from marginal to the story of slaves' eighteenth-century civil lawsuits. The writings of Lima jurist Bravo de Lagunas reveal larger jurisprudential shifts in understandings of the precise civil rights slaves possessed to liberate themselves, as well as the ultimate meaning of "freedom."

Bravo de Lagunas points to a rising debate over whether slavery was an intrinsic state or, instead, a stage of life. By capitalizing on some of the unique social features of slavery in Spanish America—principally, slave-initiated sales to new owners in cases of abuse as well as the high prevalence of conditional liberty— slave litigants and their lawyers advanced a vision of freedom as a staged process. Their vision of human progression toward freedom, of liberty as a positive stage of becoming rather than a categorical state of being, contrasted with owners' conservative attempts to fix bondage as an intrinsic condition. Ethically, slave litigants' notion of staged freedom also bucked against prevailing notions that on the other side of liberty lay disorder and lawlessness. In the end, slaves themselves were instrumental in plotting out the liberation teleology that so dominates Western thought.

The Beginning of Freedom

Historians, detecting the Enlightenment overtones of references to natural rights and liberty in late colonial Spanish American slave suits, have struggled to pinpoint their origin. Some have suggested that the ideas arrived from elsewhere, especially through news sailors brought about the American, French, and Haitian Revolutions.[6] Even so, the importance of the eighteenth century as a legal turning point for Africans in bondage in Spanish America has yet to be fully recognized in part because slaves are a common sight in a variety of types of legal documentation throughout the entire colonial period.

Most often slaves in colonial Latin America appear as objects of lawsuits. But they also show up as litigants, particularly in Church courts since Catholic tradition and canon law endowed slaves with sacramental rights as Christians.[7] Slaves sued before ecclesiastical magistrates to keep their families together and to force their masters to permit them marry.[8] They also brought charges in criminal courts when they had been victims of crimes, occasionally without a master's legal representation.[9] And they used and were subject to the tribunal of the Inquisition.[10] Slaves also possessed certain abilities to sue masters civilly, particularly for mistreatment. Sometimes, they sued over "letters of freedom" (*cartas de libertad*) and the ability to acquire documentation of owner intent to sell them (*papel* or *boleta de venta*), which they could use to find a different owner, potentially one amenable to manumission.[11]

These artifacts of slaves' active engagement with the law have presented historians something of a periodization problem, with some scholars signaling the decisive influence of nineteenth-century liberalism on slave litigation and others emphasizing medieval law the and important role the Church had played in shaping the legal consciousness of peoples of African descent during the sixteenth and seventeenth centuries.[12]

Periodization problems particularly vex specific inquiries into two customary legal practices recognized in Spanish American civil courts by the end of the eighteenth century. The first of these was the recognition of slaves' right to self-purchase, known in some regions as *coartación*, an arrangement of purchase on installment. The second was slaves' right to seek a new owner. Some historians view these "rights" as the logical outgrowth of privileges bestowed by codes in medieval and early modern Spain. Following Roman tradition, Spanish law had long "favored" freedom. One only needed to flip to a preamble on the topic of liberty in the thirteenth-century law code, the *Siete Partidas*, to find "All creatures of the world," including slaves, "naturally love and desire liberty."[13] Building on this medieval code, Spanish royal laws issued specifically for the colonies began to proliferate as human bondage reached unprecedented levels. By the late seventeenth century, slaves were becoming more visible both in local civil courts and at the high-court level of the Council of Indies.[14] Yet, as historian Alejandro de la Fuente notes, "neither *coartación* nor the possibility of changing masters appeared as slave rights in Castilian legal codes. Rather, it seems that these prerogatives emerged as a pragmatic response to the frequent litigation initiated by slaves themselves."[15]

Part of the confusion about precisely when and how slaves began to sue over self-purchase is that this customary, unwritten "right" did have partial origin in Spanish civil law—a law in the *Partidas* that mandated that masters convicted of mistreating their slaves would be punished by being forced to sell the slave.[16] Accusing a master of sevicia in a civil court and being sold to a new owner therefore was theoretically always a possibility for slaves in the Spanish empire. Slaves occasionally employed this legal strategy throughout the colonial period, but they did not fully realize its liberatory potential until the eighteenth century.

As the data from Lima shows in Table 6.1, it was during the last three or four decades of the 1700s that slaves began to sue masters in civil courts in sizeable numbers. In those suits, many slave litigants systematically sought the legally prescribed punishment for abusive masters. Some began to actively seek new owners themselves, searching for someone amenable to financial deals that could result in the slaves' freedom. In this way, they transformed a medieval law about

Table 6.1 **Slave Cases before First-Instance City Court, Lima, 18th Century**

Decade	Total Civil Cases	Slave Suing Master		Master Suing Slave		Suits over Slaves as Property		Total Slave Cases by Decade	
1700s	29	1	3.4%	0	0%	1	3.4%	2	6.9%
1710s	30	0	0%	0	0%	1	3.3%	1	3.3%
1720s	36	2	5.6%	0	0%	0	0%	2	5.6%
1730s	66	2	3%	0	0%	3	4.5%	5	7.6%
1740s	68	1	1.5%	0	0%	0	0%	1	1.5%
1750s	102	1	0.98%	0	0%	5	4.9%	6	5.9%
1760s	88	4	4.5%	1	1.1%	5	5.7%	10	11.4%
1770s	373	33	8.8%	2	0.5%	9	2.4%	44	11.8%
1780s	490	49	10%	0	0%	22	4.5%	71	14.5%
1790s	359	33	9.2%	4	1%	27	7.5%	64	17.8%
Total	**1641**	**126**	**7.7%**	**7**	**.42%**	**73**	**4.4%**	**206**	**12.6%**

Source: AGN-Perú, Cabildo, Causas Civiles

masters' punishment in cases of sevicia into the ability to find a new owner, and in turn converted this into the right to self-purchase at a fair price.

Focus on self-purchase suits should not obscure the fact that slaves also increasingly sued over practices that had long been part of the everyday civil practice of slavery. They litigated over testamentary freedom, claiming their dead owners had emancipated them in written wills or in intention. They also went to court to haggle over the details of the common practice of "conditional liberty," which was the freedom an owner bestowed upon a slave under certain conditions such as the master's death, reaching a certain age, or completing "good service." Thus, speaking in a strictly legal sense, slaves' frequent engagement with owners on civil legal grounds—whether over coartación, the ability to change masters, or any other matter—was not a perennial part of African bondage in the Spanish American colonies. It was, for the most part, an eighteenth-century event.

A total of 268 slaves initiated lawsuits against owners during the years 1700–99 in Mexico City, Lima, and Trujillo. Given the overall population of slaves in these regions, this number—even if only accounting for part of the total of all slave legal actions before judges—indicates that slaves could not take access to the courts for granted.[17] Nonetheless, by asking not what impact lawsuits had on slavery but rather what impact slaves had on lawsuits, it becomes clear that slaves were coming to play a larger part in shaping colonial civil law.

As Table 6.1 shows, in Lima the proportion of slave legal action within the overall activity of the courts is quite astounding. Even in an environment where all kinds of litigants were suing more, enslaved litigants raced ahead, doubling their claim on the percentage of cases heard by the city's civil alcaldes in the 1770s. By the end of the century, slave cases against masters consistently comprised almost 10 percent of all of the suits these local magistrates received in their civil courts. Adding the number of slave-initiated lawsuits to cases in which they figured prominently as objects of dispute, as well as the smattering of intriguing cases in which masters actually sued their own slaves, by the 1790s this municipal lower court spent almost one-fifth of its time adjudicating conflicts born of bondage.

Enslaved people turned toward the civil courts in the more elevated jurisdictions of the colonies, as well. The middle of the eighteenth century marked a transformative moment for slave litigation in the regional high court of Lima's real audiencia, just as it had in Lima's first-instance municipal court. Examining the high court hearings for three periods in the eighteenth century shows that the percentage of slave-initiated suits climbed from 1.7 percent for the period 1735–49 to 2.3, for the period 1750–75, to a staggering 10.8 percent of the court's docket in the last decade of the century.[18] Since slaves were considered part of the protected legal category of "miserables," high courts were to accept their complaints in the first instance and provide the litigants pro bono representation.[19]

But, as we will see, this was not always so easy for slaves to achieve. Although audiencias in some regions of the empire had a designated advocate known as the Protector of Slaves, it appears no such office existed in Peru or Mexico.[20] Slaves' appearance before the ministers of the high court becomes more impressive still given the jurisdiction's prestige, its increasingly full docket, and the difficulty slaves sometimes faced in getting an appeal.

Lima's late eighteenth-century slaves might have been especially active in the courts, but they were not unusual, as Table 6.2 indicates. In the viceregal capital cities of both Lima and Mexico City, slave-initiated civil lawsuits increased notably during the second half of the eighteenth century. In Trujillo, the shift happened earlier, but it was still clearly an eighteenth-century phenomenon that continued unabated into the early 1800s.[21] In fact, in a vast array of civil archives in Latin America, spanning Quito to Cuba, Bahia to Spanish Florida, slave cases are more plentiful for the eighteenth century than ever before.[22]

Slaves joined the ranks of civil litigants regardless of what was happening demographically in each region. For example, while the slave population of Lima grew in real numbers from around 7,000 in 1700 to just over 9,000 by the end of the century, the proportion of slaves in the urban population remained relatively stable at around 20 percent.[23] Likewise, the proportion of slaves in the population of Trujillo and its surrounding valley remained constant from the seventeenth to mid-eighteenth century, even as the population itself more than doubled.[24] The demographic story of slavery in eighteenth-century Mexico City differs from the stability in the Peruvian jurisdictions. Though it was home to the largest black population in Spanish America in the late sixteenth century, the slave trade into the Viceroyalty of New Spain was abolished in the mid-seventeenth century. Due to this, and undoubtedly in part due to creative action on the part of slaves themselves, the slave population—if not the population of free Afro-Mexicans—was indeed in long-term decline.[25] Even as Mexico City's

Table 6.2 **Slaves as Objects and Agents of Civil Suits, 18th Century**

	1700–49		1750–99	
	Slaves as property	*Slaves as litigants*	*Slaves as property*	*Slaves as litigants*
Mexico City	23	14	13	28
Lima	56	33	153	192
Trujillo	9	46	8	48

Data on Mexico City from AGN-M: Fiscal de lo Civil, TSJ Civil (Alcalde Ordinario), and Corregimiento Civil series. Data on Lima from AGN-P, Cabildo and Real Audiencia Civil series. Data on Trujillo from ARL, Causas Ordinarias, Corregimiento, Civil, and Intendencia Civil Series.

population swelled in the eighteenth century, the percentage of slaves in New Spain overall had fallen to just 1 percent by 1800.[26] Nonetheless, the number of slave lawsuits in civil courts thickened.

If demographics do not provide a reliable explanation for why slaves became more active in civil courts in the eighteenth century, geography and gender offer more promising terrain. Two trends not captured in the tables here are worth mentioning: the high number of urban cases and the sizeable number of lawsuits over slavery brought by women, either for their own freedom or on behalf of family members.[27] This indicates that urban inhabitants of African descent who worked for wages as street vendors, wet nurses, and artisans formed the vanguard of the suing classes because they had access to cash to put up for their own freedom or that of relatives.

Litigation involving slaves was also gendered because litigants often sued female owners. In Trujillo, for example, around half of the masters who were sued in the eighteenth century were women. This in part might be because Latin American women's propensity to manumit their slaves, especially their female slaves and their children, created expectations of freedom or clashes over the terms of liberty.[28] But owners engaged in these manumission practices long before the mid-eighteenth century, and slaves had long been money earners in colonial cities. In fact, during the lean economic years of the late colonial period, urban slave women's access to cash contracted even as their presence as litigants grew.[29] Several slaves from rural regions and remote haciendas made long journeys to the viceregal capitals to file cases against their owners, though few had a stash of cash to put up for their freedom.

Among various factors contributing to the rising number of slave-initiated civil suits in the eighteenth century in various regions of the Spanish Americas, one surely was legal culture. Slavery—in addition to being a gendered cultural, labor, and economic institution—was a legal category. For urban slaves especially, slavery did not mean living under the constant supervision of masters; it entailed some autonomy in terms of physical movement and the ability to socialize. The tyranny came, in these cases, from masters' unrelenting demand for wages (*jornales*), which the law bound slaves to submit regardless of the time and energy they spent caring for themselves and their dependents. In the end, what most separated these slaves from free wageworkers was the legal fact of dominion.

Given this, a good part of the explanation for the rise in slave civil litigation might reside within the law itself. Custom and precedent played an increasingly important and complicated role in slave cases, just as they did with the suits brought by women and indigenous litigants. Written laws also spurred slaves' civil legal actions. Multiple civil metropolitan edicts and colonial mandates were potential catalysts for slave lawsuits.[30] These include empire-wide rulings, such as a 1683 royal cédula that underscored that owners were to offer their slaves "good treatment," as well as rulings for certain regions, like the one that instructed Cuba's judges to look favorably on slave attempts to purchase their freedom.[31] Yet, notably, none of these individual laws was ever cited in slave cases aired in the courts of Trujillo, Lima, and Mexico, even though slave litigants and their lawyers based the legitimacy of their suits on a vast and fascinating array of sources.

In the last decade of the eighteenth century, slaves and their lawyers did point insistently, though often superficially, to one Bourbon initiative that they believed legitimized their suits. They cited Carlos IV's 1789 *Instruction on the Education, Treatment and Occupation of Slaves*, which, among other things, reiterated the medieval law found in the *Siete Partidas* that held that any owner found to have committed excessive cruelty could be forced to sell the slave.[32] It thus can be argued that the Bourbon Reforms undergirded some of the "rights" that slaves began to invoke in royal courts when they entered to sue their masters. After all, the royal imprimatur on any piece of legislation warning of the dangers of tyrannical masters surely served as encouragement for slaves to enter civil courts to ameliorate work or living conditions or gain freedom.[33]

Still, the growth in slave action in civil courts cannot be attributed to the promulgation of any particular Bourbon law. None of the so-called "Black Codes" of the Bourbon years, including the 1789 *Instruction*, radically innovated on the slave legislation that the crown had issued for its American colonies since the late sixteenth century. Furthermore, the 1789 *Instruction* was in effect for only six years, repealed after the planter class pressured the Council of Indies to revoke it.[34] Critically, as is clear from Tables 6.1 and 6.2, judicial activity in many civil courts clearly predated the 1789 royal order and continued unabated after its repeal. Thus Bourbon reform legislation had more of an interactive than strictly causal relationship to slave litigation. Eighteenth-century slave litigants, while using royal legislation when they could, more consistently submitted petitions that breathed life into an old sixteenth-century law compiled in the *Recopilación de Leyes de Indias*, which instructed the audiencias to hear slave complaints.[35] In other words, slave law had not drastically changed in the eighteenth century. But its interpretation had.

Jurisprudence

A change in the interpretation of rights was evident not only among litigants and their lawyers but also among judges. This is obvious in their rulings, which occasionally went slaves' way, as well as in the mere fact that they admitted cases in the first place. But because few opinions of Spanish imperial judges exist, José Pedro

Bravo de Lagunas y Castilla's commentary on slavery provides a rare glimpse of the interplay between changing jurisprudential ideas and the actual cases slaves brought during the century. His two writings on slavery point toward the areas of custom in slave cases that Spanish colonial judges found contested or murky.

Recall that the first opinion he wrote was on the right to self-purchase in the event that a slave could prove sevicia. In this 1747 opinion, the oidor considered the prevailing justice-oriented principle of "equity" as applied to slave cases. He worried that lawyers and judges interpreted the Roman emperor Justinian's injunction to "favor liberty" too broadly, applying equity, or judicial compassion, to all slave cases in a manner that was "against the law and reason, on which it is founded." Judges' interpretations of the law founded on equity, he warned, threatened to deprive owners of their property.[36] Yet, despite his rejection of casuistic legal argumentation, this was not a blanket denial of slave rights. Analogizing slaves to pueblos seeking independence, the judge ultimately decided that slaves—strictly in cases of proven abuse and only if they were to be able to purchase their own freedom by some means—should be given precedence as purchasers.

Bravo de Lagunas was about to find out that slavery was more than a metaphor. The erudite subtext and metaphorical qualities of his opinion about slaves' precedence in self-purchase was easily lost among real practitioners of law. His writings ended up assuring judges that they were on firm legal ground in permitting slaves to enter court. Indeed, just as Bravo de Lagunas privileged local practices and customs in his decision, litigants and lawyers in the courts of Peru would come to privilege his *Colección legal* as a local legal source on slave rights for their arguments in court.

The "recipient" of Bravo de Laguna's 1758 epistle reported that the number of slave suits was rising in the city. Indeed, Bravo de Lagunas himself reported in his opinion that another problematic slave case had come to the high court's bench just as his book was going to press in 1761.[37] Once again, fears of the "open door" of law in the colonies reflected the increase of new kinds of lawsuits in the colonies. The judge and his contemporaries fretted that slave suits increasingly seeped in through jurisprudential cracks in the courthouse walls.

Although the jurist had retired, the legal issue that prompted him to again pick up his plume in 1758 concerned conditional liberty. In a city where slaves were approaching the bench more frequently, this opinion was derived not from abstract jurisprudential pondering but an actual case aired before the Audiencia of Lima, a copy of which the oidor seems to have had in his possession.[38] This particular suit pivoted on the question of whether the child born to a woman who was a *statulibera*, or a female slave who had been granted conditional liberty in the future, was free or a slave.

In the 1758 opinion on conditional liberty, Bravo de Lagunas attempted to settle the question of what, exactly, slavery was. If slavery was a condition that passed through the mother, what of conditional freedom? Was there such a status as being a conditional slave? And in a slave culture where promises or expectations of freedom kept the sugar mills grinding, the fields cleared, and the wages rolling in, it was becoming increasingly unclear whether slavery was an intrinsic state or a stage that a slave could pass out of.

This issue was at the heart of the arguments that a young lawyer had advanced on behalf of the slave woman and her child in the controversial case Bravo de Lagunas was considering. The lawyer, whose opening arguments the jurist quoted from extensively but never named, had cleverly ventured that liberty was not a state but rather a stage, particularly when freedom had been offered in a will and testament. Freedom was not a "condition" as much as a "moment," re-gardless of other conditions attached. In essence, the lawyer proposed that since slavery could "expire" along with masters, slavery had a life cycle: a beginning, a middle, and an end. The intent to free the slave had triggered a movement to the middle that could not be reversed without another document.

Bravo de Lagunas sniffed that such an argument would hardly be accepted in the mock trials of law school. The lawyer had confused a certain point in time with a condition, Bravo de Lagunas pronounced, mixing up *statulibero* (person awaiting freedom) and *statu libero* (free status). To prove this, the old jurist again drew on eclectic sources ranging from Justinian's *Institutes* to the natural rights theories of derecho de gentes, or the notion of the civil laws of nations, sprinkling the pages of his letter with diverse references, ranging from Grotius to Locke, as well as his Enlightened contemporaries and working missionaries.

Bravo de Lagunas came down firmly against "the favor of liberty" and de-cided that the child was still enslaved.[39] There were, the retired judge said, only two states in which humans could find themselves: "all men are either free or not free, and there cannot be a third type, since free and servant are not contrary as much as they are contradictory, and they admit no middle ground."[40] In other words, slavery and freedom were not just opposite poles in the human condi-tion; they were mutually exclusive. But slaves in Spanish America had a different, less categorical, take on freedom.

A Multitude of Suits

Slaves in the eighteenth century did not, of course, invent the idea that they could level lawsuits against masters, but they did carve out a civil standing at law as never before. As with marital disputes, the legal activities of slaves and the notions of law that governed their interactions with social superiors had held a special place in the domain of the Church until the eighteenth century. Slave suits only trickled into the civil courts of the sixteenth and seventeenth centuries compared to the volume with which they appeared before ecclesiastical judges.

The tribunals of the Catholic Church traditionally provided slaves a space for legal action, a sphere to push back against owners to gain some control over their lives, particularly in matters of the heart and hearth.[41] Because the Church recognized the sanctity of marriage even among people in bondage, slaves often turned to priests to limit masters' authority in selling a spouse or for permission to marry. The ecclesiastical forum had a synergistic relationship with the way slaves conceived of, or at least presented, themselves before law, leading them to emphasize their standing as sacramental subjects.[42]

A sample of ecclesiastical cases concerning slaves and slavery in Lima, taken from three five-year periods across the eighteenth century, demonstrates that slaves made active use of the Church courts as litigants. Slaves figured as property, being bought, sold, or loaned by clergy or nuns, in fewer than half of the cases. In fact, cases over slaves as property were equal in number to suits over slaves' sacramental right to cohabitate with a spouse, referred to in the period as "making a married life," or "*hacer una vida maridable*." These "vida maridable" cases constituted almost a third of all slave suits. This category also includes a few petitions by owners for Church permission to separate a married slave couple, but slaves or their spouses initiated the majority, mostly to prevent owners from separating them through sale.

Ecclesiastical jurisdiction functioned for slaves at the end of the eighteenth century much in the same way as it always had. Slaves did not significantly change the content of the suits they brought before the Church over time: suits purely over abuse were split evenly, with a single case appearing in each period; and self-purchase cases—a subset of the "liberty" cases—remained steady, at two or three per period. Among the "vida maridable" cases, owners more frequently sought preemptive permission to separate slave spouses in the 1790s. This anticipatory licensing might suggest that owners, aware of the increased litigiousness of slaves in the civil realm, wanted to cover their legal bases. But other than this, there is not a dramatic change in the character of Church litigation like that found in Lima's royal tribunals.

Slave suits in the Church tribunal of Lima also displayed a numerical constancy. Unlike in the secular courts, there was no dramatic rise in the aggregate number of slave lawsuits over the course of the century. Compared to the sharp reversal in the balance between slave-initiated suits and suits over slaves as property in secular civil suits, the proportion tipped only softly in ecclesiastical cases, with cases over slaves as property dipping slightly in the period 1790–95. There was, overall, a small decline in the absolute number of ecclesiastical slave suits during the 1790s, even as the slave population grew by 2,000 people over the century. Some slave cases entering Lima's secular courts might have been

Table 6.3 **Ecclesiastical Slave Cases in Eighteenth-Century Lima**

Years	Slaves as Possessions	Marital Problems among Slaves	Vida Maridable	Forced Sale	Liberty	Abuse	Owner Suing Slave	Other	Total
1700–05	20	1	23	6	6	1	0	3	60
1750–55	14	3	11	8	6	1	0	4	47
1790–95	10	2	20	8	4	1	2	5	52
Total	44	6	54	22	16	3	2	12	169

From AAL, Causas de Negros.

simply switching jurisdictions. But if they did, only a few slaves jumped the Catholic Church's ship. Far more impactful than the actual movement of cases from one court to another was the advent of the idea among slaves that royal civil courts might serve as special harbors of freedom.

In 1791, Natividad, a slave who claimed her owner, a priest, had promised manumission when he forced her to into sexual relations with him, submitted a petition that frankly addressed why she was a rare exception in bringing a freedom suit to Church judges in Lima. Her petition announced to the *provisor* of the Church court, "I well could place my suit before the Señores of the Real Audiencia, where the Law of the Realm has directed slaves to claim their liberty whenever they want to avail themselves of the help and refuge that the law dispenses." However, not wanting "to darken the Tribunals of the secular jurisdiction" with the tale of the priest's sexual crimes, "I renounce the Indulgence of Royal Law and move [to bring] my case (*mover mis acciones*) before the just commission of Your Most Illustrious Lord."[43]

Natividad clearly presented herself as a subject with rights grounded in civil as well as canon law, and her statement construed her appearance in ecclesiastical jurisdiction as her own choice. Still, slaves continued to sue masters in Church courts over issues that were determined to be sacramental in nature, such as the issue of vida maridable. The point here is that the rise of civil litigation did not nudge aside Church authority or supplant more traditional ways of conceiving of slavery as subject to the domain of moral law, just as it did not eradicate justice-oriented gendered legal practices or eliminate native nobility. Instead, the secular subjectivity slaves fashioned in civil cases against masters ran parallel to the persistence of more traditional understandings about the sacramental rights of slaves.

Indeed, early in the century, as slaves began to increasingly enter royal jurisdiction, they brought with them many arguments that were religious or canonical in nature.[44] In 1721, Rosa Narbares, a slave freed by testament, traveled south from her home town to see the alcalde of Trujillo when her free eight-year-old daughter was sold as a slave. She drew on royal and canon law simultaneously to register her outrage, insisting that the man who sold her daughter should "incur the grave penalties established by Royal law and canon [law] of censures reserved by his Holiness against those who sell free Men."[45]

Spouses also imported sacramental identities into royal jurisdiction, protesting when masters moved toward splitting them up by sale and also when slaves were denied communication with their partner when incarcerated in workhouses.[46] At times, husbands asserted authority as protectors of their enslaved wives. For example, in 1771 a husband submitted a petition to the alcalde of Trujillo when his wife's master died and his wife was sold off as part of his estate. He, as his enslaved wife's "legitimate"—meaning married in the

Church—husband, should select a buyer who was "to [his] satisfaction and pleasure."[47]

Around a decade later, Martina Obregoso's husband, Josef Onofre, invoked canon law on marriage in an ingenious way when his wife's master sued Martina for back wages before the intendant of Trujillo. Her prior owner had instructed his executor that, upon his death, Martina should be permitted to work where and how she wished, requiring her only to pay his estate 8 pesos a month until she had submitted 200 pesos for her complete freedom. When the intendant ruled that Martina, several months behind on her payments, should either pay up or be put in prison, her husband Josef filed a statement to the intendant requesting their marriage be annulled. The judge's ruling meant that Josef had married a slave rather than a free person, which was canonical grounds for annulment based on "error of quality."[48] The trick, seemingly designed to underscore to the district judge the grave implications of his ruling, did not work. The magistrate did offer Josef the chance to pay the entire 200 pesos toward her freedom while also charging him court costs, a price that proved too steep for Josef.[49]

From Protection to Papers

In addition to such sacrament-based strategies, other aspects of slave suits, particularly those aired during the decades before the 1770s, drew from traditional early modern civil practices. Among these was the long tradition, particularly in New Spain, of approaching the high courts for writs of *amparo*, or protection.[50] These were executive, summary rulings for those individuals deemed to be of the legal category of miserables. Indigenous people in colonial New Spain frequently activated the mechanism of amparo in order to exert control over where and how they labored.[51] In the early seventeenth century, the discourses and legal practices associated with amparo had proved beneficial to slaves, as well.

In 1633, María Negra went before the corregidor of Mexico City to request his intervention on behalf of her enslaved husband, Nicolás, who was being mistreated by his owner. The master, Alonso Bueno, was a *panadero*, or the owner of a bakery, a colonial enterprise whose fires and grueling labor conditions made it a popular place of punishment for slaves in colonial Spanish America.[52] María did not seek a formal suit against Alonso. Rather, her petition stated, "Favoring me and my husband for the good treatment that he should have as we are unfortunate and humble, we have nothing other than the good protection (*bien amparo*) of Your Mercy." She then asked for summary intervention in the case, specifically that the corregidor bring Alonso before him and order him to treat her husband more benevolently. The corregidor delegated this task to his sheriff.[53]

That in 1633 María did not ask for the judge to open a formal case is crucial to understanding what changed in the practices and culture of slave law over time.[54] By the middle of the eighteenth century, slaves and freed people who litigated in royal courts had become less likely to accept extrajudicial intervention or undocumented legal solutions. Even if some slaves still sought the privilege of appealing to high courts in the first instance or for summary judgments, many had become more oriented toward formal suits against their masters that would be heard through until sentence.

The 1761 case that Margarita Francisca, a mulata slave from Mexico City, lodged in order to secure a favorable price and to change owners contrasts with María's 1633 case. The second petition in the case is a request for a pro bono defender, based on her minority of age and "so that the Lawyer defends me in my rights . . . and, since my enslavement does not permit me the faculties to pay court costs, so that the office assists me until the conclusion of the case."[55] Similarly, when María del Rosario de la Vega of Lima began to formulate a 1790 lawsuit for sexual and physical abuse against her master, she was sure to pronounce that she was a *"caso de corte,"* a privileged position based on her status as a legal "miserable." But this status did not entail seeking a summary case. She wanted a formal lawsuit, which the Real Audiencia of Lima assented to allow.[56] When she finally dropped the suit, having received assurances that she would not be forced to return to her owner's dominion and could find a new master at a rebated price, her complaint was advanced enough in the legal system to require a written petition to desist (*apartameinto*).

As slaves began to emphasize the importance of more formal proceedings resulting in written sentences, judges' interim rulings concerning the lawfulness of their suits for freedom became more crucial, and so did the written contracts specifying the arrangements they had made with owners. María Moncada was among the freed slaves who saw paper as indispensable to her enslavement. She petitioned the alcalde of Trujillo in writing in 1765, recalling that her owner had left a will freeing her for the price of 150 pesos. During an earlier verbal hearing, the judge had ruled that she could submit to the executor of her deceased owner's estate 4 pesos a month until she paid off her freedom. María's framing of the deal that the alcalde had struck for her placed it squarely within the realm of amparo. "Your Mercy," her petition reads, "protected me in amparo of free possession" (*amparo en posesión de libre*), meaning ruled in favor of her arrangement for freedom. But María decided she needed more than an unwritten arrangement. She asked for a bill showing what she had paid and what she owed to be drawn up, presumably to function as proof of her status.[57]

Pausing for a moment over María's case, it is possible to appreciate the definitional complexity slavery was beginning to pose in the eighteenth century. María had been "freed," but she still owed money toward that freedom so she was not yet "in free possession" of freedom. In this case it is unclear with whom she lived and how she earned the 4 pesos a month she was paying toward the price for dominion over her own body. It would not be unusual if María, like some manumitted slaves or slaves in the process of purchasing themselves, remained in the employment of her dead master's family or associates. What is clear, however, is that she did not seek to somehow "pass" as completely free. Rather, she sought legal documentation that would show her as party to an ongoing commercial transition to freedom.

María's attraction to the fixity of a bill as a secular contract demonstrating that she was becoming free reflected the heavy reliance slaves had on testaments, sale papers, and free papers, which served as tangible proof of status. Importantly, litigants who went to court over the issue of freedom only infrequently claimed they had been born free; most claimed that they had been freed or should be freed. Thus they tended to be heavily invested in documents that were generated in the secular sphere, such as sale papers or price appraisals, rather than by Church notaries, as would be a record of baptism.[58] The very sequence of papers in which court notaries organized the dossiers of slave lawsuits reflects the primacy of documented proof of status. Many begin not with a petition but rather with a bill of sale or will.[59]

The secularizing breeze in the colonial courts gently lifted the importance of civil contracts for slave owners as well as slave litigants. Take, as one example, Jacinta, whose name appeared in a baptismal register of free blacks in the Valley of Chicama in Peru and who in 1717 sued her presumptive master. This owner claimed that parish records had no value in civil lawsuits, "because of the sheer laxity (*mera facilidad*) with which priests may conduct themselves."[60] This was a losing argument in a larger legal culture where a person's identity—lineage, caste, marital status, age—was captured on paper during sacraments marking stages in life.[61] Jacinta was declared to be free. But however weak the master's argument, it revealed that Church evidence was losing some weight when compared to civil contractual and secular court records.

Despite the endurance of traditional discourses about religion and morality and the durability of civil practices related to miserables and amparo, eighteenth-century slave lawsuits marked a new and distinct event in Spanish colonial law by their very existence as well as in their execution and expression. Slave petitions and their lawyers' arguments might continue to base their right to sue masters in traditional notions of Christian morality and protection, but they increasingly also referred to their rights, often their right to be recognized as free or becoming free, as well as to be heard in court over the circumstances of their condition.[62]

Self-Preservation and Sevicia

As with women's civil litigation, the notion of "derecho" expressed in eighteenth-century slave cases began to split from its original meaning as "justice," or what most befitted the litigant in a distributional system. Instead, it meant "rights" in a more modern sense of the term, as a universal, natural, inviolable possession.[63] Note that in 1717 Jacinta, the woman who used her baptismal record as proof of her free status, referred to "derecho" in the more traditional sense. After submitting her evidence, she turned over a statement that announced that she had "justified my right (derecho) in the Juridical Reasons I have provided and that are in my favor."[64]

The meaning of derecho in this case differs from a 1793 statement that *pardo* Simón Rodríguez submitted to a first-instance court. He claimed that he had been living with his family, cultivating a small plot of land outside Lima, and enjoying "the peace and quiet" that "the natural right of liberty (*derecho natural de la libertad*) lent to me" when he was abducted and sold as a slave. The opening petition he submitted to the alcalde twice employed the phrase "the natural right of liberty," and it labeled the violence with which he was apprehended and enslaved as "Malevolence and Tyranny."[65] That Simón had been living as a free person undoubtedly provided the context in which "derecho" could be construed as a right over himself, and then elided with a right to "liberty." But it also increasingly planted the foundation of his "right" in the soil of "nature." The same was true of other slaves who turned to concepts of nature as well as humanity as the basis of their right to freedom.

The definitional stakes of "derecho natural" were high for slaves, as the discourses of self-preservation and inhumanity in sevicia cases demonstrate. Whereas the Roman and medieval notion of *ius naturae* emphasized how justice was revealed through relationships or the various properties of derecho, natural rights theories pointed toward a rational system of law in which rights were personal possessions. Grotius, Heineccius, and Vinnius held that rights and duties were not arbitrary nor did they depend on the authority of the judges who doled them out.[66] Rather, rights were ordered by nature and binding to all humans. Christians and non-Christians alike were entitled to the things necessary for basic survival.

The impulse toward self-preservation was central to the development of natural rights theory, since "jus," at least in Grotius's formulation, was considered, at minimum, the "power" to keep others away from what is properly one's own.[67] The Dutch philosopher Baruch Spinoza went further. Self-preservation was key to the very condition of freedom. "The more each individual strives, and is able to seek his own advantage," he wrote, "that is, conserve his being, the more he is endowed with virtue."[68] Heineccius agreed, beginning his popular *Elements of Natural Right* with the pronouncement that "what is bad destroys man [*sic*], and what is good not only preserves but also perfects him".[69] The way slaves articulated their right to freedom in eighteenth-century Spanish American courts aligned with this emergent notion that natural right to self-preservation could be construed as a right to achieve greater personal perfection through liberty.[70]

Recall that some women accusing their husbands of sevicia likewise located their right to separate from marriages—often of their own volition—in a right to "*conservarse*," or in self-preservation. This reference to self-preservation was not random; it was scripted as a basic right in natural law theory. Scripted though it was, slaves' bodies were often living proof of the legal importance of self-preservation. An eleven-year-old boy from Trujillo was admitted to the city hospital covered with open wounds from having been repeatedly whipped across his buttocks and lower back with a rope and a lash resembling a cat-o-nine-tails. He had also been hit in the face, producing a large lump over his cheekbone. Asked what he had done to merit the beating from his master, the slave youth admitted to having stolen a pair of horse bits and a hat, but also pointed out that this was his master's usual behavior, since he regularly beat a female slave in his household as well as his own wife.[71] Convicted by a local alcalde, the master was forced to sell the boy. In this case, the violence against slaves did not alone bring the case into the courts; it was special circumstance of the slave's youth and the fact that the master's blows landed on his wife. Thus, slave claims to "self-preservation" made visible in court a violence that might otherwise be expected and ordinary in master-slave relations.

Slaves did not invoke self-preservation only to protect themselves from their masters' personal violence. Though medieval Spanish laws on slavery limited bondage to certain circumstances and permitted abused slaves to be released from especially cruel masters, eighteenth-century enslaved litigants used emergent ideas about self-preservation to widen the circle of violations that masters could commit.[72] In one case, a slave even implied that her mistress's harsh words amounted to sevicia.[73]

Often, slave claims came in response to the question of where they would reside and work during the course of a suit. María Teresa del Castillo of Mexico City, for one, asked to be bonded and placed in the power of a guarantor when she sued her owner, whom she feared would incarcerate her in a penal workhouse, "since by natural derecho, this is a just fear."[74] Nicolás González de Noriega, a freed slave who had been sued for having failed to undertake the work of grinding sugar cane in exchange for a loan he used to purchase his freedom, requested that he be allowed to leave the city of Trujillo for a hacienda in the Chicama Valley. He invoked "derecho natural" as the basis for his request, "since otherwise I would stay here and perish."[75] Slave petitions to avoid being returned to their masters and instead be permitted to find someone who could guarantee their wages during the course of lawsuits frequently, almost perfunctorily, referred to natural rights. One lawyer for a slave went so far as to question the very authority of owners to place a slave in a panadería, calling it "offensive to nature law [*sic*]."[76]

Even beyond invoking the natural right to self-preservation from brutal incarceration in prisons, bakeries, and workhouses, slave suits stretched the concept to encompass a range of other rights over slaves' own bodies. Vicenta Conde y Marín objected to what she viewed to be the exorbitant price at which her new owner was attempting to sell her in 1791, and so she went to the intendant. Her opening petition pronounced that "the just price of my person (*mi individuo*) is three hundred pesos and, for the conservation of it, I should find a master of my liking, which conforms to derecho."[77] The "conservation" of her "person" was founded on not just any law. It was founded on natural law. The petition went on to explain what was meant by "de derecho." "Although it is true that the servant is reputed to be an inanimate person in terms of the [ability] of a lord to sell him without his knowledge, it is also true that when sales papers are issued, a new contract in favor of the servant results," her petition reads.

Vicenta did not want freedom but a new owner, and she believed she possessed this right because her master had written a piece of paper requesting bidders for her the year before. The sales papers, as Bravo de Lagunas would have predicted in his first opinion, endowed the slave with rights beyond that of an "inanimate person." Vicenta's argument continues, "and thus the servant can find a new owner to serve without the master being able to revoke the first permission, and since my recent mistress, Doña Rafaela Morena, gave me a sales papers, I should be able to find someone to serve under whose dominion I believe I can conserve my person . . . by natural right."[78]

Slaves' articulations of natural rights spun out into two emergent spheres of law—natural rights and the "laws of nations"—which slavery straddled. According to many natural law theorists, slavery, as a fundamentally un-natural practice, was governed not by natural law but rather by the derecho de gentes, or the laws of nations devised by humans.[79] The defending attorney in a 1741 case made this very point in response to accusations of a master's abuse and rape of a slave woman. The slave's side had drawn from a veritable potpourri of sources of law, ranging from canon law on marriage to the presiding judge's prior rulings and on to "natural, divine and positive law."[80] Indeed, at one point the slave's counsel pronounced that slavery was only legally legitimate when it was the result of a judge's sentence, the selling of one's self, or just war—conditions of medieval slave practice that were set out in the *Siete Partidas*.[81] The attorney for the master tried to forestall all of these arguments by suggesting derecho de gentes could trump all other sources of law, including natural law. He stated, "still, being permitted and established by the *Derecho de Gentes*, it cannot be doubted that servitude is True and not, as they say, intolerable."[82]

Even with this, slave litigants and their representatives began to conceive of natural rights as more universal and inclusive than seventeenth-century jurists and philosophers had intended. In fact, many of the arguments on behalf of slaves in late eighteenth-century cases began to edge toward an indictment of all bondage, a trend that in Lima would continue for decades.[83] No longer were slaves pleading only for judicial compassion or equity, no longer were parties haggling only over whether the special legal circumstances that permitted the enslavement were present in an individual case. Instead, slaves brought suits convinced that unwritten, natural law, which applied to all humans, including slaves, existed and ultimately favored them.

Vicenta Conde y Marín, who wanted a new owner, clearly benefited from the elasticity of philosophies of "natural law" and "self-preservation" by stretching them into a right to find an owner of her choosing. Yes, as the petition she submitted conceded, she was an "inanimate person" by disposition of civil law. But natural law was another matter. Similarly, in the 1791 case over abuse and material neglect that Tadeo Moreno brought against owner Don Juan de Dubois, the "rules of humanity" were set up as barriers to the reach of a master's authority. "No one doubts the extent of *potestad domínica* (the authority of master)," a filing in the case reads, "but neither can it be doubted that whenever masters exceed the rules of humanity in their mistreatment" of slaves, they forfeit that authority "so that slaves may procure their alleviation by passing to the power of others who will care for them under those rules."[84]

The concept of unwritten rules of humanity indeed began to overwrite compiled and codified Spanish laws on master abuse. In 1791, Liberata de Jesús construed her grueling work assignment as an "inhumanity." Liberata had grown old as a slave, bearing no fewer than ten children over the course of her life on the Peruvian sugar hacienda Del Valle, which had been confiscated from the Jesuits in 1776. Yet still she was assigned the task of grinding sugar cane, fitting only for a "robust man" not an old woman. Her petition claimed that this work constituted sevicia, which in turn fell under the larger category of an "inhumanity." Her petition located the legitimacy of her legal demand to be sold away from the hacienda in the natural law of self-preservation: it was "lawful, being in her natural defense."[85]

The subordination of written law protecting slaves from abuse to broader unwritten laws of humanity was a radical legal maneuver, and even the lawyers who represented slaves hesitated to see it that way. It certainly made the pro bono lawyer later assigned to Liberata nervous. He tried to amend the implications of her petitions in his later filings, reversing the relationship of laws about sevicia and inhumanity. "The immoderate work that a servant is forced to suffer, disproportionate to her natural forces, is a type of inhumanity, and consequently sevicia."[86] The lawyer preferred to view written laws as the conduit for humane treatment rather than to cast unwritten laws of humanity as rules to which Spanish laws were subject.

Yet, even as he tried to soften the implications of the slave's initial petition, the lawyer conceded there existed unwritten laws of humanity that restricted a broad range of abuses against slaves. The procurator did not bother citing any specific texts for this claim and instead only vaguely waved toward commentators and glossators on Roman and Spanish law. He did introduce a stronger case that Liberata had suffered physical punishment than she had made in her initial petition, but the focus of the witness testimony in the case involved scrutinizing common labor practices on the hacienda, including the question of why so many slaves had to tend to their own plots of land to feed themselves and whether the Jesuits formerly had assigned women to cane grinding. At issue was not sevicia, strictly and legally defined, but what constituted "inhumanity" on a plantation in particular. Liberata was sold to a new owner.

There was, however, a limit to slaves' success in stretching sevicia to encompass all of the natural or human rights they wanted to assert in battles with their owners.[87] In several cases, owners had to remind judges that abuse had to be proved for slaves to assert the legal rights to be freed or find new owners. Juana Portocarrero had tried several times to persuade her mistress, Juliana, to allow her to seek a new owner.[88] Her opening petition against her master—this was the petition penned by her former lover, the mulato barber "knowledgeable in the law"—invoked a standard refrain suggesting abuse when it claimed she would be subjected to "mistreatment, nakedness and hunger." It was nonetheless pretty clear that Juana's concern was not mistreatment but her ability to find herself a new owner and obtain a fair price. Doña Juliana had offered to sell her for 500 pesos, but Juana countered that this exorbitant price amounted to "punishment."

Doña Juliana responded with incredulity that Juana was able to move the case forward: "In law," the petition reads, "the slave is held to be, in relation to the dominion of their owners, the same as furniture or other gems, and they are not permitted to procure their sale or a price estimate, if she [*sic*] is not alleging sevicia or mistreatment."[89] Thus, in order to know what, precisely, constituted abuse, the judge would have to decide whether slaves could operate as extrinsic evaluators of their own intrinsic value in a market governed by rules. Juana's argument vested the market, not her master, with the morality to set a fair price. Doña Juliana, in contrast, defined abuse in a much more narrow sense. She emphasized the value of her slave as an object with no more capacity to recognize its own worth than a chair or emerald could possess. The judge agreed with the owner.

Even if with varied success for slaves, accusations of sevicia had become so common and so expansively rendered in lawsuits against masters that they implicated complex economic and ethical questions about markets, values, and humanity. Indeed, the question of abuse was so ubiquitous that some slaves and lawyers noted its very absence in their cases. Josefa Piñeda, whose case opened this chapter, twice pointed out she was not suing over mistreatment but over her original master's intent to sell her. In fact, her case suggested that owners offered slaves testamentary or conditional liberty precisely in order to empower slaves to control their destinies without resorting to the courts. "The objective of rebates and conditions is miserable slaves' alleviation [in order] to facilitate [their ability] to leave the power of masters who tyrannize and mistreat them," one of her statements reads, "without need for a long case of sevicia."[90]

Proving Personhood

As would be expected, masters consistently attempted to block slaves' efforts to pry the doors of the courts open on the grounds that slaves had no legal personality but were merely property, as did the owner who likened Juana Portocarrero to "furniture."[91] Technically, in order to go to court, a subordinate like a slave or wife needed the permission of a superior. To get around this required some acrobatic legal maneuvers such as those Michaela Mina employed in 1741 when she sued her female owner's husband for sevicia. She attempted to make it seem as if she had obtained his wife's permission to appear in court against the man, beginning her petition with "I, Michaela Mina, slave of Doña Luisa Luxán, legitimate wife of Don Josef Pesantes, [having] first obtained the legal permission to appear in court necessary, I ask . . ."[92] Don Josef vehemently rejected both the proposition that Michaela belonged only to his wife and that she had received permission to sue.

Yet denying slaves' right to appear in court was not masters' only tactic. Slave owners often rejected slaves' accusations of abuse not with arguments about absolute rights as property owners but rather by explaining, in detail, their benevolence toward slaves. Such explanations were often as paternalistic as they were openly cynical. Don Pedro Escandón, for example, refuted his slave's charges of abuse by pointing out that he had always treated all of his slaves well, not only out of "Christian charity, but also in consideration of the fact that they are personal capital (*caudal*)," and cruel treatment would only "dissipate them."[93] If other owners shared Don Pedro's capitalistic sentiment, they did not often say so. Instead, owners defended themselves by expressing "love" for slaves, or masters employed language that likened slaves to their own children.[94]

Many owners also were unwitting participants, just as were slaves, in the creation of a notion of a kind of contractual legal personality of slaves. A slave might be a slave, but if the proper documentation could be provided, a slave might also be a litigant. For example, one owner complained that her slave had not undertaken the "presentation, in good form, of the many instruments that are necessary to make her capable of appearing in a suit."[95] One *asesor* complained that a slave was acting as though "papel," or a written offer to sell slaves at a certain price, "legitimated" her personhood in court, and complained that the woman was cluttering the courts with "irrelevant papers."[96] In this context, nitpicking about notarial protocol and accusations of forgery were common. In the case just mentioned, the defense made a great deal of hay of a notary's erroneous reversal of a standard phrase that appeared at the beginning of a will freeing the slave. The will, dictated by the dying master of a slave, began: "Being of sound body and sick spirit."[97]

Other owners began to draw attention to procedural failings in slave suits, pointing out, for example, that slave petitions lacked the signature of a legal agent or lawyer (an oversight that slaveholders themselves also almost uniformly made in their own petitions).[98] In turn, slaves often countered by making textual demands of their own against owners. A standoff occurred in Mexico during one 1761 case when a slave's legal counsel stipulated that the slave would submit to being placed on deposit when the owner provided written proof of dominion. The owner, for her part, responded that she would provide it when the slave was put on deposit.[99] In Lima, María Tomasa Ayesta and her procurator worked out a similar paper trap for her presumed master. The procurator demanded the man show proof that he had purchased María Tomasa, since the mere fact that she worked for him did not alone prove his dominion over her. The slave then checked herself into a hospital, where masters were required to pay for their slaves' upkeep. This was a smart move. If the presumed owner financially supported her in the hospital, she was his slave; if he did not, she was not.[100] Therefore, the end result of much of the questioning of slaves' right to be in court was to drive both slave litigant and master deeper into notarial archives for documentation, creating a legal equality between the parties by subordinating the question of who they were to the contracts they had signed.

In no small part, the lack of clarity about slaves' legal personality was due to the civil contractual personality they acquired in practice, especially in and around cities, as commercial producers and consumers, selling their wares or working their own plots of land. In 1790 Francisco de la Torre saw himself as enough of a legal person, enough of a commercial individual, that he traveled 40 miles down the foothills of the Andes from Chancay to the ecclesiastical court of Lima to sue his master, a priest, over a debt. Franscisco had borrowed grass-feed from a third party to provision his masters' livestock—this was his primary task as his slave—and his master promised to compensate him. When the deadbeat priest did not pay up for over four years, Francisco came to the judge to collect his 14 pesos. The *provisor general* took care of the matter extrajudicially.[101]

In a more hotly contested case, Juana Baptista Laredo, who went to court in 1783 over the financial arrangements she had made to purchase herself from her mistress, invoked not a master's permission to appear in court but rather "the presumptive permission and grace that the law (*el derecho*) concedes me in this case."[102] The remainder of the preamble to her petition is worth considering closely since it succinctly summarizes how slaves were reinvigorating old laws to make new rights. While still claiming protected status, her petition shifted emphasis from judicial compassion to legal right: "I appear before the piety and mercy with which the law looks upon Slaves who strive for liberty, in virtue and force of the Royal Law of the *Recopiladas* of the Indies, whose words order that their cases be heard and that justice be provided them."[103]

After imbricating old notions of equity with reference to positive imperial law, Juana went on to ask for something that other slaves likewise requested: that her owner not be shown her petition and be prevented from responding.[104] The alcalde denied her request. Her second petition scathingly reacted to this perceived injustice: "I have, then, asked for freedom, so desired by natural law . . . for which I can do no more than provide the amount of my assessed price." Yet the judge had issued not one ruling favorable to her, "despite the case being delicately privileged and preferred in law." Her petition pronounced that a judge could do nothing more "horrible" than to "interpret these inviolable Laws without complying with them."[105] The reference here to new judicial norms of the application of laws and a disdain for interpretation could be no clearer.

When Juana's owner, Doña Manuela de la Sierra, finally responded to the suit, she met the level of the slave's outrage and raised it. The idea that all slave suits were privileged in law was a "crude error" in jurisprudence. There existed no law "divine, natural or positive" that stated that every slave case be admitted, and there was no example in any court of a slave suit proceeding without a master being notified. Doña Manuela's argument then veered into casuism, claiming that even if other slave cases were being admitted to court, "above all, what our Sovereign commissions in his Laws of Castile is that cases not be judged by precedent, since one instance is different from another."[106]

Juana Baptista's case against Doña Manuela, then, follows several of the legal turns that other slaves were taking in their suits against masters during the closing decades of the century. Her opening petition figures her as standing before "the piety and mercy" not of the judge but of the law, which gave her all the permission she needed. Although she pursued a more traditional vein in requesting summary execution of the case and taking refuge in her protected status, her right to challenge her owner over the terms of a financial deal for her freedom was a "natural right" buttressed by "Royal law" for the colonies. These laws were "inviolable," and judges were bound not to interpret as much as follow them. In reaction, Doña Manuela, for her part, sought shelter in older approaches to law that emphasized the value of judging each case on its merits. Precedent was dangerous for the defense in a slave case. Only casuism, with its disregard for rulings being made in similar cases, could protect mastery from being eroded by the deluge of slave lawsuits admitted to the courts of the colonies.

The Freedom that the Lawsuit Demands

Slaves' civil suits began to wear some masters down. Obviously, the case record will not capture the instances in which the threat to sue preemptively led to a resolution outside court favorable to slaves, but some of the longer suits show how litigation took a toll on some masters. Doña Inés de la Barrera argued that her sole purpose in defending herself in the suit her slave had leveled against her had become, in the end, nothing more than "to avoid lawsuits and . . . to get out of this litigation."[107] In another case, when Clara Gutiérrez was captured and imprisoned after she fled from Piura to Lima in hopes of getting the high court to accept her case for freedom against her owner, which by all appearances she was close to losing in the first instance, her owner herself petitioned for the slave's release. The lawyer for Doña Marcelina Gutiérrez encouraged the magistrates to quickly name a pro bono attorney for Clara and to get on with sentencing, "in order to avoid those tedious circles which can be expected in which the suits are transferred to and back from Piura after the sentence [has already been rendered]."[108]

Like their owners, many slaves hoped that cases would wrap up quickly, especially if freedom was the end goal. But when the slaves' primary goal was to change owners, as would be the expected result from most sevicia cases, it was certainly in the slave's interest to drag the case out, particularly if they had managed to get placed with a guarantor of their own choosing. In fact, it is in these suits, as well as conditional liberty suits, that slaves most clearly crafted a version of freedom as a staged process that stood in diametric opposition to Bravo de Lagunas's stark and reactionary proclamation that "all men are either free or not free."

Generally, the daily wages of slaves who filed cases against their masters were bonded so that owners would be certain to receive compensation for the loss of slave labor during the course of the suit, particularly if the case was judged to have no merit. The requirement for slaves to bond themselves and to be personally secured either with a person or in an institution was primarily understood to be derived from local or colonial practice, though there were laws in the *Partidas* that suggested such bonding for servants who were in court for other matters.[109]

Debates over arrangements at this interim stage therefore consumed a significant portion of slave suits. Slaves often had to find someone to bond them and,
if they could not, they would be sent back to the owner, imprisoned, or placed
in workhouses that would pay their masters a wage. For obvious reasons, most
slaves preferred a personal guarantor. But they had to be given a period of time
to find one. During that period, they were, in effect, free to move about the city
and perform tasks related to their legal defense.

Predictably, slaves petitioned over and over for more time to find financers
and custodians. In doing so, they created the status of being "in litigation" as a
unique legal state. Juana Baptista, who initiated a long suit with her mistress over
her freedom, pointed out in one petition that she was neither "a fugitive nor a
vagrant" but rather engaged in a suit.[110] The status of being "in litigation" was
also crucial to the unfortunate city slave Andrés Saturnio Matallana, who was
scheduled, according to his dead owner's will, to be freed twelve years hence.
After serving loyally for seven years, his master's heirs threatened "to bury me
in a hacienda," meaning sell him off to experience the harsh working conditions
of plantation life. Andrés was able to find someone to bond him, but the executors of his master's estate wanted to send him to the hacienda despite the suit,
"not wanting to leave me to carry out my defense, which [I am due] by right and
legal foundations."[111] Andrés's petition contrasted not slavery and freedom but
slavery and the freedom to carry out one's legal defense.

The slave Antonina Guillén argued that only she, not a legal agent, would take
the care necessary to mount such a defense. The husband of Antonina's female
owner, accused of seducing her, bitterly complained that she was permitted to
bring the suit against him at all. "Let us inquire, what is her right to appear in
court. [There is] none, since she has no legal personality," he ventured.[112] He
managed somehow to convince the alcalde not to share his response to the suit
with the slave. Antonina, in turn, appealed to Lima's audiencia, claiming that
the alcalde was preventing her from "undertaking diligences in her defense" and
"burying [her chance at] justice."[113] When her owner moved to place her in a
bakery workhouse, she feared this would further prejudice her suit since "it is
necessary to move the case forward with great care, observing the necessary filings, and as such it is better that the defense is not handled but by skillful hands,"
namely her own.[114] Her owner responded that this is what lawyers were for, but
this argument did not seem to have much impact.

This line of argumentation about slaves' need for freedom to pursue freedom
became quite common. The petition of another slave, María Antonia Hipólita,
who likewise sought for the opportunity to stay in Lima to perform the "diligences" related to her suit, captured this version of freedome with a phrase.
The petition María Antonina submitted invoked the "freedom that the lawsuit
demands."[115]

Of course, owners resented the fact that their slaves could file lawsuits and live in this period of "freedom that the lawsuit demands." As the cases wore on they complained of how the lawsuits were "leaving the slave to live without a master."[116] The always colorful commentary on behalf of slave owner Doña Juliana Portocarrero warned of the "lamentable result and common damage that would rain down on the Public if slaves, imitating [her slave] could call themselves free simply by putting in a lawsuit and taking off so that, with the course of the suit obstructed, the resolution will be eternal, yielding them the luxury of living however they become accustomed."[117]

Statements such as this show not only that a period of "freedom that the lawsuit demands" existed in legal practice but also what owners thought the implications of that freedom—or any freedom—would be. Consistently, owners worried over the threat to public order and safety that ostensibly would result from a city full of litigating slaves. A hacienda owner in Mexico even labeled the testimony on behalf of his litigious slave "rebellion-like."[118] Superficially, these accusations make sense. Fears of racial disorder and slave rebellion, particularly in the context of international news about various Atlantic revolutions, including in Saint Domingue, undoubtedly kept more than one Spanish American slave owner up at night.[119] But the concerns masters expressed when their slaves took them to court contained other, more subtle, yet in many ways more profound commentaries on the nature of human freedom.

What many slave owners meant when accusing slaves of living lives full of freedom during interim periods or transitional stages was that liberty was an opportunity to do wrong. Arguments in slave owners' defense played endlessly on the linguistic proximity between the terms *"libertad,"* freedom, and *"libertinaje,"* or licentiousness, as well as *"liviandad,"* or frivolity.[120] Such wordplay was quite serious. It engaged with larger absolutist concerns about political liberties in the age of popular revolution, and it expressed a more general ethical debate about freedom within Enlightenment thought.[121] So much was clear in one reactionary Spanish publication, which appeared in 1796, aimed at colonial inhabitants flirting with independence from Spanish rule. It proclaimed that the liberty of the "philosophers" (generally meant to be French) was really "slavery in disguise" and that "libertines believe themselves liberated."[122]

Among masters, the very utterance "libertad" connoted debauchery and limitlessness. One owner, puzzled by how her male slave had managed to level a suit against her and her husband over their supposed intent to sell him, finally put the timing and actions of the slave together in a statement: "The *negro* filed this suit in December of [1]777, the same year he had passed into *libertinaje,"* which in this case alluded to flight or living as a free person in the city.[123] Earlier in the century, Diego de la Cruz's owner complained that the slave, who had traveled Mexico City to sue him, was "directed toward liberty in order to have more liberties."[124]

Slaves apparently need not be beyond masters' supervision to take the liberty to have more liberties. Slaveholders defended themselves against accusations of abuse by portraying themselves as benevolent owners, as did one owner who reacted to his slave's move to find a new owner, "I have given my slave a Christian owner and dressed her in noble garments."[125] Some owners explained that it was precisely this, their magnanimity and permissiveness, that had let slaves loose from subjection. It was they who had given slaves the "liberty to have more liberties," and the result was a lawsuit.

Doña Ventura Alzamora recounted in court how she had taken pity on her slave, Francisco, who "convinced her" to remove him from a bakery workhouse by telling her he would "punctually give me daily wages." It was because of this that "I left him free to work wherever he wanted."[126] Doña Ventura thus herself offered up a notion of freedom within slavery. She recounted the details of this freedom: giving Francisco money to go out with his wife and celebrate the day of San Francisco (the slave's namesake), even providing him a cape and Castilian hat—sartorial signs of free status. It was precisely because she "left him free," she suggested, and not that she had him reincarcerated in the workhouse, that he believed he could sue her to change owners.

Likewise, Don Juan de Dubois believed that it was because he had so "spoiled" his slave, Tadeo—buying his enslaved wife so that she "could be at his side," permitting him to turn his nose up at silk clothes, and even providing for the rearing of Tadeo's illegitimate child—that Tadeo sued him. Indeed, he said, Tadeo and his wife, "in their bearing were no different than free people." [127]

Don Juan, like many other masters, tried to deflect attention away from the stages of freedom unfolding in this case, stalling the drive toward liberty in Tadeo's suit by calling attention to the interdependence of his slaves' status and his own behavior as a master. He stated that "as a good Christian and honorable citizen (*vecino*), I have tried to keep my slaves in subordination so that they attend to their obligations, and do not commit offenses in public."[128] Don Juan's emphasis, as with other slaveholders, was on his own authority and on the obligations rather than the rights of slaves. He implied that the more freedom he gave Tadeo and his wife the greater the slave's obligation to subordination. But this formula could easily be complicated by Spanish American masters' own participation in legal practices that defied the simple dichotomy between slave and free.

Stages of Freedom

Slaves' notion that they could inhabit a transitional stage, "getting closer to freedom" as they pursued their cases or paid off their prices, drew from a common legal experience. In particular, it drew from the practice of conditional liberty, which frequently established a temporal limit to bondage. Most often that limit was the lifetime of an owner. Sometimes it was the age of the slave. Occasionally it was another condition, such as it was with Teresa Trillo, who was to serve her dead owner's husband only as long as he did not remarry.[129] Such practices encapsulated a highly temporal notion of freedom as a transition or process not altogether different from the arguments about freedom being a "moment" that Bravo de Lagunas derided in his mid-century opinion on conditional liberty.

The idea that slaves would eventually reach freedom embedded itself in local legal culture. One price assessor in Mexico City—who undoubtedly was in collusion with an old slave woman who was seeking change owners, or, even better, to be freed—argued that time alone could liberate slaves. He evaluated María Teresa del Castillo, finding her to be over the age of 50 and "spent" (*hecha*). But then, in an unorthodox move for a price evaluator, he added his own legal opinion on the matter: "I cannot help but to say in this evaluation that what is practiced in other cases of this nature, is that—whether by law, Ordinances or Custom—the slave who has served ten continuous years should be given freedom."[130]

Despite the price evaluator's claims that it was widespread practice, slaves did not commonly automatically "time out" of slavery in the Spanish empire. Perhaps his opinion had been influenced by a few coins that old woman scraped together to facilitate evaluation at a lower price. Yet those who saw slavery as a fixed status were fighting a losing battle. Colonial inhabitants often conceived of slavery and freedom in a way that would have maddened Bravo de Lagunas—as merely contrary, not contradictory. This was so because slavery was conceived of as a phase of life rather than an intrinsic state.

Practices of conditional liberty were in fact predicated on such a notion of maturation beyond bondage. Often, conditional liberty came not only at a moment in time but also a moment in the moral development of the slave. Frequently, owners held out freedom as the end point for a slave's life well lived, even as the conditions might keep slaves in a suspended state in which they were "becoming" free.

Again, this was obviously a benefit to owners because it ensured them loyal service and tied their slaves to them as the source of their liberty. But it also held out freedom as reachable through slaves' own efforts. Consider the conditions Doña María de Torres attached to the clause in her will that freed four-year-old María Gabriela, based on the "love and will" she possessed for the girl and her mother. She freed the girl:

> with the charge that she must be subject to said Pedro Morales, who
> should have the ability to subject her and put her in a convent if he finds

it fitting for the good of her soul, but in the case that she behaves with judgment and honor, he should leave her to live freely wherever she wishes, with said Don Pedro keeping her as a free person in his power for the time that he thinks is fitting, and this is my desire.[131]

Doña María's conditions thus gave María Gabriela a liberty tethered to both time and moral behavior. If this did not make the girl's status unclear enough, the owner ended up revoking this clause when the girl was ten years old, placing her under the power of her sister, Doña Petronila, "so that she corrects her and subjects her in the way she sees fitting, directing her toward and teaching her good customs, and placing in her the holy fear of God."[132]

After María Gabriela grew into young adulthood, Doña Petronila attempted to sell her. María Gabriela protested before the alcalde of Trujillo. Though the revocation of the original will did complicate her argument, María Gabriela nonetheless submitted her baptismal certificate to "show that she was beyond the age of needing teaching" and argued that the mere fact that her new owner would try to sell her, given her original mistress's wishes, constituted "intolerable sevicia." She counted on the court to focus on the parts of her master's will that made slavery tantamount to youth and that rendered freedom the end result of rearing or education. Slavery was something she would mature out of with proper instruction.

Perhaps slaveholders' own participation in creating the notion of freedom as a natural objective in the progression of humanity accounts for the handful of suits that they themselves initiated against their own slaves at the end of the century. These owners went to court preemptively to argue that the slaves they had purchased or inherited under certain conditions had failed to display the "orderly conduct" or to live the "honest and Christian" life required of them. Not coincidentally, the incorrigibility of these slaves became clear to owners only one or two years before slaves reached the age of freedom stipulated in prior owners' wills.[133] Yet such claims laid bare the promise of natural human progress underlying the practice of conditional liberty.

Take, for example, the story of the priest who gave two young mixed-race slave boys (*mulatillos*), one named Agustín, to Don Baltázar Laya y Lano, with the hope that the man would raise them well. The priest wanted Don Baltázar to free the slaves if they displayed "good customs" after they grew up. But Don Baltázar filed a petition claiming that Agustín had turned out to be a gambler, drinker, and runaway. With this, he actually put himself in a tight position, as his witnesses had to contort to explain that Agustín had turned out bad through no fault of his caretaker.[134] Doña Ventura Alzamora was also put in a bit of a bind when she called her slave Francisco "vice-ridden": she needed to portray him in a negative light so that the court would dismiss the charge of sevicia he had leveled against her, but if she pressed the point too hard, it would lower his price were she to be forced to sell.[135]

In the end, slaveholders continued to hold the reins in determining what constituted slaves' "good behavior" and arguing that their liberty bred only licentiousness and disorder. Yet the hundreds of cases Spanish American slaves brought in the eighteenth century challenged the certainty that masters' authority was necessary to contain human freedom and bridle libertine behavior. Occasionally, slaves even attempted to speed past the ethical implications of the legal drive for liberty. Jacinto Obregoso, who was accused of failing to live by the moral standards that his dead owner had required as a condition of his freedom, submitted a legal filing that wittily addressed the gap between secular law and moral order. He admitted that he had been "no saint," but his dead master "had not demanded that I be canonized before being freed."[136]

Unlike Jacinto, most enslaved litigants came into court with a more positive moral vision of freedom as the activation of the natural right of all humans, a natural goal of human action, and a stage that could be reached, as they put it, through yearning or aspiration.[137] One slaveholder explicitly linked such yearning for freedom to ethical evil, arguing "If the principal of liberty consisted only in the malice and the desire of slaves to be free, slavery would already be extinguished."[138] Yet slaves persisted, pushing beyond the limits placed on the aspiration for freedom when owners described it as disruptive to the tidy categorical order of bondage. Instead, they construed the legal action of becoming free as a privileged stage in a moral progression.

Bernabé Flores argued that he had faithfully served his master, who, when he sold the slave, set his price at 400 pesos and stipulated that he would be freed in five years. Bernabé protested being placed to work on a hacienda seven leagues from the city of Lima, implying his faithful service earned him not just freedom in the future but the right to be treated as different than another slave in the present. His current owner's undifferentiated treatment of all slaves threatened "the just right that assists his liberty."[139] Jacinto Obregoso, of Trujillo, argued that if only the alcalde would free him from prison so he could mount a defense against re-enslavement by his former master's sister, he could gather the witnesses to his good conduct and the documents to prove that he had "managed himself as a free person," as if his good conduct could be evidence of his state of liberty.[140] Josefa Piñeda argued that if a new owner sold a slave without heeding the conditions set by a previous owner it was unjust since "the slaves are left in the same place (*quedar en la casa*) as the rest of the slaves who have not attained such conditions." The conditions were not just desired but also attained. What is more, she said, she had used being in the stage of liberty, achieved by her payments toward her freedom, in a morally good manner: to sue for freedom. Thus she transformed the act of reaching for freedom itself into a moral good.[141]

In the end, Josefa, Manuel, and Bernabé each failed to reach freedom through their suits. But perhaps they were getting closer.

Eighteenth-century slave suits poignantly illuminate the central challenge motivating this book: whether it is possible to understand the Enlightenment not in reference to the properties scholars have already assigned to it but instead by examining the limits and language generated in the historical events of the moment, by studying the practices and occurrences that make it possible to regard a slave in Trujillo to be as much an inventor of the Enlightenment as a *philosophe* in a Parisian café. Can we escape, in other words, the imperial tautologies that masquerade as accepted ontologies of the Enlightenment?

To appreciate the response that enslaved litigants provide in this chapter, it is, perhaps ironically, useful to return to the thoughts of Kant and Foucault. They are not here to lend authority to the chapter's endeavor but because the Enlightenment that slaves produced in Spanish America was not some alternate version of the one they struggled to define—not a copy, not mimicry, not emulation. Rather, it was the very movement in practice. More specifically, it was an event that embodied the very ideas Western philosophers have puzzled over for centuries.

Kant's "What Is Enlightenment?" inaugurated years of intense reflections for the eighteenth-century philosopher on the connections between freedom, history, and human progress.[142] In his 1784 essay, he famously argued that enlightenment was an emergence, a transition from immaturity. Freedom was not as much a state as a stage or process. As Kant deepened his reflections, he came to believe that progress was inherent in history. This was in part an ethical consideration; Kant gently departed from other Enlightenment thinkers who, like Spanish American slave owners, were less than sanguine about what human freedom leads to and more heavily invested in law to contain human impulses.[143] But part of Kant's argument was historical. Progress is measured not by the success or failure of events—revolutions, acts of defiance, or individual self-realization—but rather by the " 'sympathy' with which 'the non-participating spectators' " view the events.[144] Even if historical actors are not "successful" in the moment, because the event is viewed as a broadly human event, after it occurs things can never be the same.[145]

After years of critical reflections on Kant, Foucault grappled with the same question the Prussian had two hundred years before. Foucault referred to the human potential to change things as a "will to freedom." He here attempted to create a space for agency, at least within the Enlightenment construct of history, by pointing to the "will to freedom" as a mechanism by which human subjectivity can "introduce itself into history and give it a breath of life."[146] In his answer to the question at hand, Foucault further drew on places where Kant suggested that the Enlightenment was not as much a progressive historical teleology as an endless, open process that was at once individual and collective. Freedom, like humanity, is, in Kant's words, not "a categorical end . . . but a condition that is always to be found further on." Freedom is not the endpoint of modern thought; the freedom to become free is.[147]

Enslaved people of African descent, one by one and together, brought such a process of becoming into the Spanish American courts. Slaves were the agents of freedom in the courts throughout eighteenth-century Spanish America and, as such, were progenitors of the Enlightenment.[148] This was so not simply because they activated, in a very tangible form, discourses of natural rights and laws of humanity written into the books lining the libraries of jurists and stacked on the desks of law students. It is because Spanish American slaves invented themselves in civil courts in ways that escaped strict dichotomies between slave and free.[149] The legal subjectivity they forged before the law was not modern in the sense that they always argued that they were free; and it was not agency in the sense that it necessarily acted on human history. It was modern in the sense that slaves posited, through their petitions and legal initiatives, that they were becoming free; and it was agency in the sense that they embedded this becoming in a larger human process of reaching for liberty.

In order for things to never be the same, slave litigants would have to convince others, the non-participating spectators of their struggles for freedom, that they were watching a broadly human story unfold.[150] Yet many masters refused to concede that their slaves were indeed agents their own legal histories. Masters' constant complaints that their slaves were the puppets of more powerful interests and sinister forces became evidence of how the Spanish colonial Enlightenment produced its own shadow.

Conclusion

Why Not Enlightenment?

To be sure, going to court against authority figures and sustaining formal cases was not something that most slaves, wives, or native commoners the Spanish empire did in the 1700s. If similar types of civil cases in every region of the Spanish American colonies were to be collected, their number would probably not crest above two or three thousand in a sea of lawsuits whose numbers reached into the hundreds of thousands. Yet the significance of the cases examined in this book nonetheless resides in the numbers. The kinds of civil suits that women, natives, and slaves brought against their social superiors grew faster than the remarkable overall increase in colonial litigation during the century. In some instances these lawsuits radically transformed the ordinary workings of the law. By the last two decades of the century, for example, slaves suing masters placed one out of every ten cases on the docket of the first-instance judges in Lima.

Despite their social, political, and legal subordination, although they neither penned nor often could read the petitions they submitted to court, colonial litigants and their legal writings were part of a broader eighteenth-century cultural and political movement. That is, these ordinary colonial lawsuits should be understood within the historical paradigm of the Enlightenment.[1] More specifically, these litigants generated, through their actions as much as through the arguments they brought into court, a turn toward a law-oriented culture, distinguishable from the justice-oriented culture of the early modern period.

Women who entered royal jurisdiction in marital disputes wrapped themselves in discourses about natural rights and formally sued their husbands outside of Church courts. In doing so, they began to shed a relational identity dating from the Middle Ages and don a legal subjectivity that was, for all intents and purposes, a gendered variation of the modern self, a self that sprang from political contracts rather than sacraments. Indigenous litigants lodged cases that advanced new versions of history, challenging the inherited privileges of nobility in favor of meritorious participation in their pueblo republics, as well as prompting debates about whether their customs belonged to a changeless past. Slaves too evoked new temporal notions as they increasingly brought suits against masters before royal magistrates, although rather than the struggles with the past laced into native lawsuits, their innovations came in imagining the future. Like the late seventeenth-century natural rights theorists who focused on the ability of the individual to aspire to perfection, and like the Enlightenment philosophers who placed human agency at the center of history unchained, these slaves pushed the courts to recognize conditions and stages that defied the simple dichotomy of slave and free.

So, if ordinary colonial Spanish Americans produced the Enlightenment, why has it been so invisible?

The answer resides in what Michel Rolph Trouillot calls, in the case of the Haitian Revolution, its "unthinkability."[2] This unthinkability is part historical and part historiographical, and it lies at the intersection of the occurrences in the past, the way these become "events" in their own time, and the way they become history in ours.[3] In our own times, Latin American history has been characterized in ways that seem to disqualify the region as "Enlightened" or fully modern. In the times of the litigants, powerful colonial defendants responded to lawsuits by erasing them as authentic events. The two—our own ideas about who can produce Enlightenment thought and the eighteenth-century negation of ordinary, non-revolutionary litigants as independent actors—are intimately connected in ways we have yet to fully appreciate.

An ordinary legal Enlightenment is unthinkable in part because the broader Spanish American Enlightenment is, if not unthinkable, then at least hard to categorize chronologically. The expectation that the region would burst into revolutionary flames upon thinking Enlightened thoughts harbors within it a fallacy: if the Enlightenment was what caused revolution against monarchy, what did not cause revolution was not genuinely Enlightenment. Indeed, for an array of scholars, anti-monarchical revolution remains the epitome of Enlightenment in action.[4]

Of course, there were rebellions in late colonial Spanish America, some inflected by the emerging new culture of law.[5] Late colonial uprisings such as the Túpac Amaru rebellion, along with news of revolutions abroad, surely churned up defendants' fears of subversion in Peru and Mexico, especially in the last decade of the century.[6] Still, placing Enlightened litigation within the larger context of, say, an Atlantic Enlightenment does not mean that it should simply be used as the bellwether of an approaching Age of Revolution. The relative passivity of Mexico City, Oaxaca, Lima, and Trujillo—the colonial regions studied in this book—makes them ideal for understanding popular legal action outside of revolutionary models. If Enlightenment ideas later led the charge during the Spanish American wars for independence, they were flanked by strong intervening events, not least of which was the destabilization of the monarchy after Napoleon invaded Spain.

The kind of Enlightenment that litigants produced in the courts of the Spanish empire did not, in fact, grow in opposition to monarchy but rather was cultivated inside its institutions. Indeed, law-oriented legal practices could draw ordinary subject and king closer together than ever.[7] "Enlightened absolutism" might seem to be the perfect phrase to capture this phenomenon. Yet the top-down quality of the concept fails to capture the dynamic nature of legal change in the Spanish empire.[8] Law-oriented cases often preceded—even prompted— royal policy supporting them. Metropolitan measures to centralize and ration-alize legal practice were as much a product as the cause of colonial litigation that attached natural rights, merit, and freedom to secular law. Each maneuver by subject and sovereign cumulatively curtailed the authority of the political inter-mediaries that stood between them, including caciques, masters, and husbands. The view from the Spanish colonies, therefore, reveals that ordinary people found it surprisingly easy to invoke rights without revolutions, freedom without emancipation, and custom without tradition.

The Spanish imperial Enlightenment's awkward fit into existing historical par-adigms calls into question stories in which Enlightenments—radical, counter, moderate, absolute—vie until the strongest emerges in its purest form, liberal democracy. The region's continued attachment to colonial rule in the eighteenth century demands a different narrative about the rise of new forms of political culture in general and legal culture in particular, one that must account for the fact that Enlightened law-oriented culture did not immediately become domi-nant or drive out other ways of thinking about the law in Spanish colonial courts. To insist that this made it no less Enlightenment is to insist on the uneven nature of most historical change, even change that has as one of its primary features the call to break with the past.[9] Put differently, it is to write a more complete history of the incomplete nature of modernity, not just in Latin America but everywhere.[10]

Because of the obvious problem of properly defining modernity (even when it is considered as distinct from modernization or modernism), historians' concep-tualizations of it, like their definitions of Enlightenment, have become "infinitely elastic."[11] Even if we accept that the Enlightenment inaugurated the "modern" in terms of concepts of rights, self, freedom, and history, it was not the totalizing ex-perience that it was once made out to be.[12] As legal historian Knud Haakonssen explains, most of the elements associated with the "Enlightenment," including individualism and subjective rights, were only modestly advanced among most Enlightenment thinkers and more tethered to seventeenth-century concepts than we have recognized. This observation aligns with the argument here that jusrationalist natural rights theories certainly "count" as Enlightenment, and they count even more when litigants and lawyers harnessed them to new conflicts aired in the eighteenth-century civil court cases of the Spanish colonies.[13]

That law-oriented culture did not erase older versions of justice is a reminder that the Enlightenment's universalizing pretensions were just that: pretensions. The king might sign a royal edict to harmonize law school education across all imperial universities, make all native officials speak Spanish, or standardize sentencing procedures. Yet at the same time he would send out a cédula encouraging local judges to rule extrajudicially or demand that audiencias investigate the customs of a native community before deciding on a contested local election. Even in a 1790 lawsuit disparaging the obsolescence of medieval Church law and invoking the power of contemporary precedent in Mexico City, a woman's lawyer made a flowery closing argument strewn with references to obscure canonists and Bible stories.[14] There is ample evidence of the persistence of justice-oriented legal practices among all legal practitioners. Lawyers still argued in the casuistic fashion and relied heavily on Roman law; renters still appealed to medieval laws that permitted judges to rule individually and equitably; and, crucially, many, perhaps most, women, natives, and slaves who submitted petitions to the courts did so to force an extralegal outcome rather than a formal sentence. Satisfied with the socially embedded, flexible, and pluralistic nature of legal practice characteristic of the early modern period, these historical actors kept alive a legal culture where the "law" was merely one among many paths to justice.

Thus another factor in the unthinkability of the Spanish colonial legal Enlightenment is its coexistence with older justice-oriented ideologies, which seems to render the ordinary legal Enlightenment somehow partial or "hybrid."[15] In fact, the argument that Latin America as a region possesses a kind of world-historical hybridity has long undergirded cultural studies approaches to the region.[16] One of the canonical figures in Latin American postmodernism, Néstor García Canclini, began his 1989 *Hybrid Cultures* with the observation that Latin America was a space in which "traditions have not yet disappeared and modernity has not yet completely arrived."[17]

García Canclini's work perhaps has been surpassed by ever-deepening reflection on Latin America's "condition," but the quotation is worth pondering because it concisely captures how thinking about the place of Latin America inevitably involves thinking about time in Latin America.[18] In part, the hybrid condition means that Western modernity creates Latin American tradition. But there is more.[19] Modernity is forever "not yet" in Latin America. Mark Thurner has written precisely about this "not yet" in Peru's history, showing that although it seems to refer to the future, in fact "not yet," as a fundamental feature of modern historicist thought, and actually refers to a present condition. Peru's historians, Thurner shows, produced a "not yet" both within and in defiance of the chronological confines of the rise of the West paradigm.[20] This holds out promise for writing histories—however historicist they must be to resonate with modern understandings of the past—that do not simply nourish Eurocentrism.[21]

Just as García Canclini's quotation raises the question of time, it also raises the question of place, particularly the place of ideas. It summons a version of modern ideas as foreign imports that must "arrive" from elsewhere. But while top-down intellectual and policy changes related to law in the colonies were part of larger imperial and Western trends, there is no evidence that the lawsuits or the arguments in them had European origins as such. Heineccius's eclectic text-book, *Elements of Natural Law*, may have been assigned to all law students in the Spanish empire, but the key practices and ideas associated with law-oriented cul-ture seem to have originated (and I use this word with caution) in the colonies, from the everyday "entanglements and discords" between non-literate litigants and the men and masters who ruled them.

The appearance of these Enlightenment legal practices becomes even more striking when compared to a relative absence of law-oriented practices in penin-sular Spain. This observation is borne out by the contrast between the civil liti-gation boom in colonial Spanish America and the stable number of suits heard in Spain. And it is supported by the contrast between the social standing of parties in disputes between Trujillo, Peru, where subordinates increasingly sued superi-ors, and the Montes de Toledo, Spain, where litigation mostly remained between social equals or was brought by more socially powerful litigants against weaker defendants.

This is not to say that there was no change in lawsuits or legal culture in Spain during the century. To take just one example, the chapter on marital dis-putes turned up an important intensification of appeals to the Chancellería of Valladolid to use the recurso de fuerza to shove marital disputes back onto re-luctant Church judges during the latter part of the century. But this shift was different from the changes women in the cities of Spanish America produced when they forced secular courts to become the supreme arbitrators of alimony and court-cost cases, even deciding in some instances to bypass the Church courts entirely. Nonetheless, the peninsula was often quick to follow the col-onies' lead. Perhaps there is no better example of the reversal of assumptions about the direction of Enlightenment influence than this: In 1804 peninsular judges were instructed to follow the 1787 cédula on royal jurisdiction over al-imony and court fees, which had been prompted by the legal maneuvers of di-vorce-seeking Peruvian women and originally applicable only to the Indies.[22] The intention behind extending it to Spain was to create more homogeneous, universal legal practice in the empire.

Aside from inverting assumptions about the Western flow of ideas, the al-imony ruling also illustrates that law-oriented practices were not executed in some grand synchronicity. Trujillo lagged around a decade or so behind Mexico

City, Oaxaca, and Lima in its civil litigation "boom." Women in rural regions did not embrace law-oriented culture with the same zeal as their urban counterparts. But the presence or absence of a legal practice in any particular region of the empire at any particular time should not have any particular valence attached to it. The observation about the endurance of justice-centered culture in Spain or rural regions of the colonies is simply that—an observation, not a moral judgment about the inherent justice of any particular form of law.[23] In fact, the rise new state-centered, rights-oriented law did not necessarily translate into greater egalitarianism or fairness for many inhabitants of the hemisphere.[24]

Absence, then, is not the same as a historical shortcoming. And presence is not the same as historical value.[25] Still, writing about the relative absence of Enlightenment legal culture in peninsular Spain risks smudging a bit of Black Legend ink on this book's pages, repackaging longstanding claims about Spanish "backwardness" in general and its "deficiency" in Enlightenment in particular. Indeed, even as some historians demonstrate the surprising global dynamism of the Iberian American colonies—chronicling their contributions to religious tolerance, modern historical epistemology, the development of state bureaucracies, and political liberalism, to name just a few examples—other scholars still seem a bit stumped by the question of how Spanish Americans got their ideas since they could not have possibly come from Spain.[26] Israel, for example, solves the problem by reporting that the radical Enlightenment was transported back to America by a creole elite that increasingly took tours to France and England following their university education.[27]

This is a deeply ingrained intellectual habit that takes the Enlightenment as a history of ideas originating in Europe among a small group of individuals and then physically spread, usually through print but also by Atlantic travelers to and from Europe.[28] Ideas come to Latin Americans like finished goods manufactured in the Old World. They are instruments already forged, perhaps to be bent into useful tools for revolution, but nonetheless foreign imports. They are so many souvenirs to be packed into creoles' suitcases at the end of their Northern European vacations and smuggled through Spanish customs back into the Americas.

The notion that certain ideas—usually the most abstract and universal—have a point of origin beyond Latin America is, of course, not unique to studies of the eighteenth century. Consider the 1973 meditation of Brazilian literary critic Roberto Schwarz, "*As ideas fora do lugar*," or "ideas out of place," which was widely understood as a commentary on how imported models, methods, and modes of thoughts—Marxism, liberalism, fascism—were "alien to a Brazilian reality."[29] These abstract models were only imitations or copies when implanted on Latin American soil, transplants "inauthentic" to the region. This is an example of what one Argentine historian called the frantic search at the heart of national histories of Latin America "for an absolute autochthonous originality among [the region's] thinkers."[30]

The search for the origin of ideas thus ends up as a demand that subaltern or colonized groups display a kind of originality that would never be asked of powerful elites from beyond. This constitutes the final explanation for the unthinkability of the ordinary Spanish colonial Enlightenment in the civil courts. The relationship between origins and originality in the history of ideas circles back to the eighteenth century, in defiance of theorists like Foucault who hustle past the Enlightenment as a historical event.[31] With time to linger a bit over what happened, we can connect it to our own philosophical preoccupations with Latin American authenticity and originality in more meaningful ways. In the end, the problem of what qualifies as Enlightenment is a legacy not only of recent critical assessments of the violence of Western epistemology but also of the very dialectic involved in the formulation of Enlightenment ideas in eighteenth-century Spanish America itself.

However much Spanish American litigants' legal practices and arguments coincided with the broader phenomenon of the Enlightenment in the Atlantic World, they did not launch their suits into a stratosphere of "the history of ideas"; they lodged them in a real time and place against other people. Those they sued responded with ideas of their own. But there was often not a clean divide between Enlightened litigant and traditional defendant. It was not unusual for defendants to also employ the language or concepts of Enlightenment and turn them to their own defense, as well as participate in the jurisdictional strategies and efforts to standardize law that marked the new legal culture.

Indeed, this tendency to use modern concepts and practices to shore up opposition to the Enlightenment is the very essence of counter-Enlightenment. Historian Darrin McMahon argues that the historical actors in France who first and most lastingly defined what counted as "Enlightenment" were its critics, who called themselves the "*anti-philosophes.*" But, in an important twist, when assuming their stance against the "new philosophy," they often positioned themselves as the true moderns and denigrated their opponents as retrograde.[32]

One bookstore in Madrid seemed to specialize in printed tracts of counter-Enlightenment. The shop sat in the Puerta del Sol plaza behind the old Habsburg palace. This commercial center still thrived at the end of the century even though Carlos III had earlier moved royal operations west, to the Palacio Real, a hulking, neoclassical monument to Spanish absolutism. The bookstore had a new publication to sell in the fall of 1800, a recent translation of a short Italian tract entitled *Discourse on the True Natural and Civil Freedom of Man.* The prologue to this tract serves as an apt guide to the modern elements of Spanish imperial counter-Enlightenment thought.

The Spanish translator, Ventura Salzas, poured the keywords of the period into his prologue to the pamphlet. He argued that those who embraced "freedom without limits" "twisted" and "subverted" reason, tyrannizing and dazzling youth with too much light. He defended the pamphlet's focus on secular philosophy, arguing that it was necessary to "go down the same road . . . in the same terms and [using the same] expressions" as the radical philosophes. Beyond co-opting Enlightenment terminology, Salzas adopted a broader Old Regime critique of the aristocracy, turning it to monarchical ends. Those who were "unequal in power" would always be subjected to some form of authority, he claimed. Removing such people from the authority of the monarch would only leave them open to predations of the rich and powerful, who were less restrained by law than the king. The authority of monarchy was the political authority most "mediated by just laws" and was the "weight that balances everything" on the scales of justice.[33]

The same repurposing of familiar Enlightenment concepts to counter-Enlightenment legal purposes, particularly those serving traditional hierarchies, had a popular counterpart in the handwritten legal arguments that masters, caciques, and husbands advanced in their own defense. Like Salzas, eighteenth-century defendants in Spanish America at times tried to attach freedom to their side of legal battles. Consistently, defendants had to fight against litigants' requests to exercise what one slave litigant called the "freedom that the suits demand," or the right to be released from deposit or oversight so they could pursue their cases, often in the capital cities. Masters responded a lot like Salzas did in his prologue to the counter-Enlightenment treatise on freedom. They claimed that the slaves who sued them were not exercising liberty but were libertines and that their release from authority left them vulnerable to unscrupulous predators. Husbands did the same. This was true even in the case of the intrepid and obviously independent Doña María García, the Mexico City litigant who argued for her right to name her own counsel and who almost doomed her lawsuit by taking so much control over it. Her husband's lawyer argued that, if left to conduct her own legal business in the city without restraint, she was likely to fall under the spell of the first man she encountered.[34]

Husbands, native leaders, and slave owners did not win every case by warning of the dangers of subordinates let loose before the law. But, in a larger sense, they were able to mitigate the broader challenge that law-centered culture posed to their authority. They did this by subjecting their less powerful legal opponents to a skepticism that is similar to our impulse to view the Enlightenment as originating elsewhere, to be the property only of the powerful and the literate. Much like we do, defendants had trouble imagining unlettered litigants as the originators of the legal ideas and strategies that animated their lawsuits. Instead, they pointed the finger at more powerful patrons, whom they labeled "directors," diminishing litigants' protagonism in their own legal actions.

Defendants began to anticipate charges of "tyranny" by accusing the directors of of taking advantage of their own power over the litigants. These preemptive moves permitted defendants to articulate an Enlightened repugnance for "inhumanity" and "tyranny" even as they themselves faced charges of abuse. Take the argument a Mexico City lawyer put forward on behalf of a husband embroiled in a jurisdictional clash between Church and state ensuing from his wife's decision to file for divorce. Knowing the wife would accuse his client of mistreatment, the lawyer complained that the wife operated under the "bad influence" of her mother, who herself was guilty of "inhumanities." His repeated insistence that his client's mother-in-law was directing the case overlooked the fact that the wife herself wrote her own early petitions in the form of letters to the judge.[35]

Native defendants tapped into longstanding portrayals of commoners as too gullible to go to court alone, as accusations of "despotism" and "tyranny" flew back and forth between parties in Indian lawsuits.[36] The notion that ordinary Indians were victims of unscrupulous master manipulators was as old as colonialism itself. But as elite Indian defendants increasingly fended off lawsuits from commoners in their pueblos, they retreated ever deeper into a vision of native communities as naturally, peacefully suspended above time. Their conviction that commoners' lawsuits could only be the result of behind-the-scenes manipulation almost always carried the connotation that the suits came from "outside" the community, that litigation was somehow not "Indian."

Female litigants too were vulnerable to charges that educated male directors manipulated them, charges that often effaced not only women's legal agency but also their sexual honor. "A vile mulata prostitute reclining in an irrational right" is what the lawyer of one Lima master called the slave woman who sued him, adding to this the even more galling fact that her unnamed legal benefactor was "little versed in the Laws and their practice."[37] In a 1782 civil complaint related to the divorce of Mexico City resident Don Joseph, the defendant submitted a petition arguing that his wife's lawsuit against him was being driven by a sinister "director." He went further, claiming that she was having a sexual affair with this legal Svengali.[38]

In this case, the "director" was named: he was a procurator that the wife had hired. In others, suspicious anonymous directors too were court personnel or professional writers-for-hire. They also could be literate subjects to whom—if the defendants' charges were at all founded—litigants had some extralegal tie, such as priests, parents, or former slave owners. Other times the relationship was all business. Recall that the case of the African Agustín Carabeli—who spoke no Spanish yet found a fellow drinker to pen an opening petition in his suit for freedom—resulted in a concrete investigation into who, exactly, was doing his legal writing. Most of the time, however, defendants remained vague about whom they suspected of directing their opponents' suits. When slave owner Doña Marcelina Gutiérrez asked the judge of the high court of Lima to "cut at the root the entanglements that are machinating on behalf of the protectors of this slave," this was a request more dramatic than detailed.[39]

There was a reason for this elusiveness. Most defendants could no more easily claim to be the owners of their legal arguments than could subordinate litigants. Surely many defendants had friends in high places that they called upon for support. And very few defendants did their own writing, with the majority using their own unnamed legal agents for at least some of their defense. All parties' right to use such writers-for-hire was a policy endorsed by the Bourbon king Carlos IV himself in 1795. That ruling contained a more generic version of a slave's invocation of the "freedom that the lawsuit demands," referring more generally to the "liberty that that those of my Kingdoms enjoy" to use any legal writer of their choosing when entering civil courts.

Keeping this in mind, one defendant's signature deserves another look. This was a petition submitted in the middle of a case by slave master Don Antonio Arburúa, from Lima. He had taken control of his own defense and had a legal agent write up an interim petition, to which Don Antonio himself affixed his officially appointed procurator's name with the words "for my procurator" (*por mi procurador.*) Even though he never had to discuss the identity of his own rogue legal writers or the reasons for bypassing his court-appointed procurator, and even though he surely never penned a single petition himself, Don Antonio successfully pressed to find out who was writing the petitions that Andrea Arburúa submitted against him for cruelty to his slave. When interrogated by the court scribe, Andrea admitted in spoken testimony that the husband of her former owner was writing the petitions, but she adamantly claimed that this was simply because she did not know how write and could not afford a professional, insisting that she was in charge of the complaint and that the filing was hers alone.[40]

Andrea suggested that her inability to write did not make her legally illiterate.[41] It was true that she needed access to the more educated, literate men of the Lettered City to pursue formal suits, which surely accounts for the fact that women brought relatively few civil cases against their husbands in places like rural Oaxaca. But Don Antonio too apparently needed someone else to do the writing for him. His mastery of his legal papers and the arguments they contained was really not all that different from Andrea's claim to a non-literate command of her own suit.

Perhaps it was this similarity that kept most slave owners and other defendants so ambiguous about their claims of influence. Perhaps it was this that fed their fears that ideas could spread beyond writing and stoked their concern that

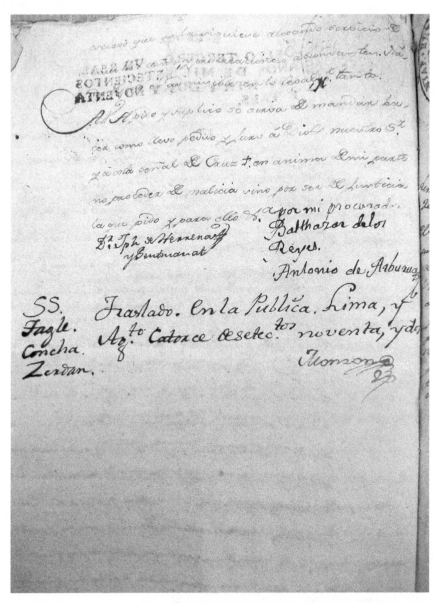

Figure C.1 This petition, first presented in Chapter 1, was not written by procurator Baltazar de los Reyes, but instead signed by the litigant on his own and his procurator's behalf. The color of the ink indicates that Dr. Joseph de Herrera y Sentaranat [?], whose signature appears on the upper left—perhaps the court receptor or the agent—provided the quill and ink that litigant Arburúa used to sign the document for his procurator and himself (top right), probably at the same time that the court officially accepted the petition during one of the Audiencia of Lima's open hearings (*traslado en la Pública*). The court notary, Miguel Monzón, officially signed the document in yet another hand, and placed the high court judges' last names in the left margin. From Autos seguidos por don Antonio Arburúa con su esclava, Andrea Escalante (*sic*; Arburúa), sobre la libertad de ésta (*sic*; su hija), AGN-P RA Civ., Leg. 203, C. 2616,1791, 19v.

eighteenth-century civil judges were "opening the door" not just to more law-suits but to new legal ideas generated by newly fashioned secular legal subjects.[42] One of the petitions that another slave master, Doña Marcelina, submitted to the court in her defense shared fears that slaves were poaching and passing around the idea that they were legal subjects with rights. The petition claimed that, if the high court of Lima accepted her slave's lawsuit against her, slaves would merely have to "forge the artifice of enchanted liberty in their ideas" and they could dash off to the courts to find out if they could be declared free, living free for months or years as they pursued their cases. If admitted to the court, the suit would serve as an example for countless others who would try to "imitate" it. As much as defendants might try to deny that the petitions of wives, slaves, and native commoners could be possible without the patronage of mysterious, behind-the scenes directors, Doña Marcelina's statement indicates that the object of worry was not just what was transpiring on paper but also what was happening in minds.[43] All that was left to do was to dismiss litigants' ideas of rights, freedom, and law as mere "artifice" rather than the real thing.[44]

Doña Marcelina's comments share much in common with those of many other defendants, including an indigenous noble from Piura who accused another native of stirring up legal trouble in his community by "taking the voice" of his community, meaning representing its commoners in court. It was easy, he said, for his opponent to sway Indians to sue since natives, "because of their rusticity," could not understand that they were being manipulated. But gullibility was not really the problem; it was the commoners' certainty in their own ideas. He claimed that "Indians have acquired a sizable sense of *joredominio* [*sic; jure dominio*]," a term suggesting a kind of ownership of the law, "and they go around sure in their ideas."[45]

A haughty but mistaken sense of a command over the law, the artifices and misplacement of ideas, the appearance of models and imitators, and the endless search for originals—in these respects the arguments that defendants raised in the civil courts of the Spanish colonies made a lasting impact. They certainly found their equivalents in the nineteenth century, when the anonymous writer of the *Complaints of the Americans* called colonial representatives in Cádiz plagiarists who misunderstood natural law. And they merge with our own historical habits in thinking about ideas in the broader Spanish empire. The argument that any Enlightenment knowledge that unlettered colonial litigants possessed was not their own, or wrong, or both, should serve as a warning about the kinds of standards to which subaltern historical actors are subjected.

The intellectual history of unlettered Spanish colonial litigants and their role in making the Enlightenment, in the end, cannot be told without also recounting defendants' arguments. It is the telling together that responds directly to the call to historians of modernity not just to uncover new facts and stories from outside Europe but also to think about how they were missed in the first place.[46] By revealing change in legal culture women, Indians, and slaves in Spanish America generated, this book has tried to outline a way we can think *about* the Enlightenment as an event without thinking only *with* the Enlightenment as an ethos.[47] Like a lawyer pacing before the judges of the high court, the book has exhausted its evidence and cited mountains of authorities to argue that ordinary colonial litigants produced, rather than reproduced, a modern way of thinking about law. The book has put the Enlightenment, as both a history and a way of thinking about that history, on trial.

Appendix I

ARCHIVAL METHODS

All statistical observations in this book derive from a broad analysis of eighteenth-century litigation in six general regions, at various levels and in diverse spheres of jurisdiction. Some of this analysis also derives from statistics generated from eighteenth-century counts of court activities, such as the report the Audiencia of Lima submitted to the Council of Indies concerning its case loads in the early years of the 1790s and the records court notaries in Oaxaca left. But much of the statistical information comes from my own analysis of the holdings of civil cases in archives in Mexico, Peru, and Spain. Readers will find an exhaustive list of the repositories consulted in the Bibliography, and I express my deep appreciation to staffs of these archives for assisting me in compiling these numbers in the Acknowledgements.

The data analysis of civil suits held in various archives required that I adjust my methods depending on the way the archive was organized and the type of finding aids that were available. Below is a discussion of all archives and methods employed to produce numerical data, organized alphabetically, by location.

- **Lima, Peru.** I compiled statistics from the civil case card catalogs of the Archivo General de la Nación-Perú, focusing mostly on the holdings in the Cabildo and Real Audiencia series, which are both divided into Causas Civiles and Causas Criminales. In Archivo Arzobispal de Lima, I analyzed the series entitled Divorcios and Causas de Negros, sampling cases in the eighteenth century using what some social scientists call a "systematic" or "arbitrary" (as opposed to random) sampling method (reviewing all cases for five-year periods from three different intervals over the 1700s).
- **Mexico City, Mexico**: I drew statistical counts of cases by using a search of the electronic catalogs of the Archivo General de la Nación-México (AGN-M) provided by Linda Arnold, which were compiled by herself and others. By using a key-term search (for example, for "alimentos," "esclavo," etc.) I was

able to search all cataloged holdings in the archive at once, providing me a panoramic view of this massive repository's holdings. This led me to multiple series for civil cases, as well as to ecclesiastical and criminal cases of various jurisdictions (Audiencia, Corregidor, Bienes Nacionales, Sala de lo Civil, and Alcaldías Mayores, which appears to contain cases heard by the viceroy in the Juzgado de Indios, or General Indian Court). The archives' administration also kindly provided me access to the Tribunal Superior de Justicia cases while they were still being cataloged in 2005.

- **Oaxaca, Mexico**: I examined all civil cases from the district of Teposcolula in the Archivo Histórico Judicial de Oaxaca, using an older, handwritten catalog, a physical count of files, and a newer archival database. In that archive I also undertook a sample from ten-year periods of civil cases from the district of Villa Alta. The way I categorized and analyzed these suits is discussed in the notes to Chapter 5. I also undertook key-term searches of criminal cases for both regions using the computer database. In the Archivo General del Poder del Estado de Oaxaca, I reviewed all cases in the Alcaldía Mayor Oaxaca (Valley of Oaxaca) section for comparative purposes, and the Real Intendencia series for Teposcolula and Villa Alta series. My review of the ecclesiastical cases of the Archivo Histórico del Arzobispado de Oaxaca did not yield any divorce disputes.

- **Toledo, Castilla-La Mancha, Spain**: In the Archivo Municipal de Toledo, I read and categorized uncataloged materials in the sections "Fiel del Juzagdo," and "Pleitos," "Ejecutorías," and "Civiles" and "Instancias" for the eleven pueblos of the Montes de Toledo during 2005 and 2008 trips. Those uncataloged materials were presented in "cajas" that contained diverse materials. For those series, my case numbers are based on my calculation that the aveage "caja," or box, of materials contained 16 actual civil cases (fragments or whole cases.) When I returned in 2010, I studied all cases in the civil and criminal sections in the newly cataloged sections of five select pueblos of the Montes de Toledo Fiel del Juzgado series. I also undertook a broad sampling of the uncataloged ecclesiastical cases in the Archivo Diocesano de Toledo, reopened one month before my 2010 visit after decades of being closed. There, the patient archive manager, Padre Dionisio, dragged out a rolling cart containing between 75 and 100 boxes of an unknown total number of discrete cases, each filled with materials loosely labeled as "Procesos," which contained anywhere from four to twenty individual suits or actions. My analytical focus on cases could not be statistically based. But as I opened long-shut boxes that puffed dust as I carefully removed papers, I concentrated on marriage and jurisdictional disputes.

- **Trujillo, Peru**: Statistics are based on the excellent published catalog descriptions of the Archivo Regional de La Libertad (ARL), which permitted me to examine all jurisdictions and series for all four centuries of Spanish rule. Research assistants María Carolina Zumaglini and Paula de la Cruz Fernández coded and entered data for these series. In the Archivo Arzobispal de Trujillo, I was permitted access to all divorce cases that were locatable for the eighteenth century.

- **Valladolid, Castilla-León, Spain:** I examined all civil cases from the Real Chancellería de Valladolid using a computer search database, which permitted me to search for the occurrence of cases by key-term. I was provided statistics on all the archive's holdings of civil cases facilitated by the director and archivist Carmen Cuevas Blanco. I also performed an arbitrary sample of the Cartas Ejecutorías and Reales Provisiones series in that archive, examining cases in 20-year blocks to follow up on observations Kagan made in *Lawsuits and Litigants*.

Appendix II

ANALYSIS OF CIVIL LITIGATION OVER TIME

Various observations about rising and falling volumes of litigation, including analysis of data compiled in the eighteenth century itself on litigation rates, is narrated throughout the book and especially in Chapter 3. The discussion of my attempts to squeeze hard numbers on civil cases out of the archives is described in Appendix I. Below is an overall description of findings, organized by regional type, followed by 11 figures representing the results of my analysis.

Spanish Colonial Capital Cities

Both lower court and high court records in Lima and Mexico City demonstrate a sizeable growth in civil action over the eighteenth century. These lower court activities are captured in the court records of judges called *alcaldes de lo civil*, who administered first-instance justice, also known throughout the empire as "*justicia ordinaria*." High court cases were overseen by the oidores, or ministers, of the Real Audiencia. The Audiencia of Lima's expansive jurisdiction extended through the Andes, reaching its limits in modern-day Ecuador and Bolivia; the Mexico's Audiencia covered the vast area extending onto the tip of the Yucatán peninsula and north into dynamic mining areas.

Peru's national archive contains a far greater number of civil cases for the eighteenth century than for earlier centuries. For example, the average number of civil suits per year heard by Lima's two alcaldes ordinarios (magistrates of the Cabildo, ruling in a jurisdiction known as "ordinary justice") rose from 1.7 in the 1600s, to 16.22 in the 1700s, to 32.85 in the early 1800s (see Figure A.1). Disaggregating the number of records of these magistrates for the eighteenth century helps to pinpoint the decades of change more precisely. The most re- markable growth in the amount of litigation housed in the archive is to be found after 1770 (Figure A.2). In no decade prior to 1770–79 do the number of civil

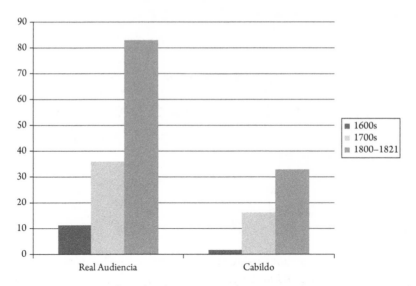

Figure A.1 Average number of civil cases per year by century, Lima. From AGN-P, Real Audiencia and Cabildo Civil series.

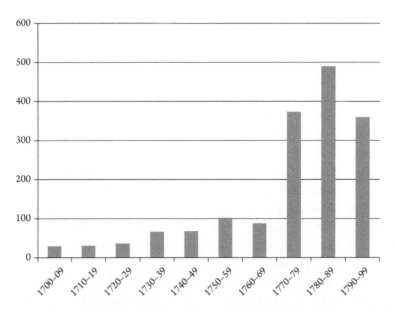

Figure A.2 Civil suits by decade, Lima, Cabildo, 1700–99. From AGN-P.

suits heard by the judges of ordinary justice reach 100, but they consistently surpass 300 in each of the last three decades of the century.

The growth of first-instance civil cases in Lima parallels an explosion in civil litigation beyond Peru's capital city. The records of civil cases heard by the

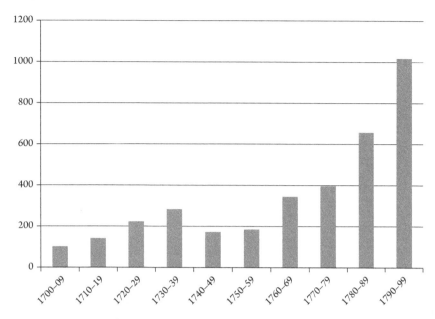

Figure A.3 Civil suits by decade, Lima, Real Audiencia, 1700–99, From AGN-P.

Audiencia of Lima, which primarily took appeals from provincial cities and rural regions, suggests that the amount of civil litigation this tribunal heard also grew significantly in the eighteenth century. In the growth of civil cases in this high court is somewhat more evenly distributed across the century than the growth in lower-instances cases (see Figure A.3). But it too is concentrated in century's final decades.

An examination of civil case series housed in the Archivo General de la Nación in Mexico City indicates, with some caveats, that an increase in civil cases also occurred at the end of the eighteenth century in the Audiencia of Mexico, the other major pole of Spanish colonial governance in the New World where, as in the Audiencia of Lima, court boundaries remained relatively stable, if not un-affected by other jurisdictional reforms of the period during the administrative reorganization of the Bourbon period.

The national archive of Mexico presents a challenge in gauging the volume of cases heard by the courts because civil cases of the same jurisdictional prov-enance are divided into several series. A good place to begin, therefore, is by analyzing a series known as the Ramo de Civil, capitalizing on the work that historian Linda Arnold and Mexican investigators have undertaken in cata-loging approximately 85 percent of all these cases. This series is extracted from the archive of the *fiscal de lo civil* (or crown's attorney) in the Audiencia de México as well as from a select number of first-instance cases brought

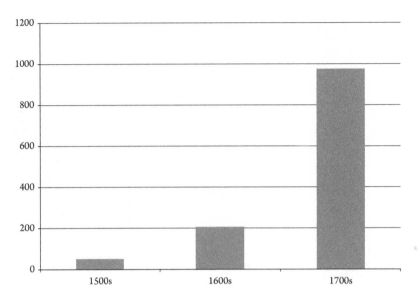

Figure A.4 Civil suits by century, Audiencia and first-instance, Mexico City. From AGN-M, Ramo de lo Civil.

before ordinary and military courts in the capital city. According to my count, 9,758 of the 12,321 cases in the series, or almost 80 percent, were heard in the eighteenth century (Figure A.4). These numbers, however, are certainly somewhat swollen since the first-instance civil cases that appear in this series, added during nineteenth-century archival reform, date only from 1720 onward.[1]

Even if the creation and re-creation of national archives led to the addition of lower-instance civil suits to this series, and thus explains some of the increase in cases in this series, another series of first-instance cases in the Mexican national archive further indicates growth in first-instance civil suits in eighteenth-century Mexico. The number of first-instance civil cases heard by Mexico City's alcaldes that are now held in the Tribunal Superior de Justicia series reaches its apogee in the last two decades of the eighteenth century. These figures, however, are somewhat inconclusive because a transitory rise during the period 1720–40 creates the impression of fluctuating, rather than consistently growing, litigation over the course of the century.

The civil case record from Mexico City's corregidor, who was a middling-level judge responsible for both appeals and first-instance cases in a jurisdiction radiating out of Mexico City through its central valley, provides another piece of evidence concerning the growing tendency to litigate during the late colonial period. The corregidor's caseload rises at the end of the century, making it unlikely that the increases in case volumes in the Mexico City alcaldes' series are

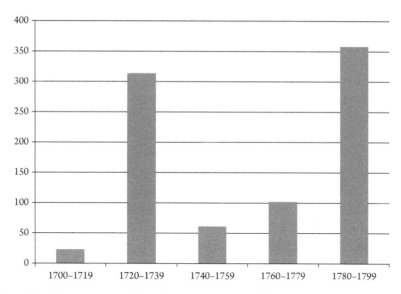

Figure A.5 First-instance civil suits by twenty-year periods, Mexico City, 1700–99. From AGN-M, Tribunal Superior de Justicia, Alcalde Ordinario, Civil.

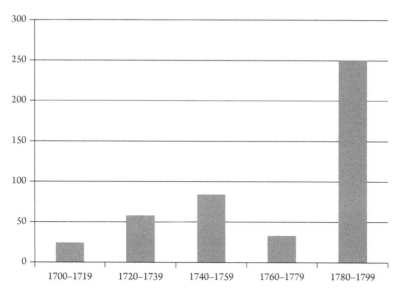

Figure A.6 Civil Suits by 20-year period, Corregimiento de México, 1700–99. From AGN-M, Tribunal Superior de Justicia, Corregidor de México, Civil.

an anomaly (Figure A.6). Thus, although each must be used with caution, in all three civil series for Mexico City in the national archive—Ramo de lo Civil, Tribunal Superior de Justicia, and the Corregidor de México—the number of civil cases climbs at a remarkable rate after 1780.

Colonial Provinces

The viceregal capitals drew into their orbit not only increasing numbers of city dwellers but also more rural litigants seeking justice, many of whom would trek hundreds of miles on horseback, guarding mounds of paper affixed with royal stamps that held autos, or proceedings of cases first brought before local judges. Yet, even as we move out of the capital cities and closer to these rural folks' homes, a similar pattern of increased litigation among provincial colonial inhabitants emerges. The alcaldía mayor districts (equivalent to the corregimiento) of Villa Alta and Teposcolula in the heavily indigenous regions of Oaxaca, Mexico, too show clear evidence of increased civil litigiousness in the second half of the 1700s (Figures A.7 and A.8). The growth in both Oaxacan jurisdictions, overwhelmingly comprised of an ethnically diverse indigenous population, demonstrates a remarkable consistency.

But, as with most matters in history, the story is not so simple. Not every archive follows the exact same pattern. The rise in litigation in the colonies was not always as concentrated at the end of the eighteenth century as it was in Mexico City, Oaxaca, and Peru. In the local and appeals courts of Trujillo, Peru, it was not until the early 1800s that civil litigation exploded. During the 1700s, at the level of the city first-instance court, civil cases only slightly increased. Yet, in the first decades of the eighteenth century, first-instance local justicia ordinaria cases begin to soar (Figure A.9).

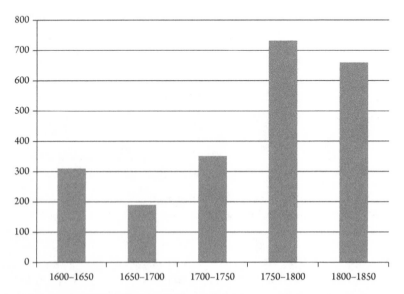

Figure A.7 Civil suits by half-century, Teposcolula, Oaxaca, Mexico, 1650–1850. From AHJO, Alcaldía Mayor, Teposcolula, Civil.

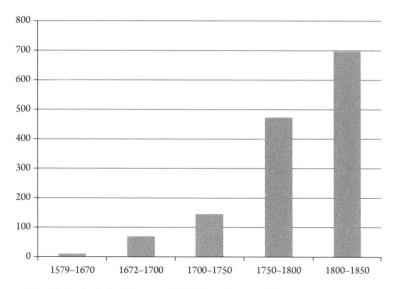

Figure A.8 Civil suits by half-century, Villa Alta, Oaxaca, Mexico, 1579–1850. From AHJO, Alcaldía Mayor, Villa Alta, Civil.

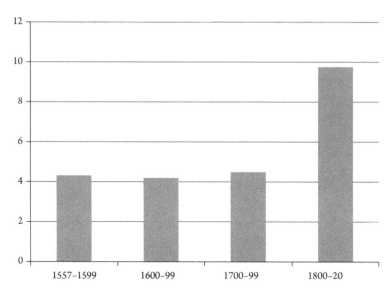

Figure A.9 Average number of first-instance civil suits per year, by century, Trujillo, Peru, 1557–1820. From ARL, Cabildo, Justicia Ordinaria.

Outside the provincial city of Trujillo, in the region's predominantly rural corregimiento, civil cases in fact declined between the seventeenth and eighteenth century, a trend that continued even when the larger jurisdictional unit of the Intendancy of Trujillo was created in 1787 and absorbed the corregimiento. Because of the incongruity in size of these two jurisdictions, I have refrained

from presenting them together in a chart, but when the civil cases from corregimiento and intendancy are added together, the average number of civil cases
slides from 12.75 per year in the 1600s to 10.97 in the 1700s. Nonetheless,
the number of cases heard at this level did, like urban cases heard in the city of
Trujillo, soar in the first two decades of the 1800s. More pointedly, the number
of cases the Intendant of Trujillo heard from throughout his large jurisdiction
increased threefold beginning in 1800 (from an average of 10.97 per year in the
previous century to a staggering 33.75 per year).

Spain

According to legal historian Richard Kagan's 1985 work on lawsuits and litigants
in early modern Spain, litigation rates in Castile were at their highest during the
period 1500–1700 but dropped in the eighteenth century, at the same time they
exploded in three of the four regions examined in Spanish America.[2] To be fair,
Kagan was not as concerned with the eighteenth century as with the high wa-
termark of litigation in the sixteenth, and thus his remarks about the devolution
of formal litigation to local authority in Castile was impressionistic. But his argument quite understandably intrigued me, so I went into Spain's archives to
follow in his footsteps, examining the same archival series as he did, but for the
eighteenth century.

The lawsuits from the Montes de Toledo were not cataloged during my first
three visits, but I analyzed the contents of boxes for four series—Pleitos, Civiles,
Fiel del Juzgado, Ejecutivos and Instancias— that contained what can be considered "civil cases." [3] (Figure A.10). As Kagan predicted, there was indeed a
boom, or "revolution," in civil legal activity in the Montes during the sixteenth
and seventeenth centuries. But by the eighteenth century, the inhabitants of the
Montes became half as likely to file civil suits or present petitions before the Fiel
del Juzgado than they had been in the 1600s. And, in the nineteenth century,
they were half as likely to sue as they had been one hundred years before.

The civil suit (*pleitos*) series housed in the upper-level court of the Real
Chancillería in Valladolid, which served the greater jurisdiction of New Castile
as a high court and appellate court, suggests that the eighteenth-century litigation "boom" was indeed a colonial, not imperial, phenomenon. The story told by
this archival series varies somewhat from Kagan's narrative of declining Spanish
litigiousness in formal royal courts; it is more one of stability across the 1700s.
An analysis of the three court notary offices that were conferred with civil cases
brought to the Chancillería—including cases in which a sentence was passed as
well as those that were settled or abandoned—reveals that the highest amount

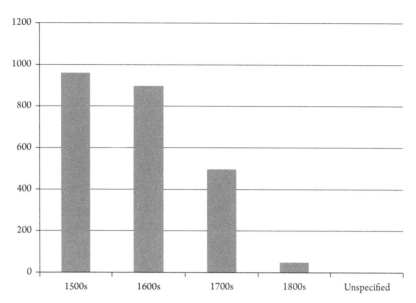

Figure A.10 Projected total of civil suits by century, Montes de Toledo, 1500–1800s. From uncataloged boxes in AMT series Fiel del Juzgado, Civiles, Ejecutivos, Pleitos.[*]
[*]The papers in these boxes included petitions from twelve pueblos, one not typically identified as belonging to the Montes (Cuevas). It was estimated that, among the papers in the boxes, around 16 can be labeled as civil lawsuits or opening petitions.

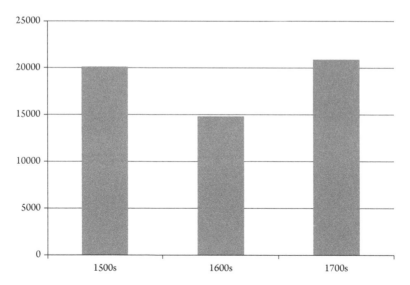

Figure A.11 Civil suits by century, Real Chancellería de Valladolid, 1500–1800. From RCV-Civil, Notarial Offices of Alonso R.; Fernández A.; and Pérez R.

of civil activity captured in the archive took place during the eighteenth century (Figure A.11). Even so, the actual numbers of cases are roughly the same for the eighteenth century as for the sixteenth century, around 20,000 cases. Thus, within this high-level court of Spain, we find a chronological pattern of civil litigation nothing like the phenomenal increase that is evident in the number of civil cases brought before late colonial judges in Spanish America.

There is other evidence from the Chancellería of Valladolid not represented in the figures that provides further evidence of a decline in civil litigation in Spain during the eighteenth century. I, like Kagan, examined the court's cartas ejecutorías, documents that were "executive writs," or short summaries of judged cases, primarily appeals brought to the Chancellería.[4] As Kagan points out, these documents were too expensive for many litigants, probably costing up to four times as much as an ordinary case heard by the Fiel del Juzgado, making them biased in favor of wealthy litigants who won significant sums of money. My analysis of these cases indicates that they declined significantly from a high in the 1570s. The period of greatest decline came in the later seventeenth century, with a bit of a rebound in the mid-eighteenth century, but never reaching even half of the volume that they had reached at their apex in the sixteenth century. My brief and limited analysis of royal provisions, which were writs similar to cartas ejecututorías but cheaper, suggests that they too declined; I found half as many provisions (112) issued on cases heard in 1750 as I did in 1700 (286).

ABBREVIATIONS

AAL	Archivo Arzobispal de Lima
AAT	Archivo Arzobispal de Trujillo
ADT	Archivo Diocesano de Toledo
AGI	Archivo General de Indias (Seville)
AGN-M	Archivo General de la Nación-México (Instituciones Coloniales)
AGN-P	Archivo General de la Nación- Perú (Sección Colonial)
AHJO	Archivo Historico de Justicia de Oaxaca
AHN	Archivo Nacional Histórico de España (Madrid)
AM	Alcaldías Mayores
AMT	Archivo Municipal de Toledo, Fondo Histórico
AO	Alcalde Ordinario
APGEO	Archivo del Poder Ejecutivo del Estado de Oaxaca
ARL	Archivo de la Region del Departamento de la Libertad (Trujillo, Peru)
BN	Bienes Nacionales
BNE	Bibiloteca Nacional de España
BNP	Biblioteca Nacional del Perú
C.	Cuaderno (case)
Cab.	Cabildo
Caja	box
Civ.	Civil
C.O.	Causas Ordinarias
Correg.	Corregimiento
Crim.	Criminal
DI	Derecho Indígena
Eje.	Causas ejecutivas
Exp.	Expediente (file)
f., ff.	foja/fojas

Intend.	Intendencia
JCB	John Carter Brown Library
Leg.	Legajo (dossier)
MS	Manuscritos
n/p	no publisher
olv.	Olvidados (abandoned suits)
RA	Real Audiencia
RCV	Real Audiencia y Chancellería de Valladolid
s/f	sin foja (without pagination)
s/t	sin título (no title)
Tepos.	Teposcolula
TSJ	Tribunal Superior de Justicia
v.	verso
VA	Villa Alta
Vol.	volumen

NOTES

Introduction

1. As I was completing this book, I discovered Paul B. Miller's *Elusive Origins: The Enlightenment in the Modern Caribbean Historical Imagination* (Charlottesville, VA: University of Virigina Press, 2010), in which he credits the great historian C.R.L. James with observing that, in order to understand the Enlightenment in all of its contradictions, one must understand Goya, 1. For a contemporary view of the frenzy of requests, proposals, and demands that Americans brought to Cádiz in order to "solve all the problems at once," see Blanco White, *El Español* (London: Imprenta de Junigné, 1811–12), tomo IV no. 23, (30 marzo, 1812), 338. Also see Scott Eastman and Natalia Sobrevilla Perea, eds., *The Rise of Constitutional Government in the Iberian Atlantic World* (Tuscaloosa: University of Alabama, 2015).

2. *Quexas de los Americanos* (Cádiz: Imprenta de la Junta de Provincia, Casa de Misericordia, 1812), 1–2. The famous Spanish American independence thinker Fray Servando Teresa de Mier published an acerbic response to this tract under the same title as the original, *Quejas de los Americanos* (1813[?]; reprint, Mexico City: Universidad Aútonoma de México, 1979), which also launched immediately into the issue of natural rights by discussing Hugo Grotius.

3. Surely this formulation drew from Montesquieu's widely known description of the Indies and Spain as "two powers under the same master, but the Indies is the principal and Spain the secondary," Ann M. Cohler, Basia C. Miller, and Harold S. Stone, eds., *Montesquieu: The Spirit of the Laws* (1989; reprint, New York: Cambridge University Press, 2013), Book 22, Chapter 22.

4. *Quexas*, 27.

5. Ibid. For another take, in which a pro-peninsular liberal polemicist rhetorically pointed out that Spain's own popular classes were equally as undeserving as were colonial inhabitants of political representation because they were unenlightened, see "Segunda representación del consulado de Méjico," attributed to Don Francisco Javier Lambarri in Andrés Cavo and Carlos María de Bustamante, *Los tres siglos de Méjico durante el gobierno español:Hasta la entrada del ejército trigarante* (Jalapa:Tipografía Veracruzana d A. Ruiz, 1870), 874, 882–905; and particularly, "And what is the plebe of Spain? What is that of Madrid? . . . How far does its popular enlightenment reach when the parish priest has to read the Gazette from the pulpit because he is the only one in the village who knows how to read?," 900, fn. 2.

6. Giambattista Vico quoted in Foucault, "What Is Enlightenment?," in *The Foucault Reader*, ed. Paul Rabinow (New York: Pantheon, 1984), 44.

7. On law as a "global institution" produced from repeated cultural interactions see Lauren Benton, *Law and Colonial Cultures: Legal Regimes in World History, 1400–1900* (New York; Cambridge University Press, 2002), 4. On the Enlightenment as a practice, see Jeremy L. Caradonna, *The Enlightenment in Practice: Prize Contests and Intellectual Culture in France, 1670–1794* (Ithaca: Cornell University Press, 2012).

8. An excellent summary of the state of the field is Dorinda Outram, *The Enlightenment* (1995; reprint, Cambridge University Press, 2013).

9. Immanuel Kant, *An Answer to the Question: "What Is Enlightenment?*," trans. H. B. Nisbet (1970; reprint, New York: Penguin Books, 1991), 1.

10. Foucault, "What Is Enlightenment?," 43.

11. Ibid., 42. Karen Stolley zeroes in on the same Foucault quotation in her study of eighteenth-century Hispanic Enlightenment literature, which, like this book, seeks to think beyond the nineteenth-century insistence that the colonies be placed outside the European Enlightenment, *Domesticating Empire: Enlightenment in Spanish America* (Nashville: Vanderbilt University Press, 2013), 178.

12. Max Horkheimer and Theodor Adorno, *Dialectic of Enlightenment* (1944; reprint, New York: Herder and Herder, 1972). In Indian history, two particular works stand out in this vein, Ranajit Guha, *Elementary Aspects of Peasant Insurgency in Colonial India* (Delhi: Oxford University Press, 1983) and Dipesh Chakrabarty, *Provincializing Europe: Postcolonial Thought and Historical Difference* (Princeton: Princeton University Press, 2000). For a sampling of Latin Americanists who are part of, or reflect on, the contributions of post-colonial scholarship to Latin American history, see, in addition to works mentioned in the conclusion, Florencia Mallon, "The Promise and Dilemma of Subaltern Studies: Perspectives from Latin American History," *American Historical Review* 99 (December 1994): 1491–1515; *Peasant and Nation: The Making of Postcolonial Mexico and Peru* (Berkeley: University of California, 1995); and "Pathways to Postcolonial Nationhood: The Democratization and Difference of Latin America," in *Postcolonial Studies and Beyond*, ed. Ania Loomba, Suvir Kaul, et al. (Durham: Duke University Press, 2005), 273; Walter Mignolo, *The Darker Side of the Renaissance: Literacy, Territoriality, and Colonization* (1995; 2nd ed., Ann Arbor: University of Michigan Press, 2006) and *Local Histories/Global Designs: Coloniality, Subaltern Knowledge and Border Thinking* (Princeton: Princeton University Press, 2001); Alvaro Félix Bolaños and Gustavo Verdesio, *Colonialism Past and Present: Reading and Writing about Colonial Latin America Today* (Stony Brook: SUNY Press, 2002); Mabel Moraña, Enrique Dussel, and Carlos A. Juáregui, eds., *Coloniality at Large: Latin America and the Postcolonial Debate* (Durham: Duke University Press, 2008).

13. James Schmidt, "What Enlightenment Project?," *Political Theory* 28, no. 6 (2000): 734–757; Sebastian Conrad, "Enlightenment in Global History: A Historiographical Critique," *American Historical Review* 117, no. 4 (2012); 1007.

14. Mark Thurner, "After Spanish Rule: Writing Another After," in *After Spanish Rule: Postcolonial Predicaments of the Americas*, eds, Mark Thurner and Andrés Guerrero, 12–57 (Durham: Duke University Press, 2003), 25. For one of the earliest delineations of the chronological dissonance between the New Imperialism and Latin American history, see Frederick Cooper and Laura Ann Stoler, "Preface," in *Tensions of Empire: Colonial Cultures in a Bourgeois World*, ed. Frederick Cooper and Laura Ann Stoler (Berkeley: University of California Press, 1997), xi.

15. Chakrabarty, *Provincializing*, 3.

16. Daniel Gordon, "Introduction," in *Postmodernism and the Enlightenment: New Perspectives in Eighteenth-Century French Intellectual History*, ed. Daniel Gordon (New York: Routledge, 2001), 1–3.

17. AHA Roundtable, "New Perspectives on the Enlightenment," *American Historical Review* 15, no. 5 (2010), especially Karen O'Brien, "The Return of the Enlightenment"; Robert C. Bartlett, *The Enlightenment: A Post-Mortem Study* (Toronto: University of Toronto Press, 2011).

18. Some scholars earnestly wrestled with the philosophical challenges of understanding the Enlightenment in the context of twentieth-century liberal demands for diversity, while others frankly hoped to "rescue" it from critics. See Keith Michael Baker and Peter Hanns Reill, eds., *What's Left of Enlightenment? A Postmodern Question* (Stanford: Stanford University Press, 2001); Gertrude Himmelfarb, *The Roads to Modernity: The British, French and American Enlightenments* (New York: Vintage, 2004); Tvestan Todorov, *In Defence of the Enlightenment* (London: Atlantic Books, 2010); Anthony Pagden, *The Enlightenment and Why It Still Matters* (New York: Random House, 2013). Also see James Schmidt, "Introduction: What

Is Enlightenment: A Question, Its Context and Some Answers," in *What Is Enlightenment? Eighteenth-Century Answers and Twentieth-Century Questions*, ed. James Schmidt, 1–44, (Berkeley: University of California Press, 1996), 1–2.

19. See Sankar Muthu, *Enlightenment Against Empire* (Princeton: Princeton University Press, 2003); Malick W. Ghachem, "Montesquieu in the Caribbean: The Colonial Enlightenment between Code Noir and Code Civil," in Gordon, *Postmodernism and the Enlightenment*, 7–30; Suzanne Desan, "What's after Political Culture? Recent French Revolutionary Historiography," *French Historical Studies* 23, no.1 (Winter 2000): 185–187.

20. Darrin McMahon, *Enemies of the Enlightenment: The French Counter-Enlightenment and the Making of Modernity* (New York: Oxford University Press, 2001); John Roberston, *The Case for the Enlightenment* (Cambridge: Cambridge University Press, 2005); Laurent Dubois, "An Enslaved Enlightenment: Rethinking the Intellectual History of the French Atlantic," *Social History* 31, no. 1 (2006): 1–14; Charles W. J. Withers, *Placing the Enlightenment: Thinking Geographically about the Age of Reason* (Chicago: University of Chicago Press, 2007); Susan Manning and Francis D. Cogliano, eds., *The Atlantic Enlightenment* (Burlington, VT: Ashgate, 2008); Daniel Carey and Lynn Festa, eds., *Postcolonial Enlightenment* (New York: Oxford University Press, 2009).

21. Clifford Siskin and William Warner, eds., *This is Enlightenment* (Chicago: University of Chicago Press, 2010).

22. Knud Haakonssen, "The History of Eighteenth-Century Philosophy: History or Philosophy?" in *The Cambridge History of Eighteenth-Century Philosophy*, vol. 1, ed. Knud Haakonssen (New York: Cambridge University Press, 2006), 3–4. For popular attempts to pare the concept down, see the author decrying the usurpation of the term by solipsistic yoga-peddling US elites, urging ordinary people to learn about the "real," historical Enlightenment lest they lose hold of its gift of democracy, Dominic Green, "Choose Your Own Enlightenment," *Atlantic Monthly*, March 12, 2015, accessed on 7/7/15, http://www.theatlantic.com/politics/archive/2015/03/choose-your-own-enlightenment/387355/.

23. Jonathan Israel, *Radical Enlightenment: Philosophy and the Making of Modernity 1650–1750* (New York: Oxford University Press, 2001); *Enlightenment Contested: Philosophy, Modernity, and the Emancipation of Man* (New York: Oxford University Press, 2006); *Democratic Enlightenment: Philosophy, Revolution and Human Rights 1750–1790* (New York: Oxford University Press, 2011). In a recent survey of the field, John Roberston eschews the globalizing impulse, *The Enlightenment: A Very Short Introduction* (New York: Oxford University Press, 2015), 11–13.

24. Samuel Moyn estimates that only about seventy or so philosophers in the Western world would make Israel's cut, "Mind the Enlightenment," *The Nation* (May 12, 2010), accessed 7/7/15, http://www.thenation.com/article/mind-enlightenment/. There were, Israel details, absolutist and moderate species of Enlightenments. And there is, he concedes, another Enlightenment still, the one that "carries an ideological baggage and resonances often superimposed later and not part of the original phenomenon," Israel, *Democratic*, 4. But the new philosophy, which "by definition is closely linked to revolution," not only can but must be distinguished from the meanings that "academics, politicians and social theorists" give the term today. Also see Robertson, *The Case*, 5–7.

25. This is the title of the more readable, popular text redacting his expansive ideas, Jonathan Israel, *A Revolution of the Mind* (Princeton, NJ: Princeton University Press, 2010).

26. On this method, described as "pushing upstream to a source," see Vincenzo Ferone: *The Enlightenment: History of an Idea* (2010; English translation, Princeton, NJ: Princeton University Press, 2015), 62–63. Also see Margaret Jacobs, "Spinoza Got it," *London Review of Books* 34, no 21 (2011): 26–27.

27. Israel, *Democratic*, 4–5.

28. See Moyn, "Mind the Enlightenment," and Israel's response, "What Samuel Moyn Got Wrong in His *Nation* Article," originally a letter to *The Nation*'s editors but expanded in the version on the History News Network, 6/27/2010, accessed 7/7/15, http://historynewsnetwork.org/article/128361.

29. For the history of ideas in Latin America, see José Elías Palti, "Beyond Revisionism: The Bicentennial of Independence, The Early Republican Experience, and Intellectual History in

Latin America," *Journal of the History of Ideas* 70, no. 4 (2009): 593–614. For new directions in intellectual history, see Samuel Moyn and Anthony Sartori, eds., *Global Intellectual History* (New York: Columbia University Press, 2013); Darrin McMahon and Samuel Moyn, *Rethinking Modern European Intellectual History* (New York: Oxford University Press, 2014).

30. Ferone, *The Enlightenment*, xi. Also see Margaret Jacobs, *Living the Enlightenment: Freemasory and Politics in Eighteenth-Century Europe* (New York: Oxford University Press, 1991).

31. To be fair, Foucault calls for the same, a "series of historical inquiries that are as precise as possible." By this he does not mean studies that seek out " 'the essential kernel of rationality," but rather that aim toward "what is and is not or is no longer indispensable for the constitution of ourselves as historical subjects." I interpret this to mean producing believable stories about the human ability to effect historical change; Foucault, "What Is Enlightenment?," 43.

32. Ibid., 65–66. Here, he is citing fellow Italian historian Arnaldo Momigliano.

33. Historians call for a return to "hard empirical modes of analysis" armed with cultural history's "epistemological reflexiveness" in the dialog in the AHR Conversation, "Explaining Historical Change; or The Lost History of Causes," Participants: Emmanuel Akeyampong, Caroline Arni, Pamela Kyle Crossley, Mark Hewitson, and William H. Sewell, Jr., *American Historical Review* 120, no. 4 (2015): 1369–1423. The call is especially resonant in the comments of Arni, 1390, Sewell, 1393, and Crossely, 1394.

34. Gustavo Verdesio, "Colonialism Now and Then," in Bolaños and Verdieso, *Colonialism*, 11.

35. Marcello Carmagnani, *The Other West: Latin America from Invasion to Globalization* (Berkeley: University of California Press, 2011).

36. The post-colonial turn gave conquest and early Spanish American history and literature new urgency. For example, three of the four scholars debating "colonial discourse" in the *Latin American Research Review* 29, no. 3 (1993): 113–56 worked on periods prior to the eighteenth century in Spanish America. Also see Mignolo, *Darker Side* and Ricardo D. Salvatore, "Imperial Revisionism: US Historians of Latin America and the Colonial Spanish Empire (ca. 1915–1945), *Transnational American Studies* 5, no. 1 (2013): 1–54, https://escholarship.org/uc/item/30m769ph, accessed 7/15/15.

37. Mignolo continued to refine his periodization of modernity, and the eighteenth century (when modern notions of Universal History and the chronological ordering of time become more manifest) figured more prominently in his new afterward to the 2nd edition of the *Darker Side*.

38. Angel Rama, *The Lettered City*, trans. John Charles Chasteen (Durham: Duke University Press, 1996), 6.

39. Thurner, "After Spanish Rule"; Stolley, *Domesticating Empire*. Historicism, as post-colonialists understand it, did its own exclusionary work inside of Europe as well. Germany's Enlightenment was long portrayed as a "poor imitation of a western model," even as eighteenth-century German historians laid the groundwork for nineteenth-century historicism. See Peter Hanns Reill, *The German Enlightenment and the Rise of Historicism* (Berkeley: University of California Press, 1975); 1, 31–36. Also see Larry Wolf, *Inventing Eastern Europe: The Map of Civilization on the Mind of the Enlightenment* (Stanford: Stanford University Press, 1994); Ian McNeely, *The Emancipation of Writing: German Civil Society in the Making, 1790s–1820* (Berkeley: University of California Press, 2003), 241.

40. Michael Iarroci, *The Properties of Modernity: Romantic Spain, European Modernity, and the Legacies of Empire* (Nashville: Vanderbilt University Press, 2006), xi. Also see Jorge Cañizares-Esguerra, *Nature, Empire, and Nation: Science and Exploration in the History of Science in the Iberian World* (Stanford: Stanford University Press, 2006), esp. ch. 5; Mariselle Meléndez and Karen Stolley, "Introduction: Enlightenments in Latin America," *Colonial Latin American Research Review* 24, no. 1 (2015): 1–16.

41. Jeremy Adelman, "The Problem of Persistence in Latin American History," in *Colonial Legacies: The Problem of Persistence in Latin American History*, ed. Jeremy Adelman, (New York: Routledge, 1999), 1–13. Also see Antonello Gerbi, *The Dispute of the New World: The History of a Polemic, 1750–1900* (1955; reprint, Pittsburgh: University of Pittsburgh Press, 2010).

42. Ruth MacKay, *"Lazy, Improvident People:" Myth and Reality in the Writing of Spanish History* (Ithaca: Cornell University Press, 2006).

43. This is Israel's portrait of Spain (though, as discussed in the Conclusion, not of Spanish America). He is in good company. See Richard Herr, *The Eighteenth-Century Revolution in Spain* (Princeton: Princeton University Press, 1958); see John Lynch, "The Origins of Spanish American Independence," in *The Cambridge History of Latin America* I, ed. Leslie Bethell (Cambridge: Cambridge University Press, 1984), 3–50, esp. 43–47; Equipo Madrid, ed., *Carlos III, Madrid y la ilustración* (Madrid: Siglo Veintiuno, 1988); I. L. McClelland, *Ideological Hesitancy in Spain, 1700–1750* (Liverpool: Liverpool University Press, 1991); Charles Noel, "Charles III of Spain," in *Enlightened Absolutism: Reform and Reformers in Later Eighteenth-Century Europe,* ed. H. M. Scott (Ann Arbor: University of Michigan Press, 1990), 119–43; Stanley and Barbara Stein, *Apogee of Empire: Spain and New Spain the Age of Charles III, 1759–1789* (Baltimore: Johns Hopkins University Press, 2003), and in literary studies by Francisco Sánchez-Blanco, *El Absolutismo y las Luces en el Reinado de Carlos III* (Madrid: Marical Pons, 2002).

44. Gabriel Paquette, *Enlightenment, Governance, and Reform in Spain and Its Empire, 1759–1808* (New York: Palgrave Macmillan, 2008), 18. Also see Arthur P. Whitaker, "The Dual Rôle of Latin American in the Enlightenment," in *Latin America and the Enlightenment,* ed. Arthur P. Whitaker (1942; reprint, Ithaca: Cornell University Press, 1961), 3–21; 5; Brian Hamnett, "The Medieval Roots of Spanish Constitutionalism," in Eastman and Sobrevilla, *The Rise,* 19. For more on the historiographical underpinnings of US scholarly views on the reception of the Enlightenment, see Salvatore, "Imperial Revisionism."

45. Jorge Cañizares-Esguerra, *How to Write the History of the New World: Histories, Epistemologies, and Identities in the Eighteenth-Century Atlantic World* (Stanford: Stanford University Press, 2001).

46. Mounting research on the production of scientific knowledge in the Spanish empire also has made the notion its "deficiency" of Enlightenment untenable. See, for example, Cañizares-Esguerra, *Nature, Empire,* Neil Safier, *Measuring the New World: Enlightenment Science and South America* (Chicago: University of Chicago Press, 2008); Daniela Bleichmar, Paula De Vos, Kristine Huffine, and Kevin Sheehan, eds., *Science in the Spanish and Portuguese Empires, 1500–1800* (Stanford: Stanford University Press, 2009); Adam Warren, *Medicine and Politics in Colonial Peru: Population Growth and the Bourbon Reforms* (Pittsburgh: University of Pittsburgh Press, 2010); Daniela Bleichmar, *Visible Empire: Botanical Expeditions and Visual Culture in the Hispanic Enlightenment* (Chicago: University of Chicago Press, 2012); Emily Berquist-Soulé, *The Bishop's Utopia: Envisioning Improvement in Colonial Peru* (Philadelphia: University of Pennsylvania Press, 2014).

47. *Plan de una memoria sobre las causas de la ociosidad* (Madrid: Don Antonio Sancha, 1787), xviii–xix. Susan Deans-Smith pursues another avenue for connecting Enlightenment sensibilities and ordinary people in her work on the artisans involved in royal arts academies in Mexico City, "*Buen Gusto* and Manuel Tolsá's Equestrian Statue of Charles IV in Late Colonial Mexico," in *Buen Gusto and Classicism in Late Eighteenth- and Nineteenth-Century Latin America,* ed. Paul B. Niell and Stacie G. Widdifield (Albuquerque: University of New Mexico Press, 2013), 3–24; "'A Natural and Voluntary Dependence': The Royal Academy of San Carlos and the Cultural Politics of Art Education in Mexico City, 1786–1797," *Bulletin of Latin American Research,* special issue on *Mexican Visual Culture* 29, no. 3 (2010): 1–18.

48. Quoted in Dena Goodman, *The Republic of Letters: A Cultural History of the French Enlightenment* (Ithaca: Cornell University Press, 1994), 32. Also see Voltaire's dismissive comment that "someone must plough the fields," quoted in Robert Darnton, *George Washington's False Teeth: An Unconventional Guide to the Eighteenth Century* (New York: Norton, 2003), 5.

49. Rama, *Lettered City,* 6.

50. José Rabasa rejects the employment of orality/writing binary for sixteenth-century Latin America, "Thinking Europe in Indian Categories, or 'Tell me the story of how I conquered you,'" in Moraña et al., eds. *Coloniality at Large,* 51.

51. Kathryn Burns, *Into the Archive: Writing and Power in Colonial Peru* (Durham: Duke University, 2010), 3.

52. José Ramón Jouve-Martín, *Esclavos de la ciudad letrada: Esclavitud, escritura y colonialismo en Lima, 1650–1700* (Lima: Instituto de Estudios Peruanos, 2005); Alcira Dueñas: *Indians and Mestizos in the Lettered City: Reshaping Justice, Social Hierarchy, and Political Culture in Colonial*

Peru (Boulder: University Press of Colorado, 2010); Joanne Rappaport and Tom Cummins, *Beyond the Lettered City: Indigenous Literacies in the Andes* (Durham: Duke University Press, 2012).

53. Pilar Gonzalbo Aizpurú, "De escrituras y escribanos," *Anuario de Historia de Derecho Mexicano* 77 (1989): 77–93; Tamar Herzog, *Mediación, archivo y ejercicio: Los escribanos de Quito (siglo XVI–XVIII)* (Frankfurt: V. Klostermann, 1996); Renzo Honores, "Una sociedad legalista: Abogados, procuradores de causas y la creación de una cultura legal colonial en Lima y Potosí, 1540–1670," PhD dissertation, Florida International University, 2007; Victor Gayol, *Laberintos de justicias: Procuradores, escribanos y oficiales de la Real Audiencia de México (1750–1812)*, vol. 1, *Las reglas del juego* (Zamora: Colegio de Michoacán, 2007) and *Labertintos de justicias: Procuradores, escribanos y oficiales de la Real Audiencia de México (1750–1812)*, vol. 2, *El juego de las reglas* (Zamora: Colegio de Michoacán, 2007); Burns, *Into the Archive*; Enrique Vilalba Pérez and Emilio Torné, *El Nervio de la República: el oficio de escribano en el Siglo de Oro* (Madrid: Calumbur, 2011). On native mediators in particular see Yanna Yannakakis, *The Art of Being In-Between: Native Intermediaries, Indian Identity, and Local Rule in Colonial Oaxaca* (Durham: Duke University Press, 2008); Gabriela Ramos and Yanna Yannakakis, eds., *Indigenous Intellectuals: Knowledge, Power and Colonial Culture in Mexico and the Andes* (Durham: Duke University Press, 2014); Kathryn Burns, "Making Indigenous Archives: The Quilcaycamayoc of Colonial Cuzco," *Hispanic American Historical Review* 91, no. 4 (2011): 665–685. On cultural mediators more generally, see Scarlett O'Phelan Godoy and Carmen Salazar-Soler, *Passuers, mediadores culturales, y agentes de la primera globalización en le Mundo Ibérico, siglos XVI–XIX* (Lima: PUCP-Instituto Riva Agüero, 2005). On the important role of scribes and notaries in other settings, see Julie Hardwick, *The Practice of Patriarchy: Gender and the Politics of Household Authority in France* (University Park: Pennsylvania State University Press, 1999); Caroline Castiglione, *Patrons and Adversaries: Nobles and Villagers in Italian Politics, 1640-1760*. New York. Oxford University Press, 2005; and McNeely, *The Emancipation*. In many respects, the focus on the everyday world of lower-level legal agents and litigants is a deepening of the pioneering work on laywers and the French Revolution undertaken by David A. Bell, *Lawyers and Citizens: The Making of a Political Elite in Old Regime France* (New York: Oxford University Press, 1994).

54. Carlos Estenssoro Fuchs, "La plebe illustrada: El pueblo en las fronteras de la razón," in *Entre la retórica y la insurgencia. Las ideas de los movimentos sociales en los Andes, Siblo XVIII*, ed. Charles Walker (Cuzco: Centro Bartolomé de las Casas, 1995), 33–66; Alberto Flores Galindo, *La ciudad sumergida: Aristocracia y plebe en Lima, 1760–1830* (1988; reprint, Lima: Editorial Horizonte, 1991); Michael Scardaville, "(Hapsburg) Law and (Bourbon) Order: State Authority, Popular Unrest, and the Criminal Justice System in Bourbon Mexico City," *The Americas* 50, no. 4 (April 1994): 501–26; Gabriel Haslip-Viera, *Crime and Punishment in Late Colonial Mexico City, 1692–1810* (Albuquerque: University of New Mexico Press, 1999); Juan Pedro Viqueira Albán, *Propriety and Permissiveness in Bourbon Mexico* (1987; reprint, Wilmington: Scholarly Publications, 1999); Pamela Voekel, "Peeing on the Palace: Bodily Resistance to the Bourbon Reforms in Mexico City," *Journal of Historical Sociology* 5, no. 2 (June 1992): 181–207; Silvia M. Arrom, *Containing the Poor: The Mexico City Poor House, 1776–1871* (Durham: Duke University Press, 2000); Chad Thomas Black, *The Limits of Gender Domination: Women, the Law, and Political Crisis in Quito, 1765–1830* (Alburquerque: University of New Mexico Press, 2011), esp. ch. 2.

55. The works are numerous but three should be highlighted because they share, in certain respects, an agenda with this book: James Sanders, *Contentious Republicans: Popular Politics, Race and Class in Nineteenth-Century Colombia* (Durham: Duke University Press, 2004); Karen D. Caplan, *Indigenous Citizens: Local Liberalism in Early National Oaxaca and Yucatan* (Stanford: Stanford University Press, 2009); Marcela Echeverri, *Indian and Slave Royalists in the Age of Revolution: Reform, Revolution, and Royalism in the Northern Andes, 1780–1825* (New York: Cambridge University Press, 2016). Other examples include Mallon, *Peasant and Nation*; Christine Hünefeldt, *Liberalism in the Bedroom* (University Park: Pennsylvania State University Press, 1999); Sarah Chambers, *From Subjects to Citizens: Honor, Gender and Politics in Arequipa, Peru, 1780-1854* (University Park: Pennsylvania State University Press, 2000); Kirsten Schultz, *Tropical Versailles: Empire, Monarchy and the Portuguese Royal Court in Rio,*

1808–21 (New York: Routledge, 2001); Ricardo Salvatore, *Wandering Paysanos: State Order and Subaltern Experience in Buenos Aires during the Rosas Era* (Durham: Duke University Press, 2003); Aline Helg, *Liberty and Equality in Caribbean Colombia, 1770–1835* (Chapel Hill: University of North Carolina Press, 2004); Arlene J. Díaz, *Female Citizens, Patriarchs, and the Law in Venezuela, 1789–1904* (Lincoln: University of Nebraska, 2004); Cecelia Méndez, *The Plebeian Republic: The Huanta Rebellion and the Making of the Peruvian State, 1820–1850* (Durham: Duke University Press, 2005); Reuben Zahler, *Ambitious Rebels: Remaking Honor, Law, and Liberalism in Venezuela, 1780–1850* (Tucson: University of Arizona Press, 2013).

56. Stuart Schwartz, *All Can Be Saved: Religious Tolerance and Salvation in the Iberian Atlantic World* (New Haven: Yale University Press, 2008); Pamela Voekel, *Alone before God: The Religious Origins of Modernity in Mexico* (Durham: Duke University Press, 2002). On the centrality of religion to the gendered Enlightenment in Spain, see Theresa Ann Smith, *The Emerging Female Citizen: Gender and Enlightenment in Spain* (Berkeley: University of California Press, 2006).

57. Ulrich L. Lehner, "What is 'Catholic Enlightenment'?," *History Compass* 8, no. 2 (2010): 166–178.

58. As just one example, William B. Taylor noted the rising number of lawsuits among peasant parishioners in eighteenth-century Mexico, and also noted that this seemed to contrast with trends of declining litigiousness in Spain, in *Magistrates of the Sacred: Priests and Parishioners in Eighteenth-Century Mexico* (Stanford: Stanford University Press, 1996), 722, n. 129.

59. Sibylle Fischer, *Modernity Disavowed: Haiti and the Cultures of Slavery in the Age of Revolution* (Durham: Duke University Press, 2004); David Scott, *Conscripts of Modernity: The Tragedy of Colonial Enlightenment* (Durham: Duke University Press, 2004); Sunil Agnani, *Hating Empire Properly: The Two Indies and the Limits of Anti-Enlightenment Colonialism* (New York: Oxford University Press, 2013). Notable here, too, is Matt Childs, *The 1812 Aponte Rebellion in Cuba and the Struggle against Atlantic Slavery* (Chapel Hill: University of North Carolina Press, 2006).

60. Michel-Rolph Trouillot, *Silencing the Past: Power and the Production of History* (New York: Beacon, 1995); Laurent Dubois, *A Colony of Citizens: Revolution and Slave Emancipation in the French Caribbean, 1787–1804* (Chapel Hill: University of North Carolina Press, 2004).

61. Trouillot, *Silencing the Past*, 73.

62. Malick W. Ghachem, *The Old Regime and the Haitian Revolution* (New York: Cambridge University Press, 2012), 25.

63. This term is Mignolo's via Johannes Fabian, *Time and the Other: How Anthropology Makes its Object* (1957; reprint, New York: Columbia University Press, 1983); *The Darker Side*, ix, 249–50; *Local Histories*, 120. Also see Reinhart Koselleck, *The Practice of Conceptual History: Timing History, Spacing Concepts* (Stanford: Stanford University Press, 2002), 154–169.

64. David Armitage, "Three Types of Atlantic History," in *The British Atlantic World*, ed. David Armitage and Michael J. Braddick (London: Palgrave, 2002), 20.

65. On the genesis of "ideas" in Latin American history, and the inheritance of liberalism in particular as variously attributed to Thomism, Machievellian realism, "civic humanism," and French and British Enlightenment thought, see Palti, "Beyond Revisionism."

66. See the justification for studying Paris as epicenter of Enlightenment in McMahon, *Enemies of the Enlightenment*, 10; and Darnton, *George Washington's False Teeth*, 6–8. Mallon refers to this type of historical thinking as the problem of "not France" in "The Promise and Dilemma."

67. On the constructed and constructive nature of periodizing, see Koselleck, *Practice*, 159, 169.

68. Xavier Gil Pujol, "Pensamiento político español y europeo en la Edad Moderna. Reflexiones sobre su estudio en una época post-*whig*," in *A vueltas con el pasado. Historia, memoria y vida*, ed. J.Ll. Palos and F. Sánchez Costa, 207–222 (Barcelona: Publicacions de la Universitat de Barcelona, 2013), 214; Smith, *Emerging Female Citizen*, 6–9.

69. Even John Tate Lanning's staunch mid-twentieth-century defense of Spanish America's "receptiveness" to Enlightenment ideas had it lagging a generation behind Europe, *Academic Culture in the Spanish Colonies* (London: Oxford University Press, 1940). I owe this observation to Salvatore, "Imperial Revisionism."

70. Ann Twinam similarly emphasizes the interactive, rather than top-down, nature of Bourbon policy in *Purchasing Whiteness: Pardos, Mulattos, and the Quest for Social Mobility in the Spanish Indies* (Stanford: Stanford University Press, 2015), esp. 78; as do Adrian Pearce, *The Origins*

of the Bourbon Reforms in Spanish South America, 1700–1763 (New York: Palgrave Macmillan, 2014); and Paquette, *Enlightened Reform.*

71. Of course, contemporaries did reflect on the degree to which inhabitants in the Spanish empire adhered to "French" ideas, but this discussion penetrated everyday lawsuits very subtly, and the concept of *"afrancemiento"* would be mostly a nineteenth-century development, reaching its peak in the post-Napoleonic years in Spain. See Gerard Dufour, "Los afrancesados o una cuestión política: los límites del despotismo ilustrado," *Cuadernos de la Historia Moderna* VI (2007): 269–277; Claudia Rosas Lauro, *Del trono al guilotina: El impacto de la revolución francesa en el Perú* (Lima: Instituto Francés del Estudios Andinos/Pontificia Universdad Católica del Perú, 2006).

72. See Rogelio Pérez-Perdomo, *Latin American Lawyers: A Historical Introduction* (Stanford: Stanford University Press, 2006), 35–36.

73. Important works at the regional or national level documenting civil case numbers include Honores, "Una sociedad legalista"; María José Gandásegui Aparicio, "Los Pleitos Civiles en Castilla, 1700–1835," PhD diss., Universidad Complutense de Madrid, 1998; Renzo Honores, "Estudios sobre la litigación y la litigiosidad colonial," *Revista de Historia del Derecho Privado* (Santiago de Chile) 2 (1999): 121–135; Díaz, *Female Citizens*; Black, *Limits of Gender Domination*; and Zahler, *Ambitious Rebels.*

74. Micol Siegel, "Beyond Compare: Comparative Method after the Transnational Turn," *Radical History Review* 91 (2005): 62–90; Ricardo Salvatore, ed., *Los lugares del saber: Contextos locales y redes transnacionales en la formación del conocimiento moderno* (Buenos Aires: Beatriz Viterbo, 2007). Also see Mignolo, *Local Histories.*

75. Lauren Benton calls for "open-ended comparisons," which I take to mean between places within the same span of time, rather than comparisons separated across time, "No Longer Odd Region Out: Repositioning Latin America in World History," *Hispanic American Historical Review* 84, no. 3 (2004): 423–430; 429. This involves a disciplinary perspective that privileges contemporaneousness and departs from experimental versions that demand cases be independent and equivalent. Also see William Hamilton Sewell, *The Logics of History: Social Theory and Social Transformation* (Chicago: University of Chicago Press, 2005), 100; 93–6; Gil Pujol, "Pensamiento."

76. Alejandro Cañeque, *The King's Living Image: The Culture and Politics of Viceregal Power in Colonial Mexico* (New York: Routledge, 2004), esp. 8–9; Alejandra Osorio, *Inventing Lima: Baroque Modernity in Peru's South Sea Metropolis* (London: Palgrave Macmillan, 2008).

77. See Emily Berquist-Soulé, *Bishop's Utopia.*

78. Richard Kagan, *Lawsuits and Litigants in Early Modern Spain* (Chapel Hill: University of North Carolina Press, 1981), 79, 252–253. Kagan believes that this might have been because the Spanish tradition of *residencia* meant that the written records often were destroyed after a review of the outgoing magistrate was complete. It might also have to do with the lively extrajudicial culture of rural regions. This is not to say that such records have been lost everywhere. For example, Cosme Gómez Carrasco studied a similar run of first-instance civil cases for the city of Albacete, in Castilla-La Mancha, in "Tensión familiar y mentalidad social en el Antiguo Régimen. Notas sobre la conflictividad en la villa de Albacete en el siglo XVIII," *Revista Historia Social de las Mentalidades* (Chile) (2005): 11–36. What is more, the historiography of litigation as *"conflictividad"* in Spain has yielded a series of important regional studies that examine everyday justice. See Tomás Antonio Mantecón Movellán, *Conflictividad y disciplinamiento social en la Cantabria rural del antiguo regimen* (Santander: Universidad de Cantabria, Fundación Marcelino Botín, 1997); Jesús Marina Barba, *Justicia y gobierno en España en el siglo XVIII: el compendio del territorio de la Chancillería de Granada* (Granada: Universidad de Granada, 1995); José I. Fortea, Juan E. Gelabert, and Tomás A. Mantecón, eds., *Furor et rabies: Violencia, conflicto y marginación en la Edad Moderna* (Santander: Universidad de Cantabria, 2003).

79. Antonio Palomeque Torres. "El Fiel del Juzgado de los Propios y Montes de la Ciudad de Toledo," *Cuadernos de Historia de España,* LV–LVI (1972): 322–399.

80. Michael R. Weisser, *The Peasants of the Montes: The Roots of Rural Rebellion in Spain* (Chicago: University of Chicago Press, 1972), 24–26.

81. Yannakakis, *Art.*

82. William Sewell calls on scholars "to trace out how novel happenings inflect and transform but also are absorbed and interpreted by the pre-existing categories . . . continuity and disconti- nuity are not categorically opposed states but mutually constituting 'moments' in an ongoing temporal process," in AHR Conversation, "Explaining Historical Change," 1392. Also note the sensitivity with which Victor Uribe-Uran approaches the centuries-long process by which punishment was ultimately "humanized" in the late colonial Spanish Atlantic in *Fatal Love: Spousal Killers, Law, and Punishment in the Late Colonial Spanish Atlantic* (Stanford: Stanford University Press, 2016), esp. 243.

83. Seán Patrick Donlan and Dirk Heirbut, "A Patchwork of Accommodations—An Introduction," in *The Law's Many Bodies: Studies in Legal Hybridity and Jurisdictional Complexity, c. 1600– 1900*, ed. Seán Patrick Donlan and Dirk Heirbut (Berlin: Duncker and Humblot, 2015), 15. I have also been influenced by the "Law as . . ." movement in legal history, which seeks to deconstruct the idea that law is partitioned off from other realms of life. See " 'Law As . . .' Theory and Method in Legal History," *UC Irvine Law Review* 1, no. 3 (2013): 239–512; " 'Law As . . .' II, History As Interface for the Interdisciplinary Study of Law," *UC Irvine Law Review* 4, no 1 (2014): 1–493; " 'Law As . . .' III, Glossolalia: Toward A Minor (Historical) Jurisprudence," *UC Irvine Law Review* 5, no. 2 (June 2015): 519–1079.

84. Tamar Herzog, *Upholding Justice: Society, State and the Penal System in Quito (1650–1750)* (Ann Arbor: University of Michigan Press, 2004), 8. Also see António Manuel Hespanha, *Como so juristas viam o mundo, 1550–1750: Direitos, estados, pessoas, coisas, contratos, ações e crimes* (Lisbon, CreateSpace Independent Publishing Platform 2015), 2.

85. See Benton, *Law and Colonial Cultures*, 27; also see 24–28, esp. n. 31, 24.

86. For suggestive comments on the mix of continuity and change in legal culture in Mexico be- tween the seventeenth and nineteenth century, see Gonzalbo Aizpuru, "Escrituras," 81.

87. Jane Burbank and Frederick Cooper, "Rules of Law, Politics of Empire," in *Legal Pluralism and Empires, 1500–1850*, ed. Lauren Benton and Richard Ross (New York: New York University Press, 2013), 287.

88. Paolo Grossi, *Mitología jurídica de la modernidad* (Madrid: Editorial Trotta, 2003).

89. Kagan, *Lawsuits*. There remains a relative paucity of studies of civil litigation, especially com- pared to criminal cases, for Europe, and little attention to the social profile of litigants. Readers interested in this historiography should consult Griet Vermeesch, "The Social Composition of Plaintiffs and Defendants in the Peacemaker Court, Leiden, 1750–4," *Social History* 40, no. 2 (2015): 208–229, who provides an outstanding overview of the state of legal studies of liti- gation in Europe.

90. Kagan, *Lawsuits*, 112–15. Also see Vermeesch, "Social Composition."

91. This reference to agency heeds warnings from historians like Walter Johnson, who points out that the concept itself is "saturated in liberalism," and "smuggles a notion of the universality of a liberal notion of selfhood," "On Agency," *Journal of Social History* 37, no. 1 (2003), 115. Yet rather than focus on how scholars make "modern" liberal categories today, this book also concerned with how slaves, together with other legal agents, created these categories in their own times.

92. Though the distinction between cases brought *de oficio* and those brought *de parte* could be vague, it is clear that state intervention in criminal lawsuits in the form of police action and de oficio prosecution make them far less representative of "popular" litigation strategies than are civil suits; Herzog, *Upholding Justice*, 24. Criminal prosecutions generally rise along with civil litigation in the late colonial period, yet, critically, many scholars view this boom in legal activity not as a "revolution" among litigants but instead as the very opposite, arguing that a late colonial state crackdown on crime, combined with urban residents' easier access to courts to accuse their neighbors of crimes, actually tamped out potential sparks of revolt in major urban areas. See Colin MacLachlan, *Criminal Justice in Eighteenth-Century Mexico: A Study of the Tribunal of the Acordada* (Berkeley: University of California Press, 1974), 21–22; Eric van Young, "Islands in the Storm: Quiet Cities and Violent Countrysides in the Mexican Independence Era," *Past & Present* 118 (1988): 130–155; Scardaville, "(Hapsburg) Law and (Bourbon) Order"; Haslip-Viera, *Crime and Punishment*. In her study of Indian civil litiga- tion in Central Mexico, Susan Kellogg, *Law and the Transformation of Aztec Culture, 1500– 1700* (Norman: University of Oklahoma Press, 1985) reaches similar conclusions about the

role of law in ensuring the relative colonial tranquility of Mexico City. For a variant on this argument for peasant communities, see Aguirre and Walker, *Bandoleros*; William B. Taylor, *Drinking, Homicide and Rebellion in Colonial Mexican Villages* (Stanford: Stanford University Press, 1979).

Part I

1. AMT, Civiles, caja 1881, Arroba, Zivil ordinario, Herraz v. Villares y Carnicero, 1789, s/f.
2. Kagan, *Lawsuits*. For a similar trajectory, see Christopher J. Brooks, *Lawyers, Litigation and English Society, 1450–1900* (London: Hambledon, 1998); Christopher Brooks and Michael Lobban, eds., *Communities and Courts in Britain, 1150–1900* (London: Hambledon, 2003).
3. Kagan, *Lawsuits*, 17–19; Roberto González Echevarría, *Myth and Archive: A Theory of Latin American* Narrative (Ithaca: Cornell University Press, 1990), 49–50. For ambivalences about contracts as proof of truth in particular, see Kathryn Burns, "Notaries, Truth, and Consequences," *American Historical Review* 110, no. 2 (April 2005): 350–379.
4. Patricia Seed, *Ceremonies of Possession in Europe's Conquest of the New World, 1492–1640* (New York: Cambridge University Press, 1995). For a historiographic appraisal of Peruvian litigiousness see, see Honores, "Estudios sobre la litigación."
5. Kagan, *Lawsuits*, 19; James Lockhart, *Spanish Peru, 1532–1560: A Colonial Society* (Madison: University of Wisconsin Press, 1968), 61–62.
6. Important works on Indian justice include Woodrow Borah, *Justice by Insurance: The General Indian Court of Colonial Mexico* (Berkeley: University of California Press, 1983); Steve J. Stern, *Peru's Indian Peoples and the Challenge of Spanish Conquest: Huamanga to 1650* (Madison: University of Wisconsin Press, 1982); Kellogg, *Law and the Transformation*; Brian Owensby, *Empire of Law and Indian Justice in Colonial Mexico* (Stanford: Stanford University Press, 2008).
7. Only recently have historians of Spanish America begun to pay special attention to how and why the legal documents that we read today were generated, to read these papers "along the archival grain." See Ann Laura Stoler, *Along the Archival Grain: Epistemic Anxieties and Colonial Common Sense* (Princeton: Princeton University Press, 2010).

Chapter 1

1. Linati describes this legal writer as a "public scribe" (*escribano público*), *Trajes Civiles*, pl. 9. Still, as explained below, given the informal office set-up and the caste characteristics of the writer, one wonders if either he confused an unlicensed "*agente*" with a public notary.
2. The examples of works on the law that take on the question of agency are numerous, but among the earliest and most classic examples is Stern, *Peru's Indian Peoples* and Kellogg, *Law and the Transformation*. For comments on agency and the law in the case of women, see Bianca Premo, "Before the Law: Women's Petitions in the Eighteenth-Century Spanish Empire," *Comparative Studies in Society and History* 53, no. 2 (2011): 261–289.
3. Tamar Herzog, *Mediación*; Burns, *Into the Archive*; Vilalba Pérez and Torné, *El Nervio*; Black, *Limits*. For European studies of law's narratives, see Natalie Zemon Davis's *Fiction in the Archives: Pardon Tales and their Tellers in Sixteenth-Century France* (Stanford: Stanford University Press, 1987); and the introductory comments to Suzanne Desan, Jeffery Merrick, et al., eds., *Family, Gender and Law in Early Modern France* (University Park: Pennsylvania State University Press, 2009). For a kind of reverse analysis of legalism's effect on literature in Latin America, see González Echevarría, *Myth and Archive*.
4. "F. de tal, vecino de tal parte, parezco ante V.md. y como mas haya lugar en Derecho digo: Que N. vecino de eta Ciudad, ò Villa, fe obligò de pagarme, dar, hacer, ò complerme tal, y tal cofa por tal razon; y haviendole requerido repetidas vefef para fu cumplimiento, no lo he podido confeguir: Por lo que à V.md. pido, y fuplico mande comparecer ante sì al dicho N. y que jure, y declare al tenor de este pedimiento. . . ."; Josef Juan y Colom, *Instrucción de Escribanos* (1736; reprint, Madrid: Francisco Javier Guerra, 1777), 7.
5. Burns, for example, draws on William Hanks to refer to "intertexts," *Into the Archive*, 126. Honores, "Una sociedad legalista," makes a similar point, and in forthcoming work theorizes

that this is the "polyphonic" nature of law. Also see Jouve-Martín, *Esclavos*, passim; Chad T. Black, "Between Prescription and Practice: Licenture and Women's Legal Identity in Bourbon Quito, 1765–1810," *Colonial Latin American Review* 16, no. 2 (2007): 273–298; Premo, "Before the Law," esp. 263–264; Jeremy Mumford, "Litigation as Ethnography in Sixteenth-Century Peru," *Hispanic American Historical Review* 88, no. 1 (2008): 5–40. On lawsuits as processes, see Rappaport and Cummins, *Beyond the Lettered City*, 17.

6. Luz Peralta Apaza, *El papel sellado en el Perú colonial, 1640–1824* (Lima: Seminario de Historia Rural Andina-UNMSM, 2007), 42–43; María del Carmen Hidalgo Brinquis, "La fabricación del papel en España e Hispanoamerérica en el siglo XVII," in *Jornadas científicas sobre documentación de Castilla e Indias en el siglo XVII*, ed. Juan Carlos Galende Díaz (Madrid: Universidad Complutense, 2006), 207–224. By the end of the century, *autos* in the Indies could be rendered on fourth-grade paper, "Cédula de 20 de enero [1795] sobre el uso del papel sellado en los Tribunales y Juzgados Eclesiásticos de estos Reynos, inclusos los de Inquisición," reprinted in Sánchez Santos, *Colección de todas la Pragmáticas, Cédulas, Provisiones, Circulares . . . publicadas en el actual reynado del Señor Don Carlos IV*, vol. 2 (Madrid: Viuda e Hijo de Marín, 1793), 88.

7. "Cédula . . . sobre el uso de papel sellado."

8. Peralta Apaza, *El papel*, 42.

9. "Cédula . . . sobre el uso de papel sellado."

10. Los alcaldes Juan Gregorio y Joaquín Lucas de la cabecera de Santa María Asumpción Tontontepec y demás principales . . . sobre el cobro de aranceles por el parroco, AGPEO, Intend., VA, Leg. 1, no, 30, 1794 [sic, 1807].

11. In addition to drawing on the published legal manuals cited below, these procedures are derived from my own reading of hundreds of cases, and have been detailed, with different emphases, by various historians, including Kagan, *Lawsuits*; Charles Cutter, *The Legal Culture of Northern New Spain, 1700–1810* (Albuquerque: University of New Mexico Press, 1995); Javier Barrientos Grandón, *La cultura jurídica en la Nueva España* (México City: Universidad Nacional Aútonoma de México, 1993); Gandásegui Aparicio, "Los Pleitos Civiles,"; Gayol, *Laberintos de justicia* 2; Honores, "Una sociedad legalista," 239–240; Herzog, *Upholding Justice*; Brian Owensby, "How Juan and Leonor Won Their Freedom," *Hispanic American Historical Review* 85, no. 1 (Feb. 2005): 39–79; Burns, *Into the Archive*, esp. 130–135; Black, *The Limits*

12. José Hipólito Unanue, *Guía política, eclesiástica y militar del virreynato del Perú para el año de 1794* (Lima: Imprenta Real de los Niños Huérfanos, 1794), 61. A similar guide to lawyers in the city, complete with their street addresses, is found in the 1817 publication of the newly created "bar" in Lima, Bernardo Ruiz, *Colegio de Abogados de Lima (Peru). Abogados del ilustre Colegio de la excma. ciudad de Lima, con expresión de las calles y casas en que viven, año de 1817* (Lima: n/p, 1817).

13. As the *Siete Partidas* put it, "the summons [of the defendant] is the root and beginning of every suit." 3:7, Robert I. Burns, S.J., ed., *Las Siete Partidas* vols. 1–5, trans. Samuel Parsons Scott (Philadelphia: University of Pennsylvania Press, 2001).

14. These figures come from my own analysis of the duration of all civil suits in the first-instance court of *justicia ordinaria* in Trujillo (ARL-Civ., C.O. for the years 1700–20 and 1780–99—many of which presumably did not reach formal sentence—and from Kagan's analysis of the duration of suits heard through to sentence in the Chancellería of Valladolid from 1540–1620, *Lawsuits*, 43. Interestingly, there was relatively little difference in the proportion of suits of varying durations between the two courts and the two periods.

15. M. C. Mirow, *Latin American Law: The History of Private Law and Institutions in Spanish America* (Austin: University of Texas Press, 2004), 23; Carta del Regente de la Audiencia de Lima, acompañado certificaciones de las causas despachadas por aquella Audiencia en los años de 1793 y 4, AGI, Gobierno, Lima, 956, no. 62, 1795.

16. In fact, manual author Pedro Melgarejo y Manrique de Lara claimed that a civil complaint transformed from a petition (*pedimiento*) to a an actual suit (*demanda*) only after the plaintiff complained of rebeldía of the defendant, *Compendio de contratos públicos, autos de particiones, executivos, recopilado y corregido y enmendado en esta última impresión* ([1647] reprint, Madrid: n/p 1791], 294. On "dilatory pleas" and avoidance of suits, see *Siete Partidas* 3:3:8

and 9. For an imprisonment for contempt, see Antonio de Mora, Yntendente, encarga the-
niente general haga cumplir diligencias al regidor y principales del pueblo de San Pedro de
Molinos y al Cacique principal, preso, APGEO, Intend. Caja 1, no. 10, 1788.

17. There were technically three, and in reality six, opportunities for a defendant to delay responding to a summons in Castilian practice. Only after a reaching a certain number of rebeldías
and exhibiting other kinds of avoidance behavior would a party be consider exhibiting "contempt" (*contumacia*), Gandásegui Aparicio, "Los pleitos," 2, 129–134.

18. Kagan, *Lawsuits*, 82–83.

19. Details about plaintiffs and subordinates suing superiors appear in *Siete Partidas* 2:3:5–11.

20. Andrew M. Riggsby, *Roman Law and the Legal World of the Romans* (New York: Cambridge
University Press, 2010), 91.

21. *Siete Partidas*, 3:23:20; 3:18:41; Bianca Premo, *Children of the Father King: Youth, Authority
and Legal Minority in Colonial Lima, 1650–1820* (Chapel Hill: University of North Carolina
Press, 2005); Cynthia Milton, *The Many Meanings of Poverty: Colonialism, Social Compacts,
and Assistance in Eighteenth-Century Ecuador* (Stanford: Stanford University Press,
2007), 60–69.

22. On the impact of the American experience on this legal category see, Caroline Cunill, "El
indio miserable: nacimiento de la teoría legal en la América colonial del siglo XVI," *Cuadernos
Intercambio* 8, no. 9 (2011): 229–248; Magdalena Díaz, "La identitad de los esclavos negros
como miserables en Nueva España: Discursos y acciones (siglos XVI–XVIII)" in *Esclavitudes
hispánicas (siglos XV al XXI): Horizontes socioculturales*, ed. Aurelia Martín Casares
(Granada: Universidad de Granada, 2014), 42–57.

23. Borah, *Justice by Insurance*; Charles R. Cutter, *The Protector de Indios in Colonial New Mexico*
(Albuquerque: University of New Mexico Press, 1986).]

24. *Recopilación de las Leyes de los Reynos de las Yndias, Mandadas Imprimir, Y Publicar por la
Magestad Católica del Rey, Don Carlos II* (Madrid: Julian de Paredes, 1681), 2:6:1; 6:5:3. On
the long road of experimentation leading to the establishment of the Mexican office of the
Juzgado de Indios and fee collection for legal services in Indian communities, see Borah,
Justice by Insurance, 54–73.

25. For a summary study, see Pérez-Perdomo, *Latin American Lawyers*. Also see Gayol, *Laberintos*,
1:262–270.

26. *Recopilación de Indias*, 2:28:13.

27. See Sebastian Covarrubias's third definition of "*auto*," "los autos" as "things of the case" (*los
del proceso*), *Tesoro de la Lengua Castellana o Española*, ed. Felipe C.R. Maldocnado, revised by
Manuel Camarero (1611; reprint, Madrid: Editorial Castalia, 1995), 140.

28. Gayol, *Laberintos*, 2:333–343; Christopher Peter Albi, "Contested Legalities in Colonial
Mexico: Francisco Xavier Gamboa and the Defense of *Derecho Indiano*," PhD diss., University
of Texas at Austin, 2009, 35. For England, see John Brewer, *Sinews of Power: War, Money and
the English State, 1688–1783* (1988; reprint, Cambridge: Harvard University Press, 1990),
66–69.

29. Burns, *Into the Archive*, 132, states that notaries were "explicitly barred" from penning petitions. I have not been able to identify any specific ban on public notaries writing pedimientos,
though surely court notaries, responsible for compiling both parties' papers into the autos,
were not to advocate for litigants. Gayol estimates that around half or more of the procuradores of the Audiencia of Mexico held "escribanía" offices, though he finds it rare that they
exercised both functions at once, *Laberintos*, 2:365. Outside of the capitals, the overlap was
more common. See Provisión Real de Fuero y caso de Corte declarado a doña Isabel de
Larejuela para que en su virtud de corregidor o qualesquiera de las justicias de la ciudad de
Truxillo remitan a esta Real Audiencia, ARL, Cab. C.O., Leg. 55, C. 965, 1782.

30. For two examples from Trujillo of lack of scribes and procurators, see Autos seguidos por
don Mathías Monzón, marido legítimo y conjunta persona de Francisca Hurtado, parda
esclava, contra doña María Josefa de Rojas, ama de la dicha, sobre que le otorgue papel de
venta, ARL, Cab. C.O., Leg. 52, C. 913, 1771; Expediente por Rita Palacios, con Don Antonio
Sanz, su marido, moradores del pueblo de Santiago de Cao, sobre calificar que al tiempo de
su matrimonio no trajo bienes conocidos y lo demás deducido, ARL, Correg., C.O., Leg. 234
C. 2109, 1780.

31. Los naturales del pueblo de Choapan piden se anulen las elecciones de alcaldes que se llevo a cabo ya que éste fue impuesto y no fue electo por pueblo, AHJO, VA,Civ., Leg. 11, Exp. 13, 1742, f. 4.

32. James Lockhart, *The Nahuas after the Conquest: A Social and Cultural History of the Indians of Central Mexico, Sixteenth through Eighteenth Centuries* (Stanford: Stanford University Press, 1992), 41–42.

33. Kevin Terraciano, "Crime and Culture in Colonial Mexico: The Case of the Mixtec Murder Note," *Ethnohistory* 45, no. 4 (Autumn 1998): 709–745; Yanna Yannakakis, "Making Spanish Law Zapotec: Local Legal Culture and Jurisdiction in Colonial Oaxaca," paper presented at the XXX Congress of the Latin American Studies Association, May 2012.

34. Real Provisión, AHJO, VA, Civ., Leg. 25, no. 1, 1783, f. 8. Also note that this was a response to a provision by the region's alcalde mayor, who had to "receive" his own order because there was no court notary in the region, f. 7v.

35. Burns, "Making Indigenous Archives," 655–689. Also see Tamar Herzog, "Los escribanos en las Américas: entre memoria española y memoria indígena" in Vilabla and Torné, *El nervio*, 337–349; Yannakakis, *Art*.

36. Burns, *Into the Archive*, 13–15; 20–23. The artistic depiction of unscrupulous scribes extended from the Golden Age through the Age of Enlightenment and into the national period. The protagonist of Mexican José Joaquín Férnandez de Lizardi's 1816 *The Mangy Parrot* (*El periquillo sarniento*), called "Latin America's first novel," and Spain's "last picaresque," was a shyster creole notary, Jean Franco, *Historia de la literatura hispanoamericana* (Barcelona: Ariel, 1981), 48–50.

37. Victor Uribe-Uran, *Honorable Lives: Lawyers, Family and Politics in Colombia* (Pittsburgh: University of Pittsburgh Press, 2000), esp. 9–44. Also see Pérez-Perdomo, *Latin American Lawyers*, 38–41; Haslip-Viera, *Crime and Punishment*, 82–84.

38. On the proliferation of manuals, see Black, *Limits*, 128–129.

39. Also note both the emphasis on the use of procurators in *Recopilación de Indias*, 2:28:1 and 2, followed by permission to use educated men in their stead if necessary, 2:28:3.

40. Juan y Colom, *Instrucción de Escribanos* (1761), 4–5.

41. Juan Ricardo Jiménez Gómez, *Un formulario notarial méxicano del siglo XVIII. La* Instrucción de escribanos *de Juan Elías Ortiz de Logroño* (Mexico City: Universidad Aútonoma de Querétaro, 2005).

42. Alonso de Villadiego Vascuñana y Montoya, *Instrucción política y práctica judicial conforme al estilo de los Consejos* (1612; reprint, Madrid: Antonio Marín, 1766), 2. He indicated that not only should a petitioner request a procurator but also that the court should name one and, indeed, the power of attorney to the procurator was to appear as the next element of the suit directly after the defendant's response.

43. Though they would not personally be responsible for court costs during the suit, indigenous tribute payers did pay a half-*real* fee for the Indian court. See Borah, *Justice by Insurance*.

44. For "jurisdictional jockeying," see Benton, *Law and Colonial Cultures*, 3, 13, 19. Benton's references to jurisdiction shows that she is concerned with the way that various authorities— officials of the Church, the royal state, indigenous authorities—laid claim to jurisdiction. Other scholars focus instead on how litigants and imperial subjects exploited the competition between jurisdictions or sought favorable forums. See Borah, *Justice by Insurance*, 305; Michelle A. McKinley, "Fractional Freedoms: Slavery, Legal Activism, and Ecclesiastical Courts in Colonial Lima, 1593–1689," *Law and History Review* 28, no. 3 (2010): 769–770; Black, *Limits*, esp. 20. While these were obviously related processes in everyday law and politics, these two processes should be conceptually distinguished. For a similar comment on the limits of the term "jurisdictional jockeying" for discussing litigant action in colonial settings, see Mitra Sharafi, "The Marital Patchwork of Colonial South India: Forum Shopping from Britain to Baroda," *Law and History Review* 28, no. 4 (2010), 981.

45. Benton, *Law and Colonial Cultures*, 100–101.

46. Juan y Colom, *Instrucción de Escribanos*, 6. Also note *Siete Partidas* 3:2:40 and 41, which divides the *libellus* into written and oral types, conceding that the "one made in writing is more certain" but also allows that small claims should be heard orally.

47. Gayol, *Laberintos*, 1:137.

48. The petition opening the suit slave Antonio Zavala brought against his master was folded into a square so small that it indicates that it was probably hidden on its way to the magistrate in Lima, Autos seguidos por Antonio Zavala, negro esclavo de D. Pedro Escandón, sobre su libertad y sevicia, AGN-P, RA Civ., Leg. 103, C. 867, 1746.

49. Autos seguidos por el Marqués de Casa Concha contra D, Juan Antonio Espineira, sobre pago de los alquileres de la casa en que habita, AGN-P RA Civ., Leg. 380, C. 3490, 1799. Note also that his landlord accused Espineira of collaboration with the escribano de cámara of the Audiencia, making it possible that the immigrant also received legal advice from this official.

50. The jurisdictional levels I was able to examine in the Montes de Toledo and elsewhere in Spain make it difficult to say whether litigants used official writers more frequently than did their colonial counterparts. Because petitions to the Fiel del Juzgado were theoretically at a second jurisdictional level of appeals, they almost universally were written by court scribes of the Ayuntamiento of Toledo. Similarly, appeals from the Arzobispado of Toledo were always written by procuradores of the Church court. I did not find many "esquelitas" or "memoriales" in the case files of the Chancellería of Valladolid, but many of these cases, which were appeals, contained copyists' re-writing of petitions from the originating court.

51. There were exceptions. For example, José Alejandro de Miranda, a distinguished lawyer in Antequera, Oaxaca, used the first person when writing an argument on behalf of the community for his clients in the Indian town council. See Juan López principal del pueblo de Santa María Yaviche se queja de que los naturales de su pueblo lo quieren despojar de las garantías de las que gozan los principales, AHJO, VA., Civ., Leg. 17, no. 16, 1760, f. 14.

52. See, for example, Manuel de la Trinidad Parolo esclavo, sobre su libertad, AHJO, Tepos. Civ., Leg. 31, Exp. 15, 1744, f. 2.

53. See the signature then the claim to not know how to read of the Indian Jacinto Puemape in Superior orden del Señor Obispo Dr. Don Bernardo de Arbiza y Ugarte, despachando censuras generales hasta la de Anathena, para que se lean y publiquen en el pueblo de San Pedro Lloc, a pedimiento de Francisco Xavier Lloc, Cacique de dicho pueblo, por la usurpación de los títulos del cacicasgo, ARL, Correg, C.O., Leg. 53, C. 2843, 1756, ff.6–6v.

54. Rama, *Lettered City*. For a treatment of the participation of illiterate people in creating the "lettered city," see Jouve-Martín, *Esclavos de la ciudad*.

55. Villadiego, *Instrucción política*, 5. This quote appears in a 1761 edition.

56. Kagan, *Lawsuits*, 53–57. According to a mid-nineteenth-century Spanish legal scholar, the "agente de negocio" was the equivalent of the "pleittese" mentioned in the *Siete Partidas* and the "solicitador" in the *Recopilación de Castilla*. But the author makes note of the fact that the Indies surpassed the peninsula in efforts to control and systematize this office in the eighteenth century, with a formal Colegio de Agentes only established in Madrid in 1847, "Agentes de Negocios," Don Patricio de la Escosura, *Diccionario universal del derecho español constituido*, vol. 4 (Madrid: Publicaciones de Ultramar, 1853), 185–186.

57. The insistence on clear origins for petitions is obvious in the sixteenth-century *Recopilación de Castilla*, which states that attorneys should take responsibility early in the case, state how they will argue the case and what "*excepciones*," or special jurisdictional prerogatives, the litigant might have, and that they should leave the signing up to the litigant or, if the litigant was illiterate, to someone other than the lawyer, *Recopilación de Castilla*, 2:16:13 and 14. In the eighteenth century, a Spanish colonial district official tried to force the identification of the writers in a contentious dispute in a native community, Sobre las elecciones de principales en el pueblo Tabaá, AHJO, Civil, Leg. 24, Exp. 11, 1784, 6v. Also see Mirow, *Latin American Law*, 28. In the nineteenth century, the newly formed Colegio de Abogados in Lima included in their own statutes a call for the clear identification of the lawyer at the beginning of the case in Ruiz, *Colegio de Abogados*, 15.

58. Gayol, *Laberintos*, 2:336.

59. Ibid., 401.

60. Los Religiosos y Sacerdotes seculares no sean agentes ni solicitadores de causas agenas . . . D. Carlos II, en Madrid, por dec. de 13 de Agosto de 1668, y en 1 de Dic. de 675 a cons. de Consejo, recompiled in the *Nueva Recopilación* 1, 184.

61. Burns, *Into the Archive*, 94.

62. Autos seguidos por Agustín Carabeli [sic], esclavo de Dna. Mariá Perales, sobre sevicia, AGN-P, RA, Civ., Leg. 289, C. 2568-B, 1790, f. 4.

63. Autos seguidos por don Antonio Arburúa con su esclava, Andrea Escalante [sic Arburúa], sobre la libertad de ésta (sic. su hija), AGN-P, RA, Civ., Leg. 203, C. 2616, 1791, f. 21v-22.

64. Michel Foucault, "What Is an Author?," in Rabinow, *Foucault Reader*, 101–20. Foucault insists that the "author function" is a more modern creation; I would also argue that it emerged precisely from the space that the "I" occupied in these opening petitions of lawsuits. In Spanish imperial practice, the petition writer was always secondary in the narrative to the litigant. Also see Robert Folger, *Writing as Poaching: Interpellation and Self-Fashioning in Colonial* relaciones de méritos y servicios (Boston: Brill, 2011).

65. Da. María Josefa de Arizaga, vecina de Tehuacán contra su marido don Fernando Monteagudo sobre malos tratamientos, AGN-M, Civ., Vol. 1500, Exp. 2, 1793.

66. Note the case in which the wife of a cacique in Ymilxapan, Mexico, was presumed by officials to be having an affair with the local *alguacil* simply because she complained to him about her husband (she was, it turned out, having an affair with someone else), Delito: malos; Acusado: Nicolas Lorenzo de los Reyes; Afectada: Efigenía María (Su Mujer); Lugar: Ixmiquilpan, AGN-M, Crim, Vol. 105, Exp. 9. ff: 302–306., 1748. Also see Quexa de Don Joseph e Maria Aicardo contra su muger y la persona que adentro se expresa, AGN-M, Civ. Vol. 2107, Exp. 4, 5, and 6, 1782.

67. Autos seguidos por Juana Portocarrero contra su ama, doña Juliana Portocarrero sobre sevicia, AGN-P, RA Civ., Leg. 292, C. 2608, 1790, f. 38.

68. On the meaning of the first person in the more socially-embedded space of pre-modernity, and the emergence of the sovereign subject and its relationship to concepts of freedom from social hindrance, see Elizabeth Povinelli, "A Flight from Freedom," in *Postcolonial Studies and Beyond*, ed. Ania Loomba et al. (Durham: Duke University Press, 2005), 145–165.

69. Folger, *Writing as Poaching*, 3. Also see McNeeley on how early modern Germans stood before scribes more as "legal personages" than as modern individuals, *Emancipation*, 45.

70. Sometimes, the advocate would actually combine a "poder" with what was actually a repetition of a first-person petition from the plaintiff. See, for example, Autos eclesiásticos hecho en esta Chanza, Ledezma, año 1781, de Da. Antonia Godínez de Paz . . . con su marido, RCV Pleitos civiles Pérez Alonso (olv.), 1215.3,1781, f. 13.

71. Da. María Josefa de Arizaga . . . AGN-M, Civil, Vol. 1500, Exp. 2, 1793.

72. Autos criminales que siguen Dn Antonio Ruiz de Luna contra Doña Catalina Gómez su mujer legítima, Lima 1800, BNP, MS, D5930, 1800. There is a pagination problem in this file. The document to which I refer can be found between the pages numbered 99 and 78–79.

73. Malinalco. Expediente formado a pedimiento de Da. María Josefa Bermúdez, vecina de Tenancingo sobre que Don Francisco Cecilia le de alimentos, AGN-M, Civ., Vol. 981, Exp. 5, 1799, f. 1.

74. Expediente seguido por Alberto Chosop, Procurador de Naturales, en nombre de los naturales del Pueblo de Santiago de Cao sobre ortogación de libertad de los 12 indios que se hallan presos, ARL, Correg., C.O., Leg. 231, C. 2025, 1769, f. 2.

75. This string is from Diligencias criminales fechas por Mariana Vidarte contra su marido, D. Fernando Trelles, vecinos de Xochimilco, AGN-M, BN, vol. 1090, exp. 15, 1776, f. 3.

76. Diligencias practicadas para la división de tierras entre el pueblo de San Pedro Cajonos y San Miguel Cajonos y descontento de los naturales de San Pedro sobre la forma en que se realize la division, APGEO, Intend., Leg. 3, Exp. 16, 1791, 7v.

77. Autos seguidos por Clara Gutiérrez, negra, contra doña Marcelina Gutiérrez de Coz sobre su libertad, AGN-P, RA, Civ., Leg. 287, C. 2554, 1790, f. 6.

78. The examples in these cases are criminal and often involve domestic violence, perhaps due to the fact that men often took the lead in complaining about other abusive men and the criminal courts wanted to ensure that the female victim would follow through on the case before proceeding: Criminal de querrella de María Josefa Cisneros contra Domingo Olivero su marido por malos tratamientos y otros excesos, AGN-M, TSJ, Correg. Crim. Vol. 17, Exp. 6, 1795, f. 2: "*leído de verbo ad verbum*," Josefa Dolores, contra Bartolomé López, vecinos del pueblo de Chilapa, por golpearla y vivir amancebado con Maria del Rosario, AJHO, Tepos, Criminal, Leg. 43, no. 4, 1797, f. 4. For more on gender, violence, and dropped cases, see Bianca Premo,

"Felipa's Braid: Women, Culture and the Law in Eighteenth-Century Oaxaca," *Ethnohistory* 61, no. 3 (2014): 497–523.

79. Sobre el divorcio que pide Don Francisco Pila, del matrimonio que contrajo con Doña María García, México, AGN-M, BN, Vol. 292, Exp. 1, 1790, f. 57.

80. See Honores, "Una sociedad legalista," 191–199.

81. Carta del Regente de la Audiencia de Lima, acompañado certificaciones de las causas despachadas por aquella Audiencia en los años de 1793 y 4, AGI, Gobierno, Lima, 956, no. 62, 1795.

82. In this respect, the Spanish cases share something in common with civil cases in late eighteenth-century England, though in the latter case there was more reason for optimism since, although juries could saddle litigants with costs for malicious prosecution, they could still hope to have the verdict overturned on grounds that the amount awarded was excessive. See James Oldham, "Only Eleven Shillings: Abusing Public Justice in England in the Late Eighteenth Century (Part 1 of 3)," *Green Bag* 15, 2D (2012): 175–188.

83. Benito Jerónimo Feijóo, "Sobre la grave importancia de abreviar las Causas Judiciales," Carta 22, in *Cartas eruditas y curiosas*, tomo 3 (reprint, 1742. Madrid: Impresa Real de la Gaceta, 1776), 246.

84. See, for example, APGEO, AM, Leg. 23, Exp. 9, 1743. Also see, ARL Intend., Civ., Leg. 447, C. 316, 1796. In late eighteenth-century Spain, an appeal to the Chancellería of Valladolid over the matter of alimony cost 259 pesos, RCV, Pleitos Civiles, Pérez Alonso, 803.0001, 1797. For the Montes, see Olivo v. Sánchez, AMT, Eje. 1915, 1791 (192 pesos); Alcalde Blanco v. Fernández, AMT, Eje, 1915, 1795, (232 reales; 33.5 pesos).

85. Slave prices are derived from BNP, Z388, 1752 [sic 1792]. Salary and commodity prices come from Pablo Macera, ed., *Los precios del Perú, siglos XVI–XIX*, tomo I (Lima: Banco Central, 1992), xxiv.

86. For indebtedness in Spain due to litigiousness, see Kagan, *Lawsuits*, 17–18.

87. For general prices, see the official "price list" (or *arancel*) for civil cases at midcentury in Mexico in AGN-M, Audiencias, Aranceles, Julio 12 de 1741; AGN-M, Bandos, vol. 3, Exps. 23–27, 1741.

88. Juan Francisco Udaeta con María Josefa Molero, su consorte, sobre divorcio a orden de la demanda que le puso ésta. Una pieza. Guadalajara, AHN, Consejos, 29387, Exp. 12.

89. Autos seguidos por D. José Moreno contra D. Felipe Uzeda por cantidad de posos, provenientes de alquileres impagados, AGN-P, RA, Civ., Leg. 378. c 3473,1799.

90. S/t, APGEO, VA, Civ., Leg. 11, Exp. 8, 1714.

91. Delito: Robo y malos tratos a su mujer; Acusado: Santiago Antonio; Afectados: Josefa Teodora y Juan de Dios Tlatic; Lugar: Xochimilco, AGN-M, Crim. Vol. 41 Exp. 3: 46–91, 1776.

92. AGN-M, Crim., Vol. 122, Exp. 11, 1778, ffs. 293–305.

93. Owensby, *Empire of Law*, esp. 88; José de la Puente Brunke, "Notas sobre la Audiencia de Lima y la 'protección de naturales' (siglo XVII)," in *Passuers, mediadores culturales y agentes de la primera globalización en e Mundo Ibérico, siglos XVI–XIX*, ed. Scarlet O'Phelan Godoy and Carmen Salazar-Soler (Lima: PUCP/Riva Aguero, 2005), 231–248; esp. 232–235.

94. Juan Carlos de Barberena Teniente de Villa Alta remite al intendente de Oaxaca Antonio de Mora el informe que hace el Bachiller Santiago Mariano Villanueva cura de Totontepec sobre la situación que guardan los naturales de esta cabecera . . . APGEO, Intend., VA, Doc. 3, 1788, f. 3v.

95. Alcira Dueñas, "The Lima Indian *Letrados*: Remaking the *República de Indios* in the Bourbon Andes," *The Americas* 72, no. 1 (2015), 64–65.

96. On "minority" and "poverty" as legal discourses see Premo, *Children of the Father King*, ch. 1; Milton, *Many Meanings*. Also see Rachel Sarah O'Toole, *Bound Lives: Africans, Indians and the Meaning of Race in Colonial Peru* (Pittsburgh: University of Pittsburgh Press, 2012), esp. 6–77, for the diverse ways native Andeans themselves constructed the official caste category of the protected "Indian" in the courts.

97. Juan Francisco del Pueblo de Betaza, solicita que Nicolas Fernando sea aprehendido por pedirle dinero para seguir sus diligencias y no le ha pagado, APGEO, Intend. VA, Leg. 1, no. 51, 1799.

98. Don Luis de Velasco, virrey, para que los corregidores y alcaldes mayores, procedan en el uso de sus oficios como deben . . . [y a] los jueces no quitaran vara a ninguna persona que la tenga por mandamiento, AHJO, Tepos., Civ., Leg. 21, Exp. 11, 1715, f. 1.

99. For one of many examples, note the case in Cajamarca, Peru, where an alcalde de indios dis-
puted charges that he abused his subordinates by pointing out how often he footed the bills
for lawsuits. San Pablo, Caxamarca. Autos que sigue Francisca Ramos, mujer legítima de
Antonio Coro, indio originario de la Doctrina de San Pablo de Chalaques, contra la persona
de Don Benito Chuquitas, Alcalde Ordinario de Naturales, por maltratos y azotes, ARL,
Intend. Crim, Leg. 353, C. 1344, 1788.

100. Expediente seguido por Juan Lorenzo Rizo, Protector de los Naturales del Corregimiento
de Truxillo, por lo tocante al Común de ellos del pueblo de San Pedro de Virú, contra los
Alcaldes y mandones del dicho pueblo para que no apremien a los indios de su comunidad
a pagar derramas gravosas, ARL, Correg., C.O., Leg. 224, C. 1898, 1748. Also note that *derramas,* in this case, applied to non-Indians as well. The rich irony at the end of this case is
that the scribe's assistant, who wrote everything up, ended up suing the officials who forced
others to pay for a suit, looking for 50 some pesos, and the Protector of Naturales who represented them himself won a claim of the next year's maize harvest in order to pay his bill.

101. Delito: Robo y malos tratos . . . AGN-M, Crim., Vol. 41, Exp. 3, 1776, ffs. 6–91; f. 89.

102. Orden del Sr Virrey sobre los derechos que deben pagar los caciques, comunidades y demas
indios litigando como actores o reos, BNP, C1733, s/f.

103. Delito: Robo y malos tratos . . . AGN-M Criminal, Vol. 41, Exp. 3: 46–91, 1776, 59.

104. Analysis from catalogs of ARL, Correg. C.O. For more on case analysis, see Appendix.

105. AGN-M, Crim., Vol. 41, Exp. 17, 1775, ffs. 299–304. In 1785 a reform was instituted in
the Mexican Juzgado de Indios to ensure adequate pay for court-appointed attorneys who
worked cases pro bono, Taylor, *Drinking, Homicide,* 76. For other Enlightenment-era challenges and changes to Indian jurisdiction, see Borah, *Justice by Insurance,* 382–385.

106. Delito: Robo y malos tratos . . . AGN-M, Crim., Vol. 41, Exp. 3, 1776, ffs. 46–91; f. 52.

107. Autos seguidos por Antonina Guillén contra D. Joaquín Barandiarán, su amo, sobre su libertad, AGN-P, Cab., Civ., Leg. 83, C. 1566, 1797, f. 50. It is worth noting that a rough signature
that we can presume to be hers follows almost all of her petitions, even though the handwriting of the agent who wrote for her changed throughout the suit.

108. See Kagan, *Lawsuits,* 244.

109. Autos seguidos por don Antonio Arburúa . . . , AGN-P, RA Civ., Leg. 203, C. 2616, 1791,
f. 21v–22.

Chapter 2

1. As much as the "letters" in the "Republic of Letters" referred to literacy and literature,
they also referenced printed correspondence. See Konstantin Dirks, *In My Power: Letter
Writing and Communications in Early America* (Philadelphia: University of Pennsylvania
Press, 2009); Susan Whyman, *The Pen and the People: English Letter Writers, 1660–1800*
(New York: Oxford University Press, 2010).

2. Benito Jerónimo Fejióo y Montenegro, "Balanza de Astréa o recta administración de justicia," in *Theatro Crítico Universal,* vol. 3 (1729; reprint, Madrid: Imprenta de Antonio Pérez
Soto, 1765), 287–312.

3. Mario Scattola, "*Scientia Iuris* and *Ius Naturae*: The Jurisprudence of the Holy Roman
Empire in the Seventeenth and Eighteenth Centuries," in *Treatise of Legal Philosophy and
General Jurisprudence,* vol. 9, *A History of the Philosophy of Law in the Civil Law World, 1600–
1900,* ed. Damiano Canalle, Paolo Grossi, and Hasso Hoffman, 1–42 (New York: Springer
Dordrecht Heidelberg, 2009), 11.

4. Feijóo, "Balanza de Astréa," 288.

5. Ibid., 311.

6. The definition of "equidad" underwent a subtle shift between the 1783 and 1791 versions
of the "Autoridades," or Royal Academy of the Castillian language, in which the new definition was more legal and indicated a characteristic that judges possessed rather than the
faculty of interpretation, Real Academia Española, *Diccionario de la lengua castellana, en que
se explica el verdadero sentido de las voces . . .* (Madrid, 1783), 435, cf. 1791, 384. For more on
the development of the concept and its replacement with natural law/right during the eighteenth century, see Alejandro Guzmán-Brito, *Codificación del Derecho Civil e Interpretación de*

las Leyes: Las normas sobre interpretación de las leyes en los principales Códigos civiles europeo-occidentales y americanos emitidos hasta fines del siglo xix (Madrid: Iustel, 2011), 188–221.

7. Feijóo, "Balanza de Astréa," 311–312.

8. Guzmán-Brito, *Codificación*, 230.

9. See Hespanha, *Como os juristas*, 560.

10. Miguel Luque Talaván, *Un universo de opiniones: La literatura juridical indiana* (Madrid: Biblioteca Historia de América/CSIC, 2003).

11. António Manuel Hespanha finds a stunning increase in European published authors using the term "law" around 1780, and by the early nineteenth century its use would surpass the frequency of the use of *"derecho/dereito."* Importantly, this shift was most pronounced in Spanish-language publications, "De novo, os factos em massa: uma proposta de retorno ao *serial* numa fase pós-positivista da historiografia jurídica," presented at VIII Congresso Brasileiro de História do Direito, "As astúcias da memória jurídica: métodos, teorias, balance," Curitiba, de 31 de agosto a 4 de setembro de 2015, 14–15, used by kind permission of the author.

12. Duncan Kennedy, "Legal Formalism," in *Encyclopedia of the Social and Behavioral Sciences*, vol. 13, ed. Neil J. Smelser and Paul B. Baltes, 8634–8639 (New York: Elsevier, 2001), 8634; Cañeque, *King's*, 326, n.132.

13. Quoted in Israel, *Radical*, 535.

14. Antonio López de Oliver, *Verdadero Idea de un Príncipe formada de las leyes que el reyno que tienen relación al derecho público* (Facsimile reprint. Valladolid: Imprenta Garrido, 1783. Murcia: Funcadción Séneca, n/d), 35. The tract was dedicated to the Conde de Floridablanca.

15. Manuel de Lardizábal y Uribe, *Discurso sobre las penas de España para facilitar su reforma* (Madrid: Ibarra, 1782). See also Luque Talaván, *Un universo*, 95, n. 105.

16. Víctor Tau Anzoátegui, *Casuismo y sistema: Indagación histórica sobre el espíritu del derecho moderno* (Buenos Aires: Instituto de Investigaciones de Historia del Derecho, 1992); Benton, *Law and Colonial Cultures*.

17. See Abelardo Levaggi's critique of the "antonymic" character of interpretations of the differences between absolutist and modern justice in "La Fundamentación de las sentencias en el Derecho Indiano," *Revista de Historia del Derecho* 6 (Buenos Aires, 1978): 45–73.

18. Peninsular Spain's unsuccessful campaign to produce a legal code law, which kicked off in 1776 with Carlos III's royal order to stop compiling laws, is especially illustrative of the mythic nature of "unification" theories for Europe; Antonio Masferrer, "Plurality of Laws, Legal Traditions and Codifications in Spain," *Journal of Civil Law Studies* 4, no. 2 (2011), 428.

19. António Manuel Hespanha locates the eighteenth-century shift toward state law on the plane of "meta-language," stating that the unity of state law was more a matter of "imagery" than of "fact," "Uncommon Laws: Laws in the Extreme Peripheries of an Early Modern Empire," *Zeitschrift der Savigny-Stiftung für Rechtsgeschitchte*, no. 130, v. IV (2013): 180–204. Also see Burbank and Cooper, "Rules of Law," 280.

20. Grossi, *Mitología*.

21. Pearce, *Origins*; Paquette, *Enlightened Reform*.

22. Francisco Tomás y Valiente, *Manual de Historia del Derecho Español* (1979, reprint; Madrid: Tecnos, 1987). 205–231.

23. We need to know more about the colonial impact on Spanish legislation genres. Tomás y Valiente suggests that the colonies produced an even more particularistic atmosphere for Spanish law—and perhaps an early regalism—since few laws were approved by any administrative body such as the *cortes*. Most royal dispositions for the New World actually were more administrative decrees (*provisiones*, *pragmáticas*, and *real cédulas*) rather than laws strictly defined, and they responded to particular circumstances and cases, *Manual*, 338–339. Colonial officials' zealous adoption of the mechanism of *"obedezco pero no se cumple,"* or the ability to disregard laws that did not fit the colonial situation without violating their obligations to the king, surely compounded the sense that royal commands were not necessarily law. Still, by the eighteenth century, the applicability of cédulas to the vast kingdoms of the empire was often taken for granted, a fact that might fuel Mirow's sense that historians have overstated New World casuism "and underappreciated the value of written provisions" in the region, *Latin American Law*, 46.

24. See Helen Nader, *Liberty in Absolutist Spain: The Habsburg Sale of Towns, 1516–1700* (Baltimore: Johns Hopkins University Press, 1990); Ruth MacKay, *The Limits of Royal Authority: Resistance in Seventeenth-Century Castile* (London: Cambridge University Press, 1999).

25. Barrientos Grandón, *La cultura jurídica*, 72–411; Tomás y Valiente, *Manual*, 200–204, Mirow, *Latin American Law*, 35; Albi, "Contested," 29–30.

26. Mirow, *Latin American Law* 35; Albi, "Contested," 27–28; Barrientos Grandón, *La cultura jurídica*, 125–126.

27. See Pérez-Perdomo, *Latin American Lawyers*, 12; Alejandro Guzmán-Brito, "Mos Italicus y mos Gallicus," *Revista de Derecho de la Universidad Católica de Valparaíso* 2 (1987): 11–40; Maximiliano Hernández-Marcos, "Conceptual Aspects of Legal Enlightenment in Europe," in Canelle, Grossi, et al., *History of the Philosophy of Law*, 87–88.

28. Albi, "Contested," 29–30.

29. Mirow, *Latin American Law*, 49–50; Barrientos Grandón, *La cultura jurídica*, 230.

30. Wording from the instruction, the Auto Acordado del Consejo de 4 de diceimbre de 1713, is reprinted in Tomás y Valiente, *Manual*, 385.

31. See in Javier Barrientos de Grandón, "Derecho común y derecho indiano en el Reino de Chile," in *Memoria del Congreso del Instituto Internacional de Historia del Derecho Indiano*, I (México, 1995), 158–159: 140; 143.

32. Grover Antonio Espinoza Ruiz, "La Reforma de la educación superior en Lima: el caso del Real Convictorio de San Carlos," in *El Perú en el siglo XVIII*, comp. Scarlett O'Phelan Godoy (Lima: Instituto Riva Agüero, 1990), 208; Tomás y Valiente, *Manual*, 389; Mirow, *Latin American Law*, 36.

33. Espinoza Ruiz, "La Reforma"; Albi, "Contested," 29.

34. See, for example, Tomás y Valiente, *Manual*, 388. Also note Juan Sempere y Guarinos's comments in 1789 about the continuing instruction of lawyers and judges in "Barbaric Roman law," an education "made even uglier by ridiculous and trying notes and explanations among its conservators," quoted in Antonio Álvarez de Morales, "La enseñanza del derecho natural y de gentes: el libro de Heineccio" in *Manuales y textos de la enseñanza en la universidad liberal, VII Congreso Internacional sobre la Historia de las Universidades Hispánicas* ed. Manuel Angel Bermijo Castrillo, 365–381 (Madrid: Dykinson, 2000), 367.

35. Barrientos Grandón, *La cultura jurídica*, 223.

36. Israel, *Radical*, 532. The word redacted here is "empiricist," which refers to metaphysics. Note, however, that Israel also chooses to ascribe an "eclectic spirit" to Feijóo's ideas, and calls his a "particular version of the Enlightenment" though his metaphysics were essentially empiricist and devoted to Newtonianism, 534. Israel finds jusnaturalist theorists to have been surpassed (whether he means philosophically or historically is unclear) by other theories of natural law proposed by Germans like Gottfried Wilhelm von Leibniz, *Enlightenment Contested*, 195–200. But contemporary thinkers were not so exacting; Gregorio Mayans incorrectly ascribed Leibniz's strident insistence that only nature, not God, endowed humans with the natural right to self-preservation and denial that natural law could be extrinsically imposed to earlier natural law scholars including Johann Gottfried Heineccius. Others believed Heineccius to be a Spinocist. Immanuel Kant himself misunderstood the Thomassian thinkers discussed below and "relegated [them] to the ranks of an unreconstructed scholastic faction," T. J. Hochstratter, *Natural Law Theories in the Early Enlightenment* (2000; reprint, New York: Cambridge University Press, 2004), 19.

37. Paquette, *Enlightenment, Governance*, 9, 14, passim. He also uses "amalgamated," "hybrid," and "syncretic." For more references to "eclecticism," see, for example, Richard M. Morse, *New World Soundings: Culture and Ideology in the Americas* (Baltimore: Johns Hopkins University Press, 1989), 107; Espinoza Ruiz, "La reforma," 230, Margarita Eva Rodríguez García, *Criollismo y patria en la Lima ilustrada (1732–1795)* (Buenos Aires: Miño y Dávila, 2006), 110; José Ignacio Saranyana, *Teología en America Latina / Theology in Latin America: De las Guerras de Independencia hasta finales de siglos XIX (1810–1899)* (Madrid: Iberoamericano, 2008), 377, 617, 528, 659.

38. For important observations on Pufendorf's elevation of natural law above interpretation for complete certainty in judging law, see Guzmán Brito *La codificación*, 204.

39. See Anthony Pagden's now-classic *The Fall of Natural Man: The American Indian and the Origins of Comparative Ethnology* (New York: Cambridge University Press, 1982), esp. 61–63.
40. Knud Haakonssen, "Divine/Natural Theories in Ethics" in *The Cambridge History of of Seventeenth-Century Philosophy*, vol. 2, ed. Daniel Garber and Michael Ayers, 1317–1357 (New York: Cambridge University Press, 2003), 1324.
41. Francis Oakley, *Natural Law, Laws of Nature, Natural Rights: Continuity and Discontinuity in the History of Ideas* (New York: Continuum, 2005), 99. Pagden also provides a clear description of the concept of natural law emerging from the Salamanca School: not a "codified body of precepts," it was a "theory in part epistemological, in part sociological, about the mechanisms which permit men to make moral decisions." At its base, it "consists of a number of 'clear and simple ideas,' the *prima praecepta* [first principles], implanted by God . . ." which permit humans to "'know' by 'natural reason' what the natural law forbids," *Fall*, 61. Also see Israel's description of eighteenth-century debates about natural law, though with expected focus on metaphysics, in *Radical Enlightenment*, 194–200.
42. Oakely, *Natural Law*, 99.
43. On the shifting balance over the seventeenth century in promoting individual obligation to the king rather than liberty and *pactismo*, or a contractual basis of monarchy, see Xavier Gil Pujól, "The Good Law of a Vassal: Fidelity, Obedience and Obligation in Hapsburg Spain," in *Forms of Union: The British and Spanish Monarchies of the Seventeenth and Eighteenth Centuries, RIEV Cauderdos* 5, ed. Jon Arrieta and John H. Elliot (2009): 83–108, esp. 98; 105.
44. Hochstratter, *Natural Law Theories*, esp. 135; Peter Hanns Reill and Ellen Judy Wilson, *Encyclopedia of the Enlightenment* (New York: Facts on File/Book Builders Incorporated, 1996), 417–418.
45. Scattola, "*Scientia Iuris* and *Ius Naturae*," 25.
46. Ibid.
47. I consulted the Spanish translation, Johann Gottlieb Heineccio, *Elementos del derecho natural y de gentes de Heinnecio, corregidos y reformados por el provisor Don Mariano Lucas Garrido . . .* ([1763]; reprint, Madrid: Fuentenbro a cargo de Alejandro Gómez, 1837). It should be pointed out that another textbook also came to be indispensable during educational reforms: Arnold Vinnius's commentaries on the Institutes. Many universities shifted from emphasis on the Digest to teaching students to perform analysis of the shorter entries of the Institutes. This, along with Vinnius's careful comparison between the Institutes and Dutch law, served as a model of a new, more nationalist approach to law in Western Europe, Mirow, *Latin American Law*, 35–37.
48. Javier Barrientos Grandón, "Librería de Don Sebastián Calvo de la Puerta (1717–1767), Oidor de la Real Audiencia de Guatemala," *Revista de estudios histórico-jurídicos*, 21 (1999), http://www.scielo.cl/scielo.php?script=sci_arttext&pid=S0716-54551999002100016, accessed 11/5/15. On the appearance of this book among the following generation, witnessing the transition from Spanish rule to republicanism, see Barrientos Grandón, *La cultura jurídica*, 221. The English translation by George Turnbul figured as one of the fewer than 200 books placed on the shelves the newly-built White House in Washington in the 1859. See Catherine Parisian, *The First White House Library: A History and Annotated Catalog* (Washington DC: The Bibliographic Society of America, 2010), 196.
49. Barrientos Grandón, *La cultura jurídica*, 50.
50. Gregorio Mayans y Siscar, *Filosofía Cristiana: Apuntamientos para ella*, transcription and preliminary study by Salvador Rus Rufino, collaborators Jorge Benavent and Javier Zamora (1746–1747; reprint. Valencia: Publicaciones del Ayuntamiento de Oliva, 1998), 76–77, 188–188, 198, 200, 208. Also note Mayans's reliance on Heineccius's *Elementa philosophae rationalis et moralis*, 70, n. 9; 99; 125. It is notable that Mayans did appreciate that Heinnecius was citing him frequently and increasing his international fame, Mayans a Nebot, 17 de junio de 1747, Gregorio Mayans y Siscar, *Epistolario IV, Mayans a Nebot* (Valencia, Ayuntamiento de Oliva, 1975), letter 164.
51. This included Spain (Valladolid, Granada, Sevilla); Lima, Guadalajara, Chile, and the short-lived schools of "derecho publíco" in Nueva Granada according to Espinoza Ruiz "La Reforma," 222–225; Erick Devoto Bazán, "La educación y el inicio de un Nuevo tiempo. Apuntes para la historia del mundo intelectual peruano de fines del siglo XVIII," in *El Virrey*

Amat y su tiempo, ed. Carlos Pardo-Figueroa Thays and Joseph Dager Alva, 81–158 (Lima: PUCP/Instituto Riva Agüero, 2004), 150; Barrientos Grandón, *La cultura jurídica*, 135; José Luis Peset Reig and Mariano Peset Reig, *Carlos IV y la Universidad de Salamanca* (Madrid: Consejo Superior de Investiaciones Científicas, 1983), 326; and Daniel Gutiérrez Adila, *Un nuevo reino, Geografía, pactismo, y diplomacia durante el interregno en Nueva Granada (1808–1816)* (Bogotá: Universidad Externado de Colombia, 2010), 89–91.

52. Tomás y Valiente, *Manual*, 389; Bazán, "La educación," 81–156; 134.

53. Álvarez de Morales, "La enseñanza," 368; Haakonssen, *Natural Law and Moral Philosophy*, 89–90.

54. This was the objection that the Scot George Turnbull raised when he translated the work to English, Haakonssen, *Natural Law and Moral Theory*, 90–95.

55. Oakley, *Natural Law*, esp. 100–104; Siegfried Van Duffel, "Natural Rights and Individual Sovereignty," *Journal of Political Philosophy* 12, no. 2 (2004): 147–162. Also see his essay and the others in Virpi Mäkinen, ed., *The Nature of Rights: Moral and Political Aspects of Rights in Late Medieval and Early Modern Philosophy. Acta philosophica Fennica* 87 (2010).

56. It is important to note that, especially within the emergent jurisprudential works on international law (derecho de gentes), a positivist legal approach emerged that was more centered on the authority of governments to make treaties and national customs, and it ran against the jusrationalist, more universalist, approach of Heineccius, Grotius, and others. In this respect, legal positivism such as that espoused by Jeremy Bentham mixed relatively indiscrimately with jusratonalist thought in the Spanish colonies. See Gutiérrez Ardila, *Un nuevo reino*, 82.

57. George Turnbull, trans. *A Methodical System of Universal Law, or the Laws of Nature and Nations . . . Written in the Latin by the celebrated Jo. Got. Heineccius . . .* 2 vols. (London: J. Noon, 1740–1741).

58. Talaván, *El universo*, 87.

59. In 1772, at the Third Lima Conciliar Assembly, a younger generation of regalist anti-probabilists sought a statement condemning the Jesuit's moral system in order to erase all traces of the Company's independence from the king. At the same time, works defending probabilism and satirical works condemning it circulated through the city. See Victor Ruiz de Peralta, "Las razones de la fe. Iglesia y la Ilustración en el Perú, 1750–1800," in *El Perú en el siglo XVIII: La Era Borbónica*, ed. Scarlett O'Phelan Godoy (Lima: Instituto Riva Agüero, 1999), 177–204; Pablo Macera D'Orso, "El probablismo en el Perú durante el siglo XVIII," 805–842, in *La universidad en el Perú: historia, presente y futuro. La época colonial*, vol. 2, ed. Jamie Ríos Burga, 705–732 (Surco: Asamblea Nacional de Rectores: n/d), 718–719.

60. Felipe Barreda y Laos, "La universidad en el siglo XVII," in Ríos Burga, *La Universidad*, 218–219; Espinoza Ruiz, "La Reforma," 225; Rodríguez García, *Criollismo*, 145–146. On the necessity of preceding new textbooks on Spanish laws with histories to contextualize them, see Tomás y Valiente, *Manual*, 391.

61. Tomás y Valiente, *Manual*, 390.

62. Talaván, *Un universo*, 86–89; Tau Anzoátegui, *Casuismo*, 367.

63. López de Oliver, *Verdadero Idea*, 59.

64. The tract is popularly known as the "Aviso pastoral," but the version I consulted in the Huntington Library is found as Francisco Antonio de Lorenzana, "A todos los fieles de este nuestro arzobispado" (Mexico: 1772), in the Mexico, Viceroyalty Collection, series 2, v. 1, no. 19.

65. Christopher Peter Albi, "*Derecho Indiano* vs. The Bourbon Reforms: The Legal Philosophy of Francisco Xavier de Gamboa," in *Enlightened Reform in Southern Europe and its Colonies, c. 1750–1830*, ed. Gabriel Paquette, 229–252 (London: Ashgate, 2009), 238.

66. The argument over this matter produced a rash of publications of opinions, including the speech itself, José Baquíjano y Carillo, *Alegato que en la oposición a la cátedra de prima de leyes de la Real Universidad de San Marcos de Lima* (Lima: n/p, 1788); Don Francisco Blasco Caro, *Juicio Imparcial sobre un manuscrito en que se pretende impugnar un dissertación . . . de . . . Baquíjano* (Lima: Real Casa de los Huérfanos, 1788).

67. Emphasis the author's. Francisco Alavardo, "Carta Primera," in *Cartas filosóficas que bajo el supuesto nombre de Aristóteles escribió el Rm. Padre Maestro Fray Francisco Alvarado*, tomo V (Madrid: Imprenta de E. Aguado, 1825), 6.

68. Don Doctor Vicente Fernández [Valcarce], *Desengaños filosóficos que en obsequio de la verdad, de la Religion, y de la Patria da al público* . . . tomo 3 (Madrid: Blas Román, 1790), I. For more on Valcarce, see Daniel Cépeda Calzada, "El filósofo palentino Vicente Fernández Valcarce: Crítico de Descartes," in *Publicaciones Instituciones Tello Téllez de Menenes.* (Palencia: Centro de Estudios Palentinos, 1982), 73–183. Also see Israel, *Democratic Enlightenment*, 406.

69. Fernández Valcarce, *Desengaños*, 39–40.

70. This assertion was one that drew on a long debate about "voluntarism," or the will of God in setting natural laws for humans to follow. See Haakonssen, "Divine/Natural Theories."

71. Baquíjano quoted in Rodríguez García, *Criollismo*, 191.

72. Ibid.

73. Espinoza Ruiz "La Reforma," 226–227; Carlos Daniel Valcárcel, *Reforma de San Marcos en la Epoca de Amat*, vol. 2 (Lima: Universidad de San Marcos, 1955), 22, 37.

74. Barrientos Grandón, *La cultura jurídica*,143.

75. Álvarez de Morales, "La enseñanza," 37.

76. Ibid., 72–74; Mirow, *Latin American Law*, 52.

77. Brian Hamnett, "The Medieval Roots of Spanish Constitutionalism," in Eastman and Sobrevilla Perea, *The Rise*, 28.

78. Antonio Álvarez de Morales, "La difusión del derecho natural y de gentes europea en la Universidad Española de los siglos XVIII y XIX," in *Doctores y escolares: II Congreso de la Historia de las Universidades Hispánicas*, vol. 1, ed. Universitat de Valencia, 49–60 (Valencia: Universidad de Valencia, 1995), 55.

79. José Servando Teresa de Mier Noriega y Guerra, *Historia de la revolución de Nueva España, antiguamente Anáhuac*, vol. 1 (London: Guillermo Glindon, 1813), xliv.

80. Gabriel René Moreno, comp., *Biblioteca peruana: Apuntes para un catálogo de impresos* (Santiago: Biblioteca Nacional [Chile], 1898), 115; for reference to a 1830s edition in Lima, see Haakonssen, *Natural Law and Moral Philosophy*, 95.

81. Guillermo Floris Margadant, "75 años de investigación histórico-jurídico," 63–80, in *LXVV años de investigaciones jurídicas* 27 (México, DF: UNAM, 1979), 65, 69.

82. Barrientos Grandón, *La cultura jurídica*, 270–271.

83. Bravo de Lagunas's opinions are referred to, for example, in Expediente seguido por María Gabriela Ponce de Leon, de color parda, libre esclava que fue de doña Josefa Ponce de Leon, difunta, contra doña Petronila Ponce, sobre el derecho que tiene de obtener su libertad según y como consta en lo instrumentos públicos que presenta, ARL, Cab. C.O., Leg. 54, C. 961, 1781, f. 5; and Autos seguidos por D. Baltázar de Laya y Llano sobre la revocatoria de la libertad concedida a su esclavo Agustín, AGN-P, Cab. Civ., Leg. 82, C. 1556, 1797, ffs. 8; 92.

84. José Pedro Bravo de Lagunas y Castilla, *Colección legal de cartas, dictámenes, y otros papeles de derecho* (Lima: Los Húerfanos, 1761).

85. Mirow, *Latin America Law*, 27; Kagan, *Lawsuits*, 27. Charles Cutter points to a Castilian law that prohibited judges from explaining sentences, *Legal Culture*, 36, 130. In 1768, the Spanish king reaffirmed this legal tradition and expressly forbade judges from explaining sentences, Levaggi, "La Fundamentación," 45–73. Note that the Catalonian region of Rousillon, which became French in the late seventeenth century, maintained a tradition of explaining sentences until it was abolished in the name of "fair justice" in 1750, Bernard Durand, "Pluralism in France in the Modern Era—Between the 'Quest for Justice' and 'Uniformity through the Law': The Case of Roussillon," in Donlan and Hierbut, *Law's Many Bodies*, 169–192; 174.

86. On increasing reception to the publication of judicial opinion in the civil law tradition, see Guzmán-Brito, *La codificación*, 221–226.

87. On Bravo de Lagunas as Defender of Indians, see Mauricio Novoa, *Protectors of Indians in the Royal Audience of Lima: History, Careers and Legal Culture, 1575–1775* (Boston: Brill, 2016).

88. Of course, during this period and certainly later, some creoles did set their legal ideas in opposition to reformers, particularly crafting legal defenses against measures taken by peninsular Bourbon interlopers such as José de Gálvez. For examples, see Mark Burkholder, *Politics of a Colonial Career: José Baquíjano and the Audiencia of Lima* (Wilmington: Scholarly Resources, 1980); and Christopher Albi's mastery of the Bourbon dynamics behind the ideas of Mexican jurist Franscico Xavier de Gamboa in "Contested" and "*Derecho Indiano.*"

89. Rodríguez García, *Criollismo*, 101–121.

90. Bravo de Lagunas has been portrayed as a Francophile peacock and a proto-nationalist, a typical colonial casuist and a pioneer of new criticism, Ruth Hill, *Hierarchy, Commerce and Fraud in Bourbon Spanish America: A Postal Inspector's Exposé* (Nashville: Vanderbilt University Press, 2005); 297 and passim; Guillermo Lohmann Villena, "Criticismo e Ilustración como factores formativos de la conciencia del Perú en el siglo XVIII," in *Problemas de la formación del estado y de la nación en Hispanoamérica*, ed. Inge Buisson et al., 15–31 (Köln: Böhlau Verlag, 1984), 24; Pablo Macera D'Orso, *Tres etapas en el desarrollo de la conciencia nacional* (Lima: Ediciones "Fanal," 1955).

91. Víctor Tau Anzoátegui argues in *El poder de la costumbre: Estudios sobre el derecho consuetudinario en América hispana hasta la emancipación* (Buenos Aires: Instituto de Investigaciones de Historia del Derecho, 1992), that the Bourbon reforms comprised a rising juridical hostility to custom, and particularly colonial custom. But a close reading of his argument shows this hostility was not necessarily widespread, and some influential jurists, including Francisco Antonio de Elizondo and Antonio Javier Pérez y López, were amenable to it, 253.

92. José Antonio de Lavallé y Arias de Saavedra, "Don Pedro José Bravo de Lagunas y Castilla (apuntes sobre su vida y sus obras)," in *Estudios históricos*, 147–194 (Lima: Gil, 1935). On the growing penchant for electing state functionaries to prestigious chairs such as the Cátedra de Primas Leyes, see Ruben Ugarte del Pino, *Historia de la Facultad de Derecho* (Lima: Universidad de Nacional Mayor de San Marcos, 1968), 20–21.

93. Bravo de Lagunas, "Carta en que se trata: si por el favor de la libertad pueda obligarse el Señor, a que reciba el precio de su siervo," 196, 197.

94. Bravo de Lagunas, "Discordia sobre la concordia," *Colección legal*, 92. In this opinion, the jurist's citations align him with a humanistic trend toward historically contextualizing Roman law, combining it with Bartolism (or a pragmatic school of applying Roman law) that was relatively common among working jurists. In other instances, his approach resembles *usus modernus pandectarum*, a way of viewing Roman laws not as authoritative transhistorically but rather as valid because they existed above time, with applicability based on the content of the particular Roman law invoked but not in the fact that it was venerable. See Randall Lesaffer and Jan Arriens, *European Legal History: A Cultural and Political Perspective* (New York: Cambridge University Press, 2009), 353, 359.

95. Macera, *Tres etapas*, 25.

96. The pamphlet was Alonso de la Cueva Ponze de Leon's defense of Church jurisdiction, *Concordia de la discordia. Sobre un punto grave de immunidad ecclesiástica* (Lima: Calle del Palacio, 1749).

97. In this case, the issue in question involved a convent's right to be paid in full for making a deal on a farm property that it had not maintained, and that thus was valued at less than the convent originally paid for it, "Discordia de la concordia. Manifesto jurídico apologético por la Jurisdicción Real, en respuesta de un libro, que con el título de Concordia de la Discordia . . . ," in Bravo de Lagunas, *Colección legal*.

98. Ibid., 137. The law is found in *Recopilación de Castilla*, 1:6:2.

99. Bravo de Lagunas, "Discordia," 138.

100. Bravo de Lagunas, " "Carta . . . de la libertad," in *Colección legal*. This 1746 opinion is the only one he was able to rescue from his home after Lima suffered a devastating earthquake in 1748 that destroyed most of his papers. Bravo de Lagunas, "Al que leyera," in *Colección legal*, 2; Lavallé y Arias de Saavedra, "Don Pedro José Bravo de Lagunas y Castilla," 185–186.

101. The general problem the text treated was how to balance Justian's injunction, repeated in the *Siete Partidas*, to "favor liberty" with what Bravo de Lagunas understood to be the "universal law" that held that no person could be forcefully dispossessed of his property, 4:22:1; Bravo de Lagunas, "Carta . . . de la libertad," 204, 203.

102. Bravo de Lagunas, "Carta . . . de la libertad," 226. On casuistry and equity, see Tau Anzoátegui, *Casuismo y sistema*, 530.

103. Bravo de Lagunas, "Carta . . . de la libertad," 228; the law on sevicia is found in *Siete Partidas* 4: 22:11.

104. Corradini was referring to a practice that took place during Spanish Habsburg rule of Naples, which ended in 1714 when the Bourbon dynasty assumed the throne in Madrid.

105. On the meaning of "town liberty," and local municipalities appeals to the Habsburg kings for autonomy, see Nader, *Liberty.*
106. On the use of precedent, and the imperative that it be shown to be "a living and actual reality," in Valencia, see Ancieto Masferrer, "Plurality of Laws and *Ius Commune* in the Spanish Legal Tradition: The Cases of Catalonia and Valencia," 193–222 in Donlan and Heirbut, *Law's Many Bodies,* 217.
107. On Larrea and his promotion of the influence of *letrados,* or university-trained lawyers, in the royal court, see Paola Volpini, "'Por la autoridad de los ministros': Obsevaciones sobre los letrados en una alegación de Juan Bautista Larrea, *Cuadernos de historia moderna* 30 (2005): 63–84. Barrientos Grandón traces his popularity to later in the century in *La cultura jurídica,* 73.
108. Bravo de Lagunas, "Carta . . . de la libertad," 234.
109. "Carta de Don Joseph Antonio de Borda Orosco y Perlata, Doctor de ambos Derechos de la Real Universidad de San Marcos," in *Colección legal,* 3. Note that de Borda found the idea that there could be an Indies-wide set of laws equally problematic, so by "national" law, he meant a law for Lima, s/f.
110. Ibid., 236.
111. The comment indicates that the flowering was actually taking place outside the universities: "All types of human letters, among those who are not professors, flower more in America than in Spain," / "Todo género de las letras humanas, entre los que no son Profesors, florecen más en la América, que en España," Bravo de Lagunas, "El Autor al Que Leyere," in *Colección legal,* 2.
112. Domingo José de Orrantia, s/t, in Bravo de Lagunas, *Colección legal . . . ,* 2.
113. Ibid., On the length of suits in the Portuguese empire, see Hespanha, *Como os juristas,* 553.
114. MacKay, *"Lazy, Improvident";* Paquette, *Enlightened Governance.*
115. Hernández-Marcos, "Conceptual Aspects," 84–85.
116. For a similar observation about the colonial origins of reform policy, see Pearce, *The Origins of the Bourbon Reforms.*
117. Particular cuidado de los Jueses en el breve despacho de las causas y negoicios y en la amistosa composición de las partes, excusando procesos en todo lo que no sea grave, Instrucción de Corregidores [Intendentes], 15 de mayo, 1788 cáp. 2 y 3, in *Recopilación de Castilla,* Ley X, cited in *Los códigos españoles. Concoradatos y anotados,* vol. 9 (Madrid: Imprenta de la Publicidad a cargo de DM Rivadeneyra, 1850), 173.
118. The Bourbon dynasty did not come to the Spanish throne with immediate plans to facilitate litigant access to the courts. In 1712, the crown issued an order that litigants from the colonies needed to indemnify paperwork-only litigation with 500 *ducados.* The order suggested that colonial litigants were making too ample use of the textual nature of suits, turning over autos without sufficient explanation, and often appealing without lawyers' arguments on the legitimacy of the request, "Para evitar lo de recursos, nulidad, e injusticia notoria que se introducian del as Audiencias de América . . . " in Diccionario de gobierno y legislación de Indias, AHN, Códices, Leg. 745, 24 de feb. de 1712.
119. "Para evitar los perjuicios que resultan de la práctica . . . dando lugar a cavilaciones de los litigantes, consumiendo mucho tiempo en la extensión de las sentencias," Ley VIII, Original Derogación del a Práctica de motivar las sentencias y extenderlas en latín en los tribunals, D. Carlos III por Real céd. De 13 de Junio de 1778 [*sic* 1768], cap. 5 y 6, *Novísma Recopilación de Castilla,* vol. VIII, 1805 (Madrid: n/p), VII p. 215.
120. Bando sobre la publicación de la Real Cédula en que establece que con solo una rebeldía se concluian los pleitos, AGN-M Bandos, Vol. 8 Exp. 72, ffs. 261–262, 1774.
121. Ibid., "ser notorious los perjuicios, gastos y molestias que sufre el Común de aquella República," "abuso, o corruptela." The colonial law was compiled in the *Recopilación de leyes de Indias,* 47:4:3.
122. Pleitos. Circular con inserción de real cédula para que los justicias no detengan su curso cuando se pida informe por la superioridad, AGN-M Bandos, Vol. 7, Exp. 61, f. 208. Also listed as "Habiéndo entendido el Rey los perjuicios que ocasionaba de suspender el curso de pedir informes," in Diccionario de gobierno y legislación de Indias, AHN, Códices, Leg. 745, 6 de Enero, 1770.

123. Ibid.
124. Carta de la Audiencia de Lima acompañando certificaciones de las Causas vistas en ella en el año anteriero, y de las que quedan pendientes con arreglo a lo prevenido en Rl Cédula de 20 de Marzo de 1790 de que también acompaña testimonio, AGI, Gobierno, Lima, 938, 1790.
125. Ibid., f 1 v.
126. Testimonio de la real cédula por la qual se dictan las normas para la aceleración de los procesos judiciales y otras disposiciones sobre la materia. El Pardo, Enero 29 de 1777, BNP, Colección Astete y Concha.
127. "Hecha presente el Regente de la Audiencia de Gualaxara se le permiese entre los Fiscales . . ." in *Diccionario de gobierno y legislación de Indias*, AHN, Códices, L. 745, under "Pleytos," and dated 20 de octobre de 1778. In addition to the flexibility displayed here concerning the extrajudicial nature of some cases, the king also showed jurisdictional flexiblity in the name of efficiency, encouraging criminal judges to hear civil cases in order to speed suits through the system in Guadalajara and Zaragoza, "Comunicación a la Audiencia de Zaragoza de una RV para que se suplan reciprocamente los Ministros de lo civil y de l crimena a fin de activar los pleitos," 19 de febrero de 1785, BNE, Manuscritos, 11265.
128. Gayol, *Laberintos* 2: 394, 428.
129. Imprint. *Instrucción de lo que deben observare los regentes de las Reales Audiencias de América: sus funciones, regalia, y como se han de haber con los Virreyes, Presidentes, y con estos aquellos*, Aranjuez, 20 de Junio 1, 1776 f. 5.
130. Ibid. f. 6.
131. While historians have yet to analyze the long-term consequences of the regent's jurisdiction, it is obvious that the new magistrate was not expected to hear all cases "miserable" litigants brought to the high court or viceroy in the first instance. Even after the establishment of the post of regent, in 1778, the viceroy of Peru was reprimanded for delegating first-instance cases to others for ruling rather than hearing them himself, demonstrating the viceroy's continued judicial power, "Apropiándose el Virrey del Peru Dn Manuel Guiror el conocimiento en primera instante . . ." in "Hecha presente el Regente de la Audiencia de Guadalaxara se le permiese entre los Fiscales . . ." in Diccionario de gobierno y legislación de Indias, AHN, Códices, L. 745, under "Pleytos," and dated 15 de mayo de 1778.
132. An example can be found in the language of "modern" legal opinions in the cédula "En que se declara que los Jueces no Letrados no sean responsables a las resueltas de las providencias que dieren con acuerdo de Asesor," 22 de sept. 1789, in Sánchez Santo, *Colección de todas la Pragmáticas, Cédulas, Provisiones, Circulares . . . publicadas en el actual reynado del Señor Don Carlos IV*, vol. 1 (Madrid: Viuda de Marin, 1793), 398.
133. *Novísma Recopilación de Castilla*, Ley XVIII, 183. The original law was "D. Carlos III por Real céd. de 17 de Mayo de 1766 con inserción de auto acordado del Consejo de 13 de mismo, "Los Jueces ordinarios no admitan recusaciones de Asesores, ni más que la de tres de ellos a cada parte."
134. Sobre lo resuelto por el Virrey para evitar el abuso de Asesores secretos con que los Jueces inferiores determinan las causas, AGI, Gobierno, Lima, 866, 1777. The bold and independent viceroy of Peru, Manuel Amat y Junient, obviously unhappy with the king's order, did a bit of doctoring of the cédula, and decided to interpret it differently, publishing it as a condemnation of litigants who had become too quick to formally recuse judges and their advisers.
135. See Abelardo Levaggi, "Los recursos de fuerza en el derecho indiano (Con especial referencia a la doctrina de Manuel Silvestre Martínez, oidor de la Audiencia de Guadalajara)," *Anuario Mexicano de Historia del Derecho* 4 (1992): 117–138; 118; 120. Other authors who discuss eighteenth-century colonial interpretations of the recurso de fuerza include Nancy Farriss, *Crown and Clergy in Colonial Mexico, 1759–1821: The Crisis of Ecclesiastical Privilege* (London: Athlone Press, University of London, 1968), 72–84; Dora Dávila Mendoza, *Hasta que la muerte nos separe: El divorcio eclesiástico en el arzobispado de México, 1702–1800* (Mexico: Colegio de México, 2005), 165.
136. José de Covarrubias, *Máximas sobre recursos de fuerza y protecciones con el método de introducirlos en los tribunales* (1790; 4th ed. Librería Razola, 1830), esp. 23–24.
137. Ibid., 98, 20.

138. D. A. Brading, *Church and State in Bourbon Mexico: The Diocese of Michoacán, 1749–1810* (1994; reprint, New York: Cambridge, 2002), 123.

139. "Sanción Prágmatica para evitar el abuso de contraer matrimonios desiguales," in Richard Konetzke, *Colleción de Documentos para la historia de la formación social de Hispanoamérica, 1493–1810*, Vol. 3, t. 1, no. 235 (Madrid: Consejo Superior de Investigaciones Científicas, 1964), 404; *Real Cédula de 10 de agosto de 1788, por la qual se ha servido S.M. declarar a quién toca y pertenece el conocimiento de el delito de Poligamía . . .* (Lima: Imprenta Real de los Niños Huérfanos, 1789). For more on these and other social reforms related to family, especially the complex colonial response to the Pragmatic Sanction on marriage choice, see Premo, *Children of the Father King*, ch. 5.

140. Sobre la causa de divorcio y sus incidencias seguidas por Da. María Romero con Dn Ygnacio Salgado, vecinos de Arequipa. AGI, Gobierno, 914, no.74, 1786.

141. Ibid.

142. "Real cédula declarando que los jueces eclesiásticos sólo deben entender en las causas de divorcios," listed as "Habiendo seguido causa de divorcio doña Josefa Castañeda con su marido don Rodrigo del Castillo, marques de Casa-Castillo en el Tribunal Eclesiástico de Lima . . ." in *Cedulario Américano* (n.p.), Newberry Library, Ayer Collection, 1788.

143. Severo Aguirre, *Prontuario alfabético y cronológico que comprende las cédulas, resoluciones, etc., expedidas el año de 1804 y algunas de las anteriores*, edited by Josef Garriga, 177 (Madrid: n/ p, 1805), cited in José M. Mariluz Urquijo, "El Derecho Prehispánico y el Derecho Indiano como modelos del Derecho Castellano," *Actas III Congreso del Instituto Internacional de Historia del Derecho Indiano Madrid, 17–23 de enero de 1972* (Madrid: Estudios Instituto Nacional de Historia del Derecho Indiano, 1978), 101–113.

144. The description of the decades-long battle between procurators and agents in Mexico is drawn from several unnumbered documents in AGI, Mexico, 1737, especially cuaderno 30, "Expediente de la Audiencia Governandora de México sobre origen en oficios vendibles y renunciables de las Agencias de Negocio de aquel reyno," which contains the contador's final decision, and cuaderno 611, "Sobre la confrimación de títulos de oficios vendibles y renunciables Secretario don Josef de Garraez."

145. Gayol, *Laberintos*, 2:405–408.

146. "Expediente de la Audiencia Governandora de México, AGI, Mexico, 1737, item 5.

147. Ibid.

148. Real cédula 21 abril, 1795, "El baylio frey don Francisco Gil de Taboada, Lemos y Villamarin . . . Para remediar los graves inconvenientes que resultan del número indefinido y arbitrario de agentes, y solicitadores para los negocios de esos mis reynos en la corte," JCB, S.7333.1795.5. For example, representing relatives within a certain degree of affinity was prohibited, and agents were to have offices, described as "open and lively houses that are self-sufficient."

149. Ibid: "my Vassals of the Indies can confer their Powers [of attorney] and charges to the subjects to their liking and confidence, as long as they are not excluded by Laws and Ordinances, using in this matter the liberty enjoyed by the inhabitants of these my Kingdoms [on the peninsula], such that my vassals of the Indies commit their Powers [of attorney] to whomever [they wish], even if they are not Numbered Agents."

150. "Discurso que en elogio del Rey nuestro Señor leyó J. Joseph de Guevara Vasconcelos, el Censor Perpetúo de la Real Sociedad Económica de Madrid . . ." in *Memorial literario instructivo y curioso de la Corte de Madrid* 13 (Madrid: Imprenta Real, 1787): 236–244; 243.

Chapter 3

1. Pérez-Perdomo, *Latin American Lawyers*, 33; Michael Scardaville, "Justice by Paperwork: A Day in the Life of a Court Scribe in Bourbon Mexico City," *Journal of Social History* 36, no. 4 (Summer 2003): 979–1007; Taylor, *Magistrates of the Sacred*, 363.

2. Hespanha, "De novo, os factos," 1. In addition to Hespanha's work with the appearance of keywords in published materials, he also has quantified the contents of libraries in *Como os juristas*, 9.

3. For the need for such work, see Pérez-Perdomo, *Latin American Lawyers*, 35–36; Gayol, *Labrintos*, 2:417.
4. While it might seem intuitive that city dwellers sued more than rural folk, in fact some historians argue that a number of factors aside from sheer population density affect litigation rates and that rural people can sometimes be more litigious than urban inhabitants, Louis Knafla, "The Geographical, Jurisdiction, and Jurisprudential Boundaries of English Litigation in the Early Modern Seventeenth Century," in *Boundaries of the Law: Geography, Gender, and Jurisdiction in Medieval and Early Modern Europe*, ed. Anthony Musson (Burlington, VT: Ashgate, 2005), 130–148, esp. 139.
5. Griet Vermeesch, "Professional Lobbying in Eighteenth-Century Brussels: The Role of Agents in Petitioning the Central Government Institutions in the Habsburg Netherlands," *Journal of Early Modern History* 16 (2012): 95–119; Vermeesch, "Social Composition." Vermeech refers to Ab Verscuren's influence on the concept of the "great decline," *The Great Council of Malines in the 18th Century: An Aging Court in a Changing World: Studies in the History of Law and Justice* 3 (Leuven: Springer Cham, 2015), 256–262.
6. For the difficulties given the incoherence of the legal archive, see Julie Hardwick, *Family Business: Litigation and the Political Economies of Everyday Life* (New York: Oxford University Press, 2009), 14.
7. See, for example, my analysis of marital annulments heard by the ecclesiastical courts, and guardianship and apprenticeship contracts in *Children of the Father King*, 66–70; 260–261. For a general decline in Church marriage litigation in the archdiocese of Lima, see Bernard Lavallè, *Amor y opresión en los Andes coloniales* (Lima: Instituto de Estudios Peruanos, 1999), 25.
8. Autos seguidos por Liberata de Jesús, contra D. Pedro Tramarría, su amo, sobre sevicia y que la venda a precio de tasación, AGN-P, Cab. Civ., Leg. 68, C. 1328, 1791.
9. "Hecha presente el Regente de la Audiencia de Gualaxara se le permiese entre los Fiscales . . ." in Diccionario de gobierno y legislación de Indias, AHN, Códices, L. 745, under "Pleytos," and dated 20 de octubre de 1778.
10. Carta de la Audiencia de Lima acompañando certificaciones de las Causas vistas en ella en el año anterior, y de las que quedan pendientes con arreglo a lo prevenido en Rl Cédula de 20 de Marzo de 1790 de que también acompaña testimonio, AGI, Gobierno, Lima, 938, 1791.
11. Ymbentario de todas la actuaciones Civiles y Criminales que existen en este Archivo y sus Protocolos deduciéndo desde el tiempo que Gobernó esta Jurisdicción dn Francisco [*sic.* Josef] Rodríguez Franco hasta el presente, AHJO, Civil, leg. 49, exp. 15, n/d [1793]. The mistake in names seems to be because the court notary mixed up the name of the alcalde mayor and his nephew, a prominent merchant in the region. The dating of Franco's tenure as alcalde mayor comes from a 1729 petition to extend his term an additional five years, which was denied. María de los Ángeles Romero Frizzi has Franco beginning his tenure in 1725, *Economía y vida de los españoles en la Mixteca Alta, 1519–1720* (Mexico City: Instituto Nacional de Antropología e Historia/Gobierno del Estado de Oaxaca, 1990), 610.
12. This is the number I found in my own count of cases, facilitated by the kind staff of the AHJO. A computer search of the archive database for the period 1725–92 yields even more cases—1212 in total—undoubtedly because the database is more likely to add administrative files that I discounted as "cases."
13. Unfortunately, the 1793 Teposcolula inventory does not list the precise dates of cases but rather the name of the alcalde mayor who adjudicated them. But the inventory is suggestive of the great variation in the volume of cases in different regions of the empire and in different courts, revealing that tribunals distant from Spanish cities had far lighter court traffic than elsewhere. Taking litigation rates as a relative constant over the period 1725–93, the Teposcolula inventory suggests a litigation distribution rate of roughly 10 cases per year (713 over 68 years). By contrast, in the city of Lima. there are 1581 cases recorded in the first-instance city tribunal for the period 1720–99, making the rate 50 per year. According to the inventory of the Real Audiencia of Lima, in 1793–94 alone, judges made a final ruling on 147 cases, interim rulings on 482, and had 296 rulings pending, Carta del Regente . . . ,1793 y 4, AGI, Gobierno, Lima, 956, no. 62, 1795. Thus, in a two-year period, the Audiencia of Lima oversaw roughly the same number of cases that the alcaldes mayores of Teposcolula heard in a 60-plus year period.

14. Note that both rates are low compared with figures from the Valley of Oaxaca in the 1760s, according to short descriptive entries on civil proceedings in that district, APGEO, Oaxaca (district), AM, Leg. 31, exp. 7, 1761–1766. This inventory puts the total of cases heard in the Valley at 233 over a period spanning from May 2, 1761 to December 21, 1767 (or 4 1/2 years) This was a rate of about 52 per year—twice as high as in Teposcolula in the 1770s, again underscoring how geographic proximity to larger Spanish colonial cities correlated to higher rates of litigation. On the population of the region, see William B. Taylor, *Landlord and Peasant in Colonial Oaxaca* (Stanford: Standford University Press, 1972), 34.

15. Sewell, *Logics*, 82.

16. AHR Conversation, "Explaining Historical Change," *American Historical Review*.

17. Note that Hespanha finds a much higher correlation between litigation rates and population for Portugal's large tribunals, but that the correlation wanes in smaller jurisdictions, and in all cases litigiousness appears affected by a series of other, circumstantial and local factors, "De novo," 8.

18. Population figures for Lima are derived from a comparison of Noble David Cook, comp. *Numeración general de todas las personas de ambos sexos, edades y calidades q[ue] se ha [h]echo en esta Ciudad de Lima, año de 1700* (Facsimile edition, Lima: COFIDE, 1985) with "Plan demostrativo de la población comprehendida en el recinto de la Ciudad de Lima," *Mercurio Peruano* 9, 30 enero, 1791.

19. The figures for Mexico City are based on a comparison of the figures of 100,000 for 1697 provided by Italian traveler Gremelli Carerri and a figure of 168,000 from a census conducted in 1811. For these figures and intervening population counts, see Haslip-Viera, *Crime and Punishment*, 19; Scardaville, "Justice by Paperwork," 981. The figures for Mexico as a whole are from Alan Knight, *Mexico: The Colonial Era* (New York: Cambridge University Press, 2002), 209. Knight has the population of Mexico City doubling over the eighteenth century, 207.

20. John K. Chance estimates a population of 36,400 in 1702 and of 42,800 in 1789, *Conquest of the Sierra: Spaniards and Indians in Colonial Oaxaca* (Norman: University of Oklahoma, 1995), 69.

21. See Shelburne Cook and Woodrow Borah, *The Population of the Mixteca Alta* (Berkeley: University of California, 1968), 54, 40.

22. Weisser, *Peasants*, 59–69; Antonio Domínguez Ortiz, *Sociedad y Estado en el siglo XVIII español* (1986; reprint, Madrid: Ariel, 1990), 192; 194. Cf. Kagan, *Lawsuits*, 91.

23. The population demonstrated only the modest growth from 104,046 inhabitants in 1751 to 106,514 in the years 1786–87 according to Ramón Sánchez González, *Los Montes de Toledo en el Siglo XVIII (Un estudio demográfico)* (Toledo: Instituto Provincial de Investigaciones y Estudios Toledanos, 1984), 25–33; 79.

24. This kind of argument is obvious in the literature on rural Mexico leading to the 1810 Hidalgo Rebellion. See John Tutino, *From Insurrection to Revolution in Mexico: Social Bases of Agrarian Violence, 1750–1940* (Princeton: Princeton University Press, 1986), esp. 4–182; Eric van Young, "Agrarian Rebellion and Defense of Community: Meaning and Collective Violence in Late Colonial and Independence-Era Mexico" *Journal of Social History* 27 (1993): 245–269, esp. 252; Arij Ouweneel and C. Bijleveld, "The Economic Cycle of Bourbon Central Mexico: A critique of the 'recaudacion del diezmo líquido en pesos'," *Hispanic American Historical Review* 69 (1989): 479–530, esp. 505; Brian Hamnett, *Roots of Insurgency: Mexican Regions, 1750–1824* (London: Cambridge University Press, 1986).

25. Juan Miguel González Fernández, *La conflictividad judicial ordinaria en la Galicia Atlántica (1670–1820)* (Vigo: Instituto de Estudios Vigueses, 1997), 22.

26. Virginia García Acosta, Juan Manuel Pérez Zavallos, et al., eds., *Desastres agrícolas en México. Catálogo histórico, Tomo I, Epocas prehispánica y colonial, 958–1822* (México DF: Centro de Investigaciones y Estudios Superiores de Antropología Social, 2003), esp. 334–347.

27. Kagan, *Lawsuits*, see esp. 2; Christopher W. Brooks, *Pettyfoggers and Vipers of the Commonwealth: The "Lower Branch" of the Legal Profession in Early Modern England* (New York: Cambridge University Press, 1986), 90–97. Also see Vermeesch's synthesis of historiography on this point for Europe and her astute comments on the fact that middling groups also occupied the ranks of so called "miserables" or needy litigants, "The Clientele," 7.

28. Michael Braddick, *State Formation in Early Modern England, c. 1550–1700* (New York: Cambridge University Press, 2000), 162. Also see Cynthia Herrup, *The Common Peace: Participation and the Criminal Law in Seventeenth-Century England* (New York: Cambridge University Press, 1987); Michael Breen, "Law, Society, and the State in Early Modern France," *Journal of Modern History* 83 (2011): 354.

29. Vermeesch, "Clientele," 5. Cf. Hardwick, who finds few very poor or very rich in the lower-level civil courts of seventeenth-century Nantes and Lyon, and a bias in favor of men as litigators except in certain types of disputes, *Family Business*, 63, 77.

30. María Pérez-Canto, *Lima en el siglo XVIII: Estudio Socioeconómico* (Madrid: Universidad Autónoma de Madrid, 1985), 89.

31. Ruiz, *Colegio de Abogados*.

32. Gayol, *Laberintos*, 2:411, 427. He admits that this is conjecture, however, since appeals procedure in the new Bourbon system was unclear.

33. See Ch. 1, note 28.

34. Pérez-Perdomo, *Latin American Lawyers*, 38–41.

35. Brooks has demonstrated convincingly for the case of England that surges in the number of lawyers followed litigation increases, *Lawyers, Litigation*, 85.

36. Scardaville, "Justice by Paperwork," 981–982.

37. Among Anglophone legal historians, Hendrick Hartog's "Pigs and Positivism" is a classic methodological primer on how to analytically privilege participants' perceptions and practices of law over written edicts and judgments, *University of Wisconsin Law Review* 4 (1985): 899–935.

38. On the role of culture in affecting perceptions of structural phenomena, see Eric van Young, *The Other Rebellion: Popular Violence, Ideology and the Mexican Struggle for Independence, 1810–1821* (Stanford: Stanford University Press, 2001), 8. Also note Taylor's observation that rebellions resulted from villagers' sense of "relative deprivation," *Drinking, Homicide*, 134–142. For the same argument see Sewell, *Logics*, ch. 10; and his contribution to AHR Conversation, Explaining Historical Change," *American Historical Review*, 1392.

39. On the cultural undertones of even debt suits, see Kagan, *Lawsuits*, 95; Scott Taylor, "Credit, Debt and Honor in Castile, 1600–1650," *Journal of Early Modern History* 7, nos. 1–2 (2003): 7–27.

40. See Scott K. Taylor, *Honor and Violence in Golden Age Spain* (New Haven: Yale University Press, 2008), passim; Kagan, *Lawsuits*, 139.

41. Navalmoral. Sobre desobediencia, AMT, Criminal, caja 6323, no. 3637, 1724.

42. Palomeque Torres, "El Fiel del Juzgado."

43. See, for example, the breach of contract consisting of "verbal orders" in the rent case in Navalucillos, López v. Montero, AMT, Ejecutivos, caja 1914, 1743.

44. William E. Christian, *Local Religion in Sixteenth-Century Spain* (Princeton: Princeton University Press, 1981), 20–21.

45. Fontanarejo. Partición de vienes por muerte de Josef Santos del Cerro, AMT, Pleitos, caja 1870, 1784, f. 1v.

46. For examples of suspicions about outsiders (*forasteros*), see Sobre incendios, San Pablo de Yébenes, AMT, Crim., caja 595, s/n, 1734; Denunciación por vender pan a precio más alta que el del pósito, San Pablo de Yébenes, AMT, Crim., caja 596, no. 20, 1764. For claims against "gypsies," see Diligencias por vida desacomodada, abiertas de oficio contra Josefa Destazaval, Juana de la Nata, Teresa de Salazar, gitanas a quienes acompaña una niña de 6 años y que van al camino a Almadén donde los maridos están condenados a las minas, Navalpino, AMT, Crim., caja 6327, no. 3751,1700. For the insult of "Jew," see Causa por injurias, incidada de oficio contra José Marco Fernández, médico, que dice publicamente que Alonso Crisanto de la Fuente (cura) es judío y otras ofensas, Navalucillos AMT, caja 6340, no. 4201, 1757. For more on attitudes toward "outsiders" in the Montes, see Weisser, *Peasants*; and in Spain in general, see Tamar Herzog, *Defining Nations: Immigrants and Citizens in Early Modern Spain and Spanish America* (New Haven: Yale University Press, 2003).

47. Note that while the ayuntamiento of Toledo traditionally confirmed the election of higher officials in the villages, lower officials (such as tax collectors, granary official, etc.) were elected locally, Antonio Palomeque Torres, "Derechos de arancel de la justicia civil y criminal

en los lugares de los propios y montes de la ciudad de Toledo anteriores al año 1500," *Anuario de Historia del Derecho Español* (1954): 89–90. However, even though all officials swore to enforce the Fiel's mandates, it is not clear that any elections were still approved by this official by the end of the eighteenth century, Palomeque Torres, "El Fiel," 377–378.

48. Novés, Don Julián Gil de Rosas, procurador síndico general del lugar de Novés, sobre que se le de testimonio de un acuerdo zelebrado por el consejo, AMT, Civiles, 1886, no. 1741.

49. Proceso por desórdenes iniciadio de oficio después de que un grupo de mozos y mujeres impidiesen a un moisario y al cura el traslado de la imagen de la Virgen a al ermita de Nuestra Señora de Herrera, Navalucillos, AMT, Criminal, caja, 6340, no. 4220, 1774, see esp. cuaderno 2, f. 46.

50. Vecinos de Navalucillos y subdelegado sobre la reintegración de los pósitos de Montes, AMT, Civiles, caja 1870, 1771.

51. See Herzog, *Upholding Justice.* On the stability that this tension produced viewed from the angle of the history of "conflict" and "consensus" in Spanish society and institutions, see my comments in Bianca Premo, "Quejas ilustradas. Litigios en la historia de España e Hispanoamérica (siglo XVIII)," *Memoria y Civilización: Anuario de Historia* (Navarra, Spain) 14 (2011): 155–173. On the tendency to use mediation that did not result in formal suits in early modern English legal culture, see Braddick, *State Formation*, 155.

52. Note the similiarity with Hespanha's observations for Portugal that educated judges more commonly issued sentences and, in comparison to criminal cases, civil regional judges were less likely to bring a case to sentence, "De novo," 9.

53. Viveros. Josef Martínez v. Josef de Pazos y Bartolomé Díaz, AMT, Pleitos, caja 1886, 1776.

54. For example, Navalmoral. Manuel Gómez Escalonilla vezino de dho lugar con Julián Gómez de la Cruz y consortes de la misma vecindad sobre que dejen libre y desembarazada unas casa, AMT, Civiles, caja 1886, 1772.

55. For two instances, see Navamoral. Paz v. López, 1756, AMT, Ejecutivos, caja 1913; Ventas, Instancia of Francisco Matheo, AMT, Ejecutivos, caja 1903, 1749.

56. In the registries of the three notarial offices of the Chancerellía of Valladolid, *casos olvidados* comprised 57.7 percent of all civil cases in the eighteenth century (12067 out of 20884). While less statistically certain, a sample of 21 divorce cases from 1700 and 23 from 1789 and 1790 in the AAL-Divorcios section shows the majority ending with no explanation (16), one case ending when a woman formally dropped the case, and one case moved to royal jurisidiction. Several cases are merely opening petitions.

57. Note that an apartamiento in the Montes entailed exonerating the accused of corporeal punishment. Taylor, *Honor and Violence*, 81–83. In Spanish America, a more common way to drop a suit was a less formal request to "*bajar*" or "*desistir*" the case, as in Sobre la reunión al matrimonio de Anastacio Baraoas y María Trinidad Delgado, AGN-M, TSJ Correg., Crim., Vol. 17 Exp. 58, 1801, f. 2.

58. Braddick, *State Formation*, 162. In the Montes, see Kagan, *Lawsuits*, 82–83; Taylor, *Honor and Violence*, 81–83.

59. Razón de causas pendientes en el Tribunal del Sr Fiel del Juzgado, AMT, Fiel del Juzgado, 1150, 1793.

60. Mantecón Movellán, *Conflictividad* and "El peso de la infrajusticialidad en el control del crimen durante la Edad Moderna," *Estudis* 28 (2002); 43–75. Mantecón calls this "infrajustice," a term with origins in criminal history of early modern France. See Benoît Garnot, "Justice, infrajustice, parajustice, et extra justice dans la France d'Ancien Régime," *Crime, Histoire, et Sociétés* 4, no. 1 (2000): 103–140.

61. Mantecón Movellán, *Conflictividad*, 457. Such legal strategies comprised a local version of a larger early modern structure of rule in which oligarchs served as intermediaries between "society in general" and the highest echelons of political power. See José Aranda Pérez, coord., *Poderes intermedios, poderes interpuestos: Sociedad y oligarquías en la España Moderna* (Ciudad Real: Universidad Castilla-La Mancha, 1999).

62. Tommaso Astarita, *Village Justice: Community, Family, and Popular Culture in Early Modern Italy* (Baltimore, MD: Johns Hopkins University Press, 1999). "Peace" as a discourse and approbation of litigious or fractious neighbors can be found from Coyoacán to Cantabria to Calabria, though the terminology used to express it could be "peace," "order," or "friendship,"

Owensby, *Empire of Law*, 236–38; Mantecón, *Conflictividad*, 124–26; Astarita, *Village Justice*, 133–36.

63. Kagan, *Lawsuits*, 87–89.

64. Ventas, Vicente Narváez Portocarrero contra los oficiales de Ventas de Peña de Alguilera, AMT, Pleitos, 1970, 1776.

65. José María Barreda Fontes and Juan Manuel Carretero Zamora, *Ilustración y reforma en La Mancha: las reales sociedades económicas de Amigos de País* (Madrid: Consejo Superior de investiagaciones Científicas, Instituto de Historia "Jerónimo Zurita," 1981), 74.

66. Regidor Vicente Narváez Portocarrero incited the investigation, which was informally referred to as an "instancia," making it vague and somewhat unofficial. On the strict forensic definition of "instancia" as "la excertación de la acción en Juicio, depués de la contestación hasta la sentencia definitiva," see Real Academia Española, *Diccionario de la lengua castellana, en que se explica el verdadero sentido de las voces . . .* (Madrid: Imprenta de Francisco del Hierro, 1734), 238. On Narváez as a member of the Economic Society, see Barreda Fontes and Carretero, *Ilustración y reforma*, 41, 104.

67. The testimony of villagers does, at a couple points, refer to earlier "papers" filed concerning this issue, but it appears that this is a reference to a case that the corrupt notary brought on behalf of the village, not their own suit, Ventas, s/t (Narváez), AMT, Pleitos, caja 1970, 1776.

68. Historian Bernard Durand observes of Rousillon, a Catalonian region under French rule, that in the 1700s "litigants increasingly sought to settle their cases and to right their wrongs out of court," creating "a whole new system distinct from the official world of tribunals," "Pluralism in France," 185–186. Also see Braddick, *State Formation*, 161–163.

69. As just one example, villages met a mid-century royal order aimed at the conservation of natural resources in the "depopulated, burned up and deforested" region with defensive withdrawal, challenging the Fiel's jurisdiction to enforce the royal order by invoking local "uses and custom." See the dispute between the alcalde of Yébenes and the Fiel discussed in Palomeque Torres, "El Fiel del Juzgado," 373–375. For more on the invocation of "custom" relative to this royal assertion of authority over resources, see the Reales Cédulas in AMT, Fiel del Juzgado, cajas 1150, 1748; 1798; 1824.

70. S/t (Letter from Juan Fernández de Palomo), AMT, Fiel del Juzgado, 1150, 1797, f. 1v.

71. Vicente Marín con Manuel Maldonado, sobre fraudes cometidos en el peso de su tienda, Los Yébenes (Toledo), AHN, Consejo, 29384, Exp.17, 1796.

72. The position of the Fiel del Juzgado was dissolved when the Constitution of 1812 rid the empire altogether of "*montes y propios*," or city-owned rural lands on which peasants paid taxes. Any montes y propios reinstated after the restoration of Fernando VII were finally appropriated by the government in 1832 in the "Ordenanzas generales de montes," passed in the Cortes on 18 Nov., 1838, reprinted in Francisco Agustín Silvela, *Colección de proyectos, ditámenes, y leyes orgánicas ó Estudios prácticos de administración* (Madrid: Imprenta Real, 1939), 364.

73. See, for example, Alan Knight, "Is Political Culture Good to Think?," in *Political Cultures in the Andes, 1750–1950*, ed. Nils Jacobsen and Cristóbal Aljovín de Losada, 25–57 (Durham: Duke University Press, 2005).

74. Benton, *Law and Colonial Cultures*, 4.

75. Catherine L. Fisk and Robert W. Gordon, "'Forward: 'Law As'. . .Theory and Method in Legal History," *UC Irvine Law Review* 1, no. 3 (2011), 525.

76. This formulation is first introduced into the AHR Conversation, "Explaining Historical Change," by Hewitson, 1374, who cites Miguel Cabrera, "On Language, Culture, and Social Actions," *History and Theory* 40 (2001): 82–100.

77. Sewell, *Logics*, 100–103. On agency in history and the importance of consciousness, see 143. I am aware that Sewell's emphasis on the recognition of an event and on historical subjects' emotional reactions to events are highly linked to Kantian articulations of history as the witnessing of events with empathy, something further explored in Chapter 6 and the Conclusion. On the Enlightenment and agency in history, see Maurizio Passerin d'Entrèves, "Critique of Enlightenment: Michel Foucault on '*Was isst Aufklärung?*'" In *The Enlightenment and Modernity*, ed. Norman Geras and Robert Wokler, 184–203 (New York: St Martins, 2000), esp. 191. On the rise of a "public" for the courts (as opposed to passive "audiences" for theaters) and for legal cases as events to be participated in through reading, see Sarah Maza, *Private*

Lives and Public Affairs: The Cause Célèbres of Prerevolutionary France (Berkeley: University of California Press, 1993); on the notion of spectatorship as an Enlightenment development in which the humanity of the observed must be conceded, see, Lynn Hunt, *Inventing Human Rights: A History* (New York, WW Norton, 2007), 65–66.

78. Lynn Hunt, "The Self and Its History," *American Historical Review* 119, no. 5 (2014): 1576–1586; esp. 1582; Tatasuya Sato, Tomo Hidaka, and Mari Fukada, "Depicting the Dynamics of Living the Life: The Trajectory Equifinality Model," in *Dynamic Process Methodology in the Social Sciences and Developmental Sciences*, ed. Jann Valsiner, Peter C. M. Mollenar et al., 217–240 (New York: Springer, 2009), 223.

79. Beyond the scholars just mentioned, it is worth noting that historians from diverse fields seem to be moving toward a kind of post- (or never) cultural- historical moment in which historians read legal documents specifically for bottom-up perceptions of historical change in concepts of law. This move has an established genealogy in legal history, summarized in Dylan C. Penningroth, "Law as Redemption: A Historical Comparison of the Way Marginalized People Use Courts," *Law and Social Inquiry* 40, no. 3 (2015): 793–796. Also see Hardwick, *Family Business*, 14. For a bit of a different take on the same issue, but in terms of concepts of race, see Twinam's comments on method in *Purchasing Whiteness*, 36–38.

80. Expediente seguido por Michaela Mina, esclava de doña Luisa Luxán Alfaro contra don Joseph Pesantes, marido de esta última sobre que se le venda a otro amo por padecer de abuso excesivo e intolerable sevicia, ARL, Cab. C.O., Leg. 44, C. 791, 1741, f. 11.

81. Expediente seguido por Juan Lorenzo Rizo, Protector de los Naturales del Corregimiento de Truxillo, por lo tocante al Común de ellos del pueblo de San Pedro de Virú, contra los Alcaldes y mandones del dicho pueblo para que no apremien a los indios de su comunidad a pagar derrames gravosas, ARL, Correg., C.O., Leg. 224, C. 1898, 1748, f. 1.

82. Autos seguidos por Segunda Montejo, contra su marido Escolástico Paredes, sobre divorcio, AAT-Divorcios, 1789.

83. Kagan, *Lawsuits*, 102–104.

84. It should be noted that less powerful defendants made slightly greater use of legal action of the "instancia," which is a brief petition that does not necessarily have to take place within a lawsuit proper. This is what happened to the legal testimony of the peasants from the town of Ventas who complained of the "*ricos.*" Less powerful petitioners involved in conflicts with social superiors submitted 10 of the 51 legal actions I identified as non-lawsuit requests for the Fiel de Juzgado to take summary executive action in the form of instancias or another genre of legal civil action known as "ejecutivos." Technically, "ejecutivos" were requests to carry out a sentence previously handed down and "instancias" were actions within a formal case. However, most documents in the Ejecutivos series of the AMT are sui generis actions with a range of relationships to formal cases. The mixing of genres is undoubtedly because some cajas are clearly not categorized by type of legal instrument but rather consist of the records of court notaries. For example, AMT, Ejecutivos, caja 1903 seem derived from the offices of notary Felix Bonillo and procurator Manuel Felix Arroyo. The sample was derived from an examination of the contents of the AMT, Ejecutivos, cajas 1903, 1906, 1908, 1909, 1913, 915 1915; and Civiles, cajas 1870, 1883, 1885.

85. I chose to analyze Trujillo 1800–19 here because of the clear upward trajectory of suits, the first-instance nature of the cases, and the availability of case descriptions for analysis in the ARL's published catalog.

86. I categorized cases that the Defender of Minors brought on behalf of minors of age for inheritance as "subordinates suing superiors" based on the age imbalance in the suits, even though the minors were sometimes of the same social standing as their progenitors or other inheritors, and sometimes were not illegitimate. Excluding those cases leaves 12 cases, or 17.9 percent of all suits, a lighter upward tilt of subordinate-initiated disputes but still the inverse of the proportion in the Montes de Toledo in the eighteenth century. For the changing character of disputes involving minors, see Premo, *Children of the Father King*.

87. Combining the records of the Corregimiento and the Intendancy of Trujillo demonstrates that rent cases comprised 5.6 percent (41 out of 731) during the period 1700–99 and did not increase proportionally during the period 1800–20, comprising 4.6 (16 out 356 cases) during the region's litigation boom. In the first instance court of the Cabildo there were 32 rent

cases brought from 1558–1700 (5 percent of all cases), 5 in the 1700s (1 percent of all cases) and 1 for the period 1800–20 (0.5 percent) making their proportion to all cases either highly variable or possibly indicative of a proportional decline in the number of superiors suing subordinates during litigation growth.

Part II

1. Autos seguidos por D. Felipe Sancho Dávila contra D. José Tomás Carillo sobre incumplimiento de un contracto de alquiler, AGN, Cab., Civ., Leg. 70, C. 1365, 1791. Note that the landlord seems to have written his own petitions and signed one "por mi procurador," Baltazar de los Reyes, who is the same procurador discussed in Chapter 1 and the Conclusion, for whom another litigant, Arburúa, also signed.
2. Ibid., 9; 9v.
3. Autos seguidos por D. José Moreno contra D. Felipe Uzeda por cantidad de posos, provenientes de alquileres impagados, AGN P, RA Civ, Leg. 378. C. 473, 1799, f. 3.
4. Ibid.
5. *Siete Partidas*, 5:8:6.
6. See the contract for a new renter in Autos seguidos por D. Juan Silverio Boto contra Ventura Garrido, sobre que desocupe la casa, AGN-P. Cab., Civ, Leg. 22, C. 366, 1767, f. 2.
7. Autos seguidos por D. José Moreno, f. 36 and passim.
8. Autos seguidos por D. Juan Silvero Boto, f. 5.
9. The landlord lists a series of disputes in ibid., f. 8. Another man, driven out of a room in a boarding house for debt, repeatedly jurisdiction-shopped and encountered judges who sided with the owner of the institution. He too tried to appeal to common practice if not precedent, claiming that the administrator of the rooming house often made far more lenient arrangements with other boarders, to which the administrator responded that the landlord's right to evict the tenant was simply legally incontestable, Autos seguidos por el Marqués de Casa Concha contra D. Juan Antonio Espineira, sobre pago de los alquileres de la casa en que habita, AGN-P, RA, Civ, Leg. 380, C. 3490, 1799, ff. 11–13.
10. Autos seguidos por D. José Moreno, f. 42.

Chapter 4

1. "*Pleito*," in Real Academia Española, *Diccionario de la lengua castellana, en que se explica el verdadero sentido de las voces* . . . (Madrid: Impenta de Francisco del Hierro, 1737). For the word's civil legal connotations, compare to the more specific terms for criminal suits, *querella* and *causa*, ibid., 464 and Real Academia Española, *Diccionario de la lengua castellana, en que se explica el verdadero sentido de las voces* . . . (Madrid: Impenta de Francisco del Hierro, 1727), 236.
2. Causa formada a pedim[ien]to de Don José María Olaeta contra su muger Da. María Monzón, AGN, TSJ, Correg., Crim., Vol. 17, Exp. 59, 1801; Don Antonio de la Cruz, cacique y principal de San Francisco Yovego, contra Sebastián Contreras, indio, natural de Yovego, por golpear a Maria Antonia de la Cruz, su mujer, AHJO, VA Crim., Leg. 22, Exp. 6, 1797. For similar usage see AGN-M, Inquisición, Vol. 1292, Exp. 12, 1788, f. 87–92; AGN-M, Crim., Vol. 131, Exp. 37, 1769, ff. 421–423.
3. The domestic discord at the base of *procesos* brought before the tribunals of the Holy Office of the Inquisition, as well as cases filed by the wives or relatives of military personnel who enjoyed special legal prerogatives in military tribunals (*fuero militar*) would also prove illuminating. But the uneven nature of these sources for the regions under study, and simple constraints of research resources, confined me to Church and royal cases.
4. For more on this, see Premo, "Before the Law," 261–289.
5. Ana Lidia García, *El fracaso del amor: Género e individualidad en México del siglo XIX* (México DF: Colegio de México/Universidad Nacional Aútonoma de México, 2006).
6. Jessica Delgado, "*Sin temor de Dios*: Women and Ecclesiastical Justice in Eighteenth-Century Toluca," *Colonial Latin American Review* 18, no. 1 (2009): 99–121; 101–103.
7. See, for example, "Sanción Prágmatica para evitar el abuso de contraer matrimonios desiguales," in Konetzke, *Colleción de Documentos* 3, 404; *Real Cédula de 10 de agosto de 1788*,

por la qual se ha servido S.M. declarar a quién toca y pertenece el conocimiento de el delito de Poligamía . . . (Lima: Imprenta Real de los Niños Huérfanos, 1789).

8. Silvia Marina Arrom, *The Women of Mexico City, 1700–1820* (Stanford: Stanford University Press, 1985); Patricia Seed, *To Love, Honor and Obey in Colonial Mexico: Conflicts over Marriage Choice, 1574–1821* (Stanford: Stanford University Press, 1988); Dávila Mendoza, *Hasta que la muerte*; Javier Juan Pescador, "Entre la espada y el olvido: pleitos matrimoniales en el provisorato eclesiástico de México, siglo XVIII," in *La familia en el mundo iberoamericano*, ed. Pilar Gonzalbo Aizpuru (Mexico City: Instituto de Investigaciones Sociales, UNAM, 1994), 373–386.

9. Of these, "*acciones*" were the most rooted in judicial rights, or the right to sue, until the end of the eighteenth century. Joaquín Escriche y Martín defines acción as "the right to sue over something," in *Diccionario razonado de legislación y jurisprudencia* (Paris: Librería de Rósa, Bouret y Cia., 1851), 175. For women's rights in Spanish law see Arrom, *Women of Mexico City*; Uribe-Uran, *Fatal Love*, 29–38. Also see Kimberly Gauderman, *Women's Lives in Colonial Quito: Gender, Law and Economy in Spanish America* (Austin: University of Texas Press, 2003), 144–145; and Viviana Kluger, *Escenas de la vida conyugal: Los conflictos matrimoniales en la sociedad virreinal rioplatense* (Buenos Aires: Editorial Quoram, 2003).

10. For the generally elite nature and female nature of annulment and divorce litigation throughout Spanish America, see Arrom, *Women of Mexico City*; 219 (though she finds the process, while expensive, nonetheless "accesible"); Bernard Lavallé, *Amor y opresión en los Andes coloniales* (Lima: Instituto de Estudios Peruanos, 1999), 88; Kluger, *Escenas*, 238; Natalia León, *La primera alianza: El matrimonio criollo: Honor y violencia conyugal* (Quito: Nueva Editorial, 1997); Nancy van Deusen, *Between the Sacred and the Worldly: The Institutional and Cultural Practice of Recogimiento* (Stanford: Stanford University Press, 2000), Dávila Mendoza, *Hasta que la muerte*; Jonathan Bird, "For Better or For Worse: Divorce and Annulment Lawsuits in Colonial Mexico (1544–1799)," PhD diss., Duke University, 2013. For Spain, see the works cited in María José de la Pascua Sánchez "Violencia y familia en la Espanã del Antiguo Régimen," *Estudis* 28 (2002): 77–100; 81, n. 32–34.

11. See, for example, AGI, Gobierno, 914, no.74, 1786. Similarly, see ARL, Intend., Civ., Leg. 447, C. 316, 1796.

12. For example, Martha Few finds that in the Guatemalan Holy Office Inquisition trials against women constitute 36 percent of all of those on file from 1650–1750, *Women Who Lead Evil Lives: Gender, Religion and the Politics of Power in Colonial Guatemala* (Austin: University of Texas Press, 2002), 142.

13. Allyson M. Poska, *Women and Authority in Early Modern Spain: The Peasants of Galicia* (New York: Oxford University Press, 2005), 176. Also see María José de la Pascua Sánchez, "Women Alone in Enlightenment Spain," in *Eve's Enlightenment: Women's Experience in Spain and Spanish America, 1726–1839*, ed. Catherine M. Jaffe and Elizabeth Franklin Lewis (Baton Rouge: Louisiana State University Press, 2009), 128–142.

14. In a sample of 74 suits before the Fiel del Juzgado (*civiles* and *ejecutorías*) from the 1700s, only two were filed by married women, and one was a case brought by a remarried widow against her second husband for dissipating the property she brought into the marriage. See Arroba, Jazinta de Paz, muger de Antonio García Fernández, alias el Pabo, sobre se le abilite por la administración de sus bienes, AMT, Civiles, Caja 1881, 1771.

15. Kagan finds that one-fifth of Montes civil cases in the period 1500–1650 involved widows, *Lawsuits*, 86.

16. For the argument that in the criminal courts of the Montes de Toledo pueblo of Yébenes honor among seventeenth-century women was only in part defined by gender or sexuality, see Taylor, *Honor and Violence*; and "Credit, Debt." Also see the concept of "domestic power" in Poska, *Women and Authority*, 10–13.

17. See, for example, the central role of women in the 1774 *motín* in the pueblo of Navalucillos, Proceso por desórdenes iniciadio de oficio después de que un grupo de mozos y mujeres impidiesen a un moisario y al cura el traslado de la imagen de la Virgen a la Hermita de Nuestra Señora de Herrera, AMT, Criminal, Navalucillos, caja. 6340, no. 4220, 1774.

18. About one-fifth of the population of Horcajo possessed "*vecino*" status in the mid eighteenth century. See Sánchez González, *Los Montes*, 91; and the list of vecinos in the Testimonio de

Vecindario associated with the 1748 *Real Cédula sobre la conservacíon montes and aumento de plantíos*, AMT, Fiel del Juzgado, caja 1150, 1749. On the meaning of *vecindad* see Herzog, *Defining Nations*.

19. Antonio García, vezino de Orcajo contra María Rodríguez de la misma vezindad, AMT, Civiles, caja 1885, 1778, " . . . *de su propia autoridad*."

20. This corresponds to Lisa Mary Sousa's observation that Zapotec women in Villa Alta served less frequently as witnesses in criminal trials than did Mixtec women, "Women and Crime in Colonial Oaxaca: Evidence of Complementary Gender Roles in Mixtec and Zapotec Societies," in *Indian Women of Early Mexico*, ed. Susan Schroeder, Stephanie Wood, et al. (Norman: University of Oklahoma Press, 1997), 199–221; 208.

21. Women were litigants in 45 of 661 of all civil disputes and were sued in 44 cases.Ymbentario de todas la actuaciones Civiles y Criminales . . . AHJO, Civil, Leg. 49, Exp. 15, s/f [1793]. For statistical patterns of women's suit in indigenous Oaxaca in depth, see Premo, "Felipa's Braid."

22. Knafla, "Geographical," 139.

23. Population numbers are derived from "Plan demostrativo de la población comprehendida en el recinto de la Ciudad de Lima," *Mercurio Peruano* 9, 30 January, 1791; Cook and Borah, *Population of the Mixteca Alta*, 54. Litigation rates derive from my own analysis of the AGN-P, Cab., Civ. series.

24. Observations are based on ARL, Cab., C.O. It should be noted that in the city of Trujillo and other cities, elite women, widows, and single women also predominated as litigants. Only 15 of the 40 female litigants were listed as married, and a staggering 85 percent (119 out of 140) were listed as "doñas."

25. Women made up 132 out of 549 litigants in the civil court Corregimiento series of the, which heard cases from 1700–84. Seventy-four percent of these women (n = 95) were doñas; 31 percent (n = 42) were widowed.

26. See Ch. 3, n. 13 and 14.

27. Gertrudis Herrera, española, pide que su marido se haga cargo de ella, de su manutención, y le deje en la casa de su habitación, AHJO, Tepos., Civ., Leg. 43, Exp. 9, 1778. For population see Kevin Terraciano, *The Mixtecas of Colonial Oaxaca: Ñudzahui History, Sixteenth through Eighteenth Centuries* (Stanford: Stanford University Press, 2001), 4–5.

28. The contrast with civil cases is statistically modest but notable nonetheless. For example, I identified 5 cases of *malos tratos*, or abuse, brought in women's name in 211 criminal cases before the Fiel del Juzgado from five pueblos during the period from roughly the 1690s–1799. I identified 17 *malos tratos* cases for the eighteenth century in Teposcolula, and 10 for Villa Alta.

29. Of the 313 cases of sixteenth- and seventeenth-century violent crimes prosecuted in the Montes pueblo of Yébenes and examined by Scott K. Taylor, women were involved in 83 and accounted for about 34 percent of the victims, *Honor and Violence*, 164. This proportion matches those Steve. J. Stern presents for Mexico City, Morelos, and Villa Alta, Oaxaca, where he finds women comprising roughly 30 percent of victims of violent crimes and between 7–12 percent of assailants, *The Secret History of Gender: Women, Men and Power in Late-Colonial Mexico* (Chapel Hill: University of North Carolina Press, 1995), 371. I did not separate the 211 criminal disputes for the five Montes de Toledo pueblos that I examined by violent crime or gender-based violence (which can include crime based on same-sex jealousy or the defense of gender-based honor). Nonetheless, I found disputes between men and women over gender obligations in marriage or sexual relations, including seduction, paternity, abuse, and adultery cases, to comprise fewer than 10 percent of all criminal cases (17/211 cases.) My investigations into the Cabildo court of Lima also revealed a relatively light presence of women as accusers, comprising only 15 percent of all crime victims (52 of 334 cases).

30. See, for example, the distinction in the anonymous 1764 legal manual, Charles Cutter, trans. *Libro de los principales rudimentos tocante a todos juicios, civil, criminal y executivo: Año de 1764* (Mexico City: Universidad Nacional de México, 1994).

31. Herzog, *Upholding Justice*, 46, 60. In the Portuguese empire, during an earlier phase of "deformalization," judges examined the detail of complaints to determine jurisdiction, whereas in the seventeenth century more "modern judges" applied general rules and propositions to determine where a suit belonged, Hespanha, *Como os juristas*, 557–558.

32. Only 30 of 267 criminal cases in Teposcolula were listed as being brought forward by individuals through instruments such *"pedimientos"* (requests) and *"querellas"* (legal complaints), Ymbentario de todas la actuaciones Civiles y Criminales, AHJO, Civil, Leg. 49, Exp. 15, n/d [1793]. In the Corregimiento of Trujillo series in the ARL, 43 of 100 cases were brought *de oficio*. In 1793 report on the criminal cases pending before the Fiel del Juzgado in the Montes de Toledo, of 20 cases, nine were brought *"de oficio,"* ten were brought by Toledo's *"guardia,"* which patroled the region looking for infractions against city property, and only one was registered by an inhabitant, AMT, caja 1150, 1793.

33. Causa por malos tratos de oficio contra Juan Gómez Gordo, acusado de maltratar a María López su esposa, a quien escuchan llora los alcaldes en su casa una noche que van haciendo la ronda, AMT, Navalmoral, Crim., caja 6324, no. 3643, 1736, f. 1v.

34. Ibid., f. 14v.

35. Stern, *Secret History*, 101.

36. In this respect the Montes pueblos had changed little from centuries earlier. See Taylor's comments on de oficio cases, *Honor and Violence*, 76–7.

37. On the public nature of divorce cases in Lima, see van Deusen, *Between the Sacred*, 82; 89.

38. S/t, AMT, Yébenes, Criminal, caja 545, no. 20, 1722, f. 1v.

39. Divorcio de Da. María Fernández, vecina de Toledo contra Dn. Antonio Fariñas, su marido, vecino de la Villa de Aloforín, ADT, 1793, f. 3.

40. Usually the "honor" was related to the fact that the woman was married, and thus this could be seen as protection of her husband's honor, not hers. But single women's names too were shielded from the record. See Promotor fiscal contra Gabriel García por trato ylícito con una muger casada, Salvanes, ADT, 1720; Promotor fiscal contra Josef Sánchez por trato ylícito con una muger casada, Pantoja, ADT, 1720; and Criminal. El Promotor Fiscal contra el Lizdo. Don Eugenio Rodrique Bravo Presbítero de Guardarrama, Guadarrama, AAT, 1729; Recurso de declinatoria de fuero de Doña Juana María Niño Ladron de Guevara, contra el Juez Eclesiástico y que remita al Juzgado Civil la causa que contra ella hubiese formado, alzando el arresto de su persona, ARL, Intend. C.O., Leg. 305, c. 242, 1792. Also see the secret "extrajudicial" process against a woman having an affair with a priest; and De oficio contra el Alcalde de Colmenar del Arroyo, Don Manuel Fernández Gago, ADT, 1757.

41. Marjaliza, s/t, AMT, Crim., 219, 1781.

42. Ymbentario de todas la actuaciones Civiles y Criminales, AHJO, Civil, Leg. 49, Exp. 15, n/d [1793]. My analysis of the Trujillo corregimiento cases, which span the years 1700–84, is similar: of 100 criminal cases, 19 involved gender-based disputes between men and women, with most brought de oficio. For example, three of the four murders of women were prosecuted de oficio, and half of the six cases of assault against women.

43. On the subtle but critical interplay of native understandings and practices of authority and Spanish legal structure in the suits of colonial Villa Alta, see María de los Ángeles Romero Frizzi, "The Power of the Law: The Construction of Colonial Power in an Indigenous Region," in *Negotiation with Domination: New Spain's Indian Pueblos Confront the Spanish State*, ed. Ethelia Ruiz Medrano and Susan Kellogg (Boulder: University Press of Colorado, 2010), 107–136.

44. Maria de Yllescas, india, natural del pueblo de San Miguel Talea, vecina de San Juan Yaee, contra Franscio de los Reyes. su marido, por haberla gopeado en la cabeza con la piedra del metate . . . , AHJO, VA, Crim., Leg. 2, Exp. 9, 1707-9, 1 v.

45. Taylor, *Drinking, Homicide*, 74; Uribe-Uran, *Fatal Love*, 14–15. On biases toward violent crime in Oaxaca's criminal records, see Ronald Spores, *Mixtecs in Ancient and Colonial Times* (Norman: University of Oklahoma Press, 1984), 199. Nonetheless it is clear that local town officials investigated violent matters in advance of reporting to Spanish authorities, especially in the early part of the century. See, for example, El gobernador y alclade del pueblo de Teotongo . . . contra Juan López . . . por haber dado muerte a Manuel de la Cruz . . . y por las heridas que le causó a María Santiago . . . su mujer, AJPO, Tepos, Crim., Leg. 20, Exp. 3, 1738 [*sic*. 1698].

46. María de Yllescas, india . . . AHJO, VA, Crim., Leg. 2, Exp. 9, 1707-9 1v- 2.

47. On female networks and gossip in the gender disputes of late colonial Mexico, see Stern, *Secret History*, 103–107, 142–150.

48. Juana Sánchez, mujer legítima de Felipe Bazán [por sevicia], AHJO, Tepos., Crim., Leg. 42, Exp. 8, 1793, f. 2.

49. AAT, Divorcios.

50. See for example, the priest who sent Doña Antonia Leiva of Trujillo back to her husband no fewer than three times, s/t (Leiva) AAT, Divorcios, 1759. Also see Delgado, "*Sin temor de Dios*," 102, whose observation about rural women's use of priests draws from Pescador, "Entre la espada." My investigation in the Archivo Histórico Diocesano of Oaxaca yielded no marital disputes. My thanks to Daniela Traffano for sharing her expertise on the archive. For priests as first resorts among Spanish female litigants, see Margarita Ortega López, "Protestas de las mujeres castellanas contra el orden patriarcal privado durante el siglo XVIII," *Cuadernos de Historia Moderna* 19 (1997): 65–89; 78.

51. See, for example, María Gertrudis Sanches, india, natural del barrio de Analco . . . contra Lorenzo Santiago, indio, su marido, y Dominga Bernal india, por adulteros, AJPO, VA, Crim., Leg. 22, Exp. 13, 1798.

52. APGEO, AM, Oaxaca, Leg. 2, C. 17, 1731.

53. For another case in which a woman presented an "*escrito*" a year before a formal criminal accusation (*querella*), see Teresa Pérez, AHJO, Tepos. Crim., Leg. 29, Exp. 24, 1741.

54. Diligencias criminales fechas por Da. Inés María Fernández de Allende, contra su marido, D. Toribio Agüero Campuzano, México, AGN-M, BN, Vol. 1090, Exp. 15, 1776, f. 1.

55. Ibid., 1; 40v–41.

56. Such was the case in divorce suits as well. See, for example, Doña María Josefa Durán contra Antonio de la Torre, AAL, Divorcios, 1700. And it could be true among male litigants as well as women. Don Pedro Crosco of Trujillo admitted that he filed his 1761 divorce suit in order to shock his wife into reconciling with him, an intention that he had apparently openly shared with the ecclesiastical judge before filing divorce papers, Autos de demanda sobre el divorcio interpuesta por don Pedro Crosco contra su esposa doña Gregoria Daza, AAT, Divorcios, 1761.

57. Josefa Dolores, contra Bartolome López, vecinos del pueblo de Chilapa, por golpearla y vivir amancebado con Maria del Rosario, AHJO, Tepos, Crim., Leg. 43, Exp. 4, 1797, f. 4.

58. María Antonia Díaz de la Cruz contra Pedro Ximénez Peralo. Yévenes, ADT, 1755.

59. See, for example, Delito: Malos tratos; Acusado: Nicolas Lorenzo de los Reyes; Afectada: Efigenía María (su mujer); Lugar: Ixmiquilpan, AGN- M, Crim., Vol. 105, Exp: 9, 1748, ff. 302–306.

60. See Doña Petronila de Muñar y Puente vecina de la ciudad de Antequera solicita se le ordene a su marido no tome ninguno de sus bienes por pertenecerles todos a ella de su primer matrimonio, APGEO, Oaxaca, AM, Leg. 2, C. 17, 1731; Autos de demanda de divorcio por doña Rosa de los Angeles, contra su esposo don Pedro de Medina, AAT, Divorcios, 1747. On the overall trend toward reunion in divorce disputes, see Dávila Mendoza, *Hasta que la muerte*, 261.

61. Diligencias criminales fechas por Da. Inés María Fernández de Allende, AGN-M, BN, Vol. 1090, Exp. 15, 1776, f. 36v. Also see the case the wife withdrew in Mariano Rodríguez, sobre el matrimonio que contrajo su hijo Manuel con María del Carmen, y malos tratamientos. Mexico, AGN- M, BN, Vol. 526, Exp. 6., 1774, f. 13.

62. See Pascua Sánchez, "Women Alone," 136.

63. Maria Olayza Pérez natural y vecina de Yanhuitlan . . . dice que Juan Montesinos, su marido, a dado en embriagarse, resultando de esto que la maltrata, AHJO, Tepos., Crim., Leg. 42, Exp. 43, 1797, f. 5-5v. Also see Yllescas, AHJO, VA, Crim., Leg. 2, Exp. 9, 1707–1709.

64. Cecilia Juárez, india, contra Juan Sánchez, mestizo, su Marido, AGN-M, BN, Vol. 526. Exp. 3., 1774.

65. On "*apartamientos*," or private pardons that halted suits, among the peasants of the Montes de Toledo, see Taylor, *Honor and Violence*, 81–82.

66. Petición de Maria Asunción de Elormendi para que Pedro Ignacio de Izaguirre, su marido, le asigne una cantidad por almientos mientra se sentencia el pleito de separación pendiente entre ambos, RCV, Pleitos civiles, Pérez Alonso (olv.), 0740.0006, 1796–98 (*hilador de oro*); Criminal contra Mariano Pliego a pedido de su Muger M[aría] Carmona por cevicia y malos tratamientos, AGN-M, TSJ, Correg., Crim., Vol. 17, Exp. 14, 1796; Autos seguidos por doña

Juana de Luna contra don Antonio Moreno, sobre alimentos de una hija, AGN-P, RA, Civ., Leg. 343, C. 3100, 1795.

67. Juana Luna, AGN-P, RA, Civil, Leg. 342, C. 3100, 1795, f. 3.

68. A standard phrasing is found in Girón v. Muñoz, Muñoz et al., AMT, Civil, caja 1883, 1771, where the litigant says the petition can be considered either a *querella* or *queja*, "*como mas había lugar.*" Also see Zivil ordinario Herraz contra Villares y Carnicero, AMT, Civil, caja 1881, 1789: "*ante VS en la forma que mas haia lugar, bajo las protextas combienientes*" and in González Zaravez contra Juárez de Cuerba, AMT, Civil, caja 1883, 1771: "*con la protexta de usar de las demas acciones cibiles o criminales que me competan como quando y contra quien había lugar.*"

69. Queja De Felipa Huesca, vecina de Xicochimalco contra su marido Pedro Colorado, por malos tratos, AGN-M, Civ., Vol. 1760, Exp. 7, 1795.

70. Sobre la causa de divorcio y sus incidencias seguidas por Da. María Romero con Dn Ygnacio Salgado, vecinos de Arequipa. AGI, Gobierno, 914, no.74, 1786.

71. Note the increasing number of cédulas on competencias and jurisdiction in the late eighteenth century recorded in Santos Sánchez, *Colección*.

72. When *alimentos* did refer to spousal suits aired in civil court, they tended to involve absent husbands, often linking the two sides of the Atlantic together when men who left to make their name or fortune in the New World had to be prodded into fulfilling their obligations to peninuslar women, as did Mariá Antonia Rodríguez, mujer de Manuel Alonso Portugués, alcalde mayor en el distrito de Nueva España con el dho su marido, sobre alimentos, AGI, Escribanía, 1064B, 1759. For more on the importance of financial obligations in the Spanish Atlantic, see Jane Mangan, *Transatlantic Obligations: Creating the Bonds of Family in Conquest-Era Peru and Spain* (New York: Oxford University Press, 2016); on republican alimentos, see Sarah Chambers, "The Paternal Obligation to Provide: Political Familialism in Early Nineteenth-Century Chile," *American Historical Review* 117, no. 4 (2012): 1123–1148.

73. In medieval Spanish civil law, *alimentos* referred to the support and nourishment of children whose parents were separating. See *Siete Partidas* 4: 19: 3 and 5; yet in civil practice, the term's association with inheritance cases, where it referred to the parceling out of bits of legacy to a family member, crowded out its definition as basic child support. Also see Viviana Kluger, "Los alimentos entre cónyuges: Un estudio sobre los pleitos en la época de la Segunda Audiencia de Buenos Aires (1785–1812)," *Revista de Historia del Derecho* [Buenos Aires] 18 (1990): 183–213.

74. As Juan y Colom explained, women's suits over dowries or alimony technically fell into the category of "*executivos*," or summary cases that required no formal process of litigation and which need not be recorded, *Instrucción de escribanos*, 72.

75. "Deposit" was a multifaceted practice that women might regard as much as a haven from an abusive or unhappy marriage as a punishment or imprisonment. See Lee M. Penyack, "Safe Harbors and Compulsory Custody: *Casas de Depósito* in Mexico, 1759–1865," *Hispanic American Historical Review* 79, no. 1 (1999): 83–99; Arrom, *Women*, 212–217. In sixteenth- and seventeenth- century Lima over two-thirds of divorcing women were able to successfully choose their own place of enclosure, with most elite women choosing private homes, van Deusen, *Between the Sacred*, 93–96.

76. Don Antonio Catalán contra Manuela Miejes, AAL, Divorcios, Leg. 75, 1786. His salary was 27 pesos a month, plus 16 pesos in earnings from renting out a house.

77. Gertrudis Herrera, . . . AHJO, Tepos., Civ., Leg. 43, Exp. 9, 1778.

78. For changes in litigation over children, and specifically the shift from inheritance to daily support in *alimentos* cases in Lima, see Premo, *Children of the Father King*, 184.

79. These cases were relatively easy to identify in Peru's national archive, given the organization of the archive by type of case and provenance, and, ironically, by its old-fashioned card catalog finding aids, which permit the researcher to read each entry. In contrast, in Mexico's national archive, the complexities of archival holdings, discussed in the Appendices, made the search somewhat less comprehensive. Finding Mexican alimentos suits was made even more complex by the addition of ecclesiastical cases or mixed-jurisdiction cases in the Bienes Nacionales and Matrimonios sections of the archive (and the fact that some of the marital suits in the Inquisition series also were heard not by that tribunal but rather by the *provisor*

general of the archbishopric). I was able to perform a key-term search of the electronic document descriptions of the holdings made available to researchers by Linda Arnold. What is certain is that, in the Mexican archives, the upward trajectory of the number of spousal alimentos suits continues in the nineteenth century, where I identified an additional 22 cases for the period 1800–50. In fact, in the nineteenth century after independence, a Juez de Alimentos was established dedicated to hearing child support suits, and a second archive kept for the cases until 1998, when the records were transferred to another archive. Ana Lidia García Peña was able to study these records, finding over 200 cases, "Madres solteras, pobres y abandonadas: Ciudad de México, Siglo XIX," *Historia Mexicana* 53, no. 3 (2004): 646–692.

80. There are 177 alimentos suits in the Pleitos series of the Archivo de la Real Chancellería de Valladolid for the 1600s, and 167 for the 1700s, meaning that they made up a marginally smaller percentage of suits over time, since there was a slight rebound in the overall number of civil cases aired before the Chancellería in the eighteenth century. Of those, I was able to identify only two that were conflicts between living spouses in the 1600s and ten in the 1700, all related to ecclesiastical divorce cases. I also counted six alimentos cases wrapped into cases of seduction (*estupro*) brought before the ministers of Valladolid during the 1700s.

81. José Febrero, *Febrero novísimo o Libreria de jueces, abogados y escribanos* . . . , vol. 10 (reprint, Valencia: Idelfonso Mompié, 1831), 162.

82. In fact, a couple of these cases suggest that Spanish women, along with judges, customarily recognized a kind of secular separation—one that could bypass Church courts altogether and permit married women to live on their own. There were two kinds of divorce in canon law: *quoad vinculum*, or anullment, and *quoad thorum et mensum*, or separation, see Daisy Rípodaz Ardanaz, *El matrimonio en Indias: Realidad social y regulación juridical* (Buenos Aires: Fundación para la Educación, la Ciencia y la Cultura, 1977), 388. For cases in which separation without divorce or anulment was accepted by Church and royal authorities, see Demanda de doña María Antonio Fernández de la Cuesta muger lexma de Don Manuel Benito del Valle vznos de la Villa de Canales con Dho, sobre diborcio y separación de matrimonios (Burgos), RCV, Pleitos Civiles Alfonso Rodriguez (olv.) 1421.0022, 1755; Pago a Josefa Pablos Nebreda y Bernabé Bayona Duque, sombrero, de las cantidades debidas por Antonio Bayona Duque, boticario, su marido y hermano respectivamente, por alimentos debidos tras la separación de su matrimonio y otras deudas, RCV, Pleitos Civiles, Pérez Alonso (Olv.) 803.00, 1797. For a similar case in the Montes de Toledo, see Navamoral, Dos cartas al Fiel, AMT, Crim., caja. 3769, no. 337, 1784. For discussion of another case, contextualized within the Enlightenment, see Pascua Sánchez, "Women Alone," 136.

83. In the Chancellería, there was a marginal but nonetheless significant uptick in the number of litigants who turned to the high court to appeal ecclesiastical alimony resolutions—for example, six of the ten recurso de fuerza cases involving divorce that I was able to identify in the Chancellería dated from the final decades of the eighteenth century, suggesting some litigant movement toward secular intervention in divorce suits in the region. But missing from most of these disputes were women's assertions of "natural rights" to sue men in civil court, understandable given that the cédula on alimony issued for the colonies was not extended to Spain until 1804. The Spanish cases remained firmly ensconced in ecclesiastical jurisdiction. In one unusual jurisdictional dispute, it was clear that Spanish authorities were familiar with the notion that alimony might be considered "purely profane" and beyond the reach of Church judges, Francisco de Lara y Zúñiga, vecino y regidor perpetuo de la villa de Aranda de Duero (Burgos) con Manuela Navarrete, su mujer, de la misma vecindad, sobre el aumento en la contribución de alimentos, RCV, Pleitos Civiles, Fernando Alonso (D), 370.0001, 1798. Also note that, at least in the tribunals of the diocese of Toledo, Church judges still adjudicated alimentos and litis expensas matters into the end of the century. See, for example, Divorcio de Da María Fernández . . . ADT, 1793, f. 80. Again, this is certainly not to say there was no "Enlightenment" in Spain, but rather that I did not find evidence of it connected to lawsuits there as I did in Spanish colonial cities. For women's lettered Enlightenment, see Mónica Bolufer Peruga, *Mujeres e ilustración: La construcción de la feminidad en la Ilustración Española* (Valencia: Artes Gráficas, 1998); Mónica Bolufer Peruga and Isabel Morant Deusa, "On Women's Reason, Education, and Love: Women and Men of the Enlightenment in Spain and France," *Gender and History* 10 no. 2 (1998): 183–216; Smith, *Emerging Female Citizen*.

84. On recursos de fuerza in Mexico, see Dávila Mendoza, *Hasta que la muerte*, 165–166.
85. This is based on a review of the cases in the Corregimiento series (1 case) and Intendencia series (3 cases).
86. I was unable to locate a single civil alimentos case between spouses in the Montes de Toledo and only one in rural Oaxaca in the alcaldía mayor records (housed in the AHJO) and intendancy districts (housed in the APGEO) of Teposcolula and Villa Alta.
87. One of the largest requests was from the wife of a pharmacist (*boticario*) in Mexico City, who initially requested 100 pesos a month from her husband, but whose request was crossed out and replaced with the phrase "*una cantidad prudente*," probably reflecting the advice of a more conservative legal counselor after her petition was first drawn up, Doña María Guadalupe Velasques sobre que su marido don José Cassillas le ministre para alimentos y litis expensas, AGN-M, TSJ, Correg., Civ., caja 16, Exp. 6, 1796. Institutions seemed to charge around 10 to 12 pesos a month for women's upkeep; see Provinica: Expte. promovido por Da. Gertrudis Hernández con don José Eslava su esposo, sobre que le ministre para alimentos y litis expensas, AGN-M, Civ., Leg. 1, Exp. 1, 1788. For those outside institutions, the cost was usually a bit higher; a middling-class "doña" was awarded 18 pesos a month in Mexico City in the 1790s, Asuntos del divorcio promovido por Doña Inés de Matamoros contra su marido Don José Antonio Sotomayor, México, AGN-M, BN, Vol. 292, Exps 19, 20, and 21, 1790. There seemed to be little change in the average amount awarded to women over the course of the century or with the shift to secular jurisdiction. For example, women were awarded 30 pesos in cases aired before the ecclesiastical tribunal of Lima in 1700; see Zavala v Lozano and Flores v. Rodríguez, AAL, Divorcios, 1700.
88. Autos que sige Doña María Guadalupe Blengua y Asudillo contra don Juan Parada, su marido, sobre alimentos, AGN-M, Civ., Leg. 18, Exp. 84, 1793, f. 4v; s/t (María Guadalupe del Valle), AGN-M, TSJ, AO, Civ., caja 23, Exp. 17, 1780, f. 1.
89. On discourses of "poverty" among the elite, see Cynthia Milton, *Many Meanings*.
90. Stern, *Secret History*, 256, 258–168. Anecdotally, middling-class couples in which women found employment in new Bourbon-era tobacco factories (at least six) or whose husbands pawned family property (at least five) at the new official pawnshop seemed inclined to legal disputes, raising the question of how broader regal economic institutions like the Monte de Piedad in Mexico City and the tobacco monopolies contributed to gender trouble. See Arrom, *Women*, 193; Marie Eileen Francois, *A Culture of Everyday Credit: Housekeeping, Pawnbroking, and Governance in Mexico City, 1750–1920* (Lincoln: University of Nebraska Press, 2006), 45–46. Examples include Doña Inés de Matamoros contra su marido Don José Antonio Sotomayor, México, AGN-M, BN, Vol. 292, exps. 19, 20, 21, 1790; Josefa Ayala contra su Marido Bernardo Elizalde por malos tratamientos, AGN-M, Civ. Vol. 1496, Exp. 19, 1794; Don Isidrio Manuel Váldez v. Josefa Anachuvi, AAL, Divorcios, Leg. 76, 1790.
91. Similarly, in Quito, one particular *alcalde de barrio* was responsible for a high number of concubinage detentions in the 1760s according to Black, *Limits*, 87. On the Bassoco family see David Brading, *Miners and Merchants in Bourbon Mexico, 1763–1810* (1971; reprint, New York: Cambridge University Press, 2008), 209.
92. Note that summary criminal cases in late colonial Mexico also were recorded in an extensive "*libro de reos*," while no such recordings have been found for the Audiencia of Lima. See Scardaville, "(Hapsburg) Law and (Bourbon) Order"; Haslip-Viera, *Crime and Punishment*, 82–84.
93. For brevity, I omit titles here: AGN-M, TSJ, Corr., Crim., Vol. 17 Exp. 58, 1801; AGN TSJ, Corr., Crim. Vol. 17, Exp. 59, 1801; AGN-M, TSJ Corr., Crim., Vol. 17, Exp. 77. 1802.
94. Gertrudis Herrera, española . . . , AHJO, Tepos., Civ., Leg. 43, Exp. 9, f. 177.
95. Ibid.
96. The lawyer was Manuel Josef Ruiz, Da. María Antonia Camacho, española, mujer legítima de Joseph Muñoz, presenta demanda de divorcio por malos tratos, AGN-M, Civ., Vol. 1669, Exp. 2, 1754.
97. Da. María Luisa de Ynojosa casica mujer lexitima de Don Joseph Gaspar Díaz govr de los Naturales de la Villa de Quernabaca con el dho Don Joseph Gaspar por malostratm[ien]tos que las da a la susd[ic]ha, AGN-M, Civ., Vol. 1627 Exp. 2, 1727. Another mid-century Mexican case, this one over the support of the illegitimate children of a priest, was brought

from ecclesiastical court to civil authorities but was thrown out by the Audiencia, Da. Francisca Xavier de Aguilar con Fernando de Bargas sobre Alimentos, AGN-M, Civ., Vol. 384, Exp. 11744, 1744.

98. This was basically a judicial mechanism to put another person on the hook for the husband's actions. See "Fianza de indemnidad," in Escriche, *Diccionario razonado*, 533.

99. Delito: Recurso de fuerza que interpuso Fco. de Villavendas, sobre el divorcio [sic] que entabló don Joseph Vicente con su mujer María Ana Rosel; Lugar: Sta. Ma. Tlamimilolpa, AGN-M, Crim., Vol. 221, Exp: 6, 1768, ffs 179–208.

100. Autos seguidos por doña Mercedes Zegarra contra don Miguel Luque, sobre alimentos, AGN-P, RA, Civ., Leg. 338, C. 3080, 1795, f. 1 v; 42.

101. Ibid., f. 26v.

102. Autos seguidos por Da. Mariana Duárez, contra D. Jose Nuñez, su marido, sobre la entrega de una esclava, AGN-P, Cab. Civ., Leg. 78, C. 1479, 1795 (told that her case was of too "small entity" [*pequeña emnidad*] for a suit); and Quexa de Don Joseph e María Aicardo contra su muger y la persona que adentro se expresa, AGN-M, Civ., Vol. 2107, Exp. 4, 5, and 6, 1782.

103. Puebla. Dona Petra Guadalupe de la Cal, se queja de que su Marido Don Lorenzo Sando vive en incontinencia con escándalo resultándole a ella malostratamientos sin darle pa. su sustencia y el de sus hijos, AGN-M, Civ., Vol. 2045, 19 b, 1794.

104. For example, see the comments of one woman dropping charges and requesting her husband's release from prison, Diligencias criminales fechas por Da. Inés María Fernández de Allende, AGN-M, BN, Vol. 1090, Exp. 15, 1776, f. 36v.

105. Ibid.

106. Compare Diligencias criminales fechas por Da. Inés María Fernández de Allende, contra su marido, D. Toribio Agüero Campuzano, México, AGN-M, BN, Vol. 1090, Exp. 15, 1776, f. 48 and Sobre el divorcio que pide Don Francisco Pila, del matrimonio que contrajo con Doña María García, México, AGN-M, BN, Vol. 292 Exp. 1, 1790.

107. ARL, Intend. Civ., Leg. 447, C. 316, 1796. Also see Delito: Malos tratos y falta de cumplimiento en sus obligaciones; Acusado: Jorge [*sic*. George] Antonio; Afectada: Maria Manuela Najera; Lugar: Mexico, AGN-M Crim., Vol. 131. Exp. 37, 1769, ff. 421–424. Also see the following (titles omitted for brevity): AGN-M, Crim., Vol. 221, Exp. 6, 1768, ffs. 179–208; AGN-M BN, Vol., 523, Exp. 14, 1773; AGN-M, Inquisición, Vol. 1336 Exp. 2, 1791, ffs. 21–31; and Don Víctor Josef Marina, contra Juliana Arnaiz sobre vida maridable, ADT, 1798.

108. Querella presentada por Doña Teresa Exhanojuáregui contra su marido, Jose Francisco Delgado, por malos tratamientos, Puebla, AGN-M, Inquisición, Vol. 476, Exp. 8, 1794, ff. 223–282.

109. Autos seguidos por Doña Melchora Oyos, mujer de Pedro Francisco Albarez, residente en la Maygosbamba jurisdicción de Chota, contra Don Pedro, sobre demanda de pensión de alimentos, ARL, Intend., C.O., Leg. 447, C. 316, 1796.

110. Autos seguidos por Segunda Montejo, contra su marido Escolástico Paredes, sobre divorcio, AAT, Divorcios, 1789.

111. Autos seguidos por doña Mercedes Zegarra . . . , AGN-P, RA, Civ., Leg. 338, C. 3080, 1795, f. 1v; 42.

112. Autos de divorcio que sigue Josef Marcelina Medina contra su mujer Gregoria Gonzales. Doctrina de Trujillo, AAT, Divorcios, 1799. There are countless other examples, but for two, see Autos seguidos por Da. Mariana Duárez, contra D. Jose Núñez, su marido, sobre la entrega de una esclava, AGN-P Cab. Civ., Leg. 78, C. 1479, 1795; Lara y Talabera v. Oquendo, AAL, Divorcios, Leg. 76, 1790.

113. Asuntos del divorcio promovido por Doña Inés de Matamoros . . . , AGN-M, BN, Vol. 292, Exps. 19, 20, and 21, 1790, 21 v.

114. Causa criminal que sigue María de las Nieves contra Gervasio Ortiz por maltratos, ARL, Intend, C. Crim, Leg. 353, C. 1329, 1787.

115. Autos de demanda de divoricio perpetuo que tiene interpuesta dona Ana Teresa Cárdenas contra su esposo don Francisco Javier de León, Trujillo, AAT, Divorcios, 1790, 3v.

116. Querella presentada por Doña Teresa Exhanojuáregui contra su marido, José Francisco Delgado, por malos tratamientos. Puebla, AGN-M, Inquisición, Vol. 476, Exp. 8, 223–282,

179: Also see Autos seguidos por Segunda Montejo, contra su marido Escólastico Paredes, sobre divorcio, AAT-Divorcios, 1789.

117. Autos seguidos por doña Trinidad Guzmán contra don Andres Zanudo [*sic*], sobre alimentos, AGN-P, RA, Civ., Leg. 282, c. 2497, 1789. Her divorce case can be found in Dona Trinidad Enrriques de Gusmán v Don Andes Zamudio, AAL, Divorcios, Leg. 75, 1789. For other direct discussions of the cédula see Provincia: Expte promovido por Da Gertrudis Hernández, AGN-M, Civ., Leg. 1, Exp. 1, 1788; Sobre el divorcio que pide Don Francisco Pila . . . , AGN-M, BN, Vol. 292, Exp. 1, 1790; Recurso de declinatoria de fuero de Doña Juana María Niño Ladron de Guevara, contra el Juez Eclesiástico y que remita al Juzgado Civil la cuasa que cnra ella hubiese formado, alzando el arresto de su persona, ARL, Intend. C.O., Leg. 305, C. 242, 1792. Note that the argument could work to the advantage of men as well, as when Lima lawyer José Dávila admitted that while women had "derechos" to preserve their dowries, nothing was "written" about the goods they brought into the marriage (*parafernales*), Autos seguidos por doña Josefa Rodríguez, con D. Francisco Jimeno, su marido, sobre que le asigne una pension alimenticia y se le impida la venta de una casa propiedad de la demandante, AGN-P, RA, Civ., Leg. 355, C. 3228, 1796.

118. Para que los eclesiásticos no conozcan de concubinato, Real cédula para España e Indias de 1777 y diciembre de 1787, reproduced in Rafael Digo-Ferñandez Sotelo and Marina Mantilla Trolle, eds., *La Nueva Galicia en el ocaso del Imperio Español: Los papeles de derecho de la audiencia de la Nueva Galicia del licenciado Juan José Ruiz Moscoso, su agente fiscal y regidor del Ayuntamiento de Guadalajara, 1780–1810*, Vol. 3 (Jalisco: Colegio de Michoacán, 2003), 270.

119. "Recurso de declinatoria de fuero de Doña Juana María Niño Ladrón de Guevara, ARL, Intend. C.O., Leg. 305, C. 242, 1792.

120. Note that the case, like others, claimed her two-month stay in the home had been like being "buried alive," and reflected a rising concern in the Enlightenment scientific community and popular culture about mistaken burial. See Peter Hanns Reill, *Vitalizing Nature In The Enlightenment* (Berkeley: University of California Press, 2005), 172–180.

121. Recurso de declinatoria de fuero . . . ARL, Intend. C.O., Leg. 305, C. 242, 1792.

122. Doña Trinidad Enrriques de Gusmán, AAL, Divorcios, Leg. 75, 1789.

123. Sobre el divorcio que pide Don Francisco Pila . . . , AGN-M, BN, Vol. 292, Exp. 1, 1790. For the juxtaposition of marriage and "liberty," also see Autos criminales que siguen Dn. Antonio Ruiz de Luna . . . BNP, MS, D5930, 1800, f. 12.

124. S/t (Pino v. Pino), AAL, Divorcios, Leg. 76, 1799.

125. Teresa Quiróz v. Antonio Aciego, AAL, Divorcios, Leg. 75, 1789. Note that contractualization did find its way into cases in peninsular Spain, at least in one rare case I identified in the Audiencia of Granada, where a woman agreed to reunite with her husband only if he agreed to renounce every one of the rights over her property and person that he enjoyed as a married man. The contract she had drawn up—a stunning historical document consisting of twelve individual points—stipulated that her husband would be stripped of the right to administer her dowry, sought a blanket license for her to appear in court, and asked him to renounce his right to force her to live with him. See María del Carmen Barrena, viuda, sobre divorcio y entrega de su dote, AHN, Consejos, 29245, Exp. 15, 1773.

126. S/t (Doña Juana María de Hora), AGN-M, TSJ, Civ., Exp. 58, 1790, 1v; 4.

127. Autos seguidos por Doña Melchora Oyos, mujer de Pedro Francisco Albarez, residente en la Maygosbamba jurisdicción de Chota, contra Don Pedro, sobre demanda de pensión de alimentos, ARL, Intend., C.O., Leg. 447, C. 316, 1796.

128. Expte promovido por Da. Gertrudis Hernández, 1788, AGN-M, Civ., Leg. 1, Exp. 1. Also see a husband's argument that alimentos and litis expensas should be administered only to poor women, in Autos seguidos por doña Trinidad Guzmán, AGN-P RA Civil, Leg. 282, C. 2497, 1789.

129. Sobre el divorcio que pide Don Francisco Pila . . . AGN-M, BN, Vol. 292, Exp. 1, 1790.

130. On the connections between narratives in court cases and the *comedias*, see Bianca Premo, "An Old Father in a New Tragedy: Fatherhood in the Legal Theater of the 18th-Century Spanish Atlantic," *Clio: A Journal of Literature, History, and Philosophy of History* 41, no. 1 (2010): 109–130.

131. The move of another Mexican woman in selecting her own procurador, a priest, also became a point of contention in a case detailed in the Conclusion. See Quexa de Don Joseph e María Aicardo . . . , AGN-M, Vol. 2107, Exp. 4, 5, and 6, 1782.

132. Ibid., f. 39.

133. Autos seguidos por doña Josefa Rodríguez, AGN-P, RA, Civ., Leg. 355, C. 3228, 1796.

134. Autos criminales que siguen Dn. Antonio Ruiz de Luna . . . BNP, MS, D5930, 1800.

135. Sobre lo representado por el Subdelegado del Partido del Cercado de Lima acerca del despojo de jurisdicción que le ha hecho el Fiscal Protector de Yndios, avocándose el conocimiento de la causa que se seguía en su Juzgado para la unión del Matrimonio de Joaquín Jordán y su Muger María Tomasa Maldonado, AGI, Gobierno, Lima, 967, 1798.

136. Ibid.; Autos seguidos por Doña Melchora Oyos, ARL Intendencia, Causas Ordinarias, Leg. 447, C. 316, 1796. Among many other examples, see Guzmán v Zamudio, AAL, Divorcios, Leg. 75,1789. Also see another woman's move from Tehuacán to Mexico City because of a biased judge in Da. María Josefa de Arizaga, vecina De Tehuacán contra su marido don Fernando Monteagudo sobre malos tratamientos, AGN-M, Civ., Vol. 1500, Exp. 2 1793.

137. Quexa de Don Joseph e María Aicardo . . . . AGN, Civ., Vol. 2107, Exp. 4, 5, and 61782.

138. Asuntos del divorcio promovido por Doña Inés de Matamoros, AGN-M, BN, Vol. 292, Exps. 19, 20, 21,1790.

139. On the changing meaning of "administration" and its "polarization" from distributive justice, with which it had been united in early modern legal thought, see Víctor Gayol, "El régimen de los oficios vendibles y renunciables como garantía para el desempeño de los oficios públicos al final del periodo colonial. Estudio del caso," *Anuario Mexicano de Historia del Derecho* 18 (2006), 199.

140. Asuntos del divorcio promovido por Doña Inés de Matamoros, AGN-M, BN Vol. 292, Exps. 19, 1790, s/f.

141. Autos seguidos por dona Paula Soriano contra su marido, D. Manuel Barrena y López, sobre sevicia, adulterio, y devolución de cantidad de pesos, AGN-P, Leg. 341, C. 3172, 1796. Also see Sarah Chambers, "To the Company of a Man Like My Husband, No Law Can Compel Me': The Limits of Sanctions against Wife Beating in Arequipa, Peru, 1780–1850," *Journal of Women's History* 11, no. 1 (1999): 31–52.

142. Autos de demanda de divoricio perpetuo que tiene interpuesta dona Ana Teresa Cárdenas contra su esposo don Francisco Javier de Leon, Trujillo, AAT Divorcios, 1790.

143. For example see Autos seguidos por dona Mercedes Zegarra . . . , AGN-P, RA, Civ., Leg. 338, C. 3080, 1795, 1 v.

144. Sobre el divorcio que pide Don Francisco Pila . . . , AGN-M BN, Vol. 292, Exp. 1, 1790, f. 39v.

145. Ibid., f. 54.

146. Ibid., f. 42.

147. Autos seguidos por Doña Melchora Oyos, ARL Intend., C.O., Leg. 447, C. 316, 1796. Note that Doña Melchora claimed that she had hoped to turn her case over to a representative so that she could return to her hometown of Magoysobamba but was unable to; she did sign a poder naming an official of the royal treasury as her representative, but only right before the case ended, f. 13.

148. For a close study of how women flouted licenture requirements in colonial Quito, see Black, "Between Prescription."

149. The cited case was "Juicio que siguió el P. Risco de Sn Agustín contra el pulpero," Oyos . . . ARL Intend., C.O., Leg. 447, C. 316, 1796, 12v.

150. Da. María Antonia Camacho, española, mujer Legítima de Joseph Muñoz, resenta demanda de divorcio por malos tratos, AGN-M., Civ., Vol. 1669 Exp. 21754, f. 154. Also see the argument over the applicability, based on practice, of the law mandating the death sentence for any man who had sex with a slave in Expediente de Rita Palacios . . . , ARL, Correg., Civ., Leg. 234 C. 2109, 1780. The law cited was *Recopilación de las Leyes de Castilla*, 6:20:8.

151. Scattola, "*Scientia Iuris* and *Ius Naturae*," 1.

152. See especially Voekel, *Alone before God* and Smith, *Emerging Female Citizen*, 6. Beyond the Spanish empire, see Dale van de Kley, *The Religious Origins of the French Revolution* (New Haven: Yale University Press, 1996).

153. Covarrubias, *Máximas*, "El juez eclesiástico oprime al vasallos, privándole de la liberatad, y derecho natural de apelación," 98; "Nacen hombres Ciudadanos; y no cesan de serlo haciéndose Eclesiásticos," 20.
154. García Peña, *El fracaso*, 38.
155. Key to the development of modern "categorical identity" is the mediation of state institutions. See Craig C. Calhoun, *Nationalism* (Minneapolis: University of Minnesota, 1997), ch. 2.
156. Rogers Brubaker and Frederick Cooper argue that modern subjectivity does not necessarily "imply a distinctively modern or Western sense of the self as a homogenous, bounded or unitary entity," "Beyond Identity," *Theory and Society* 29 (2000): 1–27; 17.
157. Charles Taylor, *Sources of the Self: The Making of Modern Identity* (New York: Cambridge University Press, 1989), 311, 313.
158. Palacios, ARL, Correg., Civ., Leg. 234, C. 2109, 1780, 63v–64.

Chapter 5

1. See Michel de Certeau's comments on Spanish colonial natives and the law, and his call for studies that examine not just the language of law but its use, *The Practice of Everyday Life*, trans. Steven Rendall (Berkeley: University of California Press, 1984).
2. For one example, see Stern, *Peru's Indian Peoples*, 132.
3. Marshall Sahlins, "What Is Anthropological Enlightenment? Some Lessons of the Twentieth Century," *Annual Review of Anthropology* 28 (1999): i–xxiii. Overviews of recent historiography can be found in R. Douglas Cope, "Indigenous Agency in Colonial Spanish America," *Latin American Research Review* 45, no. 1 (2010): 203–214; José Carlos de la Puente Luna, "Into the Heart of the Empire: Indian Journeys to the Habsburg Royal Court," PhD diss., Texas Christian University, 2010; Yanna Yannakakis, "Indigenous Peoples and Legal Culture," *History Compass* 11, no. 11 (2013): 931–994, Alcira Dueñas, "Introduction: Andeans Articulating Colonial Worlds," *The Americas* 72, no. 1 (2015): 1–8.
4. For example, Yannakakis, *Art*, 17–18; O'Toole, *Bound Lives*, 66; Sergio Serúlnikov, *Subverting Colonial Authority: Challenges to Spanish Rule in Eighteenth-Century Southern Andes* (Durham: Duke University Press, 2003), 11.
5. Notable here are Kellogg, *Law and the Transformation*; Owensby, *Empire of Law*; Yanna Yannakakis, "Custom: A Language of Negotiation in Eighteenth-Century Oaxaca," 137–171; and María de los Ángeles Romero Frizzi, "The Power of the Law: The Construction of Colonial Power in an Indigenous Region," in *Negotiation within Domination: Colonial New Spain's Indian Pueblos Confront the Spanish State*, ed. Ethelia Ruiz Medrano and Susan Kellogg (Boulder: University Press of Colorado, 2010); Tamar Herzog, "Colonial Law and 'Native Customs': Indigenous Land Rights in Colonial Spanish America," *The Americas* 69, no. 3 (2013): 303–321.
6. Van Young, *Other Rebellion*, 523, 29. Also see Taylor, *Drinking, Homicide*; Lockhart, *Nahuas*. For an argument that contrasts Indian notions of belonging to those emerging during the Age of Revolution, see Eric Van Young, "Limits of Atlantic World Nationalism in a Revolutionary Age," in *Empire to Nation*, ed. Joseph Eshrick et al. (New York: Rowman and Littlefield, 2006), 34–67.
7. See, for example, Owensby's discussion of "liberty" within the context of seventeenth-century native legal arguments about coerced labor and servitude in Chapter 5 of *Empire of Law*, esp. 114–116. For more on the deceptive nature of Indian continuity, see Caplan, *Indigenous Citizens*.
8. For a commentary on the problematics of conceiving of Native American thought as uniquely "hybrid," see Gabriela Ramos and Yanna Yannakakis, "Introduction," 1–17, in Ramos and Yannakakis, *Indigenous Intellectuals*, 6.
9. Laura Nader, *Harmony Ideology: Justice and Control in a Zapotec Mountain Village* (Stanford: Stanford University Press, 1990).
10. Nader herself has vacillated on the question of whether this principle was a legacy of Spanish Catholicism or of Zapotec notions of balance (*erj goonz*), Nader, *Harmony Ideology*, 216, 389, 391; Nader, "The Crown, The Colonists and Zapotec Village Law,"

in *History and Power in the Study of Law: New Directions in Legal Anthropology*, ed. June Starr and Jane F. Collier (Ithaca: Cornell, 1989), 330–344, esp. 334; and Laura Nader, "Styles of Court Procedure: To Make the Balance," in *Law in Culture and Society*, ed. Laura Nader (1969; reprint, Berkeley: University of California Press, 1997), 69–91. Also see Peter Just, "History, Power, Ideology, and Culture: Current Directions in the Anthropology of Law," *Law & Society Review* 26, no. 2 (1992): 373–412; 392.

11. Yannakakis, *Art*; Ramos and Yannakakis, *Indigenous Intellectuals*; Burns, "Making Indigenous Archives."

12. As but one example, see the question of paternal over maternal descent in Villa Alta in Juan, Nicolás y Tomas Hernández del pueblo de San Juan Yaeé piden se les reconsca los privilegios de principales que siempre han gozados, AHJO, VA, Crim., Leg. 20, Exp. 4, 1768, f. 10v; and the discussion of "fracturing" norms of lineage in Chance, *Conquest of the Sierra*, 131.

13. Lockhart shows that even as early as the late sixteenth century, a quarter of the conceptual terms that Nahautl speakers from Culhuacán borrowed from Spanish were legal in nature, *Nahuas*, Tables 7.13 and 7.14, 290–91; 305.

14. Tomas López Flores y sus hermanos contra la autoridad de San Juan Yaeé, sobre privilegios de nobleza, AHJO, VA, Civ., Leg. 18, Exp. 15, 1764, f. 9.

15. On the problem of distance, see Jeremy Baskes, *Indians, Merchants and Markets: Spanish-Indian Economic Relations in Colonial Oaxaca* (Stanford: Stanford University Press, 2000); Yannakakis, *Art*, 23.

16. See the case of a death, which technically should have been brought to Spanish authorities, that was concealed by officials in the Mixe pueblo of Tepuxtepec, s/t, AHJO, VA, Crim., Leg. 9, Exp. 9, 1707. Also see Kevin Terraciano, "Crime and Culture," 715–716; Spores, *Mixtecs*, 170; ch. 8.

17. On the independence of native jurisdiction in Mexico, see Arturo Gümez Pinedo, "El poder de los cabildo mahoas y la venta de propriedades privadas a través del tribunal de indios, Yucatán," *Historia Mexicana* 54, no. 5 (2004): 697–759, and Matthew Restall, Lisa Sousa, and Kevin Terraciano, eds., *Mesoamerican Voices: Native-Language Writings from Colonial Mexico, Oaxaca, Yucatan and Guatemala* (2005; reprint, New York: Cambridge University Press, 2008), 158.

18. For a comparison of jurisdiction and legal representation for natives in Mexico and Peru, see Woodrow Borah, "Juzgado General de Indios del Peru or Juzgado Particular de Indios de el Cercado," *Revista Chilena de Historia del Derecho* 6 (1970): 29–42.

19. Debates about this right, and sensitivity on the part of elected officials about the use of corporal punishment, grew during the century. See, for example, Queja de los vecinos del pueblo de Lalopa contra sus autoridades, quienes les imponen multas y latigos por no asistir a los tequíos, AHJO, VA, Civ., Leg. 13, Exp. 17, 1750 [1748]; Calisto Ayala, indio tributario del pueblo de Simbál, marido y conjunta persona de María Cosme, contra Juan Anselmo Saona, Alcalde ordinario del pueblo, sobre azotes as su mujer. ARL, Intend. C. Crim., Leg. 353, C. 1833, 1784, 1v; 12v; Sobre elecciones de principales en el pueblo de Tabaá, AHJO, VA, Civ., Leg. 27, Exp. 4, 1789, f. 16.

20. See Sinclair Tompson, *We Alone Will Rule: Native Andean Politics in the Age of Insurgency* (Madison: University of Wisconsin Press, 2002), 43; Yannakakis, *Art*, 120–121. While the cacique and, over time, the cabildo were to provide the "voice" of the pueblo in legal matters, in practice the issue of who was writing (and translating) was more complicated, as discussed in Chapter 1. For native scribes and procurators, see Burns, "Making Indigenous Archives;" and Yanna Yannakakis, "Making Law Intelligible: Networks of Translation in Mid-Colonial Oaxaca," 79–103, in Ramos and Yannakakis, *Indigenous Intellectuals*; Karen Graubart, "Competing Spanish and Indigenous Jurisdictions in Early Colonial Lima," *Oxford Research Encyclopedias, Latin American History* (Oxford University Press, 2016), http://latinameri-canhistory.oxfordre.com/view/10.1093/acrefore/9780199366439.001.0001/acrefore-9780199366439-e-365?rskey=l231vL&result=1, accessed 5/10/2016.

21. Diego de la Cruz, natural del pueblo de San Agustín Tlalotepec, de la jurisdicción de Yanhuitlán, vecino del pueblo de Chaluapa ... contra los naturales del pueblo, por decir gastaba grandes cantidades de pesos (como alcalde). Yanhuitlan, AHJO, Tepos., Civ., Leg. 19, Exp. 1, 1707. In Villa Alta, it was reported that almost all outgoing officials ended their tenures

"*adelantados*," or in debt, Queja de los vecinos del pueblo de Lalopa, AHJO, VA, Civ., Leg. 13, Exp. 17, 1750 [1748].

22. Petición que hace Jerónimo García, Juan Joseph y Lorenzo López, naturales y vecinos de San Pedro Apostól, de esta jurisdicción, para que ningun masahual deje asistir a los tequios, APGEO, AM, Oaxaca, Leg. 42, Exp. 761, 1736, f.14.

23. Tomas López Flores y sus hermanos contra la autoridad de San Juan Yaeé, sobre privilegios de nobleza, AHJO, VA, Civ., Leg. 18, Exp. 15, 1764, f. 9.

24. Don Luis de Velasco, virrey, para que los corregidores y alcaldes mayores, procedan en el uso de sus oficios como deben . . . [y a] los jueces no quitaran vara a ninguna persona que la tenga por mandamiento, AHJO, Tepos. Civ., Leg 21, 1715, f. 11.

25. Real Provisión del Superior Gobierno al Corregidor y demás justicias de Truxillo para que se pongan en posesión de la vara del Alcalde Ordinario del las parroquias unidas de Santa Ana y San Sebastián a Pascual Carlos, ARL, Asuntos de Gobierno, Leg. 107. C. 1916, 1723. Also see El gobernador del pueblo de Talea se queja que el comiciado Jose Evendulain lo despojo del mando y vara que tenía, AHJO, VA, Civ., Leg. 18, Exp. 7, 1764.

26. Expediente seguido por Juan Lorenzo Rizo, Protector de los Naturales del Corregimiento de Truxillo, por lo tocante al Común de ellos del pueblo de San Pedro de Virú, contra los Alcaldes y mandones del dicho pueblo para que no apremien a los indios de su comunidad a pagar derrames gravosas, ARL, Correg., C.O., Leg. 224, C. 1898, 1748, 1–1v; Los naturales del pueblo de Choapan piden se anulen las elecciones de alcaldes que se llevo a cabo ya que éste fue impuesto y no fue electo por pueblo, AHJO, VA, Civ., Leg. 11, Exp. 13, 1742, 2v–3.

27. Tomás y Valiente, *Manual*, 328.

28. The document is found in Las justicias del pueblo San Juan Tanetze contra Joseph de Iescas por faltas cometidas a la autoridad, AHJO, VA, Civ., Leg. 3, Exp. 3, 1690, 4–5.

29. Stephanie Wood, *Transcending Conquest: Nahua Views of Spanish Colonial Mexico* (Norman: University of Oklahoma Press, 1997), 133. Also see Yanna Yannakakis, "Witnesses, Spatial Practices, and a Land Dispute in Colonial Oaxaca," *The Americas* 65, no. 2 (Oct. 2008): 161–192.

30. Las justicias del pueblo San Jan Tanetze contra Joseph de Iescas por faltas cometidas a la auto-ridad, AHJO, VA, Civ., Leg. 3, Exp. 3, 1690. Note that there is an impressive ongoing "wiki" project of transcribing native-language documents from throughout Mesoamerica. It includes the "memoria," as well a final piece of Zapotec writing in this case—a petition for release from prison by the youth who offended Juan de Illescas—transcribed alongside their Spanish translation from the period, Wiki Filología, http://132.248.101.214/wikfil/index.php/AVA-Civil_3-3(3r),_Tanetze,_10-VIII-1683; and http://132.248.101.214/wikfil/index.php/Zapoteco_%28ticha_zaa%29, last accessed DATE. The analysis of the meaning of the Zapotec originals and Spanish translations, as well as the transcription of the opening petition is my own, and was pieced together from various Zapotec dictionaries as well as the important work of María de los Ángeles Romero Frizzi, coord., *Escritura zapoteca. 2,500 años de historia* (Mexico City: Centro de Investigación y Estudios Superiores en Antropología Social, 2003).

31. Yannakakis, *Art*, 23; also see comments on the "language ideology" at play within Spanish courts, 111–112.

32. On hair cutting, see Taylor, *Magistrates*, 234.

33. For more on how non-Spanish-speaking subjects interacted with the law via interpreters, see Yannakakis, "Making Law Intelligible," 81, n. 6, 99–100.

34. On the complex overlay of Castilian notions of community membership and Spanish American equivalents, particularly in regard to native populations, see Herzog, *Defining Nations*, esp. 62–63.

35. Yanna Yannakakis is currently working on this seemingly unique local genre of legal doc-ument, finding a number within a larger florescence of native-language documents dating from roughly 1650–1750, Yannakakis, "Making Law Intelligible"; Yanna Yannakakis and Marina Schrader-Kniffki, "Between the 'Old Law' and the New: Christian Translation, Indian Jurisdiction, and Criminal Justice in Colonial Oaxaca," *Hispanic American Historical Review*, 96, no. 3 (2016): 517–538.On ceremony in the region, see Nancy Farriss, *Libana: El discurso ceremonial mesoamericano y el sermón Cristiano* (Mexico City: Artes de México, 2011).

36. The text of the complaint about his inherited status reads: "niaquee bati çie ofiçio audiençi bene [gente] yetze [pueblo] naca [representar or colindador] xotao [antepasado] hue [one who] leni [aquí] xoçie [?] /no tiene ningún derecho a tener ofizio audiencia que es masehual su/abuelo y su padre," Las justicias del pueblo San Jan Tanetze . . . AHJO, VA, Civ, Leg. 3, Exp. 3, 1690, 4v, 5v. The repeated use of the term "audiencia" in place of "cabildo" here is notable; it was was also common among the Mixtecs, according to Terraciano, *Mixtecs*, 191, 196. Elected officials seemed to elide royal authority with their own or the community as an entity, speaking as "yoo la hui audiencia li rey ni gaa yetze San Juo. Tanetze/ la comunidad y Audiencia del Rey aquí en este Pueblo de San Juan Tanetze," f. 4; 5. For a similar elision between king and community, see S. Elizabeth Penry "The '*Rey Común*': Indigenous Political Discourse in Eighteenth-Century Alto Perú," in *The Collective and the Public in Latin America: Cultural Identities and Political Order*, ed. Luis Roniger and Tamar Herzog (Sussex: Sussex Academic Press, 2000), 219–237.

37. See the discussion of Nahautl terms for disorder or damage, which was more overtly moralized when translated into "sin" by Spanish missionaries, in Louise M. Burkhart, *The Slippery Earth: Nahua-Christian Moral Dialog in Sixteenth-Century Mexico* (Tucson: University of Arizona Press, 1989), 28–29.

38. Martina Schrader-Kniffki and Yanna Yannakakis, "Sins and Crimes: Zapotec-Spanish Translations in Catholic Evangelization and Spanish Law," in *Missionary Linguistics V/Lingüística misionera; Translation Theories and Practice*, ed. Otto Zawartjes et al., 161–196 (Bremen, Germany: John Benjamins Publishing, 2014).

39. Lockhart, *Nahuas*, 5.

40. See, for example, San Pablo, Caxamarca. Autos que sigue Francisca Ramos, mujer legítima de Antonio Coro, indio originario de la Doctrina de San Pablo de Chalaques, contra la persona de Don Benito Chuquitas, Alcalde Ordinario de Naturales, por maltratos y azotes, ARL, Intend. C. Crim, Leg. 353, C. 1344, 1788. On the flourishing of legal writing despite Toledan restrictions, see Burns, "Making Indigenous Archives."

41. Sobre lo representado por el Subdelegado del Partido del Cercado de Lima acerca del despojo de jurisdicción que le ha hecho el Fiscal Protector de Yndios, avocándose el conocimiento de la causa que se seguía en su Juzgado para la unión del Matrimonio de Joaquín Jordan y su Muger María Tomasa Maldonado, AGI, Gobierno, Lima, 967, 1798.

42. See, for example, Fragmento (parte final) de un expediente promovido por Dn. José Temoche, indio noble y principal que dice ser del Pueblo de Lambayeque, Provincia de Saña, sobre que se declare como sucesor de la Pachaquía del Ayllu Viejo de Lambayeque, por derecho de sangre. AGN-P, DI, Leg. 40, C. 832, 1780.

43. Serúlnikov, *Subverting*, 11.

44. Sinclair Tompson places the democratization of indigenous communities outside of the Reforms altogether and within an "Age of Revolution" paradigm, *We Alone*. Also see Penry, "The *Rey Común*." Scholars of the Southern Andes have been at the forefront of the tendency to place Indian actions, from lawsuits to rebellion, in a trans-regional context, arguing that the Bourbon Reforms created opportunities to reshape custom, envision an alternative to Spanish colonialism itself, or institute more democratic processes. Much of that literature attempts to explain why the power of caciques increased in the Southern Andes while elsewhere, such as in Cuzco, cacical power waned. See David Garrett, *Shadows of Empire: The Indian Nobility of Cusco, 1750–1825* (New York: Cambridge University Press, 2005), 150, ch. 5; Serúlinkov, *Subverting*, 218.

45. Chance, *Conquest of the Sierra*, 140, Table 17.

46. Ibid., 138.

47. Ymbentario de todas la actuaciones Civiles y Criminales que existen en este Archivo . . . , AHJO, Tespos., Civ., Leg. 49, Exp. 15, n/d [1793].

48. I conducted a thorough analysis of litigation by type for all cases in the 1700s in Villa Alta, and for Teposcolula during the intervals of 1700–9, 1750–59, and 1790–99. Categorizing cases into six different "types," of which intra-community conflicts over status, elections, and community service constituted one, I found no other significant trends that could account for the overall increase in litigation. Indeed, the numbers of these types of lawsuits fluctuate over the course of the century in no clear pattern. The other categories of suits analyzed include

corporate suits brought by the entire pueblo against other corporate bodies or individuals outside the community; suits between individuals (including inheritance matters); complaints against non-Indian officials; general legal instruments; and colonial authorities' correspondence and edicts.

49. My analysis of the motivation of civil suits derives from the archive's older, handwritten catalogs, which permitted an easier review of the general content of suits than does the archive's newer computerized database. By examining short descriptions of the cases in the catalog for Villa Alta, I found the number of suits to be remarkably close to Chance's, particularly considering that he includes six cases from the criminal series and some from national archive in Mexico City.

50. Judging by the published catalog descriptions of cases in the ARL, the Corregidor of Trujillo received civil cases initiated by native communities at an average of .05 cases per year in the 1600s and 1.31 suits per year in the 1700s. In its last four years from 1780–84, this official received over three such cases per year.

51. There were 35 community-led disputes in the civil jurisdiction of the Intendant of Trujillo from 1785–1810, and 11 were against caciques. Only five cases were brought by caciques as litigants.

52. Chance, *Conquest*, 157, 173; Yannakakis, *Art*, 89–95.

53. Susan Ramírez, *Provincial Patriarchs: Land Tenure and the Economics of Power in Colonial Peru* (Albuquerque: University of New Mexico Press, 1986), esp. 212–217.

54. The provision is reproduced in Para que celebren elecciones los pueblos de Achutla, San Agustín Tlacotepeque primero deben comparacer ante el Intendente provincial y traer las nuevas tasaciones para darles a conocer a los individuos de que se deveran componer las nuevas repúblicas, APGEO, Intend., Tepos., Caja 1, no. 2, 1787.

55. Ibid.

56. On the difficulty in finding a unified "Bourbon" project in Oaxaca, see Peter Guardino, *The Time of Liberty: Popular Political Culture in Oaxaca, 1750–1850* (Durham: Duke University Press, 2005), 91–96.

57. Charles Gibson, *The Aztecs under Spanish Rule: A History of Indians in the Valley of Mexico* (Stanford: Stanford University Press, 1964).

58. William Taylor, "Cacicazgos coloniales en la valle de Oaxaca," *Historia Mexicana* 20, no. 1 (1970): 1–41; and *Landlord and Peasant*, esp. 53; Scarlet O'Phelan, *Kurakas sin sucesiones: Del cacique al alcalde de indios (Perú y Bolivia, 1750–1835)* (Cuzco: Centro de Estudios Regionales Andinos Bartolomé de las Casas, 1997), 46. Susan E. Ramírez suggests that merit was always a defining feature of cacique status on the north coast, "'El Dueño de Indios': Thoughts on the Shifting Bases of Power under the *curaca de los viejos antiguos* under the Spanish in Sixteenth-Century Peru," *Hispanic American Historical Review* 67, no. 4 (1987): 575–610.

59. Margarita Menegus Bornemann refers to this as the "macehualization" of power (*macehual* being the Nahuatl term for commoner), "El cacicazgo en Nueva España," in *El cacicazgo en Nueva España y Filipinas*, coord. Margarita Mengus Bornemann and Roldolfo Aguirre Salvador (Mexico City: Universidad Nacional Autónoma de México, 2005), 13–69. Also see in the same volume the essays by Rodolfo Aguirre Salvador, "Un cacicazgo en disputa: Panoaya en el siglo XVIII," 87–163 and Norma Angelica Castillo Palma and Francisco González-Hermosillo Adams, "Nobleza indígena y cacicazgos en Cholula, siglos XVI–XVIII," 289–354. Specifically on merit in Upper Peru, see Serúlnikov, *Subverting*, 34.

60. "Nosotros los hijos," "los hijos de VM," Los naturales del pueblo de Choapan . . . , AHJO, VA, Civ., Leg. 11, Exp. 13, 1742. On the increasing number of individuals claiming noble status, see Chance, *Conquest*, ch. 5.

61. Los naturales del pueblo de Choapan . . . , AHJO, Villa Alta, Civil, Leg. 11, Exp. 13, 1742, f. 1.

62. Ibid.,1v; 3.

63. Francie R. Chassen-López, *From Liberal to Revolutionary Oaxaca: The View from the South, Mexico 1867–1911* (University Park: Pennsylvania State University Press, 2004), 282; Chance, *Conquest*, 152.

64. For various takes on community conflict with caciques, see Guardino, *Time of Liberty*, 54–56; Taylor, *Magistrates*, 347; Serúlnikov, *Subverting*, 21–26. Arij Ouweneel observes, as I also found, that native leaders often initiated litigation against the community rather than

the other way around, though Ouweneel sees caciques using invented "pre-hispanic" traditions in the context of a new Bourbon order to increase their sphere of economic authority, "From Tlahtocayotl to Goberdnadoryotl: A Critical Examination of Indigenous Rule in 18th-Century Central Mexico," *American Ethnologist* 22, no. 4 (1995): 756–785, esp. 774, 778–779.

65. Los naturales del pueblo de San Juan de Yaee que las elecciones que se celebraron para elegir a las nuevas autoridades, AHJO, VA, Crim., Leg. 23, Exp. 2, 1775, 3 v.

66. Ibid., 6. Also see Chassen-López, *From Liberal*, 283.

67. Serúlnikov, *Subverting*, 53.

68. S/t Pueblo de Teposcolula, AGN-M, AM, Vol. 7, Exp. 334, 1777.

69. Terraciano, *Mixtecas*, 195–196.

70. V. Exa. mandó al Alcalde Mayor de Tepsocolula notifique al de Teposcolula el que pena de dos cientos ps le exhiba en el acto de la Diligen las que se el de bolverion en virtud de decreto . . . y la averigucaión de los excesos pro que se quexaron los principales, y Ancianos del Pueblo contra Dn. Juan Manuel Vásquez, AGN-M, AM, Leg. 7, Exp. 47, 1770.

71. Penry, "The '*Rey Común*,'" 227.

72. Juan López, AHJO, VA., Civ., Leg. 17, Exp. 16, 1760; Juan, Nicolás y Antonio Yescas, caciques del pueblo de San Juan Yaeé, piden se les exima de trabajos bajos que sólo efectuan los macehuales, AHJO, VA, Civ., Leg. 19, Exp. 14, 1766; Sobre elecciones de nuevas justicias del pueblo de Yagallo. AHJO, VA Civ., Leg. 27, exp, 17, 1791; Dionisio Olivero, vecino de Chilapa, residente en la cabecera de Teposcolula, ante el Alclade Mayor, pidio se le libre despacho a la república y cura del pueblo de Chilapa para que no se metan con el y pueda salir y entrar libremente a su rancho, de igual formal pidió que Angel Cisneros, vecino de Chilapa, presentar las pruebas necesarias y justificara la demanda que le hizo respecto a la supuestas relaciones que tuvo con su esposa, AHJO, Civ., Tepos., Leg. 51, Exp. 33, 1797.

73. Expediente seguido por Juan Ramos Bello, Alcalde de Aguas del pueblo de Guanchaco, en nombre del común de dho pueblo, sobre no se confirmen las elecciones de Alcaldes y demás ministros con los vicios que menciona en su escrito, ARL, Correg. C.O., Leg. 233, C. 2093, 1778, 2; 9v.

74. A copy of the cédula can be found in Para que celebren elecciones, APGEO, Intend., Tepos. caja 1, no. 2. 1787.

75. Autos que promueve Jasinto Asavache, indio principal del pueblo de Santa Lucía de Moche, contra el Alcalde Don Manuel Delgado, sobre despojo de tierras, ARL, Intend. C.O., Leg. 318, C. 479, 1797.

76. The cédula is summarized in Memorial que el Cabildo de la ciudad de los naturales de los Reyes . . . acompañando un traslado de la real Cédula . . . de 1735, habilitando a los indios para ejercer en las audiencias el cargo de Procuradores en los asuntos concernientes a los de su nación, AGN-P, DI, Leg. 17, C. 302, 1762. See Alcira Dueñas's rich discussion of the position of the procurador and the struggle for native representatives, including this case, in "Lima's Indian *Letrados*." The reach and meaning of the cédula would have to be revisited periodically, as they were in this case. See Paul Charney, *Indian Society in the Valley of Lima, Peru, 1532–1825* (Lanham, MD: University Press of America, 2001), 99.

77. Traslado de los autos que d. Mateo y Martínez, como apoderado del Cabildo de Naturales de la ciudad de los Reyes, promovió en la Corte de Madrid, sobre que se separase del Cargo de Procurador de los Naturales a Toribio Ramos, por no ser indio entero, sino sambaigo; y sobre se le acordase a los naturales, AGN-P, DI, Leg. 23, C. 402, 1782, f. 23 v. Note that this case also involved the cabildo's power to name employees to the hospital of the Indian district, Santa Ana. This was not the native cabildo's first use of the phrase "scarcity of lights." See the petition dated 1762 in Autos que promovió el Cabidlo de los naturales de indios nobles de la cuidad de los Reyes contra los procuradores españoles de los indios. . ., DI, C. 311, Leg. 18, 1762-77.

78. Traslado de los autos que d. Mateo y Martínez. . ., AGN-P, DI, Leg. 23, C. 402, 1782., f. 23.

79. Ibid., 92–92v.

80. On the new connotations and ubiquity of the term "utility" in late eighteenth-century Spanish thought, see MacKay, *Lazy, Improvident*, 121.

81. See Brian Owensby, "Between Justice and Economics: Indians and Reformism in Eighteenth-Century Imperial Thought," in Benton and Ross, eds., *Legal Pluralism and Empires*, 143–169.

82. Los caciques y principales del pueblo de Tlacochuaya, contral los maceguales de dhico pueblo, sobre los servicios personales, APGEO, AM, Oaxaca, 1734.

83. For a similar case, and one in which the litigants founded exemptions in the "Leyes de Reynos" and Christian behavior rather than heredity, see Juan, Nicolás y Antonio Yescas, caciques del pueblo de San Juan Yaeé, piden se les exima de trabajos bajos que sólo efectuan los macehuales, AHJO, VA, Civ., Leg. 19, Exp. 14, 1766.

84. For this, he gathered priests as witnesses to provide a kind of legal document, called a "*certificación*." The priests, in turn, said they received their information from "*ancianos*" of various villages, attempting to create a tangible legal text that would capture and freeze a kind of generalized Zapotec custom that applied to all pueblos in the area known as "the Rincón," Juan López, AHJO, VA., Civ., Leg. 17, Exp. 16, 1760.

85. For more on the career of Miranda, see "Méritos, José Alejandro de Miranda," AGI, Indiferente, 253, n. 26, 1751.

86. On the employment of these various terms such as "style," "use," and "practice" for custom and their origins in the writings of the jurist Solórzano, see Yannakakis, *Art*, 123; Tau Anzoátegui, *El poder*, 318–322.

87. Juan López principal del pueblo de Santa María se queja de que los naturales de su pueblo lo quieren despojar de las garantías de las que gozan los principales, AHJO, VA, Civ., Leg. 17, Exp. 16, 1760, f. 15. Guardino notes this case and believes that the lawyer's argument elided cacique and principal status, *Time of Liberty*, 55.

88. Juan López . . . AHJO, VA., Civ., Leg. 17, Exp. 16, 1760, 14v.

89. Petición que hace Jerónimo García . . . AM, Oaxaca, Leg. 42, Exp. 761, 1736.

90. Juan, Nicolas y Antonio Yescas, caciques del pueblo de San Juan Yae, piden se les exima de trabajos bajos que solo efectuan los macehuales, AHJO, VA, Civ, Leg. 19, Exp. 14, 1766.

91. Superior orden del Señor Obispo Dr. Don Bernardo de Arbiza y Ugarte, despachándo censuras generales hasta la de Anathena, para que se lean y publiquen en el pueblo de San Pedro Lloc, a pedimiento de Francisco Xavier Lloc, Cacique de dicho pueblo, por la usurpación de los títulos del cacicaso, ARL, Correg, C.O., Leg. 53, C. 2843, 1756.

92. Real Provisión del Superior Gobierno al Corregidor y demás justicias de Truxillo para que se pongan en posesión de la vara del Alcalde Ordinario del las parroquias unidas de Santa Ana y San Sebastián a Pascual Carlos Quilca, ARL, Asuntos de Gobierno, Leg. 107. C. 1916, 1723.

93. The historiography is too vast to list here, but see historiographical discussions in Herzog, "Colonial Law"; Yannakakis, "Custom"; Owensby, *Empire of Law*.

94. Paola Miceli "El Derecho consuetudinario en Castilla: una Crítica a la matriz romántica de las interpretaciones sobre la costumbre," *Hispania* 63, no. 1 (2002): 9–28. Also see her "Entre memoria y olvido. El tiempo de la costumbre en un conflicto medieval," *Bulletin du centre d'études médiévales d'Auxerre* 2 (2008): 2–10. Also see Yannakakis, *Art*, 119, 123.

95. Scarlet O'Phelan Godoy, "Tiempo Inmemorial, Tiempo Colonial: Un estudio de casos," *Procesos. Revista Ecuatoriana de Historia*, no. 4 (1993): 3–20.

96. For more on the movement to measure Roman time, see Paola Miceli, "Medir y clasificar el tiempo de la costumbre: la obstinada tarea de los juristas medievales," *Mirabili* [Argentina] 11 (2010): 211; Lesaffer and Arriens, *European Legal History*, 353, 359. On the importance of Rome, history, and eschatology in the Andes, see Sabine MacCormack, *On the Wings of Time: Rome, the Incas, Spain, and Peru* (Princeton: Princeton University Press, 2007).

97. See the comments on how this legal branch of history, derived from Grotius, Pufendorf and Bodin, morphed into the "spirit of the laws" Enlightenment of Montesquieu and Voltaire, in "History," Reill and Wilson, *Encyclopedia of the Enlightenment*, 198–199.

98. Miceli, "Entre memoria y olvido," 3.

99. Sobre el pleito seguido en Lima entre Dn Eugenio Victorio Temoche Farrochumbi Puy Consoli y Don Pedro Fayso Farrochumbi, sobre pertenencia del Cacicazgo de Lambayque y Ferrañafe; y dudas ocurridas a la Audiencia con motivo de la concesión de Cacicazgos—Se expedió Cédula general el 9 de Mayo de 1790 participando reservadamente a las Audiencias lo resuelto sobre nombramiento de Caciques y declaración de Nobleza a los naturales de Yndias, AGI, Gobierno, Lima 932, Leg. 2, 1790, f. 7.

100. D. José Damaso Temoche sobre el cacicazgo de Lambayeque, BNP C4419, 1794, f. 1. Also see O'Phelan, *Kurakas sin sucesiones*, 46.

101. Sobre el pleito seguido en Lima entre Dn Eugenio Victorio Temoche Farrochumbi Puy Consoli y Dn Pedro Fayso Farrochumbi, Areche, AGI, Gobierno, Lima 932, Leg. 2, 1782, s/f.

102. Suits which indigenous litigants cleverly accused Indian opponents of *lesa magestad* or of obstructing Bourbon royal financial interests include Autos que sigue Bartola Bayona contra su marido Cipriano Dias por malos tratamientos y amancebamiento, ARL, Intendente, C. Crim, Leg. 35, C. 1347, 1788; Bernardo de las Casas y Luis de la Cruz, naturales, principales y caciques del pueblo de Yanhuitlan, ante el juez comisionado por su majestad . . . pidieron se mande notificar Pedro Sánchez, actual gobernador del pueblo, no les moleste ni a ellos ni a sus familias cobrándoles, los cuatros tercios de la real tribute, AHJO, Tepos., Civ., Leg. 48, Exp. 11, 1790. On this strategy as a specifically eighteenth-century development, see Serúnikov, *Subverting*, 109–113.

103. Sobre el pleito seguido en Lima entre Dn Eugenio Victorio Temoche Farrochumbi Puy Consoli y Dn Pedro Fayso Farrochumbi, AGI, Gobierno, Lima 932, Leg. 2, 1790, Council to King, 1787, s/f.

104. Fiscal's statement 9 sept., 1789, AGI, Gobierno, Lima 932, Leg. 2, 1790.

105. This phrasing invokes Cañizares-Esguerra's revalorization of native sources and Spanish patriotic historiography in the development of modern history, *How to Write the History*.

106. Miguel Ángel González Crespo, *Juristas de la Universidad de Huesca en La Audiencia de México (Siglos XVI–XIX)* (Mexico City: Universidad Nacional Autónoma de México: Instituto de Investigaciones Jurídicas, 1992), 232–234; Twinam, *Purchasing Whiteness*, 173, provides evidence that I believe indicates that Cistué y Coll similarly elevated precedent and practiced new law-centered culture in considering petitions to achieve "*limpieza de sangre*," or genealogical Spanishness.

107. On the eighteenth-century edition of the *Comentarios reales* and its place in Spanish imperial thought, see Fernanda Macchi, *Incas ilustrados: Reconstrucciones imperiales en la segunda mitad del siglo XVIII* (Madrid: Vervuert/Iberamericana, 2009), esp. ch. 1.

108. Sobre el pleito seguido en Lima entre Dn Eugenio Victorio Temoche Farrochumbi Puy Consoli y Dn Pedro Fayso Farrochumbi, AGI, Gobierno, Lima 932, Leg. 2, 1790, Fiscal's statement, 9 sept., 1789, s/f. The Fiscal undoubtedly had political motivations himself for discrediting the Comentarios, since it was thought to have inspired Tupac Amaru II to rebellion, Charles Walker, *The Tupac Amaru Rebellion* (Cambridge, MA: Harvard University Press, 2014), 28–29.

109. Yannakakis, *Art*, 126.

110. For this method in action, see Petición que hace Jerónimo García, Juan Joseph y Lorenzo López . . . AGPEO, AM, Oaxaca, Leg. 42, Exp. 761, 1736, f. 11.

111. Ibid., f. 37.

112. Farriss, *Libana*.

113. Expediente seguido por Pablo Céspedes Tito Yupanqui, Capitán de Infantería de los Indios forasteros de la Parroquia de Truxillo y don Pedro García Herrera, Capitán de los Indios de la Pomalca del Batallón de esta plaza, con el capitán de los indios criollos Pascual Gerónimo Gómez, sobre amparo en la antigüedad como Capitanes antiguos, ARL, Correg. C.O., Leg. 221, C. 1804, 1733.

114. Traslado de los autos que d. Mateo, AGN-P, DI, Leg. 23, C. 402, 1787, f. 13.

115. Ibid, f. 12v.

116. Ibid., f. 28.

117. Also note the use of the expression "*costumbre mal puesta*," or "misused custom," in Los alcaldes Juan Gregorio y Joaquón Lucas de la Cabecera de Santa María Asumpción Tontontepeque y demás principales del común . . . sobre el cobro de aranceles por el parroco, APGEO, Intend., VA, Leg. 1, no. 30, 1807, and a cacique's reference to "*antiguos disórdenes*" and a clever alteration of the phrase "*uso y costumbre*" to "*abuso o costumbre*" to refer to a pernicious land sale practice among his subject people in Autos que sigue Juan Manuel Céspedes Tito, en nombre del Juez Territorial en el partido de Guancabamba (Piura), contra Vicente Culquicondor, indio, por calumnias sobre el desempeño de su función, 15 f., ARL, Intend. C. Crim, Leg. 353, C. 1327, 1787, 5; 6–6v.

118. Reill, *German Enlightenment*, 145; Jay Smith, *The Culture of Merit: Nobility, the Royal Service and the Making of the Absolute Monarchy in France 1600–1789* (Ann Arbor: University of

Michigan Press, 1996); Cañizares-Esguerra, *How to Write*. More philosophically, I follow Jonathan Knudson's definition of historicism as "the belief that all reality is historical and explanation lies in life in its becoming," "Historicism and Enlightenment," in Baker and Reill, *What's Left of Enlightenment?*, 39–70; 40. Of course, later nineteenth-century historians tried to uproot romantic historicism from its eighteenth-century origins, but as Knudson and others point out, Enlightenment thinkers were largely responsible for working out a historicist method of understanding the past. Also see Sara Henary, "De Toqueville and the Challenge of Historicism," *Review of Politics* 78 (2014): 467–494.

119. Smith, *Culture of Merit*, 3. Smith is deepening the influential thesis of Guy Chaussinand-Nogaret, *The French Nobility in the Eighteenth Century*, trans. William Doyle (New York: Cambridge University Press, 1985). It bears keeping in mind that even cautious European Enlightenment reformers who rejected revolution, such as the Scots, engaged in radical reconsiderations of social rank during the eighteenth century, such as John Millar's *The Origin of the Distinction of Ranks* (1771). See Israel, *Democratic Enlightenment*, 18; 766; 938.

120. Christian humility and ideals of meaningful labor likewise had their place in the hierarchal Baroque culture of honor by birthright in Spain as well, MacKay, *Lazy, Improvident*, 86. But, much like the French revolutionaries rewriting the French past, eighteenth-century Spanish royal reformers forgot such subtleties.

121. Paquette, *Enlightened Governance*; MacKay, *Lazy, Improvident*.

122. Quoted in MacKay, *Lazy, Improvident*, 121.

123. On honor among plebeians and natives, see Stern, *Secret History*; the essays in Lyman Johnson and Sonya Lipsett-Rivera, eds., *The Faces of Honor: Sex, Shame and Violence in Colonial Latin America* (Albuquerque: University of New Mexico Press, 1998); Chambers, *From Subjects to Citizens*; Marixa Lasso, *Myths of Harmony: Race and Republicanism during the Age of Revolution, Colombia, 1795–1831* (Pittsburgh: University of Pittsburgh Press, 2007), 26–40; Aline Helg, *Liberty and Equality in Caribbean Colombia, 1770–1835* (Chapel Hill: University of North Carolina Press, 2004; Peter Guardino, "Gendering, Soldiering and Citizenship in the Mexican-American War of 1846–1848," *American Historical Review* 119, no. 1 (2014), esp. 30–31.

124. This offers a twist on Europe-centered theorizing about inheritance and history offered by the likes of J. G. A. Pocock and Slavoj Žižek. Ian Baucom summarizes how, for Žižek, the Enlightenment moment involved overthrowing "virtue as allegiance in exchange for award" and for Pocock the replacement of "heritable property by abstract property," in *Specters of the Atlantic: Finance Capital, Slavery and the Philosophy of History* (Durham: Duke University Press, 2005). Here we see a variant of inheritance as heritable property whose value must be constantly reaffirmed by the state.

125. Bianca Premo, "Custom Today: Temporality, Law, and Indigenous Enlightenment," *Hispanic American Historical Review* 94, no. 3 (2014): 355–379.

126. Eliás José Palti, "Time, Modernity and Time Irreversibility," *Philosophy & Social Criticism* 23, no. 5 (1997): 25–62; 35; Koselleck, *Practice*, 154–169.

127. Koselleck also attributes to *"Neutzeit"* the sense of an open future and epochal beginning, as well as the "non simultaneity of diverse but, in a chronological sense, simultaneous histories," *Practice*, 165–167.

128. Trouillot, *Silencing the Past*, Chakrabarty, *Provinicializing Europe*, 22–23.

129. "Deseo Literario a fin de que en Burgos y en otros Ciudades se publique en cada mes ó semna un escrto periodico," *Memorial literario, instructive y curioso de la Corte de Madrid*, tomo XIII (Madrid: Imprenta Real, 1788), abril de 1788, 535–550, 539.

130. This scarcity was not the fault of the region's inhabitants, the writer generously granted, because Extremadura was unfortunately located in the "posterior of Spain," "Discurso pronunciado en la apertura la real audiencia de Extemadura, instalada en Cáceres, en 1791," *Continuación del almacén de frutos literarios o Semanario de obras inéditas*, tomo III (Madrid: Imprente de Repullés, 1818), 189.

131. 2nd Session, 13 de diciembre de 1826, *Actas del Congreso Constituyente del estado libre de Mexico: revisadas por el mismo*, tomo XI (Mexico City: Imprenta del gobierno del estado, 1829), 240. Also see the catechism of Luis de Mendizábal in which he decried the "three hundred years of subjection by the Spanish," Dorothy Tanck de Estrada, *Independencia y educación: Cultura cívica, educación indígena, y literatura infantil* (Mexico City: El Colegio de Mexico, 2013).

132. Autos que siguieron los indios del pueblo de Morrope, en el Corregimiento de Zaña, contra Dn. Tomás Domínguez, justicia mayor de aquella provincial ... por haberse desestimado en la Real Audiencia de Lima los derechos que alegaba su contendor, Don Lorenzo Cususoli, AGN-P, DI, Leg. 20, C. 338, 1771; Expediente seguido por Juan Fermín Mondragón, Santiago Saona ... naturales del pueblo de San Juan Bautista de Simbal, en nombre de dicho común sobre recepción de información de los perjuicios que recibe dicho común al haberseles grabado en dos pesos en el pago del tributo y los derechos exigidos por el derecho de posesión de las minas de cal y yeso y otros asuntos. ARL, Correg. C.O., Leg. 232, C. 2054, 1774.

133. See, for example, Bartolomé de la Cruz, alcalde segundo, Gregorio Vásquez, alguacil mayor ... por ellos y en nombre del pueblo San Marcos Monte de León ... dijieron que Agustín Martín, alcalde reelecto del pueblo de San Marcos es notorio y público vicio de embriaguez y usurpa juridicción, por lo que piden mande sea depuesto de la vara que ostenta, AJPO, Tepos. Civ., Leg. 34, Exp. 24, 1759.

134. Accusations against native leaders or legal officials for tyranny picked up pace and intensity during the century. A sampling of such accusations follows: "*tiranias y ynjustias*," Los principales y comunes del pueblo de Lalopa piden se cambien a los alcaldes actuales por no convenir a sus intereses, AHJO, VA, Civ., Leg. 13, Exp. 15, 1750, f. 1v; "*estamos prontos a venir abotarse a los pies de VS a find de que nos liberte de la oppression de este tirano*," Bello, ARL, Correg. C.O., Leg. 233, C. 2093, 1778, ff. 7–7v; "*su espíritu denegativo y odioso pues después de amarrada que estuve de un modo tirano e indecoroso de mi sexso me asotó*," Autos que sigue Francisca Ramos, ARL, Intend. C. Crim, Leg. 353, C. 1344, 1788, f. 5; "*el despotismo y codicio ...*," "*con tirania y rigor ...*," "*el despotismo de este tirano*," Los naturales de Santo Domingo Tepustepec dela Jurisidición de Villa Alta solicitan que Juan Antonio Vázquez intepete de idioma Mixe, sea castigado por ocasionare perjuicios y extorciones, APGEO, Intendencia, VA, Leg. 1, Exp. 53, 1799, s/f. Also see Guardino, *Time of Liberty*, 72. Similar claims were leveled against Spanish officials, though perhaps in smaller proportion. See, for example, "*no con otro objecto que satifacer su crueldad y tirania, cuio carácter lo constitue especialmente haciéndose terrible entre los Indios*," Don Jose María Arellano solicitador de Yndios por Gabriel Antonio Bernal, tributario del Pueblo de Sta María de la Asumpción Totontepec ... contra el subdelegado por estar preso, APGEO, Intend, VA, Leg. 1, 55, 1800, f, 1.

135. Autos que sigue Juan Manuel Céspedes Tito, en nombre del Juez Territorial en el partido de Guancabamba (Piura), contra Vicente Culquicondor, indio, por calumnias sobre el desempeño de su función, ARL-Intend., Crim, Leg. 353, C. 1327, 1787, f. 2v–3.

136. Autos criminales seguidos por Calisto Ayala, indio tributario del pueblo de Simbal, ARL, Intend.m Crim., Leg. 353, C. 1833, 1784, ff. 1v; 12v.

137. Autos que promovió Tomás Collazos, indio del pueblo de San Pedro de los Chorrillos, jurisdicción de la ciudad de los Reyes sobre que se le mantuviese en el cargo de quiopcamayo perpetua de aquel pueblo del que lo habián despojado los Alcaldes y Cabildo sin causa alguna, nombrado en su lugar a Casimiro Laynes, AGN-P, DI, C. 389, Leg. 23, 1778.

138. Cuaderno de los autos promovidos por el subdelgado del partido de ... por el Cabildo de Lambayque, sobre que se remobiese y separase del cargo de Protector Sustituto de los Naturales a D. Manuel Sararredo no obstante de que el Fiscal Protector General D. Jose Pareja le había prorrogado el ejercicio de dicho cargo, AGN-P DI, Leg. 25, C. 459, 1795, ff. 3–3v. For the longer history of conflict around this post in Lambayeque and the Audiencia of Lima's earlier preference for a non-elite representative named Teodoro Daza, see Ramírez, *Provincial*, 251–253.

139. Autos que sobre la nulidad de las elecciones practicado por el Cabildo de Naturales del pueblo de Chocope, que promovió el Teniente Gobernador [*sic*] de Trujillo, D. Juan Bazo Berry, quien señalaba como autor de los disturbios que turbaban al referido pueblo a D. Agustin Chumbi Huamán, alcalde ordinario, indio discolo, revoltoso y mal intencionado, AGN-P, DI, Leg. 29, C. 558, 1800.

140. Sobre los perjuicios que los Hacendados de Lambayeque causan a los Yndios del Partido de Saña y extinción del Empleo de Protector partidario, AGI, Gobierno, Lima, 967, 1798, ff. 4; 14–15.

141. Sahlins,"What Is Anthropological," xv.
142. Note a similar emphasis on the peaceful and "humane" nature of independent Indians and the condemnation of (unexplained) "warring" neighbors who turned them violent in the Enlightened report from the 1789 Malaspina expedition, in David J. Weber, *Bárbaros: Spaniards and their Savages in the Age of Enlightenment* (New Haven: Yale University Press, 2005), 38, 43.
143. Los principales y comunes del pueblo de Lalopa, AHJO, VA, Civ., Leg. 13, Exp. 15, 1750, ff. 1v; 3.
144. For a similar argument see the royal notary's argument that his intervention in a Teposcolula election was only to ensure the representation of commoner Indians in the vote and to guard "that custom not be interrupted," V. Exa mandó al Alcalde Mayor de Tepsocolula, AGN-M, AM, Leg. 7, Exp. 47, 1770.
145. Sobre elecciones de principales en el pueblo de Tabaá, AHJO Villa Alta Civ, Leg. 27, Exp. 4, 1789. Earlier versions of this dispute, which originated in a split within the community over whether to litigate over labor conscription to a new mine in the area, are found in Real Provisión, AHJO, VA, Civ., Leg. 25, no. 1, 1783; Sobre elecciones de prinicipales en el pueblo de Tabaá, AHJO, VA Civ., Leg. 25, Exp. 11, 1784; Sobre que abstengan de hacer demandas de dinero en el pleito contra Francisco Echarri, AHJO, VA, Leg. 25, Exp. 8, 1784.
146. Sobre elecciones . . . , AHJO VA Civil, Leg. 25, Exp. 11, 1784, ff. 3–3v; 14.
147. Sobre elecciones de principales, AHJO, VA, Civ, Leg. 27, Exp. 4, 1789, f. 16.
148. Ibid., 17v.
149. Ibid., 3v.

Chapter 6

1. Autos seguidos por Josefa Piñeda, esclava de dona María Gallegos, contra ésta sobre que la venda, AGN-P, RA, Civ., Leg. 293, C. 2614, 1791, f. 1v.
2. The very titles of recent histories of slaves in Peru, as one example, underscore its analytical centrality. See Carlos Aguirre, *Agentes de su propia libertad. Los esclavos de Lima y la desintegración de la esclavitud, 1821–1854* (Lima: Pontificia Universidad Católica del Perú, 1993); Christine Hünefeldt, *Paying the Price of Freedom: Family and Labor among Lima's Slaves, 1800–1854* (Berkeley: University of California Press, 1994); McKinley, "Fractional Freedoms," 749–790.
3. Isaiah Berlin, *Four Essays on Liberty* (1958; reprint, Oxford: Oxford University Press, 1969). Also see Povinelli, "A Flight from Freedom"; Jerome Schneewind, *The Invention of Autonomy: A History of Modern Moral Philosophy* (New York: Cambridge University Press, 1989); David Schmidtz and Jason Brennan, *A Brief History of Liberty* (Malden, MA: Wiley-Blackwell, 2010). On indigenous notions of liberty in colonial Mexico, see Owensby, *Empire of Law*.
4. Frank T. Proctor argues that prior to the mid 1700s, most slaves sought autonomy rather than liberty, *"Damned Notions of Liberty": Slavery, Culture, and Power in Colonial Mexico, 1640–1769* (Albuquerque: University of New Mexico Press, 2011); "Slavery Rebellion and Liberty in Colonial Mexico," in *Black Mexico: Race and Society from Colonial to Modern Times*, ed. Ben Vinson and Matthew Restall, 21–50 (Albuquerque: University of New Mexico Press, 2009). This might set the bar for modern "freedom" prohibitively high, but the point about how infrequently slaves made freedom an express goal in the courts is well taken. Cf. Owensby, "How Juan and Leonor," who sees clear notions of liberty—particularly founded on the concepts set out by the seventeenth-century jurist Juan Solórzano de Pereira—at work in two Inquisition slave cases from Mexico; and Herman L. Bennett, *Colonial Blackness: A History of Afro-Mexico* (Bloomington: Indiana University Press, 2009), 11, who observes the "emergence" of concepts of freedom in Mexico through a methodology centered on personal stories, "in the absence of a history that tracks the legal opportunities and restrictions Africans and their descendants faced in trying to achieve freedom."
5. On the nineteenth-century shift to contractual self-ownership in the US slave system, see Amy Dru Stanley, *From Bondage to Contract: Wage Labor, Marriage, and the Market in the Age of Slave Emancipation* (New York: Cambridge University Press, 1998). For comparisons

of legal regimes and slave actions in the Atlantic context, see Ariela Gross and Alejandro de la Funte, "Slaves, Free Blacks, and Race in the Legal Regimes of Cuba, Louisiana, and Virginia: A Comparison," *North Carolina Law Review* 91, no. 5 (2013): 1699–1756.

6. On the Enlightenment in slave cases, see Lavallé, *Amor y opresion*, ch. 7; Camila Townsend, "'Half My Body Free, the Other Half Enslaved': The Politics of the Slaves of Guayaquil at the End of the Colonial Era," *Colonial Latin American Review* 7, no. 1 (1998): 105–128, 122; Lyman Johnson, "A Lack of Legitimate Obedience and Respect: Slaves and Their Masters in the Courts of Late Colonial Buenos Aires," *Hispanic American Historical Review* 87, no. 4 (2007): 631–657; Renée Soludré-La France, "*Esclavos de su magestad*: Slave Protest and Politics in Colonial New Granada," in *Slaves, Subjects and Subversives: Blacks in Colonial Latin America*, ed. Jane Landers and Barry M. Robinson, 175–208 (Albuquerque: University of New Mexico Press, 2006); see Pierre Tardieu, *El negro en la Real Audiencia de Quito (Ecuador) ss. XVI–XVIII* (Quito: IFEA, 2006), 318–320; Helg, *Liberty and Equality*, 113–117. On sailors and slavery in general in the revolutionary Atlantic, see Peter Linebaugh and Marcus Rediker, *The Many Headed Hydra: Sailors, Slaves, Commoners and the Hidden History of the Revolutionary Atlantic* (New York: Beacon, 2001).

7. Frank Tannenbaum, *Slave and Citizen* (1947; reprint, New York: Beacon, 1992). For a fine summary of Tannenbaum's legacy see McKinley, "Fractional Freedoms." Tannenbaum's thesis still can generate heat; see "What Can Frank Tannenbaum Still Teach Us about the Law of Slavery?," *Law and History Review* 24 (2004), particularly Alejandro de la Fuente, "Slave Law and Claims-Making in Cuba Revisited," 339–369; María Elena Díaz, "Beyond Tannenbaum," 371–387.

8. See especially Bennett, *Colonial Blackness*, ch. 6.

9. For example, slaves acting without masters' intervention brought two criminal complaints before the criminal alcalde of Trujillo in the seventeenth century, and at least four cases before Lima's criminal alcalde, including for wife-beating, physical injuries, and the murder of a spouse; abbreviated citations include: AGN-P, Cab., Crim., Leg. 6, C. 15; Leg. 7, C. 12; Leg. 8, C. 1. In the Lima cases, slaves do begin to appear as criminal accusers with somewhat more frequency at the end of the eighteenth century, indicating the growth of a more generalized sense of legal personality.

10. Technically, freedom suits were to be heard by the Audiencia, but slaves nonetheless used the Inquisition courts creatively in the seventeenth century. See Frank Trey Proctor, "Afro-Mexican Slave Labor in the *Obrajes de Paños* of New Spain, Seventeenth and Eighteenth Centuries," *The Americas* 60, no. 1 (2003): 33–58; Joan Cameron Bristol, *Christians, Blasphemers, and Witches: Afro-Mexican Ritual Practice in the Seventeenth Century* (Albuquerque: University of New Mexico Press, 2007). Owners also could be denounced in the Inquisition for being abusive, but these cases were rare, Owensby, "How Juan and Leonor," 52; Colin Palmer, *Slaves of the White God: Blacks in Mexico, 1560–1650* (Cambridge, MA: Harvard University Press), 105.

11. Alejandro de la Fuente, ed., "*Su único derecho: Los esclavos y la ley"Debate y Perspectivas* no. 4 (2004); Alejandro de la Fuente, "Slaves and the Creation of Legal Rights in Cuba: *Coartación* and *Papel*," *Hispanic American Historical Review* 87, no. 4 (2007): 663.

12. For the nineteenth century see Aguirre, *Agentes de su propia libertad*, 184; Fernando de Trazegnies, *Ciracio de Urtecho. Litigante por amor* (Lima: Pontifícia Universidad Católica, 1981); Peter Blanchard, *Slavery and Abolition in Early Republican Peru* (Wilmington: Scholarly Resources, 1992), 41–42; Hünefeldt, *Paying the Price*, 118; 7; Seth Meisel, "The Fruit of Freedom: Slaves and Citizens in Early Republican Argentina, in *Slaves Subjects and Subversives: Blacks in Colonial Latin America*, ed. Jane Landers and Barry M. Robinson (Albuquerque: University of New Mexico Press, 2006), 273–306. For earlier Church-centered considerations see Herman L. Bennett, *Africans in Colonial Mexico* (Bloomington: Indiana University Press, 2003), 34 and *Colonial Blackness*, 11; Sherwin K. Bryant, "Enslaved Rebels, Fugitives, and Litigants: The Resistance Continuum in Colonial Quito," *Colonial Latin American Review* 13, no. 2 (2004): 7–46; 9–10. Also see Mc Kinley, "Fractional Freedoms."

13. *Siete Partidas*, 4:22.

14. See, for example, Herbert Klein, *African Slavery in Latin America and the Caribbean* (New York: Oxford University Press, 1996), 194; David S. Chandler, "Slave over Master in Colonial

Colombia and Ecuador," *The Americas* 38, no. 3 (1982): 315–326. María Elena Díaz she argues that the practice of *coartación* originated in Cuba, and traces it to a 1673 crown law issued for the island, *The Virgin, the King, and the Royal Slaves of El Cobre: Negotiating Freedom in Colonial Cuba, 1670–1780* (Stanford: Stanford University Press, 2001), 175, 361 n. 2; Manuel Lucena Salmoral, *Leyes para esclavos: El ordenamiento jurídico sobre la condición, tratamiento, defensa y represión de los esclavos en las colonias de la América española* (Madrid: Fundación Ignacio Larramendi/MAPFRE Tavera, 2005), http://www.larramendi.es/en/consulta/registro.cmd?id=1151. On the presence of slaves in the seventeenth-century courts, see O'Toole, *Bound Lives*, 134; Lucena Salmoral, *Leyes*, 227.

15. Alejandro de la Fuente, "Slaves and the Creation of Legal Rights," 663. Also his "La esclavitud, la ley y la reclamación de derechos en Cuba," in Alejandro de la Fuente, ed. *Su único derecho: Los esclavos y la ley. Debate y Perspectivas* no. 4 (2004), 37–68; 42.

16. *Siete Partidas*, 4:21:6.

17. For similar arguments stressing the legal importance, alongside the overall social importance, of slave suits see Rebecca Scott, *Slave Emancipation in Cuba: The Transition to Free Labor, 1860–1899* (1985; reprint, Pittsburgh: University of Pittsburgh Press, 2000), 14, 74–77; Maribel Arrelucea Barrantes, *Replanteando la esclavitud: Estudios de etnicidad y género en Lima borbónica* (Lima: Centreo de Desarrollo Étnico, 2009), 71–73.

18. By my count, in the Real Audiencia, Causas Civiles series of the AGN-Perú, slave cases against owners comprise 5 of 291 for the years 1735–1749, 18 of 727 during the period 1750–75, and 54 of 508 for the period 1791–1804. Arrelucea Barrantes examines slave lawsuits in the same period in Lima with particular attention to gender in *Replanteando*.

19. On slaves as "miserables," see Premo, *Children of the Father King*, esp. chs. 1 and 7. Also see Johnson, "A Lack of Legitimate Obedience"; Magdalena Díaz, "La identidad de los esclavos negros como miserables en Nueva España: Discursos y acciones (siglos XVI–XVIII)," in *Esclavitudes hispánicas (siglos XV al XXI): Horizontes socioculturales*, ed. Aurelia Martín Casares (Granada: Universidad de Granada, 2014), 42–57.

20. It should be noted, however, that the Defensor de Menores did take a more active, and intrusive, role in suits involving slave children over the course of the eighteenth century. For more on "defenders of slaves," see de la Fuente, "Su único derecho," and Johnson, "Lack of Legitimate."

21. In the entire case series for the civil alcade, or *justicia ordinaria*, in Trujillo's ARL, there are only three slave cases specifically against masters until 1700 (one for general liberty; one to force a sale; and one for sevicia), whereas 40 cases were primarily about slaves as property. There are only two slave cases for the period 1675–95 in the Corregimiento civil series (one for liberty and one for sevicia). The eighteenth-century growth of slave cases seems to have held, more or less, into the nineteenth century, where before the intendent, slave cases made up around 6.6 percent (13) of all civil suits (195) for the period 1800–20. During these two later decades, it does seem that slaves preferred the intendency to justicia ordinaria; they brought only five cases against owners in the same period before the alcalde (of 195, or 2 percent).

22. On Quito, see Tardieu, *El negro*, 318–320; Bryant, "Enslaved Rebels," 9; Lavallé, *Amor y opresión*, 214. On the active use of the courts in late eighteenth-century Spanish Florida see Jane Landers, *Black Society in Spanish Florida* (Chicago: University of Illinois Press, 1999); on the growth of coartación cases in Cuba, and the generally urban nature of these demands, see the comments of Alejandro de la Fuente "La esclavitud, la ley," 56. Keila Grinberg's fascinating work on slave suits in Brazil unfortunately begins in 1808, but she does note that, contrary to progressive histories that claim that freedom lawsuits grow with the practice of slavery, in Brazil they were more common under Portuguese royal rule, "La manumisión, el género y la ley en el Brasil del siglo XIX: el proceso legal de Liberata por su libertad," in de la Fuente, *Su único derecho*, 94–96.

23. The numbers and percentages of Lima's slave population are derived from my analysis of a sample of 659 households in 1700 from Cook, *Numeración general* (21.4 percent of the total population, or a projected total of 6882 slaves in the city) and the 1791 "Plan demostrativo" in the *Mercurio Peruano* (19.4 percent of the total population, or 9229 slaves).

24. O'Toole, *Bound Lives*, 8–9.

25. This was the foundational thesis of Gonzalo Aguirre-Beltrán, *La población negra de México. Estudio etnohistórico* (MéxicoCity: Fonda de Cultura Económica, 1946); Bennett, *Africans*, 5; Bennett, *Colonial Blackness*, 5. Proctor argues that natural reproduction among slaves might have been able to sustain New Spain's slave population, at least until the mid eighteenth century, "*Damned Notions,*" 22–25.

26. George Reid Andrews, *Afro-Latin America, 1800–2000* (New York: Oxford University Press, 2004), 41. For the decline narrative also see Robert McCaa, "The Peopling of Mexico from Origins to Revolution," in *A Population History of North America*, ed. Michael R. Haines and Richard H. Stewart (New York: Cambridge University Press, 2000), 241–304.

27. Arrelucea Barrantes counts twice as many cases in the Audiencia and ecclesiastical tribunal of Lima brought by slave women as opposed to men (123 to 60), *Replanteando*, 59.

28. Frank "Trey" Proctor III, "Gender and the Manumission of Slaves in New Spain," *Hispanic American Historical Review* 86, no. 2 (2006): 309–336. Also see Premo, *Children of the Father King*, 219–220; n. 19, 309; and "Familiar: Thinking beyond Lineage and across Race in Spanish Atlantic Family History," *William & Mary Quarterly* 70, no. 2 (April 2013): 295–316.

29. On early colonial manumissions, see Kris Lane, "Captivity and Redemption: Aspects of Slave Life in Early Colonial Quito and Papayán," *The Americas* 57, no. 2 (2000): 225–246. On urban conditions and female slave wage labor, see Hünefeldt, *Paying the Price*, 214–215.

30. Lucena Salmoral, *Leyes*, 3; Alejandro de la Fuente, "Su único derecho: Los esclavos y la ley," in de la Fuente, *Su único derecho*, 7–22; 16.

31. The 1683 oreder, Real cédula recomendando a las audiencias y gobernadores el buen tratamiento de los esclavos y castigar la sevicia de los amos, Buen Retiro, 12 de octubre de 1683, is discussed and reproduced in Lucena Salmoral, *Leyes*, 227, 928–929. Díaz cites a 1673 Cuba edict for Cuba as the first official recognition of the practice of *coartación* in *The Virgin, the King*, 175, 361 n. 2.

32. The *Instruction* is reprinted in Konetzke, *Colección* 3, 643–652. On the longer history of "códigos negros" for the Spanish colonies, see Manuel Lucena Salmoral, *Los Códigos Negros de la América Española* (Alcalá: Universidad de Alcalá, 1996).

33. For slaves and expressions of loyalty to Spanish royalty, see Bennett, *Colonial Blackness*, 31 n. 21; Díaz, *The Virgin, the King*, 14 and passim.

34. On the innovations in the 1789 "Real Instrucción," see Premo, *Children of the Father King*, 216. For repeal, see Lucena Salmoral, *Los Códigos*, 21, 112–123. Also see Ana Hontanilla, "Sentiment and the Law: Inventing the Category of the Wretched Slave in the *Real Audiencia* of Santo Domingo, 1783–1812," *Eighteenth-Century Studies* 48, no. 2 (2015): 181–200.

35. *Recopilación de leyes de indias*, 7:5:8. The original order dates from Madrid a 15 de abril de 1540 and reads "Ordenamos anuestras Reales Audiencias, que si algun Negro ó Negra, ú otros qualesquiera tenidos por esclavos, proclamaren a la libertad, los oygan, y hagan justicia, y provean que por esto no sean maltratados de sus amos."

36. Bravo de Lagunas, "Carta . . . de la libertad," 226. For this kind of argument by a lawyer in seventeenth-century Mexico, see Owensby, "How Juan and Leonor," esp. 49. For more on the "favor of liberty," see Bianca Premo, "An Equity against the Law: Slave Rights and Creole Jurisprudence in Spanish America," *Slavery & Abolition* 32, no. 4 (2011): 495–517.

37. Bravo de Lagunas, "Carta en que se trata: si lo que nace de la statulibera, sea libre, esclavo; y si pueda ser statulibera la manumitada desde cierto tiempo," in *Colección legal*, 143.

38. The lawsuit does not appear to have survived to be housed today in the AGN-P but Bravo de Lagunas quotes extensively from the lawyer's closing argument (*auto de vista*), "Carta en que se trata . . . *statulibera*," 107–112. It is noteworthy that the core of the young lawyer's argument rests on "doubts" and "possibilities," two hallmarks of probabilistic argumentation.

39. This was a problem not easily resolved; its persistence is evident in a 1788 royal ruling on the issue of whether the children of mothers who had made payments toward their own liberty were free or enslaved. Like Bravo de Lagunas, the Council of Indies decided that they remained in bondage. General, Resolución del Consejo se Indias sobre que la coartación de la madre no afecta al hijo de la esclava, Madrid, 5 de diciembre de 1788, AGI, Audiencia de Santo Domingo, 1142; Konetzke, *Colección*, 3, 631–635.

40. Bravo de Lagunas, "Carta en que se trata de . . . *statulibera*," 115.

41. For the importance of Church law, as opposed to civil law, as both a framework for slave autonomy and as a site of discipline, see Bennett, *Africans*, esp. ch. 2; 196; *Colonial Blackness*, esp. ch. 2.

42. Bennett, *Africans*, 81–82.

43. Autos seguidos por Natividad, esclava del licenciado don Juan de la Reinaga [*sic*: Zuñaga], presbítero domicilario del arzobispado, sobre que la reconozca su libertad por concubinato que tuvo con su amo, AAL, Causas de Negros, Leg. 33, Exp. 3, 1792–1793.

44. On the religious origins of slave "rights" in Santo Domingo, see Richard Lee Turits, "Raza, esclavitud y libertad en Santo Domingo," in de la Fuente, *Su único derecho*, 69–88.

45. Expediente seguido por Juana de la Rosa Narbaes parda libre, natural de la ciudad de Loxa en voz y en nombre de Paula Ursula, su hija natural contra Ana Ludeñas Canela, vecina de Truxillo sobre despojo de su libertad, ARL, Cab., C.O., Leg. 39, C. 731, 1721, 8v.

46. For a case in which incarceration in a panadería was cited as separating a married slave couple, see Autos seguidos por Francisco Castillo contra da. Ventura Alzamora, su ama, sobre que la venda, AGN-P, Cab. Civ., Leg. 37, C. 664, 1777.

47. Autos seguidos por don Mathías Monzón, marido legítimo y conjunta persona de Francisca Hurtado, parda esclava, contra doña María Josefa de Rojas, ama de la dicha, sobre que le otorgue papel de venta, ARL Cab., C.O., Leg. 52, C. 913, 1771, f. 1. Also see Autos hechos a pedimiento de Juan José de la Higuera, pardo libre, sobre la libertad de Lorenza Iriarte, esclava de don Pedro Iriarte, para casarse con ella, AGN-M, Civil Vol. 1474 Exp. 29, 1757.

48. Canon 1097, "*Error in personam invalidum reddit matrimonium*," in *Marriage in Canon Law: Texts and Comments. Reflections and Questions*, ed. Ladislas Orsy, SJ (1935; reprint, New York: Michael Glasier, 1988), 134.

49. Autos promovidos por el Capitán Don Carlos Flores, vecino de esta ciudad, albacea de Bartolomé Obregoso, contra Martina Orbegoso, esclava, sobre pago de 200 pesos que vale su hipoteca o prisión de dicha esclava, ARL, Intend. C.O., Leg. 299, C. 199, 1788.

50. For a similar argument about slave appeals to "mercy" and "insider status," see Sherwin K. Bryant, *Rivers of Gold, Lives of Bondage: Governing through Slavery in Colonial Quito* (Chapel Hill: University of North Carolina Press, 2014), 118–119, 124–128.

51. Owensby, *Empire of Law*, 20, 51–53.

52. Arrelucea Barrantes, *Replanteando*, 77–90.

53. Juez: Fernando de Sausa Suárez. María negra, mujer legitima de Nicolas, negro, esclavo de Alonso Bueno, panadero, por maltrato continuamente [sic] a su esclavo, AGN-M, TSJ, Corr., Crim., Vol. 16, Exp. 38, 1633, f. 1.

54. It is noteworthy that in the 1660 Mexican Inquisition case of Leonor de los Reyes, a case Owensby analyzed for the meaning of liberty to slaves in the seventeenth century, the slave initially requested that her Inquisition case *not* be treated as formal, and that the court *not* force her to litigate, "How Juan and Leonor," 61.

55. Civiles de pedimiento de Margarita Francisca mulata esclava sobre que su ama Da. Manuela Pérez de las Cuevas, demuestre la escriptura, y nombre abaluador como dentro se expresa, AGN-M, Civ., Vol. 1959, Exp. 11, 1761, f. 3.

56. Autos seguidos por María del Rosario Vega, mulata, esclava contra su amo, Dn. Juan Rodamonte, sobre sevicia y relaciones ilícitas a la que la obligó, AGN-P, RA Civ., Leg. 292, C. 2607, 1790.

57. Autos seguidos por María Moncada, de casta chala, esclava que fue del Licenciado don Alonso Moncada, sobre se le declare persona libre y no sujeta a servidumbre dando cumplimiento a la última voluntad de su amo como consta en una claúsula de su testamento, ARL, Cab., C.O., Leg. 51, C. 893, 1765, f. 8.

58. Of course, as Chapter 1 details, "paper" had always been important in the Spanish empire, and to slaves no less than others. See Jouve-Martín, *Esclavos de la ciudad letrada*. The point here, however, is that for slaves the civil contract, including contracts of an innovative type such as the bill of debt that would serve as proof of pending freedom discussed above, assumed increasing importance with their entrance into civil courts.

59. There are countless examples, so here I will list some cases to give a sense of the variety of civil documents other than wills that slaves presented: Autos que sigue Theresa Trillo, negra criolla, residente en esta ciudad sbore la libertad que debe gozar como esclava que fue de

Antonia Trillo, mujer de Mathías Martel, difunto, ARL, Correg. C.O., Leg. 235, C. 2123, 1781 (begins with a poorly handwritten offer to sell slave. Note that in this case, the slave calls for a handwriting analysis to prove that her dead master's intent was to free her); Autos que sigue Juana Baptista Laredo, esclava, de la vecindad de Truxillo, contra doña Manuela de la Sierra, su ama sobre oblación de 300 pesos para la obtención de su libertad, ARL Cab. C.O., Leg. 56, C. 970, 1783 (begins with a receipt of sale); Mexico. María Manuela de Jesus Ortega, parda libre, contra Don Joan Pezaza sobre su hermana María Gertrudis, esclava de su esposa, sobre la libertad, AGN-M, Civ., Leg. 18, Exp. 45, 1771-5 (begins with price appraisal).

60. Expediente seguido por María Jacinta, negra libre contra María de la Garza, parda, sobre pretender privarle de su libertad que estaba gozando, ARL, Correg. C.O., Leg. 220, C. 1777, 1730, 14v–15.

61. María Elena Martínez, *Genealogical Fictions: Limpieza de Sangre, Religion, and Gender in Colonial Mexico* (Stanford: Stanford University Press, 2008).

62. Sometimes slaves mixed expressions of right and protections, as in the case of María Jacinta in Trujillo, who claimed "the right (*derecho*) to my freedom in which I aim to be protected" (*amparada*)," Expediente seguido por María Jacinta, ARL, Correg. C.O., Leg. 220, C. 1777, 1730, f. 12.

63. Oakley, *Natural Law*, 18–19.

64. Expediente seguido por María Jacinta, ARL, Correg. C.O., Leg. 220, C. 1777, 1730, f. 33.

65. Autos seguido por Simón Rodríguez, pardo libre, contra don Maríano Arias, sobre su libertad, AGN-P, Cab., Civ., Leg. 316, C. 2869, 1793.

66. Schmidz and Brennan, *Brief History of Liberty*, 107–109; Knud Haakonssen, "Hugo Grotius and the History of Political Thought," *Political Theory* 13, no. 2 (1985), 136.

67. Haakonssen, "Hugo Grotius," 136. Also note the importance of John Locke's natural rights theory, particularly his articulation of self-preservation, to slave uprisings in the United States, Jack Shuler, *Calling Out Liberty: The Stono Slave Rebellion and the Universal Struggle for Human Rights* (Jackson: University of Mississippi Press, 2009), 33, 91. Georg Wilhelm Hegel later provided a twist when it came to slavery and self-preservation: he sees slaves' choice to preserve their lives in bondage rather than to be killed in war to be the root of their very status as slaves, Susan Buck-Morss, "Hegel and Haiti," *Critical Inquiry* 26, no. 4 (Summer 2000), 849.

68. Quoted in Israel, *Radical Enlightenment*, 259. The quote is from *Ethics* VI, Proposition XX.

69. Heinnecius, *Elementos del derecho natural y de gentes*. 1. "BUENO para el hombre todo lo que le conserva y perfecciona; y MALO lo que le destruye y deteriora."

70. See Knud Haakonssen, *Natural Law and Moral Philosophy: From Grotius to the Scottish Enlightenment* (New York: Cambridge University Press, 1996), 329: "This right is commonly referred to as the right to property, though, strictly speaking, as an inalienable right it can never be more than a right to *seek* property (plus, according to some, a right to subsistence)," 329. On modernity as speculation about value in the future, see J. G. A. Pocock, "Authority and Property: The Question of Liberal Orgins," in *Virtue, Commerce, and History*, by J. G. A. Pocock, 51–72 (1980; reprint, New York: Cambridge University Press, 1985); Baucom, *Specters of the Atlantic*.

71. Expediente seguido por . . . don Simón de Laballe y Cuadra, Alcalde Ordinario . . . contra León Gattica, vecino de esta ciudad, por haber herido con crueles y rigurosas azotes al mulatillo Joseph Reymundo, su esclavo, ARL, Cab., Crim., Leg. 84, C. 1507, 1744.

72. See Burns, "Introduction to the Fourth Partida," xxiv, *The Siete Partidas* 4.

73. De la Fuente, "Slaves and the Creation of Legal Rights," makes the same observation about late eighteenth-century Cuba.

74. María Teresa del Castillo, esclava, contra Manuel de Gradillas que le venda a otra amo, AGN-M, TSJ, Civ., AO, Vol. 16, Exp., 49, 1731, 11v–12.

75. Autos de demanda que sigue doña Nicolasa González de Noriega, mujer legítima de Don Esteban de la Torre, contra Joseph Ponciano, pardo, por pago de 141 pesos suplidos para efectos de su libertad, ARL, Correg, C.O., Leg. 232, C. 2056, 1774, f. 12.

76. Autos seguidos por Francisco Castillo contra da. Ventura Alzamora, su ama, sobre que la venda, AGN-P, Cab. Civ., Leg. 37, C. 664, 1777, f. 5.

77. Expediente seguido por Vicenta Conde y Marín, esclava, contra Doña Rafaela Moreno, mujer legítima de don Félix José de Xaramillo, sobre moderación del precio en que ha de pasar a servir a otro dueño, ARL, Intendente, C.O., Leg. 299, C. 115, 1788, f. 1.

78. Ibid.
79. In general this was true, but it was not without debate. For an intriguing argument that Locke's placement of slavery within international law contained a critique of contemporary African bondage, see William Uzgalis, " . . . The Same Tyrannical Principle: Locke's Legacy on Slavery," in *Subjugation and Bondage: Critical Essays on Slavery and Social Philosophy*, ed. Tommy L. Lott (New York: Rowman & Littlefield, 1998), 49–78.
80. Expediente seguido por Michaela Mina, ARL, Cab., C.O., Leg. 44, C. 791, 1741, f. 16v.
81. These were derived from "ancient" provisions that appeared in the *Siete Partidas*, 4:21:1. However, the law notes that "being born of a slave woman" was another way of becoming a slave, a point on which this argument was silent. Note that Alfonso X's law also connects "servitude" to the Latin "*servare*," or "to preserve." For more on the development of Spanish ideas about slavery among Indians, see Nancy E. van Deusen, *Global Indios: The Indigenous Struggle for Justice in Sixteenth-Century Spain* (Durham: Duke University Press, 2015).
82. Expediente seguido por Michaela Mina, ARL, Cab., C.O., Leg. 44, C. 791, 1741, f. 25v.
83. See Premo, *Children of the Father King*, ch. 7; Aguirre, *Agentes de su propia libertad*; Hünefeldt, *Paying the Price*; and Carlos Aguirre, "Working the System: Black Slaves and the Courts in Lima, 1821–1854," in *Crossing Boundaries: Comparative History of Black People in Diaspora*, ed. Darlene Clark and Jacqueline McCloud (Bloomington: University of Indiana Press, 1999), 202–222.
84. Autos seguidos por Tadeo Moreno y Manuela Juáregui, esclavos de Juan de Dubois, sobre que los venda, AGN-P, Cab., Civ., Leg. 57, C. 118, 1786, f. 9v–10.
85. Autos seguidos por Liberata de Jesús, contra D. Pedro Tramarría, su amo, sobre sevicia y que la venda a precio de tasación, AGN-P, Cab., Civ., Leg. 68, C. 1328, 1791, f. 2.
86. Ibid., f. 13.
87. María Antonia Hipólita, negra criolla esclava de D. Tomás Bustillos, en autos contra éste demandando libertad que le hubo ofrecido por el "trato ilícito," AGN-P, RA, Civ., Leg. 103, C. 866, 1746, f. 1v. It should be noted that this slave also alleged having been seduced by her master, so verbal abuse was not the only grounds.
88. Autos seguidos por Juana Portocarrero contra su ama, doña Juliana Portocarrero sobre sevicia, AGN-P, RA, Civ., Leg. 292, C. 2608.
89. Ibid., f. 9 v.
90. Autos seguidos por Josefa Piñeda . . . AGN-P, RA, Civ., Leg. 293, c. 2614, 1791 f. 7v.
91. See, for example, Diego de la Cruz, mulato esclabo originario del pueblo de Guichiapa . . . AGN-M, TSJ, Civ., AO, Leg. 14, no. 22, 1733, s/f.
92. Expediente seguido por Michaela Mina, ARL, Cab., C.O., Leg. 44, C. 791, 1741, f. 1.
93. Autos seguidos por Antonio Zavala, negro esclavo de D. Pedro Escandón, sobre su libertad y sevicia, AGN-P, RA, Civ., Leg. 103, C. 867, 1746, f. 4 6v.
94. See, for example, Autos seguidos por Lorenzo de Aguilar contra Don Manuel de Orejuela sobre su libertad, AGN-P, Cab., Civ., Leg. 37, C. 663, 1755; Autos seguidos por doña [*sic*] María Josefa Balcazar contra doña Juana de de Balcazar sobre su libertad, AGN-P, RA, Civ., Leg. 70, C. 549, 1738.
95. Expediente seguido por Juana de la Rosa Narbaes parda libre, natural de la ciudad de Loxa en voz y en nombre de Paula Ursula, su hija natural contra Ana Ludeñas Canela, vecina de Truxillo sobre despojo de su libertad, ARL, Cab., C.O., Leg. 39, C. 731, 1721, s/f.
96. Autos seguidos por Clara Gutiérrez, negra, contra doña Marcelina Gutiérrez de Coz sobre su libertad, AGN-P, RA, Civ., Leg. 287, C. 2554, 1790, f. 7.
97. Ibid., 1v.
98. Autos seguidos por Juana Portocarrero contra su ama, doña Juliana Portocarrero sobre sevicia, AGN-P, RA., Civ., Leg. 292, C. 2608, f. 3: "el escrito que se admitio sin firma de Abogado;" Autos seguidos por Antonina Guillén contra D. Joaquín Barandiarán, su amo, sobre su libertad, AGN-P, Cab., Civ., Leg. 83, C. 1566, 1797, ff. 1v, 2.
99. Civiles de pedimiento de Margarita Francisca mulata esclava sobre que su ama Da. Manuela Perez de las Cuevas, demuestre la escriptura, y nombre abaluador como dentro se expresa, AGN-M, Civ., Vol. 1959, Exp. 11, 1761.
100. Autos seguidos por María Tomasa Ayesa contra Don Isidro Antonio Zeballos sobre que la venda, AGN-P, RA, Civ., Leg. 162, C. 1356, 1767.

101. Lima. Solicitud del esclavo Francisco de la Torre, mulatillo, pidiendo que ese ordene a don Maríano Villar, cura del partido de Chancay, que le pague los 14 pesos que le debe por los 4 años que le sirvió alimentando sus animales, AAL, Causas de Negros, Leg. 34, Exp. 24, 1790.

102. Autos que sigue Juana Baptista Laredo, esclava, de la vecindad de Truxillo, contra doña Manuela de la Sierra, su ama sobre oblación de 300 pesos para la obtención de su libertad, ARL, Cab. C.O., Leg. 56, C. 970, 1783, f. 3.

103. Ibid.

104. Autos seguidos por Tadeo Moreno y Manuela Juáregui, esclavos de Juan de Dubois, sobre que los venda, AGN-P, Cab. Civ., Leg. 57, C. 118, 1786.

105. Ibid., f. 6.

106. Ibid, f. 11v; f. 12v.

107. Autos seguidos por Tomasa Rayo, negra libre con Doña Inés de la Barrera sobre que se le otorgue Carta de Libertad, AGN-P, RA, Civ., Leg. 108, C. 914, s/f.

108. Autos seguidos por Doña Marcelina Gutiérrez contra su esclava, sobre su libertad AGN-P, RA, Civ., Leg. 311, C. 2811, 1792, f. 3. Also see Autos seguidos por Clara Gutiérrez, negra, contra doña Marcelina Gutiérrez de Coz sobre su libertad, AGN-P, RA, Civ., Leg. 287, C. 2554, 1790.

109. *Siete Partidas*, 3:5:4.

110. Autos que sigue Juana Baptista Laredo . . . ARL, Cab. C.O., Leg. 56, C. 970, 1783, f. 7.

111. Autos que sigue Andrés Saturnio Matallana, esclavo por tiempo determinado, contra doña Josefa Matallana y Matos, sobre justiprecio de persona y cuota moderada para solicitar amo a quien server, ARL, Intend. C.O., Leg. 321, C. 535, 1798, f. 4.

112. Autos seguidos por Antonina Guillén contra D. Joaquín Barandiarán, su amo, sobre su libertad, AGN-P, Cab., Civ., Leg. 83, C. 1566, 1797, 7v.

113. Ibid.

114. Ibid.

115. Autos seguidos pr María del Rosario Vega, mulata, esclava contra su amo, Dn Juan Rodamonte, sobre sevicia y relacines ilícitas a la que la obligó, AGN-P, RA, Civ., Leg. 292, C. 2607, 1790, f. 1v; María Antonia Hipólita, negra criolla esclava de D. Tomás Bustillos, en autos contra éste demandando libertad que le hubo ofrecido por el "trato ilícito," AGN-P, RA, Civ., Leg. 103, C. 866, 1746, 1 v: *"la libertad que requiere los juicios."*

116. Autos que sigue Theresa Trillo, negra criolla, residente en esta ciudad sbore la libertad que debe gozar como esclava que fue de Antonia Trillo, mujer de Mathías Martel, difunto, ARL, Correg. C.O., Leg. 235, C. 2123, 1781, f. 25.

117. Autos seguidos por Juana Portocarrero contra su ama, doña Juliana Portocarrero sobre sevicia, AGN P, RA Civ., Leg. 292, C. 2608, 46v.

118. Diego de la Cruz, mulato esclabo originario del pueblo de Guichiapa . . . AGN-M, TSJ, AO, Leg. 14, no. 22, 1733, s/f. The case was, he said, brought *"tulmutariamente,"* underscoring how owners viewed litigation a spectrum of rebellion and flight, according to Bryant, *Rivers of Gold*, esp. 120.

119. For Peru, see Scarlett O'Phelan Godoy, "La construcción del miedo a la plebe en el siglo XVIII a través de las rebeliones sociales," 123–138; and Claudia Rosas Lauro, "El miedo de la revolución. Rumores y temores desatados por la Revolución Francesa en el Perú, 1790–1800," in *El Miedo en el Perú, siglos XVI al XXX*, ed. Claudia Rosas Lauro, 139–166 (Lima: Pontificia Universdad Católica del Perú, 2005).

120. Autos seguidos por Juana Portocarrero . . . AGN-P, RA, Civ., Leg. 292, C. 2608, f. 44.

121. Here, I refer in particular to the debate in Spain about the movement of the French *libertins*. On the negative connotations assigned to the word "*libertino*," and its failure to capture a more morally postitive meaning which might include the notion of "freethinker," see Ignacio Elizalde Amerndáriz, "Feijoo y la influencia de los libertinos eruditos franceses," in *II Simposio sobre el padre Feijoo y su siglo*, vol. 2 (Oviedo: Centro de Estudios del Siglo XVIII, 1980), n. 2, 407.

122. *Desengaños sobre las preocupaciones del día. Discursos polémicos entre un Americano, y un Español, sobre la Libertad, Gobiernos, Revoluciones, y Religion 2 tomos* (Rome, n/p 1796), t. 1, 228; 278.

123. Autos seguidos por Bernabé Flores contra D. Bernadino Otero, su amo, sobre que se proceda a su tasación y se le ortogue papeleta de venta, AGN-P, Cab. Civ., Leg. 37, C. 663, 1777, f. 7.

124. Diego de la Cruz, mulato esclabo originario del pueblo de Guichiapa . . . AGN-M, TSJ, AO, Leg. 14, no. 22, 1733, s/f.
125. Expediente seguido por Vicenta conde y Marín esclava, contra Doña Rafaela Moreno, mjuer legítima de don Felix José de Xaramillo, sobre moderacion del precio en que ha de pasa a servir a otro dueño, ARL, Intendente, C.O., Leg. 299, C. 115, 1788, 13f. For the importance of clothing and status among slaves, see Tamara Walker, "'He outfitted his family in noble decency': Slavery, Honour, and Dress in Eighteenth-Century Lima," *Slavery and Abolition* 30, no. 3 (2009): 383–402.
126. Autos seguidos por Francisco Castillo contra da. Ventura Alzamora, su ama, sobre que la venda, AGN-P, Cab. Civ., Leg. 37, C. 664, 1777, 3v.
127. Autos seguidos por Tadeo Moreno y Manuela Juáregui, esclavos de Juan de Dubois, sobre que los venda, AGN-P, Cab. Civ., Leg. 57, C. 118, 1786, 8v.
128. Ibid., f. 8.
129. Autos que sigue Theresa Trillo, negra criolla, residente en esta ciudad sbore la libertad que debe gozar como esclava que fue de Antonia Trillo, mujer de Mathías Martel, difunto, ARL, Correg. C.O., Leg. 235, C. 2123, 1781.
130. María Teresa del Castillo, esclava contra Manuel de Gradillas que le venda a otra amo, AGN-M, TSJ, Civil, AO Vol. 16, Exp., 49, 1731, f 1. The *asesor* might have referring to law in the *Siete Paritidas* that put time limits on slavery, for example indicating that if a master was missing for ten years, a slave was free, William D. Phillips, *Slavery in Medieval and Early Modern Iberia* (Philadelphia: University of Pennsylvania Press, 2014), 128.
131. Expediente seguido por María Gabriela Ponce de Leon, de color parda, libre esclava que fue de doña Josefa Ponce de Leon, difunta, contra doña Petronila Ponce, sobre el derecho que tiene de obtener su libertad según y como consta en lo instrumentos públicos que presenta, ARL Cab. C.O., Leg. 54, C. 961, 1781, s/f.
132. For the Enlightenment context of "good customs," or *buenas costumbres*, see Premo, *Children of the Father King*, 294, n. 33.
133. Autos seguidos por D. Juan de Prado, contra su esclava Agustina, sobre su libertad, AGN-P, Cab. Civ., Leg. 31, C. 527, 1774; Autos seguidos por D. Nicolás López Molero contra José Inosciente, sobre la revocatoria de su libertad, AGN-P, Cab. Civ., Leg. 37, C. 665, 1777.
134. Autos seguidos por D. Baltazar de Laya y Llano sobre la revocatoria de la libertad concedida a su esclavo Agustín, AGN-P, Cab. Civ., Leg. 82, C. 1556, 1797.
135. Autos seguidos por Francisco Castillo contra da. Ventura Alzamora, su ama, sobre que la venda, AGN-P, Cab. Civ., Leg. 37, C. 664, 1777, f. 4v.
136. Autos que sigue Juana Josefa de Obregoso, parda libre, ausente en la hacienda de San Pedro y San Pablo de Cuquizongo, Partido de Guamachuco, contra Jacinto Obregoso, sobre el excesivo precio que le ha puesto sobre su persona, ARL, Intend. C.O., Leg. 321, C. 534, 1798.
137. Autos promovidos por el Capitán Don Carlos Flores, vecino de esta ciudad, albacea de Bartolomé Obregoso, contra Martina Orbegoso, esclavo, sobre pago de 200 pesos que vale su hipoteca o prisión de dicha esclava. 20 f., RL, Intend. C.O., Leg. 299, C. 199, 1788; Lima. Autos seguidos por María Mercedes Olávide contra su amo el licenciado don Pablo Barrón y Pérez, presbítero, sobre que le reconozca su libertad cumpliendo con lo prometido durante el tiempo que fueron concubinos, AAL, Causas de Negros, Leg. 33, no. 9, 1792–1797, s/f.
138. Lima. Autos seguidos por María Mercedes Olávide, AAL, Causas de Negros, Leg. 33, no. 9, 1792–1797, s/f.
139. Autos seguidos por Bernabé Flores . . . , AGN-P, Cab. Civ., Leg. 37, C. 663, 1777, f. 2.
140. Autos que sigue Juana Josefa de Orbegoso . . . ARL, Intend. C.O., Leg. 321, C. 534, 1798, 2v.
141. For another example of "merited" or "earned" freedom, see Autos seguidos por Lorenzo de Aguilar contra Don Manuel de Orejuela sobre su libertad, AGN, Cab., Civ., Leg. 37, C. 663, 1755, f. 1.
142. It should be clear by now that I am aware of the irony of using Kant, whose thoughts on race have made him a special target of postcolonialists. See Gayatri Chakravorty Spivak, *A Critique of Postcolonial Reason: Toward a History of the Vanishing Present* (Cambridge, MA: Harvard University Press, 1999).

143. Haydyn Mason, "Optimism, Progress, and Philosophical History," in Goldie and Wokler, *Cambridge History of Eighteenth-Century Political Thought*, 195–217; 202. On liberty and license in Spanish thought, see Paquette, *Enlightement, Governance*, 61.

144. Michel Foucault, "What Is Enlightenment?," 44. On sympathy and spectatorship, note that Hunt views empathy, à la Rousseau, as the touchstone of modern human rights, *Inventing Human Rights*; whereas Dror Wahrman emphasizes the empathy's outward orientation, *The Making of the Modern Self: Identity and Culture in Eighteenth-Century England* (New Haven: Yale University Press, 2004); 185–186, and Taylor, *Sources of the Self*, 12–13, shifts the attention to the recognition of human "dignity."

145. I owe most of my intepretation of this interplay between Kant and Foucault to the insightful essay by Passerin d'Entrèves, "Critique of Enlightenment." For time's place in modern thought, see Palti, "Time, Modernity," 25–62 and Elías Palti, "The Return of the Subject as a Historico-Intellectual Problem," *History and Theory* 43, no. 1 (2004): 57–82, esp. 64. Also see Koselleck, *Practice*, 162; and Mark Thurner, *History's Peru: The Poetics of Colonial and Postcolonial Historiography* (Gainesville: University of Florida Press, 2013), 241–242.

146. Michel Foucault, "Is It Useless To Revolt?," trans. J. Beranuer, *Philosophy and Social Criticism* 8, no. 1 (1981): 1–9.

147. Immanuel Kant, *Critque of the Power of Judgement*, ed. Paul Guyer (1790; reprint, New York: Cambridge University Press, 2000), 234, quoted in Daniel Carey and Sven Trakulhun, "Universalism, Diversity and the Postcolonial Enlightenment," 243–280 in Carey and Festa, *Postcolonial Enlightenment*, 258. On the open-ended nature of historical becoming, see Palti, "Time, Modernity," 29. On emancipation as progression, see Koselleck, *Practice*, 256.

148. See also Buck-Morss, "Hegel and Haiti," on the desire for freedom as an emergent "universal" in world history, esp. 846.

149. For the "creative" power of colonialism and slavery, which provides a crude framework for undertanding the possibilities as well as the limits that the law entailed for slaves, see Scott, *Conscripts of Modernity*, esp. 111; 116.

150. Muthu, *Enlightenment Against Empire*, 122–123. Also note that Buck-Morss, "Hegel and Haiti," summarizes Hegel's *Phenomenology of the Mind* thus: "Then the slaves (again, collectivizing the figure) achieve self-consciousness by demonstrating that they are not things, not objects, but subjects who transform material nature," 849.

Conclusion

1. On the "paradigm of the Enlightenment" as historical narrative that searches for commonality, see F. R. Ankersmit, *History and Tropology: The Rise and Fall of Metaphor* (Berkeley: University of California Press, 1992), 79–80.

2. Trouillot, *Silencing the Past*, esp. 70–106.

3. Sewell, *Logics*.

4. On the romantic apotheosis of revolution in contemporary historiography, see Scott, *Conscripts of Modernity*, 7; Ferrone, *Enlightenment*, viii and 79–86. For this view in European history, particularly France, see Israel, *Radical Enlightenment*, esp. 71–81; Keith Michael Baker, ed., *The French Revolution and the Creation of Modern Political Culture*, vol. 1, *The Political Culture of the Old Regime* (New York: Pergamon Press, 1987); and *Inventing the French Revolution: Essays on French Political Culture in the 18th Century* (New York: Cambridge University Press, 1990); Robert Darnton, *The Literary Underground of the Old Regime* (Cambridge, MA: Harvard University Press, 1982); and *The Revolution in Print, 1775–1800* (Berkeley: University of California Press, 1987); Dubois, *Colony of Citizens*; Peter Fritzche, *Stranded in the Present: Modern Time and the Melancholy of History* (Cambridge, MA: Harvard University Press, 2004); and his bibliographic comments in Gordon W. Wood, "The American Enlightenment," in *America and Enlightened Constitutionalism*, ed. Gary L. McDowell and Jonathan O'Neil (New York: Palgrave Macmillan 2006), 159–175; and Wood, *Empire of Liberty: A History of the Early Republic, 1789–1815* (New York: Oxford University Press, 2007), 742; Lynn Hunt, *Inventing Human Rights: A History* (New York: WW Norton, 2007). To be fair, there are many historians of the eighteenth century for

whom revolution is not the culmination of Enlightenment, exactly, but more of a turn with in it. These include Maza, *Private Lives*; Goodman, *Republic of Letters*; Dror Wahrman and Colin Jones, eds., *The Age of Cultural Revolutions: Britain and France, 1750–1820* (Berkeley: University of California Press, 2002). Cultural historians of England and early America do not seem drawn to the concept of the Enlightenment. See, for example, Warhman, *Making*; Dirks, *In My Power*.

5. On legal culture and late colonial rebellion, see Serúlnikov, *Subverting*.

6. News of revolution certainly affected elite colonial Latin Americans' sense of what the "new philosophy" might mean for the traditional caste order. For Peruvian news about the French Revolution, see Rosas Lauro, *Del trono al guilotina*; for fears about Haiti in the Spanish Caribbean, see Ada Ferrer, *Freedom's Mirror: Cuba and Haiti in the Age of Revolution* (New York: Cambridge University Press, 2014).

7. See Eric Van Young for factors present in France and the US but "absent" in Mexican Independence movement, *Other Rebellion*, 495–521. Note the importance he ascribes to popular loyalty to the monarch after Fernando VII's exile, a phenomenon I would argue was cultivated by Bourbon policy on law. See also Van Young, "Limits of Atlantic." Note, however, that even in the French colonies, the revolution marked the "end, rather than the beginning of a process of liberation" that slaves had effected through law since the seventeenth century, Ghachem, *The Old Regime and the Haitian Revolution*, 6.

8. Outram finely details the long history of critiques of this nineteenth-century concept in *Enlightenment*, 96–101, and Paquette addresses its inadequacy for Spain in *Enlightenment, Governance*, 14–18.

9. On "persistence" as a particular problem in Latin American history, see Adelman, "Problem."

10. Dilip Parameshwar Gaonkar, "On Alternative Modernities," in *Alternative Modernities*, ed. Dilip Parameshwar Gaonkar (Durham: Duke University Press, 2001), 1–23. Also see several of the essays in *American Historical Review* Roundtable on Modernity (vol. 116, no. 3, June 2011), including the Introduction, 631–637; Gurminder K. Bhambra, "Historical Sociology, Modernity, and Postcolonial Critique," 653–663; Dipesh Chakrabarty, "The Muddle of Modernity," 663–675; Carol Gluck, "The End of Elsewhere: Writing Modernity Now," 676–687.

11. Bernard Yack, *The Fetishism of Modernities: Epochal Self Consciousness in Contemporary Social and Political Thought* (South Bend, IN: Notre Dame University Press, 1997); Grossi, *Mitología*; "Introduction," to AHR Roundtable on Modernity, *American Historical Review*, 632. This phrase is the same used by Koselleck, *Practice*, 155.

12. For an argument about the limited role of universalism in eighteenth-century thought, see Daniel Carey and Sven Trakulhun, "Universalism, Diversity and the Postcolonial Enlightenment," in Carey and Festa, *Postcolonial Enlightenment: 243–280.*

13. Quoted in Schmidt, "What Enlightenment Project?," 735.

14. Sobre el divorcio que pide Don Francisco [sic] Pila, del matrimonio que contrajo con Doña María García, México, AGN-M, BN, Vol. 292, Exp. 1, 1790.

15. Certainly, postcolonial scholars of Latin America tell us that what marks the region as unique is its hybridity, perhaps especially or originally in its temporal condition. See, among many, the works of Walter Mignolo, particularly his *The Darker Side of Western Modernity: Global Futures, Decolonial Options* (Durham: Duke University Press, 2011).

16. The notion of the West as universal and the non-West as particular has inspired many of the cultural theorists of Latin America. See for example, the reflections on the "universal" as nothing but a conglomerate of "common particularities," in Alberto Moreiras, *The Exhaustion of Difference: The Politics of Latin American Cultural Studies* (Durham: Duke University Press, 2001).

17. Nestor García Canclini, *Hybrid Cultures: Strategies for Entering and Leaving Modernity* (Gainesville: University of Florida Press (1990; reprint, Minneapolis: University of Minnesota, 1995), 1.

18. Peter Wade, "Modernity, Tradition, Shifting Boundaries, Shifting Contexts," in *When Was Latin America Modern?*, ed. Nicole Miller and Stephen Hart, 49–68 (New York: Palgrave, 2007), 55–56. For the inescapable geographic underpinnings of the concept of modernity in the region, see Sarah Radcliffe, "Geographies of Modernity in Latin America: Uneven and

Contested Development," in Miller and Hart, *When Was Latin America Modern?*, 21–48. Also see See Fernando Coronil, "Beyond Occidentalism: Toward Nonimperial Geohistorical Categories," *Cultural Anthropology* 11, no. 2 (Feb. 1996), 74.

19. Wade, "Modernity, Tradition," 49–68.

20. Thurner, *History's Peru*. On this he is inspired by the mediations on periodizations and the concept of "beforehand not yet" advanced by Koselleck in *Practice*, esp., 154–169.

21. Thurner, *History's Peru*, 257. Michael Hanchard makes a similar argument about African diasporic history, but with less suggestion of the sui generis nature of thought outside Europe, in "Afro-Modernity: Temporality, Politics, and the African Diaspora," in Gaonkar, *Alternative Modernities*, 272–298. Also see Miller, *Elusive Origins*.

22. Severo Aguirre, *Prontuario alfabético y cronológico por orden de materias de las Instrucciones, Ordenanzas, Reglamentos, Pragmáticas y demás reales resoluciones no recopiladas que han de observarse para la administración de justicia y gobierno en los pueblos del Reino. . .* (Madrid,: Benito Caro, 1794), 277.

23. Chakrabarty, "Muddle," 670.

24. Laura F. Edwards, *The People and their Peace: Legal Culture and the Transformation of Inequality in the Post-Revolutionary South* (Chapel Hill: University of North Carolina Press, 2008).

25. As Frederick Cooper formulates it, the problem with "reducing non-Western history to the lack of what the West had" is that such a formulation assumes "that the West actually had itself," "Postcolonial Studies and the Study of History," in *Postcolonial Studies and Beyond*, ed. Ania Loomba, Suvir Kaul, et al. (Durham: Duke University Press, 2005), 403.

26. For an example, consider that a recent volume on the "modernity" of Iberoamerica begins with a section on the "opening" of Iberia into a pre-existing entity called "the Western world" in the sixteenth century, Francisco Colom González, ed. *Modernidad iberoaméricano: Cultura, política y cambio social* (Madrid: Iberomericano/Vervuert, 2009). On religious tolerance, see Schwartz, *All Can Be Saved*; on historical epistemology, see Cañizares Esguerra, *How to Write the History*; on liberalism, see Schultz, *Tropical Versailles*.

27. Israel, *Radical Enlightenment*, 509.

28. Also see Robertson on it as a "European phenomenon . . . that extended across the Atlantic," in *Enlightenment*, 13. On the premise of origins in the history of ideas and the normative sense of "belonging" and "fit" that they generate, see Samuel Moyn, "Contexualism and Criticism in the History of Ideas," in McMahon and Moyn, *Rethinking*, 37–38. The tensions in viewing the Enlightenment as both historical topic and historical agent is familiar in Latin Americanists, and were encapsulated in Arthur Whitaker, "The Dual Rôle of Latin American in the Enlightenment," in Whitaker, *Latin America and the Enlightenment*, 5.

29. Schwarz's notion of ideas is discussed in Elias Palti, "The Problem of 'Misplaced Ideas' Revisited: Beyond the 'History of Ideas' in Latin America," *Journal of the History of Ideas* (2006): 149–179. Also see Richard M. Morse, *El espejo de Próspero: Un studio de la dialéctica del Nuevo Mundo* (1982; reprint, Mexico: Siglo Veintiuno, 1999), esp. 112–113.

30. José Carlos Chiramonte, *Ensayos sobre la "Ilustración" argentina* (Paraná: Facultad de Ciences de la Educación, Universidad del Litoral, 1962), 81. Also note Chirimonte's dismantling of the claim that Argentine independence was more a product of *suarecismo* than Enlightenment thought, 76–78, an argument that gained even more popularity when enshrined in John Leddy Phelan's study of the comunero revolt in Colombia, *The People and the King: The Comunero Revolt in Colombia, 1781* (1978; reprint, Madison: University of Wisconsin Press, 2011).

31. Foucault, "What Is Enlightenment?," 39.

32. McMahon, *Enemies of the Enlightenment*, 196. Also see Thurner, *History's* 254; and note Foucault on "countermodernity," in "What Is Enlightenment?," 39.

33. Ventura Salzas, trans., *Discurso sobre la verdadera libertad natural y civil del hombre: escrito en italiano* (Madrid: Administración de la Rifa, 1798). The sale of the book in the Librería del Castillo in Madrid, as well as in other Castilian cities including Zaragoza and Talavera, was announced for October 14, 1800 in the *Gaceta de Madrid*, no. 84 (14 de octubre de 1800), 965.

34. Sobre el divorcio que pide Don Francisco [*sic*] Pila, 1790, f. 52.

35. Asuntos del divorcio promovido por Doña Inés de Matamoros, AGN-M, BN, Vol. 292, Exp. 19, 20, 21,1790, f. 20.

36. See Chapter 5, n. 134.
37. Autos seguidos por Antonina Guillén contra D. Joaquín Barandiarán, su amo, sobre su libertad. AGN-P, Cab., Civ., 6–7v. 1797.
38. Quexa de Don Joseph e María Aicardo contra su muger y la persona que adentro se expresa, AGN-M, Civ, Vol. 2107, exp. 4, 5, and 6, 1782, f. s/f.
39. Autos seguidos por Clara Gutiérrez, negra, contra doña Marcelina Gutiérrez de Coz sobre su libertad, AGN-P, RA, Civ., Leg. 287, C. 2554, 1790, f. 5.
40. Ibid., f. 3.
41. Jouve-Martín, *Esclavos en la ciudad letrada*; Rappaport and Cummins, *Beyond the Lettered City*. On the accumulation of modern forms of knowledge in specific places, see Ricardo Salvatore, "Introducción," in Salvatore, *Los lugares del saber*, 9–34.
42. In addition to Conclusion, n. 9, see Rosas Lauro, *El miedo*.
43. Autos seguidos por Clara Gutiérrez, AGN-P, RA, Civ., Leg. 287, C. 2554, 1790, ff. 12–13.
44. The claims to imitation, while referencing the passing of practices from one slave to the next, might be fruitfully thought of along the lines of the colonial mimicry so feared by British colonials in India, Homi Bhabha, "Of Mimicry and Man," in *Tensions of Empire: Colonial Cultures in a Bourgeois World*, ed. Frederick Cooper and Ann Stoler (Berkeley: University of California Press, 1997), 152–160. Also see Serúlnikov, *Subverting*, 5, 155.
45. Autos que sigue Juan Manuel Céspedes Tito, en nombre del Juez Territorial en el partido de Guancabamba (Piura), contra Vicente Culquicondor, indio, por calumnias sobre el desempeño de su función, ARL-P, Intend., Crim, Leg. 353, C. 1327, 1787, f. 2.
46. Bhambra, "Historical Sociology," 633; Foucault, "What Is Enlightenment?," 50. Also see the calls of Conrad, "Enlightenment in Global History."
47. On "decolonizing," see Mignolo, "The Geopolitcs of Knowledge and the Colonial Difference,"223–258 in Moraña, Dussel, et al., *Coloniality at Large*, 230–233. Scott, in *Conscripts of Modernity*, calls for something a bit different, a kind of "recolonizing" of our thinking in order to understand not just the restraints of Enlightenment, modernity, and colonialism but also their generative power.

Appendix II

1. In a private communication with Linda Arnold, she postulates that these first-instance civil cases are from the bench of one of the two alcaldes ordinarios who worked in colonial Mexico City, and that they were collected in the judicial archive that court notary Alberto Acosta inherited and turned over to the Archivo Hístorico de Notarias in the 1890s. The civil case records from the bench of the city's other alcalde ordinario seem to have been incorporated into the Tribunal Superior de Justicia series following a presidential mandate by Santa Anna in the 1840s. Thus there should be no difference in the jurisdictional levels of the first-instance cases, only in their archival histories.
2. Kagan, *Lawsuits*; also see Taylor's comments on this contrast in *Magistrates*, 722, n. 129.
3. During a 2010 visit, I also consulted a newly cataloged series of "Demandas," in which cases were a bit jurisdictionally slippery (since the Fiel heard both criminal and civil cases). The genre was, in the main, criminal but some instances in the series can be considered civil. They included a relatively high number of gender-based conflict (such as charges of *amancebamiento*, or sexual relations outside of marriage), and women appeared as the criminally accused more than in other types of cases. These cases are much more voluminous in the eighteenth century than any other kind of case, but since demandas are, in the main, criminal, I have not included them here. Had I done so, this would make the volume of civil cases stable from 1600–1800, dropping off very precipitously in the early nineteenth century. This is not impossible since the region broke away from the city during the period of "*desamortación*" beginning in 1827, severing the jurisdiction of the Fiel. If denunicas are added to the "criminal" series of the region, a pattern of gradual decline of both civil and criminal cases is consistent.
4. Kagan, *Lawsuits*, 94–118.

BIBLIOGRAPHY

Primary Sources

Actas del Congreso Constituyente del estado libre de Mexico: revisadas por el mismo. Tomo XI. Mexico City: Imprenta del Gobierno del Estado, 1829.

Aguirre, Severo. *Prontuario alfabético y cronológico por orden de materias de las Instrucciones, Ordenanzas, Reglamentos, Pragmáticas y demás reales resoluciones no recopiladas que han de observarse para la administración de justicia y gobierno en los pueblos del Reino. . .* Madrid. Benito Caro, 1794.

Alavardo, Francisco. "Carta Primera." In *Cartas filosóficas que bajo el supuesto nombre de Aristóteles escribió el Rm. Padre Maestro Fray Francisco Alvarado*, tomo V. Madrid: Imprenta de E. Aguado, 1825.

Amerndáriz, Ignacio Elizalde. "Feijoo y la influencia de los libertinos eruditos franceses." In *II Simposio sobre el padre Feijoo y su siglo*, vol. 2, 407–418. Oviedo: Centro de Estudios del Siglo XVIII, 1980.

Baquíjano y Carillo, José. *Alegato que en la oposición a la cátedra de prima de leyes de la Real Universidad de San Marcos de Lima.* Lima: s/p, 1788.

Bravo de Lagunas y Castilla, José Pedro. *Colección legal de cartas, dictámenes, y otros papeles de derecho.* Lima: Los Húerfanos, 1761.

Burns, Robert I. S.J., ed., *Las Siete Partidas* vols. 1–5, translated by Samuel Parsons Scott. Philadelphia: University of Pennsylvania Press, 2001.

Caro, Don Francisco Blasco. *Juicio Imparcial sobre un manuscrito en que se pretende impugnar un dissertación . . . de . . . Baquíjano.* Lima: Real Casa de los Huérfanos, 1788.

Continuación del almacén de frutos literarios o Semanario de obras inéditas. Tomo III. Madrid: Imprente de Repullés, 1818.

Cook, Noble David, ed. *Numeración general de todas las personas de ambos sexos, edades y calidades q[ue] se ha [h]echo en esta Ciudad de Lima, año de 1700.* Facsimile edition. Lima: COFIDE, 1985.

Covarrubias, Sebastian. *Tesoro de la Lengua Castellana o Española*, edited by Felipe C.R. Maldocnado, revised by Manuel Camarero. 1611. Reprint, Madrid: Editorial Castalia, 1995.

Los códigos españoles. Concordatos y anotados. Tomo IX. Madrid: Imprenta de la Publicidad a cargo de DM Rivadeneyra, 1850.

Covarrubias, José de. *Máximas sobre recursos de fuerza y protecciones con el método de introducirlos en los tribunales.* 1790. Reprint, 4th ed. Librería Razola, 1830.

Cueva Ponze de Leon, Alonso de la. *Concordia de la discordia. Sobre un punto grave de immunidad ecclesiástica.* Lima: Calle del Palacio, 1749.

Cutter, Charles, trans. *Libro de los principales rudimentos tocante a todos juicios, civil, criminal y executivo: Año de 1764*. Mexico City: Universidad Nacional de México, 1994.

Desengaños sobre las preocupaciones del día. Discursos polémicos entre un Americano, y un Español, sobre la Libertad, Gobiernos, Revoluciones, y Religion 2 tomos. Rome: n/p, 1796.

"Error in personam invalidum reddit matrimonium." In *Marriage in Canon Law: Texts and Comments. Reflections and Questions*, edited by Ladislas Orsy, SJ. 1935. Reprint, New York: Michael Glasier, 1988.

Escosura, Don Patricio de la. "Agentes de Negocios." *Diccionario universal del derecho español constituido*. Tomo IV. Madrid: Publicaciones de Ultramar, 1853.

Escriche y Martín, Joaquín. *Diccionario razonado de legislación y jurisprudencia*. Paris: Librería de Rósa, Bouret y Cia., 1851.

Febrero, José. *Febrero novísimo o Libreria de jueces, abogados y escribanos . . .* Vol. 10. Reprint, Valencia: Idelfonso Mompié, 1831.

Feijóo, Benito Jerónimo. "Sobre la grave importancia de abreviar las Causas Judiciales." In *Cartas eruditas y curiosas*, tomo 3, 245–254. 1750. Reprint, Madrid: Impresa Real de la Gaceta, 1776.

Fejióo y Montenegro, Benito Jerónimo. "Balanza de Astréa o recta administración de justicia." In *Theatro Crítico Universal*, tomo 3. 1729. Reprint, Madrid: Imprenta de Antonio Pérez Soto, 1765.

Gaceta de Madrid, no. 84 (14 de octubre de 1800).

Heineccio, Johann Gottlieb, trans. *Elementos del derecho natural y de gentes de Heinnecio, corregidos y reformados por el provisor Don Mariano Lucas Garrido . . . 1763*. Reprint, Madrid: Fuentenbro a cargo de Alejandro Gómez, 1837.

Instrucción de lo que deben observar los regentes de las Reales Audiencias de América: sus funciones, regalia, y como se han de haber con los Virreyes, Presidentes, y con estos aquellos, Aranjuez, 20 de Junio 1, 1776.

Jiménez Gómez, Juan Ricardo. *Un formulario notarial méxicano del siglo XVIII. La Instrucción de escribanos de Juan Elías Ortiz de Logroño*. Mexico City: Universidad Aútonoma de Querétaro, 2005.

Juan y Colom, Josef. *Instrucción de escribanos en orden a lo judicial, tomo II, 1761–73*. Madrid: Hijo de Marín, 1763.

Kant, Immanuel. *An Answer to the Question: "What Is Enlightenment?"* 1970. Reprint, translated by H. B. Nisbet. New York: Penguin Books, 1991.

Kant, Immanuel. *Critique of the Power of Judgement*. 1790. Reprint, edited by Paul Guyer. Cambridge, New York: Cambridge University Press, 2000.

Konetzke, Richard. *Colleción de Documentos para la historia de la formación social de Hispanoamérica, 1493–1810*. 4 vols. Madrid: Consejo Superior de Investigaciones Científicas, 1964.

Lambarri, Don Francisco Javier. "Segunda representación del consulado de Méjico." In *Los tres siglos de Méjico durante el gobierno español:Hasta la entrada del ejército trigarante*, edited by Andrés Cavo and Carlos María de Bustamante, 874–905. Jalapa: Tipografía Veracruzana d A. Ruiz, 1870.

Lara, Pedro Melgarejo y Manrique de. *Compendio de contratos públicos, autos de particiones, executivos, recopilado y corregido y enmendado en esta última impresión*. 1647. Reprint, Madrid: 1791.

Linati, Claudio. *Trajes Civiles, militares y religiosos de México*. Mexico City, Distrito Federal: Instituto de Investigaciones Estéticas, Universidad Nacional Aútonoma de México, 1956.

Lardizábal y Uribe, Manuel de. *Discurso sobre las penas de España para facilitar su reforma*. Madrid: Ibarra, 1782.

López de Oliver, Antonio. *Verdadero Idea de un Príncipe formada de las leyes que el reyno que tienen relación al derecho público*. Murcia: Funcadción Sénca, n/d. Facsimile reproduction, Valladolid: Imprenta Garrido, 1783.

Lorenzana, Francisco Antonio de. "A todos los fieles de este nuestro arzobispado." Mexico, 1772.

Mayans y Siscar, Gregorio. *Epistolario IV, Mayans a Nebot*. Valencia: Ayuntamiento de Oliva, 1975.

Mayans y Siscar, Gregorio. *Filosofía Cristiana: Apuntamientos para ella*, transcription and preliminary study by Salvador Rus Rufino, collaborators Jorge Benavent and Javier Zamora. 1746–47. Reprint, Publicaciones del Ayuntamiento de Oliva: Valencia, 1998.

Memorial literario, instructivo y curioso de la Corte de Madrid, 13. Madrid: Imprenta Real, 1788.

Mier, Fray Servando de Teresa. *Quejas de los Americanos.* 1813[?]. Reprint, Mexico City: Universidad Nacional Aútonoma de México, 1979.

Moreno, Gabriel René, comp. *Biblioteca peruana: Apuntes para un catálogo de impresos.* Santiago: Biblioteca Nacional [Chile], 1898.

Noriega y Guerra, José Servando Teresa de Mier. *Historia de la revolución de Nueva España, antiguamente Anáhuac,* vol. 1. London: Guillermo Glindon, 1813.

Para que los eclesiásticos no conozcan de concubinato, Real cédula para España e Indias de 1777 y diciembre de 1787. Reproduced in *La Nueva Galicia en el ocaso del Imperio Español: Los papeles de derecho de la audiencia de la Nueva Galicia del licenciado Juan José Ruiz Moscoso, su agente fiscal y regidor del Ayuntamiento de Guadalajara, 1780–1810,* vol. 3, 270, edited by Rafael Digo-Ferñandez Sotelo and Marina Mantilla Trolle. Jalisco, Colegio de Michoacán, 2003.

Plan de una memoria sobre las causas de la ociosidad. Madrid: Don Antonio Sancha, 1787.

"Plan demostrativo de la población comprehendida en el recinto de la Ciudad de Lima." *Mercurio Peruano* 9, no. 30. January, 1791.

Quexas de los Americanos. Cádiz: Imprenta de la Junta de Provincia, Casa de Misericordia, 1812.

Real Academia Española. *Diccionario de la lengua castellana, en que se explica el verdadero sentido de las voces* . . . Madrid: Impenta de Francisco del Hierro, 1727.

Real Academia Española. *Diccionario de la lengua castellana, en que se explica el verdadero sentido de las voces* . . . Madrid: Imprenta de Francisco del Hierro, 1734.

Real Academia Española. *Diccionario de la lengua castellana, en que se explica el verdadero sentido de las voces* . . . Madrid: Impenta de Francisco del Hierro, 1737.

Real Academia Española. *Diccionario de la lengua castellana, en que se explica el verdadero sentido de las voces* . . . Madrid: Impenta de Francisco del Hierro, 1783.

Real Cédula de 10 de agosto de 1788, por la qual se ha servido S.M. declara a quien toca y pertenece el conocimiento de el delito de Poligamía . . . Lima: Imprenta Real de los Niños Huérfanos, 1789.

Recopilación de las Leyes de los Reynos de las Yndias, Mandadas Imprimir, Y Publicar por la Magestad Católica del Rey, Don Carlos II. Madrid: Julian de Paredes, 1681.

Ruiz, Bernardo. *Colegio de Abogados de Lima (Peru). Abogados del ilustre Colegio de la excma. ciudad de Lima, con expresión de las calles y casas en que viven, año de 1817.* Lima: n/p, 1817.

Saavedra, José Antonio de Lavallé y Arias de. "Don Pedro José Bravo de Lagunas y Castilla (Apuntes sobre su vida y sus obras)." *Estudios históricos.* Lima: Gil, 1935.

Salzas, Ventura, trans. *Discurso sobre la verdadera libertad natural y civil del hombre: escrito en italiano.* Madrid: Administración de la Rifa, 1798.

Sánchez, Santos. *Colección de todas la Pragmáticas, Cédulas, Provisiones, Circulares* . . . *publicadas en el actual reynado del Senor Don Carlos IV.* Madrid: Viuda e Hijo de Marín, 1793.

Silvela, Francisco Agustín. *Colección de proyectos, ditámenes, y leyes orgánicas ó Estudios prácticos de administración.* 1838. Madrid: Imprenta Real, 1939.

Turnbull, George, trans. *A Methodical System of Universal Law, or the Laws of Nature and Nations* . . . *Written in the Latin by the celebrated Jo. Got. Heineccius* . . . 2 vols. London: J. Noon, 1740–1741.

Unanue, José Hipólito. *Guía política, eclesiástica y militar del virreynato del Perú para el año de 1794.* Lima: Imprenta Real de los Niños Huérfanos, 1794.

[Valcarce] Fernández, Don Doctor Vicente. *Desengaños filosóficos que en obsequio de la verdad, de la Religion, y de la Patria da al público* . . . tomo 3. Madrid: Blas Román, 1790.

Villadiego Vascuñana y Montoya, Alonso de. *Instrucción política y práctica judicial conforme al estilo de los Consejos.* 1612. Reprint, Madrid: Antonio Marín, 1766.

White, Blanco. *El Español* 4, no. 23. (London: Imprenta de Junigné), 30 marzo, 1812.

Secondary Sources

Adelman, Jeremy. "The Problem of Persistence in Latin American History." In *Colonial Legacies: The Problem of Persistence in Latin American History,* edited by Jeremy Adelman, 1–13. New York: Routledge, 1999.

Albán, Juan Pedro Viqueira.. *Propriety and Permissiveness in Bourbon Mexico*. 1987. Reprint, Wilmington: Scholarly Publications, 1999.

Agnani, Sunil. *Hating Empire Properly: The Two Indies and the Limits of Anti-Enlightenment Colonialism*. New York: Oxford University Press, 2013.

Aguirre, Carlos. "Working the System: Black Slaves and the Courts in Lima, 1821–1854." In *Crossing Boundaries: Comparative History of Black People in Diaspora*, edited by Darlene Clark and Jacqueline McCloud, 202–222. Bloomington: University of Indiana Press, 1999.

Aguirre, Carlos. *Agentes de su propia libertad. Los esclavos de Lima y la desintegración de la esclavitud, 1821–1854*. Lima: Pontificia Universidad Católica del Perú, 1993.

Aguirre-Beltrán, Gonzalo. *La población negra de México. Estudio etnohistórico*. México City: Fonda de Cultura Económica, 1946.

Aguirre Salvador, Rodolfo. "Un cacicazgo en disputa: Panoaya en el siglo XVIII." In *El cacicazgo en Nueva España y Filipinas*, coord. Margarita Mengus Bornemann and Roldolfo Aguirre Salvador, 87–163. Mexico City: UNAM, 2005.

AHR Roundtable, "New Perspectives on the Enlightenment." *American Historical Review* 15, no. 5 (2010): 1340–1425.

AHR Conversation, "Explaining Historical Change; or The Lost History of Causes." *American Historical Review* 120, no. 4 (2015): 1369–1423.

Albi, Christopher Peter. "Contested Legalities in Colonial Mexico: Francisco Xavier Gamboa and the Defense of *Derecho Indiano*." PhD dissertation, University of Texas at Austin, 2009.

Albi, Christopher Peter. "*Derecho Indiano* vs. The Bourbon Reforms: The Legal Philosophy of Francisco Xavier de Gamboa." In *Enlightened Reform in Southern Europe and its Colonies, c. 1750–1830*, edited by Gabriel Paquette, 229–252. London: Ashgate, 2009.

Álvarez de Morales, Antonio. "La difusión del derecho natural y de gentes europea en la Universidad Española de los siglos XVIII y XIX." In *Doctores y escolares: II Congreso de la Historia de las Universidades Hispánicas*, vol. 1, edited by Universitat de Valencia, 49–60. Valencia: Universidad de Valencia, 1995.

Álvarez de Morales, Antonio. "La enseñanza del derecho natural y de gentes: el libro de Heineccio." In *Manuales y textos de la enseñanza en la universidad liberal, VII Congreso Internacional sobre la Historia de las Universidades Hispánicas*, edited by Manuel Angel Bermijo Castrillo, 365–381. Madrid: Dykinson, 2000.

Andrews, George Reid. *Afro-Latin America, 1800–2000*. New York: Oxford University Press, 2004.

Ankersmit, F. R. *History and Tropology: The Rise and Fall of Metaphor*. Berkeley: University of California Press, 1992.

Aranda Pérez, José, coord. *Poderes intermedios, poderes interpuestos: Sociedad y oligarquías en la España Moderna*. Ciudad Real: Universidad Castila-La Mancha, 1999.

Armitage, David. "Three Types of Atlantic History." In *The British Atlantic World*, edited by David Armitage and Michael J. Braddick, 11–27. London: Palgrave, 2002.

Arrelucea Barrantes, Maribel. *Replanteando la esclavitud: Estudios de etnicidad y género en Lima borbónica*. Lima: Centro de Desarrollo Étnico, 2009.

Arrom, Silvia Marina. *The Women of Mexico City, 1700–1820*. Stanford: Stanford University Press, 1985.

Arrom, Silvia. *Containing the Poor: The Mexico City Poor House, 1776–1871*. Durham: Duke University Press, 2000.

Astarita, Tommaso. *Village Justice: Community, Family, and Popular Culture in Early Modern Italy*. Baltimore: Johns Hopkins University Press, 1999.

Baker, Keith Michael, ed. *The French Revolution and the Creation of Modern Political Culture*. Vol. 1, *The Political Culture of the Old Regime*. New York: Pergamon Press, 1987.

Baker, Keith Michael, ed. *Inventing the French Revolution: Essays on French Political Culture in the 18th Century*. New York: Cambridge University Press, 1990.

Baker, Keith Michael, and Peter Hanns Reill, eds. *What's Left of Enlightenment? A Postmodern Question*. Stanford: Stanford University Press, 2001.

Barba, Jesús Marina. *Justicia y gobierno en España en el siglo XVIII: el compendio del territorio de la Chancillería de Granada*. Granada: Universidad de Granada, 1995.

Barreda Fontes, José María, and Juan Manuel Carretero Zamora. *Ilustración y reforma en La Mancha: las reales sociedades económicas de Amigos de País*. Madrid: Consejo Superior de Investigaciones Científicas, Instituto de Historia "Jerónimo Zurita," 1981.

Barreda y Laos, Felipe. "La universidad en el siglo XVII." In *La universidad en el Perú: historia, presente y futuro. La época colonial*, vol. 2, edited by Jamie Ríos Burga, 218–219. Surco: Asamblea Nacional de Rectores: n/d.

Barrientos Grandón, Javier. "Librería de Don Sebastián Calvo de la Puerta (1717–1767), Oidor de la Real Audiencia de Guatemala." *Revista de estudios histórico-jurídicos* 21 (1999). Accessed November 5, 2015. http://www.scielo.cl/scielo.php?script=sci_arttext&pid=S0716-54551999002100016.

Barrientos Grandón, Javier. "Derecho común y derecho indiano en el Reino de Chile." In *Memoria del Congreso del Instituto Internacional de Historia del Derecho Indiano*, 133–159. México, 1995.

Barrientos Grandón, Javier. *La cultura jurídica en la Nueva España*. México City: Universidad Nacional Aútonoma de México, 1993.

Bartlett, Robert C. *The Enlightenment: A Post-Mortem Study*. Toronto: University of Toronto Press, 2011.

Baskes, Jeremy. *Indians, Merchants and Markets: Spanish-Indian Economic Relations in Colonial Oaxaca*. Stanford: Stanford University Press, 2000.

Baucom, Ian. *Specters of the Atlantic: Finance Capital, Slavery and the Philosophy of History*. Durham: Duke University Press, 2005.

Bazán, Erick Devoto. "La educación y el inicio de un Nuevo tiempo. Apuntes para la historia del munco intellectual peruano de fines del siglo XVIII." In *El Virrey Amat y su tiempo*, edited by Carlos Pardo-Figueroa Thays and Joseph Dager Alva, 81–158. Lima: Pontificia Universidad Católica del Perú/ Instituto Riva Agüero, 2004.

Bell, David T. *Lawyers and Citizens: The Making of a Political Elite in Old Regime France*. New York: Oxford University Press, 1994.

Bennett, Herman L. *Africans in Colonial Mexico*. Bloomington: Indiana University Press, 2003.

Bennett, Herman. *Colonial Blackness: A History of Afro-Mexico*. Bloomington: Indiana University Press, 2010.

Benton, Lauren. *Law and Colonial Cultures: Legal Regimes in World History, 1400–1900*. New York: Cambridge University Press, 2002.

Benton, Lauren. "No Longer Odd Region Out: Repositioning Latin America in World History." *Hispanic American Historical Review* 84, no. 3 (2004): 423–430.

Benton, Lauren, and Richard Ross, eds. *Legal Pluralism and Empires, 1500–1850*. New York: New York University Press, 2013.

Berlin, Isaiah. *Four Essays on Liberty*. 1958. Reprint, Oxford: Oxford University Press, 1969.

Berquist-Soulé, Emily. *The Bishop's Utopia: Envisioning Improvement in Colonial Peru*. Philadelphia: University of Pennsylvania Press, 2014.

Bhabha, Homi K. "Of Mimicry and Man." In *Tensions of Empire: Colonial Cultures in a Bourgeois World*, edited by Frederick Cooper and Ann Stoler, 152–160. Berkeley: University of California Press, 1997.

Bhambra, Gurminder K. "Historical Sociology, Modernity, and Postcolonial Critique." *American Historical Review* 116, no. 3 (June 2011): 653–663.

Bird, Jonathan. "For Better or For Worse: Divorce and Annulment Lawsuits in Colonial Mexico (1544–1799)." PhD dissertation, Duke University, 2013.

Black, Chad T. "Between Prescription and Practice: Licenture and Women's Legal Identity in Bourbon Quito, 1765–1810." *Colonial Latin American Review* 16, no. 2 (2007): 273–298.

Black, Chad Thomas. *The Limits of Gender Domination: Women, the Law, and Political Crisis in Quito, 1765–1830*. Alburquerque: University of New Mexico Press, 2011.

Blanchard, Peter. *Slavery and Abolition in Early Republican Peru*. Wilmington: Scholarly Resources, 1992.

Bleichmar, Daniela. *Visible Empire: Botanical Expeditions and Visual Culture in the Hispanic Enlightenment*. Chicago: University of Chicago Press, 2012.

Bleichmar, Daniela, Paula De Vos, Kristine Huffine, and Kevin Sheehan, eds. *Science in the Spanish and Portuguese Empires, 1500–1800*. Stanford: Stanford University Press, 2009.

Bolaños, Alvaro Félix, and Gustavo Verdesio, eds. *Colonialism Past and Present: Reading and Writing about Colonial Latin America Today*. Stony Brook: State University of New York Press, 2002.

Borah, Woodrow. "Juzgado General de Indios del Peru or Juzgado Particular de Indios de el Cerado." *Revista Chilena de Historia del Derecho* 6 (1970): 29–42.

Borah, Woodrow. *Justice by Insurance: The General Indian Court of Colonial Mexico*. Berkeley: University of California Press, 1983.

Braddick, Michael. *State Formation in Early Modern England, c. 1550–1700*. New York: Cambridge University Press, 2000.

Brading, D. A. *Church and State in Bourbon Mexico: The Diocese of Michoacán, 1749–1810*. 1994. Reprint, New York: Cambridge University Press, 2002.

Brading, David. *Miners and Merchants in Bourbon Mexico, 1763–1810*. 1971. Reprint, New York: Cambridge University Press, 2008.

Breen, Michael. "Law, Society, and the State in Early Modern France." *Journal of Modern History* 83 (2011): 346–386.

Brewer, John. *Sinews of Power: War, Money and the English State, 1688–1783*. 1988. Reprint, Cambridge, MA: Harvard University Press, 1990.

Bristol, Joan Cameron. *Christians, Blasphemers, and Witches: Afro-Mexican Ritual Practice in the Seventeenth Century*. Albuquerque: University of New Mexico Press, 2007.

Brooks, Christopher W. *Pettyfoggers and Vipers of the Commonwealth: The "Lower Branch" of the Legal Profession in Early Modern England*. New York: Cambridge University Press, 1986.

Brooks, Christopher W. *Lawyers, Litigation and English Society, 1450-1900*. London: Hambledon, 1998.

Brooks, Christopher, and Michael Lobban, eds. *Communities and Courts in Britain, 1150–1900*. London: Hambledon, 2003.

Brubaker, Rogers, and Frederick Cooper. "Beyond Identity." *Theory and Society* 29 (2000): 1–27.

Bryant, Sherwin K. "Enslaved Rebels, Fugitives, and Litigants: The Resistance Continuum in Colonial Quito." *Colonial Latin American Review* 13, no. 2 (2004): 7–46.

Bryant, Sherwin K. *Rivers of Gold, Lives of Bondage: Governing through Slavery in Colonial Quito*. Chapel Hill: University of North Carolina Press, 2014.

Buck-Morss, Susan. "Hegel and Haiti." *Critical Inquiry* 26, no. 4 (Summer 2000): 821–865.

Burbank, Jane, and Frederick Cooper. "Rules of Law, Politics of Empire." In *Legal Pluralism and Empires, 1500–1850*, edited by Lauren Benton and Richard Ross, 279–293. New York: New York University Press, 2013.

Burkhart, Louise M. *The Slippery Earth: Nahua-Christian Moral Dialog in Sixteenth-Century Mexico*. Tucson: University of Arizona Press, 1989.

Burkholder, Mark. *Politics of a Colonial Career: José Baquíjano and the Audiencia of Lima*. Wilmington: Scholarly Resources, 1980.

Burns, Kathryn. "Notaries, Truth, and Consequences." *American Historical Review* 110, no. 2 (April 2005): 350–379.

Burns, Kathryn. *Into the Archive: Writing and Power in Colonial Peru*. Durham: Duke University, 2010.

Burns, Kathryn. "Making Indigenous Archives: The Quilcaycamayoc of Colonial Cuzco." *Hispanic American Historical Review* 91, no. 4 (2011): 665–685.

Cabrera, Miguel. "On Language, Culture, and Social Actions." *History and Theory* 40 (2001): 82–100.

Calhoun, Craig C. *Nationalism*. Minneapolis: University of Minnesota, 1997.

Calzada, Daniel Cepeda. "El filósofo palentino Vicente Fernández Valcarce: Crítico de Descartes." In *Publicaciones Instituciones Tello Téllez de Menenes*, 73–183. Palencia: Centro de Estudios Palentinos, 1982.

Caplan, Karen D. *Indigenous Citizens: Local Liberalism in Early National Oaxaca and Yucatan*. Stanford: Stanford University Press, 2009.

Cañeque, Alejandro. *The King's Living Image: The Culture and Politics of Viceregal Power in Colonial Mexico*. New York: Routledge, 2004.

Cañizares-Esguerra, Jorge. *How to Write the History of the New World: Histories, Epistemologies, and Identities in the Eighteenth-Century Atlantic World*. Stanford: Stanford University Press, 2001.

Cañizares-Esguerra, Jorge. *Nature, Empire, and Nation: Science and Exploration in the History of Science in the Iberian World*. Stanford: Stanford University Press, 2006.

Caradonna, Jeremy L. *The Enlightenment in Practice: Prize Contests and Intellectual Culture in France, 1670–1794*. Ithaca: Cornell University Press, 2012.

Carey, Daniel, and Lynn Festa, eds. *The Postcolonial Enlightenment*. New York: Oxford University Press, 2009.

Carey, Daniel, and Sven Trakulhun. "Universalism, Diversity and the Postcolonial Enlightenment." In *The Postcolonial Enlightenment*, edited by Daniel Carey and Lynn Festa, 243–280. Oxford: Oxford University Press, 2009.

Carmagnani, Marcello. *The Other West: Latin America from Invasion to Globalization*. Berkeley: University of California Press, 2011.

Castiglione, Caroline. *Patrons and Adversaries: Nobles and Villagers in Italian Politics, 1640-1760*. New York. Oxford University Press, 2005.

Castillo Palma, Norma Angelica, and Francisco González-Hermosillo Adams. "Nobleza indígena y cacicazgos en Cholula, siglos XVI–XVIII." In *El cacicazgo en Nueva España y Filipinas*, coord. Margarita Menegus Bornemann and Roldolfo Aguirre Salvador, 289–354. Mexico City: Universidad Nacional Aútonoma de México, 2005.

Cépeda Calzada, Daniel. "El filósofo palentino Vicente Fernández Valcarce: Crítico de Descartes." In *Publicaciones Instituciones Tello Téllez de Menenes*, 73–183. Palencia: Centro de Estudios Palentinos, 1982.

Certeau, Michel de. *The Practice of Everyday Life*, translated by Steven Rendall. Berkeley: University of California Press, 1984.

Chakrabarty, Dipesh. *Provincializing Europe: Postcolonial Thought and Historical Difference*. Princeton: Princeton University Press, 2000.

Chakrabarty, Dipesh. "The Muddle of Modernity." *American Historical Review* 116, no. 3 (2011): 663–675.

Chambers, Sarah C. *From Subjects to Citizens: Honor, Gender and Politics in Arequipa, Peru, 1780–1854*. University Park: Pennsylvania State University Press, 1999.

Chambers, Sarah C. "'To the Company of a Man Like My Husband, No Law Can Compel Me': The Limits of Sanctions against Wife Beating in Arequipa, Peru, 1780-1850." *Journal of Women's History* 11, no. 1 (1999): 31–52.

Chambers, Sarah. "The Paternal Obligation to Provide: Political Familialism in Early Nineteenth-Century Chile." *American Historical Review* 117, no. 4 (2012): 1123–1148.

Chance, John K. *Conquest of the Sierra: Spaniards and Indians in Colonial Oaxaca*. Norman: University of Oklahoma, 1995.

Chandler, David S. "Slave over Master in Colonial Colombia and Ecuador." *The Americas* 38, no. 3 (1982): 315–326.

Charney, Paul. *Indian Society in the Valley of Lima, Peru, 1532–1825*. Lanham, MD: University Press of America, 2001.

Chassen-López, Francie R. *From Liberal to Revolutionary Oaxaca: The View from the South, Mexico 1867–1911*. University Park: Pennsylvania State University Press, 2004.

Chaussinand-Nogaret, Guy. *The French Nobility in the Eighteenth Century*, translated by William Doyle. New York: Cambridge University Press, 1985.

Childs, Matt. *The 1812 Aponte Rebellion in Cuba and the Struggle against Atlantic Slavery*. Chapel Hill: University of North Carolina Press, 2006.

Chiramonte, José Carlos. *Ensayos sobre la "Ilustración" Argentina*. Paraná: Facultad de Ciences de la Educación, Universidad del Litoral, 1962.

Christian, William E. *Local Religion in Sixteenth-Century Spain*. Princeton: Princeton University Press, 1981.

Cohler, Ann M., Basia C. Miller, and Harold S. Stone, eds. *Montesquieu, The Spirit of the Laws*. 1989. Reprint, New York: Cambridge University Press, 2013.

Colom González, Francisco, ed. *Modernidad iberoaméricano: Cultura, política y cambio social.* Madrid: Iberomericano/Vervuert, 2009.

Conrad, Sebastian. "Enlightenment in Global History: A Historiographical Critique." *American Historical Review* 117, no. 4 (2012): 999–1027.

Cook, Shelburne, and Woodrow Borah. *The Population of the Mixteca Alta.* Berkeley: University of California Press, 1968.

Cooper, Frederick. "Postcolonial Studies and the Study of History." In *Postcolonial Studies and Beyond,* edited by Ania Loomba, Suvir Kaul, et al., 401–422. Durham: Duke University Press, 2005.

Cooper, Frederick, and Laura Ann Stoler, eds. *Tensions of Empire: Colonial Cultures in a Bourgeois World.* Berkeley: University of California Press, 1997.

Cope, R. Douglas. "Indigenous Agency in Colonial Spanish America." *Latin American Research Review* 45, no. 1 (2010): 203–214.

Coronil, Fernando. "Beyond Occidentalism: Toward Nonimperial Geohistorical Categories." *Cultural Anthropology* 11, no. 2 (Feb. 1996): 51–87.

Crespo, Miguel Ángel González. *Juristas de la Universidad de Huesca en La Audiencia de México (Siglos XVI–XIX).* Mexico City: Universidad Nacional Autónoma de México: Instituto de Investigaciones Jurídicas, 1992.

Cunill, Caroline. "El indio miserable: nacimiento de la teoría legal en la América colonial del siglo XVI." *Cuadernos Intercambio* 8, no. 9 (2011): 229–248.

Cutter, Charles. *The Legal Culture of Northern New Spain, 1700–1810.* Albuquerque: University of New Mexico Press, 1995.

Cutter, Charles. R. *The* Protector de Indios *in Colonial New Mexico.* Albuquerque: University of New Mexico Press, 1986.]

Darnton, Robert. *The Literary Underground of the Old Regime.* Cambridge, MA: Harvard University Press, 1982.

Darnton, Robert. *The Revolution in Print, 1775–1800.* Berkeley: University of California Press, 1987.

Darnton, Robert. *George Washington's False Teeth: An Unconventional Guide to the Eighteenth Century.* New York: Norton, 2003.

Dávila Mendoza, Dora. *Hasta que la muerte nos separe: El divorcio eclesiástico en el arzobispado de México, 1702–1800.* Mexico City: Colegio de México, 2005.

Davis, Natalie Zemon. *Fiction in the Archives: Pardon Tales and their Tellers in Sixteenth-Century France.* Stanford: Stanford University Press, 1987.

de la Fuente, Alejandro, ed. Special Issue, "Su único derecho: Los esclavos y la ley." *Debate y Perspectivas. Cuadernos de Historia y Ciencias Sociales* 4 (2004).

de la Fuente, Alejandro. "Su único derecho." In "Su único derecho: Los esclavos y la ley." *Debate y Perspectivas. Cuadernos de Historia y Ciencias Sociales* 4 (2004), ed. de la Fuente, 7–22.

de la Fuente, Alejandro. "La esclavitud, la ley y la reclamación de derechos en Cuba." In "Su único derecho: Los esclavos y la ley." *Debate y Perspectivas. Cuadernos de Historia y Ciencias Sociales* 4 (2004), ed. de la Fuente, 37–68.

de la Fuente, Alejandro. "Slave Law and Claims-Making in Cuba Revisited." *Law and History Review* 24 (2004): 339–369.

de la Fuente, Alejandro. "Slaves and the Creation of Legal Rights in Cuba: *Coartación* and *Papel.*" *Hispanic American Historical Review* 87, no. 4 (2007): 659–692.

de la Puente Brunke, José. "Notas sobre la Audiencia de Lima y la 'protección de naturales' (siglo XVII)." In *Passuers, mediadores culturales y agentes de la primera globalización en e Mundo Ibérico, siglos XVI–XIX,* edited by Scarlet O'Phelan Godoy and Carmen Salazar-Soler, 231–248. Lima: PUCP/Riva Aguero, 2005.

de la Puente Luna, José Carlos. José Carlos. "Into the Heart of the Empire: Indian Journeys to the Habsburg Royal Court." PhD dissertation, Texas Christian University, 2010.

de la Puente Luna, José Carlos. "The Many Tongues of the King: Indigenous Language Interpreters and the Making of the Spanish Empire." *Colonial Latin American Review* 23, no. 2 (2014): 143–147.

Delgado, Jessica. "*Sin temor de Dios*: Women and Ecclesiastical Justice in Eighteenth-Century Toluca." *Colonial Latin American Review* 18, no. 1 (2009): 99–121.

Desan, Suzanne. "What's after Political Culture? Recent French Revolutionary Historiography." *French Historical Studies* 23, no. 1 (2000), 185–187.

Desan, Suzanne, and Jeffery Merrick, eds. *Family, Gender and Law in Early Modern France.* University Park: Pennsylvania State University Press, 2009.

Díaz, Arlene J. *Female Citizens, Patriarchs, and the Law in Venezuela, 1789–1904.* Lincoln: University of Nebraska, 2004.

Díaz, Magdalena. "La identitad de los esclavos negros como miserables en Nueva España: Discursos y acciones (siglos XVI–XVIII)." In *Esclavitudes hispánicas (siglos XV al XXI): Horizontes socio-culturales*, edited by Aurelia Martín Casares, 42–57. Granada: Universidad de Granada, 2014.

Díaz, María Elena. *The Virgin, the King, and the Royal Slaves of El Cobre: Negotiating Freedom in Colonial Cuba, 1670–1780.* Stanford: Stanford University Press, 2001.

Díaz, María Elena. "Beyond Tannenbaum." *Law and History Review* 24 (2004): 371–387.

Dirks, Konstantin. *In My Power: Letter Writing and Communications in Early America.* Philadelphia: University of Pennsylvania Press, 2009.

Deans-Smith. Susan. "'A Natural and Voluntary Dependence': The Royal Academy of San Carlos and the Cultural Politics of Art Education in Mexico City, 1786–1797." *Bulletin of Latin American Research*, Special Issue on *Mexican Visual Culture* 29, no. 3 (2010): 1–18.

Deans-Smith. Susan."*Buen Gusto* and Manuel Tolsá's Equestrian Statue of Charles IV in Late Colonial Mexico." In *Buen Gusto and Classicism in Late Eighteenth- and Nineteenth-Century Latin America*, edited by Paul B. Niell and Stacie G. Widdifield, 3–24. Albuquerque: University of New Mexico Press, 2013.

Domínguez Ortiz, Antonio. *Sociedad y Estado en el siglo XVIII español.* 1986. Reprint, Madrid: Ariel, 1990.

Donlan, Seán Patrick, and Dirk Heirbut. "A Patchwork of Accommodations—An Introduction." In *The Law's Many Bodies: Studies in Legal Hybridity and Jurisdictional Complexity, c. 1600–1900*, edited by Seán Patrick Donlan and Dirk Heirbut, 9–34. Berlin: Duncker and Humblot, 2015.

Dubois, Laurent. *A Colony of Citizens: Revolution and Slave Emancipation in the French Caribbean, 1787–1804.* Chapel Hill: University of North Carolina Press, 2004.

Dubois, Laurent. "An Enslaved Enlightenment: Rethinking the Intellectual History of the French Atlantic." *Social History* 31, no. 1 (2006): 1–14.

Dueñas, Alcira. *Indians and Mestizos in the Lettered City: Reshaping Justice, Social Hierarchy, and Political Culture in Colonial Peru.* Boulder: University Press of Colorado, 2010.

Dueñas, Alcira. "Introduction: Andeans Articulating Colonial Worlds." *The Americas* 72, no. 1 (2015): 1–8.

Dueñas, Alcira."The Lima Indian *Letrados*: Remaking the *República de Indios* in the Bourbon Andes." *The Americas* 72, no. 1 (2015): 55–75.

Dufour, Gerard. "Los afrancesados o una cuestión política: los límites del despotism ilustrado." *Cuadernos de la Historia Moderna* 6 (2007): 269–277.

Durand, Bernard. "Pluralism in France in the Modern Era—Between the 'Quest for Justice' and 'Uniformity through the Law': The Case of Roussillon." In *The Law's Many Bodies: Studies in Legal Hybridity and Jurisdictional Complexity, c. 1600–1900*, edited by Seán Patrick Donlan and Dirk Heirbut, 169–192. Berlin: Duncker and Humblot, 2015.

Eastman, Scott and Natalia Sobrevilla Perea, eds. *The Rise of Constitutional Government in the Iberian Atlantic World.* Tuscaloosa: University of Alabama, 2015.

Echeverri, Marcela. *Indian and Slave Royalists in the Age of Revolution: Reform, Revolution, and Royalism in the Northern Andes, 1780–1825.* New York: Cambridge University Press, 2016.

Edwards, Laura F. *The People and Their Peace: Legal Culture and the Transformation of Inequality in the Post-Revolutionary South.* Chapel Hill: University of North Carolina Press, 2008.

Elizalde Amerndáriz, Ignacio. "Feijoo y la influencia de los libertinos eruditos franceses." In *II Simposio sobre el padre Feijoo y su siglo*, vol. 2, 407–418. Oviedo: Centro de Estudios del Siglo XVIII, 1980.

Equipo Madrid, ed. *Carlos III, Madrid y la ilustración.* Madrid: Siglo Veintiuno, 1988.

Espinoza Ruiz, Grover Antonio. "La Reforma de la educación superior en Lima: el caso del Real Convictorio de San Carlos." In *El Perú en el siglo XVIII*, compiled by Scarlett O'Phelan Godoy, 242–262. Lima: Instituto Riva Agüero, 1990.

Estenssoro Fuchs, Carlos. "La plebe illustrada: El pueblo en las fronteras de la razón." In *Entre la retórica y la insurgencia: Las ideas de los movimentos sociales en los Andes, Siblo XVIII*, edited by Charles Walker, 33–66. Cuzco: Centro de Estudios Regionales Andinos Bartolomé de las Casas, 1995.

Fabian, Johannes. *Time and the Other: How Anthropology Makes Its Object*. 1957. Reprint, New York: Columbia University Press, 1983.

Farriss, Nancy. *Crown and Clergy in Colonial Mexico, 1759–1821: The Crisis of Ecclesiastical Privilege*. London: Athlone Press, University of London, 1968.

Farriss, Nancy. *Libana: El discurso ceremonial mesoamericano y el sermón Cristiano*. Mexico City: Artes de México, 2011.

Ferrone, Vincenzo. *The Enlightenment: History of an Idea*. 2010. Translated by Elisabetta Tarantino. Princeton: Princeton University Press, 2015.

Ferrer, Ada. *Freedom's Mirror: Cuba and Haiti in the Age of Revolution*. New York: Cambridge University Press, 2014.

Few, Martha. *Women Who Lead Evil Lives: Gender, Religion and the Politics of Power in Colonial Guatemala*. Austin: University of Texas Press, 2002.

Fischer, Sibylle. *Modernity Disavowed: Haiti and the Cultures of Slavery in the Age of Revolution*. Durham: Duke University Press, 2004.

Fisk, Catherine L. and Robert W. Gordon. "Forward: 'Law As'. . .Theory and Method in Legal History," *UC Irvine Law Review* 1, no.3 (2011). 519–41.

Folger, Robert. *Writing as Poaching: Interpellation and Self-Fashioning in Colonial relaciones de méritos y servicios*. Boston: Brill, 2011.

Fortea, José I., Juan E. Gelabert, and Tomás A. Mantecón, eds. *Furor et rabies: Violencia, conflicto y marginación en la Edad Moderna*. Santander: Universidad de Cantabria, 2003.

Foucault, Michel. "What Is Enlightenment?" In *The Foucault Reader*, edited by Paul Rabinow, 32–50. New York, Pantheon, 1984.

Foucault, Michel. "What Is An Author?" In *The Foucault Reader*, edited by Paul Rabinow, 101–120. New York, Pantheon, 1984.

Foucault, Michel. "Is It Useless To Revolt? " Translated by J. Beranuer. *Philosophy and Social Criticism* 8, no. 1 (1981): 1–9.

Franco, Jean. *Historia de la literatura hispanoamericana*. Barcelona: Ariel, 1981.

Francois, Marie Eileen. *A Culture of Everyday Credit: Housekeeping, Pawnbroking, and Governance in Mexico City, 1750–1920*. Lincoln: University of Nebraska Press, 2006.

Fritzche, Peter. *Stranded in the Present: Modern Time and the Melancholy of History*. Cambridge, MA: Harvard University Press, 2004.

Galindo, Alberto Flores. *La ciudad sumergida: Aristocracia y plebe en Lima, 1760–1830*. 1988. Reprint, Lima: Editorial Horizonte, 1991.

Gandásegui Aparicio, María José. "Los Pleitos Civiles en Castilla, 1700–1835." PhD dissertation, Universidad Complutense de Madrid, 1998.

Gaonkar, Dilip Parameshwar. "On Alternative Modernities." In *Alternative Modernities*, ed. Dilip Parameshwar Gaonkar, 1–23. Durham: Duke University Press, 2001.

Gaonkar, Dilip Parameshwar, ed. *Alternative Modernities*. Durham: Duke University Press, 2001.

García Acosta, Virginia, Juan Manuel Pérz Zevallos, and América Molina de Villar, eds. *Desastres agrícolas en México. Catálogo histórico, Tomo I, Epocas prehispánica y colonial, 958–1822*. México CITY: Centro de Investigaciones y Estudios Superiores de Antropología Social, 2003.

García Canclini, Néstor. *Hybrid Cultures: Strategies for Entering and Leaving Modernity*. Gainesville: University of Florida Press, 1990. Reprint, Minneapolis: University of Minnesota, 1995.

García Peña, Ana Lidia. "Madres solteras, pobres y abandonadas: Ciudad de México, Siglo XIX." *Historia Mexicana* 53, no. 3 (2004): 646–692.

García Peña, Ana Lidia. *El fracaso del amor: Género e individualidad en México del siglo XIX*. México CITY: Colegio de México/UNAM, 2006.

Garnot, Benoît. "Justice, infrajustice, parajustice, et extra justice dans la France d'Ancien Régime." *Crime, Histoire, et Sociétés* 4, no. 1 (2000): 103–140.

Garrett, David. *Shadows of Empire: The Indian Nobility of Cusco, 1750–1825.* New York: Cambridge University Press, 2005.

Gauderman, Kimberly. *Women's Lives in Colonial Quito: Gender, Law and Economy in Spanish America.* Austin: University of Texas Press, 2003.

Gayol, Víctor. "El régimen de los oficios vendibles y renunciables como garantía para el desempeño de los oficios públicos al final del periodo colonial. Estudio del caso." *Anuario Mexicano de Historia del Derecho* 18 (2006): 197–214.

Gayol, Victor. *Laberintos de justicias: Procuradores, escribanos y oficiales de la Real Audiencia de México (1750–1812).* Vol. 1, *Las reglas del juego.* Zamora: Colegio de Michoacán, 2007.

Gayol, Victor. *Laberintos de justicias: Procuradores, escribanos y oficiales de la Real Audiencia de México (1750–1812).* Vol. 2, *El juego de las reglas.* Zamora: Colegio de Michoacán, 2007.

Gerbi, Antonello. *The Dispute of the New World: The History of a Polemic, 1750–1900.* 1955. Reprint, Pittsburgh: University of Pittsburgh Press, 2010.

Ghachem, Malick W. "Montesquieu in the Caribbean: The Colonial Enlightenment between Code Noir and Code Civil." In *Postmodernism and the Enlightenment: New Perspectives in Eighteenth-Century French Intellectual History*, edited by Daniel Gordon, 7–30. New York: Routledge, 2001.

Ghachem, Malick W. *The Old Regime and the Haitian Revolution.* New York: Cambridge University Press, 2012.

Gibson, Charles. *The Aztecs under Spanish Rule: A History of Indians in the Valley of Mexico.* Stanford: Stanford University Press, 1964.

Gil Pujól, Xavier. "The Good Law of a Vassal: Fidelity, Obedience and Obligation in Hapsburg Spain." In *Forms of Union: The British and Spanish Monarchies of the Seventeenth and Eighteenth Centuries, Revista Internacional de Estudios Vascos. Cuadernos* 5, edited by Jon Arrieta and John H. Elliot (2009): 83–108.

Gil Pujol, Xavier. "Pensamiento político español y europeo en la Edad Moderna. Reflexiones sobre su estudio en una época post-*whig*." In *A vueltas con el pasado. Historia, memoria y vida*, edited by J. Ll. Palos and F. Sánchez Costa, 207–222. Barcelona: Publicacions de la Universitat de Barcelona, 2013.

Gluck, Carol. "The End of Elsewhere: Writing Modernity Now." *American Historical Review* 116, no. 3 (June 2011): 676–687.

Godoy, Scarlet O'Phelan. "Tiempo Inmemorial, Tiempo Colonial: Un estudio de casos." *Procesos. Revista Ecuatoriana de Historia*, no. 4 (1993): 3–20.

Gómez Carrasco, Cosme. "Tensión familiar y mentalidad social en el Antiguo Régimen. Notas sobre la conflictividad en la villa de Albacete en el siglo XVIII." *Revista Historia Social de las Mentalidades* [Chile] (2005): 11–36.

Gonzalbo Aizpuru, Pilar. "De escrituras y escribanos." *Anuario de Historia de Derecho Mexicano* 77 (1989): 77–93.

Gonzalbo Aizpuru, Pilar, ed. *La familia en el mundo iberoamericano.* Mexico City: Instituto de Investigaciones Sociales, UNAM, 1994.

González Echevarría, Roberto. *Myth and Archive: A Theory of Latin American Narrative.* Ithaca: Cornell University Press, 1990.

González Fernández, Juan Miguel. *La conflictividad judicial ordinaria en la Galicia Atlántica (1670–1820).* Vigo: Instituto de Estudios Vigueses, 1997.

Gordon, Daniel, ed. *Postmodernism and the Enlightenment: New Perspectives in Eighteenth-Century French Intellectual History.* New York: Routledge, 2001.

Green, Dominic. "Choose Your Own Enlightenment." *Atlantic Monthly*, March 12, 2015. Accessed July 7, 2015. http://www.theatlantic.com/politics/archive/2015/03/choose-your-own-enlightenment/387355/.

Goodman, Dena. *The Republic of Letters: A Cultural History of the French Enlightenment.* Ithaca: Cornell University Press, 1994.

Graubart, Karen. "Competing Spanish and Indigenous Jurisdictions in Early Colonial Lima." *Oxford Research Encyclopedias, Latin American History* (Oxford University Press, 2016). Accessed May 10, 2016. http://latinamericanhistory.oxfordre.com/view/10.1093/acrefore/9780199366439.001.0001/acrefore-9780199366439-e-365?rskey=l231vL&result=1.

Grinberg, Keila. "La manumisión, el género y la ley en el Brasil del siglo XIX: el proceso legal de Liberata por su libertad." In "Su único derecho: Los esclavos y la ley." *Debate y Perspectivas. Cuadernos de Historia y Ciencias Sociales* 4 (2004), ed. Alejandro de la Fuente, 89–104.

Gross, Ariela, and Alejandro de la Feunte. "Slaves, Free Blacks, and Race in the Legal Regimes of Cuba, Louisiana, and Virginia: A Comparison." *North Carolina Law Review* 91, no. 5 (2013): 1699–1756.

Grossi, Paolo. *Mitología jurídica de la modernidad.* Madrid: Editorial Trotta, 2003.

Guardino, Peter. "Gendering, Soldiering and Citizenship in the Mexican-American War of 1846-1848." *American Historical Review* 119, no. 1 (2014): 23–46.

Guardino, Peter. *The Time of Liberty: Popular Political Culture in Oaxaca, 1750–1850.* Durham: Duke University Press, 2005.

Guha, Ranajit. *Elementary Aspects of Peasant Insurgency in Colonial India.* Delhi: Oxford University Press, 1983.

Gutiérrez Ardila, Daniel. *Un nuevo reino, Geografía, pactismo, y diplomacia durante el interregno en Nueva Granada (1808–1816).* Bogotá: Universidad Externado de Colombia, 2010.

Guzmán-Brito, Alejandro. "Mos Italicus y mos Gallicus." *Revista de Derecho de la Universidad Católica de Valparaíso* 2 (1987): 11–40.

Guzmán-Brito, Alejandro. *La Codificación del Derecho Civil e Interpretación de las Leyes: Las normas sobre interpretación de las leyes en los principales Códigos civiles europeo-occidentales y americanos emitidos hasta fines del siglo xix.* Madrid: Iustel, 2011.

Haakonssen, Knud. "Hugo Grotius and the History of Political Thought." *Political Theory* 13, no. 2 (1985): 239–265.

Haakonssen, Knud. *Natural Law and Moral Philosophy: From Grotius to the Scottish Enlightenment.* New York: Cambridge, 1996.

Haakonssen, Knud. "Divine/Natural Theories in Ethics." In *The Cambridge History of Seventeenth-Century Philosophy,* vol. 2, edited by Daniel Garber and Michael Ayers, 1317–1357. New York: Cambridge University Press, 2003.

Haakonssen, Knud. "The History of Eighteenth-Century Philosophy: History or Philosophy?" In *The Cambridge History of Eighteenth-Century Philosophy,* vol. 1, edited by Knud Haakonssen, 1–25. New York: Cambridge Univeristy Press, 2006.

Hamnett, Brian. *Roots of Insurgency: Mexican Regions, 1750–1824.* London: Cambridge University Press, 1986.

Hamnett, Brian. "The Medieval Roots of Spanish Constitutionalism." In *The Rise of Constitutional Government in the Iberian Atlantic World,* edited by Scott Eastman and Natalia Sobrevilla Perea, 19–41. Tuscaloosa: University of Alabama, 2015.

Hanchard, Michael. "Afro-Modernity: Temporality, Politics, and the African Diaspora." In *Alternative Modernities,* ed. Dilip Parameshwar Gaonkar, 272–298. Durham: Duke University Press, 2001.

Hardwick, Julie. *The Practice of Patriarchy: Gender and the Politics of Household Authority in France.* University Park: Pennsylvania State University Press, 1999.

Hardwick, Julie. *Family Business: Litigation and the Political Economies of Everyday Life.* New York: Oxford University Press, 2009.

Hartog, Hendrick. "Pigs and Positivism." *University of Wisconsin Law Review* 4 (1985): 899–935.

Haslip-Viera, Gabriel. *Crime and Punishment in Late Colonial Mexico City, 1692–1810.* Albuquerque: University of New Mexico Press, 1999.

Helg, Aline. *Liberty and Equality in Caribbean Colombia, 1770–1835.* Chapel Hill: University of North Carolina Press, 2004.

Henary, Sara. "De Toqueville and the Challenge of Historicism." *Review of Politics* 78 (2014): 467–494.

Hernández-Marcos, Maximiliano. "Conceptual Aspects of Legal Enlightenment in Europe." In *Treatise of Legal Philosophy and General Jurisprudence*. Vol. 9, *A History of the Philosophy of Law in the Civil Law World, 1600–1900*, edited by Damiano Canelle, Paolo Grossi, and Hasso Hoffman, 87–88. New York: Springer Dordrecht Heidelberg, 2009.

Herr, Richard. *The Eighteenth-Century Revolution in Spain*. Princeton: Princeton University Press, 1958.

Herrup, Cynthia. *The Common Peace: Participation and the Criminal Law in Seventeenth-Century England*. New York: Cambridge University Press, 1987.

Herzog, Tamar. *Mediación, archivo y ejercicio: Los escribanos de Quito (siglo XVI–XVIII)*. Frankfurt: V. Klostermann, 1996.

Herzog, Tamar. *Defining Nations: Immigrants and Citizens in Early Modern Spain and Spanish America*. New Haven: Yale University Press, 2003.

Herzog, Tamar. *Upholding Justice: Society, State and the Penal System in Quito (1650–1750)*. Ann Arbor: University of Michigan Press, 2004.

Herzog, Tamar. "Los escribanos en las Américas: entre memoria española y memoria indígena." In *El Nervio de la República: el oficio de escribano en el Siglo de Oro*, edited by Enrique Vilalba Pérez and Emilio Torné, 337–349. Madrid: Calumbur, 2011.

Herzog, Tamar. "Colonial Law and 'Native Customs': Indigenous Land Rights in Colonial Spanish America." *The Americas* 69, no. 3 (2013): 303–321.

Hespanha, António Manuel. "Uncommon Laws. Laws in the Extreme Peripheries of an Early Modern Empire." *Zeitschrift der Savigny-Stiftung für Rechtsgeschichte*, no. 130, v. IV (2013): 180–204.

Hespanha, António Manuel. *Como so juristas viam o mundo, 1550–1750: Direitos, estados, pessoas, coisas, contratos, ações e crimes*. Lisbon: CreateSpace Independent Publishing Platform, 2015.

Hespanha, António Manuel. "De novo, os factos em massa: uma proposta de retorno ao *serial* numa fase pós-positivista da historiografia jurídica." Presented at VIII Congresso Brasileiro de História do Direito, "As astúcias da memória jurídica: métodos, teorias, balanço." Curitiba, de 31 de agosto a 4 de setembro de 2015.

Hidalgo Brinquis, María del Carmen. "La fabricación del papel en España e Hispanoamérica en el siglo XVII." In *Jornadas científicas sobre documentación de Castilla e Indias en el siglo XVII*, edited by Juan Carlos Galende, 207–224. Madrid: Universidad Complutense, 2006.

Hill, Ruth. *Hierarchy, Commerce and Fraud in Bourbon Spanish America: A Postal Inspector's Exposé*. Nashville: Vanderbilt University Press, 2005.

Himmelfarb, Gertrude. *The Roads to Modernity: The British, French and American Enlightenments*. New York: Vintage, 2004.

Hochstratter, T.J. *Natural Law Theories in the Early Enlightenment*. 2000. Reprint, New York: Cambridge University Press, 2004.

Honores, Renzo. "Estudios sobre la litigación y la litigiosidad colonial." *Revista de Historia del Derecho Privado* [Santiago de Chile] 2 (1999): 121–135.

Honores, Renzo. "Una sociedad legalista: Abogados, procuradores de causas y la creación de una cultura legal colonial en Lima y Potosí, 1540–1670." PhD dissertation, Florida International University, 2007.

Hontanilla, Ana. "Sentiment and the Law: Inventing the Category of the Wretched Slave in the *Real Audiencia* of Santo Domingo, 1783–1812." *Eighteenth-Century Studies* 48, no. 2 (2015): 181–200.

Horkheimer, Max, and Theodore Adorno. *Dialectic of Enlightenment*. 1944. Reprint, New York: Herder and Herder, 1972.

Hünefeldt, Christine. *Paying the Price of Freedom: Family and Labor among Lima's Slaves, 1800–1854*. Berkeley: University of California Press, 1994.

Hünefeldt, Christine. *Liberalism in the Bedroom*. University Park: Pennsylvania State University Press, 1999.

Hunt, Lynn. *Inventing Human Rights: A History*. New York: WW Norton, 2007.

Hunt, Lynn. "The Self and Its History." *American Historical Review* 119, no. 5. (2014): 1576–1586.

Iarroci, Michael. *The Properties of Modernity: Romantic Spain, European Modernity, and the Legacies of Empire*. Nashville: Vanderbilt University Press, 2006.

Israel, Jonathan. *Radical Enlightenment: Philosophy and the Making of Modernity 1650–1750.* New York: Oxford University Press, 2001.

Israel, Jonathan. *Enlightenment Contested: Philosophy, Modernity, and the Emancipation of Man.* New York: Oxford University Press, 2006.

Israel, Jonathan. *A Revolution of the Mind.* Princeton, NJ: Princeton University Press, 2010.

Israel, Jonathan. *Democratic Enlightenment: Philosophy, Revolution and Human Rights, 1750–1790.* New York: Oxford University Press, 2011.

Israel, Jonathan. "What Samuel Moyn Got Wrong in His *Nation* Article." Expanded reprint, *History News Network,* June 27, 2010. Accessed July 7, 2015. http://historynewsnetwork. org/article/128361.

Jacobs, Margaret. *Living the Enlightenment: Freemasory and Politics in Eighteenth-Century Europe.* New York: Oxford University Press, 1991.

Jacobs, Margaret. "Spinoza Got it." *London Review of Books* 34, no 21 (2011), 26–27.

Johnson, Lyman. "A Lack of Legitimate Obedience and Respect: Slaves and Their Masters in the Courts of Late Colonial Buenos Aires." *Hispanic American Historical Review* 87, no. 4 (2007): 631–657.

Johnson, Lyman, and Sonya Lipsett-Rivera, eds. *The Faces of Honor: Sex, Shame and Violence in Colonial Latin America.* Albuquerque: University of New Mexico Press, 1998.

Johnson, Walter. "On Agency." *Journal of Social History* 37, no.1 (2003): 113–124.

Jouve Martín, José Ramón *Esclavos de la ciudad letrada: Esclavitud, escritura y colonialismo en Lima, 1650–1700.* Lima: Instituto de Estudios Peruanos, 2005.

Just, Peter. "History, Power, Ideology, and Culture: Current Directions in the Anthropology of Law." *Law & Society Review* 26, no. 2 (1992): 373–412.

Kagan, Richard. *Lawsuits and Litigants in Early Modern Spain.* Chapel Hill: University of North Carolina, 1981.

Kellogg, Susan. *Law and the Transformation of Aztec Culture, 1500–1700.* Norman: University of Oklahoma Press, 1985.

Kennedy, Duncan. "Legal Formalism." In *Encyclopedia of the Social and Behavioral Sciences,* vol. 13, edited by Neil J. Smelser and Paul B. Baltes, 8634–8639. New York: Elsevier, 2001.

Klein, Herbert. *African Slavery in Latin America and the Caribbean.* New York: Oxford University Press, 1996.

Kluger, Viviana. "Los alimentos entre cónyuges: Un estudio sobre los pleitos en la época de la Segunda Audiencia de Buenos Aires (1785–1812)." *Revista de Historia del Derecho* [Buenos Aires] 18 (1990): 183–213.

Kluger, Viviana. *Escenas de la vida conyugal: Los conflictos matrimoniales en la sociedad virreinal rioplatense.* Buenos Aires: Editorial Quoram, 2003.

Knafla, Louis. "The Geographical, Jurisdiction, and Jurisprudential Boundaries of English Litigation in the Early Modern Seventeenth Century." In *Boundaries of the Law: Geography, Gender, and Jurisdiction in Medieval and Early Modern Europe,* edited by Anthony Musson, 118–130. Burlington, VT: Ashgate, 2005.

Knight, Alan. *Mexico: The Colonial Era.* New York: Cambridge University Press, 2002.

Knight, Alan. "Is Political Culture Good to Think?" In *Political Cultures in the Andes, 1750–1950,* edited by Nils Jacobsen and Cristóbal Aljovín de Losada, 25–57. Durham: Duke University Press, 2005.

Konetzke, Richard, comp. *Colección de Documentos para la Historia de la Formación Social de Hispanoamérica, 1493–1810,* vols 1–3. Madrid: Consejo Superior de Investigaciones Científicas, 1953–1964.

Koselleck, Reinhart. *The Practice of Conceptual History: Timing History, Spacing Concepts.* Translated by Todd Presner et al. Stanford: Stanford University Press, 2002.

Landers, Jane. *Black Society in Spanish Florida.* Chicago: University of Illinois Press, 1999.

Lane, Kris. "Captivity and Redemption: Aspects of Slave Life in Early Colonial Quito and Papayán." *The Americas* 57, no. 2 (2000): 225–246.

Lanning, John Tate. *Academic Culture in the Spanish Colonies.* London: Oxford University Press, 1940.

Lasso, Marixa. *Myths of Harmony: Race and Republicanism during the Age of Revolution, Colombia, 1795–1831*. Pittsburgh: University of Pittsburgh Press, 2007.

Lavallé, Bernard. *Amor y opresión en los Andes coloniales*. Lima: Instituto de Estudios Peruanos, 1999.

Lavallé y Arias de Saavedra, José Antonio de. "Don Pedro José Bravo de Lagunas y Castilla (apuntes sobre su vida y sus obras)." In *Estudios históricos*, 147–194. Lima: Gil, 1935.

"'Law As . . .' Theory and Method in Legal History." *UC Irvine Law Review* 1, no. 3 (2013): 239–512.

"'Law As . . .' II, History As Interface for the Interdisciplinary Study of Law." *UC Irvine Law Review* 4, no 1 (2014): 1–493.

"'Law As . . .' III, Glossolalia: Toward A Minor (Historical) Jurisprudence." *UC Irvine Law Review* 5, no. 2 (June 2015): 519–1079.

Lehner, Ulrich L. "What is 'Catholic Enlightenment'?" *History Compass* 8, no. 2 (2010): 166–178.

León, Natalia. *La primera alianza: El matrimonio criollo: Honor y violencia conyugal*. Quito: Nueva Editorial, 1997.

Lesaffer, Randall, and Jan Arriens. *European Legal History: A Cultural and Political Perspective*. New York: Cambridge University Press, 2009.

Levaggi, Abelardo. "La Fundamentación de las sentencias en el Derecho Indiano." *Revista de Historia del Derecho* [Buenos Aires] 6 (1978): 45–73.

Levaggi, Abelardo. "Los recursos de fuerza en el derecho indiano (Con especial referencia a la doctrina de Manuel Silvestre Martínez, oidor de la Audiencia de Guadalajara)." *Anuario Mexicano de Historia del Derecho* 4 (1992):117–138.

Linebaugh, Peter, and Marcus Rediker. *The Many Headed Hydra: Sailors, Slaves, Commoners and the Hidden History of the Revolutionary Atlantic*. New York: Beacon, 2001.

Lockhart, James. *Spanish Peru, 1532–1560: A Colonial Society*. Madison: University of Wisconsin Press, 1968.

Lockhart, James. *The Nahuas after the Conquest: A Social and Cultural History of the Indians of Central Mexico, Sixteenth through Eighteenth Centuries*. Stanford: Stanford University Press, 1992.

Lohmann Villena, Guillermo. "Criticismo e Ilustración como factores formativos de la conciencia del Perú en el siglo XVIII." In *Problemas de la formación del estado y de la nación en Hispanoamérica*, edited by Inge Buisson et al., 15–31. Köln: Böhlau Verlag, 1984.

López, Margarita Ortega. "Protestas de las mujeres castellanas contra el orden patriarcal privado durante el siglo XVIII." *Cuadernos de Historia Moderna* 19 (1997): 65–89.

Lucena Salmoral, Manuel. *Los Códigos Negros de la América Española*. Alcalá: Universidad de Alcalá, 1996.

Lucena Salmoral, Manuel. *Leyes para esclavos: El ordenamiento jurídico sobre la condición, tratamiento, defensa y represión de los esclavos en las colonias de la América Española*. Madrid: Fundación Ignacio Larramendi/MAPFRE Tavera, 2005. http://www.larramendi.es/en/consulta/registro.cmd?id=1151].

Lynch, John. "The Origins of Spanish American Independence." In *The Cambridge History of Latin America*, vol. 1, edited by Leslie Bethell, 3–50. Cambridge: Cambridge University Press, 1984.

Macchi, Fernanda. *Incas ilustrados: Reconstrucciones imperiales en la segunda mitad del siglo XVIII*. Madrid: Vervuert/Iberamericana, 2009.

MacCormack, Sabine. *On the Wings of Time: Rome, the Incas, Spain, and Peru*. Princeton: Princeton University Press, 2007.

Macera D'Orso, Pablo. "El probablismo en el Perú durante el siglo XVIII." In *La universidad en el Perú: historia, presente y futuro. La época colonial*, vol. 2., edited by Jamie Ríos Burga, 705–732. Surco: Asamblea Nacional de Rectores, s/d.

Macera D'Orso, Pablo. *Tres etapas en el desarrollo de la conciencia nacional*. Lima: Ediciones "Fanal," 1955.

Macera, Pablo, ed. *Los precios del Perú, siglos XVI–XIX*, tomo I. Lima: Banco Central, 1992.

MacKay, Ruth. *The Limits of Royal Authority: Resistance in Seventeenth-Century Castile*. London: Cambridge University Press, 1999.

MacKay, Ruth. *"Lazy, Improvident People": Myth and Reality in the Writing of Spanish History.* Ithaca: Cornell University Press, 2006.

MacLachlan, Colin. *Criminal Justice in Eighteenth-Century Mexico: A Study of the Tribunal of the Acordada.* Berkeley: University of California Press, 1974.

Mäkinen, Virpi. ed. *The Nature of Rights: Moral and Political Aspects of Rights in Late Medieval and Early Modern Philosophy. Acta Philosophica Fennica* 87 (2010).

Mallon, Florencia. "The Promise and Dilemma of Subaltern Studies: Perspectives from Latin American History." *American Historical Review* 99 (Dec. 1994): 1491–1515.

Mallon, Florencia. *Peasant and Nation: The Making of Postcolonial Mexico and Peru.* Berkeley: University of California, 1995.

Mallon, Florencia. "Pathways to Postcolonial Nationhood: The Democratization and Difference of Latin America." In *Postcolonial Studies and Beyond,* edited by Ania Loomba, Suvir Kaul, Matti Bunzi, Antoinette Burton, and Jed Esty. Durham: Duke University Press, 2005, 272–292.

Mangan, Jane. *Transatlantic Obligations: Creating the Bonds of Family in Conquest-Era Peru and Spain.* New York: Oxford University Press, 2016.

Manning, Susan, and Francis D. Cogliano, eds. *The Atlantic Enlightenment.* Burlington, VT: Ashgate, 2008.

Mantecón Movellán, Tomás Antonio. *Conflictividad y disciplinamiento social en la Cantabria rural del antiguo regimen.* Santander: Universidad de Cantabria, Fundación Marcelino Botín, 1997.

Mantecón Movellán, Tomás Antonio. "El peso de la infrajusticialidad en el control del crimen durante la Edad Moderna." *Estudis* 28 (2002): 43–75.

Margadant, Guillermo Floris. "75 años de investigación histórico-jurídico." In *LXVV años de investigaciones jurídicas 27,* 63–80. México CITY: Universidad Nacional Aútonoma de México, 1979.

Martínez, María Elena. *Genealogical Fictions: Limpieza de Sangre, Religion, and Gender in Colonial Mexico.* Stanford: Stanford University Press, 2008.

Masferrer, Ancieto. "Plurality of Laws, Legal Traditions and Codifications in Spain." *Journal of Civil Law Studies* 4, no. 2 (2011): 419–447.

Masferrer, Ancieto. "Plurality of Laws and *Ius Commune* in the Spanish Legal Tradition: the Cases of Catalonia and Valencia." In *The Law's Many Bodies: Studies in Legal Hybridity and Jurisdictional Complexity, c. 1600–1900,* edited by Seán Patrick Donlan and Dirk Heirbut, 193–222. Berlin: Duncker and Humblot, 2015.

Mason, Haydyn. "Optimism, Progress, and Philosophical History." In *The Cambridge History of Eighteenth-Century Political Thought,* edited by Mark Goldie and Robert Wokler, 195–217. New York: Cambridge, 2006.

Maza, Sarah. *Private Lives and Public Affairs: The Causes Célèbres of Prerevolutionary France.* Berkeley: University of California Press, 1993.

McCaa, Robert. "The Peopling of Mexico from Origins to Revolution." In *A Population History of North America,* edited by Michael R. Haines and Richard H. Stewart, 241–304. New York: Cambridge University Press, 2000.

McClelland, I. L. *Ideological Hesitancy in Spain, 1700–1750.* Liverpool: Liverpool University Press, 1991.

McKinley, Michelle A. "Fractional Freedoms: Slavery, Legal Activism, and Ecclesiastical Courts in Colonial Lima, 1593–1689." *Law and History Review* 28, no. 3 (2010): 749–790.

McMahon, Darrin. *Enemies of the Enlightenment: The French Counter-Enlightenment and the Making of Modernity.* New York: Oxford University Press, 2001.

McMahon, Darrin, and Samuel Moyn. *Rethinking Modern European Intellectual History.* New York: Oxford University Press, 2014.

McNeely, Ian. *The Emancipation of Writing: German Civil Society in the Making, 1790–1820s.* Berkeley: University of California Press, 2003.

Meléndez, Mariselle, and Karen Stolley. "Introduction: Enlightenments in Latin America." *Colonial Latin American Research Review* 24, no. 1 (2015): 1–16.

Méndez, Cecelia. *The Plebeian Republic: The Huanta Rebellion and the Making of the Peruvian State, 1820–1850*. Durham: Duke University Press, 2005.

Menegus Bornemann, Margarita. "El cacicazgo en Nueva España." In *El cacicazgo en Nueva España y Filipina*, coord. Margarita Menegus Bornemann and Roldolfo Aguirre Salvador, 13–69. Mexico City: Universidad Aútonomo de México, 2005.

Miceli, Paola. "El Derecho consuetudinario en Castilla: una Crítica a la matriz romántica de las interpretaciones sobre la costumbre." *Hispania* 63, no. 1 (2002): 9–28.

Miceli, Paola. "Entre memoria y olvido. El tiempo de la costumbre en un conflicto medieval." *Bulletin du centre d'études médiévales d'Auxerre* 2 (2008): 2–10.

Miceli, Paola. "Medir y clasificar el tiempo de la costumbre: la obstinada tarea de los juristas medievales." *Mirabili* [Argentina] 11 (2010): 211.

Miesel, Seth. "The Fruit of Freedom: Slaves and Citizens in Early Republican Argentina." In *Slaves, Subjects and Subversives: Blacks in Colonial Latin America*, edited by Jane Landers and Barry M. Robinson, 273–306. Albuquerque: University of New Mexico Press, 2006.

Mignolo, Walter. *Local Histories/Global Designs: Coloniality, Subaltern Knowledge and Border Thinking*. Princeton: Princeton University Press, 2001.

Mignolo, Walter. *The Darker Side of the Renaissance: Literacy, Territoriality, and Colonization*. 1995. Reprint, Ann Arbor: University of Michigan Press, 2006.

Mignolo, Walter. "The Geopolitcs of Knowledge and the Colonial Difference." In *Coloniality at Large: Latin America and the Postcolonial Debate*, edited by Mabel Moraña, Enrique Dussel, and Carlos A. Juáregui, 223–258. Durham: Duke University Press, 2008.

Mignolo, Walter. *The Darker Side of Western Modernity: Global Futures, Decolonial Options*. Durham, Duke University Press, 2011.

Miller, Nicole, and Stephen Hart, eds. *When Was Latin America Modern?* New York: Palgrave, 2007.

Miller, Paul B. *Elusive Origins: The Enlightenment in the Modern Caribbean Historical Imagination*. Charlottesville, VA: University of Virigina Press, 2010.

Milton, Cynthia. *The Many Meanings of Poverty: Colonialism, Social Compacts, and Assistance in Eighteenth-Century Ecuador*. Stanford: Stanford University Press, 2007.

Mirow, M. C. *Latin American Law: The History of Private Law and Institutions in Spanish America*. Austin: University of Texas Press, 2004.

Moraña, Mabel, Enrique Dussel, and Carlos A. Juáregui, eds. *Coloniality at Large: Latin America and the Postcolonial Debate*. Durham: Duke University Press, 2008.

Moreiras, Alberto. *The Exhaustion of Difference: The Politics of Latin American Cultural Studies*. Durham: Duke University Press, 2001.

Morse, Richard M. *New World Soundings: Culture and Ideology in the Americas*. Baltimore: Johns Hopkins University Press, 1989.

Morse, Richard M. *El espejo de Próspero: Un studio de la dialéctica del Nuevo Mundo*. 1982. Reprint, Mexico: Siglo Veintiuno, 1999.

Moyn, Samuel. "Mind the Enlightenment." *The Nation*, May 12, 2010. Accessed July 7, 2015. http://www.thenation.com/article/mind-enlightenment/.

Moyn, Samuel. "Contexualism and Criticism in the History of Ideas." In *Rethinking Modern European Intellectual History*, edited by Darrin McMahon and Samuel Moyn, 32–55. New York: Oxford University Press, 2014.

Moyn, Samuel, and Anthony Sartori, eds. *Global Intellectual History*. New York: Columbia University Press, 2013.

Mumford, Jeremy. "Litigation as Ethnography in Sixteenth-Century Peru." *Hispanic American Historical Review* 88, no. 1 (2008): 5–40.

Muthu, Sankar. *Enlightenment Against Empire*. Princeton: Princeton University Press, 2003.

Nader, Helen. *Liberty in Absolutist Spain: The Habsburg Sale of Towns, 1516–1700*. Baltimore: Johns Hopkins University, 1990.

Nader, Laura. "Styles of Court Procedure: To Make the Balance." In *Law in Culture and Society*, edited by Laura Nader, 69–91. 1969; reprint. Berkeley: University of California Press, 1997.

Nader, Laura. "The Crown, The Colonists and Zapotec Village Law." In *History and Power in the Study of Law: New Directions in Legal Anthropology*, edited by June Starr and Jane F. Collier, 330–344. Ithaca: Cornell University Press, 1989.

Nader, Laura. *Harmony Ideology: Justice and Control in a Zapotec Mountain Village*. Stanford: Stanford University Press, 1990.

Noel, Charles. "Charles III of Spain." In *Enlightened Absolutism: Reform and Reformers in Later Eighteenth-Century Europe*, edited by H. M. Scott, 119–143. Ann Arbor: University of Michigan Press, 1990.

Novoa, Mauricio. *Protectors of Indians in the Royal Audience of Lima: History, Careers and Legal Culture, 1575–1775*. Boston, Brill, 2016.

Oakley, Francis. *Natural Law, Laws of Nature, Natural Rights: Continuity and Discontinuity in the History of Ideas*. New York: Continuum, 2005.

Oldham, James. "Only Eleven Shillings: Abusing Public Justice in England in the Late Eighteenth Century (Part 1 of 3)." *Green Bag* 15, 2D (2012): 175–188.

O'Phelan, Scarlet. *Kurakas sin sucesiones: Del cacique al alcalde de indios (Perú y Bolivia, 1750–1835)*. Cuzco: Centro de Estudios Regionales Andinos Bartolomé de las Casas, 1997.

O'Phelan Godoy, Scarlett. "La construcción del miedo a la plebe en el siglo XVIII a través de las rebeliones sociales." In *El Miedo en el Perú*, edited by Claudia Rosas Lauro, 123–138. Lima: Pontificia Universdad Católica del Perú, 2005.

O'Phelan Godoy, Scarlett, and Carmen Salazar-Soler. *Passuers, mediadores culturales, y agentes de la primera globalización en le Mundo Ibérico, siglos XVI–XIX*. Lima: Pontificia Universidad Católica del Perú-Instituto Riva Agüero, 2005.

Osorio, Alejandra. *Inventing Lima: Baroque Modernity in Peru's South Sea Metropolis*. London: Palgrave Macmillan, 2008.

O'Toole, Rachel Sarah. *Bound Lives: Africans, Indians and the Meaning of Race in Colonial Peru*. Pittsburgh: University of Pittsburgh Press, 2012.

Outram, Dorinda. *The Enlightenment*. 1995. Reprint, New York: Cambridge University Press, 2013.

Ouweneel, Arij. "From Tlahtocayotl to Goberdnadoryotl: A Critical Examination of Indigenous Rule in 18th-Century Central Mexico." *American Ethnologist* 22, no. 4 (1995): 756–785.

Ouweneel, Arij, and C. Bijleveld. "The Economic Cycle of Bourbon Central Mexico: A Critique of the 'recaudacion del diezmo líquido en pesos.'" *Hispanic American Historical Review* 69 (1989): 479–530.

Owensby, Brian. "How Juan and Leonor Won Their Freedom." *Hispanic American Historical Review* 85, no. 1 (Feb. 2005): 39–79.

Owensby, Brian. *Empire of Law and Indian Justice in Colonial Mexico*. Stanford: Stanford University Press, 2008.

Owensby, Brian. "Between Justice and Economics: Indians and Reformism in Eighteenth-Century Imperial Thought." In *Legal Pluralism and Empires, 1500–1850*, edited by Lauren Benton and Richard Ross, 143–169. New York: New York University Press, 2013.

Pagden, Anthony. *The Fall of Natural Man: The American Indian and the Origins of Comparative Ethnology*. New York: Cambridge University Press, 1982.

Pagden, Anthony. *The Enlightenment and Why It Still Matters*. New York: Random House, 2013.

Palmer, Colin. *Slaves of the White God: Blacks in Mexico, 1560–1650*. Cambridge, MA: Harvard University Press.

Palomeque Torres, Antonio. "Derechos de arancel de la justicia civil y criminal en los lugares de los propios y montes de la ciudad de Toledo anteriores al año 1500." *Anuario de Historia del Derecho Español* (1954): 87–94.

Palomeque Torres, Antonio. "El Fiel del Juzgado de los Propios y Montes de la Ciudad de Toledo." *Cuadernos de Historia de España* LV–LVI (1972): 322–399.

Palti, Elías José. "Time, Modernity and Time Irreversibility." *Philosophy & Social Criticism* 23, no. 5 (1997): 25–62.

Palti, Elías. "The Return of the Subject as a Historico-Intellectual Problem." *History and Theory* 43, no. 1 (2004): 57–82.

Palti, Elías. "The Problem of 'Misplaced Ideas' Revisited: Beyond the History of Ideas in Latin America." *Journal of the History of Ideas* (2006): 149–179.

Palti, Elías José. "Beyond Revisionism: The Bicentennial of Independence, The Early Republican Experience, and Intellectual History in Latin America." *Journal of the History of Ideas* 70, no. 4 (2009): 593–614.

Paquette, Gabriel. *Enlightened Reform in Southern Europe and its Colonies, c. 1750–1830*. London: Ashgate, 2009.

Paquette, Gabriel. *Enlightenment, Governance, and Reform in Spain and Its Empire, 1759–1808*. New York: Palgrave Macmillan, 2008.

Parisian, Catherine. *The First White House Library: A History and Annotated Catalog*. Washington DC: The Bibliographic Society of America, 2010.

Passerin d'Entrèves, Maurizio. "Critique of Enlightenment: Michel Foucault on '*Was isst Aufklärung?*'" In *The Enlightenment and Modernity*, edited by Norman Geras and Robert Wokler, 184–203. New York: St Martins, 2000.

Pearce, Adrian. *The Origins of the Bourbon Reforms in Spanish South America, 1700–1763*. New York: Palgrave Macmillan, 2014.

Penningroth, Dylan C. "Law as Redemption: A Historical Comparison of the Way Marginalized People Use Courts." *Law and Social Inquiry* 40, no. 3 (2015): 793–796.

Penry, Elizabeth S. "The '*Rey Común*': Indigenous Political Discourse in Eighteenth-Century Alto Perú." In *The Collective and the Public in Latin America: Cultural Identities and Political Order*, edited by Luis Roniger and Tamar Herzog, 219–237. Sussex: Sussex Academic Press, 2000.

Penyack, Lee M. "Safe Harbors and Compulsory Custody: *Casas de Depósito* in Mexico, 1759–1865." *Hispanic American Historical Review* 79, no.1 (1999): 83–99.

Peralta, Victor Ruiz de. "Las razones de la fe. Iglesia y la Ilustración en el Perú, 1750–1800." In *El Perú en el siglo XVIII: La Era Borbónica*, edited by Scarlett O'Phelan Godoy. Lima: Instituto Riva Aguero, 1999.

Peralta Apaza, Luz. *El papel sellado en el Perú colonial, 1640–1824*. Lima: Seminario de Historia Rural Andina-UNMSM, 2007.

Pérez-Canto, María. *Lima en el siglo XVIII: Estudio Socioeconómico*. Madrid: Universidad Autónoma de Madrid, 1985.

Pérez-Perdomo, Rogelio. *Latin American Lawyers: A Historical Introduction*. Stanford: Stanford University Press, 2006.

Peruga, Mónica Bolufer. *Mujeres e ilustración: La construcción de la feminidad en la Ilustración Española*. Valencia: Artes Gráficas, 1998.

Peruga, Mónica Bolufer, and Isabel Morant Deusa. "On Women's Reason, Education, and Love: Women and Men of the Enlightenment in Spain and France." *Gender and History* 10, no.2 (1998): 183–216.

Pescador, Javier Juan. "Entre la espada y el olvido: pleitos matrimoniales en el provisorato eclesiástico de México, siglo XVIII." In *La familia en el mundo iberoamericano*, edited by Pilar Gonzalbo Aizpurú, 373–386. Mexico City: Instituto de Investigaciones Sociales, UNAM, 1994.

Peset Reig, José Luis, and Mariano Peset Reig. *Carlos IV y la Universidad de Salamanca*. Madrid: Consejo Superior de Investiaciones Científicas, 1983.

Phelan, John Leddy. *The People and the King: The Comunero Revolt in Colombia, 1781*. 1978. Reprint, Madison: University of Wisconsin Press, 2011.

Phillips, William D. *Slavery in Medieval and Early Modern Iberia*. Philadelphia: University of Pennsylvania Press, 2014.

Pinedo, Arturo Gümez. "El poder de los cabildo mahoas y la venta de propriedades privadas a través del tribunal de indios, Yucatán." *Historia Mexicana* 54, no. 5 (2004): 697–759.

Pocock, J. G. A. "Authority and Property: The Question of Liberal Orgins." In *Virtue, Commerce, and History*, by J. G. A. Pocock, 51–72. 1980. Reprint, New York: Cambridge University Press, 1985.

Poska, Allyson M. *Women and Authority in Early Modern Spain: The Peasants of Galicia*. New York: Oxford University Press, 2005.

Povinelli, Elizabeth. "A Flight from Freedom." In *Postcolonial Studies and Beyond*, edited by Ania Loomba, Suvil Kaul, Matti Bunzl, Antoinette Burnton, and Jed Esty, 145–165. Durham: Duke University Press, 2005.

Premo, Bianca. *Children of the Father King: Youth, Authority, and Legal Minority in Colonial Lima, 1650–1820*. Chapel Hill: University of North Carolina Press, 2005.

Premo, Bianca. "An Old Father in a New Tragedy: Fatherhood in the Legal Theater of the 18th-Century Spanish Atlantic." *Clio: A Journal of Literature, History, and Philosophy of History* 41, no. 1 (2010): 109–130.

Premo, Bianca. "Before the Law: Women's Petitions in the Eighteenth-Century Spanish Empire." *Comparative Studies in Society and History* 53, no. 2 (2011): 261–289.

Premo, Bianca. "An Equity against the Law: Slave Rights and Creole Jurisprudence in Spanish America." *Slavery & Abolition* 32, no. 4 (2011): 495–517.

Premo, Bianca. "Quejas ilustradas. Litigios en la historia de España e Hispanoamérica (siglo XVIII)." *Memoria y Civilización: Anuario de Historia* [Navarra, Spain] 14 (2011): 155–173.

Premo, Bianca. "Familiar: Thinking beyond Lineage and across Race in Spanish Atlantic Family History." *William & Mary Quarterly* 70, no. 2 (April 2013): 295–316.

Premo, Bianca. "Custom Today: Temporality, Law, and Indigenous Enlightenment." *Hispanic American Historical Review* 94 no. 3 (2014): 355–379.

Premo, Bianca. "Felipa's Braid: Women, Culture and the Law in Eighteenth-Century Oaxaca." *Ethnohistory* 61, no. 3 (2014): 497–523.

Proctor, Frank "Trey." "Afro-Mexican Slave Labor in the *Obrajes de Paños* of New Spain, Seventeenth and Eighteenth Centuries." *The Americas* 60, no. 1 (2003): 33–58.

Proctor III, Frank "Trey." "Gender and the Manumission of Slaves in New Spain." *Hispanic American Historical Review* 86, no. 2 (2006): 309–336.

Proctor, Frank Trey. "Slavery Rebellion and Liberty in Colonial Mexico." In *Black Mexico: Race and Society from Colonial to Modern Times*, edited by Ben Vinson and Matthew Restall, 21–50. Albuquerque: University of New Mexico Press, 2009.

Proctor, Frank. *"Damned Notions of Liberty": Slavery, Culture, and Power in Colonial Mexico, 1640–1769*. Albuquerque: University of New Mexico Press, 2011.

Rabasa, José. "Thinking Europe in Indian Categories, or 'Tell me the story of how I conquered you.'" In *Coloniality at Large: Latin America and the Postcolonial Debate*, edited by Mabel Moraña, Enrique Dussel, and Carlos A. Juáregui, 43–77. Durham: Duke University Press, 2008.

Rabinow, Paul. *The Foucault Reader*. New York, Pantheon, 1984.

Radcliffe, Sarah. "Geographies of Modernity in Latin America: Uneven and Contested Development." In *When Was Latin America Modern?*, edited by Nicole Miller and Stephen Hart, 21–48. New York: Palgrave, 2007.

Rama, Angel. *The Lettered City*. Translated by John Charles Chasteen. Durham: Duke University Press, 1996.

Ramírez, Susan. *Provincial Patriarchs: Land Tenure and the Economics of Power in Colonial Peru*. Albuquerque: University of New Mexico Press, 1986.

Ramírez, Susan E. "'El Dueño de Indios': Thoughts on the Shifting Bases of Power under the *curaca de los viejos antiguos* under the Spanish in Sixteenth-Century Peru." *Hispanic American Historical Review* 67, no. 4 (1987): 575–610.

Ramos, Gabriela, and Yanna Yannakakis, eds. *Indigenous Intellectuals: Knowledge, Power and Colonial Culture in Mexico and the Andes*. Durham: Duke University Press, 2014.

Rapaport, Joanne, and Tom Cummins. *Beyond the Lettered City: Indigenous Literacies in the Andes*. Durham: Duke University Press, 2012.

Reill, Peter Hanns. *The German Enlightenment and the Rise of Historicism*. Berkeley: University of California Press, 1975.

Reill, Peter Hanns. *Vitalizing Nature in the Enlightenment*. Berkeley: University of California Press, 2005.

Reill, Peter Hanns, and Ellen Judy Wilson. *Encyclopedia of the Enlightenment*. New York: Facts on File/Book Builders Incorporated, 1996.

Restall, Matthew, Lisa Sousa, and Kevin Terraciano, eds. *Mesoamerican Voices: Native-Language Writings from Colonial Mexico, Oaxaca, Yucatan and Guatemala.* 2005. Reprint, New York: Cambridge University Press, 2008.

Riggsby, Andrew M. *Roman Law and the Legal World of the Romans.* New York: Cambridge University Press, 2010.

Rípodas Ardanaz, Daisy. *El matrimonio en Indias: Realidad social y regulación juridical.* Buenos Aires: Fundación para la Educación, la Ciencia y la Cultura, 1977.

Robertson, John. *The Case for the Enlightenment.* Cambridge: Cambridge University Press, 2005.

Roberston, John. *The Enlightenment: A Very Short Introduction.* New York: Oxford University Press, 2015.

Rodríguez García, Margarita Eva. *Criollismo y patria en la Lima ilustrada (1732–1795).* Buenos Aires: Miño y Dávila, 2006.

Romero Frizzi, María de los Ángeles. *Economía y vida de los españoles en la Mixteca Alta, 1519–1720.* Mexico City: Instituto Nacional de Antropología e Historia/Gobierno del Estado de Oaxaca, 1990.

Romero Frizzi, María de los Ángeles, coord. *Escritura zapoteca. 2,500 años de historia.* Mexico CITY: Centro de Investigación y Estudios Superiores en Antropología Social, 2003.

Romero Frizzi, María de los Ángeles. "The Power of the Law: The Construction of Colonial Power in an Indigenous Region." In *Negotiation within Domination: Colonial New Spain's Indian Pueblos Confront the Spanish State,* edited by Ethelia Ruiz Medrano and Susan Kellogg, 107–136. Boulder: University Press of Colorado, 2010.

Rosas Lauro, Claudia, ed. *El miedo en le Perú, siglos XVI al XXX.* Lima: Pontificia Universdad Católica del Perú, 2005.

Rosas Lauro, Claudia. "El miedo de la revolución. Rumores y temores desatados por la Revolución Francesa en el Perú, 1790–1800." In *El Miedo en el Perú,* edited by Claudia Rosas Lauro, 139–166. Lima: Pontificia Universdad Católica del Perú, 2005.

Rosas Lauro, Claudia. *Del trono al guilotina: El impacto de la revolución francesa en el Perú.* Lima: Instituto Francés del Estudios Andinos/Pontificia Universdad Católica del Perú, 2006.

Safier, Neil. *Measuring the New World: Enlightenment Science and South America.* Chicago: University of Chicago Press, 2008.

Sahlins, Marshall. "'What Is Anthropological Enlightenment?' Some Lessons of the Twentieth Century." *Annual Review of Anthropology* 28 (1999): i–xxiii.

Salvatore, Ricardo D. *Wandering Paysanos: State Order and Subaltern Experience in Buenos Aires during the Rosas Era.* Durham: Duke University Press, 2003.

Salvatore, Ricardo D. "Introducción." In *Los lugares del saber: Contextos locales y redes transnacionales en la formación del conocimiento modero,* edited by Ricardo Salvatore, 9–34. Buenos Aires: Beatriz Viterbo, 2007.

Salvatore, Ricardo D. "Imperial Revisionism: US Historians of Latin America and the Colonial Spanish Empire (ca. 1915–1945)." *Transnational American Studies* 5, no. 1 (2013): 1–54. Accesed on July 15, 2015. https://escholarship.org/uc/item/30m769ph.

Sánchez, María José de la Pascua. "Violencia y familia en la Espanã del Antiguo Régimen." *Estudis* 28 (2002): 77–100.

Sánchez, María José de la Pascua. "Women Alone in Enlightenment Spain." In *Eve's Enlightenment: Women's Experience in Spain and Spanish America, 1726–1839,* edited by Catherine M. Jaffe and Elizabeth Franklin Lewis, 128–142. Baton Rouge: Louisiana State University Press, 2009.

Sánchez-Blanco, Francisco. *El Absolutismo y las Luces en el Reinado de Carlos III.* Madrid: Marical Pons, 2002.

Sánchez González, Ramón. *Los Montes de Toledo en el Siglo XVIII (Un estudio demográfico).* Toledo: Instituto Provincial de Investigaciones y Estudios Toledanos, 1984.

Sánchez González, Ramón. *Sexo y violencia en Los Montes de Toledo.* Toledo: Asociación para el Desarrollo de Territorio "Montes Toledanos," 2006.

Sanders, James. *Contentious Republicans: Popular Politics, Race and Class in Nineteenth-Century Colombia.* Durham: Duke University Press, 2004.

Saranyana, José Ignacio. *Teología en America Latina / Theology in Latin America: De Las Guerras de Independencia hasta finales de siglos XIX (1810–1899).* Madrid: Iberoamericano, 2008.

Sato, Tatasuya, Tomo Hidaka, and Mari Fukada. "Depicting the Dynamics of Living the Life: The Trajectory Equifinality Model." In *Dynamic Process Methodology in the Social Sciences and Developmental Sciences,* edited by Jann Valsiner, Peter C. M. Mollenar, et al., 217–240. New York: Springer, 2009.

Scardaville, Michael. "(Hapsburg) Law and (Bourbon) Order: State Authority, Popular Unrest, and the Criminal Justice System in Bourbon Mexico City." *The Americas* 50, no. 4 (April 1994): 501–526.

Scardaville, Michael. "Justice by Paperwork: A Day in the Life of a Court Scribe in Bourbon Mexico City." *Journal of Social History* 36, no. 4 (Summer 2003): 979–1007.

Scattola, Mario. "*Scientia Iuris* and *Ius Naturae*: The Jurisprudence of the Holy Roman Empire in the Seventeenth and Eighteenth Centuries." In *Treatise of Legal Philosophy and General Jurisprudence.* Vol. 9, *A History of the Philosophy of Law in the Civil Law World, 1600–1900,* edited by Damiano Canalle, Paolo Grossi, and Hasso Hoffman, 1–42. New York: Springer Dordrecht Heidelberg, 2009.

Schmidt, James. "Introduction: What Is Enlightenment: A Question, Its Context and Some Answers." In *What Is Enlightenment? Eighteenth-Century Answers and Twentieth-Century Questions,* edited by James Schmidt, 1–44. Los Angeles: University of California, 1996.

Schmidt, James. "What Enlightenment Project?" *Political Theory* 28, no. 6 (2000): 734–757.

Schmidtz, David, and Jason Brennan. *A Brief History of Liberty.* Malden, MA: Wiley-Blackwell, 2010.

Schneewind, Jerome. *The Invention of Autonomy: A History of Modern Moral Philosophy.* New York: Cambridge University Press, 1989.

Schrader-Kniffki, Martina, and Yanna Yannakakis. "Sins and Crimes: Zapotec-Spanish Translations in Catholic Evangelization and Spanish Law." In *Missionary Linguistics V/ Lingüística misionera; Translation Theories and Practice,* edited by Otto Zawartjes, Klaus Zimmermann, and Martina Schrader-Kniffki, 161–196. Bremen, Germany: John Benjamins Publishing, 2014.

Schultz, Kirsten. *Tropical Versailles: Empire, Monarchy and the Portugeuse Royal Court in Rio, 1808– 21.* New York: Routledge, 2001.

Schwartz, Stuart. *All Can Be Saved: Religious Tolerance and Salvation in the Iberian Atlantic World.* New Haven: Yale University Press, 2008.

Scott, David. *Conscripts of Modernity: The Tragedy of Colonial Enlightenment.* Durham: Duke University Press, 2004.

Scott, Rebecca. *Slave Emancipation in Cuba: The Transition to Free Labor, 1860–1899.* 1985. Reprint, Pittsburgh: University of Pittsburgh Press, 2000.

Seed, Patricia. *To Love, Honor and Obey in Colonial Mexico: Conflicts over Marriage Choice, 1574–1821.* Stanford: Stanford University Press, 1988.

Seed, Patricia. *Ceremonies of Possession in Europe's Conquest of the New World, 1492–1640.* New York: Cambridge University Press, 1995.

Serúlnikov, Sergio. *Subverting Colonial Authority: Challenges to Spanish Rule in Eighteenth-Century Southern Andes.* Durham: Duke University Press, 2003.

Sewell, William Hamilton. *The Logics of History: Social Theory and Social Transformation.* Chicago: University of Chicago Press, 2005.

Sharafi, Mitra. "The Marital Patchwork of Colonial South India: Forum Shopping from Britain to Baroda." *Law and History Review* 28, no. 4 (2010): 979–1009.

Shuler, Jack. *Calling Out Liberty: The Stono Slave Rebellion and the Universal Struggle for Human Rights.* Jackson: University of Mississippi Press, 2009.

Siegel, Micol. "Beyond Compare: Comparative Method after the Transnational Turn." *Radical History Review* 91 (2005): 62–90.

Siskin, Clifford, and William Warner, eds. *This is Enlightenment.* Chicago: University of Chicago Press, 2010.

Smail, Daniel Lord. *The Consumption of Justice: Emotions, Publicity, and Legal Culture in Marseille, 1264–1423.* Ithaca: Cornell University Press, 2003.

Smith, Jay. *The Culture of Merit: Nobility, the Royal Service and the Making of the Absolute Monarchy in France, 1600–1789.* Ann Arbor: University of Michigan Press, 1996.

Smith, Theresa Ann. *The Emerging Female Citizen: Gender and Enlightenment in Spain.* Berkeley: University of California Press, 2006.

Soludré-La France, Renée. *"Esclavos de su magestad:* Slave Protest and Politics in Colonial New Granada." In *Slaves, Subjects and Subversives: Blacks in Colonial Latin America,* edited by Jane Landers and Barry M. Robinson, 175–208. Albuquerque: University of New Mexico Press, 2006.

Sousa, Lisa Mary. "Women and Crime in Colonial Oaxaca: Evidence of Complementary Gender Roles in Mixtec and Zapotec Societies." In *Indian Women of Early Mexico,* edited by Susan Schroeder, Stephanie Wood, and Robert Haskett, 199–221. Norman: University of Oklahoma Press, 1997.

Spivak, Gayatri Chakravorty. *A Critique of Postcolonial Reason: Toward a History of the Vanishing Present.* Cambridge, MA: Harvard University Press, 1999.

Spores, Ronald. *Mixtecs in Ancient and Colonial Times.* Norman: University of Oklahoma Press, 1984.

Stanley, Amy Dru. *From Bondage to Contract: Wage Labor, Marriage, and the Market in the Age of Slave Emancipation.* New York: Cambridge University Press, 1998.

Stein, Stanley, and Barbara Stein. *Apogee of Empire: Spain and New Spain the Age of Charles III, 1759–1789.* Baltimore: Johns Hopkins University Press, 2003.

Stern, Steve J. *Peru's Indian Peoples and the Challenge of Spanish Conquest: Huamanga to 1650.* Madison: University of Wisconsin Press, 1982.

Stern, Steve J. *The Secret History of Gender: Women, Men and Power in Late-Colonial Mexico.* Chapel Hill: University of North Carolina Press, 1995.

Stoler, Ann Laura. *Along the Archival Grain: Epistemic Anxieties and Colonial Common Sense.* Princeton: Princeton University Press, 2010.

Stolley, Karen. *Domesticating Empire: Enlightenment in Spanish America.* Nashville: Vanderbilt University Press, 2013.

Talaván, Miguel Luque. *Un universo de opiniones: La literatura juridical indiana.* Madrid: Biblioteca Historia de América/CSIC, 2003.

Tanck de Estrada, Dorothy. *Independencia y educación: Cultura cívica, educación indígena, y literatura infantil.* Mexico City: El Colegio de Mexico, 2013.

Tannenbaum, Frank. *Slave and Citizen.* 1947. Reprint, New York: Beacon, 1992.

Tardieu, Pierre. *El negro en la Real Audiencia de Quito (Ecuador) ss. XVI–XVIII.* Quito: IFEA, 2006.

Tau Anzoátegui, Víctor. *Casuismo y sistema: Indigación histórica sobre el espíritu del derecho moderno.* Buenos Aires: Instituto de Investigaciones de Historia del Derecho, 1992.

Tau Anzoátegui, Víctor. *El poder de la costumbre: Estudios sobre el derecho consuetudinario en América hispana hasta la emancipación.* Buenos Aires: Instituto de Investigaciones de Historia del Derecho, 1992.

Taylor, Charles. *Sources of the Self: The Making of Modern Identity.* New York: Cambridge University Press, 1989.

Taylor, Scott K. "Credit, Debt and Honor in Castile, 1600–1650." *Journal of Early Modern History* 7, no. 1–2 (2003): 7–27.

Taylor, Scott K. *Honor and Violence in Golden Age Spain.* New Haven: Yale University Press, 2008.

Taylor, William B. "Cacicazgos coloniales en la valle de Oaxaca." *Historia Mexicana* 20, no. 1 (1970): 1–41.

Taylor, William B. *Landlord and Peasant in Colonial Oaxaca.* Stanford: Stanford University Press, 1972.

Taylor, William B. *Drinking, Homicide and Rebellion in Colonial Mexican Villages.* Stanford: Stanford University Press, 1979.

Taylor, William B. *Magistrates of the Sacred: Priests and Parishioners in Eighteenth-Century Mexico.* Stanford: Stanford University Press, 1996.

Terraciano, Kevin. "Crime and Culture in Colonial Mexico: The Case of the Mixtec Murder Note." *Ethnohistory* 45, no. 4 (Autumn 1998): 709–745.

Terraciano, Kevin. *The Mixtecas of Colonial Oaxaca: Ñudzahui History, Sixteenth through Eighteenth Centuries.* Stanford: Stanford University Press, 2001.

Thurner, Mark. "After Spanish Rule: Writing Another After." In *After Spanish Rule: Postcolonial Predicaments of the Americas,* edited by Mark Thurner and Andrés Guerrero, 12–57. Durham: Duke University Press, 2003.

Thurner, Mark. *History's Peru: The Poetics of Colonial and Postcolonial Historiography.* Gainesville: University of Florida Press, 2013.

Todorov, Tvestan. *In Defence of the Enlightenment.* London: Atlantic Books, 2010.

Tomás y Valiente, Francisco. *Manual de Historia del Derecho Español.* 1979. Reprint; Madrid: Tecnos, 1987.

Tompson, Sinclair. *We Alone Will Rule: Native Andean Politics in the Age of Insurgency* Madison: University of Wisconsin Press, 2002.

Townsend, Camila. "'Half My Body Free, the Other Half Enslaved': The Politics of the Slaves of Guayaquil at the End of the Colonial Era." *Colonial Latin American Review* 7, no. 1 (1998): 105–128.

Trazegnies, Fernando de. *Ciracio de Urtecho. Litigante por amor.* Lima: Pontificia Universidad Católica, 1981.

Trouillot, Michel-Rolph. *Silencing the Past: Power and the Production of History.* New York: Beacon, 1995.

Turits, Richard Lee. "Raza, esclavitud y libertad en Santo Domingo." In "Su único derecho: Los esclavos y la ley." *Debate y Perspectivas. Cuadernos de Historia y Ciencias Sociales* no. 4 (2004), ed. Alejandro de la Fuente, 69–88.

Tutino, John. *From Insurrection to Revolution in Mexico: Social Bases of Agrarian Violence, 1750–1940.* Princeton: Princeton University Press, 1986.

Twinam, Ann. *Purchasing Whiteness: Pardos, Mulattos, and the Quest for Social Mobility in the Spanish Indies.* Stanford: Stanford University Press, 2015.

Ugarte del Pino, Ruben. *Historia de la Facultad de Derecho.* Lima: Universidad de Nacional Mayor de San Marcos, 1968.

Uribe-Uran, Victor. *Honorable Lives: Lawyers, Family and Politics in Colombia.* Pittsburgh: Penn State University Press, 2000.

Uribe-Uran, Victor. *Fatal Love: Spousal Killers, Law, and Punishment in the Late Colonial Spanish Atlantic.* Stanford: Stanford University Press, 2015.

Urquijo, José M. Mariluz. "El Derecho Prehispánico y el Derecho Indiano como modelos del Derecho Castellano." In *Actas III Congreso del Instituto Internacional de Historia del Derecho Indiano Madrid, 17–23 de enero de 1972,* 101–113. Madrid: Estudios Instituto Nacional de Historia del Derecho Indiano, 1978.

Uzgalis, William. " . . . The Same Tyrannical Principle: Locke's Legacy on Slavery." In *Subjugation and Bondage: Critical Essays on Slavery and Social Philosophy,* edited by Tommy L. Lott, 49–78. New York: Rowman & Littlefield, 1998.

Valcárcel, Carlos Daniel. *Reforma de San Marcos en la Epoca de Amat,* vol. 2. Lima: Universidad de San Marcos, 1955.

van de Kley, Dale. *The Religious Origins of the French Revolution.* New Haven: Yale University Press, 1996.

van Deusen, Nancy E. *Between the Sacred and the Worldly: The Institutional and Cultural Practice of Recogimiento.* Stanford: Stanford University Press, 2000.

van Deusen, Nancy E. *Global Indios: The Indigenous Struggle for Justice in Sixteenth-Century Spain.* Durham: Duke University Press, 2015.

van Duffel, Siegfried. "Natural Rights and Individual Sovereignty." *Journal of Political Philosophy* 12, no. 2 (2004): 147–162.

Van Young, Eric. "Islands in the Storm: Quiet Cities and Violent Countrysides in the Mexican Independence Era." *Past & Present* 118 (1988): 130–155.

Van Young, Eric. "Agrarian Rebellion and Defense of Community: Meaning and Collective Violence in Late Colonial and Independence-Era Mexico." *Journal of Social History* 27 (1993): 245–269.

Van Young, Eric. *The Other Rebellion: Popular Violence, Ideology and the Mexican Struggle for Independence, 1810–1821*. Stanford: Stanford University Press, 2001.

Van Young, Eric. "Limits of Atlantic World Nationalism in a Revolutionary Age." In *Empire to Nation*, edited by Joseph Eshrick, Hasan Kayali, and Eric van Young, 34–67. New York: Rowman & Littlefield, 2006.

Verdesio, Gustavo. "Colonialism Now and Then." In *Colonialism Past and Present: Reading and Writing about Colonial Latin America Today*, edited by Alvaro Félix Bolaños and Gustavo Verdesio, 1–133. Stony Brook: State University of New York Press, 2002.

Verscuren, Ab. *The Great Council of Malines in the 18th Century: An Aging Court in a Changing World: Studies in the History of Law and Justice* 3. Leuven: Springer Cham, 2015.

Vermeesch, Griet. "Professional Lobbying in Eighteenth-Century Brussels: The Role of Agents in Petitioning the Central Government Institutions in the Habsburg Netherlands." *Journal of Early Modern History* 16 (2012): 95–119.

Vermeesch, Griet. "The Social Composition of Plaintiffs and Defendants in the Peacemaker Court, Leiden, 1750–4." *Social History* 40, no. 2 (2015): 208–229.

Vilalba Pérez, Enrique, and Emilio Torné. *El Nervio de la República: el oficio de escribano en el Siglo de Oro*. Madrid: Calumbur, 2011.

Voekel, Pamela. "Peeing on the Palace: Bodily Resistance to the Bourbon Reforms in Mexico City." *Journal of Historical Sociology* 5, no. 2 (June 1992): 181–207.

Voekel, Pamela. *Alone before God: The Religious Origins of Modernity in Mexico*. Durham: Duke University Press, 2002.

Volpini, Paola. "'Por la autoridad de los ministros': Obsevaciones sobre los letrados en una alegación de Juan Bautista Larrea." *Cuadernos de historia moderna* 30 (2005): 63–84.

Wade, Peter. "Modernity, Tradition, Shifting Boundaries, Shifting Contexts." In *When Was Latin America Modern?*, edited by Nicole Miller and Stephen Hart, 49–68. New York: Palgrave, 2007.

Wahrman, Dror. *The Making of the Modern Self: Identity and Culture in Eighteenth-Century England*. New Haven: Yale University Press, 2004.

Wahrman, Dror, and Colin Jones, eds. *The Age of Cultural Revolutions: Britain and France, 1750–1820*. Berkeley: University of California Press, 2002.

Walker, Charles. *The Tupac Amaru Rebellion*. Cambridge, MA: Harvard University Press, 2014.

Walker, Tamara. "'He outfitted his family in noble decency': Slavery, Honour, and Dress in Eighteenth-Century Lima." *Slavery and Abolition* 30, no. 3 (2009): 383–402.

Warren, Adam. *Medicine and Politics in Colonial Peru: Population Growth and the Bourbon Reforms*. Pittsburgh: University of Pittsburgh Press, 2010.

Weber, David J. *Bárbaros: Spaniards and Their Savages in the Age of Enlightenment*. New Haven: Yale University Press, 2005.

Weisser, Michael R. *The Peasants of the Montes: The Roots of Rural Rebellion in Spain*. Chicago: University of Chicago Press, 1972.

Whitaker, Arthur P. "The Dual Rôle of Latin American in the Enlightenment." In *Latin America and the Enlightenment*, edited by Arthur P. Whitaker, 3–22. 1942. Reprint, Ithaca: Cornell University Press, 1961.

Whyman, Susan. *The Pen and the People: English Letter Writers, 1660–1800*. New York: Oxford University Press, 2010.

Withers, Charles W. J. *Placing the Enlightenment: Thinking Geographically about the Age of Reason*. Chicago: University of Chicago Press, 2007.

Wolf, Larry. *Inventing Eastern Europe: The Map of Civilization on the Mind of the Enlightenment*. Stanford: Stanford Univeristy Press, 1994.

Wood, Gordon W. "The American Enlightenment." In *America and Enlightened Constitutionalism*, edited by Gary L. McDowell and Jonathan O'Neil, 159–175. New York: Palgrave Macmillan, 2006.

Wood, Gordon W. *Empire of Liberty: A History of the Early Republic, 1789–1815.* New York: Oxford, 2007.

Wood, Stephanie. *Transcending Conquest: Nahua Views of Spanish Colonial Mexico.* Norman: University of Oklahoma Press, 1997.

Yack, Bernard. *The Fetishism of Modernities: Epochal Self Consciousness in Contemporary Social and Political Thought* (South Bend, IN: Notre Dame University Press, 1997.

Yannakakis, Yanna. "Witnesses, Spatial Practices, and a Land Dispute in Colonial Oaxaca." *The Americas* 65, no. 2 (October 2008): 161–192.

Yannakakis, Yanna. *The Art of Being In-Between: Native Intermediaries, Indian Identity, and Local Rule in Colonial Oaxaca.* Durham: Duke University Press, 2008.

Yannakakis, Yanna. "Custom: A Language of Negotiation in Eighteenth-Century Oaxaca." In *Negotiation within Domination: Colonial New Spain's Indian Pueblos Confront the Spanish State*, edited by Ethelia Ruiz Medrano and Susan Kellogg, 137–171. Boulder: University Press of Colorado, 2010.

Yannakakis, Yanna. "Making Spanish Law Zapotec: Local Legal Culture and Jurisdiction in Colonial Oaxaca." Paper presented at the XXX Congress of the Latin American Studies Association, May 2012.

Yannakakis, Yanna. "Indigenous Peoples and Legal Culture." *History Compass* 11, no. 11 (2013): 931–994.

Yannakakis, Yanna, and Marina Schrader-Kniffki. "Between the 'Old Law' and the New: Christian Translation, Indian Jurisdiction, and Criminal Justice in Colonial Oaxaca." *Hispanic American Historical Review* 96, no. 3 (2016): 517–548.

Zahler, Reuben. *Ambitious Rebels: Remaking Honor, Law, and Liberalism in Venezuela, 1780–1850.* Tuscon: University of Arizona Press, 2013.

INDEX

CPSIA information can be obtained
at www.ICGtesting.com
Printed in the USA
BVHW030003140819
555817BV00002B/8/P